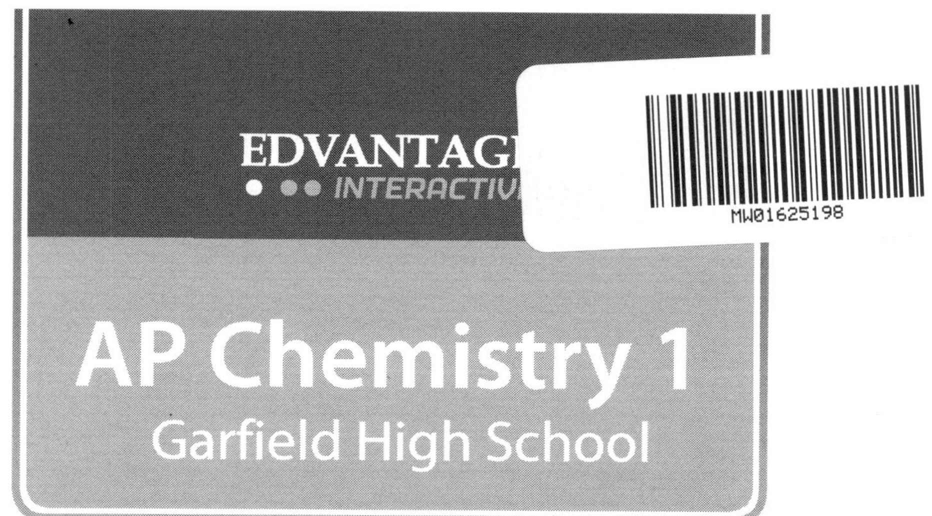

Development Team

Authors

Cheri Smith
Yale Secondary
School District 34 Abbotsford

Gary Davidson
School District 22 Vernon

Megan Ryan
Walnut Grove Secondary
School District 35 Langley

Chris Toth
St. Thomas More Collegiate
Burnaby, British Columbia

Program Consultant

Lionel Sandner
Edvantage Interactive

COPIES OF THIS BOOK MAY BE OBTAINED BY CONTACTING:

Edvantage Interactive

E-MAIL:
info@edvantageinteractive.com

TOLL-FREE FAX:
866.275.0564

TOLL-FREE CALL:
866.422.7310

EDVANTAGE INTERACTIVE

AP Chemistry 1

ISBN 978-1-77249-279-8

Garfield High School

Vice-President of Marketing: *Don Franklin*
Director of Publishing: *Yvonne Van Ruskenveld*
Design and Production: *Donna Lindenberg*
Proofreading: *Eva van Emden*
Editorial Assistance: *Rhys Sandner*
Index: *Noeline Bridge*
Photos: *p. 33, K. Jung; p. 34, Bureau international des poids et mesures (BIPM)*

The AP Big Ideas at the beginning of each chapter are quoted from AP Chemistry: Course and Exam Description, revised edition, effective Fall 2013, published by the College Board, New York, NY. Advanced Placement, AP, and College Board are registered trademarks of the College Board.

QR Code — What Is This?

The image to the right is called a QR code. It's similar to bar codes on various products and contains information that can be useful to you. Each QR code in this book provides you with online support to help you learn the course material. For example, find a question with a QR code beside it. If you scan that code, you'll see the answer to the question explained in a video created by an author of this book.

You can scan a QR code using an Internet-enabled mobile device. The program to scan QR codes is free and available at your phone's app store. Scanning the QR code above will give you a short overview of how to use the codes in the book to help you study.

Note: We recommend that you scan QR codes only when your phone is connected to a WiFi network. Depending on your mobile data plan, charges may apply if you access the information over the cellular network. If you are not sure how to do this, please contact your phone provider or us at: info@edvantageinteractive.com

Contents

Welcome to AP Chemistry 1

AP Chemistry 1 is a print and digital resource for classroom and independent study, aligned with the AP curriculum. You, the student, have two core components — this write-in textbook or WorkText and, to provide mobile functionality, an interactive Online Study Guide.

AP Chemistry 1 WorkText

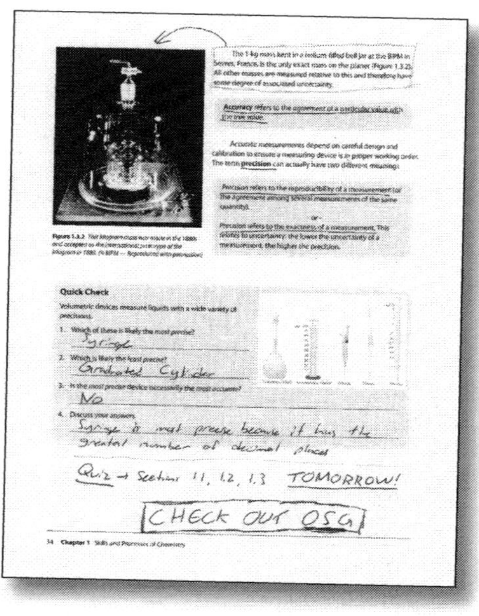

What is a WorkText?

A WorkText is a write-in textbook. Not just a workbook, a write-in **textbook**.

Like the vast majority of students, you will read for content, underline, highlight, take notes, answer the questions — all in this book. **Your book.**

Use it as a textbook, workbook, notebook, AND study guide. It's also a great reference book for post secondary studies.

Make it your own personal WorkText.

Why a write-in textbook?

Reading is an extremely active and personal process.

Research has shown that physically interacting with your text by writing margin notes and highlighting key passages results in better comprehension and retention.

Use your own experiences and prior knowledge to make meaning, not take meaning, from text.

How to make this book work for you:

1. Scan each section and check out the shaded areas and bolded terms.
2. Do the Warm-Ups to activate prior knowledge.
3. Take notes as required by highlights and adding teacher comments and notes.
4. Use Quick Check sections to find out where you are in your learning.
5. Do the Review Questions and write down the answers. Scan the **QR codes** or go to the **Online Study Guide** to see YouTube-like video worked solutions by *AP Chemistry 1* authors.
6. Try the **Online Study Guide** for online quizzes, PowerPoints, and more videos.
7. Follow the six steps above to be successful.

For more information on how to purchase your own personal copy
info@edvantageinteractive.com

AP Chemistry 1 Online Study Guide (OSG)

What is an Online Study Guide?

It's an interactive, personalized, digital, mobile study guide to support the WorkText.

The **Online Study Guide** or OSG, provides access to online quizzes, PowerPoint notes, and video worked solutions.

Need extra questions, sample tests, a summary of your notes, worked solutions to some of the review questions? It's all here!

Access it where you want, when you want.

Make it your own personal mobile study guide.

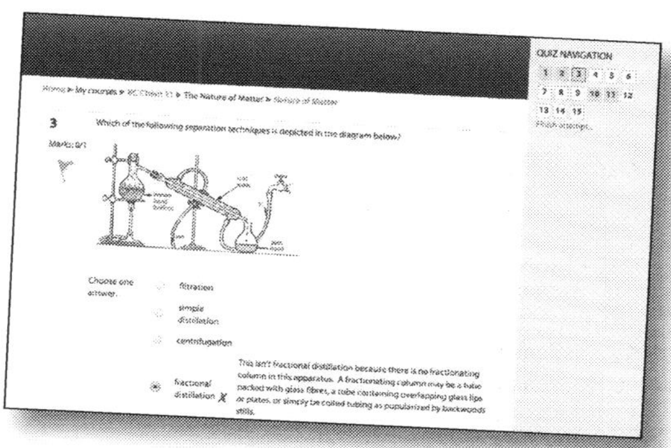

What's in the Online Study Guide?

- Online quizzes, multiple choice questions, exam-like tests with instant feedback
- PowerPoint notes: Key idea summary and student study notes from the textbook
- Video worked solutions: Select video worked solutions from the WorkText

If you have a smart phone or tablet, scan the QR code to the right to find out more. Colour e-reader WorkText version available.

Scan this code for a quick tour of the OSG

Where is the Online Study Guide located?

www.edvantagescience.com

Should I use the Online Study Guide?

YES... if you want to do your best in this course.
The OSG is directly LINKED to the activities and content in the WorkText.
The OSG helps you learn what is taught in class.

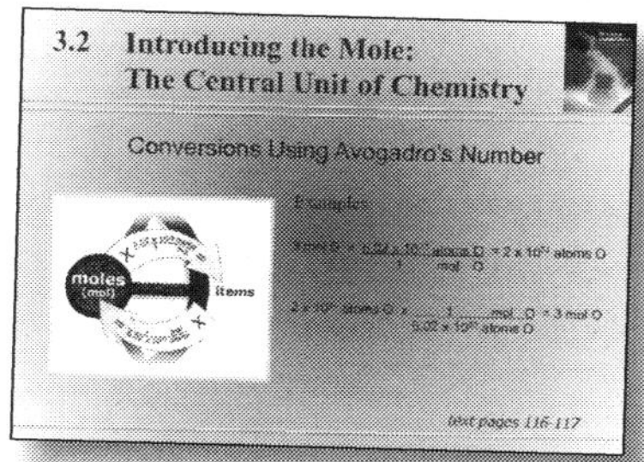

If your school does not have access to the Online Study Guide and you'd like more information — info@edvantageinteractive.com

1 Skills and Processes of Chemistry

This chapter focuses on the following AP Big Idea from the College Board:

Big Idea 1: The chemical elements are fundamental building materials of matter, and all matter can be understood in terms of arrangements of atoms. These atoms retain their identify in chemical reactions.

By the end of this chapter, you should be able to do the following:

- Demonstrate appropriate safety techniques and proper use of protective equipment
- Demonstrate skills in measuring and in recording data
- Communicate results and data in clear and understandable forms

---

By the end of this chapter, you should know the meaning of these **key terms**:

- accuracy
- analysis
- interpretation
- observation
- precision
- SI unit
- significant figures
- unit

In this chapter, you'll learn about the range of tools, skills, and techniques you'll be using as you study chemistry.

1.1 Staying Safe Around Matter

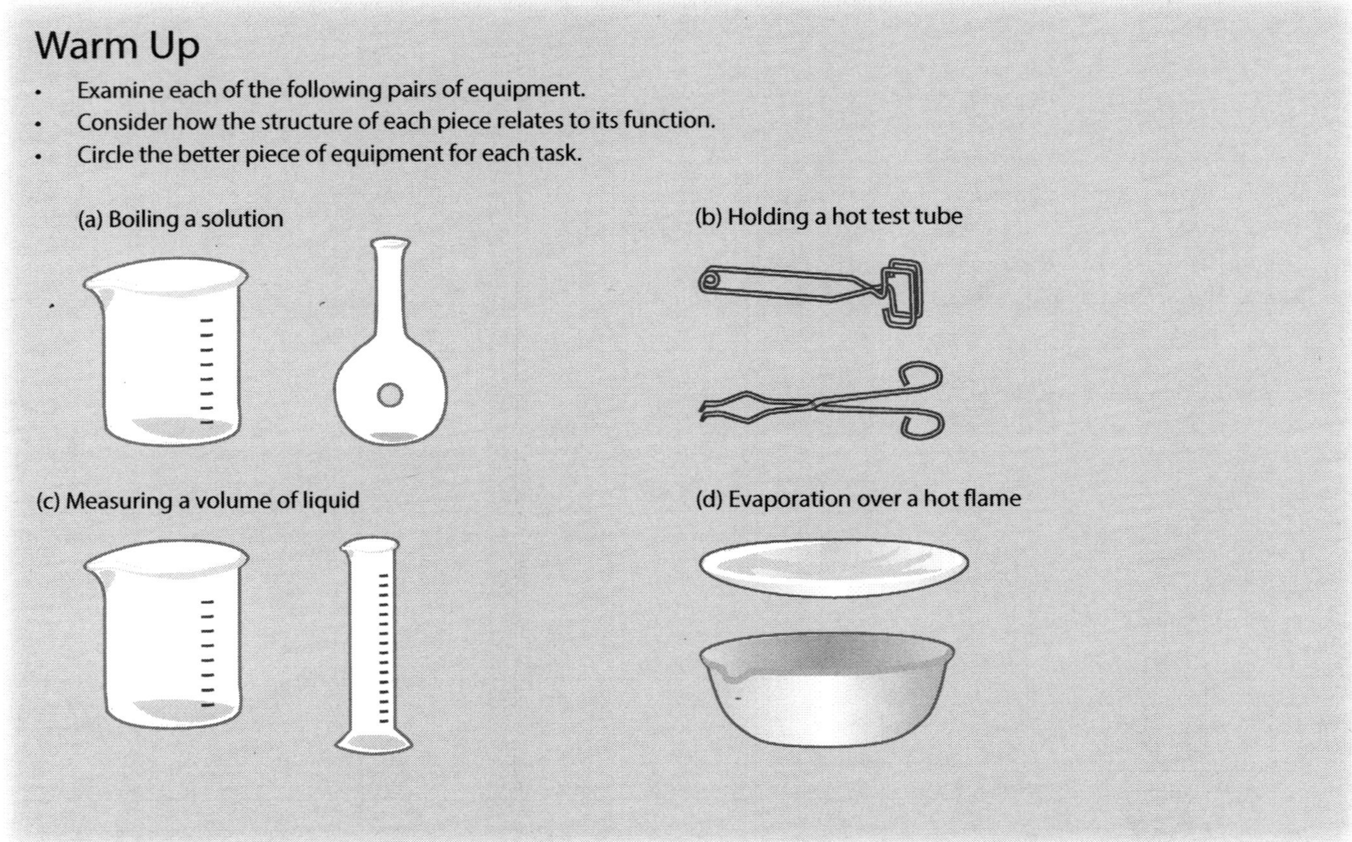

Chemistry Equipment and Its Uses

The equipment used for manipulating and measuring chemicals can be classified in a variety of ways. One of the most common methods of classification is based on the material it is made from. Tables 1.1.1 and 1.1.2 divide equipment into glassware and hardware.

Most of the glassware found in the laboratory is made of a special type of glass with a low *coefficient of expansion*. This simply means the glass expands so slowly as it is heated that it is unlikely to break. Two common brand names for this type of glassware are Pyrex® and Kimax®. Some glassware is made of ceramic material. It may be heated to red-hot temperatures without breaking or melting. Hardware is made of various types of metal including wrought iron, stainless steel, aluminum, and brass.

Table 1.1.1 *Commonly Used Glassware in the Chemistry Lab*

Glassware	Name	Use
	beaker	Holding liquids • may be graduated (sometimes in two directions) • has a white spot for labeling • various sizes including 50, 150, 250, 450, 650, and 1000 mL
	Erlenmeyer flask	Holding liquids • shape avoids loss due to splashing • used for titration • common sizes include 125, 250, and 500 mL
	Florence flask	Heating liquids • shape allows even distribution of heat while boiling • never graduated • common sizes include 250 and 500 mL
	test tubes	Holding liquids or solids • can be heated directly or in a water bath • may be used to mix small quantities of chemicals • large variety of sizes
	fluted funnel	Funneling liquids • useful for pouring liquids through small openings • can contain filter paper for separating solids from suspensions by filtration
	evaporating dish	Evaporating solvent • evaporation from a solution • can be used to dry a damp product • ceramic material allows direct heat to high temperatures
	watch glass	Holding or covering • useful for holding a sample of chemical • may cover a beaker or flask to prevent evaporation • holds chemicals while drying
	crucible	Heating to high temperatures • heating covered or partially covered samples • ceramic material may be directly heated until red hot

	pipe stem triangle	Providing a base to hold a crucible • sits atop a wrought-iron ring • stems are made of ceramic material
	graduated cylinder	Measuring volumes of liquids • sizes vary • commonly 10, 25, 50, 100, and 250 mL
	burette	Measuring volumes of liquids • delivers various volumes through a valve called a stop cock • more precise (exact) than the graduated cylinder
	pipette	Measuring volumes of liquids • may be graduated • may be volumetric (designed to deliver one specific volume) • liquid is drawn up with a pipette bulb or suction device
	thermometer	Measuring temperatures • bulb should be submerged in the fluid being measured • temperature ranges vary • most contain dyed alcohol • more precise thermometers contain mercury • commonly measure temperature in degrees Celsius

Quick Check

Working with a partner, design a classification scheme and use it to put the glassware into groups according to common characteristics.

Compare your classification scheme with that of another pair of students.

Table 1.1.2 *Commonly Used Hardware in the Chemistry Lab*

Hardware	Name	Use
	ring stand	Providing a post to attach • ring clamps, burette clamps, extension clamps, etc. • also called a utility stand
	ring clamp	Attaching to a ring stand • supports a ceramic pad, a pipe stem triangle, or an evaporating dish • may surround a beaker as a safety ring
	burette clamp	Attaching to a ring stand • holds a burette • may hold a test tube in a stationary position • may support the neck of a flask
	flint striker	Lighting a Bunsen burner • provides a spark by moving a flint across a file
	bunsen burner	Providing heat • adjusts flame temperature by addition of air through the barrel • adjusts flame height by turning the regulator valve
	test tube holder	Holding hot test tubes • used for heating test tubes over flame • used for removing test tubes from water baths
	beaker tongs	Lifting hot beakers • rubber cover allows tongs to firmly grasp and move beakers of all sizes
	crucible tongs	Holding hot crucibles • may remove or adjust crucible lid • holds hot evaporating dishes • NOT designed for lifting beakers or test tubes
	ceramic pad	Providing a base to hold glassware • sits atop a wrought-iron ring • provides a flat surface for beakers or flasks • sometimes called a wire gauze
	scoopula	Moving samples of solids • sometimes called a spatula • should NOT be used as a stirring rod (stirring rods should be glass)

Quick Check

Working with a partner, design a classification scheme and use it to put the hardware into groups according to common characteristics.

Compare your classification scheme with that of another pair of students.

Labelling Chemicals

Workplace Hazardous Materials Information System

The **Workplace Hazardous Materials Information System (WHMIS)** is the Canadian system for communicating information about the safety requirements for working with chemicals. The main components of WHMIS are:

- a labelling system consisting of eight specialized safety icons (see below)
- training programs for people who work with chemicals
- **Material Safety Data Sheets (MSDS)** providing information about chemicals

compressed gas

flammable and combustible material

oxidizing material (increases risk of fire)

poison and infectious material causing immediate and serious toxic effects

poison and infectious material causing other toxic effects

biohazardous infectious material

dangerously reactive material

corrosive material

People who work with chemicals are required to take WHMIS training with varying frequencies depending on their jobs. It is possible that you or some of your classmates may have taken WHMIS training for a part-time job. Your chemistry teacher has certainly had WHMIS training.

As a condition of sale, a Material Safety Data Sheet (MSDS) must be provided with every chemical purchased in Canada. Your chemistry teacher has a binder full of these sheets containing hazard information and safety procedures associated with each and every chemical in your science stock rooms and elsewhere in the school.

Quick Check

An excerpt from an MSDS for hydrochloric acid solution follows the questions below. This is only an excerpt. An actual MSDS may contain more than 15 sections, each of which may be quite detailed. Read this abbreviated excerpt carefully and answer these questions.

1. What WHMIS labels would you expect to find on hydrochloric acid?

   ____

2. Give a synonym for hydrochloric acid.

   ____

3. What are the chemicals that make up hydrochloric acid?

   ____

4. What are the hazards of spilling hydrochloric acid on the skin?

   ____

5. How should you treat a person who has ingested hydrochloric acid?

   ____

Material Safety Data Sheet

1. Product Identification

- Hydrochloric Acid
- Synonym: Muriatic Acid

2. Composition/Information on Ingredients

- Hydrogen Chloride 38% by weight
- Water 62% by weight

3. Hazards Identification

- Potential acute health effects
  - Skin Contact: Corrosive, irritant, permeation causing itching, reddening, scaling, or blistering
  - Eye Contact: Corrosive, irritant causing redness, watering, and itching
  - Inhalation: Irritation of respiratory tract, coughing, choking, or shortness of breath
- Potential chronic health effects
  - May be toxic to: kidneys, liver, mucous membranes, upper respiratory tract, skin, eyes, circulatory system, and teeth

4. First Aid Measures

- Eye contact: Remove contact lenses, rinse with cold water for 15 minutes, get medical attention immediately.
- Skin contact: Remove effected clothes, rinse with cold water for 15 minutes, get medical attention immediately.
- Inhalation: Remove to fresh air, if breathing is difficult; give oxygen, if not breathing; give artificial respiration.
- Ingestion: If swallowed, do not induce vomiting, loosen tight clothing, get medical attention immediately.

5. Handling and Storage

- Storage: Keep container tightly closed in a cool, well-ventilated area.

6. Stability and Reactivity Data

- Is highly reactive with metals.
- Reactive with oxidizing agents, organic materials, alkalis and water

Household Hazardous Products Labels

The Consumer Chemicals and Containers Regulations (CCCR) require specific packaging and labeling of **household products**. There are only four different household labels. These labels may be bordered in two different ways. The border indicates whether the label refers to the *container* or the *contents* within the container. The octagonal border refers to the contents of the labelled container while the triangular border refers to the container itself. The latest household labels are as follows:

corrosive product

flammable product

poisonous product

explosive container

Quick Check

What household labels would you expect to find on a container of muriatic acid?

Safety in the Chemistry Lab

Safety Equipment

Every chemistry laboratory has a number of items "built in" to the facility for use in case of an accident or simply to ensure the safest laboratory operation possible. It is important to know the location and instructions for operation of each of these items. Table 1.1.3 summarizes important information on each of these important pieces of equipment.

If you think you might need to use any of the equipment in this table for an emergency, don't hesitate. Call out to inform others of the situation and immediately use the equipment as instructed. Note that any accident requiring the use of the eyewash station, safety shower, or fire blanket is likely serious enough that medical attention should be sought quickly after using the equipment.

Table 1.1.3 *Laboratory Safety Equipment*

Safety Equipment	Information Regarding Operation
Fume hood	• Enclosed area equipped with fans to draw vapours out of the hood and vent them outside • May contain gas jets, sinks, lights, and electrical outlet • Enclosed by a sliding safety glass window • May store chemicals emitting toxic fumes • Useful for venting odours, smoke, and toxic fumes
Eyewash station	• If a chemical is splashed or spilled into the eyes, they should be held open and rinsed continuously for 10 to 15 min. Contact lenses should be removed. • Eyewash stations may be operated by pushing on a hand bar and/or a foot pedal. • Some labs may use a squeeze bottle apparatus or a piece of rubber tubing attached to a sink.
Safety shower	• Spills over a large portion of the body require removal of clothing and washing of the entire region for 10 to 15 min under the safety shower. • Safety showers are operated by pulling on a ring that will begin the flow of some 200 L of water over a drained area of the lab.

Fire extinguisher	• Small fires such as those that occur in a beaker or a crucible usually may be smothered by placing a ceramic pad or cover on top.
	• If a larger fire occurs, pull the safety pin from the top of the extinguisher, point the hose at the base of the fire, and squeeze. Extinguishers operate by depriving the fire of oxygen and by lowering the temperature.
	    • There are five classes of fires:
	    • Type A: wood or paper
	    • Type B: oil or grease (most chemicals)
	    • Type C: electrical equipment
	    • Type D: metals (such as magnesium)
	    • Type E: radioactive materials
	• Most extinguishers contain carbon dioxide and are good for class A, B, and C fires.

Fire blanket	• A fire extinguisher should *never* be used on a person. • *STOP, DROP, and ROLL* is the best way to extinguish a fire involving a person. A fire blanket may be used in combination with this process to smother the fire. • Fire blankets may be enclosed in a box or a cylindrical container attached to a wall, or they may be upright. An upright blanket may be wrapped around the victim while he or she is standing.
Emergency gas shut off	• The emergency gas shut off valve allows *all* gas outlets in the laboratory to be shut off at once. • To use the shut off, turn a handle so it is perpendicular to the gas line or simply push a large red button. • At the end of the day, this valve should always be left in the off position.
Spill control station	• Spill control stations contain absorbent pillows to soak up spills, safety goggles and gloves, and chemicals to neutralize acid and base spills. • Some labs simply have the neutralizing chemicals stored in a dedicated area. • Acid spills should be neutralized with sodium bicarbonate or baking soda. • Base spills should be neutralized with acetic acid or vinegar. • Neutralization is only necessary for large spills of concentrated reagents. Smaller spills may simply be diluted with water and wiped up with paper towel.

First aid kit	• All labs should have access to a first aid kit. The kit may be stored in a common storage area adjacent to the lab so that all teachers have easy access. • Such a kit should contain an antibiotic cream or ointment and plenty of bandages. • Burns are the most common injury in the chemistry lab. While ice followed by cold water is generally enough, the kit may contain a topical anesthetic cream. It is critical to ensure a student has no anesthetic allergies before using such a product. • Avoid burns from hot glass or metal by bringing your hand near the object first to test for heat. • Small cuts closely follow burns on the list of chemistry lab injuries. These may be treated with the antibiotic cream and a bandage.
Glass disposal container	• Broken glass should never be placed in the garbage can as this presents a hazard to the custodian. • A plastic bucket or a specially designated recyclables box can be found on a counter or the floor for the disposal of broken glassware or glass tubing.
Chemical disposal	• Containers clearly marked "Chemical Disposal" should be used for disposing solutions or precipitates containing heavy metals or any other toxic chemicals. • Some organic waste may release toxic fumes. Such waste often warrants its own container, which may be covered and/or placed in the fume hood. • Some chemicals such as dilute solutions of acids and bases and non-toxic salts may be flushed down the sink with plenty of water. • The ultimate judge of correct chemical disposal is, of course, your lab instructor.
Fire alarm	• Though it may be in the hall outside of your lab, you must know where the fire alarm is located.

Quick Check

1. How would you deal with each of the following accidents should it occur during a lab you are performing this year?

   (a) While heating a small amount of alcohol in a beaker, it bursts into flame.

   (b) Your partner hands you a piece of hot glass they've just bent after heating over a Bunsen burner.

   (c) A test tube full of concentrated hydrochloric acid is dropped and broken on the floor.

2. How could you have prevented each accident from happening to begin with?

Safety Procedures

Any time you know you will be working in the laboratory, it is important to arrive fully prepared to perform all work as safely as possible. We call this *lab preparedness*. The following are some things you should always do *before* you begin doing a lab.

- Read the entire experiment carefully, paying close attention to any safety issues. Prepare any data tables that may be required. Your teacher may ask you to prepare an abstract (summary) or a flow chart before you arrive for lab.
- Clear all binders, backpacks, book bags, coats, etc. away from your work area.
- Always wear eye protection during the laboratory period.
- Wear lab aprons or lab coats if available.
- Tie back long hair to keep it away from flames or chemicals.
- Secure loose sleeves or jewellery to keep them away from flames or chemicals.
- Consider wearing clothing made of natural fibres such as cotton and wool, as those are the most fire resistant fibres.
- Do not wear open-toed shoes during laboratory work.
- Be sure all equipment is in good working order. Do not use chipped glassware or damaged electrical equipment.
- Never attempt laboratory procedures without your instructor's permission and direct instruction.

Laboratory Technique

There are several things that all good chemists know about using equipment and chemicals in the lab. We refer to these things as *proper laboratory technique*.

- Always approach lab work with a business-like attitude and keep voices kept to a reasonable volume.
- Do not consume food or drink or chew gum during laboratory period.
- Never touch or taste chemicals.
- Never inhale chemicals directly. Use your hand to sweep odours toward you.
- Bring your hand near metal or glass to test for heat. Handle hot equipment with appropriate tongs, test tube holders, or mitts.
- Never use open flames around flammable materials. Use a hot plate or mantle.
- Clamp test tubes near the top and hold at a 45° angle with constant motion and the end pointed away from everyone during heating.
- Never pipette liquids directly by mouth.
- Never leave heat sources unattended. Turn off Bunsen burners and hot plates when not in use.
- Read the labels on all chemicals at least twice. Always grasp bottles on the label side so that drips do not obscure the label.
- Always use an appropriate lubricant such as glycerin or saliva when inserting glass tubing or thermometers into rubber stoppers.
- When diluting chemicals, always begin with water. It is particularly important to add acid to water, never the other way around.

Laboratory Clean Up

Last, but not least, there are a number of things that relate to **laboratory clean up**. Some of these things may be related to accidents that occur in the lab. Others simply relate to leaving the lab in as good, or better, condition than you found it.

- Sweep broken glassware into a dustpan and place it in the proper disposal container. Always notify neighbours of any broken glass.
- Clean up spilled chemicals immediately as outlined in Table 1.1.3. Be sure to notify neighbours of any chemical spill.
- Never return unused chemical to the original stock bottle. Either share it with another student or properly dispose of any excess.
- Always wash glassware well with soap and a proper brush, then rinse it, and leave it to air dry.
- Rinse your hands well following the use of any chemicals. Wipe your lab bench with a damp paper towel when you have completed your lab.
- Clean up should begin with a reasonable amount of time to allow all equipment to be washed well and replaced in the appropriate spot.
- For experiments that run for more than one period, clearly label all materials and leave them in the appropriate place as instructed by your teacher.

1.1 Activity: Safety in the Laboratory

Question

Where is the safety equipment located in your chemistry laboratory?

Procedure

1. In the space below, draw an outline map of your chemistry laboratory, including every item in Table 1.1.3.

2. Add at least five more items that contribute to safety in your lab.

1.1 Review Questions

1. Where is the closest fire alarm to your chemistry laboratory?

2. Outline the route you should follow in case of a fire alarm while you are in chemistry class.

3. How many fire extinguishers are in your laboratory? What are their classifications?

4. Knowing you have lab on a particular school day, describe how you should dress.

5. Give the *name* and *use* of each of the following pieces of equipment:

6. List three things you should do before beginning any chemistry experiment.

7. Give three uses for the fume hood.

8. What is the most common injury in the chemistry lab? How might you avoid this injury? How would you treat this injury?

9. How would you assist your lab partner in each of the following cases?
   (a) Partner has spilled a chemical into his or her eyes.

   (b) Partner's clothing has caught fire.

   (c) Partner has spilled concentrated acid onto the floor.

   (d) Partner took more chemical than required for the lab.

   (e) Partner has broken a test tube on the floor.

10. What is the meaning of each of the following labels?

11. Outline a three-step procedure for cleaning glassware at the end of the period.

12. Why should long hair always be secured back during lab?

13. Why do you suppose food and drink are not allowed during lab?

14. What do you think is safer: the laboratory or your kitchen? Explain why.

15. Give the name and use of each of the following pieces of equipment:

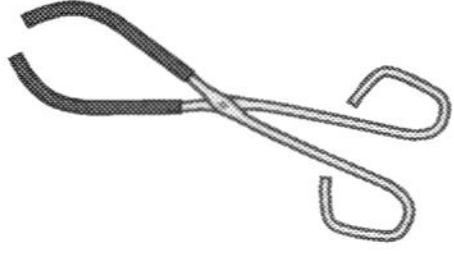

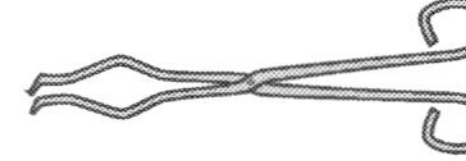

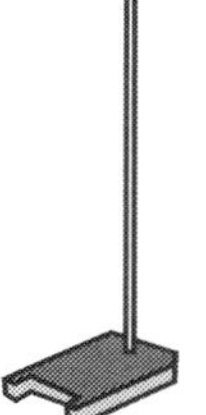

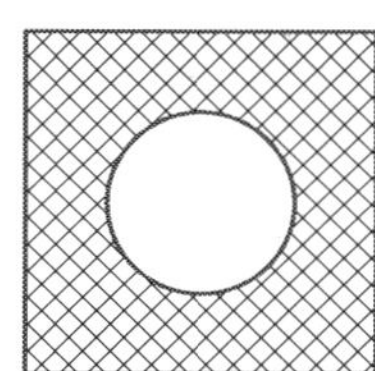

16. Where should binders, book bags, and backpacks be stored during the lab?

17. What is an MSDS? Where might an MSDS be found in your school?

18. Where would you dispose of each of the following?
(a) a few milliliters of excess dilute acid

(b) a sample of heavy metal precipitate

(c) an excess piece of glass tubing

(d) used litmus paper

(e) a few milliliters of excess acetone (nail polish remover)

19. What is the meaning of each of the following labels?

20. Give four things to keep in mind while heating a test tube half-filled with liquid.

1.2 Laboratory and Reporting Skills

Warm Up

Classify the following observations as *quantitative* or *qualitative* by placing a checkmark in the correct column. Hint: Look at each syllable of those words: *quantitative* and *qualitative*. What do they seem to mean?

Observation	Quantitative	Qualitative
The melting point of paradichlorobenzene is 53.5°C.		
Mercury(II) oxide is a deep red powder.		
The density of scandium metal is 2.989 g/cm^3.		
Copper metal may be pulled into a wire. (It is ductile.)		
Silver metal forms a black layer of tarnish over time.		
Zinc has a specific heat capacity of 388 J/(kg·K).		
Oxygen gas supports combustion.		

The Scientific Method

How do you approach the problems you encounter in everyday life? Think about beginning a new class at the start of the school year, for example. The first few days you make observations and collect data. You might not think of it this way, but in fact, when you observe your classmates, the classroom and your instructor, you actually are making observations and collecting data. This process will inevitably lead you to make some decisions as you consider the best way to interact with this new environment. Who would you like for a partner in this class? Where do you want to sit? Are you likely to interact well with this particular teacher? You are drawing conclusions. This tried and true method of solving problems is called the **scientific method**.

Figure 1.2.1 *Robert Boyle*

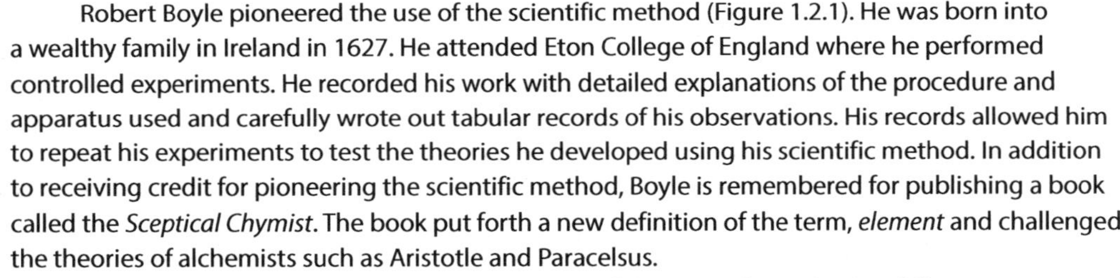

Robert Boyle pioneered the use of the scientific method (Figure 1.2.1). He was born into a wealthy family in Ireland in 1627. He attended Eton College of England where he performed controlled experiments. He recorded his work with detailed explanations of the procedure and apparatus used and carefully wrote out tabular records of his observations. His records allowed him to repeat his experiments to test the theories he developed using his scientific method. In addition to receiving credit for pioneering the scientific method, Boyle is remembered for publishing a book called the *Sceptical Chymist*. The book put forth a new definition of the term, *element* and challenged the theories of alchemists such as Aristotle and Paracelsus.

Different groups of scientists outline the parts of the scientific method in different ways. Here is one example, illustrating its steps.

Steps of the Scientific Method

1. **Observation**: Involves collecting data. **Quantitative** has numbers or quantities associated with it. **Qualitative** data describes qualities or changes in the quality of matter including a substance's colour, odour, or physical state. Observations may also be categorized as **physical**, related to the colour, the temperature at which the substance changes state or the density. Or they may be **chemical**, related to the substance's chemical reactivity or its behaviour during a chemical change.
2. **Statement of a hypothesis**: The formulation of a statement in an "if…then…" format that explains the observations.
3. **Experimentation**: After making a set of observations and formulating a hypothesis, scientists devise an experiment to determine whether the hypothesis accurately explains the observations. Depending on the results, the hypothesis may be adjusted and experiments repeated collecting new observations a multitude of times.
   Frequently the results of an experiment differ from what was expected. There are a variety of reasons this might happen. Things that contribute to such differences are called **sources of error**. Sources of error are different from mistakes. Rather, they are things we have *no control over*.
4. **Statement of a Theory**: Once enough information has been collected from a series of experiments, a coherent set of explanations called a theory may be deduced. This theory may lead to a **model** that helps us explain a collection of observations. (Sometimes the scientific method leads to a **law**, which is a general statement of *fact*, without an accompanied set of explanations.)

Quick Check

1. What is the difference between a law and a theory?

____

2. What are the fundamental steps of the scientific method?

____

____

____

____

3. Place a checkmark in the appropriate column to indicate whether each of the reasons for determining an incorrect mass is a mistake or a source of error.

Event	Mistake	Source of Error
The balance used to weigh the product was not zeroed.		
The product being weighed was damp.		
The balance used to weigh the product only reads to the nearest centigram.		
Your partner read the value for a mass incorrectly.		
You made a subtraction error when determining the mass.		

Using Scientific Notation

Because it deals with atoms, and they are so incredibly small, the study of chemistry is notorious for using very large and very tiny numbers. For example, if you determine the total number of atoms in a sample of matter, the value will be very large. If, on the other hand, you determine an atom's diameter or the mass of an atom, the value will be extremely small. The method of reporting an ordinary, expanded number in scientific notation is very handy for both of these things.

Scientific notation refers to the method of representing numbers in *exponential form*. Exponential numbers have two parts. Consider the following example:

24 500 becomes 2.45×10^4 in scientific notation

Convention states that the first portion of a value in scientific notation should always be expressed as a number **between 1 and 10**. This portion is called the **mantissa** or the **decimal portion**. The second portion is the base 10 raised to some power. It is called the **ordinate** or the **exponential portion**.

mantissa → $\underline{2.45} \times 10^4$ and $2.45 \times \underline{10^4}$ ← ordinate

A positive exponent in the ordinate indicates a *large number* in scientific notation, while a negative exponent indicates a *small number*. In fact the exponent indicates the number of 10s that must be multiplied together to arrive at the number represented by the scientific notation. If the exponents are negative, the exponent indicates the number of tenths that must be multiplied together to arrive at the number. In other words, the exponent indicates the number of places the decimal in the mantissa must be moved to correctly arrive at the **expanded notation** (also called standard notation) version of the number.

A *positive exponent* indicates the number of *places* the decimal must be moved to the *right*, while a *negative exponent* indicates the number of *places* the decimal must be moved to the *left*.

Quick Check

1. Change the following numbers from scientific notation to expanded notation.
   (a) 2.75×10^3 = 2750

   (b) 5.143×10^{-2} = .05143
2. Change the following numbers from expanded notation to scientific notation.
   (a) 69 547 = 6.9547×10^4

   (b) 0.001 68 = 1.68×10^{-3}

don't round unless it says to

Multiplication and Division in Scientific Notation

To *multiply* two numbers in scientific notation, we *multiply the mantissas* and state their product multiplied by 10, raised to a power that is the *sum of the exponents*.

$$(A \times 10^a) \times (B \times 10^b) = (A \times B) \times 10^{(a+b)}$$

To *divide* two numbers in scientific notation, we divide one mantissa by the other and state their quotient multiplied by 10, raised to a power that is the *difference* between the exponents.

$$(A \times 10^a) \div (B \times 10^b) = (A \div B) \times 10^{(a-b)}$$

Sample Problems — Multiplication and Division Using Scientific Notation

Solve the following problems, expressing the answer in scientific notation.

1. $(2.5 \times 10^3) \times (3.2 \times 10^6) =$
2. $(9.4 \times 10^{-4}) \div (10^{-6}) =$

What to Think about	How to Do It
Question 1	
1. Find the product of the mantissas.	$2.5 \times 3.2 = 8.0$ (the new mantissa)
2. Raise 10 to the sum of the exponents to determine the ordinate.	$10^{(3+6)} = \underline{10^9}$ (the new ordinate)
3. State the answer as the product of the new mantissa and ordinate.	$(2.5 \times 10^3) \times (3.2 \times 10^6) = 8.0 \times 10^9$
Question 2	
1. Find the quotient of the mantissas. When no mantissa is shown, it is assumed that the mantissa is 1.	$9.4 \div 1 = \underline{9.4}$ (the new mantissa)
2. Raise 10 to the difference of the exponents to determine the ordinate.	$10^{(-4-(-6))} = \underline{10^2}$ (the new ordinate)
3. State the answer as the product of the mantissa and ordinate.	$(9.4 \times 10^{-4}) \div (10^{-6}) = 9.4 \times 10^2$

Practice Problems — Multiplication and Division Using Scientific Notation

Solve the following problems, expressing the answer in scientific notation, *without* using a calculator. Repeat the questions using a calculator and compare your answers. Compare your method of solving with a calculator with that of another student.

1. $(4 \times 10^3) \times (2 \times 10^4) =$ ________________
2. $(9.9 \times 10^5) \div (3.3 \times 10^3) =$ ________________
3. $[(3.1 \times 10^{-4}) \times (6.0 \times 10^7)] \div (2.0 \times 10^5) =$ ________________
4. $10^9 \div (5.0 \times 10^6) =$ ________________
5. $[(4.5 \times 10^{12}) \div (1.5 \times 10^4)] \times (2.5 \times 10^{-6}) =$ ________________

Addition and Subtraction in Scientific Notation

Remember that a number in proper scientific notation will always have a mantissa between 1 and 10. Sometimes it becomes necessary to *shift* a decimal in order to express a number in proper scientific notation.

The *number of places* shifted by the decimal is indicated by an *equivalent change* in the *value of the exponent*. If the decimal is shifted *LEFT*, the *exponent* becomes *LARGER*; shifting the decimal to the *RIGHT* causes the *exponent* to become *SMALLER*.

Another way to remember this is if the *mantissa becomes smaller* following a shift, the *exponent becomes larger*. Consequently, if the *exponent becomes larger*, the *mantissa becomes smaller*. Consider AB.C × 10^x: if the decimal is shifted to change the value of the mantissa by 10^n times, the value of x changes $-n$ times.

For example, a number such as 18 235.0 × 10^2 (1 823 500 in standard notation) requires the decimal to be shifted 4 places to the left to give a mantissa between 1 and 10, that is 1.823 50. A LEFT shift *4* places, means the exponent in the ordinate becomes *4 numbers* LARGER (from 10^2 to 10^6). The correct way to express 18 235.0 × 10^2 in scientific notation is 1.823 50 × 10^6. Notice the new mantissa is $10^{\underline{4}}$ *smaller*, so the exponent becomes 4 numbers larger.

Quick Check

Express each of the given values in proper scientific notation in the second column. Now write each of the given values from the *first* column in expanded form in the third column. Then write each of your answers from the *second* column in expanded form. How do the expanded answers compare?

	Given Value	Proper Notation	Expanded Form	Expanded Answer
1.	6 014.51 × 10^2			
2.	0.001 6 × 10^7			
3.	38 325.3 × 10^{-6}			
4.	0.4196 × 10^{-2}			

When adding or subtracting numbers in scientific notation, it is important to realize that we add or subtract only the mantissa. *Do not add or subtract the exponents!* To begin, it is often necessary to shift the decimal to be sure the value of the exponent is the same for both numbers that will be added or subtracted. Once the arithmetic has been completed, the decimal may be shifted again if required to ensure that the mantissa is, indeed, between 1 and 10.

Shift the decimal to obtain the *same value for the exponent* in the ordinate of both numbers to be added or subtracted. Then simply *sum or take the difference of the mantissas*. Convert back to proper scientific notation when finished.

Sample Problems — Addition and Subtraction in Scientific Notation

Solve the following problems, expressing the answer in proper scientific notation.

1. $(5.19 \times 10^3) - (3.14 \times 10^2) =$
2. $(2.17 \times 10^{-3}) + (6.40 \times 10^{-5}) =$

What to Think about	How to Do It
Question 1	
1. Begin by shifting the decimal of one of the numbers and changing the exponent so that both numbers share the *same exponent*. For consistency, adjust one of the numbers so that *both* numbers have the *larger* of the two ordinates. The goal is for both mantissas to be multiplied by 10^3. This means the exponent in the second number should be increased by one. Increasing the exponent requires the decimal to shift to the left (so the mantissa becomes smaller).	3.14×10^2 becomes 0.314×10^3
2. Once both ordinates are the same, the mantissas are simply subtracted.	5.19×10^3 -0.314×10^3 4.876×10^3
Question 1 — Another Approach	
1. It is interesting to note that we could have altered the first number instead. In that case, 5.19×10^3 would have become 51.9×10^2.	51.9×10^2 -3.14×10^2 48.76×10^2
2. In this case, the difference results in a number that is not in proper scientific notation as the mantissa is greater than 10.	
3. Consequently, a further step is needed to convert the answer back to proper scientific notation. Shifting the decimal one place to the left (mantissa becomes smaller) requires an increase of 1 to the exponent.	48.76×10^2 becomes 4.876×10^3
Question 2	
1. As with differences, begin by shifting the decimal of one of the numbers and changing the exponent so both numbers share the same ordinate. The *larger ordinate* in this case is 10^{-3}.	2.17×10^{-3} will be left as is.
2. Increasing the exponent in the second number from –5 to –3 requires the decimal to be shifted two to the left (make the mantissa smaller).	6.40×10^{-5} becomes 0.0640×10^{-3}
3. Once the exponents agree, the mantissas are simply summed.	2.17×10^{-3} $+ 0.0640 \times 10^{-3}$ 2.2340×10^{-3}
4. The alternative approach involves one extra step, but gives the same answer.	217×10^{-5} $+ 6.40 \times 10^{-5}$ 223.40×10^{-5} becomes 2.2340×10^{-3}

Practice Problems — Addition and Subtraction in Scientific Notation

Solve the following problems, expressing the answer in scientific notation, *without* using a calculator. Repeat the questions using a calculator and compare your answers. Compare your use of the exponential function on the calculator with that of a partner.

1. 8.068×10^8
   -4.14×10^7

2. 6.228×10^{-4}
   $+4.602 \times 10^{-3}$

3. 49.001×10^1
   $+ \quad 10^{-1}$

Scientific Notation and Exponents

Occasionally a number in scientific notation will be raised to some power. When such a case arises, it's important to remember when one exponent is raised to the power of another, the exponents are multiplied by one another. Consider a problem like $(10^3)^2$. This is really just $(10 \times 10 \times 10)^2$ or $(10 \times 10 \times 10 \times 10 \times 10 \times 10)$. So we see this is the same as $10^{(3 \times 2)}$ or 10^6.

$$(A \times 10^a)^b = A^b \times 10^{(a \times b)}$$

Quick Check

Solve the following problems, expressing the answer in scientific notation, *without* the use of a calculator. Repeat the problems with a calculator and compare your answers.

1. $(10^3)^5$
2. $(2 \times 10^2)^3$
3. $(5 \times 10^4)^2$
4. $(3 \times 10^5)^2 \times (2 \times 10^4)^2$

Pictorial Representation of Data — Graphing

Often in scientific investigations, we are interested in measuring how the value of some property changes as we vary something that affects it. We call the value that responds to the variation the **dependent variable**, while the other value is the **independent variable**. For example, we might want to measure the extension of a spring as we attach different masses to it. In this case, the extension would be the dependent variable, and the mass would be the independent variable. Notice that the amount of extension depends on the mass loaded and not the other way around. The variable "time" is nearly always independent.

The series of paired measurements collected during such an investigation is quantitative data. It is usually arranged in a **data table**. Tables of data should indicate the *unit of measurement* at the top of each column. The information in such a table becomes even more useful if it is presented in the form of a **graph** ("graph" is the Greek word root meaning "picture"). The independent data is plotted on the *x*-axis. A graph reveals many data points not listed in a data table.

Once a graph is drawn, it can be used to find a mathematical **relationship** (equation) that indicates how the variable quantities depend on each other. The first step to determining the relationship is to calculate the **proportionality constant** or **slope** "***m***" for the *line of best fit*. Curved graphs must be manipulated mathematically before a constant can be determined. Such manipulation is beyond the scope of this course. First, the constant is determined by finding the change in *y* over the change in *x* ($\Delta y/\Delta x$ or the "rise over the run"). Then substitute the *y* and *x* variable names and the calculated value for *m*, including its units, into the general equation $y = mx + b$. The result will be an equation that describes the relationship represented by our data.

$y = mx + b$ is the general form for the equation of a *straight line relationship* where m represents the *slope, determined by* $m = \Delta y/\Delta x$. In scientific relationships, the slope includes units and represents the constant that relates two variables. For this reason, it is sometimes represented by a ***K***.

The three most common types of graphic relationships are shown in Figure 1.2.2.

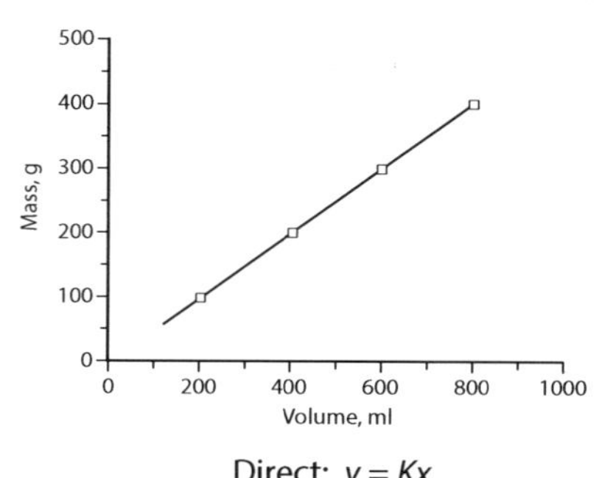

Direct: $y = Kx$

(y and x increase in direct proportion)

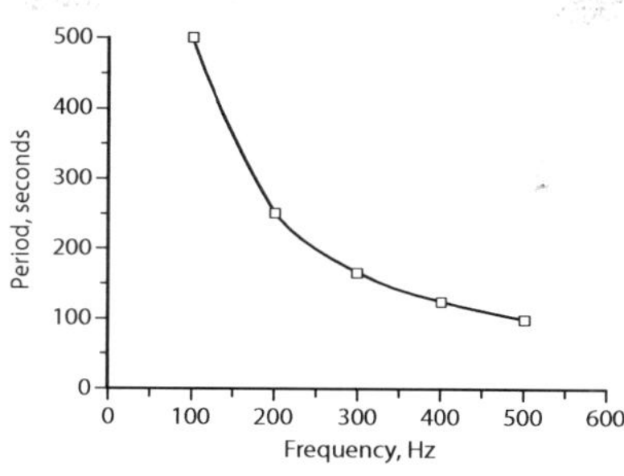

Inverse: $y = K/x$

(as x increases, y decreases)

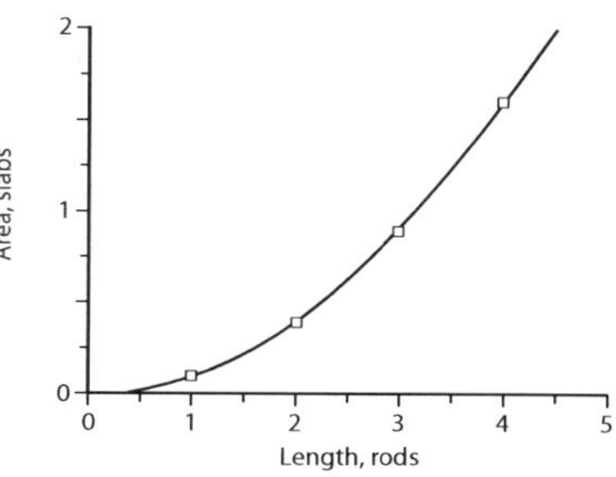

Exponential: $y = Kx^n$

(as x increases, y increases more quickly)

Figure 1.2.2 *Three common types of graphic relationships*

Sample Problem — Determination of a Relationship from Data

Find the relationship for the graphed data below:

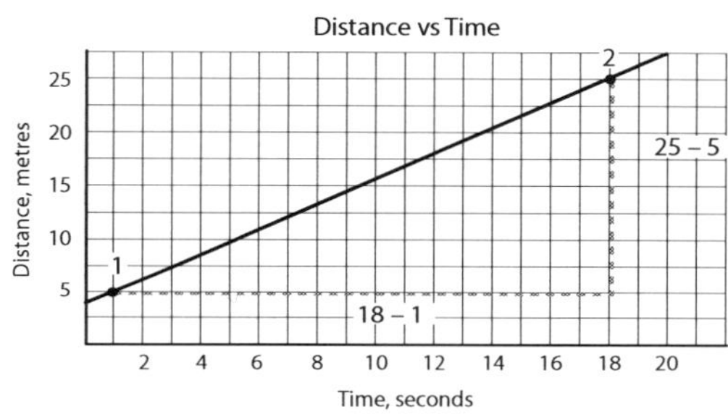

What to Think about	How to Do It
1. Determine the constant of proportionality (the slope) for the straight line. To do this, select two points on the line of best fit. These should be points whose values are easy to determine on both axes. *Do not use data points* to determine the constant. Determine the change in y (Δy) and the change in x (Δx) including the units. The constant is $\Delta y / \Delta x$.	Δy is 25–5 = 20 m Δx is 18 – 1 = 17 s 20 m/17 s = 1.18 m/s
2. The relationship is determined by subbing in the *variable names* and the constant into the general equation, $y = Kx + b$. Often, a straight line graph passes through the origin, in which case, $y = Kx$.	Distance = (1.18 m)Time + 4.0 m.

Practice Problem — Determination of a Relationship from Data

Examine the following graphs. What *type of relationship* does each represent? Give the full relationship described by graph (c).

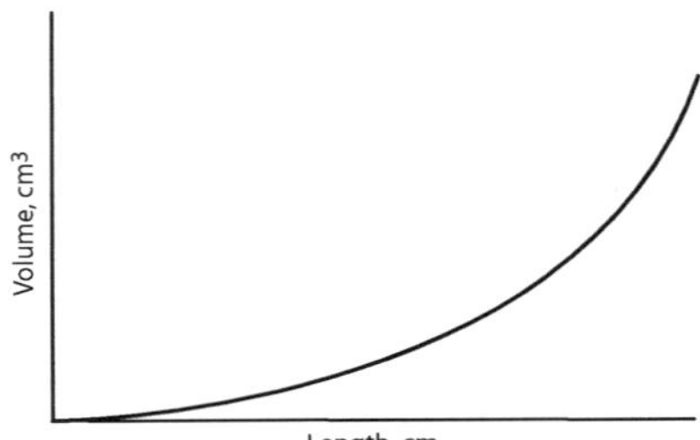

(a)

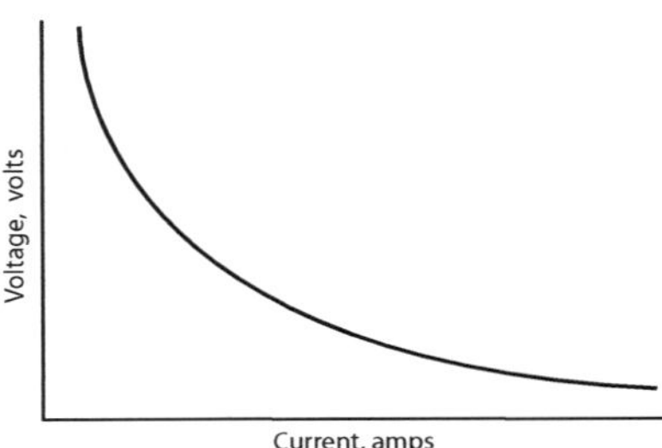

(b)

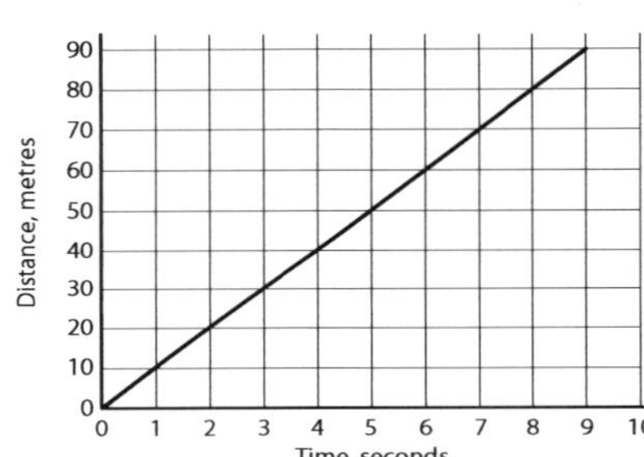

(c)

1.2 Activity: Graphing Relationships

Question

Can you produce a graph given a set of experimental data?

Background

A beaker full of water is placed on a hotplate and heated over a period of time. The temperature is recorded at regular intervals. The following data was collected.

Temperature (°C)	Time (min)
22	0
30	2
38	4
46	6
54	8
62	10
70	12

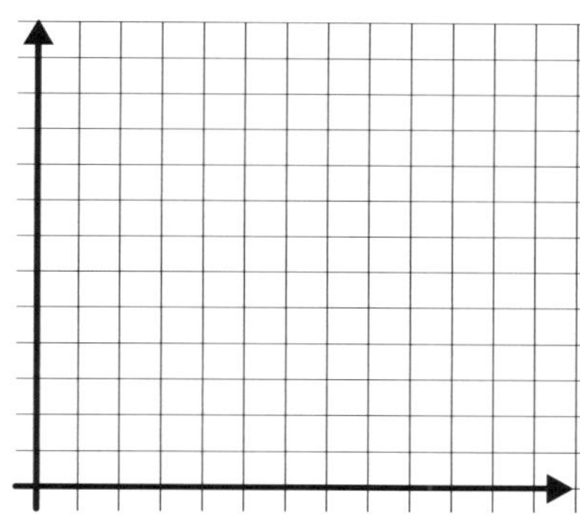

Procedure

1. Use the grid above to plot a graph of temperature against time. (Time goes on the *x*-axis.)

Results and Discussion

1. What type of relationship was studied during this investigation?

2. What is the constant (be sure to include the units)?

3. What temperature was reached at 5 minutes?

4. Use the graph to determine the relationship between temperature and time.

5. How long would it take the temperature to reach 80°C?

6. What does the *y*-intercept represent?

7. Give a source of error that might cause your graph to vary from that expected.

1.2 Review Questions

1. Use the steps of the scientific method to design a test for the following hypotheses:
   (a) If a person takes vitamin C daily, then they will get fewer colds.

   (b) If cyclists ride titanium bicycles, then they will win more races.

2. Complete the following table for the listed observations by checking the appropriate columns.

Property Observed	Qualitative	Quantitative
Freezes at 52.0°C		
Dissolves in ethylene glycol		
Fractures into cubic crystals		
5.4 mol dissolve in each litre		

3. Complete the following table for the listed observations by checking the appropriate columns.

Property Observed	Qualitative	Quantitative
Attracts to a magnet		
Changes to $Br_2(l)$ at –7.2°C		
Has a density of 4.71 g/mL		
Is a bright orange solid crystal		

4. Convert the following numbers from *scientific* notation to *expanded* notation and vice versa (be sure the scientific notation is expressed correctly).

Scientific Notation	Expanded Notation
3.08×10^4	
	960
4.75×10^{-3}	
	0.000 484
0.0062×10^5	

5. Give the product or quotient of each of the following problems (express all answers in proper form scientific notation). Do **not** use a calculator.
   (a) $(8.0 \times 10^3) \times (1.5 \times 10^6) =$

   (b) $(1.5 \times 10^4) \div (2.0 \times 10^2) =$

   (c) $(3.5 \times 10^{-2}) \times (6.0 \times 10^5) =$

   (d) $(2.6 \times 10^7) \div (6.5 \times 10^{-4}) =$

6. Give the product or quotient of each of the following problems (express all answers in proper form scientific notation). Do **not** use a calculator.

(a) $(3.5 \times 10^4) \times (3.0 \times 10^5) =$

(b) $(7.0 \times 10^6) \div (1.75 \times 10^2) =$

(c) $(2.5 \times 10^{-3}) \times (8.5 \times 10^{-5}) =$

(d) $(2.6 \times 10^5) \div (6.5 \times 10^{-2}) =$

7. Solve the following problems, expressing the answer in scientific notation, *without* using a calculator. Repeat the questions using a calculator and compare your answers.

(a) $\begin{array}{r} 4.034 \times 10^5 \\ \underline{-2.12 \times 10^4} \end{array}$

(b) $\begin{array}{r} 3.114 \times 10^{-6} \\ \underline{+2.301 \times 10^{-5}} \end{array}$

(c) $\begin{array}{r} 26.022 \times 10^2 \\ \underline{+7.04 \times 10^{-1}} \end{array}$

8. Solve the following problems, expressing the answer in scientific notation, *without* using a calculator. Repeat the questions using a calculator and compare your answers.

(a) $\begin{array}{r} 2.115 \times 10^8 \\ \underline{-1.11 \times 10^7} \end{array}$

(b) $\begin{array}{r} 9.332 \times 10^{-3} \\ \underline{+6.903 \times 10^{-4}} \end{array}$

(c) $\begin{array}{r} 68.166 \times 10^2 \\ \underline{+ \quad\quad \times 10^{-1}} \end{array}$

9. Solve each of the following problems *without* a calculator. Express your answer in correct form scientific notation. Repeat the questions using a calculator and compare.

(a) $(10^{-4})^3$ (b) $(4 \times 10^5)^3$ (c) $(7 \times 10^9)^2$ d. $(10^2)^2 \times (2 \times 10)^3$

10. Solve each of the following problems *without* a calculator. Express your answer in correct form scientific notation. Repeat the questions using a calculator and compare.

(a) $(6.4 \times 10^{-6} + 2.0 \times 10^{-7}) \div (2 \times 10^6 + 3.1 \times 10^7)$

(b) $\dfrac{3.4 \times 10^{-17} \times 1.5 \times 10^4}{1.5 \times 10^{-4}}$

(c) $(2 \times 10^3)^3 \times [(6.84 \times 10^3) \div (3.42 \times 10^3)]$

(d) $\dfrac{(3 \times 10^2)^3 + (4 \times 10^3)^2}{1 \times 10^4}$

11. Use the grid provided to plot graphs of mass against volume for a series of metal pieces with the given volumes. Plot all three graphs on the same set of axes with the independent variable (volume in this case) on the *x*-axis. Use a different colour for each graph.

Volume (mL)	Copper (g)	Aluminum (g)	Platinum (g)
2.0	17.4	5.4	42.9
8.0	71.7	21.6	171.6
12.0	107.5	32.4	257.4
15.0	134.4	40.5	321.8
19.0	170.2	51.3	407.6

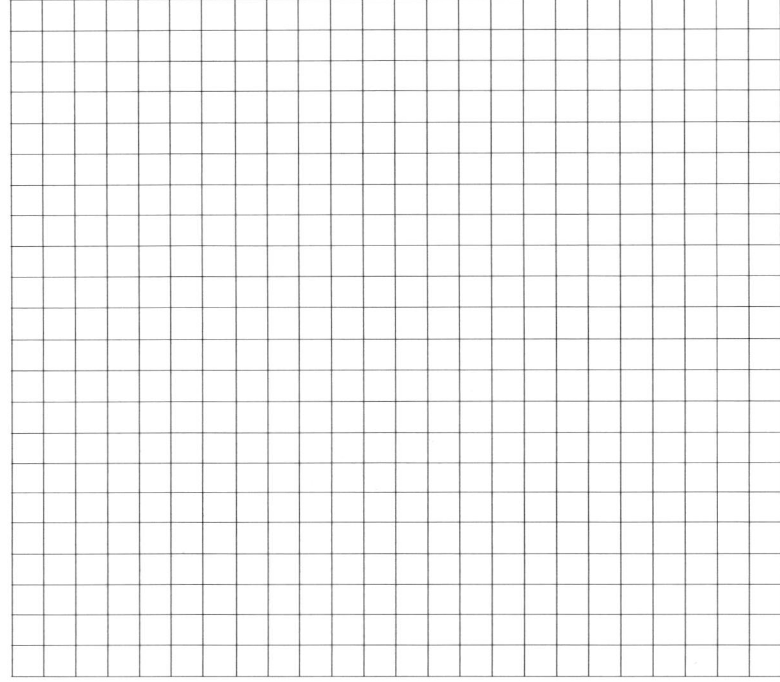

(a) Determine the constant for each metal.

(b) The constant represents each metal's density. Which metal is most dense?

12. Use the grid provided to plot two separate graphs, (a) and (b), for each the following sets of data. Be sure to draw a *smooth curve* through the points. Indicate the type of relationship represented by each graph.

Initial Rate (*y*) (mol/L/s)	Concentration (mol/L)		Volume (*y*) (L)	Pressure (kPa)
0.003	0.05		5.0	454
0.012	0.10		10.0	227
0.048	0.20		15.0	151
0.075	0.25		20.0	113
0.108	0.30		25.0	91
0.192	0.40		30.0	76

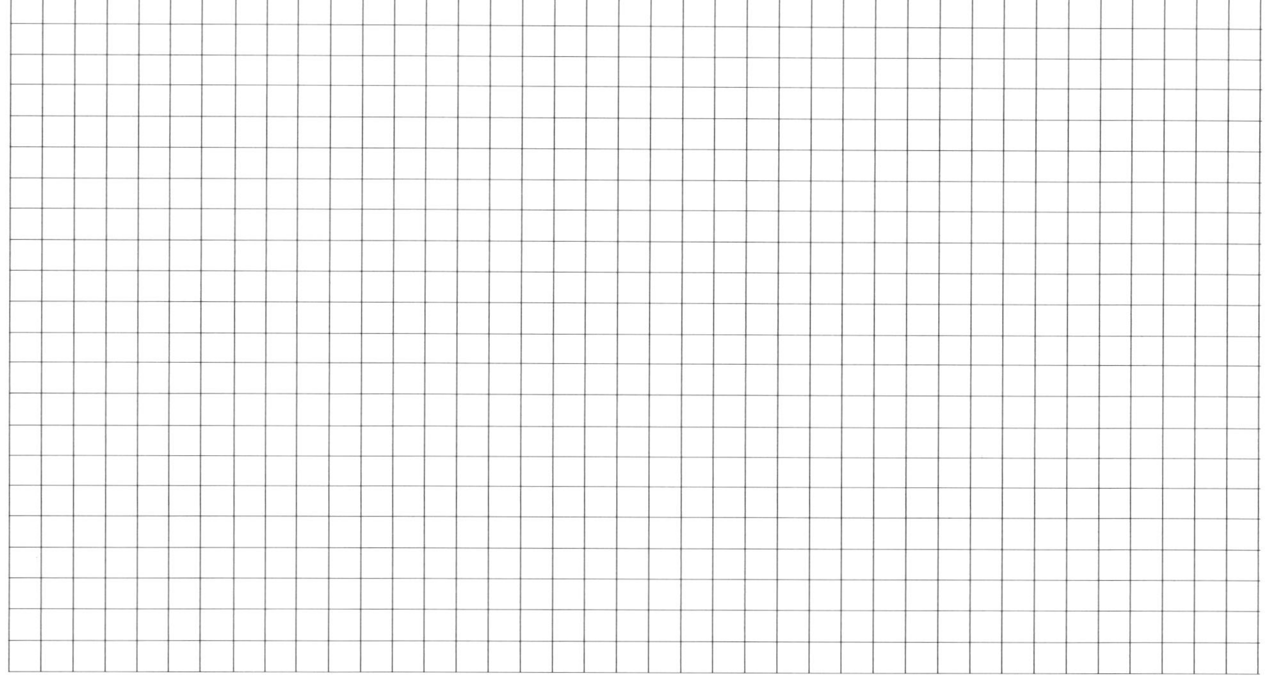

13. Many science departments use a still to produce their own distilled water. Data representing the volume of distilled water produced over a particular period of time might look like the data shown in the table.

Volume of Distilled Water (L)	Distillation Time (h)
0.8	0.4
1.6	0.8
2.4	1.2
5.0	2.5
7.2	3.6
9.8	4.9

(a) Plot this data on your own piece of graph paper. Where should time be plotted?

(b) Determine the constant for your graph. Show all work on the graph.

(c) Determine the relationship between volume and time.

(d) Assume the still was left on overnight. What volume of water would be collected if a period of 14 h passed?

(e) How long would it take to produce 12.5 L of water with this still?

1.3 Measuring and Recording Significant Data

Warm Up

Draw lines to match the following measured values, stated in SI units (International System of Units), with the appropriate everyday measurement.

SI measured value	Equivalent Everyday Measured Quantity
1 mm	width across a small fingernail
100 kPa	distance from your fingertips to your nose
1 L	pressure exerted by Earth's atmosphere
1 g	one-sixtieth of one minute in time
1 km	thickness of one dime
1 m	length of 10 football fields
1 s	volume of 1000 mL of milk
1 cm	mass of one raisin

SI Units

The **SI system (International System of Units)** is the modern metric system of measurement and the dominant system of international commerce and trade. The abbreviation SI comes from the French, Système international d'unités. The SI system was developed in 1960 and is maintained by the International Bureau of Weights and Measures (BIPM) in France. It is a non-static system devised around the seven base units listed below. Its non-static nature means SI units may be created and definitions may be modified through international agreement as measurement technology progresses and the precision of measuring devices improves. The SI system is the primary system of measurement in all but a small number of countries. The seven fundamental SI units are given in Table 1.3.1.

The following are some important SI rules or conventions:

- Unit symbols are always lower case letters unless the unit is named after a person. The one exception to this rule is L for litres. The full names of units are always written in lower case with the exception of *degrees Celsius*.
- Unit symbols should never be pluralized.
- Symbols should only be followed by a period at the end of a sentence.
- In general, the term *mass* replaces the term *weight*.
- The symbol cc should not be used in place of mL or cm^3.
- For values less than 1, use a 0 in front of the decimal point (e.g., 0.54 g not .54 g).
- A space rather than a comma should separate sets of three digits to the left *and right* of a decimal point. This practice is optional where there are only four digits involved.
- Use decimal fractions rather than common fractions (0.25 rather than ¼).
- Abbreviations such as sec, cc, or mps are avoided and only standard unit symbols such as s for second, cm^3 for cubic centimeter, and m/s for metre per second should be used.
- There is a space between the numerical value and unit symbol (4.6 g).
- Use the unit symbol in preference to words for units attached to numbers (e.g., 5.0 g/mol rather than 5.0 grams/mole). Note that 5.0 grams per mole is incorrect but five grams per mole is correct.
- A specific temperature and a temperature change both have units of degrees Celsius (°C).

Table 1.3.1 *The Fundamental SI Units*

Name	Unit Symbol	Quantity
metre	m	length
kilogram	kg	mass
second	s	time
ampere	A	electric current
kelvin	K	temperature
candela	cd	luminous intensity
mole	mol	amount of substance

Quick Check

Locate the SI error(s) in each of the following statements and correct them.

1. Ralph bought 6 kilos of potato salad. ______________________________

2. The thickness of the oxide coating on the metal was 1/2 c.m.
____

3. The weight of 1 Ml of water is exactly 1 gms at 4 °c.
____

4. My teacher bought 9.0 litres of gasoline for her 883 c.c. motorcycle.
____

5. Rama's temperature increased by .9 C°. ______________________________

Accuracy and Precision — The Quality of Measurements

Measured values like those listed in the Warm Up at the beginning of this section are determined using a variety of different measuring devices, some of which were included in section 1.1.

There are devices designed to measure all sorts of different quantities. The collection pictured in Figure 1.3.1 measures temperature, length, and volume. In addition, there are a variety of precisions (exactnesses) associated with different devices. The micrometer (also called a caliper) is more precise than the ruler while the burette and pipette are more precise than the graduated cylinder.

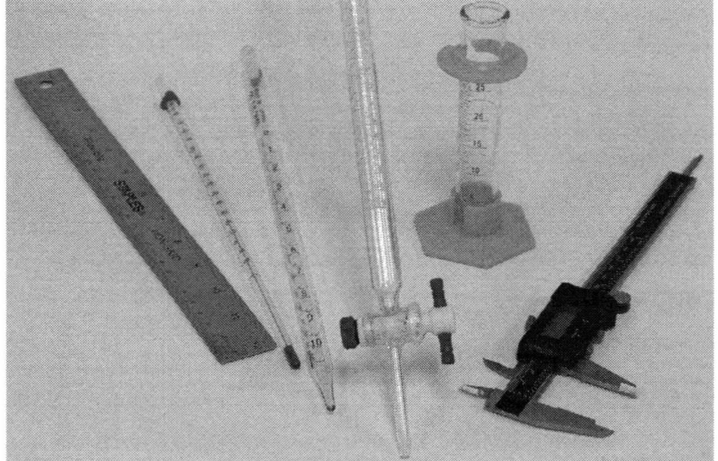

Figure 1.3.1 *A selection of measuring devices with differing levels of precision*

Despite the fact that some measuring devices are more precise than others, it is impossible to design a measuring device that gives perfectly exact measurements. All measuring devices have some degree of **uncertainty** associated with them.

The 1-kg mass kept in a helium-filled bell jar at the BIPM in Sèvres, France, is the only exact mass on the planet (Figure 1.3.2). All other masses are measured relative to this and therefore have some degree of associated uncertainty.

Figure 1.3.2 *This kilogram mass was made in the 1880s and accepted as the international prototype of the kilogram in 1889. (© BIPM — Reproduced with permission)*

Accuracy refers to the *agreement* of a particular value with the *true value.*

Accurate measurements depend on careful design and calibration to ensure a measuring device is in proper working order. The term **precision** can actually have two different meanings.

Precision refers to the reproducibility of a measurement (or the agreement among several measurements of the same quantity).

- *or* -

Precision refers to the exactness of a measurement. This relates to uncertainty: the lower the uncertainty of a measurement, the higher the precision.

Quick Check

Volumetric devices measure liquids with a wide variety of precisions.

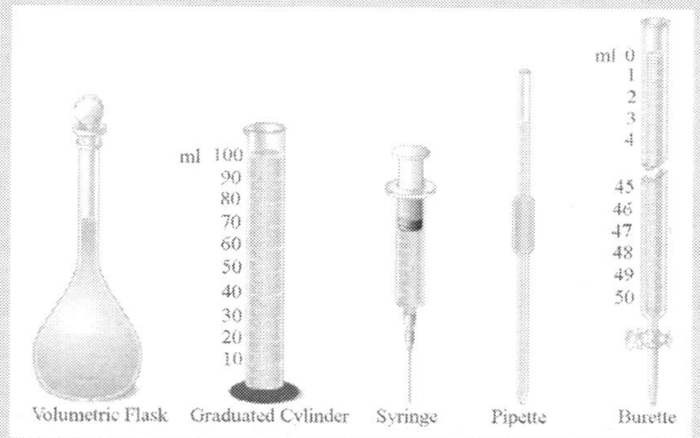

1. Which of these is likely the *most precise*?

____

2. Which is likely the *least precise*?

____

3. Is the *most precise* device necessarily the *most accurate*?

____

____

4. Discuss your answers.

____

Types of Errors

No measurement can be completely precise. In fact, all measurements must have some degree of uncertainty associated with them, so it must be true that every measurement involves some degree of error. A group of measurements may tend to consistently show error in the same direction. Such a situation is called **systematic error**. When a group of errors occurs equally in high and low directions, it is called **random error**.

Quick Check

Four groups of Earth Science students use their global positioning systems (GPS) to do some geocaching. The diagrams below show the students' results relative to where the actual caches were located.

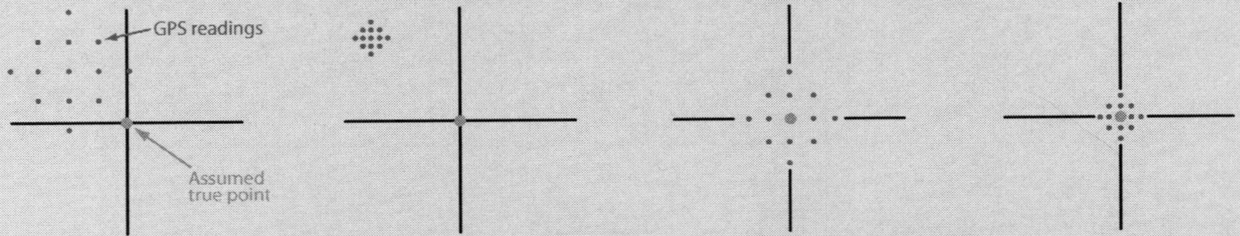

1. Comment on the precision of the students in each of the groups. (In this case, we are using the "reproducibility" definition of precision.)

   ___

2. What about the accuracy of each group?

   ___

3. Which groups were making systematic errors?

   ___

4. Which groups made errors that were more random?

   ___

Uncertainty

Every measurement has some degree of uncertainty associated with it. The uncertainty of a measuring device depends on its precision. The most precise measuring devices have the smallest uncertainties. The most common way to report the uncertainty of a measuring device is as a **range uncertainty.**

The **range uncertainty** is an *acceptable* range of values within which the true value of a measurement falls. This is commonly presented using the *plus* or *minus* notation (shown as +/–).

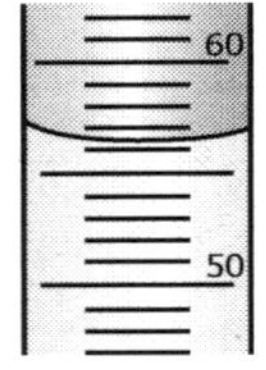

Figure 1.3.2 *A meniscus in a graduated cylinder*

An acceptable range uncertainty is usually considered plus or minus *one-tenth* to *one-half* the smallest division marked on a measuring scale. For the graduated cylinder in Figure 1.3.2, the smallest division marked on its scale is 1 mL. One-half of this division is 0.5 mL. Therefore, reading the volume from the bottom of the meniscus would give a value of 56.3 mL +/– 0.5 mL. Because it is possible to go down to one-tenth of the smallest division on the scale as a range, the volume could also be reported as 56.3 mL +/– 0.1 mL. Notice that the unit is given twice, before and after the +/– symbol. This is the correct SI convention.

When *two uncertain values* with range uncertainties are *added or subtracted*, their *uncertainties must be added*.

Quick Check

1. Sum the following values:

   27.6 mL +/− 0.2 mL
   + 14.8 mL +/− 0.2 mL

2. Subtract the following values:

   19.8 mL +/− 0.2 mL
   − 7.2 mL +/− 0.2 mL

Compare your answers with your partner. Explain to your partner why the answer to question 1 makes sense. Have your partner explain the answer to question 2.

Absolute uncertainty refers to exactly how much higher or lower a measured value is than an accepted value.

In such a case, an accepted value is the value considered to be the best measurement available. Constants such as the speed of light or the boiling point of water at sea level are accepted values. For absolute uncertainties, a sign should be applied to indicate whether the measured value is above or below the accepted value.

Another common way to indicate an error of measurement is as a percentage of what the value should be.

$$\textbf{percentage error} = \frac{\text{(measured value – accepted value)}}{\text{accepted value}} \times 100\%$$

Quick Check

A student weighs a Canadian penny and finds the mass is 2.57 g. Data from the Canadian Mint indicates a penny from that year should weigh 2.46 g.

1. What is the absolute uncertainty of the penny's mass?

   0.11g

2. What is the percentage error of the penny's mass?

   $\frac{2.57-2.46}{2.46} \cdot 100 = 4.57\%$

3. Suggest a reasonable source of the error.

   dirt accumulating on the penny

Significant Figures

When determining the correct value indicated by a measuring device, you should always record all of the **significant figures** (sometimes called "sig figs").

> The number of significant figures in a measurement includes *all* of the certain figures *plus* the *first* uncertain (estimated) figure.

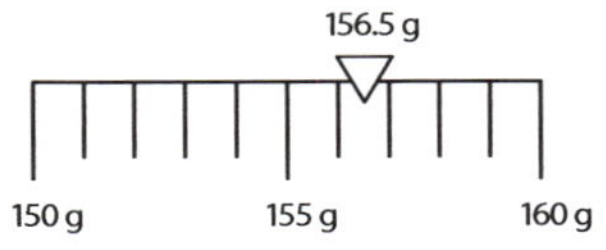

Figure 1.3.3 *Scale on a measuring device*

Say the scale on a measuring device reads as shown in Figure 1.3.3. (Note that *scale* may refer to the numerical increments on any measuring device.) The measured value has *three certain figures* (1, 5, and 6) and *one uncertain* figure (5 or is it 4 or 6?). Hence the measurement has *four significant figures*.

The following rules can be applied to determine how many figures are significant in any measurement.

Counting Significant Figures in a Measured Value

1. All non-zero digits are significant.
2. All zeros between non-zero digits are significant. Such zeros may be called *sandwiched* or *captive* zeros.
3. Leading zeros (zeros to the left of a non-zero digit) are *never* significant.
4. Trailing zeros (zeros to the right of a non-zero digit) are *only* significant if there is a *decimal* in the number.

Another way to determine the number of significant figures in a measured value is to simply express the number in scientific notation and count the digits. This method nicely eliminates the non-significant leading zeros. However, it is only successful if you recognize when to include the trailing (right side) zeros. Remember that trailing zeros are only significant if there is a decimal in the number. If the trailing zeros are significant, they need to be included when the number is written in scientific notation.

Sample Problems — Counting Significant Figures in a Measured Value

Determine the number of significant figures in each example.

1. 0.09204 g
2. 87.050 L

What to Think about	How to Do It
Question 1	
1. To begin with, apply rule 3: leading zeros are never significant. Note that the position of the zero relative to the decimal is irrelevant. These are sometimes referred to as *place holding* zeros. The underlined leading zeros are not significant.	0.09204 g
2. Apply rule 1 next: all non-zero digits are significant. The underlined digits are significant.	0.09204 g
3. Finally, apply rule 2: the captive zero is significant. The underlined zero is sandwiched between two non-zero digits so it is significant.	0.09204 g
4. A check of the number in scientific notation, 9.204×10^{-2} g, also shows four significant figures.	0.09204 g has **four** significant figures.

Continued

Sample Problems — *Continued*

Question 2

1. Apply rule 1: all non-zero digits are significant. All of the underlined digits are significant.	87.050 L
2. Apply rule 2: the captive zero is significant. The underlined zero is between two non-zero digits so it is significant.	87.050 L
3. Finally, consider the trailing or right-side zero. Rule four states that such zeros are only significant if a decimal is present in the number. Note that the position of the zero relative to the decimal is irrelevant. As this number does contain a decimal, the underlined trailing zero is significant.	87.050 L
4. Check: 8.7050×10^1 L has five sig figs (note that the right-side zero is retained).	87.050 L has **five** significant figures.

Practice Problems — Counting Significant Figures in a Measured Value

1. How many significant figures are in each of the following measured values?
   - (a) 425 mL 3
   - (b) 590.50 g 5
   - (c) 0.00750 s 3
   - (d) 1.50×10^4 L 3
   - (e) 3400 m 2

2. Round the following measurements to the stated number of significant figures.
   - (a) 30.54 s (3 sig figs) 30.5 s
   - (b) 0.2895 g (3 sig figs) 0.290 g
   - (c) 4.49 m (2 sig figs) 4.5 m
   - (d) 100.4°C (2 sig figs) 1.0×10^2

Significant Figures and Arithmetic — Multiplication and Division

The answer to a multiplication or division problem should have only as many figures as the number having the *least significant digits* in the problem.

Sample Problems — Significant Figures in Multiplication and Division Calculations

Give the answer to each of the following problems with the correct number of significant figures:

1. 8.2 m × 9.47 m =
2. 12 970.0 g ÷ 530.8 mL =

What to Think about	How to Do It
Question 1	
1. Begin by applying rules 1 to 4 to determine the number of significant figures contained in each number in the problem.	8.2 m × 9.47 m = 77.654 m^2 2 sig figs) (3 sig figs)
2. Express the answer should be expressed to *two* significant figures.	77.654 rounds to 78 m^2
Question 2	
1. The second example involves more difficult numbers. Apply rules 1 to 4 to quickly determine the number of sig figs in each value.	12 970.0 g ÷ 530.8 mL = 24.434815... g/mL (6 sig figs) (4 sig figs)
2. Express the answer to *four* significant figures.	24.434815... rounds to 24.43 g/mL

Quick Check

Give the answer to each of the following problems with the appropriate unit and the correct number of significant figures:

1. 0.14 m × 14.00 m = ____________
2. 940 g ÷ 0.850 mL = ____________
3. 0.054 g ÷ 1.10 s = ____________

Significant Figures and Arithmetic – Addition and Subtraction

The answer to an addition or subtraction problem should have only as many figures as the *least precise* (least exact) number in the problem. The number of significant figures in the answer is determined by considering the *place value* of the last significant figure in each number in the problem. (If both measurements include numbers to the right of a decimal, this means you simply round to the smallest number of decimal places.)

Sample Problems — Significant Figures in Addition and Subtraction Calculations

Give the answer to each of the following problems with the correct number of significant figures:

1. 246.812 cm + 1.3 cm =
2. 25 510 km − 7 000 km =

What to Think about

Question 1

1. In addition and subtraction problems, the most important thing is to determine the *place value* of the last significant figure in each number.
   246.812 contains non-zero digits only, so the last significant figure is the last 2, which occupies the thousandths place.
   The 3 in 1.3 is the last significant figure and occupies the tenths place.

   How to Do It

   $$\begin{array}{r} 246.81\underline{2} \\ +\quad 1.\underline{3} \\ \hline 248.\underline{1}12 \text{ cm} \end{array}$$

2. When these two place values are compared, the tenths is *less precise*; that is, it is *less exact* than the thousandths place.
   Round the final answer to the tenths place, resulting in a number with **four** significant figures. Notice that this rounded to one decimal place.

   248.$\underline{1}$12 rounds to 248.1 cm

Question 2

1. The problem involves adding and subtracting. Determine the place value of the last significant figure in each number.
   The last significant figure in 25 510 is the 1. It is in the tens place. The 7 is the last significant figure in 7000. It is in the thousands place.

   $$\begin{array}{r} 25\,5\underline{1}0 \\ -\quad \underline{7}\,000 \\ \hline 1\underline{8}\,510 \text{ km} \end{array}$$

2. Thousands are far less exact than tens so round the final answer to the thousands place resulting in an answer with two significant figures.
   Notice that the decimal place simplification does not apply in this example.

   1$\underline{8}$ 510 km rounds to → 19 000 km

Practice Problems— Significant Figures in Addition and Subtraction Calculations

Give the answer to each of the following problems with the correct number of significant figures:

1. 16.407 mL + 5.70 mL = 22.107 22.12 mL
2. 0.32 g + 0.009 g = .329 .33 g
3. 750 m + 8.001 m = ____________

Significant Figures — Summary

- When there are a series of arithmetic functions to be performed with measurements, always remember to apply the correct order of operations.
- Use the proper rules for determining the number of significant figures *in each step.*
- Remember that significant figures apply to measured values only.
- They do *not* apply to counted values or values that are defined.

Quick Check

Answer each of the following with the correct number of significant figures.

1. $\dfrac{9.825\text{g} - 9.804\text{ g}}{9.825\text{ g}} \times 100\% = \dfrac{0.021\text{ g}}{9.825\text{ g}} \times 100\% =$ .214 .21%
2. 804.08 g ÷ (424.4 mL + 42.8 mL) = 81.09 81.1 g
3. (3.202 m × 4.80 m) / (26.4 min – 17.3 min) = 1.689 1.69 m^2/min
4. 7.0×10^2 s + 6.010×10^3 s = .116 1.2×10^{-1}

1.3 Activity: Connecting Significant Figures with Uncertainty

Question

What is the uncertainty in an area calculation?

Background

A student was assigned the task of determining the area of a small Post-It® note. She was instructed to use a low-precision plastic ruler, marked in increments of centimetres. Knowing it is acceptable to use between one-tenth and one-half the smallest increments on the ruler, the student decided on a range uncertainty of +/– 0.2 cm.

Dimensions	Measurements
Height	4.6 cm +/– 0.2 cm
Width	5.5 cm +/– 0.2 cm

Procedure

1. Calculate the smallest possible area of the Post-It® (keep **all digits**).

   4.4 · 5.3 = 23.32 cm²

2. Calculate the largest possible area of the Post-It® (again, keep all digits).

   4.8 · 5.7 = 27.36 cm²

3. Determine the area as the average of the values calculated in one and two (keep all figures in your calculation).

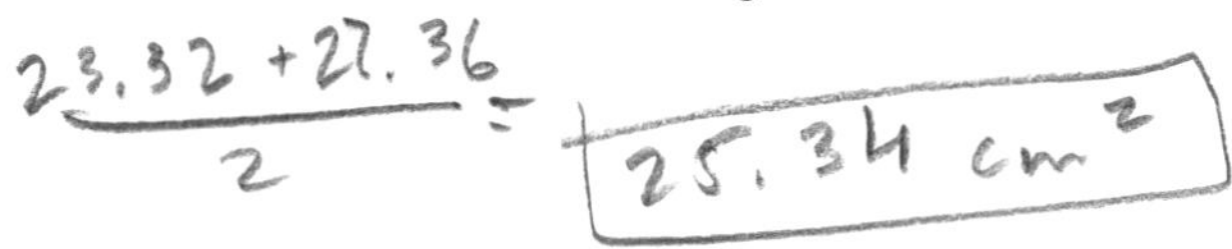

Results and Discussion

1. Determine an uncertainty that will include the smallest and largest possible areas (note that uncertainty may be expressed *in one place value only).*

   ± 2

2. The uncertain place will determine what place your area should be rounded to. Now express the area of the Post-It™ including the range uncertainty.

   25 cm² ± 2 cm²

3. How does the number of significant figures in your answer compare with what you would have expected based on what you've learned about calculating with significant figures in this section?

   It is the same as what I would've expected, which is 2 because the number in the multiplication problem with the least amount of sig figs is 2.

1.3 Review Questions

1. Determine the errors and correct them according to the SI system:

   (a) The package contained 750 Gm of linguini.

   (b) The car accelerated to 90 km per hour in 10 sec.

   (c) The recipe called for 1 ML of vanilla and 250 cc of milk.

   (d) Jordan put 250 gms of mushrooms on his 12 inch pizza.

2. A zinc slug comes from a science supply company with a stated mass of 5.000 g. A student weighs the slug three times, collecting the following values: 4.891 g, 4.901 g, and 4.890 g. Are the student's values accurate? Are they precise (consider both meanings)?

3. A student doing experimental work finds the density of a liquid to be 0.1679 g/cm^3. The known density of the liquid is 0.1733 g/cm^3. What is the absolute error of the student's work? What is the percent error?

4. Two students weigh the same object with a known mass of 0.68 g. One student obtains a mass of 0.72 g, while the other gets a mass of 0.64 g. How do their percent errors compare? How do their absolute errors compare?

5. In an experiment to determine the density of a liquid, a maximum error of 5.00% is permitted. If the true density is 1.44 g/cm^3, what are the maximum and minimum values within which a student's answer may fall into the acceptable range?

6. What is the mass, including uncertainty, arrived at as the result of summing 45.04 g +/– 0.03 g, and 39.04 g +/– 0.02 g?

7. What is the smallest number that could result from subtracting 22 m +/– 2 m from 38 m +/– 3 m?

8. The dimensions of a rectangle are measured to be 19.9 cm +/– 0.1 cm and 2.4 +/– 0.1 cm. What is the area of the rectangle, including the range uncertainty?

9. Read each of the following devices, including a reasonable range uncertainty:

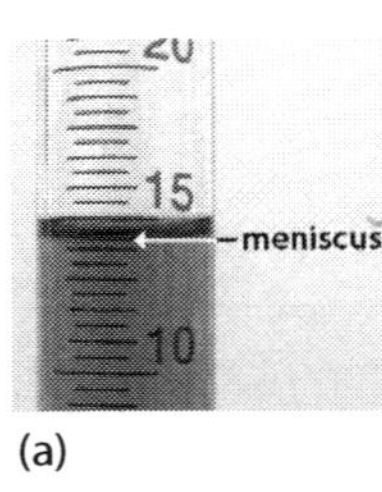

(a)

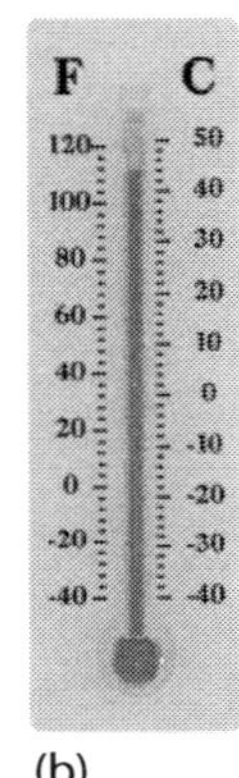

(b)

10. Determine the number of significant figures in each of the following measurements:

    (a) 0.1407 m ____________

    (b) 21.05 mg ____________

    (c) 570.00 km ____________

    (d) 0.0030 cm ____________

    (e) 250 m ____________

    (f) 10 035.00 cm^3 ____________

    (g) 2800 g ____________

    (h) 5000°C ____________

    (i) 1.1×10^2 kPa ____________

    (j) 5.35×10^{-2} m/h ____________

11. Express the following in proper form scientific notation. Then indicate the correct number of significant figures in the value.

(a) 4907 L ____________________

(b) 0.000 052 m ____________________

(c) 7900 g ____________________

(d) 0.060 30 ft ____________________

(e) 790.0 lb ____________________

12. Carry out the following operations and give the answers with the correct number of significant figures. Pay close attention to the units.

(a) 14.6 cm × 12.2 cm × 9.3 cm

(b) 28.0 m × 16.0 m × 7.0 m

13. A chunk of nickel has a mass of 9.0 g and a volume of 1.01 mL. What is its density?

14. The density of copper is 8.9 g/mL. What is the mass of a 10.8 mL piece of copper?

15. Carry out the following operations and give the answer with the correct number of significant figures.

(a) 608 g + 7 g + 0.05 g

(b) 481.33 mL − 37.1 mL

(c) 6620 s + 35.7 s + 1.00 s

(d) 0.007 m + 0.100 m + 0.020 m

16. Determine the answer with the correct number of significant figures:

$$\frac{1.415\text{ g}}{1.6\text{ mL}} + \frac{0.240\text{ g}}{0.311\text{ mL}} + \frac{40.304\text{ g}}{0.2113\text{ mL}}$$

17. Determine the answer to each the following with the correct number of significant figures:

(a) $\dfrac{8.4\text{ g} + 3.0\text{ g} + 4.175\text{ g}}{3}$

(b) $\dfrac{9.00 \times 10^{-23}\text{ units} \times 2.9900 \times 10^{-25}\text{ units}}{2.9 \times 10^{-9}\text{ units}}$

(c) $\dfrac{(5.9 \times 10^{-12}\text{ u} + 7.80 \times 10^{-13}\text{ u})}{(4 \times 10^{12}\text{ u} + 6.700 \times 10^{13}\text{ u})}$

18. The label on a bottle of mood-elevating medication states that each tablet contains 25.0 mg of imipramine. A test conducted by the bureau of standards shows a tablet to contain 28.0 mg. Legally, drug companies are allowed to be within plus or minus 5% of their labelled quantities.

(a) Give the *percentage* uncertainty for the imipramine tablets:

(b) Is the drug company within the legally allowed limits for their tablets?

1.4 Analysis of Units and Conversions in Chemistry

Warm Up

Place a check by the larger quantity in each row of the table.

Metric Quantity		Imperial Quantity	
A kilogram of butter		A pound of butter	
A five-kilometre hiking trail		A five-mile mountain bike trail	
One litre of milk		One quart of milk	
A twelve-centimetre ruler		A twelve-inch ruler	
A fifteen-gram piece of chocolate		A fifteen-ounce chocolate bar	
A temperature of 22°C		A temperature of 22°F	

Measurement Through History

Units of measurement were originally based on nature and everyday activities. The grain was derived from the mass of one grain of wheat or barley a farmer produced. The fathom was the distance between the tips of a sailor's fingers when his arms were extended on either side. The origin of units of length like the foot and the hand leave little to the imagination.

The inconvenient aspect of units such as these was, of course, their glaring lack of consistency. One "Viking's embrace" might produce a fathom much shorter than another. These inconsistencies were so important to traders and travellers that over the years most of the commonly used units were standardized. Eventually, they were incorporated into what was known as the English units of measurement. Following the Battle of Hastings in 1066, Roman measures were added to the primarily Anglo-Saxon ones that made up this system. These units were standardized by the Magna Carta of 1215 and were studied and updated periodically until the UK *Weights and Measures Act* of 1824 resulted in a major review and a renaming to the **Imperial system of measurement**. It is interesting to note that the United States had become independent prior to this and did not adopt the Imperial system, but continued to use the older English units of measure.

Despite the standardization, its development from ancient agriculture and trade has led to a rather vast set of units that are quite complicated. For example, there are eight different definitions for the amount of matter in a ton. The need for a simpler system, a system based on decimals, or multiples of 10, was recognized as early 1585 when Dutch mathematician, Simon Stevin published a book called *The Tenth*. However, most authorities credit Gabriel Mouton of Lyon, France, as the originator of the metric system nearly 100 years later. Another 100 years would pass before the final development and adoption of the metric system in France in 1795.

Recall from section 1.3 the International Bureau of Weights and Measures (BIPM) was established in Sévres, France, in 1825. The BIPM has governed the metric system ever since. Since 1960, the metric system has become the SI system. Its use and acceptance has grown to the point that only three countries in the entire world have not adopted it: Burma, Liberia, and the United States (Figure 1.4.1).

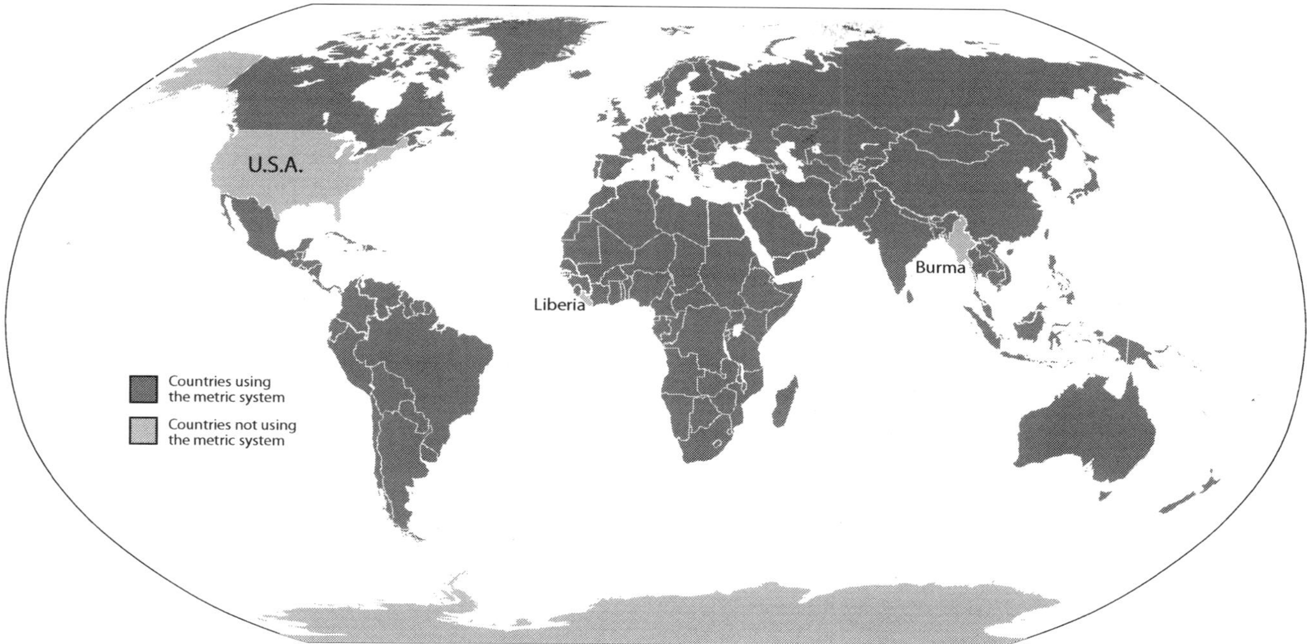

Figure 1.4.1 *Map of the world showing countries that have adopted the SI/metric system*

Dimensional Analysis

Dimensional analysis is a method that allows you to easily solve problems by converting from one unit to another through the use of conversion factors. The dimensional analysis method is sometimes called the *factor label method*. It may occasionally be referred to as the use of *unitary rates*.

A **conversion factor** is a *fraction* or factor written so that the denominator and numerator are *equivalent values* with *different units*.

One of the most useful conversion factors allows the user to convert from the metric to the imperial system and vice versa. Since 1 inch is exactly the same length as 2.54 cm, the factor may be expressed as:

$$\frac{1\ \text{inch}}{2.54\ \text{cm}} \text{ or } \frac{2.54\ \text{cm}}{1\ \text{inch}}$$

These two lengths are identical so multiplication of a given length by the conversion factor will not change the length. It will simply express it in a different unit.

Now if you wish to determine how many centimetres are in a yard, you have two things to consider. First, which of the two forms of the conversion factor will allow you to *cancel* the imperial unit, converting it to a metric unit? Second, what other conversion factors will you need to complete the task? Assuming you know, or can access, these equivalencies: 1 yard = 3 feet and 1 foot = 12 inches, your approach would be as follows:

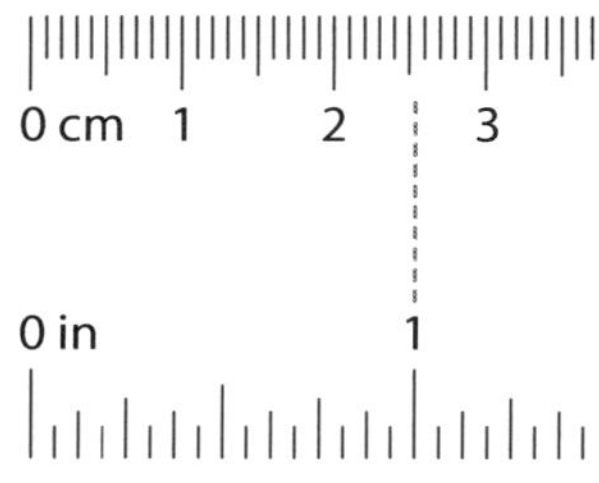

Figure 1.4.2 *A ruler with both imperial and metric scales shows that 1 inch = 2.54 cm.*

$$1.00\ \cancel{\text{yards}} \times \frac{3\ \cancel{\text{feet}}}{1\ \cancel{\text{yard}}} \times \frac{12\ \cancel{\text{inches}}}{1\ \cancel{\text{foot}}} \times \frac{2.54\ \text{cm}}{1\ \cancel{\text{inch}}} = 91.4\ \text{cm}$$

Notice that as with the multiplication of any fractions, it is possible to cancel anything that appears in both the numerator and the denominator. We've simply followed a numerator-to-denominator pattern to convert yards to feet to inches to cm.

The number of feet in a yard and inches in a foot are *defined values*. They are not things we measured. Thus they do not affect the number of significant figures in our answer. This will be the case for any conversion factor in which the numerator and denominator are in the same system (both metric or both imperial). Interestingly enough, the BIPM has indicated that 2.54 cm will be *exactly* 1 inch. So it is the only multiple-system conversion factor that will not influence the number of significant figures in the answer to a calculation. As all three of the conversion factors we used are defined, only the original value of 1.00 yards influences the significant figures in our answer. Hence we round the answer to three sig figs.

Converting Within the Metric System

The metric system is based on powers of 10. The power of 10 is indicated by a simple prefix. Table 1.4.1 is a list of SI prefixes. Your teacher will indicate those that you need to commit to memory. You may wish to highlight them.

Metric conversions require either one or two steps. You will recognize a one-step metric conversion by the presence of a *base unit* in the question. The common base units in the metric system include:

Measures	Unit Name	Symbol
length	metre	m
mass	gram	g
volume	litre	L
time	second	s

One-step metric conversions involve a *base unit* (metres, litres, grams, or seconds) being converted to a *prefixed unit* or a prefixed unit being converted to a base unit.

Two-step metric conversions require the use of two conversion factors. Two factors will be required any time there are two prefixed units in the question. In a two-step metric conversion, you must always *convert to the base unit first.*

Table 1.4.1 *SI Prefixes*

Prefix	Symbol	10^n
yotta	Y	10^{24}
zetta	Z	10^{21}
exa	E	10^{18}
peta	P	10^{15}
tera	T	10^{12}
giga	G	10^{9}
mega	M	10^{6}
kilo	k	10^{3}
hecto	h	10^{2}
deca	da	10^{1}
deci	d	10^{-1}
centi	c	10^{-2}
milli	m	10^{-3}
micro	μ	10^{-6}
nano	n	10^{-9}
pico	p	10^{-12}
femto	f	10^{-15}
atto	a	10^{-18}
zepto	z	10^{-21}
yocto	y	10^{-24}

Sample Problems — One- and Two-Step Metric Conversions

1. Convert 9.4 nm into m. 2. Convert 6.32 μm into km.

What to Think about	How to Do It
Question 1	
1. In any metric conversion, you must decide whether you need one step or two. There is a base unit in the question and only one prefix. This problem requires only one step. Set the units up to convert nm into m. Let the units lead you through the problem. You are given 9.4 nm, so the conversion factor must have nm in the denominator so it will cancel.	$9.4\ \text{nm} \times \frac{\text{m}}{\text{nm}} = \quad \text{m}$
2. Now determine the value of nano and fill it in appropriately. **1** nm = **10^{-9}** m Give the answer with the appropriate number of significant figures and the correct unit. Because the conversion factor is a defined equality, only the given value affects the number of sig figs in the answer.	$9.4\ \cancel{\text{nm}} \times \frac{10^{-9}\ \text{m}}{1\ \cancel{\text{nm}}} = 9.4 \times 10^{-9}\ \text{m}$
Question 2	
1. This problem presents with two prefixes so there must be two steps. The first step in such a problem is always to convert to the base unit. Set up the units to convert from μm to m and then to km.	$6.32\ \mu\text{m} \times \frac{\text{m}}{\mu\text{m}} \times \frac{\text{km}}{\text{m}} = \quad \text{km}$
2. Insert the values for 1 μm and 1 km. 1 μm = 10^{-6} m 1 km = 10^{3} m	
3. Give the answer with the correct number of significant figures and the correct unit.	$6.32\ \cancel{\mu\text{m}} \times \frac{10^{-6}\ \cancel{\text{m}}}{1\ \cancel{\mu\text{m}}} \times \frac{1\ \text{km}}{10^{3}\ \cancel{\text{m}}} = 6.32 \times 10^{-9}\ \text{km}$

Practice Problems — One- and Two-Step Metric Conversions

1. Convert 16 s into ks.
2. Convert 75 000 mL into L.
3. Convert 457 ks into ms.
4. Convert 5.6 × 10^{-4} Mm into dm.

Derived Unit Conversions

A **derived unit** is composed of more than one unit.

Units like those used to express rate (km/h) or density (g/mL) are good examples of derived units.

Derived unit conversions require *cancellations in two directions* (from numerator to denominator as usual AND from denominator to numerator).

Sample Problem — Derived Unit Conversions

Convert 55.0 km/h into m/s

What to Think about

1. The numerator requires conversion of a prefixed metric unit to a base metric unit. This portion involves one step only and is similar to sample problem one above.
2. The denominator involves a time conversion from hours to minutes to seconds. The denominator conversion usually follows the numerator. Always begin by putting all conversion factors in place using *units only*. Now that this has been done, insert the appropriate numerical values for each conversion factor.
3. As always, state the answer with units and round to the correct number of significant figures (in this case, three).

How to Do It

$$\frac{55.0\ \text{km}}{\text{h}} \times \frac{\text{m}}{\text{km}} \times \frac{\text{h}}{\text{min}} \times \frac{\text{min}}{\text{s}}$$

$$= \frac{\text{m}}{\text{s}}$$

$$\frac{55.0\ \cancel{\text{km}}}{\cancel{\text{h}}} \times \frac{10^3\ \text{m}}{1\ \cancel{\text{km}}} \times \frac{1\ \cancel{\text{h}}}{60\ \cancel{\text{min}}} \times \frac{1\ \cancel{\text{min}}}{60\ \text{s}}$$

$$= \frac{15.3\ \text{m}}{\text{s}}$$

Practice Problems — Derived Unit Conversions

1. Convert 2.67 g/mL into kg/L. Why has the numerical value remained unchanged?

2. Convert the density of neon gas from 8.9994×10^{-4} mg/mL into kg/L.

3. Convert 35 mi/h (just over the speed limit in a U.S. city) into m/s. (Given: 5280 feet = 1 mile)

Use of a Value with a Derived Unit as a Conversion Factor

A quantity expressed with a derived unit may be used to convert a unit that measures one thing into a unit that measures something else completely. The most common examples are the use of rate to convert between distance and time and the use of density to convert between mass and volume. These are challenging! The keys to this type of problem are determining which form of the conversion factor to use and where to start.

Suppose we wish to use the speed of sound (330 m/s) to determine the time (in hours) required for an explosion to be heard 5.0 km away. It is always a good idea to begin any conversion problem by considering what we are trying to find. Begin with the end in mind. This allows us to decide where to begin. Do we start with 5.0 km or 330 m/s?

First, consider: are you attempting to convert a unit → unit, or a $\frac{\text{unit}}{\text{unit}} \rightarrow \frac{\text{unit}}{\text{unit}}$?

As the answer is unit → unit, begin with the single unit: km. The derived unit will serve as the conversion factor.

Second, which of the two possible forms of the conversion factor will allow conversion of a distance in km into a time in h? Do we require $\frac{330\text{ m}}{1\text{ s}}$ or $\frac{1\text{ s}}{330\text{ m}}$? As the distance unit must cancel, the second form is the one we require. Hence, the correct approach is

$$5.0\ \cancel{\text{km}} \times \frac{10^3\ \cancel{\text{m}}}{1\ \cancel{\text{km}}} \times \frac{1\text{s}}{330\ \cancel{\text{m}}} \times \frac{1\ \cancel{\text{min}}}{60\text{ s}} \times \frac{1\text{ h}}{60\ \cancel{\text{min}}} = 4.2 \times 10^{-3}\text{ h}$$

Sample Problem — Use of Density as a Conversion Factor

What is the volume in L of a 15.0 kg piece of zinc metal? (Density of Zn = 7.13 g/mL)

What to Think about	How to Do It
1. Decide what form of the conversion factor to use: g/mL or the reciprocal, mL/g. Always begin by arranging the factors using *units* only. As the answer will contain one unit, begin with one unit, in this case, kg.	$15.0\text{ kg} \times \frac{\text{g}}{\text{kg}} \times \frac{\text{mL}}{\text{g}} \times \frac{\text{L}}{\text{mL}} = \text{L}$
2. Insert the appropriate numerical values for each conversion factor. In order to cancel a mass and convert to a volume, use the reciprocal of the density: $\frac{1\text{mL}}{7.13\text{ g}}$	$15.0\ \cancel{\text{kg}} \times \frac{10^3\ \cancel{\text{g}}}{1\ \cancel{\text{kg}}} \times \frac{1\ \cancel{\text{mL}}}{7.13\ \cancel{\text{g}}} \times \frac{10^{-3}\text{ L}}{1\ \cancel{\text{mL}}} = 2.10\text{ L}$
3. Calculate the answer with correct unit and number of significant digits.	

Practice Problems — Use of Rate and Density as Conversion Factors

1. The density of mercury metal is 13.6 g/mL. What is the mass of 2.5 L?

2. The density of lead is 11.2 g/cm^3. The volumes 1 cm^3 and 1 mL are exactly equivalent. What is the volume in L of a 16.5 kg piece of lead?

3. The speed of light is 3.0×10^{10} cm/s. Sunlight takes 8.29 min to travel from the photosphere (light-producing region) of the Sun to Earth. How many kilometres is Earth from the Sun?

Conversions Involving Units with Exponents (Another Kind of Derived Unit)

If a unit is squared or cubed, it may be cancelled in one of two ways. It may be written more than once to convey that it is being multiplied by itself *or* it may be placed in brackets with the exponent applied to the *number* inside the brackets as well as to the *unit*. Hence, the use of the equivalency 1 L = 1 dm^3 to convert 1 m^3 to L might appear in either of these formats:

$$1\ \text{m}^3 \times \frac{1\ \text{dm}}{10^{-1}\ \text{m}} \times \frac{1\ \text{dm}}{10^{-1}\ \text{m}} \times \frac{1\ \text{dm}}{10^{-1}\ \text{m}} \times \frac{1\ \text{L}}{1\ \text{dm}^3} = 1\ \text{m}^3 \times \left(\frac{1\ \text{dm}}{10^{-1}\ \text{m}}\right)^3 \times \frac{1\ \text{L}}{1\ \text{dm}^3} = 1000\ \text{L}$$

Sample Problem – Use of Conversion Factors Containing Exponents

Convert 0.35 m^3 (cubic metres) into mL. (1 mL = 1 cm^3)

What to Think about	How to Do It
1. The unit cm must be cancelled three times. Do this by multiplying the conversion factor by itself three times or through the use of brackets.	$0.35\ \text{m}^3 \times \frac{\text{cm}}{\text{m}} \times \frac{\text{cm}}{\text{m}} \times \frac{\text{cm}}{\text{m}} \times \frac{\text{mL}}{\text{cm}^3} = \text{mL}$ or $0.35\ \text{m}^3 \times \left(\frac{\text{cm}}{\text{m}}\right)^3 \times \frac{\text{mL}}{\text{cm}^3} = \text{mL}$
2. Once the units have been aligned correctly, insert the appropriate numerical values.	$0.35\ \text{m}^3 \times \frac{1\ \text{cm}}{10^{-2}\ \text{m}} \times \frac{1\ \text{cm}}{10^{-2}\ \text{m}} \times \frac{1\ \text{cm}}{10^{-2}\ \text{m}} \times \frac{1\ \text{mL}}{1\ \text{cm}^3}$ $= 3.5 \times 10^5\ \text{mL}$
3. Calculate the answer with the correct unit and number of significant figures.	or $0.35\ \text{m}^3 \times \left(\frac{1\ \text{cm}}{10^{-2}\ \text{m}}\right)^3 \times \frac{1\ \text{mL}}{1\ \text{cm}^3} = 3.5 \times 10^5\ \text{mL}$

Practice Problems — Use of Conversion Factors Containing Exponents

1. Convert 4.3 dm^3 into cm^3.

2. Atmospheric pressure is 14.7 lb/in^2. Convert this to the metric unit, g/cm^2. (Given 454 g = 1.00 lb)

3. Convert a density of 8.2 kg/m^3 to lb/ft^3 using factors provided in this section.

Measurement of Temperature

Temperature is a measure of the intensity of heat. It is the average kinetic energy of the particles is sample of matter. Heat is the energy transferred between two objects in contact with one another at different temperatures. There are several different scales for measuring temperature. Three of these scales are commonly used, two in physical sciences and one in engineering. The earliest instrument for measuring the intensity of heat involved measuring the expansion and contraction of water and was called a *thermoscope*. This device was invented by an Italian, named Santorio in the late 1500's. The thermoscope, later called the thermometer, was refined around the same time by Galileo Galilei.

It wasn't until the early 1700s that the Swede Andres Celsius and the German Daniel Gabriel Fahrenheit applied measured scales of temperature to tubes containing alcohol and later, for more precision, mercury. Celsius devised a scale of temperature giving the value of 0°C to the temperature at which water freezes and 100°C to the temperature at which water boils. Fahrenheit, apparently in an attempt to avoid the use of negative numbers on really cold German days, used the coldest temperature he could produce with rock salt and ice as his zero point. His original scale was later adjusted so that the freezing point of water was 32°F and the boiling point of water was 212°F.

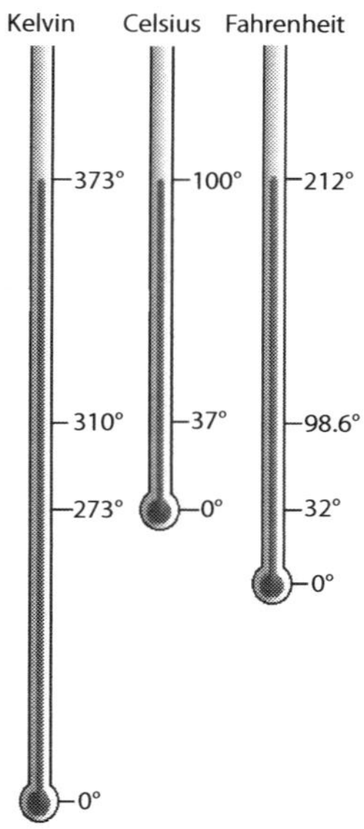

Figure 1.4.3 *The three commonly used temperature scales*

In the mid 1800s, Lord William Thomson Kelvin of Scotland, a student at Cambridge University who eventually became a professor at the University of Glasgow, developed the idea of an absolute temperature scale. His theory was that there was an absolute coldest temperature that could ever be attained. This temperature was called **absolute zero** and would be 273.15°C colder than the freezing point of water. The boiling point of water on the absolute scale would be 100°C *and* 100 Kelvin units hotter than the freezing point.

Comparison of these scales helps you see how to convert from one scale to another (Figure 1.4.3). Not only are the conversion factors of 100°C/180°F and 100°C/100 K degrees, which result in 1°C /1.8°F and 1 °C/1 K important, but the difference at the freezing point of water is also important. This requires the addition or subtraction of 32°F and 273.15 K (or slightly less precisely, 273 K) as well.

Consequently, you could simply memorize the following equations for conversion:

$$T_F = \frac{1.8°F}{1°C}(T_C) + 32\,°F \quad \text{and} \quad T_C = (T_F - 32°F) \times \frac{1°C}{1.8°F}$$

Or, even easier (your teacher may elect to use 273 exactly as the addition/subtraction factor):

$$T_K = T_C\frac{(1\text{ K})}{(1°C)} + 273.15\text{ K} \quad \text{and} \quad T_c = (T_k - 273.15\text{ K}) \times \frac{1°C}{1\text{ K}}$$

The number of significant figures in a temperature is generally determined by using the rule of precision. That is, if the given temperature is good to the *tenths*, the temperature in the new units is good to the *tenths*. Similarly, if the given temperature was a whole number (good to the ones place), the new temperature should also be stated to the ones place. It is interesting to note by convention there is no degree symbol (°) placed before K.

Some people prefer to memorize formulas and apply them. However, it is nearly always easier to apply logic to derive a method for converting from one unit to another. Notice this method of derivation in the next sample problem.

Sample Problem — Conversion of the Celsius to Fahrenheit Temperature Scale

Convert a warm day temperature from 25.2°C to °F.

What to Think about

1. Is the Fahrenheit temperature bigger or smaller than 25.2°C?
   Based on our common sense understanding, °F should be larger. This means the difference of 32°F should be added to the 25.2°C.

2. Should the 32°F be added to 25.2°C *now*, or following a conversion to °F?
   Units of different types *cannot* be added to one another, so the conversion *must* be completed first.

3. The conversion to °F must occur first and then 32°F should be added on. There are
   1.8 F degrees for each 1 C degree.
   Needless to say, the answer is calculated to the *tenths place* as that is the precision of the original temperature given in the problem!
   The final temperature is rounded to the *TENTHS* of a degree.

How to Do It

$25.2°C \times \frac{°F}{°C}$

$25.2°C \times \frac{1.8\ °F}{1\ °C}\ (+\ 32°F) = 77.4\ °F$

Practice Problems — Conversion Between Units of Temperature

1. Cesium metal is very soft. It has a melting point below body temperature. Convert cesium's melting point of 28.4°C to °F.

2. Air can be liquefied at a temperature of –319°F. Convert this to °C.

3. Convert absolute zero (the coldest possible temperature) from 0 K to °F. Hint: convert to °C first.

1.4 Activity: Our Life in the Metric System

Question

How does our everyday life measure up in the metric system?

Background

Use a measuring tape, a bathroom scale, an odometer on the family car (or an estimate of the distance to school), and be aware of the number of students in your school.

Procedure

1. Measure your height in inches and record it in the table below.
2. Measure the width of your classroom in feet. Convert a fraction of a foot to tenths of a foot. For example, 6 inches or ½ of a foot would be 0.5 ft, 3 inches would be 0.25 foot, etc.
3. Measure the weight of your body in pounds (lb) on a bathroom scale.
4. Determine the distance from your house to your school in miles. If you have to estimate, assume 10 blocks equals 1 mile. Convert fractions of a block to decimals as suggested in procedure two above.

Results and Discussion

Using the space below, calculate the missing distances in the following table. Compare the distances with the units you are familiar with. Show the conversions required.

Measurement	Imperial Measurement	Metric Measurement
Your height	in	cm
Room width	ft	m
Body weight	lb	kg
Home distance	mi	km

1.4 Review Questions

1. Show your work and the result for each of the following conversions.

Measurement	Given Unit	Calculation	Required Unit
Grain of salt's mass	415 μg		g
Earth to the Moon's distance	384.4 Mm		m
Mass of a nickel	3.976 g		μg
Volumetric pipette length	4.5 dm		m
Smoke particle's mass	1.05×10^{-12} g		ng
Distance from UBC to SFU	24.99 km		m

2. Show your work and the result for each of the following conversions.

Measurement	Given Unit	Calculation	Required Unit
Energy to heat a grande latte to 65°C	83.60 kJ		MJ
Mass of a college chemistry text	2.54 kg		cg
Average light bulb wattage	600.0 dW		nW
Volume of a can of soda	355 mL		cL
Average time to send one text message	185 das		ms
Distance from Prince George to Trail	987 km		dm

3. The official Mini web site states that the Mini Cooper gets 14.25 km/L fuel economy. Express this value in miles per gallon. (Given 5280 ft = 1 mile, 1 gal = 4.546 L)

4. The maximum highway speed limit in British Columbia is 110 km/h. Express this speed in units of metres per second.

5. The density of tantalum (a heavy metal used in cell phone production) is 16.7 g/mL. What is this value in units of lb/L? (Given 1.00 kg = 2.21 lb)

6. The average energy consumption for a new Samsung refrigerator is 5.47×10^2 kWh/year. What is the average energy consumption of this refrigerator in gigajoules per day? (Given 1 GJ = 277.8 kWh, 1year = 365 days)

7. The density of pure iridium metal is 22.68 kg/dm^3. Express this density in units of g/cm^3.

8. The density of mercury metal is 13.6 g/mL. What is the mass of 1.00 L of mercury? Express your answer in kg.

9. Use the Mini Cooper mileage rate in question 3 above to determine how many metres a Mini could travel if its tank contained 120 dL of fuel.

10. Silver has a density of 10.5 g/cm^3. If you have a pure silver coin with a mass of 6.00 g (about the same as a Canadian quarter), what is the volume of silver in the coin? Express your answer in units of mL. (1 mL = 1 cm^3)

11. Isopropyl alcohol (also called rubbing alcohol) has a density of 8.34 lb/gal. A large jug of rubbing alcohol weighs 2.3 kg. Determine the volume of this jug in mL. (Given 454 g = 1 pound. Check question 3.)

12. The planet of Bark is fond of dogs of all types. The inhabitants trade the animals much as art collectors on Earth trade sculptures and paintings: 1 pit bull is worth 3 collies; 2 collies are worth 5 poodles; 3 poodles are worth 7 dobermans; 1 doberman is worth 9 german sheep dogs. An inhabitant of Bark (often called a "Bow-wow") owns 4 pit bulls. How many German sheep dogs may she obtain?

13. The planet of Purr is fond of cats of all types. The inhabitants trade the animals with one another: 1 calico is worth 5 Siamese; 2 Siamese are worth 7 Persians; 3 Persians are worth 8 tabbies; 1 tabby is worth 6 Heinz Fifty-Sevens. An inhabitant of Purr (often called a "Purrsian") owns 2 calico cats. How many Heinz Fifty-Sevens may she obtain?

14. What is the engine piston displacement in litres of an engine whose displacement is listed at 325 in^3? (Given: 1 L = 1dm^3)

15. Standard atmospheric pressure on a cold day (0°C) at sea level is 14.7 lb/in^2 (this unit is sometimes written as psi). Determine this atmospheric pressure in units of kg/cm^2. (Given: 1.00 lb = 454 g)

16. If a gallon of paint can cover 400. square feet what is this paint coverage expressed in square metres per litre (1 gal = 4.546 L)?

17. The ignition temperature is the temperature at which something catches fire and burns on its own. The ignition temperature of paper is 451°F. What is this value in °C?

18. In Geneva, on the April 10, 2007, the first sector of CERN's Large Hadron Collider (LHC) was cooled to reach a temperature of 1.9 K. That is colder than deep outer space! What was the temperature of this sector of the LHC expressed in °F?

19. The coldest temperature recorded in Antarctica, the home of the Emperor penguin, was recorded to be –89°C at the Voskok Station on July 21, 1983. An American scientist converted –89°C to °F for the benefit the media in the United States. What temperature did the media report to the American public expressed in °F?

20. A springlike day in Denver Colorado in February may register a temperature of 9.0°C. Convert to °F.

2 The Nature of Matter

This chapter focuses on the following AP Big Ideas from the College Board:

Big Idea 1: The chemical elements are fundamental building materials of matter, and all matter can be understood in terms of arrangements of atoms. These atoms retain their identify in chemical reactions.
Big Idea 2: Chemical and physical properties of materials can be explained by the structure and the arrangement of atoms, ions, or molecules and the forces between them.

By the end of this chapter, you should be able to do the following:

- Relate the observable properties and characteristics of elements, compounds, and mixtures to the concept of atoms and molecules
- Write the names and formulae for ionic and covalent compounds, given appropriate charts or data tables
- Describe the characteristics of matter
- Differentiate between physical and chemical changes
- Select an appropriate way of separating the components of a mixture

---

By the end of this chapter, you should know the meaning of these **key terms**:

- acid
- atom
- base
- boiling point
- chemical change
- chemical property
- chemical reactivity
- chromatography
- compound
- distillation
- element
- evaporation
- filtration
- freezing point
- gas
- ion charge
- ion/ionic
- kinetic molecular theory
- liquid
- mass
- matter
- melting point
- metal
- mixture
- molecular formula
- molecule
- monatomic ions
- non-metal
- physical change
- physical property
- pure substance
- salt
- solid

Your cellphone, your food, your books, your school, you — everything is made up of matter. How matter can be combined into compounds that form all the different parts of your cellphone depends on physical and chemical properties and physical and chemical changes. In this chapter, you'll learn about the nature of matter and its properties.

2.1 Properties of Matter

Warm Up

1. List four properties of snow.

   ______________________ ______________________

   ______________________ ______________________

2. Name or describe two different types of snow.

   ______________________ ______________________

3. Suggest why there are different types of snow. Hint: Think about why snow can have different properties.

   ____

Classifying Material Properties

Chemistry is the science concerned with the properties, composition, and behaviour of matter. **Matter** is anything that has mass and occupies space. **Mass** is the amount of matter contained in a thing. Usually the mass of common things is measured in grams (g) or kilograms (kg).

Properties are the qualities of a thing, especially those qualities common to a group of things. The relationship between matter and its properties is a very important aspect of chemistry. Properties are classified as being extensive or intensive.

Extensive properties are qualities that are or depend on the amount of the material. Examples of extensive properties are mass, volume, the electrical resistance of a copper wire (which depends on its diameter and length), and the flexibility of a metal sheet (which depends on its thickness).

Intensive properties are qualities that do not depend on the amount of the material. Melting point and density are examples of intensive properties. The gold in Figure 2.1.1 has a melting point of 1064°C and a density of 19.3 g/cm^3. Put another way, gold's melting point and density are the same for all samples of gold. These properties can therefore be used to identify that material. Other intensive properties such as temperature, concentration, and tension differ from sample to sample of the same material.

Figure 2.1.1 *Gold's melting point and density are two intensive properties that can be used to identify samples.*

Every material possesses a unique set of intensive properties that can be used to identify it.

You may be familiar from previous science courses with the alchemist's four elements of matter: earth, air, fire, and water. These elements were not equivalent to matter in modern chemistry. For the alchemists, earth, air, fire, and water represented four fundamental properties of matter. Alchemists believed that these properties existed independent of matter and could be added to matter or removed from matter to transform it. In other words, the alchemists had it backwards: they believed that a material depends on its properties rather that the properties depending on the material.

Physical Properties versus Chemical Properties

The properties of matter are also classified as being either physical properties or chemical properties. Physical changes are changes of state or form. A **physical property** is one that describes a physical change or a physical quality of a material. Melting point, boiling point, color, and hardness are examples of physical properties. Chemical changes are those in which a new substance(s) or species is formed. A **chemical property** is one that describes a chemical change or the tendency of a chemical to react. Chemical properties include stability, flammability, toxicity, and reactivity with other chemicals.

Most chemical properties describe relationships or interactions between different forms of matter. A material's electrical properties, magnetic properties, thermal properties, optical properties, acoustical properties, radiological properties, and mechanical properties (various indicators of strength) are all classified as physical properties. For example, a material can be classified as opaque, transparent, or translucent by how it interacts with light. Other physical properties you may have learned about include temperature, density, viscosity, and surface tension. In this section we'll focus on thermal properties (those related to thermal energy and heat).

> Physical properties describe physical changes.
> Chemical properties describe chemical changes.

Figure 2.1.2 *The wood that is burning to heat the pot is undergoing chemical changes. The boiling soup in the pot is undergoing a physical change.*

Particle Relationships

Matter is composed of basic units or particles that move independently. In some forms of matter, these particles are atoms while in others these particles are groups of atoms called molecules or polyatomic ions. Physical changes involve the repositioning of a material's own independent particles. Chemical changes involve the regrouping of one or more substances' atoms.

Physical properties depend solely on the relationships between the material's own independent particles. Chemical properties depend on how the existing relationships between a substance's atoms contrast with those of other groupings, either with the same or different atoms. For molecular substances, physical changes alter intermolecular relationships (those between the molecules) while chemical changes alter intramolecular relationships (those within molecules). Physical changes generally involve less energy than chemical changes. Changing the positions of molecules relative to one another involves less energy than changing the positions of atoms within molecules. Nature forms hierarchies or levels of organization. Subatomic particles (protons, neutrons and electrons) form atoms which in turn may form molecules which in turn form materials. New properties emerge at and describe each new level of organization.

Quick Check

1. What is matter?

   ____

2. What is a property?

   ____

3. What is an extensive property?

   ____

4. What is a chemical property?

   ____

Kinetic Energy

Kinetic energy is any form of energy that cannot be stored. The greater an object's speed and mass, the greater its kinetic energy. The particles of matter possess a type of kinetic energy called **mechanical energy** because of their continuous motion. Independent atoms and molecules have three forms of mechanical energy or types of motion: translational (movement from place to place), rotational (movement about an axis), and vibrational (a repetitive "back and forth" motion).

Thermal Energy, Temperature, and Heat

Thermal energy is the total mechanical energy of an object's or a material's particles. It is an extensive property as it depends on the size of the object or the amount of the material. Within any substance there is a "normal" distribution of kinetic energy among its particles due to their random collisions. This is very similar to the "normal" distribution of marks among the members of a class. **Temperature** is the average mechanical energy of the particles that compose a material and is therefore an intensive property. An increase in a material's temperature indicates that the average speed of its particles has increased.

A bathtub full of cold water has more thermal energy than a cup of boiling water because the bathtub contains so many more molecules even though they are moving more slowly. Consider the following analogy. Which contains more money, a bathtub full of $5 bills or a cup full of $20 bills? Despite the greater denomination of the bills in the cup, the bathtub still contains more money because it contains so many more bills.

A physical property is largely defined by the instrument used to measure it. Thermometers are used to measure temperature. There are many kinds of thermometers. All thermometers work by correlating some other property of a material to its temperature. Some electronic thermometers contain a small semiconductor, the electric resistance of which correlates to its temperature. Some medical thermometers contain liquid crystals that change colour with varying temperature. Some thermometers correlate the temperature of a material to the infrared radiation it emits. Scientists can infer the temperature of luminous materials from the visible light the materials emit. The standard laboratory thermometer uses the expansion of a column of liquid, usually tinted alcohol or mercury, as an index of its temperature. As a natural consequence of moving faster, the thermometer's particles (atoms or molecules) strike each other harder and spread farther from each other. The expansion of the thermometer fluid is proportional to the average kinetic energy of its particles.

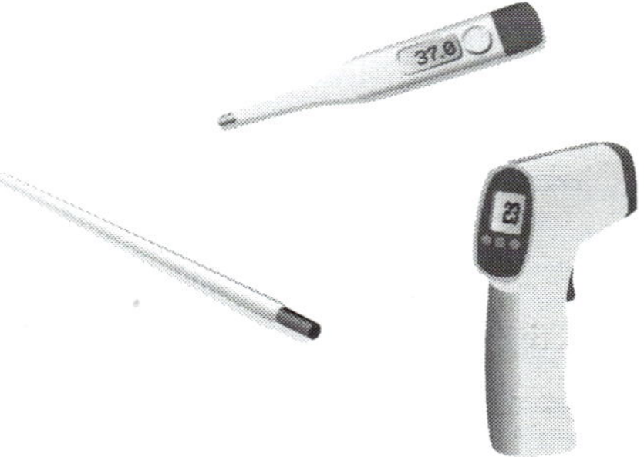

Figure 2.1.3 *Some different types of thermometers*

Most thermometers, including the standard laboratory thermometer, actually display the temperature of the thermometer itself rather than that of the fluid it is immersed in. The scientific definition of **heat** is the energy transferred from one body to another because of a difference in temperature. An object immersed in a fluid will transfer or exchange thermal energy with the fluid until both arrive at the same temperature thus the thermometer ultimately becomes the same temperature as the fluid it is immersed in. This however introduces a "Catch-22" into measuring temperature: the thermometer can't measure the temperature without altering it. When a cold thermometer is placed into hot water, the thermometer heats up and the water cools down until they are at the same temperature. For this reason, chemists include thermometers in their apparatus at the beginning of experiments so they will not have to introduce them into the fluid later.

Quick Check

1. What is temperature? ____________________
2. What is thermal energy? ____________________
3. What is heat? ____________________

The States of Matter

Under normal conditions, matter exists in three states: solid, liquid, or gas. The three states can be defined using both an operational definition and a conceptual definition as in Table 2.1.1. An **operational definition** consists of observable characteristics that help us classify things as belonging or not belonging to the defined group. **Conceptual definitions** explain what operational definitions describe.

Table 2.1.1 *The States of Matter*

State	Operational Definition		Conceptual Definition
	Shape	Volume	
solid	fixed	fixed	Each particle bounces around pushing the ones surrounding it outward. The particles have not spread far enough apart for any particle to fit through a gap between the particles surrounding it so the structure remains intact.
liquid	adopts its container's	fixed	The particles are travelling faster and striking each other harder. As a result they have spread apart to an extent where they can slip by one another.
gas	adopts its container's	adopts its container's	The particles have been struck with enough force to escape their attractions to the other particles in the liquid. They are now either too far apart or moving too fast for their attractions to affect their movement.

The Kinetic Molecular Theory

The **kinetic molecular theory** explains what happens to matter when the kinetic energy of particles changes. The key points of the kinetic molecular theory are:

1. All matter is made up of tiny particles.
2. There is empty space between these particles.
3. These particles are always moving. Their freedom to move depends on whether they are in a solid, liquid, or gas, as described in Table 2.1.1 above.
4. The particles move because of energy. The amount of energy the particles have determine how fast the particles move and how much or far they move.

Figure 2.1.4 identifies the three states of matter and the terms for each phase change. These phase changes depend on temperature. The following terms describe changes from one state to another.

- **freezing:** liquid to solid
- **melting**: solid to liquid
- **evaporation** (also known as vaporization): liquid to gas — special: boiling
- **condensation**: gas to liquid
- **sublimation**: solid to gas
- **deposition**: gas to solid

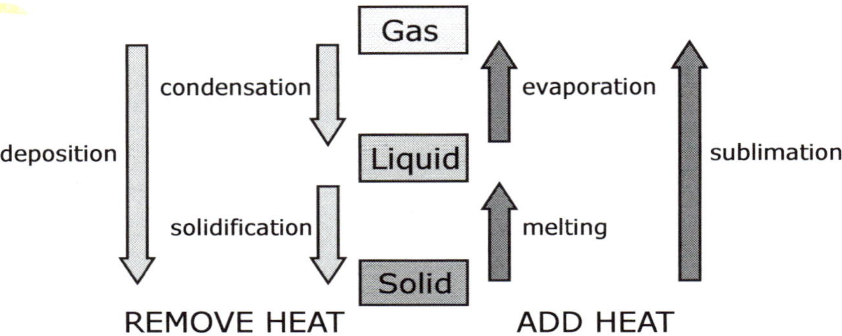

Figure 2.1.4 *Changes of state*

Quick Check

1. Explain the difference between the operational and conceptual definition of a liquid.

 ____

2. Describe the differences in kinetic energy between the particles in a cube of ice and a glass of water.

 ____

3. How does heat contribute to a phase change?

 ____

Some Physical Properties of Pure Substances

Melting Point

A material's **melting point** is the temperature of its solid as it changes to a liquid. Melting occurs because the independent particles (atoms, molecules, or ions) have spread far enough apart so that they can just slip through the gaps between the atoms surrounding them. The melting point of a substance depends on the strength of the attractive forces (bond strength) between its independent particles as well as the mass and symmetry of the particles. The freezing point and melting point of most substances are the same. Thus, the melting point may also be described as the temperature at which a solid can be immersed indefinitely in its own liquid because its rate of melting equals its rate of freezing.

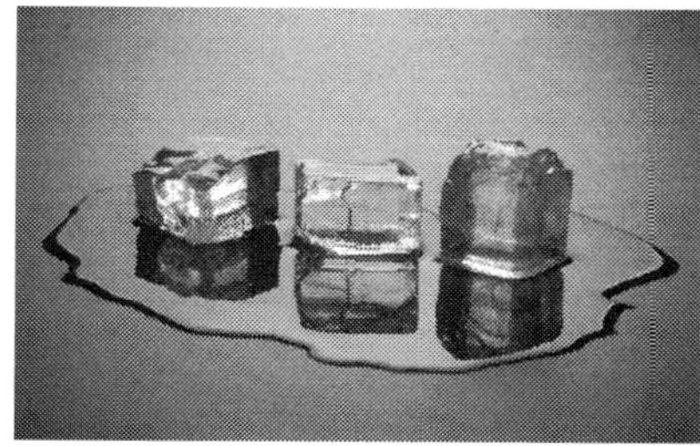

Figure 2.1.5 *At the melting point, a substance can exist in both the solid and liquid states.*

Boiling Point

Boiling is a special case of evaporation. Any particle in the liquid state may evaporate. The puddles on your street evaporate but you've never seen a puddle boil. The gas formed by a substance that boils above room temperature is called **vapour**.

Boiling is the vigorous bubbling that occurs within the body of a liquid as it vaporizes internally. A bubble is a quantity of gas or vapour surrounded by liquid. Imagine a pot of water being heated (Figure 2.1.6). Some molecules at the bottom of the pot are receiving so much heat and consequently moving so fast that they bounce around pushing other water molecules away from them. This produces a bubble. The vapour pressure inside the bubble acts to inflate the bubble while the weight of the water and air above the bubble creates an opposing pressure that acts to collapse the bubble. As the bubble rises, the water vapour molecules transfer energy to the water molecules around the bubble. This causes the vapour molecules to lose energy so the bubble shrinks and collapses before it reaches the surface.

Figure 2.1.6 *Vigorously boiling water. The bubbles are rising to the surface without collapsing.*

The entire pot of water is not yet boiling because it has not yet reached the boiling point. This process continues, transferring energy from the bottom of the pot to the top until all of the water molecules are moving as fast as possible without entering the gas phase. Only at this point, when the bubbles rise to the surface of the water without collapsing is the entire pot of water boiling. Just before breaking through the water's surface the bubble is only opposed by the atmospheric pressure above the liquid. One definition of boiling point is the temperature at which the substance's vapour pressure (the pressure inside that bubble) equals the surrounding air pressure. The air pressure above the sample could be lowered by placing the sample in a vacuum chamber or by taking it to a higher elevation. This would lower the substance's boiling point because the bubbles would have less opposing pressure.

Boiling point is also defined as a substance's highest possible temperature in the liquid state at any given atmospheric pressure. It therefore represents the highest kinetic energy the substance's particles can possess in the liquid state. As the temperature of the water approaches 100°C, more and more of the molecules have their maximum kinetic energy in the liquid state until at 100°C all the molecules are moving at the same maximum speed in the liquid state.

Boiling point, vapour pressure, and volatility are three closely related properties that are all relevant to boiling. **Volatile** substances are substances that readily evaporate or evaporate at high rates. They have high vapour pressures and low boiling points.

Heat of Fusion (H_f)

The **heat of fusion** is the amount of heat required to melt a specified amount of a substance at its melting point. It represents the difference of potential energy between the solid and liquid states since only the substance's state, not its temperature, is changing. **Potential energy** is stored energy. Objects have stored energy by virtue of their position or shape. The heat of fusion is released when the specified quantity of the substance freezes. Heat of fusion is measured in joules per gram.

Heat of Vaporization (H_v)

The **heat of vaporization** is the amount of heat required to evaporate a specified amount of a substance at its boiling point. It represents the difference of potential energy between the liquid and gas states since only the substance's state, not its temperature, is changing. The heat of vaporization is released when the specified quantity of the substance condenses. The heat of vaporization indicates the strength of the force holding the liquid particles together in the liquid state. Heat of vaporization is measured in units such as joules per gram.

Quick Check

1. What is melting? ______________________________

2. What is boiling? ______________________________

3. What is the heat of fusion? ______________________________

Reading a Heating Curve

As energy is added to a solid, the temperature changes. These changes in temperature can be illustrated in a graph called a heating curve. Figure 2.1.7 illustrates an ideal heating curve for water. Note the first plateau in the graph. As a solid melts slowly in its own liquid, the temperature of the liquid will not rise if the melting converts kinetic energy into potential energy as fast as the heat is being added. As the amount of solid decreases, it becomes less able to remove the heat as fast as it is being added. This usually causes the melting segment on the graph to curve upward on the right, rather than remaining horizontal as shown on the ideal heating curve (Figure 2.1.7). The amount of heat needed to melt the ice is the heat of fusion. Once all the ice has melted the water's temperature will begin to increase.

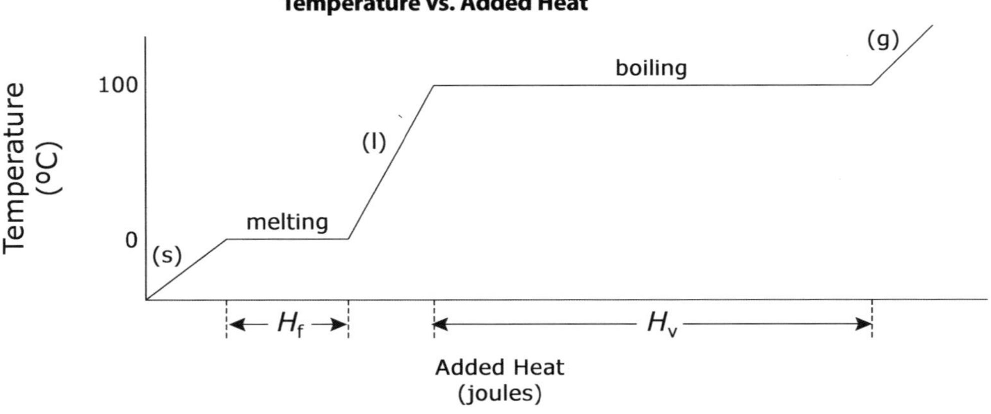

Figure 2.1.7 *Ideal heating curve of water (not to scale)*

Some Chemical Properties of Substances

Reactivity

Reactivity refers to whether a substance reacts or to its reaction rate. Both of these properties are temperature dependent but otherwise depend on different underlying factors. Reaction rates depend on the path from reactants to products, particularly which reactant bonds require breaking. Reaction rates also depend on properties such as reactant concentration. On the other hand, whether or not a reaction will occur depends only on the beginning and end states. Chemical reactions occur because the organization and potential energy of the atoms in the products are favoured over those in the reactants.

Heat of Formation

The **heat of formation** is the heat released when a substance is formed from its elements. The heat of formation is measured in joules per gram.

Heat of Combustion

The **heat of combustion** is the heat released when a specified amount of a substance undergoes complete combustion with oxygen. It is usually measured in units such as joules or kilojoules per gram.

Table 2.1.2 *Some Thermal Properties of Selected Substances*

Substance	Melting Point (°C)	Boiling Point (°C)	Heat of Fusion (J/g)	Heat of Vaporization (J/g)	Heat of Combustion (J/g)	Heat of Formation (J/g)
methane	−182.5	−161.6	69	511	54 000	4 679
ammonia	−77.7	−33.3	333	1 374	22 471	2 710
water	0.0	100.0	334	2 259	—	13 400
magnesium	650	1091	349	5 268	12 372	—

2.1 Activity: The Thickness of Aluminum Foil

Question

What is the thickness of a sheet of aluminum foil?

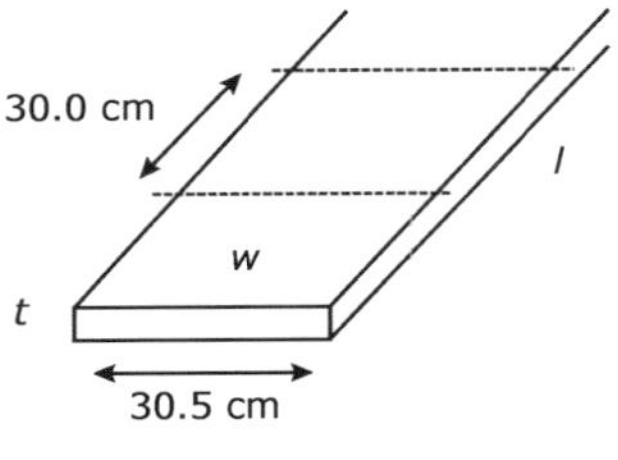

Not to scale

Background

The thickness of a sheet of aluminum foil is an extensive property that is difficult to measure directly with reasonable precision and accuracy. The thickness of the foil can however be derived by dividing its volume by the surface area of one side as proven below:

$$\frac{\text{volume}}{\text{surface area}} = \frac{\cancel{\text{length} \times \text{width}} \times \text{thickness}}{\cancel{\text{length} \times \text{width}}} = \text{thickness}$$

Obviously you can't calculate the volume of the sheet using the formula $V = lwt$ because you don't know the foil's thickness. You will have to calculate its volume by dividing its mass (another extensive property) by its density (an intensive property).

Procedure

1. Mark two points 30 cm apart on one edge of a piece of aluminum foil (see diagram).
2. Repeat step 1 on the parallel edge.
3. Draw a straight line between adjacent points on the opposite edges.
4. Use a razor blade or scissors to carefully cut out your marked section of foil.
5. Scrunch up your piece of foil and weigh it on a milligram scale.

Results and Discussion

Length (cm)	Width (cm)	S. Area (cm^2)	Mass (g)	Density (g/cm^3)	Volume (cm^3)	Thickness (cm)
30.0	30.5			2.702		

1. Calculate the surface area of one side of the foil (length × width). The standard width of a roll of aluminum foil is 30.5 cm, as indicated on the box.

2. Calculate the volume of the piece of foil.

   $$\text{volume} = \_\_\_\_\_\_\_\_ \text{ g Al} \times \frac{1 \text{ cm}^3 \text{ Al}}{2.702 \text{ g Al}} = \_\_\_\_\_\_\_\_ \text{cm}^3$$

3. Calculate the thickness of the sheet of foil.

   $$\text{thickness} = \frac{\text{volume}}{\text{surface area}} = \frac{\_\_\_\_\_\_\_\_ \text{cm}^3}{\_\_\_\_\_\_\_\_ \text{cm}^2} = \_\_\_\_\_\_\_\_ \text{ cm}$$

4. Aluminum atoms have a diameter of 0.286 nm. If aluminum atoms were stacked linearly, one on top of the other, how many atoms thick would this sheet of Al foil be?

5. This technique is remarkably reliable. Compare your results to those of the other groups.

2.1 Review Questions

1. In each pair of items below, which is a form of matter and which is a property?
   (a) vapour, vapour pressure
   (b) freezing point, solid

2. What are two properties shared by all matter?

3. How was the alchemists' view of matter and its properties different from ours today?

4. Describe three general properties that would be desirable for a material(s) being used for the outer sole of tennis shoes. durable, sticky, slightly flexible

5. You sometimes choose one brand over another because it has properties that you prefer. List three properties of paper towels that might influence your choice of which brand to purchase.

6. Whether a property is intensive or extensive often depends on how it is expressed. State whether each of the following physical properties is intensive or extensive.
   (a) temperature
   intensive
   (b) thermal energy
   extensive
   (c) thermal expansion (the change in volume in response to a change in temperature)
   extensive
   (d) coefficient of thermal expansion (the fractional change in volume per degree Celsius change in temperature)
   extensive
   (e) specific heat capacity (the joules of heat required to raise 1 g of the material by 1°C)
   intensive
   (f) heat capacity (the joules of heat required to raise the temperature of the object 1°C)
   intensive

7. State whether each phrase refers to a physical or a chemical property.
   (a) changes of state or form
   physical
   (b) relationships or interactions between matter and energy
   physical
   (c) only evident through a chemical reaction or a lack thereof
   chemical
   (d) dependent solely on the relationships between the material's own particles
   physical
   (e) relationships or interactions between different forms of matter
   chemical

8. State whether each of the following properties is physical or chemical.

   (a) heat of vaporization
   physical

   (b) heat of formation
   chemical

   (c) corrosion resistance
   chemical

   (d) electrical resistance
   chemical

   (e) flammability (how easily something will burn or ignite)
   chemical

   (f) speed of sound through the material
   physical

9. Composite materials (or just composites) consist of two or more constituent materials that adhere to each other but remain separate and distinct (e.g. the materials could be layered on each other). Why do you think manufacturers sometimes use composite materials in their products?

10. What two properties of particles affect the temperature of the material they compose?

11. Density is mass per unit volume, commonly the amount of matter in one cubic centimetre of the material. What two properties of particles affect the density of the material they compose?

12. Briefly explain what causes materials to expand at the particle level when heated.

13. List the defining physical properties of each phase of matter; solids, liquids, and gases.

14. Does an individual atom or molecule have a melting point? Explain.

15. Describe what is occurring at the molecular level when a material melts.

16. Why doesn't the temperature of an ice water bath (a mixture of ice and water) increase as it absorbs heat from a classroom?

17. Under what condition do all the particles of a liquid have the same kinetic energy?

they're all at absolute zero.

18. Provide an operational (what to look for) and a conceptual (an explanation) definition of boiling point.

operational: look for vapor or bubbles in liquid
explanation: the temp at which a liquid turns to vapor

19. (a) Which is greater, a substance's heat of fusion or its heat of vaporization?

heat of vaporization.

(b) Explain in terms of relationships why this would be expected.

because it's harder to turn liquid to gas than solid to liquid

20. (a) Which is greater, a substance's heat of vaporization or its heat of combustion?

(b) Explain in terms of relationships why this would be expected.

21. Sensorial properties describe our senses of a material. Rather than being the properties of something, they are actually the properties of our interaction with that thing. Are sensorial properties such as taste and odour physical properties or are they chemical properties?

22. Label and describe briefly a physical change and a chemical change on the drawing of the lit candle.

23. Students change classes at designated times throughout the day in most secondary schools. How is this event like a chemical change or reaction?

2.2 The Classification of Matter

Warm Up

Most sentences or paragraphs in your textbooks could be classified as a definition, a description, an explanation, a comparison, a sequence, an example, or a classification.

1. Give an example of a sport. ____________________

2. Name a class of sports. ____________________

3. What is the difference between an example of something and a class of something?

____

Classifying Matter

We currently classify everything in the physical world as either a form of energy or a form of matter. Early chemists failed to distinguish between forms of energy and forms of matter. They identified light, heat, electricity, and magnetism as substances. Any solid, liquid, or gas is a form of matter. Matter can be further classified as shown in Figure 2.1.1.

Recall from section 2.1 that there are different types of definitions that describe concepts. An operational definition is more descriptive, providing an operation that helps us classify things as belonging or not belonging to the defined group. Conceptual definitions explain what operational definitions describe. Table 2.2.1 shows operational and conceptual definitions that distinguish between a pure substance and a mixture.

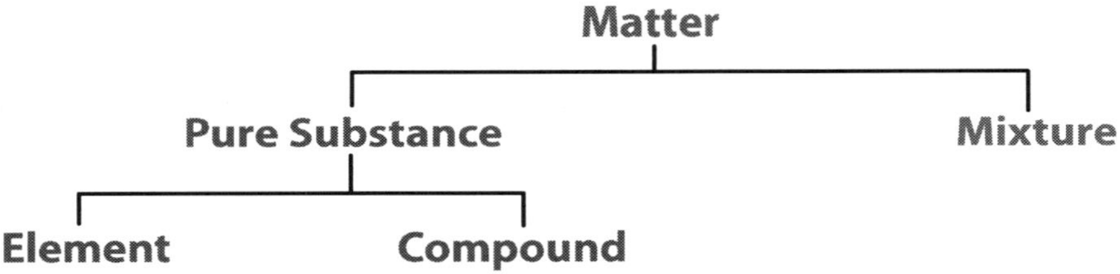

Figure 2.2.1 *Classification of matter*

Table 2.2.1 *Distinguishing Between a Pure Substance and a Mixture*

Material	Operational Definition	Conceptual Definition
pure substance	• all samples have the same proportions of components • a material with only one set of properties	• a material with atoms that are chemically combined in a fixed ratio • a material which in the solid phase has only one pattern and/or grouping of atoms throughout
mixture	• a material with components that retain their own individual identities and can thus be separated • the same components may be mixed in different proportions	• a material composed of more than one substance
element	• a pure substance that cannot be decomposed	• a pure substance composed of only one type of atom
compound	• a pure substance that can be decomposed	• a pure substance composed of more than one type of atom

The particles that make up materials are also forms of matter. Chemists refer to all the particles of matter collectively as **chemical species**. Just as materials are classified, so are chemical species. Chemical species can be classified as neutral atoms, molecules, or ions. These in turn can be further classified as types of atoms, molecules, and ions. Atoms are composed of particles that can be classified as well. The initial classification of chemical species will be discussed later in this section and the rest will be left to later sections and later courses.

Quick Check

1. Use the words, *substance* and *element* in a sentence that describes how the two terms are related.

   ____

2. Use the words, *substance* and *mixture* in a sentence that describes how the two terms are related.

   ____

3. Give an example of an element, a compound, and a mixture.

   ____

Elements

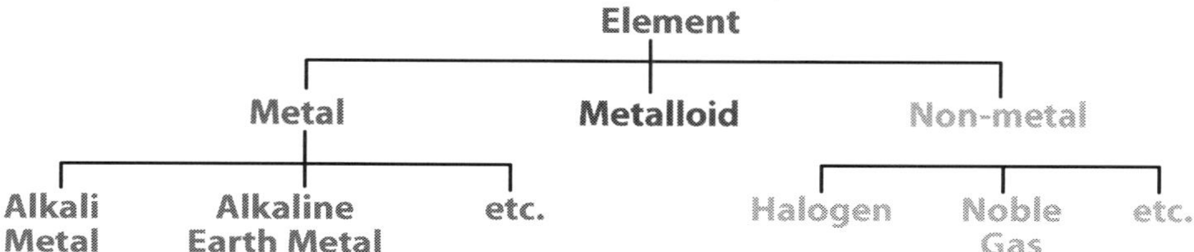

Figure 2.2.2 *Classification of elements*

The elements are further classified as metals, non-metals, and metalloids (Figure 2.2.2). About 80% of the elements are metals. The metals are separated from the non-metals on the periodic table of the elements by a staircase beginning between boron and aluminum as shown in Figure 2.2.3. The elements shaded in grey are generally considered to be metalloids because they are intermediate in properties between the metals and the non-metals. Hydrogen also has properties that are in-between those of the metals and the non-metals. Although it has some chemical properties of metals, it has more in common with non-metals and is classified as a non-metal for most purposes. Hydrogen is such a unique element that it is usually considered to be in a group of its own.

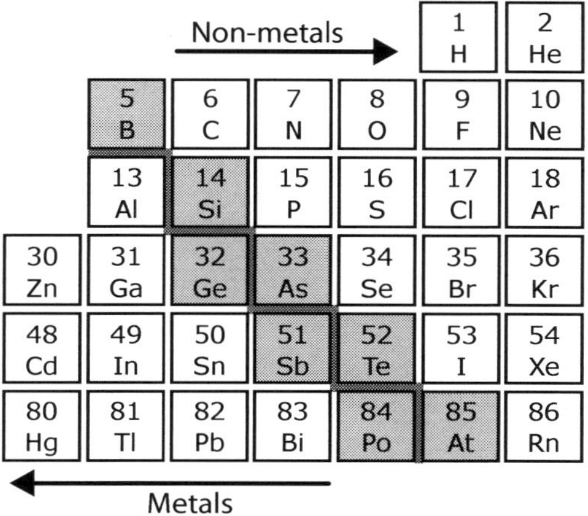

Figure 2.2.3 *The location of metals, non-metals, and metalloids in the periodic table of the elements*

Metals are good conductors of both heat and electricity. They are also malleable (can be pounded into thin sheets), ductile (can be drawn into wires), and lustrous. Many people have the misconception that metals are hard. It is actually **alloys**, mixtures containing metals, which are hard. Metal oxides react with water to form bases (hydroxides). For example:

$Na_2O + H_2O \rightarrow 2\ NaOH$

Non-metals are poor conductors of both heat and electricity. Many are gases at room temperature but in the solid phase their crystals are brittle and shatter easily. Non-metal oxides react with water to form acids. For example:

$CO_2(g) + H_2O(l) \rightarrow H_2CO_3(aq)$ (carbonic acid)

An element is described as being more or less metallic according to the extent that it possesses these properties. Moving up and to the right in the periodic table, there is a general trend toward decreasing metallic character from one element to the next. As a consequence, there is no sharp demarcation between the metals and non-metals. Instead, there is a group of elements called metalloids that exhibit some metallic properties (although weakly) and some non-metallic properties. For example, silicon is a semiconductor meaning that it conducts electricity but poorly. Some elements have different **allotropes** meaning different groupings or arrangements of the same atoms. Some elements bordering on the metalloids have one allotrope that could be considered a metalloid and another or others that are metallic or non-metallic. For example, one allotrope of carbon called diamond is non-metallic whereas another allotrope called graphite is semi-metallic.

Both the metals and the non-metals are further classified according to more selective criteria regarding their chemical and physical properties. These different groups are easily identified and associated with a column or columns in the periodic table. For example, the elements in the first column of the periodic table are called the alkali metals.

Compounds

A compound word is one word that is made from more than one word, e.g. daycare. A compound of matter is a pure substance composed of more than one type of atom. A compound can be decompounded (we say decomposed). Decomposition is a type of chemical reaction in which a single compound reacts to produce two or more new substances. The process requires assemblages of chemically combined atoms to be disassembled and then reassembled in a different manner. Specifically, they reassemble into two or more new groupings or patterns of the atoms. For example:

$2NaCl \rightarrow 2Na + Cl_2$
$K_2CO_3 \rightarrow K_2O + CO_2$
$2H_2O \rightarrow 2H_2 + O_2$

Compounds are classified in several ways. A few of the more common ways in which a compound can be classified are as an organic or inorganic compound, as a molecular or an ionic compound, as an electrolyte or a non-electrolyte, and as a binary or non-binary compound. Some compounds are also classified as acids, bases, or salts.

Organic Compounds versus Inorganic Compounds

An **organic compound** is any compound that has carbon and hydrogen atoms. It may have other types of atoms as well. All other compounds are inorganic, meaning not organic. Organic chemistry is essentially the chemistry of carbon compounds, and inorganic chemistry is the chemistry of all the other elements' compounds. This must surely seem like an unbalanced division of the science. However, because of carbon's unique ability to form extended chain structures, there are countless billions of carbon compounds, while there are less than a thousand inorganic compounds. Living things contain many inorganic compounds but for the most part they are built out of organic compounds. Organic compounds will be covered in chapter 8.

Binary Compounds versus Non-binary Compounds

A **binary compound** is composed of only two elements. Hydrocarbons (compounds consisting of only carbon and hydrogen atoms) are thus binary compounds whereas carbohydrates are non-binary compounds because they contain carbon, hydrogen, and oxygen atoms.

Ionic Compounds versus Molecular Compounds

An **ion** is a charged atom or group of atoms. Because ions are more stable than their corresponding neutral atoms, the atoms of many elements exist almost exclusively in nature as ions. **Ionic compounds** consist of positively and negatively charged ions held together by their opposite electrical charges into long range, symmetrical packing arrangements called **ionic crystal lattices** (Figure 2.2.4). The bond or attraction between oppositely charged ions is appropriately called an **ionic bond**.

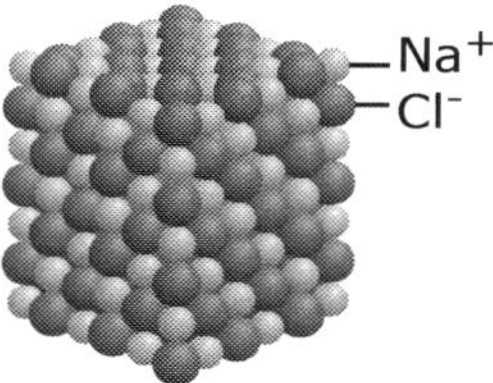

Figure 2.2.4 *An ionic crystal lattice*

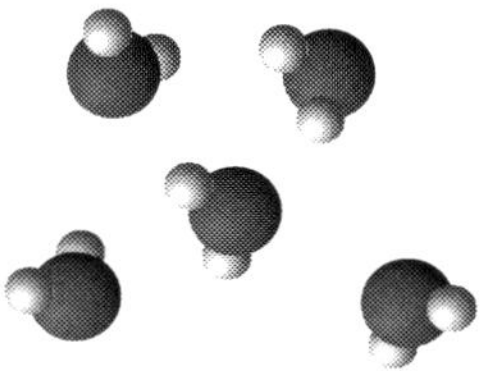

Figure 2.2.5 *A molecular compound*

Non-metal atoms can also become more stable by sharing valence (outer) electrons with each other. A shared pair of valence electrons that holds two atoms together is appropriately called a **covalent bond**. A neutral group of covalently bonded atoms is called a **molecule** and compounds consisting of molecules are called **molecular compounds**.

Non-metals form molecular compounds with other non-metals but form ionic compounds with metals.

> Any compound containing a metal is an ionic compound.
>
> Any compound containing only non-metals is a molecular compound, except compounds containing the ammonium ion (NH_4^+) which are ionic.

Sample Problem — Classifying a Compound as Ionic or Molecular

State whether each of the following is an ionic compound or a molecular compound:

(a) NaCl (b) $Cu(NO_3)_2$ (c) P_2O_5

What to Think about	How to Do It
If the compound contains a metal or the ammonium ion then it is ionic, otherwise it is molecular.	
(a) Na is a metal	(a) NaCl is an ionic compound.
(b) Cu is a metal	(b) $Cu(NO_3)_2$ is an ionic compound.
(c) P and O are both non-metals	(c) P_2O_5 is a molecular compound.

Practice Problems — Classifying a Compound as Ionic or Molecular

1. State whether each of the following is an ionic compound or a molecular compound:

(a) CO_2 ______________________ (d) $Mg_3(PO_4)_2$ ______________________

(b) CaF_2 ______________________ (e) $Li_2Cr_2O_7$ ______________________

(c) C_3H_8 ______________________ (f) NH_4Cl ______________________

Acids versus Bases versus Salts

Some compounds are also classified as acids, bases, or salts. There are both organic and inorganic acids, bases, and salts.

From its formula, an **acid** appears to be a compound having one or more H^+ ions bonded to an anion (e.g., HCl, H_2SO_4, H_3PO_4). In reality, acids are a special type of molecular compound that can be induced to form these ions. This is a complex affair you'll learn about in Chemistry 12.

Chemists actually have three different conceptual definitions of acids and bases, which they use interchangeably depending on the circumstance. The most common definition of a **base** is a hydroxide. This is any compound containing the hydroxide (OH^-) ion. Examples include NaOH, $Ca(OH)_2$, and $Al(OH)_3$.

A **salt** is any ionic compound other than a hydroxide. A salt is thus one type of ionic compound, the only other type being a base. Acids and bases react to produce a salt and water. This type of reaction is called a neutralization reaction. For example:

$$HCl + NaOH \rightarrow NaCl + H_2O$$

Quick Check

Circle the correct response.

1. Salts are (ionic or molecular).
2. $Mg(OH)_2$ is a(n) (acid, base, or salt).
3. AgBr is a(n) (acid, base, or salt).

Classification of Mixtures

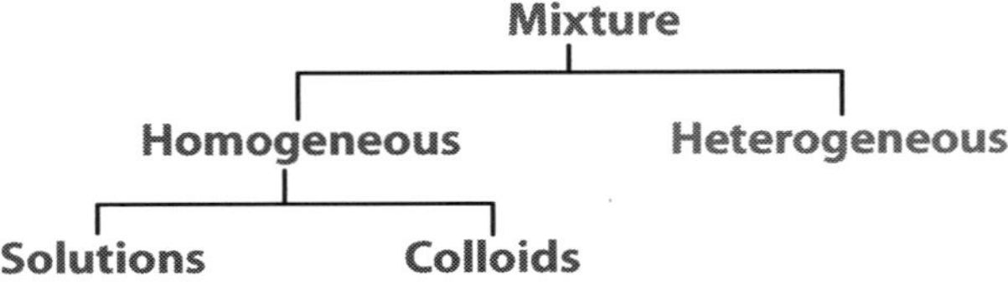

Figure 2.2.6 *Classification of mixtures*

Table 2.2.2 *Distinguishing Between Homogeneous and Heterogeneous Mixtures*

Material	Operational Definition	Conceptual Definition
Homogeneous mixture	a mixture that appears the same throughout	The individual particles are smaller than 1 μm (a micrometre).
Heterogeneous mixture	a mixture that doesn't appear the same throughout	At least some particles are larger than 1 μm (a micrometre).

There are many instances where the scientific meaning of a word conflicts with its general usage or even its literal meaning. As an example, the components of a material do not need to be mixed for it to be a chemical mixture. Any material having atoms that are not chemically combined in a fixed ratio is a chemical mixture and would be so even if those atoms were organized in a uniform pattern. Conversely, any material having atoms that have been chemically forced into a fixed ratio is a pure substance and would be so even if those atoms were mixed. As an example, molten (melted) sodium chloride is a pure substance. Even though its ions are mixed, they coexist in a chemically determined ratio and cannot be separated into pure Na^+ ions and pure Cl^- ions.

The difference between the classes of mixtures is really a matter of degree, rather than of kind. It can't be overemphasized that there is no sharp demarcation between the classes of mixtures but rather a general trend from smaller particles to larger particles in moving from solutions to colloids to heterogeneous mixtures.

A **homogeneous mixture** is one that appears the same throughout. A homogeneous mixture is not actually perfectly homogeneous. Atoms are not homogeneous and therefore nothing composed of atoms is truly homogeneous. A homogeneous mixture doesn't even have the same proportions of atoms throughout because every sample has a slightly different composition due to the random motion and mixing of the particles. It can be difficult to distinguish between a homogeneous mixture and a compound since both appear to be the same throughout. Whether or not the constituents of air for example are chemically combined was still a point of contention in the early 1800s. The French chemists, Proust and Berthollet, had an ongoing debate over this issue. What Berthollet perceived as a compound that could vary in proportion, Proust perceived as a physical mixture. As a prerequisite to his development of atomic theory, John Dalton resolved the issue in 1808 by simply declaring that any process in which elements do not combine in a fixed proportion is not a chemical process. Thus any material having constituents that do not combine in a fixed proportion became a mixture. This scheme proved to be so fruitful in advancing chemistry that it quickly found general acceptance.

Solutions

A **solution** is a type of homogeneous mixture in which the constituent chemical species do not aggregate to form any particles greater than 1 nm (nanometre). A **solute** is a minor component of the mixture, generally what has been dissolved. The **solvent** is the major component of the mixture, generally what the solute was dissolved in. Many chemicals are in **aqueous** solution (dissolved in water). Our lakes, rivers, oceans, drinks, and bodily fluids are all aqueous solutions. Chemists denote that a chemical is in aqueous solution with "*aq*" in brackets after the formula (e.g., NaCl(*aq*)).

Solutions can be produced from materials in different phases (e.g., a solid can dissolve in a liquid). Regardless of the constituents' phases when undissolved, a solution is a single phase, usually that of the solvent. If the solvent is a solid, it is melted to allow for mixing and then cooled to solidify the mixture.

Table 2.2.3 *Examples of Solutions*

	Solute		
Solvent	**Solid**	**Liquid**	**Gas**
Solid	steel, bronze	mercury in gold	hydrogen in palladium
Liquid	salt water	gasoline	oxygen in water
Gas	–	–	air

Colloids

A colloidal system consists of particles between 1 nm and 1 μm dispersed throughout a continuous medium (Table 2.2.5). The particles of the dispersed phase are large molecules (macromolecules) or aggregates of molecules that are invisible to the naked eye. Unlike a solution, the colloid particles can be in a different phase than the dispersion medium in which they are suspended. Any mixture of solid particles in a liquid, regardless of how small the solid particles are, is a colloid or a mechanical mixture.

If a liquid is translucent (cloudy) then it is a colloid or a heterogeneous mixture. A bright beam of light is not visible when shone through a solution because the particles of a solution are too small to reflect or scatter the light. A bright beam of light is visible however when shone through a colloid because the particles of the dispersed phase are large enough to scatter and reflect the light. This is called the **Tyndall effect**.

Table 2.2.4 *Names and (Examples) of Colloids*

Medium	Dispersed Phase		
	Solid (grains)	**Liquid** (droplets)	**Gas** (bubbles)
Solid	solid sol (some stained glass)	gel (jelly, butter)	solid foam (styrofoam)
Liquid	sol (blood)	emulsion (milk, mayonnaise)	foam (whipped cream)
Gas	solid aerosol (smoke)	liquid aerosol (fog)	–

Heterogeneous Mixtures

If one or more of the components of a mixture is visible then it is a **heterogeneous mixture**. The term, "mechanical mixture" is often misused as an intended synonym for "heterogeneous mixture." A mechanical mixture is a mixture of components that can be separated by mechanical means, i.e. by picking, sifting, shaking, spinning, pouring, skimming, etc. This definition includes at least some mixtures of every class. For example, the components of colloids can be separated by mechanical means such as centrifugation (spinning) and ultra-filtration. Even isotopes of the same element (atoms of the same element with different masses) can be separated by centrifugation. If the heterogeneous mixture has a dispersed phase and a continuous medium then, it is a **coarse suspension** or just a suspension.

Colloids are distinguished from suspensions by their longevity or stability. Colloids remain suspended indefinitely but the larger mass of the suspended particles in suspensions causes them to settle out or **sediment** upon standing. The dispersed phase in a suspension is usually a solid. Common examples of suspensions include silt in water, dust in air, and paint (pigments in a solvent). The component particles are all visible solid particles in some heterogeneous mixtures such as gravel.

Table 2.2.5 provides operational and conceptual definitions of solutions, colloids, and suspensions.

Table 2.2.5 *Distinguishing Solutions, Colloids, and Suspensions*

Type of Mixture	Operational Definition*			Conceptual Definition**
	Tyndall Effect	Sediments if left undisturbed	Separates by Centrifugation	
Solution	no	no	no	All particles are < 1 nm.
Colloid	yes	no	yes	Dispersed particles are between 1 nm and 1 um. Particles comprising the medium are < 1 nm.
Suspension	yes	yes	yes	Dispersed particles are > 1 μm.

* The operational definitions only provide methods of differentiating mixtures that have a liquid continuous medium.

** The sizes cited for the particles are only rough guidelines, not steadfast rules.

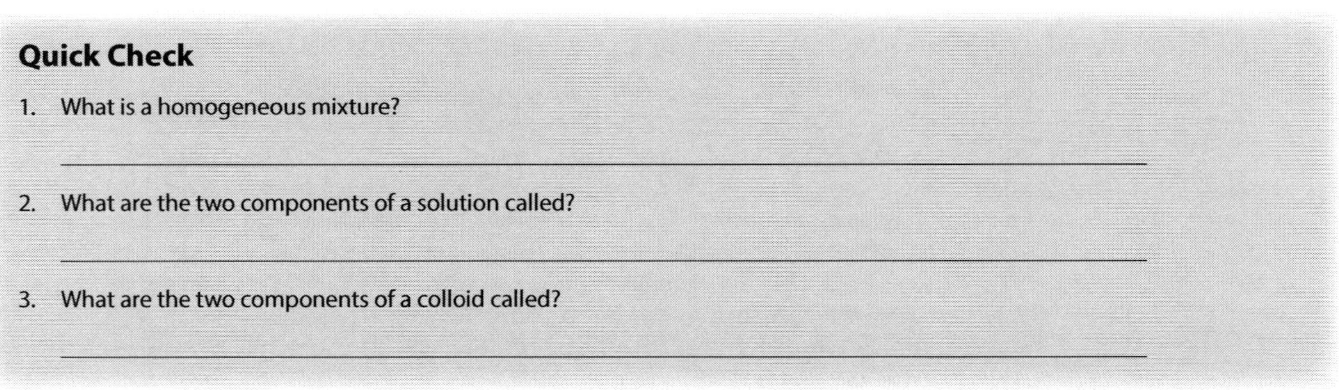

Quick Check

1. What is a homogeneous mixture?

____

2. What are the two components of a solution called?

____

3. What are the two components of a colloid called?

____

2.2 Activity: Classifying Chemical Glassware

Question

Can things be classified according to a variety of schemes?

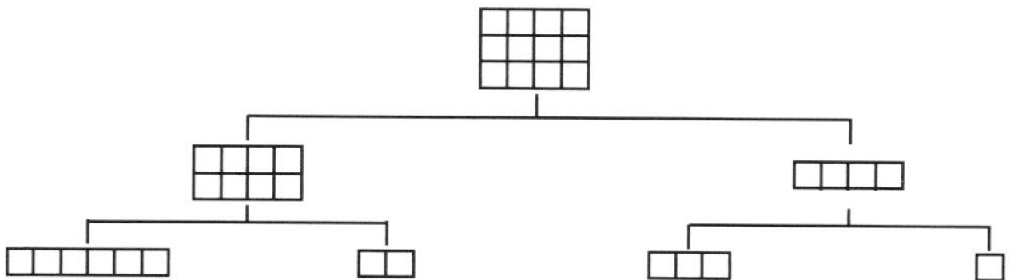

Background

In section 1.1 you were asked to classify items of safety equipment. People have a compulsion to mentally organize the world around them. Knowledge is essentially recognizing relationships. Organizing our world helps us to cope with it and allows us to think about it. The way we conceptualize or organize the world reflects both the world itself and the ways we perceive it. You are classifying something every time you call something by a name that isn't specific to that individual thing.

Procedure

1. Your teacher will display a variety of chemical glassware.
2. Divide the items into two groups based on any criterion you choose.
3. Subdivide the items in each of the two groups into two smaller groups again based on any criteria you choose.

Results and Discussion

1. Display your groupings on a piece of poster paper using a classification chart like that shown at the top of the page. Include your criteria on the chart.
2. Compare your classification scheme with those of other groups.
3. Were some classification schemes more valid than others? Explain in the space below.

2.2 Review Questions

1. Name an element, a compound, and a mixture found in your home.

2. Is it easier to prove that an unknown substance is an element or a compound? Explain.

3. Elements, compounds and mixtures are each classified into types of elements, compounds, and mixtures. Use "properties" or "composition" to correctly complete each of the following sentences:

   (a) Elements are classified on the basis of their ________________________.

   (b) Compounds are classified on the basis of their ______________________.

   (c) Mixtures are classified on the basis of their ________________________.

4. Using only white circles (○) and black circles (●) to represent different types of atoms, draw an element, a molecular compound, an ionic compound, a mixture of elements, and a mixture of compounds using at least 10 circles in each drawing.

5. Classify each of the following as an element (E), a compound (C), or a mixture (M).

   (a) potassium fluoride
   (b) eggnog
   (c) can be decomposed
   (d) can vary in proportions
   (e) carbon
   (f) seawater
   (g) substance containing only one type of atom
   (h) contains more than one substance

6. Classify each of the following elements as a metal, metalloid, or a non-metal.
   (a) germanium (b) calcium (c) iodine (d) xenon

7. Give four examples of physical properties of metals.

8. Complete the following table by classifying each of the compounds.

Compound	Organic or Inorganic	Binary or Non-Binary	Molecular or Ionic	Acid, Base, Salt or None of these
$CaCl_2$				
CH_3CH_2OH				
NH_4ClO_3				
KOH				
C_3H_8				
H_3PO_4				
$Ba(NO_3)_2$				
CO_2				
$Al(OH)_3$				

9. Suppose that chemists used nanotechnology to produce a material with two different types of metal atoms organized into alternating rows. Would this material be a substance or would it be a mixture? Explain.

10. Why is no material truly homogeneous at the atomic level?

11. Is a mixture of O_2 and O_3 (two different allotropes of the element oxygen) a chemical mixture? Explain.

12. Identify each of the following species as a neutral atom, an ion, or a molecule.

(a) N_2 (b) O (c) NO_2^- (d) H (e) NH_3 (f) K^+

13. Complete the following table by checking (✓) the type(s) of mixture each statement describes.

	Solution	Colloid	Heterogeneous Mixture
All particles are less than 1 nm in size			
Gravel			
Does not appear the same throughout			
Forms a sediment if left undisturbed			
Has a solute and a solvent			
Milk			
Exhibits the Tyndall effect			
Homogeneous mixture			
Coarse suspension			
Orange juice with pulp			
May be separated by centrifugation			

14. To diagnose an ulcer, a doctor may have the patient drink a suspension of barium sulphate which coats the patient's gastrointestinal tract allowing it to be imaged by X-rays. What is the difference between a suspension and a colloid?

15. Is dust a colloid or is it a suspension? Explain.

16. Correct each of the following sentences by replacing the underlined word.

    (a) Salt water is a denser <u>substance</u> than fresh water.

    (b) The colloid particles were <u>dissolved</u> in water.

2.3 Separating the Substances of a Mixture

Warm Up

A student scoops up a pail full of water and mud from the bottom of a pond. The mixture in the pail is a suspension of mud particles and algal cells and a solution of salts. Outline a method for separating these three components.

____

____

____

Separating Mixed Substances

Most naturally occurring objects and materials are mixtures. Our atmosphere, our natural water systems, and the ores and petroleum products (such as crude oil and natural gas) that we extract from the ground are mixtures. Just as a compound can be decompounded (decomposed), a mixture can be unmixed. Since the ingredients of a mixture are not chemically combined, they retain their individual identities. The trick to separating the substances in a mixture is to pick a property that clearly differentiates the substances.

Consider a mixture of marbles and beads. Because the marbles and beads do not form any aggregates, they can easily be separated by pouring the mixture into a colander (a bowl full of holes). It would capture the marbles but allow the beads to pass through. Laboratory technicians perform a tremendous number of separations daily in medical, forensic, and analytical chemistry laboratories to allow the substances in the mixtures to be identified. Large industrial-scale separations are performed around the world in commercial refineries (for sugar, oil, metal, etc.) to obtain the target substances for their useful properties, their intrinsic values, or more commonly to use the substances to produce useful mixtures of our own design.

Mechanical Means of Separation

In Chemistry 12, you'll examine a chemical separation technique called selective precipitation. In this course we restrict our studies to **physical separations**: those not involving chemical reaction. Physical separation techniques include centrifugation, chromatography, recrystallization, decantation, density separation, distillation, electrophoresis, evaporation, extraction, flotation, filtration, freezing, magnetic separation, reverse osmosis, and sedimentation. Physical separations may be classified as mechanical or non-mechanical. Non-mechanical means of separation include techniques that use heat, electricity, magnetism, dissolving, or sticking to separate a mixture's components. **Mechanical means of separation** use gravity, contact forces, or motion to sort the components of a mixture. Terms such as picking, sifting, filtering, shaking, spinning, pouring, and skimming, describe the type of actions involved in mechanical separations. We'll just describe some of the more common techniques in this section.

Density Separation

To **sediment** (verb) means to fall or sink to the bottom of a liquid. **Sediment** (noun) is matter that has fallen or sunk to the bottom of a liquid. As Isaac Newton deduced, an object doesn't just fall of its own accord. A force is required to change an object's state of motion. A falling object is acting under the influence of gravity. The difference between falling through a vacuum (which is essentially empty space) and falling through a medium is the medium. A medium exerts an upward force called **buoyancy** on all objects immersed in it. As an object enters a fluid, it lifts the fluid it displaces. A buoyant force equal to the weight of this displaced fluid is redirected upward on the immersed object.

Every object surrounded by a fluid (air, water, etc.) has at least some of its weight supported by buoyancy.

If the object is less dense than the fluid, then the object will float because it will displace a weight of fluid greater than its own weight. Therefore, the force of buoyancy acting on it will be greater than the force of gravity acting on it. Density separation can be used to separate solids with different densities. By adding a liquid that is more dense than one of the solids in the mixture, only that solid floats while the others sink. Conversely, by adding a liquid that is less dense than one of the solids in the mixture, only that solid sinks while the others float. The solids must be insoluble in the liquid media used to selectively float or sink them. This technique is used to separate plastics of different densities.

F_b F_b

F_g F_g

net upward force results in the particle rising

net downward force results in the particle sinking

Figure 2.3.1 *Forces acting on particles suspended in a heterogeneous mixture*

Although density separation separates the solid particles from each other, they are now mixed with the liquid(s) used to separate them. The particles that float can be skimmed off the top of the liquid and dried. The particles that sediment can be separated from the liquid by decanting off the liquid or by filtering out the sediment. **Decanting** is carefully pouring off the liquid and leaving the sediment in the bottom of the original container. A small amount of liquid is usually left in the container and care must be taken to prevent a small amount of sediment from flowing with the liquid out of the container.

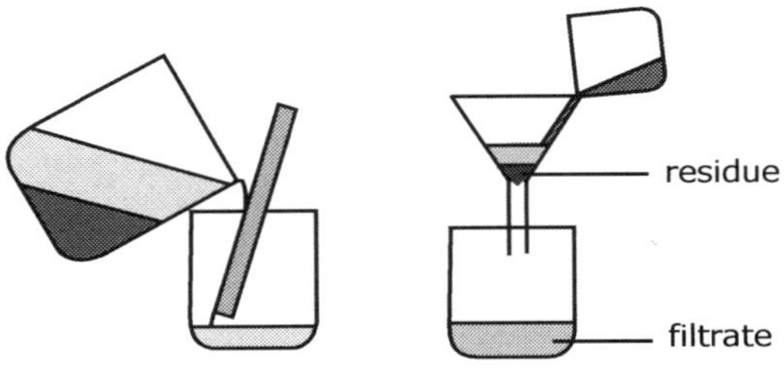

Figure 2.3.2 *Decanting (left) and filtering*

The sediment can also be separated from the liquid by filtration. In the simplest form of **filtration**, the liquid containing the sediment is poured into a folded piece of filter paper in a funnel. The material filtered out of the mixture is called the **residue**. The liquid that passes through the filter paper is called the **filtrate**. Dissolved substances and colloids are too small to be filtered out by regular filter paper but some colloids can be removed by ultra-filtration which uses filter paper with extremely small pores.

Centrifugation

Another mechanical means of separation is centrifugation or spinning. Centrifugation enhances density separation. Particles that would normally sink or rise still do so, just more rapidly.

When you are in a car that turns a sharp corner you may be "thrown" sideways. It might seem as though a force pushed you against the door. To explain this and similar phenomena, people have invented an imaginary or nonexistent force known as a centrifugal force, which is said to cause the outward motion. In fact, no force was necessary for you to keep travelling at a constant speed in a straight line. When the car turned, you didn't. Your body attempted to keep going in your original direction. All objects have a resistance to change in motion. This property is called **inertia**. The suspended particles in a mixture behave similarly in a centrifuge. As the tube changes its direction, the suspended particles initially maintain their linear motion. This process occurs continuously as the tube spins, directing the suspended particles to the bottom of the tube (Figure 2.3.3).

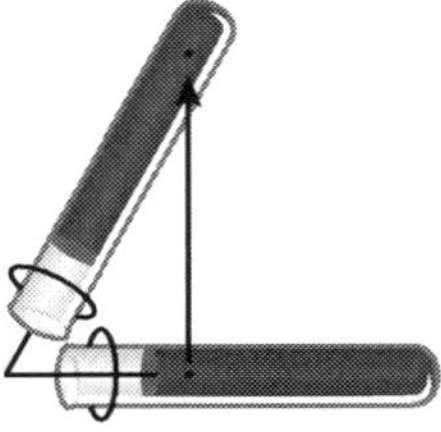

Figure 2.3.3 *The particle in the centrifuge tube continues to travel in a straight line while the tube turns. The spinning forces it to the bottom of the tube, as shown on the right.*

Quick Check

1. What force causes objects to float? ______________________
2. What is decanting?

   ____
3. How does centrifugation work? ______________________

   ____

Non-Mechanical Means of Separation

Chromatography

Chromatography is one of the most widely used techniques in scientific research today. The processes involved in the separation are generally mild ones. Chromatography has been successfully employed to separate some of the most fragile and elusive substances. Researchers have been able to devise a chromatographic method for separating all but a few mixtures.

Chromatography separates the substances in a solution by having a flowing liquid or gas carry them at different rates through a *stationary phase*. The flowing liquid or gas is called the *mobile phase*. Each substance travels through the stationary phase at its own characteristic rate, according to its relative affinities for the two phases. A substance that adheres strongly to the stationary phase but isn't very soluble in the mobile phase travels slowly through the chromatogram. Conversely, a substance that adheres weakly to the stationary phase but is very soluble in the mobile phase travels quickly through the chromatogram.

There are many forms of chromatography. These include gas chromatography, column chromatography, thin layer chromatography, and paper chromatography. In thin layer chromatography (TLC), the stationary phase is a thin layer of silica gel dried onto a glass plate. In paper chromatography, the stationary phase is a strip or sheet of paper. The mobile phase in both forms of chromatography could be water, an organic solvent such as alcohol, or a mixture of solvents. A drop of the solution to be separated is placed near the bottom of the sheet or plate and allowed to dry. Another drop of the solution is then placed on top of the first and also allowed to dry.

This process is repeated many times until there is a sufficient amount of each solute to produce a clear chromatogram. The bottom of the chromatogram is lowered into a pool of the solvent. **Capillary action** is the tendency of a liquid to rise in narrow tubes or to be drawn into small openings. Capillary action results from the adhesive forces between the solvent molecules and those of the wicking material in combination with the cohesive forces between the solvent molecules themselves. Capillary action causes the solvent to rise up the stationary medium, between the paper fibres or the grains of the gel, past the deposit of solutes, and up the remainder of the paper or glass plate.

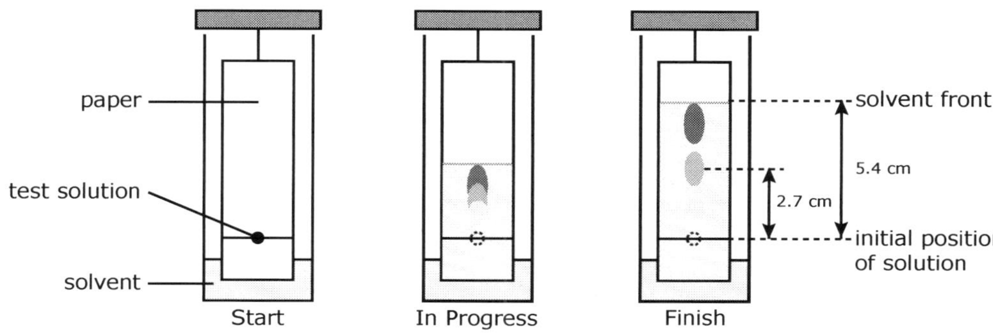

Figure 2.3.4 *Thin layer or paper chromatography*

A substance's $\boldsymbol{R_f}$ (retention factor) for any particular system is defined as its flow speed relative to that of the mobile phase. Here is an example calculation:

$$R_f = \frac{\text{distance the substance flows}}{\text{distance the solvent flows}} \quad \text{(in a given time period)}$$

$$= \frac{2.7\text{ cm}}{5.4\text{ cm}} = 0.50$$

A substance's R_f may help identify it or at least support its identification by more definitive means.

"Developing a chromatogram" is the spraying of chemicals on a chromatogram to form coloured complexes with the separated substances so they reveal their location. *Elution* is the process of rinsing the separated substances off the chromatogram. Their recovery is usually necessary so that they can be identified through further analysis. Chemists commonly run at least two chromatograms under identical conditions. One is developed to determine the location of the separated substances. The substances are then eluted from the same locations on the undeveloped chromatogram.

In column chromatography, the stationary phase is a glass tube packed with specially treated resin beads. The mobile phase is sometimes just the solution itself but another solvent may be needed to wash the solutes through. Column chromatography is an "open-ended" form of chromatography in which the separated substances flow out the bottom end of the column at different times. Periodic chemical tests or constant electronic monitoring indicates the presence of substances as they leave the column. For column chromatography, the substances' R_f values are calculated as:

$$R_f = \frac{\text{substance time}}{\text{solvent time}} \quad \text{(to travel through the column)}$$

Electrophoresis is similar to chromatography except that the stationary phase is a gel-coated slide or gel-filled dish with oppositely charged electrodes at either end. Species are separated according to their charge or polarity, mass, and size. Other separation methods that involve solubility include solvent extraction and recrystallization. In solvent extraction, one or more compounds are soluble in a particular solvent while the others are not. In recrystallization, trace amounts of impurities stay in solution as the solution is cooled

Distillation

Distillation is any process that separates a mixture of substances by using their different vapour pressures or boiling points. Distillations require a heating device, a flask containing the original mixture, a condenser to cool and condense the vapours, and something to collect the condensed substances as they leave the condenser one after the other (Figure 2.3.5). Distilled water is produced by boiling tap water, cooling its vapours, and then collecting the condensate or **distillate**. The impurities that were dissolved in the water remain as **residue** in the original flask.

Such *simple distillations* are suitable for separating dissolved solids from a solvent but there is a fundamental problem using this technique to separate two liquids. Liquids can evaporate long before boiling occurs as evidenced by the puddles on our street that come and go without ever boiling. Because of this, the initial distillate is still a mixture although it is now richer in the liquid with the lower boiling point. If you took this distillate and repeated the distillation process, the next distillate would be richer still in this liquid. If you repeated this process many times, each time the distillate would become increasingly richer in the substance with the lower boiling point but this would be a tedious process. A mixture that cannot be completely separated by simple distillation is called an azeotropic mixture.

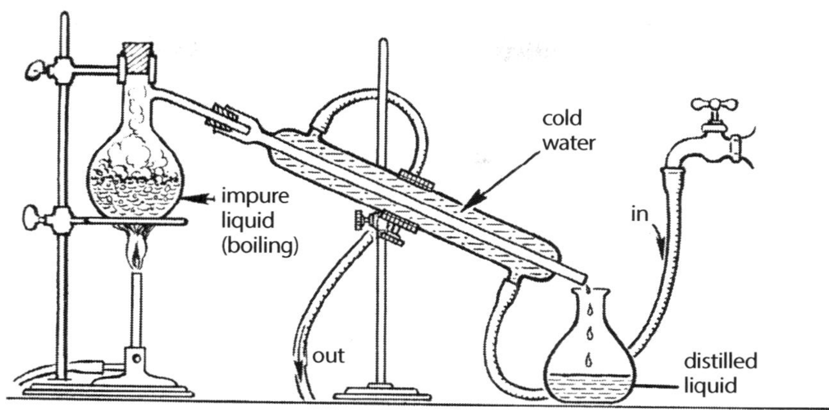

Figure 2.3.5 *Laboratory distillation apparatus*

Scientists have therefore devised a method called **fractional distillation** in which the simple distillation (vaporizing and condensing) is repeated many times within the one device. After evaporating, the vapour enters a *fractionating column*. This may be a tube packed with glass fibres, a tube containing overlapping glass lips or plates, or simply coiled tubing as popularized by backwoods stills. The idea is to provide surfaces on which the vapours can condense. As the hot vapours from below reheat the distillate, some compounds revapourize and travel farther up the column. At the same time, others with higher boiling points drip back in the opposite direction. This process is called *reflux*. The plates become progressively cooler as you move up the column. Each time the process is repeated, the distillate becomes richer in the liquid with the lower boiling point. The component liquids thus proceed at different rates up the fractionating column so as you move higher up, the mixture becomes increasing richer in the liquid with the lower boiling point. If the column is long enough, the liquid components may separate completely and enter the condenser one after the other. There are of course several variations on this same technique.

Figure 2.3.6 *Industrial distillation*

Distillation is an important laboratory and industrial process (Figure 2.3.6). Oil refineries employ distillation to separate the hundreds of different hydrocarbons in crude oil into smaller groups of hydrocarbons with similar boiling points. Chevron has an oil refinery in Burnaby and Husky has an oil refinery in Prince George. When distilling a single batch, as described and illustrated above, the temperatures within the column continuously change as the chemicals travel through the column much like solutes travelling up a piece of chromatography paper. By contrast, oil refineries continuously feed the vaporized crude oil mixture into large steel fractionating towers that electronically monitor and maintain a steady range of temperatures from 400°C at the bottom to 40°C at the top. Each compound rises until it reaches a section of the column that is cool enough for it to condense and be withdrawn from the column. For example, the gasoline fraction (meaning the fraction containing gasoline, itself a mixture) exits near the top of the tower at the 40°C to 110°C level.

Froth Flotation

BC is one of the world's major mining regions, and mining is a key contributor to the province's economy. Precious metals such as gold and silver are very stable or unreactive and are found in nature in their "native" or elemental form. This property is central to their value in jewellery. Other metal atoms such as copper are mostly found in nature in ionic compounds. Naturally occurring compounds are called **minerals**.

Rock containing a desired mineral is called **ore**. The first stage of mining is to extract the ore via blasting or drilling, depending on the kind of mine. The second stage is to mill or crush the ore into a fine powder. The third stage is to separate the target mineral(s) from the rest of the ore, called gangue. Copper compounds are separated by a technique called **froth flotation**. The powdered rock is mixed with water and then a small amount of pine oil is added that adheres to the mineral grains but not to the gangue. Oil and water don't mix so the grains are rendered **hydrophobic** or water repelling. Air is bubbled through the mixture and the hydrophobic grains of mineral escape the water by attaching to the air bubbles, which float them to the surface. The target mineral is then skimmed off, washed, dried, and shipped to a refinery where it is decomposed to recover the metal. Froth flotation is also used in wastewater treatment and paper recycling.

Quick Check

1. What is chromatography?

____

____

2. What is distillation?

____

____

3. Name three areas that use froth flotation.

____

____

2.3 Activity: Separating Stuff

Question
Can you separate a variety of objects using methods that don't rely on their appearance?

Background
Chemists separate the substances in a mixture by picking on properties that clearly distinguish the substances from one another.

Procedure
1. Design and perform a procedure to separate a mixture of marbles, paper clips, pennies and small wooden discs.
2. Record your results in the table below.

	Procedure	Items Separated from Mixture
1.		
2.		
3.		

Results and Discussion
1. What property of each item allowed you to separate it from the mixture?

2. Was the order of the procedures important in your separation scheme?

3. Discuss any complications that arose during your procedures.

4. Compare your methods with those of other groups.

2.3 Review Questions

1. What is the difference between decomposing compounds and separating mixtures?

2. Give three reasons for separating the substances in a mixture.

3. Oil floats on top of water because it is less dense. However, oil pours more slowly than water because it is more viscous. Is the ability of a fluid to suspend particles more closely correlated to its density or its viscosity?

4. Inertia plays an integral role in most mechanical separations.
   (i) What is inertia?

   (ii) Describe the role inertia plays in centrifugation.

5. Rewrite the underlined part of the following statement to correct it.
   Heavier particles centrifuge more rapidly because <u>of the greater centrifugal force exerted on them.</u>

6. Devise a simple scheme for separating a mixture of sand, sugar, and iron filings. Each material must be recovered in its original solid form.

7. Briefly describe the role of a furnace filter.

8. Briefly describe how chromatography separates the substances in a mixture.

9. What does the phrase "developing a chromatogram" refer to?

10. What is elution and what is its usual purpose?

11. Why should you mark the starting position of the deposited solution on the chromatography paper with pencil rather than pen?

12. What is the R_f of the compound shown in the diagram ?

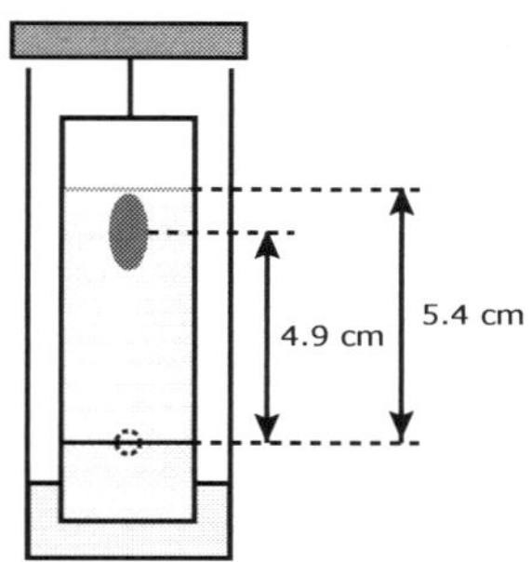

13. What is the basic problem with simple distillation?

14. Identify two factors that affect how completely the components of a solution are separated by fractional distillation.

15. Air is approximately 78% nitrogen (boiling point: –196°C) and 21% oxygen (boiling point: –183°C). Briefly describe how you would separate nitrogen and oxygen from air.

16. Which process requires more energy: chromatography or distillation? Explain.

17. Both density separations and froth flotations involve some materials floating and others sinking, yet density separations are considered a mechanical means of separation while froth flotations are not. What is the main difference between these two techniques?

2.4 Names and Formulae of Inorganic Compounds

Warm Up

Ions are charged atoms or charged groups of atoms. Ions always associate (bond) together in the ratio that results in their charges cancelling to form neutral compounds. Complete the table by providing the formulas of the compounds formed by the ions specified.

	Br^-	O^{2-}	N^{3-}	OH^-	SO_4^{2-}	PO_4^{3-}
Na^+	NaBr		Na_3N			
Ca^{2+}						$Ca_3(PO_4)_2$
Al^{3+}				$Al(OH)_3$		
NH_4^+		$(NH_4)_2O$				
Sn^{4+}					$Sn(SO_4)_2$	

Binary Ionic Compounds

Recall from section 2.2 that non-metals form molecular compounds with other non-metals but they form ionic compounds with metals. The names and formulas of these two types of compounds are handled differently.

A **binary compound** contains the atoms of only two elements, and binary ionic compounds contain only two types of **monatomic ions** (charged individual atoms).

The name of any ionic compound is simply the name of its constituent metal ion followed by the name of its constituent non-metal ion.

For example, a compound containing sodium ions and chloride ions is called sodium chloride.

The ratio of the ions formed when a particular metal and non-metal react can be predicted through the charge of their common ions, which can be found in the table of common ions at the back of this book. Positively charged ions are called **cations** (think of the letter 't" as a + sign). Negatively charged ions are called **anions.** Note that the sign of the ion charge (+ or –) is written after the numeral. For example, the aluminum ion is denoted as Al^{3+} rather than as Al^{+3}. Scientists felt that placing the plus or minus charge before the numeral might mislead people into believing that it meant greater than or less than zero. In fact, these plus and minus signs designate the type of electrical charge. The different types of electrical charge are called opposite charges because they have opposing effects. They can cancel each other. Note that there is a difference between cancelling two things and two things cancelling. Cancelling two things (e.g., magazine subscriptions) means eliminating them. By contrast, two things cancelling means they negate each other's effects. This is what happens with positive and negative ion charges. When particles with equal but opposite charges bond together, the charges cancel to yield a product with a net charge of zero.

The concept of a net property means that the property of the whole is equal to the sum of the still existing properties of its parts. Ions always associate together in a ratio that results in their charges cancelling to form neutral compounds. For example:

separate — combined

$$2Al^{3+}(aq) + 3S^{2-}(aq) \rightarrow Al_2S_3(s)$$

$$6+ \quad + \quad 6- \quad = \quad 0$$

All compounds are neutral. There is no such thing as a charged compound.

The formula Al_2S_3 means that there are $2Al^{3+}$ ions for every $3S^{2-}$ ions. Chemists know the charges but don't show the charges in the formulas of ionic compounds. The ionic nature of the compound is implicit in the combination of a metal and a non-metal. The formula of an ionic compound shows that the compound as a whole is neutral even though it contains both positively and negatively charged ions. Remember that a neutral atom also contains positively and negatively charged particles (protons and electrons) that are not evident in its symbol.

Look at the formula of aluminum sulphide shown below on the left. The number of aluminum ions equals the numerical value of the sulphide ion's charge and vice versa. This simple shortcut for determining the formula of ionic compounds is sometimes called the cross-over method. The cross-over method matches up the opposite charges so that they cancel and will always work if you reduce the formula to its simplest ratio.

Al^{3+} S^{2-} Al_2S_3

$2(3+) = 3(2-)$

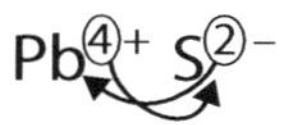

Pb^{4+} S^{2-} Pb_2S_4 which reduces to PbS_2

$2(4+) = 4(2-)$

Multivalent Ions

Some elements have two or more possible valence shell electron configurations (ways of arranging its electrons). These **multivalent** elements have more than one form of stable ion. Many of the transition metals (groups 3 to 12 in the periodic table) are multivalent. For example, iron has two stable ions, Fe^{2+} and Fe^{3+}. Rather than Fe^{2+} being called the iron two plus ion, it is simply called the iron two ion, but it is written as iron(II), bracketing the roman numeral for the numerical value of the ion's charge after the name. Likewise Fe^{3+} is called the iron(III) ion. The roman numerals only appear in the compound's name, never in its formula.

A different method for naming the ions of multivalent elements was used in the not too distant past, and you may encounter it occasionally. In that method, an *–ous* or *–ic* suffix was added to the root of the element's name from which the symbol was derived. The *–ous* suffix denoted the lesser ion charge and the *–ic* suffix denoted the greater ion charge. For example, the iron(II) ion, Fe^{2+}, was called the ferrous ion, and the iron(III) ion, Fe^{3+}, was called the ferric ion.

Sample Problem — Determining the Formula of a Binary Ionic Compound from Its Name

What is the formula of tin(IV) sulphide?

What to Think about	How to Do It
1. Write the symbols of the ions named. 2. Combine the ions in the simplest ratio that results in their charges cancelling.	Sn^{4+} S^{2-} $1\,Sn^{4+} + 2\,S^{2-} \rightarrow SnS_2$ $4+ \quad + \quad 4- \quad = \quad 0$

Sample Problem — Determining the Name of a Binary Ionic Compound from Its Formula

What is the name of Fe_2S_3?

What to Think about	How to Do It
1. Write the names of the two constituent ions. 2. Write the formulas of the possible compounds to see which one has the correct formula.	iron(II) or iron(III), sulphide iron(II) sulphide $Fe^{2+} + S^{2-} \rightarrow FeS$ ✗ iron(III) sulphide $2\,Fe^{3+} + 3\,S^{2-} \rightarrow Fe_2S_3$ ✓

Practice Problems — Determining the Names and Formulas of Binary Ionic Compounds

1. Write the formula of each of the following binary ionic compounds:

(a) lithium sulphide	(c) aluminum chloride	(e) tin(II) iodide
(b) chromium(III) oxide	(d) lead(II) sulphide	(f) zinc bromide

2. Name each of the following binary ionic compounds:

(a) ZnO ____________	(d) NaI ____________
(b) $PbCl_4$ ____________	(e) K_2S ____________
(c) $CuCl_2$ ____________	(f) CrO ____________

Polyatomic Ions

Recall that a molecule is a *neutral* group of covalently bonded atoms. A **polyatomic ion** is a *charged* group of covalently bonded atoms so it's like a molecule except that it has a charge. Polyatomic ions play an extremely important role in the environment, the laboratory, and industry. They are relatively stable species that often remain intact in chemical reactions. Many polyatomic ions are **oxyanions**, consisting of an atom of a given element and some number of oxygen atoms. Typically the element forms polyatomic ions with different numbers of oxygen atoms. When the element forms two such ions, the one with the lesser number of oxygen atoms takes an *–ite* suffix, while the one with the greater number of oxygen atoms takes an *–ate* suffix. For example:

nitrite	NO_2^-	nitrate	NO_3^-
sulphite	SO_3^{2-}	sulphate	SO_4^{2-}

When there are more than two oxyanions in a series, the prefixes *hypo-* (less than) and *per-* (more than) are used to indicate polyatomic ions with still less or still more oxygen atoms. For example:

hypochlorite	ClO^-
chlorite	ClO_2^-
chlorate	ClO_3^-
perchlorate	ClO_4^-

The prefix bi- before the name of a polyatomic ion adds an H^+ to it. For example:

carbonate	CO_3^{2-}	hydrogen carbonate or bicarbonate	HCO_3^- $(H^+ + CO_3^{2-})$
sulphate	SO_4^{2-}	hydrogen sulphate or bisulphate	HSO_4^- $(H^+ + SO_4^{2-})$

Note that there are some exceptions to these naming conventions. The hydroxide ion is the only polyatomic ion to have an *–ide* suffix. The dichromate ion has the formula $Cr_2O_7^{2-}$ and despite its prefix does not refer to two chromate ions.

Because they are charged, polyatomic ions associate with oppositely charged ions to form ionic compounds. Polyatomic ions are bracketed in formulas. For example, the formula of calcium nitrate is $Ca(NO_3)_2$. This means that the atoms within the brackets are bonded covalently to each other and as a group they are bonded ionically to the atom or atoms outside the brackets. The brackets are necessary to show that the formula ratio applies to the entire polyatomic ion, not just to its last atom. For example, the formula of calcium hydroxide is $Ca(OH)_2$ meaning that there are two hydroxide (OH^-) ions for each calcium ion. If the brackets were omitted, the formula would look like this: $CaOH_2$. In that case, the subscript 2 would apply only to the hydrogen atom. By convention, chemists omit the brackets if no subscript is required. For example, Na(OH) is written as just NaOH.

The ionic compounds that you'll encounter in this course will each have only two types of ions unless otherwise specified. Therefore, the first element in the formula will represent the cation and the remainder will represent the anion. The one exception is in ammonium compounds; the only polyatomic cation you'll encounter is the ammonium ion, NH_4^+. For example:

$ZnCr_2O_7$ must consist of Zn^{2+} ions and $Cr_2O_7^{2-}$ ions (to cancel the 2+).
$Cr_2O_7^{2-}$ is the dichromate ion so this compound is called zinc dichromate.

$NaClO_2$ must consist of Na^+ ions and ClO_2^- ions (to cancel the 1+).
ClO_2^- is the chlorite ion so this compound is called sodium chlorite.

Sample Problem — Determining the Formula of any Ionic Compound from Its Name

What is the formula of potassium sulphite?

What to Think about	How to Do It
1. Write the symbols of the ions named.	$K^+ \quad SO_3^{2-}$
2. Combine the ions in the simplest ratio that results in their charges cancelling.	$2K^+ + SO_3^{2-} \rightarrow K_2SO_3$ $2+ \quad + \quad 2- \quad = \quad 0$

Sample Problem — Determining the Name of any Ionic Compound from Its Formula

What is the name of $Cr(HSO_4)_2$?

What to Think about	How to Do It
1. Write the names of the two constituent ions.	chromium(II) or chromium(III), bisulphate
2. Write the formulas of the possible compounds to see which one has the correct formula.	chromium(II) bisulphate $Cr^{2+} + 2HSO_4^- \rightarrow Cr(HSO_4)_2$ ✓ chromium(III) bisulphate $Cr^{3+} + 3HSO_4^- \rightarrow Cr(HSO_4)_3$ ✗

Practice Problems — Determining the Names and Formulas of Ionic Compounds

1. Write the formula of each of the following ionic compounds:

(a) barium sulphate
(b) silver nitrate
(c) mercury(II) bromide
(d) tin(IV) oxalate
(e) aluminum dichromate
(f) potassium fluoride

2. Name each of the following ionic compounds:

(a) $Zn(OH)_2$ ______________________
(b) SnO ______________________
(c) $Cu(ClO)_2$ ______________________
(d) $NaCH_3COO$ ______________________
(e) MgI_2 ______________________
(f) $FeCr_2O_7$ ______________________

Names and Formulas of Binary Molecular Compounds

Any cation and anion combine in a single ratio that is easily predictable from their charges. This is why ionic compounds' names do not need to explicitly contain their formulas. On the other hand, two non-metal atoms may share electrons and combine in several ratios. Therefore, the name of the molecular compound must reveal its formula to distinguish it from the other compounds of the same two elements. The name of a molecular compound uses a prefix code to provide its formula. The prefixes used are shown in Table 2.4.1.

The names of all binary compounds have an *–ide* suffix. N_2O_4 is therefore dinitrogen tetroxide. Note that the number of atoms comes before the *name* of the element but after the *symbol* of the element. The prefix *mono-* is understood for the first element named if no prefix is stated. For example, carbon dioxide is CO_2.

Table 2.4. *Prefixes for Molecular Compounds*

Number	Prefix
1	mono-
2	di-
3	tri-
4	tetra-
5	penta-
6	hexa-
7	hepta-
8	octa-
9	nona-
10	deca-

Sample Problem — Determining the Formula of a Molecular Compound from Its Name

What is the formula of xenon tetrafluoride?

What to Think about	How to Do It
1. Write the symbols of each element and the number of atoms of each.	1 Xe and 4 F
2. Rewrite this information as a formula.	XeF_4

Sample Problem — Determining the Name of a Molecular Compound from Its Formula

What is the name of P_4S_{10}?

What to Think about	How to Do It
1. Write the names of each element and the number of atoms of each.	4 phosphorus and 10 sulphur
2. Rewrite this information using the prefix code.	tetraphosphorus decasulphide

Practice Problems — Determining the Names and Formulas of Molecular Compounds

1. Write the formula of each of the following molecular compounds:

   (a) nitrogen monoxide

   (b) nitrogen dioxide

   (c) dinitrogen tetroxide

   (d) dinitrogen trioxide

2. Name each of the following molecular compounds:

   (a) PCl_5 ______________________

   (b) SO_2 ______________________

   (c) CO ______________________

   (d) P_2O_5 ______________________

Hydrates

When many salts crystallize out of aqueous solution they incorporate water molecules in a fixed ratio and pattern into their ionic crystal lattice. These salts are called **hydrates.** Many salts are supplied as hydrates. The water in the crystal doesn't usually present a problem as most salts are destined for aqueous solutions anyway. Water is an integral part of hydrates and thus must be accounted for in both their names and their formulas. The same prefixes used for naming molecules precede the term *-hydrate* to denote the number of water molecules in the formula. This tells you the ratio of water molecules to ions.

Gently warming a hydrated salt will usually remove the water from the crystal. The term "**anhydrous**" refers to the form of the salt without ("an") water ("hydrous"). Some anhydrous salts are *hygroscopic* which means that they can absorb water from the air to form hydrates. Hygroscopic salts that are being used to keep the air dry in a container are called **desiccants**. Pouches containing silicate salts are sometimes used as desiccants in boxes or cases containing binoculars, guitars, shoes, etc. Most labs have a special airtight glass container designed to store containers of hygroscopic salts. This container is called a **desiccator**. One of the salts is poured onto the bottom of the desiccator to keep its air dry so the others are not exposed to water vapour.

Sample Problem — Determining the Formula of a Hydrate from Its Name

What is the formula of copper(II) sulphate heptahydrate?

What to Think about	How to Do It
1. Write the symbols of the ions named. 2. Combine the ions in the simplest ratio that results in their charges cancelling. 3. Tack on the appropriate number of water molecules to complete the formula.	Cu^{2+} SO_4^{2-} $Cu^{2+} + SO_4^{2-} \rightarrow CuSO_4$ heptahydrate means $7H_2O$ $CuSO_4 \cdot 7H_2O$

Sample Problem — Determining the Name of a Hydrate from its Formula

What is the name of $NaCH_3COO \cdot 3H_2O$?

What to Think about	How to Do It
1. Write the names of the two constituent ions. 2. Tack on the appropriate number of water molecules using the prefix code (–hydrate).	sodium, acetate sodium acetate trihydrate

Practice Problems — Determining the Names and Formulas of Hydrates

1. Write the formula of each of the following hydrates:
   (a) barium chloride dihydrate
   (b) sodium carbonate monohydrate
   (c) iron(III) nitrate nonahydrate
   (d) barium hydroxide octahydrate

2. Name each of the following hydrates:
   (a) $CoCl_2 \cdot 6H_2O$ ____________________
   b) $FeCl_3 \cdot 4H_2O$ ____________________
   (c) $Na_2Cr_2O_7 \cdot 2H_2O$ ____________________
   (d) $MgSO_4 \cdot 7H_2O$ ____________________

Acids

Acids have a number of interesting and unique properties. An acid can be thought of as one or more H^+ ions bonded to an anion. Remember that in ionic compounds the charges cancel (negate each other) without being cancelled (eliminated). In acids however, these ion charges are actually cancelled as the ions convert into neutral atoms and the group of atoms into a molecule. **Acids** are a special type of molecular compound that can be induced to form ions. The names of acids are based on the name of the anion formed.

The rules for naming acids depend on whether the anion contains oxygen. If the *anion doesn't contain oxygen*, the prefix *hydro-* precedes the name of the anion and the suffix *–ic* replaces the *–ide* in the anion's name. Hydrogen fluoride (HF) is hydrofluoric acid; hydrogen chloride (HCl) is hydrochloric acid; hydrogen cyanide (HCN) is hydrocyanic acid, etc. There are of course some exceptions. S^{2-} is the sulphide ion, not the sulphuride ion yet hydrogen sulphide (H_2S) is hydrosulphuric acid.

If the *anion does contain oxygen* then the suffix *–ic* replaces *–ate* in the anion's name or the suffix *–ous* replaces *–ite* in the anion's name. Hydrogen sulphate (H_2SO_4) is sulphuric acid and hydrogen sulphite (H_2SO_3) is sulphurous acid.

It bears mentioning that the term "acid" is sometimes ambiguous in that it may refer either to the compound or to its solution. For example, $H_2SO_4(l)$ and $H_2SO_4(aq)$ are both called sulphuric acid. Although the latter might be referred to as a solution of sulphuric acid, it is commonly referred to simply as sulphuric acid. Hydrogen chloride is a gas that condenses into a liquid at –85°C. Because neither the gas nor the liquid is commonly encountered, the term "hydrochloric acid" virtually always refers to an aqueous solution of hydrogen chloride.

Sample Problem — Determining the Formula of an Acid from Its Name

What is the formula of hydrobromic acid?

What to Think about	How to Do It
1. Decode the suffix to determine possible anions: bromic denotes bromide or bromate.	Br^- or BrO_3^-
2. Decode the prefix (if any) to select the anion: *hydro-* indicates that the anion doesn't contain oxygen.	Br^-
3. Determine the formula from the ion charges.	$H^+ + Br^- \rightarrow HBr$

Sample Problem — Determining the Name of an Acid from Its Formula

What acid has the formula HNO_2?

What to Think about	How to Do It
1. Write the names of the two constituent ions.	hydrogen nitrite
2. Use the code for naming acids. The anion contains oxygen so the suffix *–ous* replaces *–ite* in the anion's name.	nitrous acid

Practice Problems — Determining the Names and Formulas of Acids

1. Write the formula of each of the following acids:

(a) hydrofluoric acid

(b) hypochlorous acid

(c) phosphoric acid

(d) hydrosulphuric acid

2. Name each of the following (as) acids:

(a) HCH_3COO ____________________

(b) H_2SO_3 ____________________

(c) H_2CO_3 ____________________

(d) HI ____________________

2.4 Activity: The Ionic Compound Card Game

Question
Are students more likely to study or practise if it's fun?

Background
The basic premise of fun theory is that the easiest way to change people's behaviour is to make the desired behaviour more fun than the other options. Learning is sometimes defined as changing behaviour. From that perspective, we are testing the theory that people are more likely to learn if it's fun than simply virtuous or to our advantage. Learn more about fun theory by searching for "The Fun Theory" online.

Procedure
1. Your teacher will have made some special cards for this fun activity. Thank your teacher. (Teachers: go to bcscienceinteractions.com for stickers and instructions.)
2. Deal seven cards to each player.
3. The player to the left of the dealer flips one card face up from the deck. The player then attempts to make a compound by combining one or more cards from his or her hand with the card that is face up on the table. Each compound may only consist of two types of ions.
   If the player makes a compound then the player must correctly state the formula or name of the compound. Those cards are then removed from the game. If the player cannot make a compound or correctly state the formula or name of the compound, the player leaves the card face up on the table.
4. Play rotates clockwise around the table. A player always begins a turn by flipping over a card from the deck so there is always at least one card to combine with. A player may make only one formula per turn. Cards flipped over from the deck remain there until combined with a card or cards from a player's hand. Every time a player is unable to form a compound, the number of cards face up on the table increases by one.
5. The game continues until someone wins by having no cards remaining in his or her hand. The first player to win two hands wins the game.

Results and Discussion
1. Did you enjoy this card game? Why or why not?

2. Did it help you learn how to write chemical formulas or remember the names of ions? Why or why not?

3. Feel free to devise an ionic formula card game of your own: ionic formula rummy, ionic formula "Go Fish," etc.

2.4 Review Questions

1. In each case below, write out the chemical equation for the association of the ions that form the given binary ionic compound.
   Example: magnesium phosphide
   $3\ Mg^{2+} + 2\ P^{3-} \rightarrow Mg_3P_2$
   (a) sodium fluoride

   (b) iron(II) bromide

   (c) tin(IV) chloride

   (d) chromium(III) sulphide

2. Write the formulas of the following binary ionic compounds:
   (a) chromium(III) chloride

   (b) aluminum fluoride

   (c) magnesium iodide

   (d) tin(IV) oxide

3. Write the names of the following binary ionic compounds:
   (a) K_2O

   (b) $ZnBr_2$

   (c) PbO_2

   (d) $HgCl_2$

4. Write the name and formula of the binary ionic compound formed by:
   (a) potassium and chlorine

   (b) manganese(IV) and oxygen

   (c) iron(III) and sulphur

   (d) copper(II) and iodine

5. In each case below, write out the chemical equation for the association of the ions that form the given ionic compound,
   Example: magnesium nitrate
   $Mg^{2+} + 2\ NO_3^- \rightarrow Mg(NO_3)_2$
   (a) sodium nitrite

   (b) silver phosphate

   (c) lithium ethanoate (lithium acetate)

   (d) chromium(III) oxalate

6. Write the formulas of the following ionic compounds:
   (a) copper(I) perchlorate

   (b) calcium bisulphide

   (c) aluminum monohydrogen phosphate
   (d) magnesium hydroxide

7. Write the names of the following ionic compounds:
   (a) $Ba_3(PO_4)_2$

   (b) $Fe(HSO_3)_2$

   (c) $Pb(HC_2O_4)_4$

   (d) CuH_2PO_4

8. Many minerals contain three types of ions. In BC, we mine several minerals of copper including two forms of copper(II) carbonate hydroxide.
   malachite
   $2\ Cu^{2+} + CO_3^{2-} + 2\ OH^- \rightarrow Cu_2(CO_3)(OH)_2$
   $4+ \ + \ 2- \ + \ 2- \ = \ 0$
   azurite
   $3\ Cu^{2+} + 2\ CO_3^{2-} + 2\ OH^- \rightarrow Cu_3(CO_3)_2(OH)_2$
   $6+ \ + \ 4- \ + \ 2- \ = \ 0$
   Notice that more than one ratio of the ions results in their charges cancelling. Thus there is more than one possible compound of three ion combinations. Write a <u>possible</u> formula for:
   (a) iron(III) sodium chromate

   (b) zinc sulphate nitrate

9. Write the formulas of the following molecular compounds:
   (a) chlorine monoxide
   (b) tetraphosphorus hexaoxide
   (c) arsenic pentafluoride
   (d) nitrogen tri-iodide

10. Write the names of the following molecular compounds:
   (a) P_3Br_5
   (b) B_2H_6
   (c) SO_3
   (d) CF_4

11. Write the formulas of the following hydrated salts:
   (a) sodium sulphate decahydrate
   (b) calcium chloride dihydrate
   (c) copper(II) acetate monohydrate
   (d) chromium(III) chloride hexahydrate

12. Write the names of the following hydrated salts:
   (a) $Cd(NO_3)_2 \bullet 4H_2O$
   (b) $Na_2HPO_4 \bullet 7H_2O$
   (c) $CuSO_4 \bullet 5H_2O$
   (d) $Fe(NO_3)_3 \bullet 9H_2O$

13. Why is a hydrate not a mixture of salt and water?

14. Suggest why hydrate formulas are written in the manner they are, rather than bracketing the number of water molecules in the formula (e.g., $SrCl_2 \bullet 6H_2O$ rather than $SrCl_2(H_2O)_6$).

15. Write the formulas of the following acids:
   (a) hydrobromic acid
   (b) chromic acid
   (c) chloric acid
   (d) hypochlorous acid

16. Write the names of the following acids:
   (a) H_2S
   (b) $HClO_4$
   (c) HNO_2
   (d) HSCN

17. Write the formulas of the following variety of compounds:
   (a) potassium oxide
   (b) permanganic acid
   (c) sulphur dioxide

   (d) ammonium carbonate
   (e) iron(II) sulphate heptahydrate
   (f) hydrocyanic acid
   (g) sulphur hexafluoride
   (h) calcium acetate monohydrate
   (i) chromium(III) bisulphite
   (j) magnesium hydroxide

3 The Mole — The Central Unit of Chemistry

This chapter focuses on the following AP Big Idea from the College Board:

Big Idea 1: The chemical elements are fundamental building materials of matter, and all matter can be understood in terms of arrangements of atoms. These atoms retain their identify in chemical reactions.

By the end of this chapter, you should be able to do the following:

- Explain the significance and use of the mole
- Perform calculations involving the mole
- Determine relationships between molar quantities of gases at STP
- Perform calculations involving molecular and empirical formulas to identify a substance
- Describe concentration in terms of molarity
- Perform calculations involving molarity

By the end of this chapter you should know the meaning of these **key terms**:

- empirical formula
- molarity
- molar mass
- molar solution
- molar volume
- mole
- molecular formula
- molecular mass
- percentage composition
- relative atomic mass
- standard solution
- stoichiometry
- STP

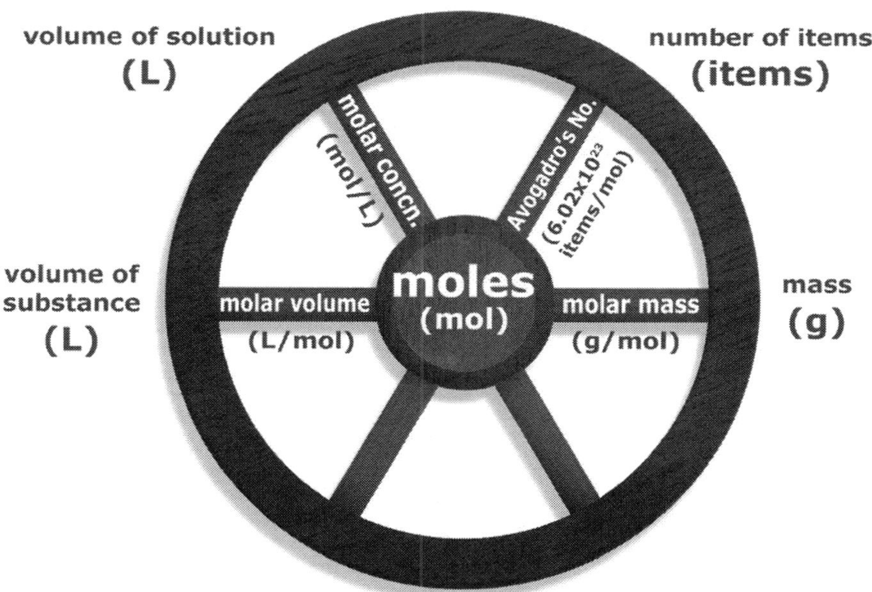

The mole is at the centre of the chemical measurement.

3.1 Relative Atomic Mass

Warm Up

1. Complete the grocery list by filling in the missing units (Figure 3.1a).
   One __________ eggs, Two __________ milk, Three __________ flour
2. From your answer to #1, what are the three ways that we typically express amounts of materials?

   (a) number of items (b) ____________________ (c) ____________________

We express amounts of materials in different ways.

Relative Mass

Experimental chemistry is essentially figuring out things about matter that cannot be observed directly. The joy of experimental chemistry lies in figuring out how to figure it out. Consider the following ingenious method for determining the relative masses of objects without needing to know their actual masses. **Mass** is the amount of matter. When you say that one object has twice as much mass as another you are expressing the object's **relative mass**. You are comparing one object's mass to the other's.

Suppose you wanted to determine the relative mass of a staple and a grain of rice, each of which is too small to register a mass on your balance (Figure 3.1.1). Why not weigh 100 of each? If 100 identical staples weigh twice as much as 100 identical grains of rice then one staple will weigh twice as much as one grain of rice. The nifty aspect of this technique is that we don't even need to know how many objects we are weighing: we just need to know that we're weighing the same number of each. If some number of staples weighs twice as much as the same number of rice grains then any number of staples will weigh twice as much as that number of rice grains.

Figure 3.1.1 *One hundred staples and one hundred grains of rice have the same mass ratio as one staple and one grain of rice, 2:1.*

This technique for determining relative mass still works even if the items being weighed are not identical. If the items being weighed for comparison are not identical, then the ratio provided is that of their average masses rather than the ratio of the masses of the individual items since this would depend on which individual items. For example, if a variety of pens weighs 1.52 times as much as the same number of a variety of pencils then the average mass of these pens is 1.52 times the average mass of these pencils.

> The mass ratio of any equal number of items equals the average mass ratio of those individual items.

While you should never confuse the terms "weight" and "mass," the word "weigh" serves double duty. To **weigh** is to find the weight or compare the weights of. Since scales work by comparing weights, you are by definition "weighing" objects and materials with a scale. In fact, a **weighing scale** is a measuring instrument for determining the mass or weight of an object.

Quick Check

1. What does "relative mass" mean? ____
2. You have two bags of candy from a bulk food store: a bag of gumdrops and a bag of jujubes. You intend to determine the relative masses of a jujube and a gumdrop by weighing the contents of each bag. What condition is necessary for this to work? ____

Law of Constant Composition

In this book, as in most chemistry textbooks, much of our current chemical knowledge will be presented in historical context. Instead of just telling you what we know (or think we know), we'll tell you how chemists came to this understanding. This is because chemistry is more than just an accumulated list of facts about matter: it is also the processes that lead us to such information. By learning and assessing these processes, as well as the facts, some of you will decide to continue this quest. In addition, people often acquire a better understanding of a concept by learning the concept in the same manner that it was originally developed.

To use the technique just described to determine the relative masses of different types of atoms, chemists needed to be able to weigh an equal number of different types of atoms. In the early 1800s, chemists discovered that all samples of a given compound have the same mass ratio of their constituent elements. For example, there are 8 g of oxygen for every 1 g of hydrogen in every sample of water. This is called the **law of constant composition**. In 1804, John Dalton, a scientist in England, argued that the law of constant composition not only supported the concept of atoms but also provided their relative masses. He reasoned that the mass ratios in which different elements combine are the mass ratios of their individual atoms or a simple multiple thereof. If one atom of magnesium weighs 1.5 times as much as one atom of oxygen then any number of magnesium atoms would weigh 1.5 times as much as the same number of oxygen atoms. Dalton argued that this was the reason all samples of a compound contained the same mass ratio of its elements.

Sample Problem — Determining Relative Atomic Mass

A chemist carefully heats 0.350 g of magnesium powder in a crucible. The magnesium reacts with atmospheric oxygen to produce 0.580 g of magnesium oxide (MgO). What is the mass of a magnesium atom relative to the mass of an oxygen atom?

What to Think about	How to Do It
1. 0.350 g Mg must have combined with 0.230 g O to produce 0.580 g MgO.	0.580 g MgO − 0.350 g Mg = 0.230 g O
2. Since magnesium oxide has the formula MgO, 0.350 g of magnesium and 0.230 g of oxygen contain equal numbers of atoms.	$\frac{\text{mass of Mg atoms}}{\text{mass of O atoms}} = \frac{0.350 \text{ g}}{0.230 \text{ g}} = 1.52$
3. If some number of Mg atoms weighs 1.52 times as much as the same number of O atoms then any number of Mg atoms weighs 1.52 times as much as the same number of O atoms, even one of each.	A Mg atom weighs 1.52 times as much as an O atom.

Practice Problems — Determining Relative Atomic Mass

1. A dozen identical AA batteries have a mass of 276 g and a dozen identical watch batteries have a mass of only 26.4 g. The mass of an AA battery is ______ times the mass of a watch battery.

2. A sample of strontium oxide (SrO) is found to contain 2.683 g Sr and 0.490 g O. What is the mass of a strontium atom relative to that of an oxygen atom?

3. A 4.218 g sample of daltonium bromide (DBr) is decomposed and 0.337 g of D is recovered.
   (a) What is the atomic mass of daltonium given that the atomic mass of bromine is 79.9 u?

   ____

   (b) This question uses the fictitious element, daltonium, so you can't just look up the element's atomic mass.

   What element does daltonium represent? ______________________________

Relative Masses of Atoms

According to the sample problem, if all the atoms of an element are identical then the mass of a magnesium atom is 1.52 times the mass of an oxygen atom. If all the atoms of an element do not have the same mass then the average mass of a magnesium atom is 1.52 times the average mass of an oxygen atom. The issue of whether all the atoms of an element are identical wasn't resolved for another century but, as described, we need only insert the word, "average" if they are not.

The element hydrogen was discovered to have the least massive atoms so its atoms were originally assigned an atomic mass of 1 u (atomic mass unit) and the mass of all the other types of atoms were expressed relative to this. The discussion of atomic mass and atomic mass units will continue in chapter 5. Oxygen's atomic mass of 16 u means that the mass of an oxygen atom is 16 times the mass of a hydrogen atom (or that the average mass of an oxygen atom is 16 times the average mass of a hydrogen atom) (Figure 3.1.2). If the mass of a magnesium atom is 1.52 times the mass of an oxygen atom then the mass of a magnesium atom is 1.52×16.0 u = 24.3 u. The periodic table of the elements confirms that magnesium has a relative atomic mass of 24.3 u.

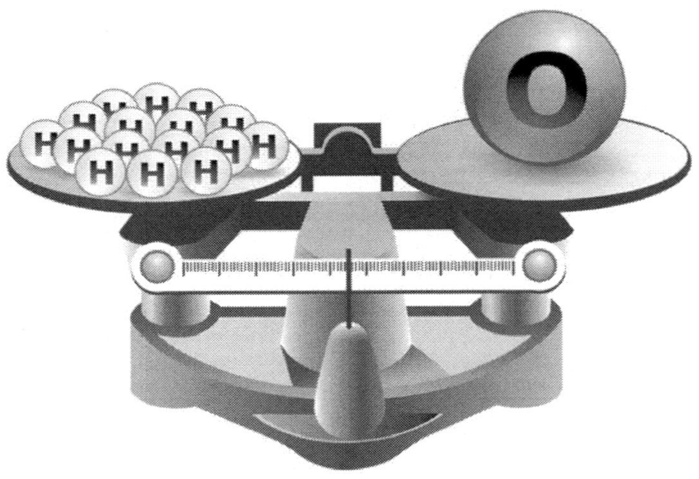

Figure 3.1.2 *The mass of an oxygen atom is equal to the mass of 16 hydrogen atoms.*

Determining the relative masses of the basic units of matter was a remarkable feat. Dalton bridged the gap between the world we experience and the invisible world of atoms by deriving the relative masses of atoms from laboratory observations. But how did Dalton know that the formula of magnesium oxide was MgO? Recall Dalton's important qualification: "or a simple multiple thereof." If the formula of magnesium oxide is MgO_2 then the mass ratio of Mg to O in the compound would need to be doubled to determine their atomic mass ratio. This is necessary because we are weighing half as many magnesium atoms. Therefore, the same number of magnesium atoms would weigh twice as much. Similar adaptations would be required for other possible formulas.

Sample Problem — Determining Relative Atomic Mass (Non 1:1 Formulas)

Barium chloride has a mass ratio of 1.934 g Ba:1.000 g Cl. Chlorine has an atomic mass of 35.5 u. What is the atomic mass of barium if the formula of barium chloride is $BaCl_2$?

What to Think about	How to Do It
If the formula is $BaCl_2$ then we need to double the mass of barium so that we can compare the masses of equal numbers of atoms.	$2(1.934) \times 35.5$ u = 137.3 u

Practice Problems — Determining Relative Atomic Mass (Non 1:1 Formulas)

Aluminum iodide has a mass ratio of 1.000 g Al: 14.100 g I. Given that the atomic mass of iodine is 126.9 u, what is the atomic mass of aluminum if the formula of aluminum iodide is:

1. AlI_3? ______________________ 2. Al_2I_3? ______________________

Cannizzaro's Paper

Dalton assumed that atoms combined in the simplest manner possible. He believed that if a pair of elements (A + B) formed only one compound, the formula for the compound would be AB. If they formed a second compound, its formula would be either A_2B or AB_2. Dalton was well aware that he had no evidence for his "rules of simplicity." He conceded that some of his formulas and resulting atomic mass determinations might be incorrect. As you may recall from Science 9 and Science 10, the formulas of ionic compounds are simple ratios, but not quite as simple as Dalton supposed.

On September 3, 1860, many of Europe's leading chemists met in Karlsruhe, Germany. At this meeting, the Italian chemist Stanislao Cannizzaro presented a remarkable paper in which he solved the mystery of atomic masses. For example, Dalton hadn't understood how two particles of hydrogen gas could react with one particle of oxygen gas to produce two particles of water vapour. He thought that couldn't happen because it would require splitting the oxygen particle, which he thought was an atom. Cannizzaro showed that Dalton's atomic model was still valid if the hydrogen and oxygen gas particles were made up of pairs of atoms. Hydrogen and oxygen molecules are called **diatomic molecules** because they are formed of two atoms of the same element ("di" means 2).

2 hydrogen molecules + 1 oxygen molecule → 2 water molecules

Figure 3.1.3 *Diatomic molecules of hydrogen and oxygen combine to form water molecules.*

Cannizzaro's paper went on to describe and explain three other techniques for determining atomic mass: one for metals, one for liquid or gaseous non-metals, and one for solid non-metals.

Dalton is called the father of the atomic theory because he explained how the law of constant composition provided support for the concept of atoms. However, additional methods were required to determine the relative atomic masses. These atomic masses were, in turn, used to determine the correct formulas of compounds. Dmitri Mendeleev, who published his first periodic table of the elements in 1869, was at Karlsruhe. The correct atomic masses were a prerequisite to Mendeleev's famous table.

3.1 Activity: The Relative Mass of Paper Clips

Question

What is the mass of a large paper clip relative to that of a small paper clip?
(We'll answer this question without weighing only one paper clip of either type.)

Background

If some number of large paper clips weighs twice as much as the same number of small paper clips then any number of large paper clips will weigh twice as much as the same number of small paper clips, including one of each. Remember we don't need to know how many paper clips we are weighing; we just need to know that we're weighing the same number of each. The mass ratio of any equal number of identical items equals the mass ratio of the individual items.

Procedure

1. Weigh a pile of small paper clips. Record this mass in the table provided below.
2. Attach a large paper clip to each small paper clip and measure the total mass of these coupled clips. Record this mass in the table provided below.
3. Calculate the total mass of the attached large paper clips and record this mass in the table below.

Results and Discussion

Objects	Mass (g)
Small paper clips	
Coupled paper clips	
Large paper clips	

1. $$\frac{\text{mass of some number of large paper clips}}{\text{mass of the same number of small paper clips}} = \frac{\_\_\_\_\_\_\_\_\_\_\ \text{g}}{\_\_\_\_\_\_\_\_\_\_\ \text{g}} = \_\_\_\_\_\_\_\_\_\_$$

   The mass of a large paper clip is ________ times the mass of a small paper clip.

2. If we assign a small paper clip a mass of 1.00 smu (stationary mass unit), what is the mass of a large paper clip?

3. Let's check this result by weighing one small paper clip and one large paper clip.

   $$\frac{\text{mass of one large paper clip}}{\text{mass of one small paper clip}} = \frac{\_\_\_\_\_\_\_\_\_\_\ \text{g}}{\_\_\_\_\_\_\_\_\_\_\ \text{g}} = \_\_\_\_\_\_\_\_\_\_$$

4. Why might the ratios calculated in steps 1 and 3 be slightly different?

3.1 Review Questions

1. A certain number of identical glass marbles has a mass of 825 g. The same number of identical steel marbles has a mass of 2245 g.
   (a) Assigning a glass marble a mass of 1.00 mmu (marble mass unit), calculate the mass of a steel marble.

   (b) Why don't you need to know the number of marbles that were weighed?

2. 1.965 g of sodium is placed in a flask containing chlorine gas. 5.000 g of NaCl is produced in the resulting reaction.
   (a) A sodium atom's mass is _______ times a chlorine atom's mass.

   (b) Chlorine has an atomic mass of 35.5 u. What is the atomic mass of sodium?

3. A 10.000 g sample of zubenium fluoride (ZuF) is decomposed and 8.503 g of Zu is recovered.
   (a) What is the atomic mass of zubenium?

   (b) This question uses the fictitious element zubenium so you can't just look up the element's atomic mass. What element does zubenium represent?

4. Zinc sulphide has a mass ratio of 2.037 g Zn: 1.000 g S. Given that the atomic mass of sulphur is 32.1 u, what is the atomic mass of zinc if the formula of zinc sulphide is:
   (a) ZnS?

   (b) ZnS_2?

   (c) Zn_3S_2?

5. A compound of copper and oxygen contains 13.073 g Cu and 1.647 g O. Oxygen has an atomic mass of 16.0 u.
   (a) What is the atomic mass of copper if the formula of the above compound is CuO?

   (b) What is the atomic mass of copper if the formula of the above compound is Cu_2O?

   (c) What is the atomic mass of copper if the formula of the above compound is CuO_2?

6. In 1819, Dulong and Petit noted a relationship between the presumed atomic mass of most metals and their specific heats. The specific heat of a metal divided into 25.0 provides the approximate atomic mass of the metal. The specific heat of a substance is the amount of heat required to raise 1 g of the substance by 1°C. The specific heat of copper is 0.3864 J/g°C.
   (a) Calculate the approximate atomic mass of copper using Dulong and Petit's method.

   (b) Knowing the approximate atomic mass of the metal allowed chemists to determine which of the more accurate atomic masses derived by composition analysis was correct. Which of the atomic masses and corresponding formulas calculated in question 5 is correct for the compound that was analyzed?

7. Determine the percent error of Dulong and Petit's method of approximating a metal's atomic mass for aluminum (0.903 J/g°C), magnesium (1.05 J/g°C) and silver (0.23772 J/g°C).

8. In 1811 Amedeo Avogadro proposed that equal volumes of any gas at the same temperature and pressure contain *the same number of particles*. Cannizzaro realized this allows scientists to weigh equal numbers of atoms of different gaseous elements and determine their relative atomic masses. Complete the following data table showing the mass of equal volumes of two different gases at the same temperature and pressure.

Element	Mass of Gas (g)	Relative Atomic Mass (u)
H	0.210	1.0
	7.455	

9. Potassium has an atomic mass of 39.1 u. What does this mean?

10. Look up the following elements in the periodic table and report each element's atomic mass.

(a) P ______________

(b) Ca ______________

(c) U ______________

11. Eight identical forks have a mass of 213.1 g. Eight identical knives have a mass of 628.2 g.

(a) What is the mass of a knife relative to that of a fork?

(b) Why did you not need to divide the supplied masses by 8 to answer 10(a)?

(c) What could you conclude from this data if the utensils of each type were not identical?

12. A mint is advertising a special set of silver coins containing a 10 g coin, a 20 g coin and a 30 g coin. One of these coins is accidentally being made 1 g lighter than its advertised mass. You have two sets of these coins and have been challenged to identify the undersized coin by weighing only one pile of coins. The single pile may include any combination of the coins that you wish. What combination of the coins would you weigh? How can you use that mass to identify the undersized coin?

3.2 Introducing the Mole — The Central Unit of Chemistry

Warm Up

1. It takes 15 gulps to drink a bottle of water. What information would allow you to calculate how many *slurps* it would take to drink an identical bottle of water?

   ____

2. If 4 slurps = 1 gulp, how many slurps would it take to consume a 15-gulp drink?

   ____

3. If 5 slurps equal 1 gulp, how many gulps would it take to consume a 20-slurp drink? ____________

The Mole Concept

What mass of oxygen has the same number of atoms as 1 g of hydrogen? An oxygen atom (16 u) weighs 16 times as much as a hydrogen atom (1 u). Therefore, it would require 16 g of oxygen to have the same number of atoms as 1 g of hydrogen. Chemists extended this reasoning to all the elements. For example, 55.8 g Fe, 35.5 g Cl, 23.0 g Na, and 12.0 g C all contain the same number of atoms since these masses are in the same ratios as their individual atomic masses. How many atoms are there in the atomic mass of any element expressed in grams? Originally chemists didn't know and even now they only have a very rough estimate but they nevertheless gave a name to that number. They called this number a "mole."

> A **mole** is a quantity equal to the number of atoms in the atomic mass of any element expressed in grams (e.g., the number of atoms in 1.0 g H, 16.0 g O, 63.5 g Cu).

The definition of the mole is under continuous review. It is "fine-tuned" periodically in response to new information about atomic structure and to changes in the definition of the atomic mass unit on which the definition of the mole is based.

Figure 3.2.1 *6.02214179 × 10^{23} carbon atoms*

The number of things in a mole is also referred to as **Avogadro's number** in honour of the Italian scientist whose insight regarding gases led to a technique for determining the relative atomic masses of non-metals. Just as the word "dozen" refers to a number of something, so does the word "mole." The chief difference is that we know that a dozen is 12 of something but we only have a rough estimate of how many things are in a mole of something. There have been many independent derivations of the number of items in a mole. Chemists currently estimate that a mole is 6.02214179 × 10^{23} give or take a few million billion (Figure 3.2.1). The actual number isn't important unless you're working at the atomic level because whatever the number is, it's the same for a mole of anything.

Just as a dozen is 12 of anything, a mole is approximately 6.02 × 10^{23} of anything. While a dozen is a fairly small number, a mole is an absurdly large number. A mole of peas would cover the entire Earth's surface with a layer over 200 m deep. Atoms are so small however that you can hold a mole of atoms in the palm of your hand. Just as a dozen is a convenient unit of quantity for a baker to group buns and doughnuts, a mole is a convenient unit of quantity for a chemist to group atoms and molecules. The number of items is one way to express the amount of a material so chemists often refer to a mole of a substance rather than a mole of the substance's particles (e.g., a mole of copper instead of a mole of copper atoms).

The mole was introduced in the early 1900s by Wilhelm Ostwald. Ironically, Ostwald developed the mole concept as an alternative to the atomic theory, which he did not accept. Today, the mole is used throughout modern chemistry as the central unit through which all other quantities of materials are related, but it was not common before the mid-1950s, just two generations of chemists ago. Before that, chemists related quantities of chemicals through their atomic masses without reference to the mole.

Quick Check

1. (a) How is a mole like a dozen?

   ____

   (b) How is a mole different than a dozen?

   ____

2. What does a mole of chlorine atoms weigh? ______________
3. What mass of sulphur has the same number of atoms that are in 1.0 g H? ______________

Conversions Using Avogadro's Number

Many chemistry problems can be solved by examining the units of the values provided and considering the units that the answer must have. This technique of manipulating units is called "dimensional analysis." While it's important to understand the mathematical operation you're performing, it's reassuring to see that the units work out (i.e., that the answer has the appropriate units).

Most chemical conversions involve the mole. The key to conversion is the conversion factor. Chemists know or know where to find the conversion factors they need. At this point in the course, we'll use only two conversion factors: Avogadro's number (the number of items per mole) and molar mass (the number of grams per mole). The items that a chemist would normally be concerned about are chemical species such as atoms, molecules, ions, and formula units. The abbreviation for the unit mole is mol (Figure 3.2.2).

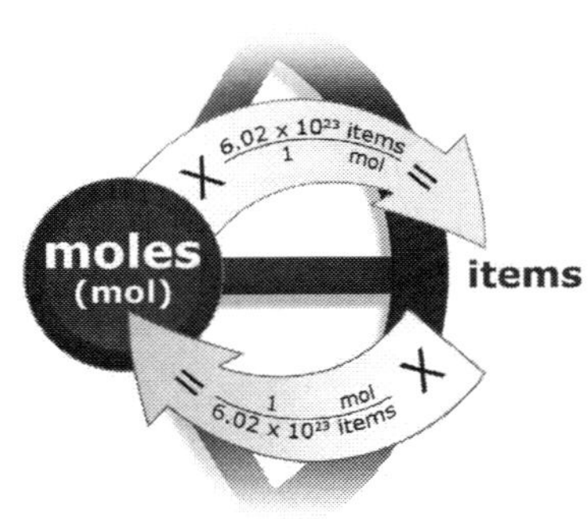

Figure 3.2.2 *Converting the moles and the number of items of a substance*

Name	Equivalence Statement	Conversion Factors	
Avogadro's number	1 mol = 6.02×10^{23} items	$\frac{6.02 \times 10^{23} \text{ items}}{1 \text{ mol}}$	$\frac{1 \text{ mol}}{6.02 \times 10^{23} \text{ items}}$

Sample Problem—Converting Moles to Number of Items

How many oxygen atoms are in 3.2 mol of oxygen atoms?

What to Think about

1. Convert: mol O → atoms O
2. Setup:
   $3.2 \text{ mol O} \times \frac{? \text{ atoms O}}{1 \text{ mol O}}$
3. Conversion factor:
   6.02×10^{23} atoms O per 1 mol O
4. Count the number of significant figures of each value in the operation and then round the answer to the least of these.

How to Do It

$3.2 \cancel{\text{mol O}} \times \frac{6.02 \times 10^{23} \text{ atoms O}}{1 \cancel{\text{mol O}}} = 1.9 \times 10^{24} \text{ atoms O}$

Note: There is no uncertainty in the 1 mol O. The uncertainty of the conversion factor is expressed in the 6.02×10^{23} atoms O.

Practice Problems—Converting Moles to Number of Items

1. Chromium ions are responsible for the beautiful colours of rubies and emeralds. How many chromium ions (Cr^{3+}) are in 3.5 mol of chromium ions?

2. 30.0 mol H_2O = ___________ molecules H_2O

3. How many atoms of sodium are in 0.023 mol Na?

Sample Problem—Converting Number of Items to Moles

7.3×10^{24} carbon monoxide molecules (CO) represent how many moles of carbon monoxide?

What to Think about	How to Do It
1. Convert: molecules CO ⟶ mol CO	
2. Setup: $(7.3 \times 10^{24} \text{ molecules CO}) \times \frac{1 \text{ mol CO}}{? \text{ molecules CO}}$	$(7.3 \times 10^{24} \text{ ~~molecules CO~~}) \times \frac{1 \text{ mol CO}}{6.02 \times 10^{23} \text{ ~~molecules CO~~}}$
3. Conversion factor: 1 mol CO per 6.02×10^{23} molecules CO	= 12 mol CO

Practice Problems — Converting Number of Items to Moles

1. Incandescent lights are filled with argon to prevent the glowing filament from burning up. How many moles of argon do 1.81×10^{22} atoms of argon represent?

2. 2.25×10^{24} molecules CO_2 = ___________ mol CO_2?

3. A 1-L intravenous bag of saline solution contains 9.27×10^{22} formula units of NaCl. How many moles of NaCl is this?

Molar Mass

The mass of one mole of an element's atoms is called that element's **molar mass** (Figure 3.2.3). It follows from simply restating the definition of a mole that the molar mass of an element is its atomic mass expressed in grams. For example, "one mole is the number of atoms in 16 g of oxygen" can be restated as "one mole of oxygen atoms weighs 16 g." The atomic masses of the elements can be found in the periodic table. The atomic mass of oxygen is 16 u and thus the molar mass of oxygen is 16 g. This is better expressed as a conversion factor for calculation purposes: 16 g per mole of oxygen or 16 g/mol O.

Figure 3.2.3 *The mass of 1 mol of a chemical depends on the atoms that make it up.*

The **molecular mass** or **formula mass** of a compound is the sum of its constituent atomic masses (e.g., H_2O: 2(1 u) + 16 u = 18 u). One mole of water molecules consists of 1 mol of oxygen atoms (16 g) and 2 mol of hydrogen atoms (2 g) and therefore weighs 18 g. Similarly, 1 mol of NaCl formula units consists of 1 mol of sodium atoms (23 g) and 1 mol of chlorine atoms (35.5 g) for a total mass of 58.5 g (Figure 3.2.4).

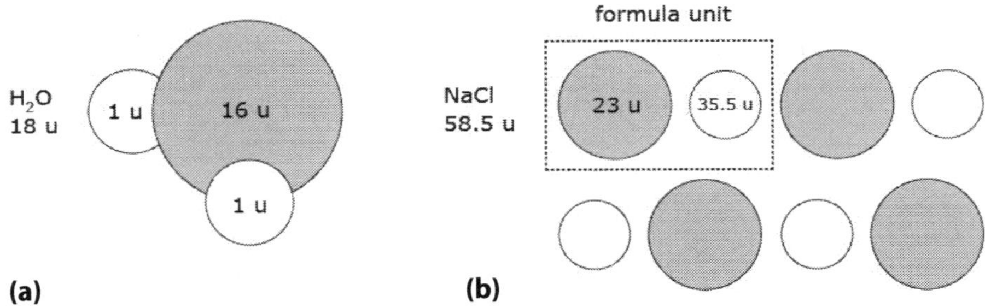

Figure 3.2.4 *(a) The molecular mass of water is the sum of the masses of the oxygen and hydrogen atoms. (b) The formula mass of NaCl is the sum of the masses of sodium and chlorine atoms.*

Just as the molar mass of an element is simply its atomic mass expressed in grams, the **molar mass** of a compound is simply its molecular or formula mass expressed in grams.

> The molar mass of a substance is its atomic, molecular, or formula mass expressed in grams.

Sample Problem — Determining a Compound's Formula Mass and/or Molar Mass

What are the formula mass and molar mass of $Al_2(SO_4)_3$?

What to Think About	How to Do It
1. 1 $Al_2(SO_4)_3$ consists of 2 Al's, 3 S's, and 12 O's.	Formula Mass = 2(27.0 u) + 3(32.1 u) + 12(16.0 u) = 342.3 u
2. 1 mol $Al_2(SO_4)_3$ consists of 2 mol Al, 3 mol S and 12 mol O.	Molar Mass = 2(27.0 g) + 3(32.1 g) + 12(16.0 g) = 342.3 g Expressed as a conversion factor, it is 342.3 g/mol.

Practice Problems — Determining a Compound's Formula Mass and/or Molar Mass

1. What is the molecular mass of nitrogen dioxide?

2. What is the molar mass of $Na_2Cr_2O_7$?

3. What is the molar mass of iron(III) sulphide?

Conversions Using Molar Mass

Name	Equivalence Statement	Conversion Factors	
Molar mass	1 mol = ? g	$\frac{?\text{ g}}{1\text{ mol}}$	$\frac{1\text{ mol}}{?\text{ g}}$
Example: H_2O	1 mol = 18.0 g	$\frac{18.0\text{ g}}{1\text{ mol}}$	$\frac{1\text{ mol}}{18.0\text{ g}}$

Sample Problem — Converting Moles to Mass

What is the mass of 3.2 mol of oxygen atoms?

What to Think about

1. Convert: mol O → g O
2. Setup:
   $3.2\text{ mol O} \times \frac{?\text{ g O}}{1\text{ mol O}}$
3. Conversion factor:
   16.0 g O per 1 mol O

How to Do It

$3.2\ \cancel{\text{mol O}} \times \frac{16.0\text{ g O}}{1\ \cancel{\text{mol O}}} = 51\text{ g O}$

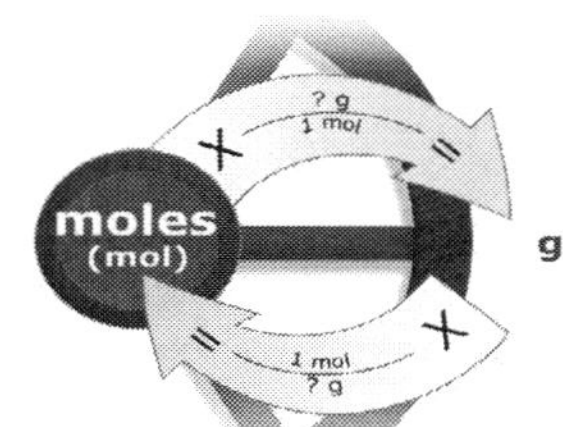

Practice Problems — Converting Moles to Mass

1. What does 2.65 mol of table salt (NaCl) weigh?

2. 0.87 mol NH_3 = ________ g NH_3?

3. Very large quantities of chemicals are produced in the chemical industry. Worldwide production of sulphuric acid (H_2SO_4) is estimated at two trillion (2.0×10^{12}) moles annually. How many tonnes of H_2SO_4 is this? (1 tonne = 1000 kg)

Sample Problem — Converting Mass to Moles

How many moles of water are in 1.8 g of water?

What to Think about	How to Do It
1. Convert: g $H_2O \rightarrow$ mol H_2O 2. Setup: $1.8 \text{ g } H_2O \times \frac{1 \text{ mol } H_2O}{? \text{ g } H_2O}$ 3. Conversion factor. 1 mol H_2O per 18 g H_2O	$1.8 \cancel{\text{g } H_2O} \times \frac{1 \text{ mol } H_2O}{18.0 \cancel{\text{g } H_2O}} = 0.10 \text{ mol } H_2O$

Practice Problems — Converting Mass to Moles

1. Gold is the most malleable metal. It can be hammered into sheets that are only several hundred atoms thick. In 2010, Vancouver's Science World covered an entire billboard with just two troy ounces (62.2 g) of gold to dramatize this fact. How many moles of gold is this?

2. 3.88 g CO_2 = ________ mol CO_2

3. Smelling salts are used to revive an unconscious athlete. A capsule of smelling salts contains 500.0 mg $(NH_4)_2CO_3$. How many moles of $(NH_4)_2CO_3$ is this?

3.2 Activity: A Mole of Pennies

Question

How long and massive would a stack of 1 mol of pennies be?

Background

The mole is a convenient and useful term for counting very large quantities of things. You know that 1 mol of pennies is approximately 6.02×10^{23} pennies but can you picture just how many that really is? Suppose you stacked 1 mol of pennies. How tall do you think that stack would be? How much would it weigh? Just for fun, try guessing by completing the tables below in pencil before you do the necessary calculations.

Procedure

1. Make a stack of 10 pennies.
2. Measure and record the stack's height in centimetres. ______________
3. Measure and record the stack's mass in grams. _________________

Results and Discussion

1. Calculate the height in kilometres of a stack of 1 mol of pennies.

2.

Would the stack reach...	Distance (km)	✔ or ✗
our Moon?	3.9×10^5	
Pluto?	5.9×10^9	
Proxima Centauri (the nearest star)?	4.1×10^{13}	
Andromeda (the nearest galaxy)?	1.9×10^{19}	

3. Calculate the mass in kilograms of 1 mol of pennies.

4.

Would the stack weigh as much as...	Mass (kg)	✔ or ✗
the U.S.S. *Ronald Reagan* (the world's heaviest aircraft carrier)?	2.1×10^7	
the total of all living things on Earth?	2×10^{15}	
our Moon?	7.4×10^{22}	
Earth?	6.0×10^{24}	

3.2 Review Questions

1. (a) What is the definition of a mole?

   (b) What is our best estimate of the number of things in a mole?

   (c) What do chemists call this number?

2. (a) What mass of carbon would have the same number of atoms as 1.0 g H?

   (b) What mass of carbon would have the same number of atoms as 3.0 g H?

   (c) What mass of sulphur would have the same number of atoms as 32.0 g O?

3. (a) What does a mole of iron weigh?

   (b) Chemists call this value the ______________________ of iron.

4. (a) What is the molecular mass of propane, C_3H_8?

   (b) What is the formula mass of calcium hydroxide, $Ca(OH)_2$?

   (c) What is the molar mass of carbon tetrachloride, CCl_4?

5. 3.2 mol C = ____________________ atoms C

6. How many molecules are in 0.0085 mol of C_2H_6?

7. 1.4×10^{18} Ag atoms represent how many moles of atoms?

8. 2.99 g Na = ___________ mol Na

9. What is the mass of 5.2 mol of fluorine?

10. Airline regulations prohibit lithium metal batteries that contain over 2.0 g of lithium on passenger aircraft. How many moles of lithium are in 2.0 g Li?

11. What is the mass of 0.32 mol of sodium nitrite?

12. A can of cola contains 58 mg of caffeine, $C_8H_{10}N_4O_2$. How many moles of caffeine are in a can of cola?

13. Carbon dioxide, produced by respiration in plants and animals, causes the slightly acidic nature of normal rain. How many molecules of CO_2 are in 0.725 mol CO_2?

14. The male luna moth can detect specialized chemicals known as pheromones in order to locate a mate. A moth can detect 1.70×10^9 molecules of the pheromone. How many moles of the pheromone is this?

15. Cycling enthusiasts often prefer bicycles made with titanium frames. Titanium is resistant to corrosion and fatigue, has a significantly lower density than steel, and seems to have a natural shock absorbing ability. Suppose a high-quality titanium frame contains 1300 g of titanium. How many moles of titanium does this frame contain?

16. Bluestone is an attractive mineral with the chemical name copper(II) sulphate pentahydrate. What is the mass of a 1.75-mol sample of bluestone?

17. An environmental assessment predicts that a coal plant would emit 8.18×10^6 mol of ammonia into the atmosphere annually. How many tonnes of ammonia is this?

18. Ammonium phosphate is a fertilizer containing nitrogen and phosphorus for healthy plant growth. How many moles of ammonium phosphate are in a bag containing 2.640 kg of it?

19. The movie *Erin Brockovich* dramatizes the efforts of the title character (played by Julia Roberts) to prove that the Pacific Gas and Electric Co. contaminated the water supply of Hinkley, California, with hexavalent chromium. Tin(II) dichromate is a hexavalent chromium compound. What is the mass of 5.925 mol of tin(II) dichromate?

3.3 The Wheel Model of Mole Conversions

Warm Up

1. Which contains more atoms, 30 g Cl or 15 g C? ________________
2. Which weighs more, 1 mol Zn or 3 mol N? ________________
3. Which contains more molecules, 34 g CH_4 or 58 g O_2? ________________

Two-Step Mole Conversions

The mole serves as a link between the invisible world of atoms and observable quantities of chemicals. The mole is to a chemist what the dollar is to an accountant. Just as the dollar is the central unit of commerce and allows us to keep track of money, the mole is the central unit of chemistry and allows us to keep track of atoms and molecules.

A quantity of a substance can only be related to another quantity of the same substance through the mole.

How would you solve the following problem?
How many atoms are in 5.0 g of copper?

You might split the problem into two parts, each of which you learned how to solve in section 3.2:

1. How many moles of copper are in 5.0 g Cu?
2. How many copper atoms is this?

This is how chemists solve this type of problem. Think of the mole as the hub of a wheel with the spokes leading out to all the other units. In our wheel model, the spokes represent the conversion factors (Figure 3.3.1).

For now, our conversions are limited to those between moles and items and between moles and grams. Mass and the number of items must be related to each other through the mole: grams to moles to items or items to moles to grams. The beauty of the wheel model is that as you learn more chemical quantities they can simply be added to the rim of the wheel. In order to relate or "connect" a new chemical quantity to all of the others you only need to connect it to the mole. In other words, if you wanted to convert grams into sneebugs, you would convert grams into moles and then moles into sneebugs.

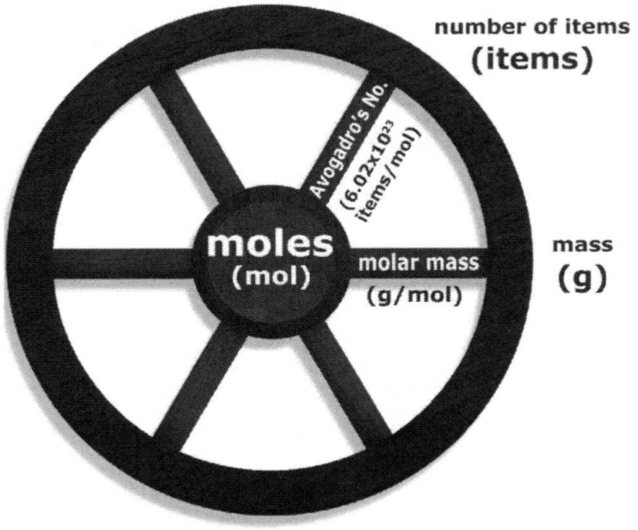

Figure 3.3.1 *The wheel is a useful model for representing conversion factors.*

Sample Problem — Two-Step Conversion: Mass to Number of Items (Atoms)

Chemists count by weighing. How many atoms are in 5.0 g of copper?

What to Think about

1. Plan your route.
   Convert: g Cu → mol Cu → atoms Cu
   Chemists usually perform these two calculations in one continuous sequence.
2. Setup: $5.0 \text{ g Cu} \times \dfrac{1 \text{ mol Cu}}{? \text{ g Cu}} \times \dfrac{? \text{ atoms Cu}}{1 \text{ mol Cu}}$

   The numerators show the route; in this case, grams to moles to atoms.
   Each numerator's unit is cancelled by the next denominator's unit until you arrive at your answer.
3. Conversion factors:
   1 mol Cu per 63.5 g Cu
   6.02×10^{23} atoms Cu per 1 mol Cu

How to Do It

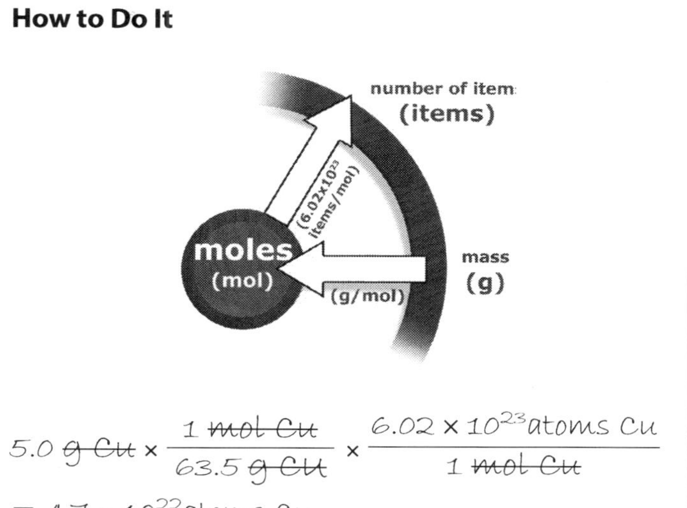

$$5.0 \text{ g Cu} \times \frac{1 \text{ mol Cu}}{63.5 \text{ g Cu}} \times \frac{6.02 \times 10^{23} \text{ atoms Cu}}{1 \text{ mol Cu}}$$

$$= 4.7 \times 10^{22} \text{ atoms Cu}$$

As Avogadro's number is an estimate, so is the above answer. Nevertheless, being able to estimate the number of atoms in any sample of a substance is remarkable. This is perhaps even more evident for the reverse conversion, which allows us to estimate the mass of a single atom in grams.

Sample Problem — Two-Step Conversion: Number of Items (Atoms) to Mass

What is the mass of an oxygen atom in grams?

What to Think about

1. Convert: atom O → mol O → g O
2. Setup: $1 \text{ atom O} \times \dfrac{1 \text{ mol O}}{? \text{ atoms O}} \times \dfrac{? \text{ g O}}{1 \text{ mol O}}$
3. Conversion factors:
   1 mol O per 6.02×10^{23} atoms O
   16.0 g per 1 mol O
4. All that we've done here is divide the mass of a mole of oxygen atoms by the number of atoms in a mole to determine the mass of each atom.
   Always check to make sure that your answer is reasonable. 2.66×10^{-23} g is a reasonable answer because an atom would have a very small mass.

How to Do It

$$1 \text{ atom O} \times \frac{1 \text{ mol O}}{6.02 \times 10^{23} \text{ atoms O}} \times \frac{16.0 \text{ g O}}{1 \text{ mol O}}$$

$$= 2.66 \times 10^{-23} \text{ g O}$$

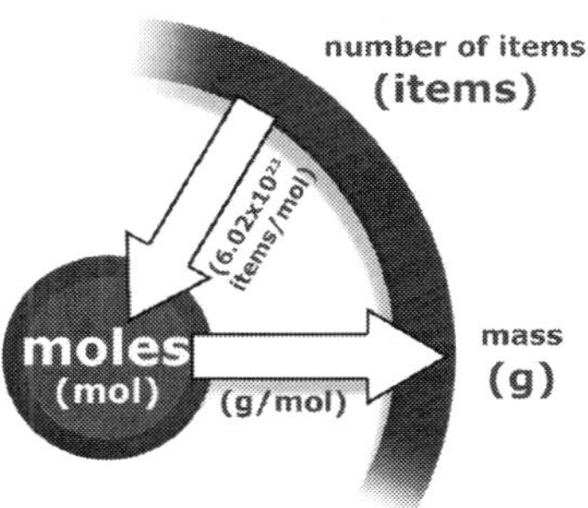

Practice Problems — Two-Step Conversions

1. Fill in the missing entries to determine the mass in grams of a billion billion (1×10^{18}) sulphur dioxide molecules.

$$(1 \times 10^{18} \text{ molecules } SO_2) \times \frac{1 \text{ mol } SO_2}{\_\_\_\_\_\_\_\_ \text{ molecules } SO_2} \times \frac{\_\_\_\_\_\_ \text{ g } SO_2}{1 \text{ mol } SO_2} = \_\_\_\_\_\_\_\_ \text{ g } SO_2$$

2. How many atoms are in 2.1 g Br?

3. What is the mass in grams of one atom of Ag?

Two Wheel Conversions (Composition Stoichiometry)

Chemists often relate a quantity of one chemical substance to a quantity of another. **Stoichiometry** is the branch of chemistry that deals with the quantitative relationships between elements in a compound (composition stoichiometry) and between the reactants and products in a chemical reaction (reaction stoichiometry). ("Stoichiometry" is from the Greek words *stoicheion* meaning "element" and *metron* meaning "measure.") Our presentation here is limited to composition stoichiometry. To accommodate such conversions, we simply add another wheel to our model. Each wheel in our model represents a different substance or species and, of course, the only functional way to connect two wheels is with an axle. An axle runs between the hubs of wheels and in our model, connects moles of one substance or species to moles of another (Figure 3.3.2).

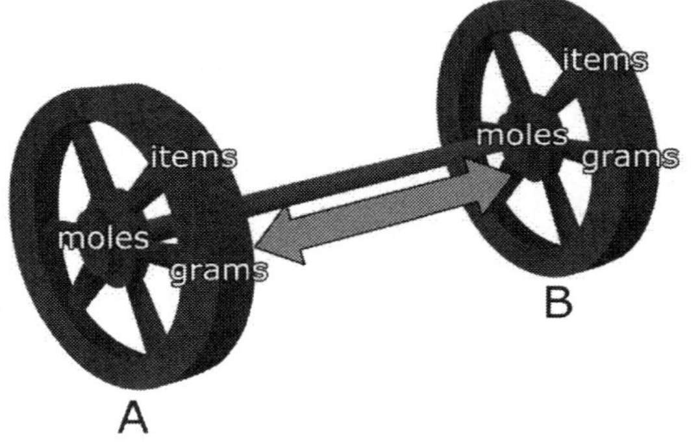

Figure 3.3.2 *The two-wheel-and-axle model for converting between species*

A quantity of a substance or species can only be related to a quantity of another substance or species through the mole.

We already know how to move about (convert units) using single wheels. The only new step added here is represented by the axle, which helps you to convert moles of one substance into moles of another. The conversion factor is found in the compound's formula. There are two oxygen atoms in a CO_2 molecule, so there are two dozen oxygen atoms in a dozen CO_2 molecules and there are… *wait for it*… 2 mol of oxygen atoms in 1 mol of CO_2 molecules.

Name	Equivalence Statement	Conversion Factors	
Chemical Formula	1 molecule A = ? atoms B ∴ 1 mol A = ? mol B	$\frac{1 \text{ mol A}}{? \text{ mol B}}$	$\frac{? \text{ mol B}}{1 \text{ mol A}}$
Example: CO_2	1 molecule CO_2 = 2 atoms O ∴ 1 mol CO_2 = 2 mol O	$\frac{1 \text{ mol } CO_2}{2 \text{ mol O}}$	$\frac{2 \text{ mol O}}{1 \text{ mol } CO_2}$

Sample Problem — One-Step Conversion: Moles of A to Moles of B

How many moles of hydrogen are in 6.0 mol of water?

What to Think about

1. Convert: mol $H_2O \rightarrow$ mol H
2. Setup: $6.0 \text{ mol } H_2O \times \frac{? \text{ mol H}}{1 \text{ mol } H_2O}$
3. Conversion factor:
   There are 2 H's in an H_2O;
   therefore there are
   2 mol of H in 1 mol of H_2O.
4. The values in the conversion factor (2 mol H per 1 mol H_2O) do not limit the significant figures in the answer as these values have no uncertainty. There are exactly 2 H's in an H_2O.

How to Do It

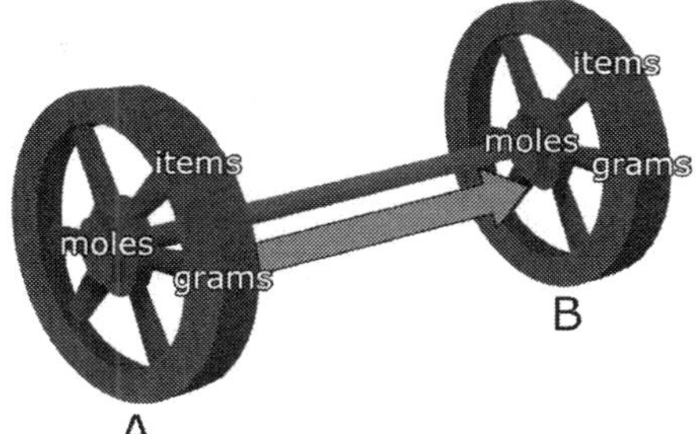

$$6.0 \text{ mol } H_2O \times \frac{2 \text{ mol H}}{1 \text{ mol } H_2O} = 12 \text{ mol H}$$

Sample Problem — Two-Step Conversion: Mass of A to Moles of B

Hydrogen fuel cells are batteries that are continually supplied or "fuelled" with reactants. Their hydrogen sometimes comes from a process that "scrubs" it off methane molecules. How many moles of methane (CH_4) are required to get 0.860 g of hydrogen?

What to Think about

1. Convert: g H $\rightarrow$ mol H $\rightarrow$ mol CH_4
2. Setup: $0.860 \text{ g H} \times \frac{1 \text{ mol H}}{? \text{ g H}} \times \frac{1 \text{ mol } CH_4}{? \text{ mol H}}$
3. Insert the conversion factors:
   1 mol H per 1.0 g H
   1 mol CH_4 per 4 mol H (given by the formula, CH_4)

How to Do It

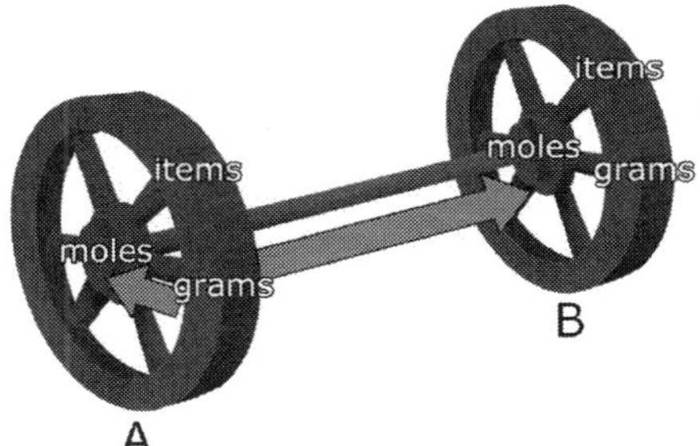

$$0.860 \text{ g H} \times \frac{1 \text{ mol H}}{1.0 \text{ g H}} \times \frac{1 \text{ mol } CH_4}{4 \text{ mol H}} = 0.22 \text{ mol } CH_4$$

Sample Problem — Three-Step Conversion: Mass of A to Mass of B

How many grams of oxygen are in 14.6 g CO_2?

What to Think about

1. Convert: g CO_2 → mol CO_2 → mol O → g O

2. Setup:

$$14.6\text{ g }CO_2 \times \frac{1\text{ mol }CO_2}{?\text{ g }CO_2} \times \frac{?\text{ mol O}}{1\text{ mol }CO_2} \times \frac{?\text{ g O}}{1\text{ mol O}}$$

3. Insert the conversion factors:
   1 mol CO_2 per 44.0 g CO_2
   2 mol O per 1 mol CO_2
   16.0 g O per 1 mol O

How to Do It

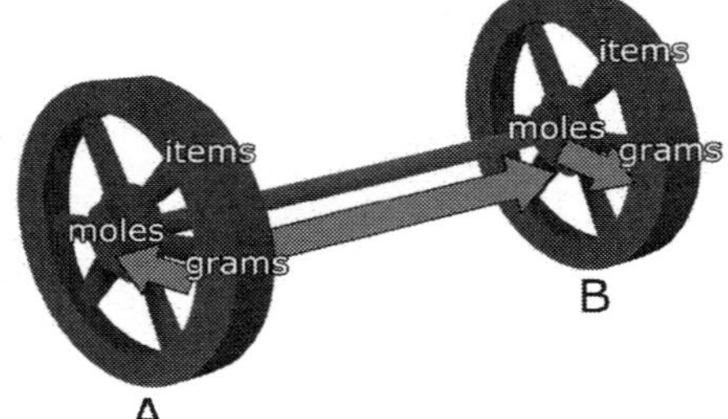

$$14.6\text{ g }CO_2 \times \frac{1\text{ mol }CO_2}{44.0\text{ g }CO_2} \times \frac{2\text{ mol O}}{1\text{ mol }CO_2} \times \frac{16.0\text{ g O}}{1\text{ mol O}}$$

$= 10.6$ g O

Practice Problems — One-, Two-, and Three-Step Conversions

1. Fill in the missing entries in these "axle" conversion factors.

   (a) $\frac{\_\_\_\_\text{ mol O}}{\_\_\_\_\text{ mol }SO_2}$ (b) $\frac{\_\_\_\_\text{ mol }C_2H_4}{\_\_\_\_\text{ mol H}}$

2. How many moles of KNO_3 contain 14 g of oxygen? ________________

3. Fill in the missing entry in each conversion factor to determine how many oxygen atoms are in 2.5 g $K_2Cr_2O_7$.

$$2.5\text{ g }K_2Cr_2O_7 \times \frac{1\text{ mol }K_2Cr_2O_7}{\_\_\_\_\text{ g }K_2Cr_2O_7} \times \frac{\_\_\_\_\text{ mol O}}{1\text{ mol }K_2Cr_2O_7} \times \frac{\_\_\_\_\_\_\_\_\text{ atoms O}}{1\text{ mol O}} =$$

4. What mass of sodium ions is contained in 1.23×10^{24} formula units of sodium sulphide?

3.3 Activity: The Evaporation Rate of Water

Question

What is the evaporation rate of water in molecules per second?

Background

Evaporation occurs when a molecule on the surface of a liquid is struck with enough force by neighbouring molecules to break away from its attractions to those around it and enter the gas phase. Evaporation is often depicted like popcorn being popped. Pop...pop, pop, pop...pop, pop, etc. Let's use the mole concept to calculate the actual rate at which water molecules evaporate.

Procedure

1. Half-fill a small beaker with water and weigh it. Record its mass and the time of day.
2. Put the beaker in a place where it won't be disturbed.
3. In about 30 min, weigh the beaker and its contents again, once more recording its mass and the time of day.

Results and Discussion

	Mass of Beaker and H_2O (g)	Time of Day
Initial		
Final		
Change		min

1. Calculate the number of water molecules evaporated during the trial.

2. Calculate the duration of the trial in seconds.

3. Calculate the water's average evaporation rate during the trial in molecules per second.

4. Be suitably amazed. Oh come on, more amazed than that!

3.3 Review Questions

1. Acticoat dressings, developed in 1995 by Robert Burrell of the University of Alberta, are impregnated with crystals of silver that are only 15 nm (nanometres) in size. These nanocrystals are remarkably more effective at healing burns and other severe wounds than any treatment previously available. Acticoat bandages are credited with saving the lives and limbs of dozens of victims of the World Trade Center attack in New York City in 2001. What is the mass of a crystal containing 1.0×10^3 silver atoms?

2. Diamond is one way of arranging carbon atoms. The "Star of Africa" diamond, displayed with the crown jewels in the Tower of London, weighs 106.0 g and has an estimated value of over $400 million. How many carbon atoms compose the "Star of Africa" diamond?

3. What is the mass in grams of a chlorine atom?

4. How many propane molecules are in 72.6 g propane, C_3H_8?

5. On a particular day, 31.1 g (1 troy ounce) of gold cost $1300.
   (a) 31 g Au = ______________atoms of Au

   (b) How many atoms of gold could you buy for 1 cent on that day?

6. Complete the following "axle" conversion factors by filling in the appropriate numbers:

   (a) $\dfrac{\_\_\_\_\_\ \text{mol O}}{\_\_\_\_\_\ \text{mol } N_2O_4}$

   (b) $\dfrac{\_\_\_\_\_\ \text{mol } NO_2}{\_\_\_\_\_\ \text{mol N}}$

7. 2.3 mol CO_2 = ____________ mol O

8. Calcium oxalate is a poisonous compound found in rhubarb leaves. How many moles of carbon are in 52.4 mg of calcium oxalate?

9. Sodium phosphate is sold as a cleaner at most hardware stores. How many moles of sodium ions are there in 6.80×10^{24} formula units of Na_3PO_4?

10. Sulphuric acid is used to produce a tremendous number and variety of materials including fertilizers, pigments, textiles, plastics, and explosives. What mass of sulphuric acid, H_2SO_4, contains 1.4 mol O?

11. How many carbon atoms are in 0.85 mol of the "pain-killer" acetaminophen, $C_8H_9NO_2$?

12. How many mercury(II) ions are in 100.0 g $HgCl_2$?

13. How many grams of chloride ions are in 8.3 g of copper(II) chloride?

14. What mass of carbon is present in 4.8×10^{26} molecules of ethanol, C_2H_5OH?

15. Hydrogen fluoride, HF, can be used to etch glass. The white lines on the glassware in your lab may have been made by this acidic gas. Determine the mass in kilograms of 3.9×10^{27} molecules of HF.

16. Up to 1.44×10^5 kg of various oxides of nitrogen are emitted by a gas-burning electrical plant in one year. Assuming this entire mass to be nitrogen dioxide, how many oxygen atoms would be present in this gas sample?

17. How many molecules are in 1.000 mg of the organic solvent, carbon tetrachloride?

18. Glycerol, $C_3H_5(OH)_3$, is a viscous, colourless liquid found in cough syrup, toothpaste, soaps, and many other household products. Calculate the number of hydrogen atoms in 4.5 mol of glycerol.

19. How many atoms are in 14.56 g of sodium hydrogen sulphate, the active ingredient in some toilet cleaners?

3.4 Molar Volume

Warm Up

Recall from section 1.4 that the prefix "milli" means one-thousandth or 1×10^{-3}.

1. A milligram (mg) is one-________________ of a gram.
2. A ________________ (_______) is 1×10^{-3} moles.
3. A millilitre (mL) is one-thousandth of a ______________.
4. 0.032 L = ___________ mL
5. 11.2 mg = ______________ g

Molar Volume

Just as the mass of a mole of a substance is called its molar mass, the volume of a mole of a substance is called its molar volume. The **molar volume** of a substance is the space occupied by a mole of its particles. A solid's or a liquid's molar volume is determined by the size and spacing of its particles. The size of the particles has little effect on a gas's molar volume because the average distance between the particles is so much greater than their size.

Solids, liquids, and gases under constant pressure all expand when heated. Kinetic molecular theory explains that matter is composed of moving particles. At a higher temperature, a substance's particles are moving faster and are thereby hitting each other harder and bouncing farther apart. Since its particles have spread farther apart, a substance's molar volume is greater at higher temperatures.

Liquids and gases are more frequently measured by volume than by mass. A substance's molar volume allows you to convert the volume of the substance into its number of moles.

Figure 3.4.1 *Gay-Lussac was an avid hot-air balloonist and conducted some of his experiments aloft.*

Quick Check

1. What does the term "molar volume" mean? ____
2. A solid's or a liquid's molar volume is determined by the ___________ and _____________ of its particles.
3. A gas's molar volume is determined mainly by the ____________ of its particles.
4. What generally happens to the molar volume of a material as it is heated? _______________

The Molar Volume of Gases

All of Dalton's evidence for the atomic theory came from combining mass ratios. During the same time period when Dalton lived, other scientists were following a separate line of research gathering data on combining volume ratios called volumetric data. In 1809, the French chemist, Joseph Gay-Lussac found that gases measured at the same temperature and pressure always reacted in whole-number volume ratios (Figure 3.4.1). For example, two volumes of hydrogen gas and one volume of oxygen gas react to produce two volumes of gaseous water.

Using Gay Lussac's findings, the Italian chemist Amedeo Avogadro hypothesized that equal volumes of different gases, measured at the same temperature and pressure, have equal numbers of particles. Modern chemists still refer to this as **Avogadro's hypothesis**.

At low pressures, the different sizes and attractive forces of different particles have little effect on the gas's volume because the particles are so far apart on average. As an example, 1 mol of any gas at 0°C and 101.3 kPa occupies approximately 22.4 L. Chemists refer to 0°C and 101.3 kPa as **standard temperature and pressure** or **STP** for short. The standard pressure 101.3 kPa is normal atmospheric pressure at sea level.

The molar volume of any gas at STP is approximately 22.4 L.

Name	Equivalence Statement	Conversion Factors	
Molar gas volume	1 mol = 22.4 L @ STP	$\frac{22.4\ L}{1\ mol}$ @ STP	$\frac{1\ mol}{22.4\ L}$ @ STP

While all gases at the same temperature and pressure have approximately the same molar volume, each solid and liquid has its own characteristic molar volume. In questions requiring volumetric conversions, you will be given either the molar volume of any solid, liquid, or gas not at STP, or you will be given a means to calculate it.

Sample Problem — Converting Moles to Volume

Atmospheric nitrogen and oxygen react during lightning storms to produce nitrogen monoxide that is quickly converted to nitrogen dioxide. What is the volume of 1.3 mol of NO_2 at STP?

What to Think about

1. Convert: mol NO_2 → L NO_2
2. Setup:
   $1.3\ mol\ NO_2 \times \frac{?\ L\ NO_2}{1\ mol\ NO_2}$
3. Conversion factor:
   22.4 L NO_2 per 1 mol NO_2

How to Do It

$1.3\ \cancel{mol\ NO_2} \times \frac{22.4\ L\ NO_2}{1\ \cancel{mol\ NO_2}} = 29\ L\ NO_2$

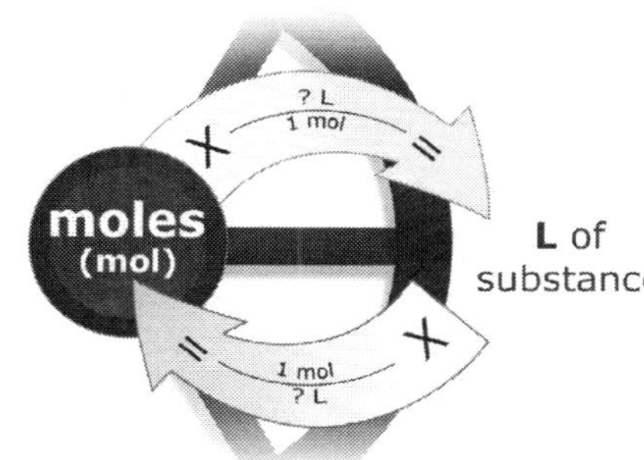

Sample Problem — Converting Volume to Moles

600.0 L of air at STP is compressed into a scuba tank. How many moles of air are in the tank?

What to Think about

1. Convert: L air → mol air
2. Setup: $600.0\ L\ air \times \frac{1\ mol\ air}{?\ L\ air}$
3. Conversion factor:
   1 mol air per 22.4 L air

How to Do It

$600.0\ \cancel{L\ air} \times \frac{1\ mol\ air}{22.4\ \cancel{L\ air}} = 26.8\ mol\ air$

Practice Problems — Converting Moles to Volume and Volume to Moles

1. What volume of oxygen gas at STP contains 1.33 mol of O_2?

2. In British Columbia, the burnt-match odor of sulphur dioxide is often associated with pulp and paper mills. How many moles of SO_2 are in 9.5 L of SO_2 at STP?

3. Silicon dioxide, better known as quartz, has a molar volume of 22.8 cm^3/mol. What is the volume of 0.39 mol of SiO_2?

Multi-Step Conversions Involving the Volume of a Substance

Recall from section 3.3 that as you learn more chemical quantities we'll add them to the rim of the wheel. You'll relate or connect the volume of a substance to the other quantities through the mole. For example, if you wanted to convert the volume of a substance into its mass, you would convert litres into moles and then moles into grams.

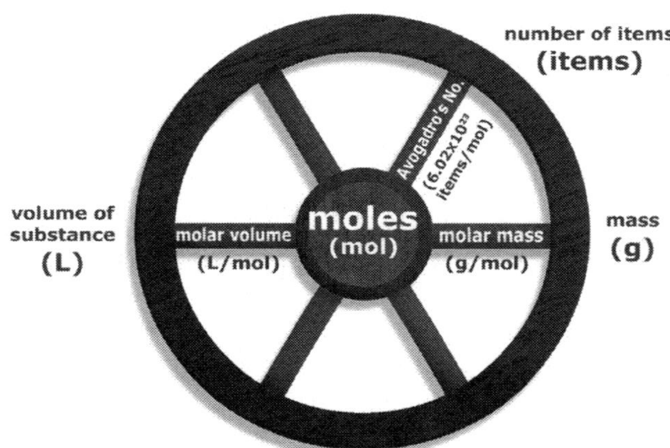

Figure 3.4.2 *Use the wheel model to help you do conversions involving the volume of a substance.*

Sample Problem — Two Step Conversion: Volume to Number of Items (Atoms)

The gas in neon signs is at extremely low pressure. How many neon atoms are present in a sign containing 75 mL of neon gas at a molar volume that is 100 times greater than the molar volume at STP?

What to Think about

1. Convert: mL → L
2. Convert: L Ne → mol Ne → atoms Ne
3. Setup:

$$0.075 \text{ L Ne} \times \frac{1 \text{ mol Ne}}{? \text{ L Ne}} \times \frac{? \text{ atoms Ne}}{1 \text{ mol Ne}}$$

4. Conversion factors:
   2240 L Ne per 1 mol Ne
   6.02×10^{23} atoms Ne per 1 mol Ne

How to Do It

$$75 \text{ ml} \times \frac{1.0 \text{ L}}{1000 \text{ mL}} = 0.075 \text{ L}$$

$$0.075 \text{ L Ne} \times \frac{1 \text{ mol Ne}}{2240 \text{ L Ne}} \times \frac{6.02 \times 10^{23} \text{ atoms Ne}}{1 \text{ mol Ne}}$$

$= 2.0 \times 10^{19}$ atoms Ne

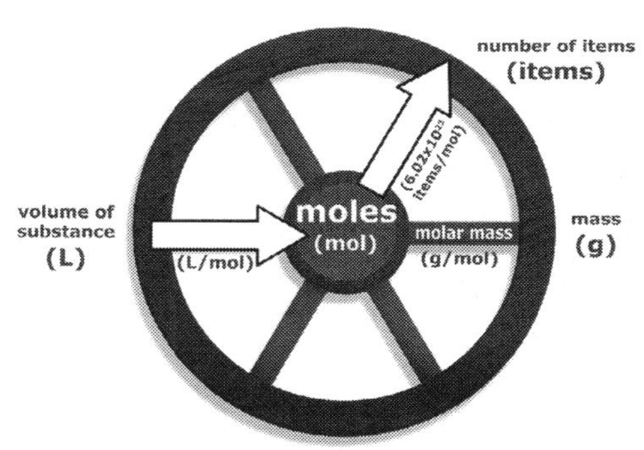

Sample Problem — Two Step Conversion: Volume to Mass

Natural gas is used to heat many homes and may fuel the Bunsen burners in your laboratory. Natural gas consists primarily of methane, CH_4. What is the mass of 8.0 L of CH_4 at STP?

What to Think about

1. Convert: L CH_4 → mol CH_4 → g CH_4
2. Setup:

$$8.0 \text{ L } CH_4 \times \frac{1 \text{ mol } CH_4}{? \text{ L } CH_4} \times \frac{? \text{ g } CH_4}{1 \text{ mol } CH_4}$$

3. Conversion factors:
   22.4 L CH_4 per 1 mol CH_4
   16.0 g CH_4 per 1 mol CH_4

How to Do It

$$8.0 \text{ L } CH_4 \times \frac{1 \text{ mol } CH_4}{22.4 \text{ L } CH_4} \times \frac{16.0 \text{ g } CH_4}{1 \text{ mol } CH_4} = 5.7 \text{ g } CH_4$$

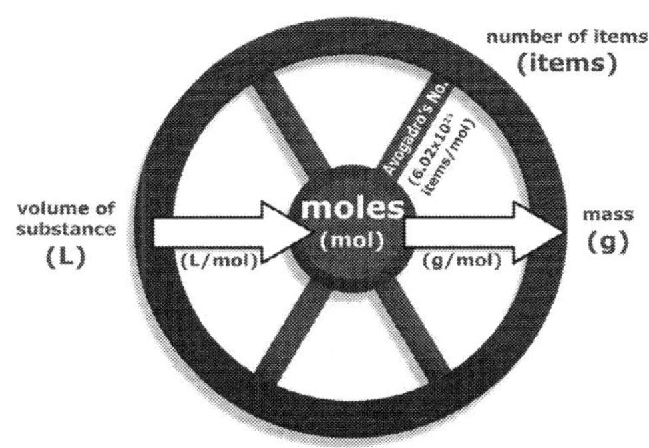

Sample Problem — Three Step Conversion: Mass of A to Volume of B

People often refer to the amount of CO_2 produced as the carbon "footprint" of a process. What volume of CO_2 at STP contains 0.20 g of carbon?

What to Think about

1. Convert:
   g C → mol C → mol CO_2 → L CO_2

2. Setup:

$$0.20 \text{ g C} \times \frac{1 \text{ mol C}}{? \text{ g C}} \times \frac{1 \text{ mol } CO_2}{? \text{ mol C}} \times \frac{? \text{ L } CO_2}{1 \text{ mol } CO_2}$$

3. Conversion factors:
   1 mol C per 12.0 g C
   1 mol CO_2 per 1 mol C
   22.4 L CO_2 per 1 mol CO_2

How to Do It

$$0.20 \text{ g C} \times \frac{1 \text{ mol C}}{12.0 \text{ g C}} \times \frac{1 \text{ mol } CO_2}{1 \text{ mol C}} \times \frac{22.4 \text{ L } CO_2}{1 \text{ mol } CO_2}$$

$= 0.37$ L CO_2

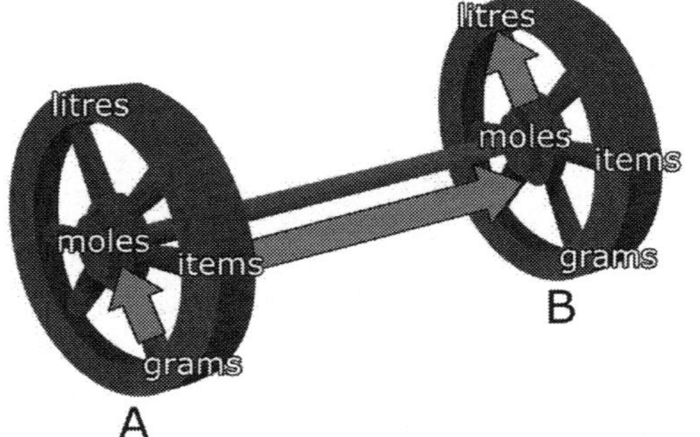

Converting mass of one substance to volume of another

Practice Problems — Conversions: Volume to Number of Items or Mass; Mass to Volume

1. H_2S gas is released from rotten eggs. What volume of H_2S gas at STP contains 17 g H_2S?

2. Fill in the missing entry in each conversion factor below to determine the mass of carbon in 1.0 L of propane, C_3H_8, at STP.

$$1.0 \text{ L } C_3H_8 \times \frac{1 \text{ mol } C_3H_8}{\_\_\_\_ \text{ L } C_3H_8} \times \frac{\_\_\_\_ \text{ mol C}}{1 \text{ mol } C_3H_8} \times \frac{\_\_\_\_ \text{ g C}}{1 \text{ mol C}}$$

3. Ethylene glycol ($C_2H_6O_2$) is widely used as an automotive antifreeze. The molar volume of $C_2H_6O_2$ is 0.0559 L/mol. How many hydrogen atoms are in 200.0 mL of $C_2H_6O_2$?

Molar Volume and Density

Density is the amount of matter in a given volume of an object or material. In other words, it is the mass per unit volume. Density is a conversion factor that relates a substance's mass directly to its volume without any reference to the mole. In terms of our wheel model, density is the section of the rim between grams and litres.

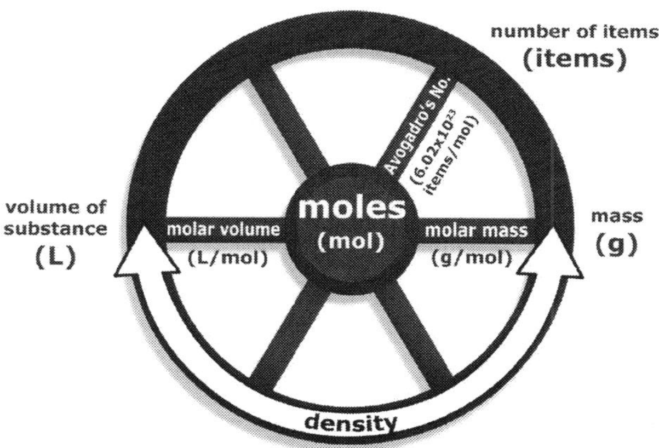

Figure 3.4.3 *Interconverting the mass and the volume of a substance*

Sample Problem — Converting Volume Directly to Mass

The density of methanol, CH_3OH, at 20°C is 0.813 g/mL. What is the mass of 0.500 L of the alcohol at 20°C?

What to Think about	How to Do It
1. Convert: L CH_3OH → g CH_3OH 2. Setup: $0.500\ \text{L } CH_3OH \times \frac{?\ \text{g } CH_3OH}{1\ \text{L } CH_3OH}$ 3. Conversion factor: 813 g/L	$0.500\ \cancel{\text{L } CH_3OH} \times \frac{813\ \text{g } CH_3OH}{1\ \cancel{\text{L } CH_3OH}} = 407\ \text{g } CH_3OH$

It is the densities of substances, rather than their molar volumes, that are usually published in reference texts and tables. Molar volume and density are related through molar mass. An examination of their units (dimensional analysis) reveals that:

$$\frac{\cancel{g}}{\text{mol}} \times \frac{\text{L}}{\cancel{g}} = \frac{\text{L}}{\text{mol}}$$

$$\text{molar volume} = \frac{\text{molar mass}}{\text{density}}$$

Sample Problem — Calculating Molar Volume from Density

In an episode of the television show "MythBusters," the team floated an aluminum foil boat on the invisible gas, sulphur hexafluoride, SF_6. SF_6 has a density of 6.00 g/L at room temperature and pressure, about six times that of air. What is the molar volume of SF_6 under these conditions?

What to Think about

1. $\text{molar volume} = \dfrac{\text{molar mass}}{\text{density}}$

2. Setup: $\dfrac{?\text{ g } SF_6}{1\text{ mol } SF_6} \times \dfrac{1\text{ L } SF_6}{6.00\text{ g } SF_6}$

3. Conversion factors:
   146.1 g SF_6 per 1 mol SF_6

How to Do It

$$\frac{146.1\ \cancel{\text{g } SF_6}}{1\text{ mol } SF_6} \times \frac{1\text{ L } SF_6}{6.00\ \cancel{\text{g } SF_6}} = 24.3\ \frac{\text{L } SF_6}{\text{mol } SF_6}$$

Practice Problems — Calculating Molar Volume and Density

1. Gold has a density of 19.42 g/cm^3. The standard gold bar held as gold reserves by central banks weighs 12.4 kg. What is the volume of the standard gold bar?

2. Mercury has a density of 13.534 g/mL at room temperature. What is the mass of 12.7 mL of mercury?

3. Although ethanol (C_2H_5OH) is best known as the type of alcohol found in alcoholic beverages, its largest use is as a fuel or fuel additive. The density of ethanol is 0.789 g/mL. What is the molar volume of ethanol?

3.4 Activity: The Atomic Radius of Aluminum

Question
What is the radius of an aluminum atom?

Background
We can't even see an individual atom with the naked eye but we can still derive an atom's radius from the molar volume and packing arrangement of a substance's atoms. Molar volume is the actual amount of space required to "house" 1 mol of the atoms and includes the space between them. In a technique called X-ray diffraction, chemists reflect X-rays off the substance. The scattering (diffraction) pattern allows chemists to determine how the atoms are arranged. Aluminum atoms are packed in such a way that 74% of the metal's volume is the volume of the atoms themselves and the rest is space.

Procedure
1. Weigh and measure the dimensions of a small aluminum block and fill in the table below.

Mass (g)	Length (cm)	Width (cm)	Height (cm)	Volume (cm^3)	Density (g/cm^3)

Results and Discussion
1. Calculate the molar volume of aluminum in cm^3/mol.

2. Calculate the volume of 1 mol of Al atoms (excluding the space between them).

   Volume = 0.74 × ____________ cm^3/mol = ______________ cm^3/mol

3. Calculate the volume of one Al atom.

   $$\text{Atomic volume} = \frac{\_\_\_\_\_\ \text{cm}^3\ \text{Al}}{1\ \text{mol Al}} \times \frac{1\ \text{mol Al}}{\_\_\_\_\_\_\_\_\_\ \text{atoms Al}} = \_\_\_\_\_\_\_\_\_\_\_\_\_\_\ \text{cm}^3/\text{mol}$$

4. Calculate the radius of a spherical aluminum atom. Given $V = {}^4/_3\, \pi\, r^3$ solve for r.

5. Convert the radius of the atoms into nanometres.

6. The accepted value for the radius of an aluminum atom is 0.143 nm. What is your percent error?

You just figured out the radius of an atom. How amazing is that! Cu (8.96 g/cm^3) atoms are packed the same way as Al atoms if you'd like to repeat this activity for copper.

3.4 Review Questions

1. Liquid octane, C_8H_{18}, has a molar volume of 82.4 mL/mol. What is the volume of 250 millimoles of C_8H_{18}?

2. How many moles of air are there in a human lung with a volume of 2.4 L at STP?

3. 2.75 L N_2 at STP = ____________ mol N_2

4. Air is approximately 21% oxygen. How many moles of oxygen are in 5.0 L of air at STP?

5. Diphosphorus pentoxide is a gas produced each time you strike a match. What is the mass of 2.57 L of this gas at STP?

6. A 525 mL flask contains 0.935 g of a noble gas at STP. Identify the gas from its molar mass.

7. Acetylene gas, C_2H_2, is used as a fuel in welding torches. How many acetylene molecules are in a cylinder that delivers 1400 L of acetylene at STP?

8. 5×10^{19} molecules PH_3 = __________ mL PH_3 at STP

9. Propane gas, $C_3H_8(g)$, is easily compressible to a storable liquid. A standard barbecue tank holds 9.1 kg of propane. How many litres of gas will the tank release at STP?

10. Soft drinks are bottled under pressure forcing CO_2 into solution. The industry expresses the amount of carbonation in volumes of CO_2 at STP per volume of solution. The carbonation of a typical soft drink is 3.7 v/v meaning that a 355 mL can contains 3.7×355 mL CO_2 at STP. What is the mass of CO_2 in a 355 mL can?

11. How many moles of hydrogen are in 83.9 L of ammonia gas, NH_3, at STP?

12. Nitrous oxide, N_2O, is commonly called "laughing gas." It is sometimes used by dentists as a partial anaesthetic. How many grams of nitrogen are in 3.84 L of N_2O at STP?

13. Dinitrogen tetroxide is one of the most important rocket propellants ever developed. How many oxygen atoms are in 27.2 L of the gas at STP?

14. Disposable lighters often contain butane, C_4H_{10} (density = 0.601 g/mL). How many grams of butane are there in a lighter containing 15 mL of the fuel?

15. Mercury is a liquid metal with a density of 13.546 g/mL at 20°C. What is the molar volume of mercury at 20°C?

16. Gold has a density of 19.42 g/cm^3. How many moles of gold are there in a 5.0 cm^3 strip?

17. Liquid bromine, Br_2, has a density of 3.53 g/mL. How many bromine molecules are in 15.0 mL of bromine?

3.5 Composition Analysis — Determining Formulas

Warm Up

Forensic investigators collect samples from crime scenes. How do technicians identify the unknown samples? An instrument called a **mass spectrometer** can identify the vast majority of compounds. Each compound has a unique mass spectrum; much like each person has a unique fingerprint. A mass spectrometer breaks most of the molecules into fragments. In so doing, it creates a variety of particles from individual atoms to the intact molecule itself, and then marks the mass of each of these particles along a graph's horizontal axis. The height of the line in the spectrum indicates the relative abundance of that particle. Below is a simplified mass spectrum of a compound called pentane (C_5H_{12}).

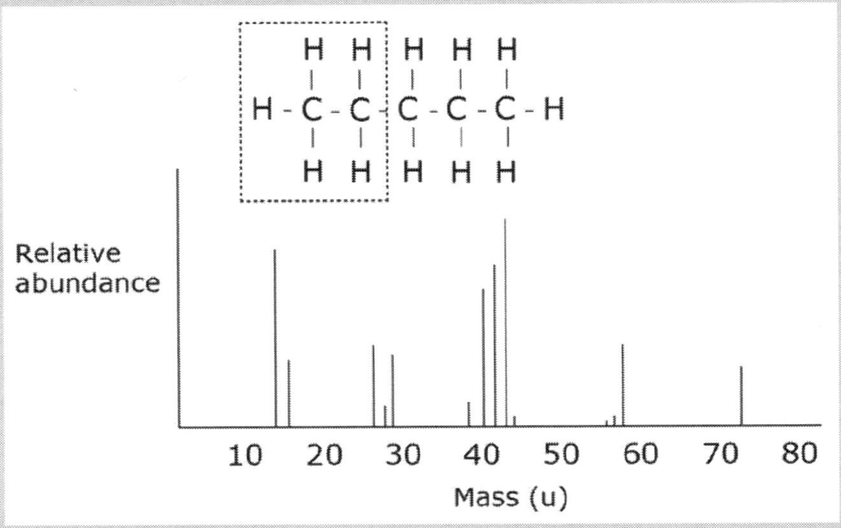

Mass spectrum analysis of pentane

1. The last spectral line represents the intact molecule. What is its molecular mass? __________
2. Draw an arrow to point to the spectral line that represents the mass of the outlined fragment.
3. Why do you think there are more of some fragments than others?

____

____

The important point here is that one of the most sophisticated tools in a chemist's arsenal identifies compounds solely from their "mass profile". In this section, you'll learn to determine a compound's formula from its composition by mass.

Percentage Composition

Percentage composition is the percent of a compound's mass contributed by each type of atom in the compound.

A compound's percentage composition can be determined theoretically from its formula.

Sample Problem — Determining Percentage Composition

What is the percentage composition of a sugar with the formula $C_{12}H_{22}O_{11}$?

What to Think about

1. Calculate the sugar's molar mass.
2. Thus one mole of this sugar contains 144 g C, 22 g H, and 176 g O.
3. Express each element's percentage of the molar mass.

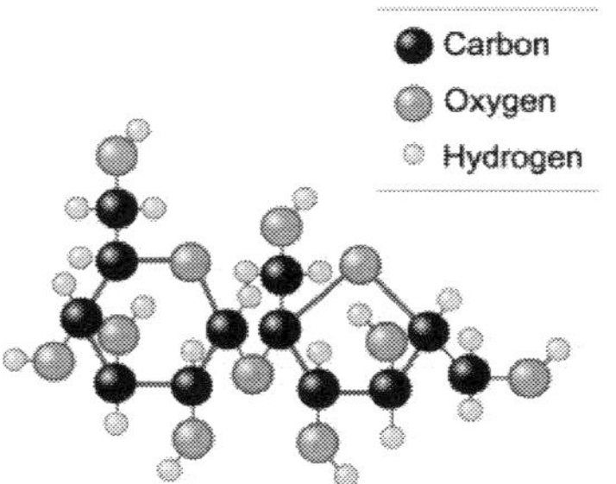

A sugar molecule with 12 carbon atoms, 22 hydrogen atoms, and 11 oxygen atoms.

How to Do It

$$\frac{12 \text{ mol C}}{1 \text{ mol } C_{12}H_{22}O_{11}} \times \frac{12.0 \text{ g C}}{1 \text{ mol C}} = \frac{144.0 \text{ g C}}{1 \text{ mol } C_{12}H_{22}O_{11}}$$

$$\frac{22 \text{ mol H}}{1 \text{ mol } C_{12}H_{22}O_{11}} \times \frac{1.0 \text{ g H}}{1 \text{ mol H}} = \frac{22.0 \text{ g H}}{1 \text{ mol } C_{12}H_{22}O_{11}}$$

$$\frac{11 \text{ mol O}}{1 \text{ mol } C_{12}H_{22}O_{11}} \times \frac{16.0 \text{ g O}}{1 \text{ mol O}} = \frac{176.0 \text{ g O}}{1 \text{ mol } C_{12}H_{22}O_{11}}$$

$$\text{Total} = 342.0 \text{ g/mol } C_{12}H_{22}O_{11}$$

$$\% \text{ C} = \frac{144.0 \text{ g C}}{342.0 \text{ g } C_{12}H_{22}O_{11}} \times 100 = 42.1\ \%$$

$$\% \text{ H} = \frac{22.0 \text{ g H}}{342.0 \text{ g } C_{12}H_{22}O_{11}} \times 100 = 6.4\ \%$$

$$\% \text{ O} = \frac{176.0 \text{ g O}}{342.0 \text{ g } C_{12}H_{22}O_{11}} \times 100 = 51.5\ \%$$

Practice Problems — Determining Percentage Composition

1. Ibuprofen is a common pain reliever and anti-inflammatory. Its formula is $C_{13}H_{18}O_2$. What is its percentage composition?

2. Ammonium sulphate, $(NH_4)_2SO_4$, is a common fertilizer used to lower the pH of soil. Calculate its percentage composition.

3. Many salts are hydrated, which means they have water molecules incorporated into their ionic crystal lattice in a fixed ratio. Magnesium sulphate heptahydrate, $MgSO_4 \cdot 7\,H_2O$, has seven water molecules incorporated into the crystal lattice for each magnesium ion and sulphate ion. Calculate the percentage of water by mass in $MgSO_4 \cdot 7\,H_2O$.

Empirical, Molecular, and Structural Formulas

Every molecular compound has three formulas; an empirical formula, a molecular formula, and a structural formula. They become more specific in that order.

- The **empirical formula** is the simplest integral ratio of the different types of atoms in the compound.
- The **molecular formula** is the actual number of each type of atom in each molecule of the compound.
- The **structural formula** shows how the atoms in a molecule are arranged. It is a diagram that shows the pattern of the atoms' connections.

Organic chemistry is the study of compounds and reactions involving carbon. There are millions of organic compounds. Glucose is an organic compound with a molecular formula of $C_6H_{12}O_6$. The subscripts 6, 12, 6 can be reduced or simplified to 1, 2, 1. We don't show the number 1 as a subscript in a formula so the empirical formula of glucose is CH_2O.

Many compounds have the same empirical formula but different molecular formulas. Their molecular formulas all reduce to the same ratio. For example, all alkenes such as ethene (C_2H_4), propene (C_3H_6), and butene (C_4H_8), have an empirical formula of CH_2 because each of their molecular formulas can be reduced to a 1 to 2 ratio.

Compounds with the same molecular formula but with different structural formulas, i.e. the same atoms are put together differently, are called structural isomers. For example, C_4H_{10} has two structural isomers. You will learn more about structural isomers in chapter 8.

Quick Check

1. Complete the following table.

<table>
<tr><th>Structural Formula</th><th>Molecular Formula</th><th>Empirical Formula</th></tr>
<tr><td>H O
| ||
H - C - C - O - H
|
H</td><td></td><td></td></tr>
<tr><td>O O
|| ||
H - O - C - C - O - H</td><td></td><td></td></tr>
</table>

Determining an Empirical Formula from Percent Composition

In section 3.1 you learned how to determine an element's relative atomic mass from a compound's percent composition and formula. Earlier in this section (3.5), you learned how to determine the percent composition of a compound from its formula and the atomic masses of its component elements. There's only one more arrangement of these variables to learn. That's how to determine the formula of a compound from its percent composition and the atomic masses of its component elements.

The word "empirical" is an adjective meaning that something is based on observation or experiment. Empirical formulas are determined from the mass ratios of a compound's component elements; in other words, from its percent composition. The most direct, but not always easiest, way to experimentally determine a compound's percent composition is to decompose a sample of the compound into its component elements.

Sample Problem — Determining an Empirical Formula

Determine the empirical formula of a compound that is 48.65% carbon, 8.11% hydrogen, and 43.24% oxygen.

What to Think about

1. In 100.0 g of the substance, there would be 48.65 g C, 8.11 g H, and 43.24 g O. Convert these amounts into moles.
2. Divide each molar quantity by the smallest one and then multiply by whatever factor is necessary to find their integral ratio (as shown in a conventional formula).

   The mole ratio and the individual atom ratio are of course the same. This means the subscripts in a formula can be read either as mole ratios or as individual atom ratios. If this compound has 3 mol of carbon atoms for every 2 mol of oxygen atoms then it has 3 dozen carbon atoms for every 2 dozen oxygen atoms, and 3 carbon atoms for every 2 oxygen atoms.

How to Do It

$$48.65\ \cancel{g\ C} \times \frac{1\ mol\ C}{12.0\ \cancel{g\ C}} = 4.0542\ mol\ C$$

$$8.11\ \cancel{g\ H} \times \frac{1\ mol\ H}{1.0\ \cancel{g\ H}} = 8.1100\ mol\ H$$

$$43.24\ \cancel{g\ O} \times \frac{1\ mol\ O}{16.0\ \cancel{g\ O}} = 2.7025\ mol\ O$$

$$\frac{C_{4.0542}H_{8.1100}O_{2.7025}}{2.7025} = C_{1.5}H_3O$$

$$2\ (C_{1.5}H_3O) = C_3H_6O_2$$

Practice Problems — Determining an Empirical Formula

1. A compound is 18.7% Li, 16.3% C, and 65.5% O. Determine its empirical formula.

2. A compound is 9.93% C, 58.6% Cl, and 31.4% F. Determine its empirical formula.

3. A sample of a compound contains 5.723 g Ag, 0.852 g S, and 1.695 g O. Determine its empirical formula.

Determining the Molecular Formula of a Compound

Recall the difference between the empirical formula and the molecular formula of a compound. The empirical formula is the simplest integral ratio of the different types of atoms in the compound. The molecular formula is the actual number of each type of atom in each molecule. A compound's molecular formula is an integral multiple of its empirical formula. Its molecular formula's molar mass is that same integral multiple of its empirical formula's molar mass. For example, butane has an empirical formula of C_2H_5
(29 g/mol) and a molecular formula of C_4H_{10} (58 g/mol). The "molecular formula's molar mass" is just another way of saying "the compound's molar mass." Therefore, we can determine the compound's molecular formula from its empirical formula and its molar mass.

$$\text{molecular formula} = \text{empirical formula} \times \frac{\text{compound's molar mass}}{\text{molar mass of empirical formula}}$$

There are many ways to experimentally derive a compound's molar mass. If the compound is volatile, meaning it is easily evaporated, then you know from section 3.4 that 1 mol of any gas occupies 22.4 L at STP. The mass of 22.4 L at STP thus provides the compound's molar mass.

Sample Problem — Determining a Molecular Formula

A compound has an empirical formula of CH_2 and a molar mass of 42.0 g/mol. Determine its molecular formula.

What to Think about	How to Do It
1. Calculate the molar mass of the empirical formula.	$\frac{1 \text{ mol C}}{1 \text{ mol } CH_2} \times \frac{12.0 \text{ g C}}{1 \text{ mol C}} = \frac{12.0 \text{ g C}}{1 \text{ mol } CH_2}$ $\frac{2 \text{ mol H}}{1 \text{ mol } CH_2} \times \frac{1.0 \text{ g H}}{1 \text{ mol H}} = \frac{2.0 \text{ g H}}{1 \text{ mol } CH_2}$ Total = 14.0 g/mol CH_2
2. Divide the molar mass of the molecular formula by the molar mass of the empirical formula.	$\frac{42.0 \text{ g/mol}}{14.0 \text{ g/mol}} = 3.00$
3. Multiply the empirical formula itself by this factor.	$3\ CH_2 = C_3H_6$

Practice Problems — Determining a Molecular Formula

1. Vinegar is a dilute solution of acetic acid. The molar mass of acetic acid is 60.0 g/mol and it has an empirical formula of CH_2O. What is the molecular formula of acetic acid?

2. A compound has an empirical formula of C_3H_4. Which of the following are possible molar masses of the compound: 20 g/mol, 55 g/mol, 80 g/mol, 120 g/mol?

3. A small sample of antifreeze was analyzed. It contained 4.51 g C, 1.13 g H, and 6.01 g O. From the elevation of water's boiling point, it was determined that the antifreeze's molar mass is 62.0 g/mol. What is the molecular formula of antifreeze?

3.5 Activity: Determining the Empirical Formula of Butane from the Percentage Composition of Its Model

Question

What is the empirical formula of butane?

Background

Recall that "empirical" is an adjective meaning "based on observation or experiment." Empirical formulas are determined from the mass ratios of a compound's component elements (i.e., from its percent composition as determined by analysis). The empirical formula is the simplest integral ratio of the different types of atoms in the compound.

Procedure

1. Use #1 (regular sized) paper clips to represent hydrogen atoms. Jumbo paper clips represent carbon atoms. As a prelude to this exercise, someone must weigh 48 of each type of paperclip and divide by 4 to obtain the mass per dozen. Provide these values to the students to enter in column 3.
2. Form a group of two to five students.
3. Each student links 4 jumbo paper clips together with 10 regular paper clips.
4. Unlink all the clips and weigh all your group's jumbo clips together. Record the mass of your group's jumbo clips as the mass of carbon in the table below.
5. Weigh all your group's regular sized clips together. Record the mass of your group's regular clips as the mass of hydrogen in the table below.

Results and Discussion

Element	Mass (g)	Mass per Dozen (g/doz)	Number (doz)	Dozen Ratio	Empirical Formula
carbon				1.0	
hydrogen					

1. Calculate how many dozens of each type of paper clip are in your group's sample.

2. Calculate the dozen ratio to find out how many dozens of hydrogen atoms there are for each dozen carbon atoms.

3. By what integer do you need to multiply this ratio in order to obtain an integral dozen ratio? ______________

4. What is the empirical formula of butane? ____

5. Given the molecular models you made, what is the molecular formula of butane?

3.5 Review Questions

1. Menthol is a strong-smelling compound that is used in cough drops. It has a formula of $C_{10}H_{20}O$. Calculate its percentage composition.

2. Sodium acetate trihydrate ($NaCH_3COO \cdot 3H_2O$) is a salt commonly used in pickling foods. Calculate the percentage of water by mass in this compound.

3. Trinitrotoluene ($C_7H_5O_6N_3$) is an explosive commonly referred to as TNT. Calculate the percentage of nitrogen by mass in this compound.

4. Complete the following table.

Structural Formula	Molecular Formula	Empirical Formula
H-C(H)(H)-C(H)(H)-C(H)(H)-C(H)(H)-H		
H-O-C(=O)-C(H)(H)-C(H)(H)-C(H)(H)-H		

5. (a) Explain why the empirical formula alone is not enough to identify a compound.

   (b) What other piece of information will allow you to determine its molecular formula?

6. A pigment on a suspected forgery is analyzed using X-ray fluorescence and found to contain 0.5068 mol Ba, 0.5075 mol C, and 1.520 mol O. Determine its empirical formula.

7. A sample of caffeine is analyzed and found to contain 1.4844 g C, 0.1545 g H, 0.4947 g O and 0.8661 g N. Determine the empirical formula of caffeine.

8. (a) In a TV series, a forensic anthropologist uses X-ray fluorescence to analyze a dental filling found in skeletal remains. The results of the analysis are provided as *atomic* percentages: 2.85% Al, 87.4% Si, and 9.75% Yb. Convert these results into mass percentages.

(b) These results identified the filling as a commercial restorative material called Heliomolar. How might identifying the material be useful in helping to identify the remains?

9. A compound has an empirical formula of NH_2 and a molar mass of 32.1 g/mol. What is the compound's molecular formula?

10. A sample of ascorbic acid, also known as vitamin C, was analyzed and found to contain 1.080 g C, 0.121 g H, and 1.439 g O. Ascorbic acid has a molar mass of 176.1 g/mol. Determine the molecular formula of ascorbic acid.

11. A hydrocarbon is a compound containing only carbon and hydrogen. One particular hydrocarbon is 92.29% carbon by mass. If the compound's molar mass is 78.0 g/mol then what is its molecular formula?

12. Cannizzaro determined that a certain compound of carbon and oxygen had a molecular mass of 44.0 u. This meant that a certain volume of this gaseous compound weighed 44.0 times as much as the same volume of hydrogen gas at the same temperature and pressure. This compound was analyzed and found to be 27.3% carbon by mass.
(a) What is the total mass of carbon in a molecule of this compound?

(b) Cannizzaro repeated this experiment on many carbon compounds. Because he never found a molecule with less carbon than this one, Cannizzaro assumed that this molecule had only one carbon atom. Was this assumption correct?

3.6 Molar Concentration

Warm Up

Examples of common household liquids

1. List three products in your refrigerator that are solutions.
   ____
2. Name some substances that are dissolved in these solutions.
   ____
3. Where else in your home are solutions kept?
   ____

Molarity — A Useful Unit of Concentration

Many chemicals are dispensed in solution and most chemical reactions occur in solution.Recall from chapter 2 that a solution is a type of mixture in which the chemical species are completely mixed. A solute is a minor component of the mixture, generally what has been dissolved. The solvent is the major component of the mixture, generally what the solute was dissolved in.

Concentration is any expression of the proportion of a chemical in a solution. Chemists need to know the amount of solute present in any volume of solution they might dispense. Therefore, concentration is most usefully expressed as an amount of solute per volume of solution rather than per volume of solvent. There are many units of concentration. Common units of concentration express the amount of solute in grams. These include grams per litre of solution, percent m/v, which is the number of grams (mass) per 100 mL (volume) of solution, and parts per million (ppm), when expressed as the number of grams per million grams of solution. A useful unit of concentration for chemists expresses the quantity of solute in moles.

Molarity (M) is the number of moles of the chemical per litre of solution.

For example, 1.8 M HCl means 1.8 mol HCl per litre of solution. Molar concentrations allow chemists to directly compare the number of particles in the same volume of different solutions. For example, 10 mL of 2 M Li^+ contains twice as many ions as 10 mL of 1 M Na^+.

Name	Equivalence Statement	Conversion Factors	
Molar concentration	1 L solution = ? mol solute	$\frac{\text{? mol solute}}{\text{1 L solution}}$	$\frac{\text{1 L solution}}{\text{? mol solute}}$
Example: 3 M HCN	1 L solution = 3 mol HCN	$\frac{\text{3 mol HCN}}{\text{1 L solution}}$	$\frac{\text{1 L solution}}{\text{3 mol HCN}}$

Quick Check

1. Give one reason why solutions are important in chemistry.

   ____

2. What does 2 M NaOH mean?

   ____

3. Why is molarity a useful unit of concentration?

   ____

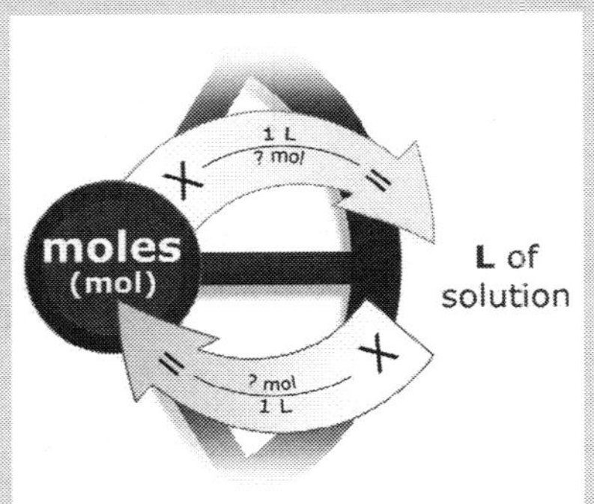

Sample Problem — Converting Volume of Solution into Moles of Solute

The average salinity (total salt concentration) of seawater is 0.60 M. How many moles of salt are in a toy bucket containing 435 mL of seawater?

What to Think about	How to Do It
1. Convert: mL → L	$435 \text{ mL} \times \frac{1.0 \text{ L}}{1000 \text{ mL}} = 0.435 \text{ L}$
2. Convert: L soln → mol salt	
3. Setup: $0.435 \text{ L soln} \times \frac{\text{? mol salt}}{1 \text{ L soln}}$	$0.435 \cancel{\text{L soln}} \times \frac{0.60 \text{ mol salt}}{1 \cancel{\text{L soln}}} = 0.26 \text{ mol salt}$
4. Conversion factor: 0.60 mol salt per 1 L soln	Note: There is no conventional abbreviation for "solution" but we will use "soln" in our calculations.

Sample Problem — Converting Moles of Solute into Volume of Solution

What volume of 3.0 M HCl should a chemist dispense to obtain 0.25 mol HCl?

What to Think about	How to Do It
1. Convert: mol HCl → L soln	
2. Setup: $0.25 \text{ mol HCl} \times \frac{1 \text{ L soln}}{\text{? mol HCl}}$	$0.25 \cancel{\text{mol HCl}} \times \frac{1 \text{ L soln}}{3.0 \cancel{\text{mol HCl}}} = 0.083 \text{ L soln}$
3. Conversion factor: 1 L soln per 3.0 mol HCl	

Practice Problems — Converting Moles of Solute to/from Volume of Solution

1. 0.72 L of 2.5 M NaOH = __________ mol NaOH

2. An intravenous bag of saline solution contains 0.154 M NaCl. How many moles of NaCl does a 500.0 mL bag contain?

3. 3.0 mol HCl = __________ L of 0.60 M HCl

4. A person's urine may have a distinct odor as soon as 15 min after eating asparagus. Methanethiol, one of the metabolic products responsible for this odor, can be detected by some people in concentrations as low as 4.0×10^{-8} M. At this concentration, what volume of urine contains 1.0 mmol of methanethiol?

Preparing a Standard Solution from a Solid

A solution of known concentration is called a **standard solution**. To prepare a 1 M NaCl(*aq*) solution, you could measure out 1 mol (58.5 g) of NaCl and then add water up to 1 L of solution so that the 1 mol NaCl is dissolved in the resulting 1 L solution. Note that you "add water up to 1 L" not "add up to 1 L of water," which means something entirely different. Adding water *up to* 1 L of solution won't quite require 1 L of water because the solute will displace a small amount of water. You won't always want 1 L of solution, however. To prepare a particular volume and concentration of solution requires calculating the mass of solute to weigh out. Chemists generally memorize the formula for this calculation through countless repetitions in the lab.

Sample Problem — Converting Volume of Solution into Mass of Solute

Describe how to prepare 0.055 L of 0.20 M KCl from the solid.

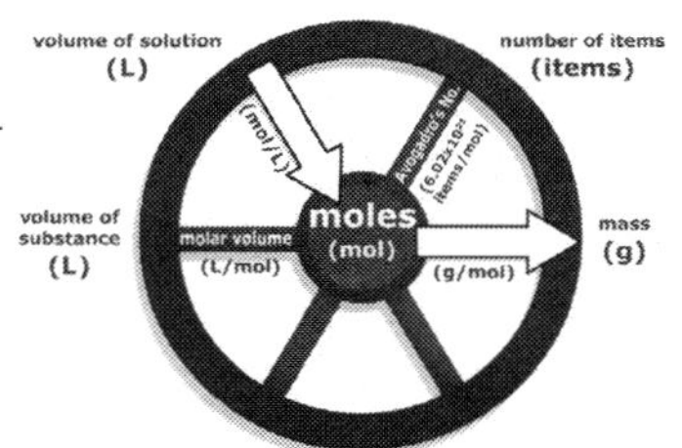

What to Think about

1. Convert: L soln ⟶ mol KCl ⟶ g KCl
2. Setup:
   $0.055 \text{ L soln} \times \frac{? \text{ mol KCl}}{1 \text{ L soln}} \times \frac{? \text{ g KCl}}{1 \text{ mol KCl}}$
3. Conversion factors:
   0.20 mol KCl per 1 L soln
   74.6 g KCl per 1 mol KCl

How to Do It

$0.055 \cancel{\text{ L soln}} \times \frac{0.20 \cancel{\text{ mol KCl}}}{1 \cancel{\text{ L soln}}} \times \frac{74.6 \text{ g KCl}}{1 \cancel{\text{ mol KCl}}}$
$= 0.82 \text{ g KCl}$

Measure out 0.82 g KCl and add water up to 55 mL (0.055 L) of solution.

Sample Problem — Determining Molar Concentration

What molar concentration of KCl is produced by measuring out 1.0 g KCl and adding water up to 0.350 L of solution?

What to Think about	How to Do It
1. Convert: g KCl → mol KCl	
2. Setup: $1.0 \text{ g KCl} \times \frac{1 \text{ mol KCl}}{? \text{ g KCl}}$	$1.0 \text{ g KCl} \times \frac{1 \text{ mol KCl}}{74.6 \text{ g KCl}} = 0.013 \text{ mol KCl}$
3. Conversion factor: 1 mol KCl per 74.6 g KCl	Molar Concentration
4. Molarity is moles per litre meaning the number of moles divided by the number of litres.	$\text{KCl} = \frac{0.013 \text{ mol KCl}}{0.350 \text{ L soln}} = 0.038M \text{ KCl}$

Practice Problems — Converting Volume of Solution into Mass of Solute and Determining Molar Concentration

1. Describe how to prepare 500.0 mL of 1.5 M $CaCl_2$ from $CaCl_2(s)$.

2. What mass of KCl would be recovered if 55 mL of 0.20 M KCl were "evaporated to dryness"? [Hint: this is the same as asking how many grams of KCl are in 55 mL of 0.20 M KCl.]

3. What molar concentration of silver nitrate is produced by measuring out 1.8 g and then adding water to make 75 mL of solution?

Ions in Solution

Recall from chapter 2 that ionic compounds have no net charge. The ions associate together in the ratio that results in their charges cancelling. For example:

$2Al^{3+}(aq) + 3SO_4^{2-}(aq) \rightarrow Al_2(SO_4)_3(s)$

The ionic compound is neutral because the ions have a net charge of zero: $2(3+) + 3(2-) = 0$. The ions, however, remain unchanged in the crystal. By convention, chemists don't show the charges of the ions in the formulas of ionic compounds. The charges are implicit (implied) rather than explicit (shown). When an ionic compound dissolves, the same ions that associated together to form the compound now **dissociate** (dis-associate) and travel independently through the solution. For example,

$Al_2(SO_4)_3(s) \rightarrow 2Al^{3+}(aq) + 3SO_4^{2-}(aq)$

Sample Problem — Two-Step Conversion: Volume of Solution to Number of Ions

Some communities fluoridate their water to reduce tooth decay. HealthLinkBC reports that the most effective F^- concentration for water supplies in B.C. is between 0.042 M and 0.053 M. How many fluoride ions would a person ingest by drinking 2.0 L of 0.047 M F^-?

What to Think about

1. Convert: L soln → mol F^- → ions F^-
2. Setup:
$$2.0 \text{ L soln} \times \frac{? \text{ mol F}^-}{1 \text{ L soln}} \times \frac{? \text{ ions F}^-}{1 \text{ mol F}^-}$$
3. Conversion factors:
0.047 mol F^- per 1 L soln
6.02×10^{23} ions F^- per 1 mol F^-

How to Do It

$$2.0 \text{ L soln} \times \frac{0.047 \text{ mol F}^-}{1 \text{ L soln}} \times \frac{6.02 \times 10^{23} \text{ ions F}^-}{1 \text{ mol F}^-}$$

$$= 5.7 \times 10^{22} \text{ ions F}^-$$

Being able to relate the concentration of dissolved ions to the concentration of their parent compound is extremely important in chemistry. Although it may be misleading, a label is not necessarily intended to indicate what is actually present in the solution. Some knowledge of chemistry is required to realize how a solute behaves in solution. 1 M $Al_2(SO_4)_3$ means that 1 mol of $Al_2(SO_4)_3$ was dissolved per litre of solution. There is no such thing as an $Al_2(SO_4)_3$ particle. The dissociation equation provides the ratio of the released ions to each other and to their parent compound; thus 1 M $Al_2(SO_4)_3$ actually contains 2 M Al^{3+} and 3 M SO_4^{2-}.

Sample Problem — Relating the Concentration of Dissolved Ions to the Concentration of Their Parent Compound

What concentrations of ions are present in 3.0 M $CaCl_2(aq)$?

What to Think about

The ratios in the dissociation equation show that 1 mol Ca^{2+} and 2 mol Cl^- are formed for each mole of $CaCl_2$ dissolved.

How to Do It

$CaCl_2(s)$	→	$Ca^{2+}(aq)$ +	$2Cl^-(aq)$
3.0 mol/L	dissolves to form	?	?
3.0 mol/L	dissolves to form	3.0 M	6.0 M

This table is shown for teaching purposes only — you don't need to show it in your work.

The molar concentration of a chemical is indicated by putting square brackets [ ] around the chemical's formula.

For example, [Na^+] means the molar concentration of Na^+. A couple of precautions:

- "M" already means "mol per L" therefore *don't write* "M per L" because that would mean "moles per litre per litre," which doesn't make sense.

- You can write "2 M Na^+" or "$[Na^+] = 2$ M" but *don't write* "2 M $[Na^+]$" because that would mean "two molar the molar concentration of Na^+," which doesn't make sense.

The dissociation equation provides the conversion factor represented by the axle in our wheel model.

Sample Problem — Three-Step Conversion: Volume of Solution to Number of Ions

Aluminum chloride can be used to produce aluminum chlorohydrate, an active ingredient in antiperspirants. How many chloride ions are in 0.025 L of 0.30 M $AlCl_3$?

What to Think about

1. Convert:
   L soln $\rightarrow$ mol $AlCl_3$ $\rightarrow$ mol Cl^- $\rightarrow$ ions Cl^-
2. Setup: $0.025 \text{ L soln} \times \frac{?\text{ mol } AlCl_3}{1 \text{ L soln}} \times \frac{?\text{ mol } Cl^-}{1 \text{ mol } AlCl_3} \times \frac{?\text{ ions } Cl^-}{1 \text{ mol } Cl^-}$
3. Conversion factors:
   0.30 mol $AlCl_3$ per 1 L soln
   3 mol Cl^- per 1 mol $AlCl_3$
   6.02×10^{23} Cl^- ions per 1 mol Cl^-

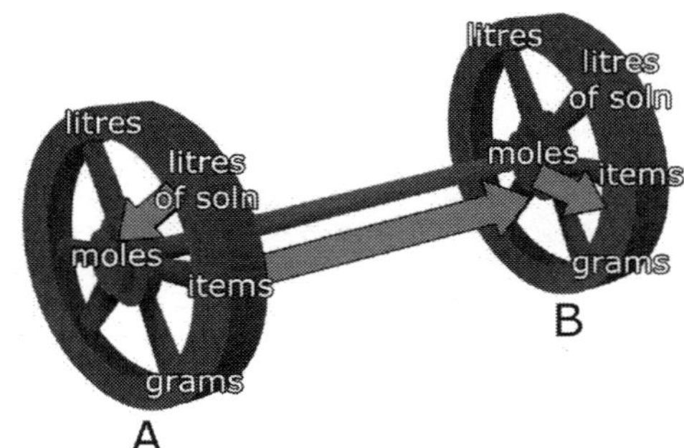

How to Do It

$$0.025 \cancel{\text{L soln}} \times \frac{0.30 \cancel{\text{mol } AlCl_3}}{1 \cancel{\text{L soln}}} \times \frac{3 \cancel{\text{mol } Cl^-}}{1 \text{ mol } \cancel{AlCl_3}} \times \frac{6.02 \times 10^{23} \text{ ions } Cl^-}{1 \cancel{\text{mol } Cl^-}} = 1.4 \times 10^{22} \text{ ions } Cl^-$$

Practice Problems — Three-Step Conversion: Volume of Solution to Number of Ions

1. What concentrations of ions are present in 1.5 M $CaCl_2(aq)$?

2. What concentration of sodium phosphate contains 0.60 M Na^+?

3. Write the relationship between the concentrations of the ions present in a solution of lithium phosphate. (Careful; this is tricky. In a $CaCl_2$ solution, $[Cl^-] = 2\,[Ca^{2+}]$).

4. What mass of potassium ions is in 0.75 L of 2.8 M K^+?

5. Iron(III) nitrate solutions are used by jewellers to etch silver. How many NO_3^- ions are dissolved in a 525 mL bath of 3.0 M iron(III) nitrate?

3.6 Activity: Building a Scale Model of a Solution

Question

What is the ratio of solute ions to water molecules in a solution of 1 M NaCl(*aq*)?

Background

Models are very important in science. A model, scientific or otherwise, is anything that represents something else. Chemists can use models to explain and predict the behaviour of matter. The American chemist, Linus Pauling, figured out the spiral structure of proteins using paper cut-outs as models. He was awarded the 1954 Nobel Prize in chemistry partly for this accomplishment. In this activity, you will construct a scale model of a solution.

Procedure

1. Calculate how many moles of H_2O molecules occupy one L. (Density of H_2O = 1000 g/L)

$$\frac{\_\_\_\_\_ \text{ g } H_2O}{1 \text{ L } H_2O} \times \frac{1 \text{ mol } H_2O}{\text{g } H_2O} = \_\_\_\_\_\_\_\_\_\_\_\_ \text{ mol } H_2O/\text{l } H_2O$$

   Although its units are moles per litre this value is not a concentration; it is not molarity. It does not describe the proportion of a chemical in a mixture. It describes the number of moles of water in 1 L of the substance and is simply the inverse of water's molar volume.

2. Determine the ion concentrations in 1.0 M NaCl(*aq*).

NaCl	→	**Na^+** +	**Cl^-**
1.0 M	dissolves to form		

3. For simplicity, let's assume that each mole of ions displaces a mole of water molecules. State the ratio of water molecules: sodium ions: chloride ions in 1 M NaCl (*aq*).

   ________ H_2O: ________ Na^+: ________ Cl^-

4. As a class, decide which kind or colour of bead will represent each chemical species.

   H_2O molecules ____________________ Na^+ ions ____________________

   Cl^- ions ____________________

5. Count out the beads in the ratio shown in step 3 and pour them into the 500-mL graduated cylinder provided by your teacher for the class.

Results and Discussion

6. State three ways your model differs from an actual 1 M NaCl solution.

3.6 Review Questions

1. What does 1.5 M HCl mean?

2. A cough syrup contains 0.011 M dextromethorphan. How many moles of the cough suppressant are in one teaspoon (5.0 mL) of the cough syrup?

3. 75.0 mmol Ca^{2+} = _______ L of 0.20 M Ca^{2+}

4. The fluid inside living cells is called cytosol. A human hepatocyte (a type of liver cell) with a volume of 500 fL (1 fL (femtolitre) = 10^{-15} L) contains 12 mM Na^+. How many sodium ions are in the cytosol of this cell?

5. Consumer products express concentrations in mg/volume or g/volume because the general public isn't familiar with molarity.
   (a) A medium-sized (296 mL) cup of Tim Horton's coffee contains 0.10 g caffeine, $C_8H_{10}N_4O_2$. Express this concentration in molarity.

   (b) A 355 mL can of pop contains 42.6 g sugar, $C_6H_{12}O_6$. What is the sugar's molar concentration?

6. Humans have an average blood volume of 5.0 L with an average blood sugar ($C_6H_{12}O_6$) concentration of 4.0 mM. What is the average mass of glucose coursing through the human bloodstream?

7. Describe how to prepare 250 mL of 0.50 M sodium nitrate. Be sure to answer in a complete sentence.

8. As a glass of cold tap water warms up, small air bubbles will come out of solution on the inner wall of the glass. A glass of cold water contains 0.45 mM O_2. How many millilitres of oxygen gas at STP are dissolved in 300.0 mL of this water?

9. What concentrations of ions are present in:
   (a) 0.35 M $Fe_2(Cr_2O_7)_3$?

   (b) 1.6 mol/L strontium cyanide?

10. In reflected light, iron(III) chloride crystals appear dark green but in transmitted light they appear maroon. What concentration of iron(III) chloride contains 0.038 M Cl^-?

11. In a solution of $Fe_2(SO_4)_3$:
(a) if the $[Fe^{3+}]$ = 1.5 M then what is the $[SO_4^{2-}]$?

(b) if the $[SO_4^{2-}]$ = 3.0 M then what is the $[Fe^{3+}]$?

12. Write the relationship between the concentrations of the ions in a solution of:
(a) zinc chromate

(b) strontium hydroxide

13. Milk has a $[Ca^{2+}]$ of about 31.4 mM. What mass of Ca^{2+} ions are in a 250 mL serving of milk?

14. How many Na^+ ions are dissolved in 1.5 L of 3.0 M Na_2CO_3?

15. It takes 145 drops from a pipette to reach the 5.0 mL mark on a graduated cylinder. How many grams of bromide ions are in one such drop of 0.10 M iron(III) bromide?

16. Phosphoric acid, H_3PO_4, is added to soft drinks to increase their tartness and to act as a preservative. The concentration of H_3PO_4 in Pepsi is proprietary (a company secret) but can be determined from its phosphorus content since H_3PO_4 is the only source of phosphorus in the beverage. There are 49 mg of phosphorus in a 355 mL can of Pepsi. What is the $[H_3PO_4]$ in Pepsi?

17. Draw the plot representing a 1.5 M NaCl solution on the graph provided.

Amount of NaCl vs. Volume of Solution

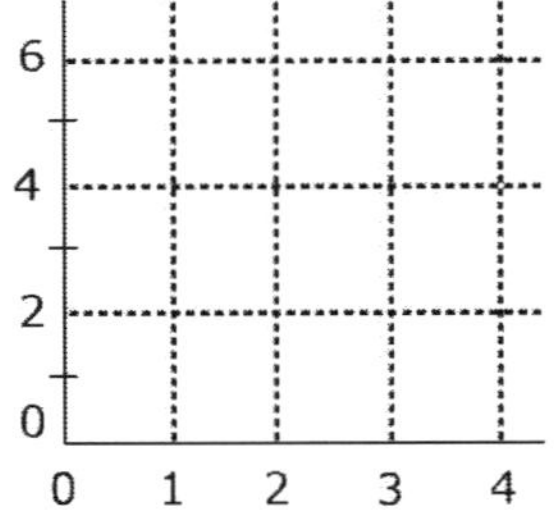

4 Expressing and Measuring Chemical Change

This chapter focuses on the following AP Big Idea from the College Board:

Big Idea 3: Changes in matter involve the rearrangement and/or reorganization of atoms and/or the transfer of electrons.

By the end of this chapter, you should be able to do the following:

- Explain chemical reactions in terms of the rearrangement of the atoms as bonds are broken and new bonds are formed
- Apply the law of conservation of mass to balance formula equations
- Devise balanced equations for various chemical reactions
- Describe reactions in terms of energy changes
- Perform stoichiometric calculations involving chemical reactions

---

By the end of this chapter, you should know the meaning of these key terms:

- acid-base neutralization
- chemical reactivity
- coefficient
- combustion reaction
- decomposition reaction
- double replacement reaction
- endothermic
- exothermic
- formula equation
- limiting reagent
- precipitate
- product
- reactant
- single replacement reaction
- stoichiometry
- synthesis reaction
- thermochemical equation

$$Zn(s) + 2HCl(aq) \rightarrow ZnCl_2(aq) + H_2(g)$$

Chemical reactions transform one set of chemicals (reactants) to completely different chemicals (products).

4.1 Writing and Balancing Chemical Equations — The Magic of Chemistry

Warm Up

Water may be broken down into its component elements, oxygen and hydrogen, by the application of electric current. This process is called electrolysis.

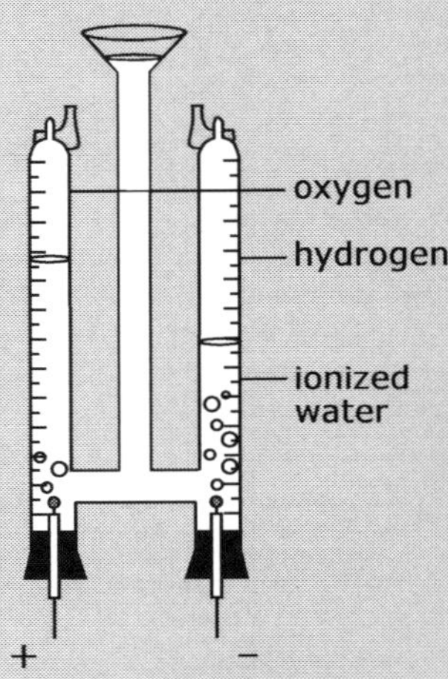

1. Use your knowledge of chemical nomenclature to write an equation showing the process occurring in the diagram. (Be sure to indicate hydrogen and oxygen as diatomic molecules.)
2. Count the total number of atoms of hydrogen and oxygen before and after the change. Make any necessary changes to ensure that these are equal.
3. Make any necessary changes to indicate the states of the substances in your equation.
4. Include anything else you feel is necessary to help your equation fully describe what is happening during this process.

Chemical Reactions Run Our World

Chemistry is the study of matter and its changes. In section 2.1, you learned how physical and chemical changes differ. Chemical changes always produce new substances with new properties and their own unique chemical formulas. Such changes involve the breaking and forming of chemical bonds. They are referred to as chemical reactions. The processes of photosynthesis and aerobic cellular respiration, for example, involve a series of chemical reactions that produce and use oxygen. These reactions are taking place right now in our bodies and in most of the living things in our world.

Another series of oxygen-requiring chemical reactions are necessary to heat our homes and move our vehicles from place to place. Chemical reactions involving oxygen can also be a problem when the metal in many human-made objects spontaneously breaks down in a chemical process called corrosion. Most people take chemical reactions for granted as if they were magic. It is important to appreciate that every waking moment of our lives, the matter of our world is continually undergoing an endless series of chemical reactions.

The Use of Chemical Shorthand

When you email or text message your friends, you probably use abbreviations or "text-speak" that makes it easier to communicate quickly (and less expensively). In mathematics, equations are often used to communicate operations involving numbers. Chemists use chemical equations to condense a large amount of information into a short expression.

In 1774, Joseph Priestley performed a famous chemical reaction that led to the discovery of oxygen. His synthesis involved the heating of a deep red powder to produce a silver liquid and a clear odourless gas (Figure 4.1.1). This chemical reaction can be represented by two different types of chemical equations:

Word equation: mercury(II) oxide → mercury + oxygen
Formula equation: $HgO\,(s) \rightarrow Hg(l) + O_2(g)$

Formula equations may sometimes be referred to as molecular equations. Both of these equations indicate a starting substance or **reactant** forming new substances or **products.** Formula equations may include italicized letters to indicate the physical state of the reactants and products:

solid (*s*), liquid (*l*), or gas (*g*). The symbol (*aq*) stands for aqueous, meaning the substance is dissolved in water.

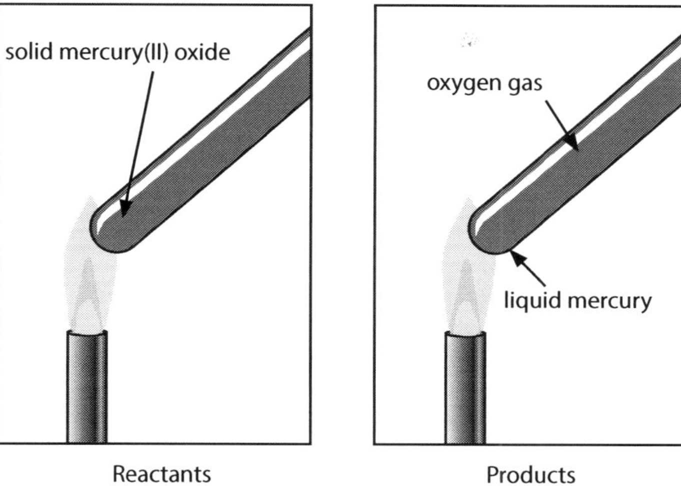

Figure 4.1.1 *Heating solid mercury(II) oxide results in the formation of liquid mercury and oxygen gas.*

You can tell that a chemical reaction has occurred by looking for evidence of chemical change. Some examples of such evidence include:

- noticeable absorption or release of heat (or sometimes light)
- a colour change
- evolution of a gas (bubbles may be visible)
- formation of a solid from two solutions. Such a solid is called a **precipitate**.

Quick Check

1. List three pieces of evidence of chemical change in the decomposition of mercury(II) oxide.

____

____

2. Convert the following from a word equation to a formula equation:
Calcium oxide powder is combined with water to form calcium hydroxide solid.

____

____

3. Convert the following from a formula equation to a word equation: $H_2CO_3(aq) \rightarrow CO_2(g) + H_2O(l)$

____

Balancing Chemical Equations

Historical evidence connects Joseph Priestley's experiments with oxygen with another famous chemist, Antoine Lavoisier. Lavoisier's experiments were more quantitative than those of Priestley. That is, Lavoisier liked to measure the volumes and masses of the chemicals he studied. Lavoisier is generally credited with formulating the **law of conservation of mass**. The law states that the mass before and after a chemical reaction occurs remains constant. Priestley and Lavoisier were both radical thinkers for the time they lived in. Englishman Priestley's support of the French Revolutionists led to his persecution, and he eventually had to flee from Europe altogether. He lived the last of his days in Pennsylvania in the United States. Lavoisier's problems were even more severe as he eventually lost his head to the guillotine at the height of the French Revolution.

A brief examination of the equation for the decomposition of mercury(II) oxide, $HgO(s) \rightarrow Hg(l) + O_2(g)$, shows that it does not obey the law of conservation of mass. The reactant, HgO contains one less oxygen atom than the products, Hg and O_2. If these atoms could somehow be placed on a balance, it would be evident that the reactant weighs less than the products (Figure 4.1.2). To show that the mass before and after a chemical reaction occurs remains constant, the formula equation has to be balanced.

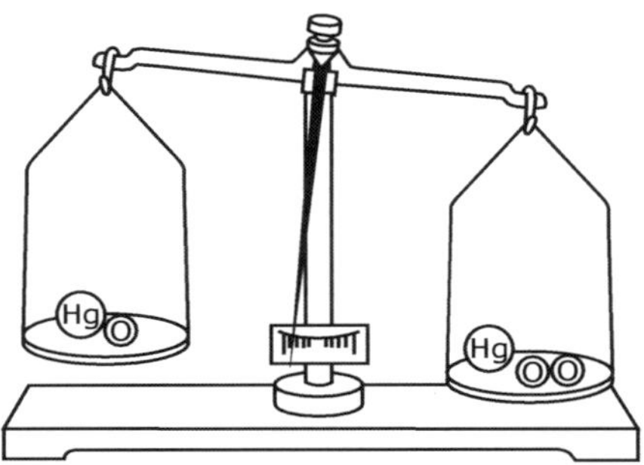

Figure 4.1.2 *The reactant in this reaction weighs less than the products.*

Balancing a chemical equation requires the placement of coefficients in front of reactant and/or product species. **Coefficients** are numbers that multiply the entire chemical species that follows them. These numbers ensure that the number of atoms of each kind on the reactant side is equal to those on the product side of the equation.

It is critical to remember balancing must always involve the placement of coefficients and never the changing of subscripts. Altering the subscripts will give an incorrect formula for a substance. Placing a coefficient 2 in front of the reactant HgO is a start, but the equation is still not balanced, $2\ HgO(s) \rightarrow Hg(l) + O_2(g)$. The balancing of the oxygen has resulted in an imbalance of the mercury (Figure 4.1.3).

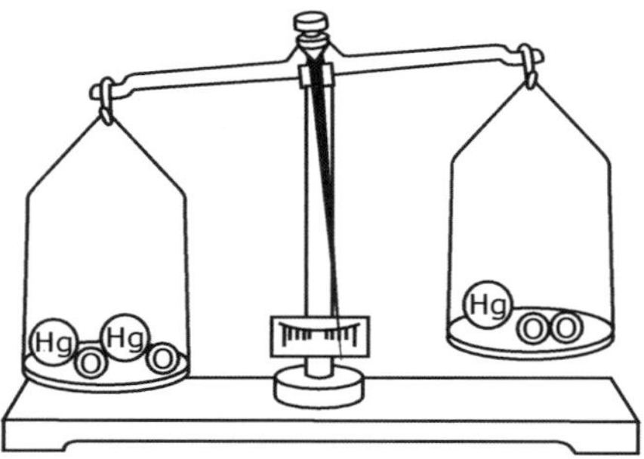

Figure 4.1.3 *Adding a coefficient to one side of the equation may not be enough to balance it.*

Placement of a coefficient 2 in front of the mercury will finally balance the entire equation, $2\ HgO(s) \rightarrow 2\ Hg(l) + O_2(g)$. By convention, a space is placed between the coefficient and the species it multiplies. It is always a good practice to check to make sure that you have accomplished your goal (Table 1).

Table 1 *Equation Balancing Check*

Atom	Reactant Side	Product Side
Hg	2	2
O	2	2

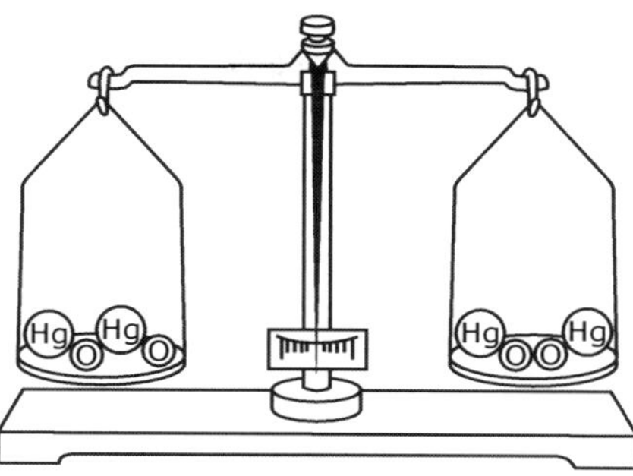

Figure 4.1.4 *This reaction required coefficients on both sides of the equation to balance it.*

Quick Check

Circle the letter of the properly balanced equations:

(a) $Na(s) + Cl_2(g) \rightarrow NaCl_2(s)$

(b) $AgNO_3(aq) + KBr(aq) \rightarrow AgBr(s) + KNO_3(aq)$

(c) $H_2O(l) + SiCl_4(l) \rightarrow SiO_2(s) + 4\,HCl(g)$

(d) $C_3H_8(g) + 5\,O_2(g) \rightarrow 3\,CO_2(g) + 4\,H_2O(l)$

(e) $3\,LiOH(aq) + Fe(IO_4)_3(aq) \rightarrow Fe(OH)_3(s) + 3\,LiIO_4(aq)$

Keeping Your Balance — Helpful Hints

Often students balance equations by simply attacking each atom in turn, moving back and forth with pencil and eraser until they accomplish their objective. Given enough time, most equations can eventually be balanced this way. However, the job can be made much easier if you follow a good plan of attack. Keep the following hints in mind when attempting to balance an equation:

- Begin by balancing atoms that appear in only one place on each side of the equation. Atoms that appear in too many places will be more difficult to balance and should always be left until last. Oxygen and hydrogen often appear in multiple places.
- Balance atoms that occur in *elemental form* last. This simply means atoms that are not grouped with any other type of atom. Examples include metals such as Zn, non-metals such as P_4 or diatomic gases such as H_2, O_2, N_2 or any halogen.
- Balance polyatomic ions such as nitrate or sulphate as a group whenever possible.
- Once a coefficient has been placed in front of a molecule or formula unit, finish balancing the rest of the atoms in that species before moving on. In other words, let your coefficients lead you through the equation.
- When balancing word equations, begin by making certain all formulas are correct. One formula error will cause a sequence of errors leading to disaster.
- It is always a good idea to perform a check such as the one shown in Table 1 above. This is particularly important with longer, more difficult equations.

Sample Problem — Balancing Formula Equations – Introductory

$Ba(s) + Al(NO_3)_3(aq) \rightarrow Ba(NO_3)_2(aq) + Al(s)$

What to Think about	How to Do It
1. Barium and aluminum must be left until last as both appear in elemental form.	
2. The nitrate ion may be balanced as a group as it is the only *aggregation* of nitrogen and oxygen in the equation. The way several atoms are combined in an equation is called their aggregation.	
Consider the lowest common multiple of nitrate's subscripts 3 and 2 to determine the first set of coefficients. That number is 6 so coefficients of 2 and 3 are required to make the number of reactant and product nitrate groups equal.	$Ba + 2\,Al(NO_3)_3 \rightarrow 3\,Ba(NO_3)_2 + Al$
3. Now it is simply a matter of balancing the elements. As the coefficient 2 is first, you could balance aluminum next.	$Ba + 2\,Al(NO_3)_3 \rightarrow 3\,Ba(NO_3)_2 + 2\,Al$
4. Complete the balance with the barium and replace the phase indicators if required.	$3\,Ba(s) + 2\,Al(NO_3)_3(aq) \rightarrow 3\,Ba(NO_3)_2(aq) + 2\,Al(s)$
5. Be sure to complete the process by checking the total number of barium, aluminum, nitrogen, and oxygen atoms on each side.	

Sample Problem — Balancing Formula Equations — Advanced

$NaOH(aq) + Cr_2O_3(s) + O_2(g) \rightarrow Na_2CrO_4(aq) + H_2O(l)$

What to Think about	How to Do It
1. Leave oxygen until last as it occurs in every species in the equation and appears in elemental form. You cannot balance hydroxide and chromate as groups because they each appear on only one side of the equation.	$2\,NaOH + Cr_2O_3 + O_2 \rightarrow Na_2CrO_4 + H_2O$
2. Begin with sodium, as it is the first atom that has not been left until last. There are two sodiums on the reactant side, so you need a coefficient of 2 on the product side.	

Continued

Sample Problem — *Continued*

What to Think about

3. The coefficient in front of sodium leads you to balance hydrogen next (remember, oxygen will be balanced last). As hydrogen is already balanced, you may proceed to chromium.
   The advantage of balancing in pencil becomes clear, as the sodium must now be rebalanced along with the hydrogen.

4. A careful count of the oxygen atoms indicates there are 9 on the reactant side and 10 in the products. The balance can be finished easily by placing a coefficient of 3/2 or 1.5 in front of the elemental oxygen molecule. Eliminate the fraction by multiplying all coefficients by a common value.

5. Always perform balancing using the smallest values of whole number coefficients, so everything must be doubled to complete the balance. If required, include the phase indicators.

How to Do It

$2\ NaOH + Cr_2O_3 + O_2 \rightarrow$
$\quad 2\ Na_2CrO_4 + H_2O$

$4\ NaOH + Cr_2O_3 + O_2 \rightarrow$
$\quad 2\ Na_2CrO_4 + 2\ H_2O$

$4\ NaOH + Cr_2O_3 + 1.5\ O_2 \rightarrow$
$\quad 2\ Na_2CrO_4 + 2\ H_2O$

$8\ NaOH(aq) + 2\ Cr_2O_3(s) + 3\ O_2(g) \rightarrow$
$\quad 4\ Na_2CrO_4(aq) + 4\ H_2O(l)$

Practice Problems — Balancing Formula Equations

1. Complete the following table to check the balancing of the sample equation above.

Atom	Reactant Side	Product Side
Na		
O		
H		
Cr		

2. Balance each of the following using the smallest possible whole number coefficients.
   (a) $Al(s) +\ \ H_2SO_4(aq) \rightarrow\ \ Al_2(SO_4)_3(aq) +\ \ H_2(g)$
   (b) $Mg_3N_2(s) +\ \ H_2O(l) \rightarrow\ \ Mg(OH)_2(s) +\ \ NH_3(g)$
   (c) $NH_3(g) +\ \ O_2(g) \rightarrow\ \ H_2O(l) +\ \ NO(g)$

Sample Problem — Writing Balanced Formula Equations from Word Equations

Butane gas burns in oxygen to produce carbon dioxide and water vapour.

What to Think about	How to Do It
1. Make sure the formulas are correct.	$C_4H_{10} + O_2 \rightarrow CO_2 + H_2O$
2. Leave oxygen until last as it appears twice on the product side and is in elemental form on the reactant side. Balance carbon first, followed by hydrogen.	$C_4H_{10} + O_2 \rightarrow \mathbf{4}\,CO_2 + \mathbf{5}\,H_2O$
3. Don't forget that oxygen is diatomic. Use a fraction initially for oxygen as there are 13 oxygen atoms on the product side. Insert 13/2 or 6.5 for the oxygen gas.	$C_4H_{10} + \mathbf{6.5}\,O_2 \rightarrow 4\,CO_2 + 5\,H_2O$
4. Butane is a four-carbon hydrocarbon whose formula might best be determined by drawing its bonding arrangement.	
5. Multiply the equation by 2 and add the appropriate phase indicators to complete the balance.	$\mathbf{2}\,C_4H_{10}(g) + \mathbf{13}\,O_2(g) \rightarrow \mathbf{8}\,CO_2(g) + \mathbf{10}\,H_2O(g)$
6. Once the balance is complete, be sure to perform a check.	

Atom	Reactant Side	Product Side
C	8	8
H	20	20
O	26	26

Practice Problems — Writing Balanced Formula Equations from Word Equations

Write balanced equations for each of the following, using the smallest possible whole number coefficients. Include appropriate phase indicators.

1. Solid iron and chlorine gas combine to form iron(III) chloride.

2. Aqueous solutions of ammonium phosphide and lead(II) bromate react to give a precipitate of lead(II) phosphide and aqueous ammonium bromate.

3. Calcium metal reacts in an aqueous solution of nickel(III) sulphate to form calcium sulfate solution and nickel metal.

4.1 Activity: Building a Balanced Equation

Question

How can you represent the chemical reaction between nitrogen dioxide gas and water to form nitric acid and nitrogen monoxide?

Materials

You may use any of the following materials:

- a series of coins of different sizes representing nitrogen, oxygen, and hydrogen atoms
- modelling clay in different colours and sizes representing the required atoms
- a chemical model kit
- a series of drawings using different colours and sizes of images to represent the required atoms

Procedure

1. Use the materials you've selected to build a model of the balanced equation that represents the reaction in the question.
2. Compare your model with models done by one or more of your classmates.

Results and Discussion

1. Sketch your model in the space provided:

2. Make a table to check the balancing in your model equation:

3. How many chemical bonds were broken during your reaction? Describe each of these bonds.

4. How many chemical bonds were formed during your reaction? Describe each.

5. Were more bonds formed or broken? What might this mean for your reaction?

4.1 Review Questions

1. State two examples of chemical change from everyday life. What evidence indicates that these are chemical changes?

2. What chemical law requires us to balance chemical equations?

   Who was responsible for formulating this law?

3. Write a word equation for each formula equation below:

   (a) $C(s) + O_2(g) \rightarrow CO_2(g)$

   (b) $CH_4(g) + 2\ O_2(g) \rightarrow CO_2(g) + 2\ H_2O(g)$

   (c) $Cl_2(g) + 2\ KI(s) \rightarrow I_2(s) + 2\ KCl(s)$

   (d) $HCl(aq) + NaOH(s) \rightarrow NaCl(aq) + H_2O(l)$

   (e) $KF(s) \rightarrow K(s) + F_2(g)$

4. Balance each of the following equations. (State indicators are not required.)

   (a) $CdF_2 + \quad NaBr \rightarrow \quad CdBr_2 + \quad NaF$

   (b) $Cr + \quad F_2 \rightarrow \quad CrF_3$

   (c) $Ca + \quad H_2O \rightarrow \quad Ca(OH)_2 + \quad H_2$

   (d) $Bi(NO_3)_3 + \quad Na_2S \rightarrow \quad Bi_2S_3 + \quad NaNO_3$

   (e) $C_2H_5OH + \quad O_2 \rightarrow \quad CO_2 + \quad H_2O$

   (f) $V + \quad S_8 \rightarrow \quad V_2S_5$

   (g) $LiNO_3 + \quad Li \rightarrow \quad Li_2O + \quad N_2$

   (h) $Ca_3(PO_4)_2 + \quad H_2SO_4 \rightarrow \quad CaSO_4 + \quad H_3PO_4$

   (i) $PH_3 + \quad O_2 \rightarrow \quad P_2O_5 + \quad H_2O$

   (j) $Ba + \quad Ag_3PO_4 \rightarrow \quad Ba_3(PO_4)_2 + \quad Ag$

   (k) $Ca(ClO_3)_2 \rightarrow \quad CaCl_2 + \quad O_2$

   (l) $C_{12}H_{22}O_{11} + \quad O_2 \rightarrow \quad CO_2 + \quad H_2O$

   (m) $Ca_2C + \quad H_2O \rightarrow \quad Ca(OH)_2 + \quad CH_4$

   (n) $NH_4Br + \quad BaO \rightarrow \quad NH_3 + \quad BaBr_2 + \quad H_2O$

   (o) $LiAlH_4 + \quad BF_3 \rightarrow \quad LiF + \quad AlF_3 + \quad B_2H_6$

5. Write a balanced formula equation for each of the following (phase indicators should be included if possible):

(a) Titanium metal reacts with selenium to produce crystals of titanium(III) selenide.

(b) Phosphoric acid is neutralized with barium hydroxide to produce a precipitate of barium phosphate in water.

(c) Nitrogen gas reacts with lead(II) oxide powder to yield lead(II) nitride and oxygen gas.

(d) Xenon hexafluoride crystals react with water to produce xenon trioxide powder and hydrofluoric acid.

(e) Aluminum carbide is reacted with water in the synthesis of methane gas. Aluminum hydroxide precipitate is also formed.

(f) Plants produce the simple sugar $C_6H_{12}O_6$ and oxygen gas from carbon dioxide and water during photosynthesis.

(g) Ammonia gas (NH_3) is formed along with a precipitate of magnesium hydroxide from the reaction of magnesium nitride powder with water.

(h) Strong heating of copper(II) nitrate trihydrate produces copper(II) oxide, nitrogen dioxide, oxygen gas, and water.

6. Balancing Bonkers: Some equations are extremely difficult to balance even with the application of the balancing hints! Later on in your chemistry career, you will learn to balance some equations using the concepts of oxidation and reduction. This will be a major stress reducer when it comes to balancing. In the meantime, try to balance a few of these exhauster equations:

(a) $Ag + HNO_3 \rightarrow NO + AgNO_3 + H_2O$
(b) $Al + NaOH + H_2O \rightarrow NaAl(OH)_4 + H_2$
(c) $HNO_3 + Zn \rightarrow Zn(NO_3)_2 + H_2O + NH_4NO_3$
(d) $H_2O + As + HClO_3 \rightarrow H_3AsO_3 + HClO$
(e) $H_2SO_4 + H_2O_2 + KMnO_4 \rightarrow MnSO_4 + O_2 + H_2O + K_2SO_4$

Hint: You may want to come back to these once you've finished section 4.3.

4.2 Classifying Chemical Changes and Predicting Products

Warm Up

Reaction Type	Reactants	Products
Synthesis (combination)	two substances	one substance
Decomposition	one substance	two substances
Single replacement	element + compound	new element + compound
Double replacement	two compounds	two new compounds
Neutralization	acid + base	salt + water
Combustion	organic compound + oxygen	carbon dioxide + water

Balance the following equations. Then use the table above to classify each as one of the major reaction types listed:

1. $Na(s) + H_2O(l) \rightarrow NaOH(aq) + H_2(g)$
2. $Li_2O(s) + H_2O(l) \rightarrow LiOH(aq)$
3. $C_6H_{14}(l) + O_2(g) \rightarrow CO_2(g) + H_2O(g)$
4. $HCl(aq) + Sr(OH)_2(aq) \rightarrow SrCl_2(aq) + H_2O(l)$
5. $AlBr_3(s) \rightarrow Al(s) + Br_2(l)$

Classification of Chemical Reactions

Reactions, much like elements and compounds, can be classified according to type. The ability to recognize and classify reactions can help us predict the products of those chemical changes. Classification can also help us predict whether a reaction is likely to occur or not.

It is not always easy to classify a reaction. Most reactions, however, can be classified according to the six major categories described in the warm up table above.

Synthesis (Combination) Reactions

A **synthesis** (or combination) reaction involves two or more simple substances (elements or compounds) combining to form one more complex substance.

Usually synthesis reactions are accompanied by the release of a significant amount of energy in the form of heat and/or light. That is they are **exothermic**. The prefix "exo" means outside, while "thermo" refers to heat. It should be noted, however, that synthesis reactions sometimes require a small amount of "start-up" energy to begin. This start-up energy is known as activation energy.

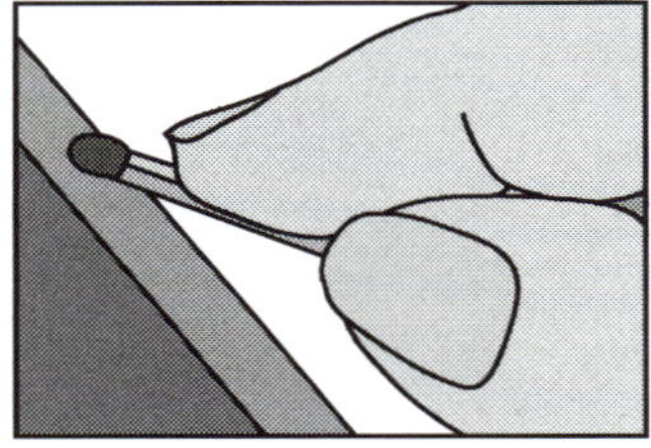
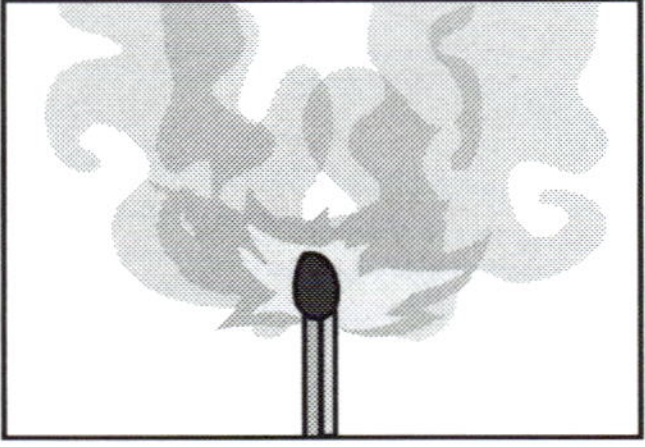
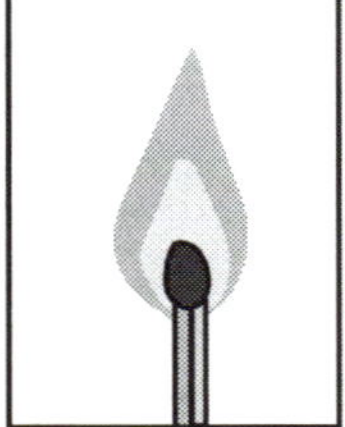

Figure 4.2.1 *Activation energy is required for both lighting and burning the match.*

An example of activation energy is shown in Figure 4.2.1. The friction in striking a match against a rough surface provides activation energy for the very exothermic reaction between the red phosphorus on the match head and the oxygen gas in the air around it. The product of this match-lighting reaction is the poof of a white gaseous oxide of phosphorus. The reaction is:

$P_4(s) + 5\ O_2(g) \rightarrow 2\ P_2O_5(g)$ + energy. This exothermic reaction in turn provides the activation energy for a second reaction involving the combustion of the wood or paper of the match stick. The combustion reaction is, of course, also exothermic.

Synthesis reactions may involve the combination of two elements to form a simple binary compound. Halides and oxides are formed in this way.

Halide example: $Ba(s) + Cl_2(g) \rightarrow BaCl_2(s)$
Oxide example: $2\ Sn(s) + O_2(g) \rightarrow 2\ SnO(s)$

Some synthesis reactions involve the combination of two compounds to form a more complex compound. The most common reactions of this type involve oxides of metals or non-metals and water. When a non-metal oxide combines with water, the product is always an acid. This type of reaction occurs in the atmosphere and is responsible for the formation of acid precipitation. The non-metal oxide is sometimes called an acidic oxide or an acid anhydride. Sulphur trioxide from factory exhaust reacts with water in the atmosphere to form sulphuric acid as follows:

$$SO_3(g) + H_2O(l) \rightarrow H_2SO_4(aq)$$

This then falls to Earth's surface in the form of acid precipitation, which is harmful to the natural environment and to objects with marble and metal surfaces in our built environment.

Metal oxides react with water to form bases. The metal oxide is sometimes called a basic oxide or a basic anhydride. When a metal oxide reacts with a non-metal oxide, the product is a complex or ternary salt. Examples of these two reaction types are:

Example of a metal oxide reacting with water: $K_2O(s) + H_2O(l) \rightarrow 2\ KOH(aq)$
Example of a metal oxide reacting with a non-metal oxide: $CaO(s) + CO_2(g) \rightarrow CaCO_3(s)$

Decomposition Reactions

A **decomposition** reaction involves a complex compound being broken down or decomposed into two or more simpler substances (elements or compounds).

Decomposition reactions are really just the opposite of synthesis reactions. Most decomposition reactions require a continuous source of energy. This energy is used to break the bonds between the elements of the starting material. Reactions that absorb more energy to break bonds than they release during bond formation are said to be **endothermic**. The prefix "endo" means inside and "thermo" is from the Greek for heat.

Decomposition reactions are commonly used in the mining industry in British Columbia to separate metals from their ores. For example, aluminum production occurs when electric current is passed through molten aluminum oxide or bauxite ore:
$2\ Al_2O_3(l) \rightarrow 4\ Al(s) + 3\ O_2(g)$. Charles Martin Hall developed this electrolysis process in 1886. Hall was a 21-year-old university student at the time. Before the development of the Hall cell, pure aluminum was very rare and it was worth nearly $100 000 a pound.

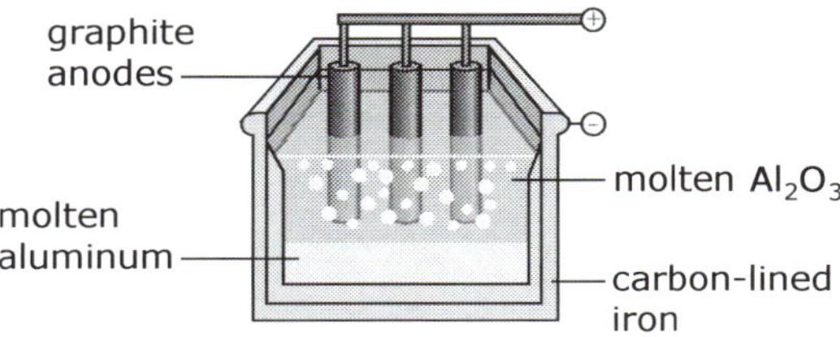

Figure 4.2.2 *The Hall cell produces aluminum metal and oxygen gas from melted bauxite ore.*

Some decomposition reactions form simple compounds instead of elements. These reactions generally involve one of the following reactions:

- acids decomposing to form water and non-metal oxides
- bases decomposing to form metal oxides and water
- ternary salts decomposing to form oxides of metals and non-metals

Examples of each of these types of reaction include:

Acid decomposition: $H_2SO_3(aq) \rightarrow H_2O(l) + SO_2(g)$

Base decomposition: $Ba(OH)_2(s) \rightarrow BaO(s) + H_2O(l)$

Salt decomposition: $Fe_2(SO_4)_3(s) \rightarrow Fe_2O_3(s) + 3\ SO_3(g)$

The relationship between various types of synthesis and decomposition reactions are summarized in Table 4.2.1.

Table 4.2.1 *Relationships between Synthesis and Decomposition Reactions*

	Reaction Direction	
Non-metal Oxide + Water	Synthesis → ← Decomposition	Acid
Metal Oxide + Water	Synthesis → ← Decomposition	Base
Non-metal Oxide + Metal Oxide	Synthesis → ← Decomposition	Complex (Ternary) Salt
Metal and Non-metal Elements	Synthesis → ← Decomposition	Simple (Binary) Salt

summary table

Combustion Reactions

A **combustion** reaction involves the reaction of a hydrocarbon (a compound made up of hydrogen and carbon) or a carbohydrate (a compound made up of hydrogen, carbon and oxygen) with oxygen gas to produce carbon dioxide gas and water.

Combustion reactions are exothermic and release a significant amount of energy in the form of heat, sometimes light, and even sound, depending on the conditions. Generally the combustion is rapid and involves the burning of an organic compound in atmospheric oxygen. Under these conditions, water will be released as vapour. The combustion of a variety of hydrocarbons such as propane, fuel oil, and natural gas provides most of the energy for our homes. The following combustion of octane in gasoline provides the energy to move most of our vehicles:

$$2\ C_8H_{18}(l) + 25\ O_2(g) \rightarrow 16\ CO_2(g) + 18\ H_2O(g)$$

Slow combustion, sometimes referred to simply as oxidation, occurs in the cells of our body to produce energy. One of the most common examples is this reaction of the simple sugar glucose with oxygen:

$$C_6H_{12}O_6(s) + 6\ O_2(g) \rightarrow 6\ CO_2(g) + 6\ H_2O(l)$$

Quick Check

Balance each of the following reactions and classify them as synthesis, decomposition or combustion.

1. $P_2O_5(g) + H_2O(l) \rightarrow H_3PO_4(aq)$ synthesis
2. $CH_4(g) + O_2(g) \rightarrow CO_2(g) + H_2O(g)$ combustion
3. $H_2CO_3(aq) \rightarrow H_2O(l) + CO_2(g)$ decomposition

Sample Problem — Predicting Products of Combination, Decomposition, and Combustion Reactions

Predict the products of the following reactions:

1. $CH_3OH(l) + O_2(g) \rightarrow$
2. $B_2O_3(s) + H_2O(l) \rightarrow$
3. $Sc(OH)_3(s) \rightarrow$

What to Think about	How to Do It
Reaction 1	
1. Classify the reaction based on the reactants provided. A carbohydrate reacts with oxygen, so this must be a combustion reaction. All combustion reactions form CO_2 and water.	$CH_3OH(l) + O_2(g) \rightarrow CO_2(g) + H_2O(l)$
2. Once the products have been determined, balance the equation.	$2\,CH_3OH(l) + 3\,O_2(g) \rightarrow 2\,CO_2(g) + 4\,H_2O(l)$
Reaction 2	
1. Reaction 2 is combining a non-metal oxide with water. This must be a combination reaction to form an acid.	
2. Determine the correct formula for the acid by combining the H^+ ion with an oxyanion of boron. To determine the oxyanion of boron, calculate the **oxidation number** (charge) on boron in the B_2O_3. As oxide is −2, boron must be +3. This indicates that borate, BO_3^{3-}, is the oxyanion in the acid.	$B_2O_3(s) + H_2O(l) \rightarrow H_3BO_3(aq)$
3. Balance the equation.	$B_2O_3(s) + 3\,H_2O(l) \rightarrow 2\,H_3BO_3(aq)$
Reaction 3	
1. Reaction 3 has only one reactant so it must be a decomposition reaction.	
2. As the reactant is a base, it must decompose to form a metal oxide and water. The metal oxide has to be an oxide of the metal in the base. As this is scandium, the products have to be scandium oxide and water	$Sc(OH)_3(s) \rightarrow Sc_2O_3(s) + H_2O(l)$
3. Balance the equation.	$2\,Sc(OH)_3(s) \rightarrow Sc_2O_3(s) + 3\,H_2O(l)$

Practice Problems — Predicting Products of Reactions

First classify the equations, then determine the products and write a balanced formula equation for each of the following:

1. 2 $Fe_2O_3(s) \rightarrow$ 4 Fe + 3 O_2 Class: decomposition
2. $C_3H_7OH(l)$ + $O_2(g) \rightarrow$ $CO_2 + H_2O$ Class: combustion
3. $Ag_2O(s)$ + $H_2O(l) \rightarrow$ AgOH Class: Synthesis
4. $Pb(OH)_4(s) \rightarrow$ $PbO_2 + H_2O$ Class: Decomposition

Single Replacement Reactions

A **single replacement** reaction (also called single displacement) involves a reaction between a compound and an element so that the element replaces an element of the same type in the compound. The result is a new compound and a new element.

During a single replacement reaction, a free, uncombined element "kicks out" a combined element and takes its place. It is important to remember that a metal element always bonds with a non-metal element. Hence metals replace metals, while non-metals replace non-metals. Active metals may also replace hydrogen, kicking out hydrogen gas, from either water (family I and II metals) or acids (family I and II and several transition elements). For example:

- metal replacement: $2\ K(s) + Cu(NO_3)_2(aq) \rightarrow 2\ KNO_3(aq) + Cu(s)$
- hydrogen replacement: $2\ Na(s) + 2\ HOH(l) \rightarrow 2\ NaOH(aq) + H_2(g)$
- non-metal replacement: $Br_2(l) + 2\ NaI(aq) \rightarrow 2\ NaBr(aq) + I_2(s)$

Notice that, when hydrogen is being replaced in water, it is a good idea to think of the water's formula as HOH. This makes it evident that the product is a hydroxide of the metal (or a base), rather than an oxide. Although water is a covalent compound, thinking of it as being composed of hydrogen and hydroxide ions, rather than hydrogen and oxide ions will help simplify these equations.

To determine whether a single replacement reaction will proceed or not, we must compare the **chemical reactivity** of the element to that of the element it will replace in the compound Table 4.2.2. Chemical reactivity is the tendency of a substance to undergo chemical change. A more reactive element will kick off a less reactive one. Periodic properties and trends such as electronegativity and ionization energy to be discussed in sections 6.1 and 6.2 are certainly useful in predicting the reactivity of chemical elements. Interestingly, however, when an element replaces another element from an aqueous solution of a compound, the series of energy changes that occur result in a somewhat different reactivity series than we might predict based on the trends we will study in chapter 6.

Table 4.2.2 *Series of Chemical Reactivity*

Two Activity Series		
Metals	Decreasing Activity	Halogens
lithium		flourine
potassium		chlorine
calcium		bromine
sodium		iodine
magnesium		
aluminum		
zinc		
chromium		
iron		
nickel		
tin		
lead		
HYDROGEN*		
copper		
mercury		
silver		
platinum		
gold		

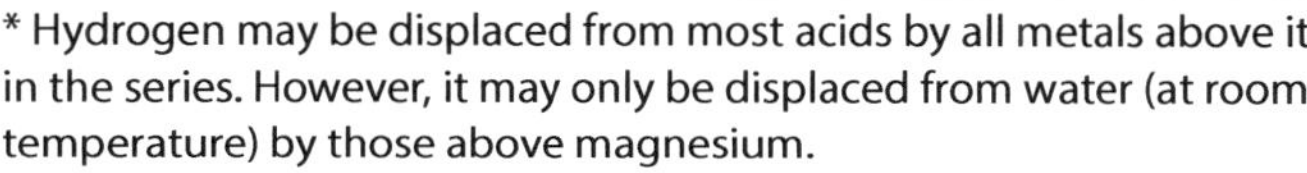

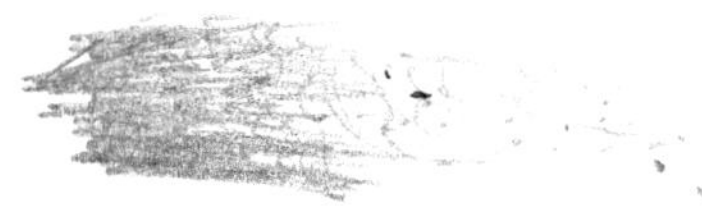

* Hydrogen may be displaced from most acids by all metals above it in the series. However, it may only be displaced from water (at room temperature) by those above magnesium.

Quick Check

Use the series of chemical reactivity in Table 4.2.2 to determine whether each of the following single replacement reactions would proceed. Predict the products for those that do proceed and balance the equations.

1. $Na(s) + AlCl_3(aq) \rightarrow$

2. $Cu(s) + KBr(aq) \rightarrow$

3. $F_2(g) + LiI(aq) \rightarrow$

4. $Ca(s) + HOH(l) \rightarrow$

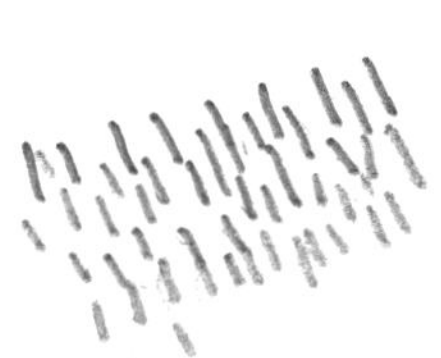

Double Replacement Reactions

A **double replacement** reaction is a chemical reaction between two compounds that trade cations (or anions) with one another.

It is important to remember that an ionic compound is made up of a positively charged ion called a **cation** bonded to a negatively charged ion called an **anion**. When these ions trade positions in their compounds, a new set of compounds is formed. As is usual in an ionic compound, the cations' and anions' charges must balance. The cation's formula will be listed first. There are three categories of double replacement reactions: precipitation, neutralization, and gas formation.

In a precipitation reaction, two freely soluble salts are combined in solution. When their ions "trade partners," two new salts are formed, at least one of which is not very soluble. This low solubility salt gives immediate evidence of chemical change as it forms a solid suspended in solution called a precipitate.

Predicting which product salt will precipitate requires information about the relative solubilities of the products. Chapter 7 will provide more information on solubility, but for now, keep in mind that compounds containing family I ions (alkali metal ions) and/or nitrate are always soluble. The precipitate is always indicated by a symbol (*s*), which indicates that a solid has been formed. The equation for the precipitation reaction in Figure 4.2.3 is:

$$NaCl(aq) + AgNO_3(aq) \rightarrow AgCl(s) + NaNO_3(aq)$$

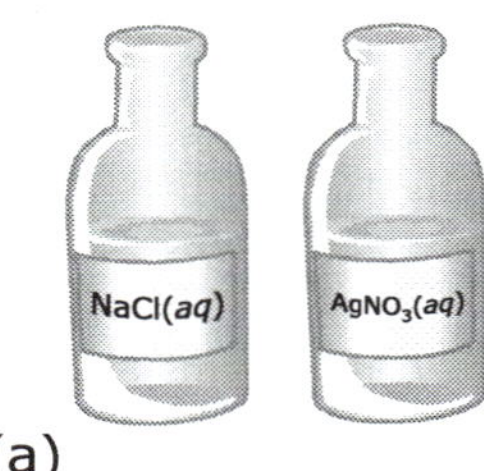

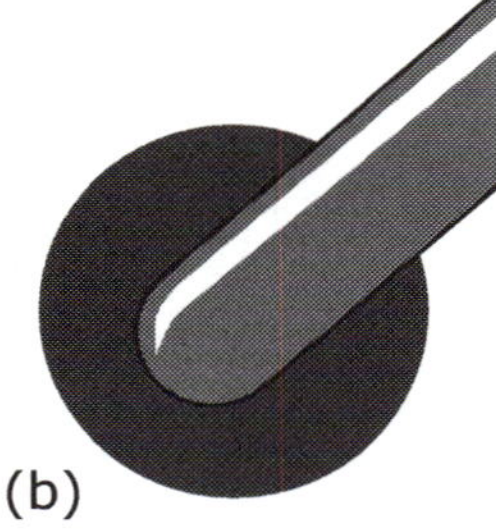

Figure 4.2.3 (a) *Solutions of sodium chloride and silver nitrate; (b) Precipitate of silver chloride suspended in a solution of sodium nitrate*

A **neutralization** reaction always occurs between an acid and a base. The products are always water and a salt.

The salt is composed of the cation from the base and the anion from the acid. The hydrogen ion from the acid and the hydroxide ion from the base combine to form the water. Evidence of chemical change is less obvious during a neutralization reaction, although detectable heat is released:

$$H_2SO_4(aq) + 2\,KOH(aq) \rightarrow K_2SO_4(aq) + 2\,H_2O(l) + \text{heat}$$

A few products of double replacement reactions are not very stable and spontaneously decompose to form water and a gas. The two most common ones are:

- carbonic acid, which decomposes to form carbon dioxide and water, and
- ammonium hydroxide, which decomposes to form ammonia gas and water

At first glance, the full equation of a neutralization reaction may not appear to represent a double replacement reaction as two compounds form three new compounds. Watch for reactions such as:

$$K_2CO_3(aq) + 2\,HCl(aq) \rightarrow 2\,KCl(aq) + H_2O(l) + CO_2(g)$$

or $$NH_4Br(aq) + NaOH(aq) \rightarrow NaBr(aq) + H_2O(l) + NH_3(g)$$

The evolution of CO_2 gas following addition of an acid to a compound is a good indication that the compound contains the carbonate anion. Similarly, the evolution of ammonia gas, with its characteristic odour, following addition of a base to a compound is indicative of the presence of the ammonium cation in the compound.

Sample Problem — Predicting Products of Replacement Reactions

Predict the products of the following replacement reactions:

1. $Br_2(aq) + KI(aq) \rightarrow$
2. $Li_2SO_3(aq) + Ca(NO_3)_2(aq) \rightarrow$
3. $Na_2CO_3(aq) + HBr(aq) \rightarrow$

What to Think about	How to Do It
Reaction 1	
1. Classify the reaction based on the reactants provided. Reaction 1 has an element and a compound and so must be a single replacement.	
2. As bromine is a non-metal, it must replace the non-metal iodine in the salt. A check of the reactivities of bromine and iodine indicates this is possible. Recall that iodine is diatomic.	$Br_2 + KI \rightarrow KBr + I_2$
3. Balance the completed equation and include phase subscripts if required.	$Br_2(aq) + 2\,KI(aq) \rightarrow 2\,KBr(aq) + I_2(s)$
Reaction 2	
1. Two reactant compounds indicate reaction 2 must be a double replacement reaction.	
2. Consider ion charges and be sure to write correct formulas. Show the results of the exchange of cations.	$Li_2SO_3 + Ca(NO_3)_2 \rightarrow LiNO_3 + CaSO_3$
3. Balance the completed equation.	$Li_2SO_3(aq) + Ca(NO_3)_2(aq) \rightarrow 2\,LiNO_3(aq) + CaSO_3(s)$
4. As the reactants are not acids and bases and neither of the products that decompose is formed, there must be precipitation. As the first product contains a family IA cation and is a nitrate, it must be soluble, so you can label $CaSO_3$ with an (*s*) if phase indicators are added.	
Reaction 3	
1. Reaction 3 appears to be a double replacement also.	
2. Show the results of the exchange of cations.	$Na_2CO_3 + HBr \rightarrow NaBr + H_2CO_3$
3. The formation of H_2CO_3 should remind you that this particular acid spontaneously decomposes into its non-metal oxide and water.	$Na_2CO_3 + HBr \rightarrow NaBr + CO_2 + H_2O$
4. Balance the equation and include phases.	$Na_2CO_3(aq) + 2\,HBr(aq) \rightarrow 2\,NaBr(aq) + CO_2(g) + H_2O(l)$

Practice Problems — Predicting Products of Replacement Reactions

First classify the equations, then determine the products and write a balanced formula equation for each of the following:

1. $HCl(aq) + Fe(OH)_3(s) \rightarrow$ Class:________________
2. $Zn(s) + AgClO_3(aq) \rightarrow$ Class:________________
3. $(NH_4)_2S(aq) + CsOH(aq) \rightarrow$ Class:________________
4. $Cl_2(g) + Li_2S(aq) \rightarrow$ Class:________________

4.2 Activity: Identifying an Unknown Substance

Question

Can you identify an unknown substance based on its chemical reactions?

Procedure

1. Working with a partner or by yourself, use the information in the table below to determine the identity of each of the four unknown substances.

Possible Identities	Added	Observation
1) $Cl_2(aq)$ or $I_2(aq)$? An unknown halogen dissolved in water contained in an opaque dropper	$NaBr(aq)$ — colourless solution	An orange-brown solution results.
2) $MgCO_3(s)$ or $Mg(OH)_2(s)$? An unknown white powder	$HNO_3(aq)$ —colourless acid solution	Bubbles of gas form as powder dissolves. Heat is released.
3) $Pb(NO_3)_2(aq)$ or $KNO_3(aq)$? An unknown compound dissolved to form a colourless solution	$NaI(aq)$ — colourless solution	Bright yellow precipitate forms.
4) $CaCl_2(aq)$ or $ZnCl_2(aq)$? An unknown compound dissolved to form a colourless solution	$Al(s)$ — freshly sanded strip of metal.	Dark grey coating forms on the shiny metal. Metal slowly disintegrates and falls apart.
5)		

Continued →

Results and Discussion

1. Use the table below to record all information and answer the questions below.

Identity of Unknown	Balanced Equation	Explanation
1)		
2)		
3)		
4)		
5)		

2. Write a balanced chemical equation, including phase indicators for each of the confirming tests performed.

3. Explain why you decided on the unknown in each equation.

4. Design a test to distinguish between a fifth pair of unknown substances. Give the substances, the test and the expected observations in the provided spaces in the table above. Complete row #5 for your identified substance in the second table above.

4.2 Review Questions

1. Balance each of the following reactions:

   (a) $CdF_2 + NaBr \rightarrow CdBr_2 + NaF$

   (b) $Na_2SO_4 + Cu \rightarrow Cu_2SO_4 + Na$

   (c) $Cr + F_2 \rightarrow CrF_3$

   (d) $Fe(OH)_3 \rightarrow Fe_2O_3 + H_2O$

   (e) $Ca + H_2O \rightarrow Ca(OH)_2 + H_2$

   (f) $Bi(NO_3)_3 + Na_2S \rightarrow Bi_2S_3 + NaNO_3$

   (g) $C_{25}H_{52} + O_2 \rightarrow CO_2 + H_2O$

   (h) $Al + H_2SO_4 \rightarrow Al_2(SO_4)_3 + H_2$

   (i) $LiClO_3 \rightarrow LiCl + O_2$

   (j) $K + Cl_2 \rightarrow KCl$

   (k) $Au + H_2S \rightarrow Au_2S_3 + H_2$

   (l) $Nb + S_8 \rightarrow Nb_2S_5$

   (m) $P_4O_{10} + H_2O \rightarrow H_3PO_4$

   (n) $HClO \rightarrow Cl_2O + H_2O$

   o) $H_3PO_4 + KOH \rightarrow K_3PO_4 + H_2O$

   (p) $Rb + Sc_2(CrO_4)_3 \rightarrow Rb_2CrO_4 + Sc$

   (q) $V(OH)_5 \rightarrow V_2O_5 + H_2O$

   (r) $Ba_3P_2 \rightarrow Ba + P_4$

   (s) $K_2C_2O_4 + Ca(NO_3)_2 \rightarrow CaC_2O_4 + KNO_3$

   (t) $BaCO_3 + HCl \rightarrow BaCl_2 + CO_2 + H_2O$

2. (a) Classify each of the reactions in question 1 as synthesis, decomposition, combustion, single replacement, double replacement, or neutralization.

   (b) Which of the single replacement reactions would *not* proceed spontaneously?

   (c) Which of the double replacement reactions involve precipitate formation?

   (d) Indicate the precipitates with an (*s*).

3. Classify each of the following reactions, using the following key: **S** = Synthesis, **D** = Decomposition, **C** = Combustion, **SR** = Single Replacement, **DR** = Double Replacement, **N** = Neutralization. Complete the equations and balance them. Indicate any precipitates that form with an (*s*).

   ___(a) $Rb + ZnF_2 \rightarrow$

   ___(b) $Sc_2O_3 + H_2O \rightarrow$

   ___(c) $Pb(NO_3)_2 + NaCl \rightarrow$

   ___(d) $H_2CO_3 \rightarrow$

   ___(e) $GeO_2 + SO_2 \rightarrow$

   ___(f) $SrCO_3 + H_2S \rightarrow$

   ___(g) $C_2H_6 + O_2 \rightarrow$

   ___(h) $Cs + NiCl_2 \rightarrow$

l (i) $Zr(OH)_4 \rightarrow$ Zr + OH

Sh (j) $Br_2 + InI_3 \rightarrow$ $InBr_3 + I_2$

Dh (k) $H_3PO_4 + Ba(OH)_2 \rightarrow$ $BaPO_4 + H_2O$

Dh (l) $AgNO_3 + Ca(CH_3COO)_2 \rightarrow$ $Ag(CH_3COO)_2 + CaNO_3$

C (m) $C_3H_5OH + O_2 \rightarrow$ $H_2O + CO_2$

___(n) ~~$N_2O_5 + H_2O \rightarrow$~~

Dh (o) $AlCl_3 + Na_2CO_3 \rightarrow$ $Al_2(CO_3)_3 + NaCl$

Dh (p) $NH_4F + LiOH \rightarrow$ $NH_4OH + LiF$

Dh (q) $HNO_3 + Sr(OH)_2 \rightarrow$ $SrNO_3 + H_2O$

___(r) ~~$F_2 + K_2S \rightarrow$~~

D (s) $Mg(OH)_2 \rightarrow$ Mg + OH

S (t) $Na + N_2 \rightarrow$ Na_3N

4. Classify each of the following chemical changes using the key from question 3. Write balanced formula equations for each, including state indicators.

S (a) A piece of magnesium ribbon on a stock shelf reacts over time with nitrogen gas in the air to form a black coating.

$Mg + N_2 \rightarrow Mg_3N_2$

Dh (b) Phosphoric acid solution removes iron(III) hydroxide stains from an old bath tub.

$H_3PO_4 + FeOH \rightarrow FePO_4 + H_2O$

C (c) Butane gas is combusted in a disposable lighter.

$C_4H_{10} + O_2 \rightarrow H_2O + CO_2$

Sh (d) A zinc strip placed in a solution of copper (II) sulphate becomes coated with brownish solid.

$Zn + CuSO_4 \rightarrow ZnSO_4 + Cu$

___(e) Sulphur dioxide emitted from industrial plants combines with water vapour to form acid rain.

___(f) Calcium carbonate in marble structures is eroded over time by nitric acid in acid rain.

$CaCO_3 + HNO_3 \rightarrow Ca(NO_3)_2 + H_2CO_3$

Sh (g) Nickel(III) hydroxide reacts with a cadmium anode in a prototype rechargeable battery.

$Ni(OH)_3 + Cd \rightarrow CdOH + Ni$

Dh (h) Solutions of gold(III) nitrate and sodium carbonate are combined.

$Au(NO_3)_3 + NaCO_3 \rightarrow Au_2(CO_3)_3 + NaNO_3$

Dh (i) Potassium chromate solution indicates the endpoint in a potato chip analysis with a standard silver nitrate solution.

$K_2Cr + AgNO_3 \rightarrow KNO_3 + Ag_2Cr$

___(j) Methanol (CH_3OH) is combusted in race car engines.

$CH_3OH + O_2 \rightarrow H_2O + CO_2$

___(k) Baking soda (sodium hydrogen carbonate) is used to neutralize a spill of hydrochloric acid.

$NaHCO_3 + HCl \rightarrow NaCl + H_2CO_3$

___(l) A bright yellow pigment once used in paints is formed from the reaction of lead(II) nitrate and sodium iodide solutions.

$Pb(NO_3)_2 + NaI \rightarrow PbI_2 + NaNO_3$

___(m) Iron(III) oxide and water combine to form a basic compound often called rust.

$Fe_2O_3 + H_2O \rightarrow Fe + H_2O$ (?)

___(n) Dark silver sulphide tarnish may be removed from knives and forks by placing them in contact with a piece of aluminum foil in a dilute ionic solution.

$Ag_2S + Al \rightarrow Al_2S_3 + Ag$

___(o) A precipitate of barium oxalate forms in a solution of sodium nitrate following the combination of two solutions.

$BaC_2O_4 + NaNO_3 \rightarrow Ba(NO_3)_2 + Na_2C_2O_4$

___(p) A precipitate of barium sulphate and hydrogen gas are formed from the combination of a metal and an acid.

$BaSO_4 + H_2 \rightarrow BaH_2 + SO_4$

___(q) Diphosphorus pentoxide gas and water are produced from the decomposition of an acid.

4.3 Another Way to Classify — Identifying Electron Transfer

Warm Up

Complete and balance the following equations.

1. $CsOH(s) \rightarrow$
2. $Al(s) + F_2(g) \rightarrow$
3. $H_2CO_3(aq) + KOH(aq) \rightarrow$
4. $K(s) + Sr(OH)_2(aq) \rightarrow$

Circle the numbers of the equations that involve a change in the oxidation number (charge) of one or more atoms during the reaction.

A Second System of Classification — To Give or Not to Give?

In section 4.2, you learned to classify reactions into five major categories based on patterns in the way the chemical species reacted to produce new products. The categories included synthesis (combination), decomposition, combustion, double replacement, and single replacement reactions. A second classification scheme results in only two major categories. This new scheme is based on the criterion of electron transfer from one atom to another during the chemical reaction.

Metathesis reactions are reactions that do not involve electron transfer.

All double replacement reactions, including neutralization, precipitation and those that involve the decomposition of one product to form a gas and water are metathesis reactions. Synthesis and decomposition reactions involving oxides of metals or nonmetals are also metathesis reactions.

Reactions that do involve electron transfer are commonly called **oxidation-reduction reactions.** Such reactions are often referred to as **redox reactions.**

Synthesis and decomposition reactions involving species in elemental form always involve electron transfer so they may be categorized as redox reactions. Single replacement and combustion reactions also fall into this category.

Quick Check

Classify the reactions 1 to 4 in the Warm Up above using the categories described in section 4.2 (synthesis (combination), decomposition, combustion, double replacement, and single replacement reactions). Which of the major reaction types involved electron transfer?

Oxidation Numbers — A System for Tracking Electrons

The easiest way to determine whether electrons have been transferred between elements during a chemical reaction is to keep track of each atom's **oxidation number** (also referred to as the **oxidation state**). In junior science, you probably referred to the oxidation state as the combining capacity. Multivalent metals such as iron, for example, may combine with chlorine to form $FeCl_2$ or $FeCl_3$, depending on the oxidation state of the iron ion involved. The compound containing iron with an oxidation state of +2 has the formula $FeCl_2$ and is called iron(II) chloride. This distinguishes it from $FeCl_3$ or iron(III) chloride containing iron with an oxidation state of +3. Notice that the charge is indicated before the number in an oxidation state.

Oxidation numbers (oxidation states) actually extend beyond combining capacities as they may be assigned to any atom in any aggregation, whether atoms exist as elements, monatomic ions, or part of a polyatomic ion or compound. The easiest way to assign oxidation states to atoms is to follow the simple set of rules in Table 4.3.1.

Table 4.3.1 *Rules for Oxidation Numbers*

Rule	Statement Regarding the Oxidation Number	Examples
1.	Atoms in elemental form = 0	Na, O_2, P_4, As, Zn
2.	Monatomic ions = the ion's charge	K^{+1},Ca^{+2}, Fe^{+2}, Fe^{+3}, Cl^{-1}
3.	Oxygen always = −2 except in peroxides (O_2^{2-}) = −1 and OF_2 = +2	Na_2O_2 and OF_2
4.	Hydrogen always = +1 except in metal hydrides = −1	CaH_2, LiH
5.	Oxidation states in compounds must sum to zero.	CuCl, $CuCl_2$ contain copper(I) and copper(II)
6.	Oxidation states in polyatomic ions must sum to the ion charge.	ClO_4^{1-}, ClO_3^{1-} contain chlorine = +7 and +5
7.	Always assign the more electronegative element a negative oxidation number.	PF_5 contains F = −1 and thus P = +5
8.	In a compound or ion containing more than two elements, the element written farthest to the right takes its most common oxidation state.	SCN^- contains N = −3 (most common), S = −2 (negative value), thus C = +4.

If the species contains oxygen and/or hydrogen, it is often best to assign their oxidation states first. For a species containing multiple types of atoms, assign the more electronegative element first. If the more electronegative element has more than one oxidation state, use its most common oxidation state.

It is important to note that we always calculate the oxidation number of *one* atom of a particular element. The subscripts that may be assigned to a particular atom have *no effect* on the oxidation number of that atom.

Sample Problem — Assigning Oxidation States

Assign the oxidation state of each atom in the following species:

1. H_2CO_3
2. PO_4^{3-}
3. $Fe(NO_3)_2$

What to Think about	How to Do It
Species 1	
1. For H_2CO_3 assign oxidation states to hydrogen and oxygen first, following the rules. Neither hydrogen nor oxygen is in elemental form. This is not an exception for oxygen (the compound is not a peroxide nor is it OF_2) or hydrogen (the compound is not a metal hydride). Consequently these two elements are assigned their usual oxidation states. Specifically, apply rule 3 for oxygen and rule 4 for hydrogen.	Hydrogen is **+1** and oxygen is **–2**. For hydrogen, (2 × +1) = a total of +2 For oxygen, (3 × -2) = a total of -6
2. Apply rule 5 to calculate the oxidation state for the middle atom in the formula, in this case, carbon.	For carbon: (+2) + ( ) + (-6) = 0 so the oxidation state must be **+4**.
Species 2	
1. For PO_4^{3-} assign the oxidation state of oxygen first, following rule 3. Oxygen is not in elemental form, nor is it in a peroxide or OF_2.	Oxygen is **–2**. For oxygen, (4 × -2) = a total of -8
2. Apply rule 6 to calculate the oxidation state for the phosphorus.	For phosphorus: ( ) + (-8) = -3 so the oxidation state must be **+5**.
Species 3	
1. For $Fe(NO_3)_2$, begin by considering the nitrate ion NO_3^- as a group and following rule 5 to calculate the oxidation state of iron. As there are two NO_3^- groups, each with an overall charge of 1–, the oxidation state of the Fe must be **+2.**	Iron is **+2.** Oxygen is a **–2**. For oxygen, (3 × -2) = a total of -6
2. Remember that subscripts have no effect on oxidation states, so rules 3 and 6 can now be applied to complete the problem.	For nitrogen: ( ) + (-6) = -1 so the oxidation state must be **+5**.

Practice Problems — Assigning Oxidation States

Assign the oxidation state of each atom in the following species:

1. H_2O
2. Li_2O_2
3. $AgMnO_4$
4. $K_2Cr_2O_7$
5. AlH_3
6. NH_4^+
7. OF_2
8. $Ca(NO_3)_2$
9. ClO_3^-
10. $(N_2H_5)_2CO_3$

Quick Check

1. Write a balanced equation for the combination of magnesium metal with oxygen gas to synthesize a metal oxide.
2. Indicate the oxidation state of each element over top of its symbol.
3. Use arrows to indicate the direction of electron transfer between the reactants.

Oxidation and Reduction

When an atom gains electrons during a reaction, its oxidation number becomes more negative. This is logical as the electrons the atom gains are negative particles. The substance whose oxidation number becomes smaller is being reduced.

A *decrease in oxidation state* is called **reduction.**

On the other hand, when an atom loses electrons during a reaction, its oxidation number becomes more positive. This is because the number of protons (positive charges) does not change, but there are fewer electrons. Consequently, the atom now has more positive protons than negative electrons and so the net charge is greater. The substance whose oxidation state increases is being oxidized.

An *increase in oxidation state* is called **oxidation.**

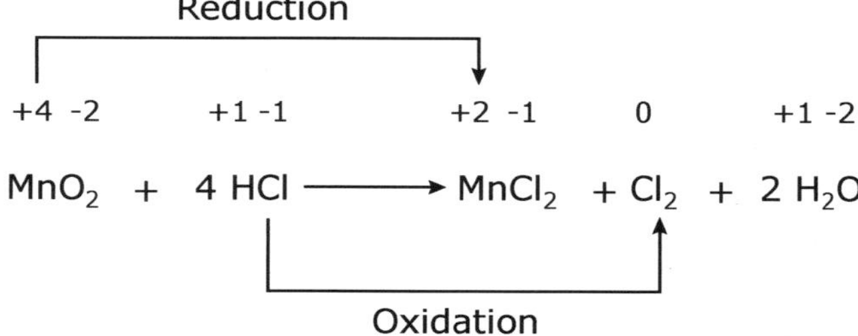

Figure 4.3.1 *Reduction and oxidation always occur together in a reaction.*

It is important to realize that reduction and oxidation always occur together in a reaction (Figure 4.3.1). If the oxidation number of one atom increases due to a loss of electrons, the oxidation number of another substance must decrease due to a gain of electrons. This is why reactions that involve electron transfer are called oxidation-reduction reactions or redox reactions for short. The oxidation number changes are entirely due to the transfer of electrons.

Remember that we always state the oxidation number for just *one* atom of a particular element, *no matter what subscript or coefficient* may be associated with the atom.

A *gain of electrons* is REDUCTION, while *a loss of electrons* is OXIDATION.

The following is a handy device to help remember what happens to electrons during the redox process:

LEO goes GER

lose electrons oxidation   gain electrons reduction

Quick Check

1. (a) How many electrons did each magnesium atom lose in the previous Quick Check? ____
   (b) How many electrons did each oxygen atom gain? _____
   (c) Which species was oxidized? __________
   Which was reduced? ____________
2. (a) In Figure 4.3.1, how many electrons did each manganese(IV) ion gain? _____
   (b) How many electrons did each chloride ion lose? _____
   Did all the chloride ions lose electrons? _____

Agents are the Cause of Electron Transfer

Examination of the two examples in the Quick Check above indicates that the number of electrons lost by the species being oxidized must always equal the number of electrons gained by the species being reduced.

So far we have examined electron transfer in terms of the species that lost or gained the electrons. Another approach is to view the reaction from the perspective of the species that cause the electron loss or gain. In this sense, the species that is oxidized causes another species to gain electrons and be reduced. Such a species may be called a reducing agent. A similar argument describes the chemical that is reduced as an oxidizing agent (Figure 4.3.2).

A substance that is reduced acts as an **oxidizing agent**, while a substance that is oxidized acts as a **reducing agent**.

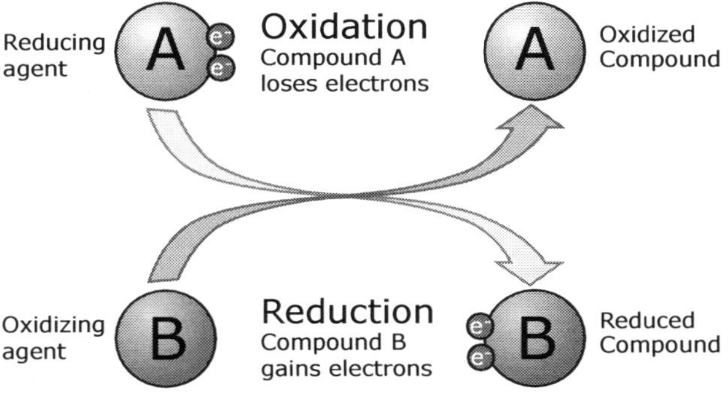

Figure 4.3.2 *Oxidizing agents and reducing agents*

Sample Problem — Recognizing Oxidizing and Reducing Agents

Indicate the oxidizing and reducing agent in each of the following reactions:

1. $Zn(s) + 2\ HCl(aq) \rightarrow ZnCl_2(aq) + H_2(g)$
2. $4\ NH_3(g) + 7\ O_2(g) \rightarrow 4\ NO_2(g) + 6\ H_2O(l)$

What to Think about

Reaction 1

1. Assign oxidation states to all elements in the equation.
2. Indicate the increase in oxidation state as an oxidation and the decrease in oxidation state as a reduction.
3. Identify the species that was oxidized as the reducing agent. Identify the one that was reduced as the oxidizing agent.

Notice that the Zn atom lost two electrons, while each H^+ ion gained one.

Reaction 2

1. The second example may appear not to fit any of the traditional five categories of classification from section 4.2. (It is the combustion of ammonia.) Often redox reactions do not fit our classic categories. You will encounter many more of these in Chemistry 12.
2. Notice that even though hydrogen is written second in the formula for ammonia, this species is not a metal hydride so hydrogen is assigned its usual oxidation state.

NOTE: When the atom that is oxidized or reduced belongs to a covalent compound, we indicate the entire species as the agent.

How to Do It

Zn: $0 \rightarrow +2$
H: $+1 \rightarrow 0$
Cl: $1 \rightarrow -1$
Zinc atom was oxidized.
Hydrogen ion was reduced.

Zinc atom is the reducing agent.
Hydrogen ion (H^+) is the oxidizing agent.

H: $+1 \rightarrow +1$
O: $0 \rightarrow -2$ (in both products)
N: $-3 \rightarrow +4$

Oxygen gas was reduced.
N in ammonia was oxidized.

Oxygen gas is the oxidizing agent.
Ammonia is the reducing agent.

Practice Problems — Recognizing Oxidizing and Reducing Agents

Determine the oxidizing and reducing agent in each of the following reactions. Begin by clearly indicating the oxidation states of all elements in each equation.

1. $Si(s) + 2\ H_2(g) \rightarrow SiH_4(g)$
2. $3\ Ca(s) + 2\ AlBr_3(aq) \rightarrow 2\ Al(s) + 3\ CaBr_2(aq)$
3. $5\ CO(g) + I_2O_5(s) \rightarrow 5\ CO_2(g) + I_2(s)$
4. $2\ NH_3(g) \rightarrow N_2(g) + 3\ H_2(g)$
5. $Mg(s) + 2\ H_2O(l) \rightarrow Mg(OH)_2(s) + H_2(g)$

4.3 Activity: Building a Table of Reduction Strengths

Question

Can you build a table of reduction strengths?

Background

It is possible to separate out the reduction and oxidation portions of a redox reaction and to represent them as half reactions. For example, the sample reaction from the previous page: $Zn(s) + 2\ HCl(aq) \rightarrow ZnCl_2(aq) + H_2(g)$ may be broken into the following half reactions: $Zn \rightarrow Zn^{2+} + 2e^-$ (oxidation) and $2H^+ + 2e^- \rightarrow H_2$ (reduction). Notice that the chloride ion is not included in either reaction, as its oxidation state does not change.

An attempt to replace zinc with hydrogen in the following single replacement reaction: $H_2(g) + ZnCl_2(aq) \rightarrow 2HCl(aq) + Zn(s)$ is *unsuccessful* because H_2 gas is too weak as a reducing agent to be oxidized to H^+. Similarly Zn^{2+} is too weak as an oxidizing agent to be reduced to Zn. Comparing these two competing reactions shows us that H^+ ion is a stronger oxidizing agent than Zn^{2+}. Consider the following data:

Attempted Reaction	Result
1. A piece of zinc metal is placed in a solution of $CuCl_2$.	Brown coating results on the zinc.
2. A piece of copper metal is placed in a $ZnCl_2$ solution.	No reaction occurs.
3. Hydrogen gas is bubbled through a solution of $CuCl_2$.	Bits of brown metal form in an acid.
4. Copper metal is placed in a solution of HCl.	No reaction occurs.
5. Manganese metal is placed in a solution of $ZnCl_2$.	Black solid forms in pink $Mn^{2+}(aq)$.
6. Manganese metal is placed in a solution of $CaCl_2$.	No reaction occurs.
7. Calcium metal is placed in a solution of KCl.	No reaction occurs.
8. A coil of zinc wire is placed in a solution of HCl.	Bubbles form as the zinc breaks up.

Procedure

1. Work with a partner or by yourself to design a table of reduction half reactions. Your table should be organized with the strongest oxidizing agent (the species most likely to be reduced) at the top. See the Results and Discussion section below for more ideas.
2. Compare your completed table with those of other groups.

Results and Discussion

1. Write a balanced equation for each attempted reaction (successful and *unsuccessful*) in the space below.

2. Write a half reaction for the reduction process that would occur in each equation.

3. Use the result of each attempted reaction to help list the reductions from the most likely to the least likely to occur.

4. Label the species at the top of your list as the "strongest oxidizing agent."

5. What role do metals always play in these reactions (oxidizing or reducing agent)?

6. Where would the strongest reducing agent be located?

4.3 Review Questions

1. Give the oxidation state for the underlined element in each of the following species:
   (a) $\underline{Ca}Br_2$
   (b) $\underline{O}F_2$
   (c) $\underline{C}_6H_{12}O_6$
   (d) $K_2\underline{O}_2$
   (e) $\underline{S}_2O_3^{2-}$
   (f) $Ba\underline{H}_2$
   (g) $\underline{Cl}O^-$
   (h) $\underline{S}_8$

2. Complete and balance each of the following reactions. (States are not required.) Indicate which involve electron transfer.
   (a) $Ca + O_2 \rightarrow$
   (b) $CaO + H_2O \rightarrow$
   (c) $Ca + H_2O \rightarrow$
   (d) $Ca(OH)_2 + HCl \rightarrow$

3. (a) What is an oxidizing agent?

   (b) What is a reducing agent?

   (c) How would you expect electronegativity to be related to the strength of each?

4. For each of the following reactions, indicate the species being oxidized and reduced and show the oxidation states above their symbols.

   (a) $2\ KClO_3(s) \rightarrow 2\ KCl(s) + 3\ O_2(g)$

   (b) $Mg(s) + 2\ AgNO_3(aq) \rightarrow Mg(NO_3)_2(aq) + 2\ Ag(s)$

   (c) $P_4(s) + 5\ O_2(g) \rightarrow 2\ P_2O_5(g)$

   (d) $NH_4NO_3(s) \rightarrow N_2O(g) + 2\ H_2O(l)$

5. In which chemical family would you expect to find:
   (a) the most readily oxidized elements? Explain.

   (b) the most readily reduced elements? Explain.

6. Determine the oxidizing and reducing agent in each of the following reactions. Then indicate the number of electrons transferred by one atom of the reducing agent.
(a) $2\ Pb(s) + O_2(g) \rightarrow 2\ PbO(s)$ OA: RA: No. e^-:
(b) $Pb(s) + 2\ Br_2(l) \rightarrow PbBr_4(s)$ OA: RA: No. e^-:
(c) $2\ Al(s) + 6\ HCl(aq) \rightarrow 2\ AlCl_3(aq) + 3\ H_2(g)$ OA: RA: No. e^-:
(d) $C_3H_8(g) + 5\ O_2(g) \rightarrow 3\ CO_2(g) + 4\ H_2O(g)$ OA: RA: No. e^-:

7. Predict the products and write balanced equations for each of the following reactions. Include state indicators. Classify each equation according to the system learned in section 4.2. Then classify each again as redox or not.

(a) Sulphur dioxide gas reacts with solid calcium oxide.

(b) Solid potassium nitrate is heated to form solid potassium nitrite and a gas.

(c) Strontium hydroxide solution reacts with nitric acid.

(d) Aluminum hydroxide solid is decomposed.

(e) Chlorine gas is bubbled through a solution of cesium iodide.

(f) Tetraphosphorus decaoxide solid is reacted with water.

(g) Aluminum metal reacts with liquid bromine.

(h) Zinc metal is placed in a solution of nickel(III) choride.

8. Give an oxidation and a reduction half reaction for each of the following redox reactions:

(a) $Sn(s) + 2\ AgNO_3(aq) \rightarrow Sn(NO_3)_2(aq) + 2\ Ag(s)$

(b) $F_2(g) + 2\ NaCl(s) \rightarrow 2\ NaF(s) + Cl_2(g)$

4.4 Energy Changes Associated with Chemical Change — Endothermicity and Exothermicity

Warm Up

Complete the following table by placing a checkmark in the appropriate energy-change column for each of the classifications of chemical change listed.

Reaction Type	Energy is Released	Energy is Absorbed
Most Synthesis (Combination) Reactions		
Most Decomposition Reactions		
Neutralization Reactions		
Combustion Reactions		

Sources of Energy

Fuels such as natural gas, wood, coal, and gasoline provide us with energy. Did you ever wonder where this energy comes from? Most of it is stored as chemical potential energy that can be converted into heat. The amount of potential energy available depends on the position of the subatomic particles making up a chemical sample and the composition of the sample. While the absolute potential energy content of a system is not really important, a change in potential energy content often is. We use changes in chemical energy to other energy forms to heat our homes and move our vehicles. Because chemical energy is most commonly converted to heat, we use the symbol ΔH to symbolize a change in energy available as heat. The symbol is sometimes read as delta *H* or an **enthalpy** change. Enthalpy is defined as potential energy that may be evolved or absorbed as heat.

All sorts of processes, both physical and chemical, have an enthalpy change associated with them. While a general change in enthalpy is symbolized as ΔH, specific types of enthalpy changes may be symbolized by a subscripted explanation attached to this symbol. Some examples include:

$$KOH(s) \rightarrow K^+(aq) + OH^-(aq) \qquad \Delta H_{solution} = -57.8 \text{ kJ/mol}$$

$$C_3H_8(g) + 5\,O_2(g) \rightarrow 3\,CO_2(g) + 4\,H_2O(l) \qquad \Delta H_{combustion} = -2221 \text{ kJ/mol}$$

$$H_2O(s) \rightarrow H_2O(l) \qquad \Delta H_{fusion} = 6.0 \text{ kJ/mol}$$

$$Fe_2O_3(s) + 2\,Al(s) \rightarrow Al_2O_3(s) + 2\,Fe(s) \qquad \Delta H_{reaction} = -852 \text{ kJ/mol}$$

$$Ca(s) + O_2(g) + H_2(g) \rightarrow Ca(OH)_2(s) \qquad \Delta H_{formation} = -986 \text{ kJ/mol}$$

What is it that causes the enthalpy stored in reactants to differ from that in the products of a physical or chemical change? What exactly is responsible for producing a ΔH value? The answer is the chemical bonds.

Quick Check

Examine each of the equations listed on the previous page. Consider the sign of the ΔH value and determine whether the reactants or products have more stored energy in each case. Put a checkmark under the side with more enthalpy.

Reaction	Reactants	Products
Dissolving potassium hydroxide		
Combustion of propane		
Melting ice		
Replacement of iron by aluminum		
Formation of calcium hydroxide		

The Energy of Chemical Bonds

Suppose your work text has fallen off your desk to the floor. When you lift it back to the desktop, you give the text potential energy because of its position above the floor. The gravitational potential energy your text now has could easily be converted into mechanical, as well as sound energy, should it happen to fall again.

In a similar way, the electrons in the atoms of the molecules of any substance have potential energy. Think of the negative electrons as being pulled away from the positive nucleus of their atom. If it were not for their high velocity, they would certainly rush toward and smash directly into the nucleus of their atom, much like your work text falling to the floor. By virtue of the position of the negative electrons in an atom relative to the positive nucleus and the other nuclei nearby in a molecule, the electrons (and the protons in the nuclei for that matter) have potential energy. This is the chemical potential energy called **bond energy.**

The bond energy just mentioned is the energy of **intramolecular bonds**. These are bonds that are formed *between atoms within a molecule.* Weaker bonds exist *between molecules* in a sample of solid, liquid, and even gaseous matter. These weak bonds hold the molecules of a solid or liquid together. These weak interactions between molecules are called **intermolecular forces.** The details of intermolecular forces relate to the polarity or lack of polarity of a molecule. The difference between the potential bond energy of reactants and products before and after a chemical or physical change is known as the enthalpy change or ΔH value.

Bond breaking requires *energy input* while *bond forming* results in *energy release.*

It's fairly intuitive to most of us that breaking something requires energy. For a karate master to break a board, he must apply energy. Similarly breaking chemical bonds requires energy. This energy is used to overcome the electrostatic forces that bind atoms or ions together. It follows from this that bond formation must result in a more stable situation in which energy is released.

If more energy is absorbed as bonds break than is released as bonds form during a chemical change, there is a net absorption of energy. As energy is required to break bonds there will be a gain in enthalpy. Reactions such as these have a positive ΔH value and are called endothermic reactions. Such a reaction may be shown graphically in an energy profile, sometimes called a *potential energy diagram* (Figure 4.4.1).

Potential Energy vs. Reaction Proceeding

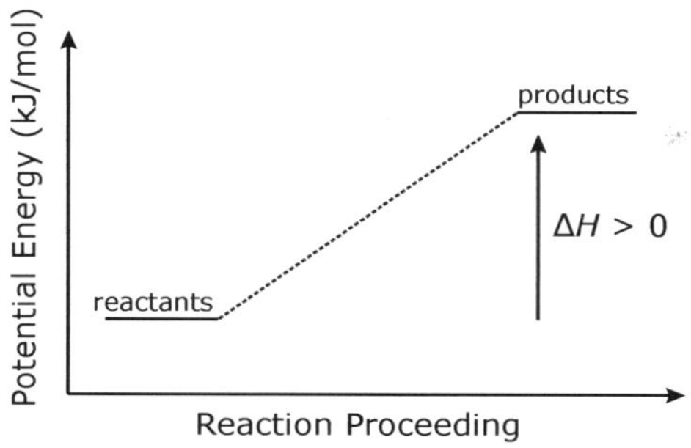

Figure 4.4.1 *Potential energy diagram for an endothermic reaction*

The energy absorbed to break bonds is greater than the energy released during bond formation in an *endothermic* reaction so they have positive ΔH values.

If, on the other hand, more energy is released as bonds are formed than is absorbed as they are broken during a chemical change, there is a net release of energy and so a decrease in enthalpy content occurs. Reactions such as these will have a negative ΔH value and may be called exothermic. Such a reaction may be represented graphically as shown in Figure 4.4.2.

Potential Energy vs. Reaction Proceeding

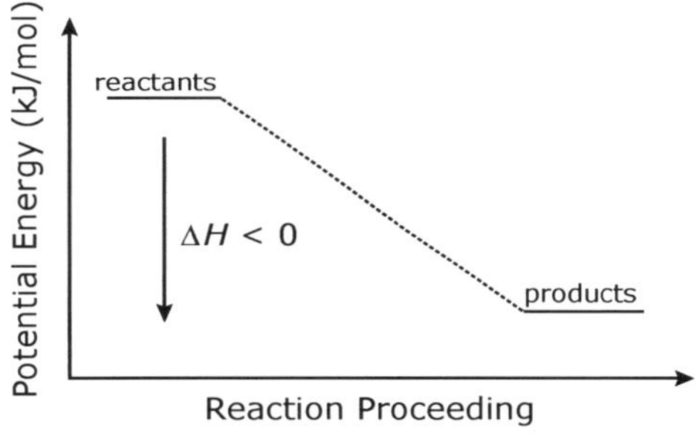

Figure 4.4.2 *Potential energy diagram for an exothermic reaction*

More energy is released during bond formation than is absorbed during bond breaking in an *exothermic* reaction so they have negative ΔH values.

Quick Check

Complete the right column in the following table by labelling each of the introductory reactions in this section as endothermic or exothermic.

Reaction	Endothermic or Exothermic
Dissolving potassium hydroxide	
Combustion of propane	
Melting ice	
Replacement of iron by aluminum	
Formation of calcium hydroxide	

Thermochemical Equations Versus ΔH Notation

There are two ways to express the ΔH value associated with a balanced chemical equation.

> A **thermochemical equation** includes the energy change as an integral part of the equation.

In an endothermic reaction, the energy absorbed by the reactants to form the products appears on the reactant side of the equation as though the energy itself is a reactant. Of course, energy is not a form a matter, so this cannot be strictly true.

Energy (enthalpy) changes are extensive properties. These are properties that depend on the quantity of material reacting and forming in a reaction. For this reason, the unit for an enthalpy change is kJ/mol. Consequently, if twice as many species react, the magnitude of the enthalpy change should be doubled. In a thermochemical equation, the mole in the denominator of the enthalpy unit actually refers to a *mole of the reaction*. The following equation shows the decomposition of water:

$$572 \text{ kJ/mol} + 2\,H_2O(l) \rightarrow 2\,H_2(g) + O_2(g)$$

It indicates that 572 kJ of energy are required per mole of this reaction. A mole of this reaction involves the decomposition of *2* mol of $H_2O(l)$ to form *2* mol of $H_2(g)$ and *1* mol of $O_2(g)$. Consequently, if 1 mol of water is decomposed, the energy requirement will be half as much, as represented in the following thermochemical equation.

$$286 \text{ kJ/mol} + H_2O(l) \rightarrow H_2(g) + \tfrac{1}{2}\,O_2(g)$$

In an exothermic reaction, the energy released by the reactants as the products are formed appears on the product side of the equation. According to what we've learned about bond energy, it should come as no surprise that the equation for the formation of water is simply the reverse of that for the decomposition, including the same magnitude of the heat change.

$$2\,H_2(g) + O_2(g) \rightarrow 2\,H_2O(l) + 572 \text{ kJ/mol}$$

The energy released by this reaction is exploited in fuel cells (Figure 4.4.3). The prototype fuel cell was used in the Apollo spacecrafts. These cells were continuously fed with hydrogen and oxygen gas and had the unique advantage of producing drinking water along with energy. The International Space Station continues to rely on fuel cells for energy production in space today.

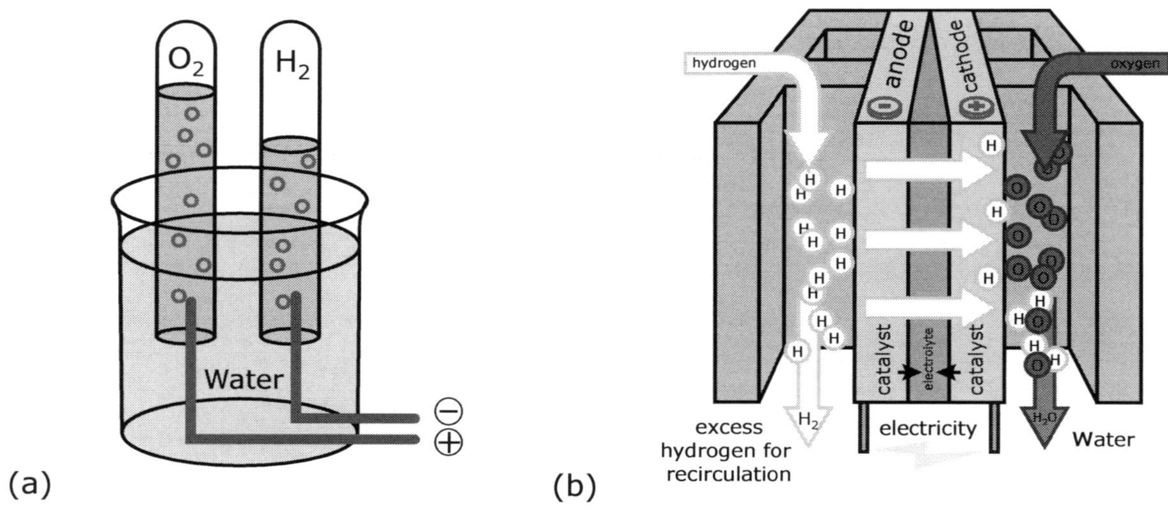

Figure 4.4.3 *The energy required to decompose 2 mol of water in an electrolysis apparatus (a) is identical to the energy released in the formation of 2 mol of water in a fuel cell (b). Fuel cells may be the most rapidly expanding form of energy production today.*

ΔH notation requires the energy change to be specified along with the equation, but written separately following a "ΔH =" symbol at the end of the equation.

Endothermic reactions are expressed with a *positive* ΔH value. Exothermic reactions are, of course, *negative*. If no sign is shown in front of a ΔH value, it is assumed to be positive.

Decomposition of water: $2\ H_2O(l) \rightarrow 2\ H_2(l) + O_2(g)$ $\quad \Delta H = +572$ kJ/mol

Formation of water: $2\ H_2(l) + O_2(g) \rightarrow 2\ H_2O(l)$ $\quad \Delta H = -572$ kJ/mol

Sample Problem — ΔH Notation and Thermochemical Equations

Given the following ΔH value, write a balanced thermochemical equation and an equation using ΔH notation with the smallest possible whole number coefficients given

$\Delta H_{decomposition}$ of $NO_2(g) = +33.9$ kJ/mol.

What to Think about

1. The decomposition of a binary compound implies the formation of its elements in their standard states (phases they are found in under room conditions). The compound $NO_2(g)$ decomposes into nitrogen and oxygen gas, both of which are diatomic.
2. This reaction involves decomposition, hence there is likely more energy required to break reactant bonds than energy is released during the formation of product bonds. This is an endothermic reaction. An endothermic reaction shows the heat of reaction as a reactant. In its unbalanced form, there are 33.9 kJ required for each mole of reactant decomposed.
3. Once this equation is balanced, there are 2 mol of nitrogen dioxide decomposed and hence twice as much heat of reaction.
4. The ΔH notation for an endothermic reaction results in a positive ΔH value. The ΔH notation shows a positive ΔH value adjusted for 2 mol of reactant.

How to Do It

$NO_2(g) \rightarrow 1/2 N_2(g) + O_2(g)$

33.9 kJ/mol $+ NO_2(g) \rightarrow 1/2 N_2(g) + O_2(g)$

2 mol NO_2 × 33.9 kJ/ mol NO_2 = 67.8 kJ 67.8 kJ/mol + $2\ NO_2(g) \rightarrow N_2(g) + 2\ O_2(g)$

$2\ NO_2(g) \rightarrow N_2(g) + 2\ O_2(g)$
$\Delta H = 67.8$ kJ/mol

Practice Problems — Representing Exothermic and Endothermic Changes

Given the following ΔH values, write a balanced thermochemical equation and an equation using ΔH notation with the smallest possible whole number coefficients for each of the following chemical changes:

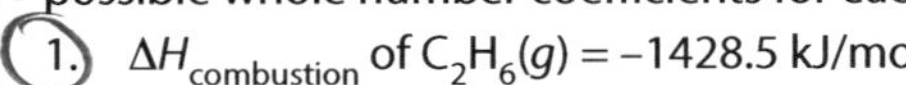

1. $\Delta H_{combustion}$ of $C_2H_6(g) = -1428.5$ kJ/mol

2. $\Delta H_{decomposition}$ of $NH_3(g) = 46.1$ kJ/mol

3. $\Delta H_{formation}$ of $HBr(g) = -36.1$ kJ/mol

4.4 Activity: Designing a Household Product

Question

How can endothermic and exothermic reactions be used to produce useful household products?

Background

The formation of iron(III) oxide, from iron powder and oxygen gas from the air is very exothermic and produces 826 kJ/mol of iron(III) oxide ore.

The dissolving of ammonium nitrate in water produces a solution of separated ammonium and nitrate ions. This physical change can be shown as

$$NH_4NO_3(s) \rightarrow NH_4^+(aq) + NO_3^-(aq) \quad \Delta H = 25.7 \text{ kJ/mol}$$

Procedure

1. Use the theoretical information provided above to design two useful products for treating athletic injuries. Present your designs in each of the following formats:
   - Describe each design in point form.
   - Provide a labeled diagram of each design.
2. Compare your designs with those of a classmate. Use your comparison to improve your designs.

Results and Discussion

1. Write a balanced thermochemical equation using the smallest possible whole number coefficients to describe the chemical change used in each of your designs.

2. Which of the two reactions is useful for cooling a warm, inflamed injury?

3. Which of the two reactions involves more bond breaking than bond forming?

4. Assume 240 g of ammonium nitrate are dissolved in the second design. How many kJ of energy are absorbed during this reaction?

4.4 Review Questions

1. Indicate whether each of the following changes is endothermic or exothermic:
   (a) Barbecuing a steak

   (b) Freezing a tray full of water to make ice

   (c) Neutralizing an acid spill with baking soda

   (d) Making a grilled cheese sandwich

   (e) Lighting a barbecue igniter

   (f) Condensing water on a mirror

2. Convert the following ΔH notation equations into thermochemical equations using the smallest whole number coefficients possible:
   (a) $\frac{1}{2}\,C_3H_8(g) \rightarrow \frac{1}{2}\,C_3H_8(l)$ $\Delta H = -175$ kJ/mol

   (b) $Li(s) + \frac{1}{2}\,CaCl_2(aq) \rightarrow LiCl(aq) + \frac{1}{2}\,Ca(s)$ $\Delta H = -362$ kJ/mol

   (c) $2\,B(s) + 3\,H_2O(g) \rightarrow B_2H_6(g) + 3/2\,O_2(g)$ $\Delta H = 762$ kJ/mol

   (d) $\frac{1}{2}\,P_4(s) + 3\,Cl_2(g) \rightarrow 2\,PCl_3(s)$ $\Delta H = -613$ kJ/mol

   (e) $NH_3(g) + 3/2\,N_2O(g) \rightarrow 2\,N_2(g) + 3/2\,H_2O(l)$ $\Delta H = -505$ kJ/mol

   (f) $\frac{1}{2}\,Fe_3O_4(s) + \frac{1}{2}\,CO(g) \rightarrow 3/2\,FeO(s) + \frac{1}{2}\,CO_2(g)$ $\Delta H = 9$ kJ/mol

3. Convert the following thermochemical equations into ΔH notation using the smallest whole number coefficients possible.
   (a) $C(s) + 2\,H_2(g) + \frac{1}{2}\,O_2(g) \rightarrow CH_3OH(l) + 201$ kJ/mol

   (b) $\frac{1}{2}\,Cu(s) + \frac{1}{2}\,H_2(g) + \frac{1}{2}\,O_2(g) \rightarrow \frac{1}{2}\,Cu(OH)_2(s) + 225$ kJ/mol

   (c) 389 kJ/mol $+ \frac{1}{2}\,Sb_4O_6(s) + 3\,C(s) \rightarrow 2\,Sb(s) + 3\,CO(g)$

   (d) 56 kJ/mol $+ NO_2(g) \rightarrow NO(g) + \frac{1}{2}\,O_2(g)$

   (e) $PCl_3(g) + \frac{1}{2}\,O_2(g) \rightarrow Cl_3PO(g) + 286$ kJ/mol

   (f) $F_2(s) + \frac{1}{2}\,O_2(g) \rightarrow OF_2(g) + 22$ kJ/mol

4. Use the equations in question 3 to answer the following questions:

(a) How much energy would be released during the formation of 4 mol of methanol?

804 kJ/mol

(b) How many moles of nitrogen dioxide could be decomposed through the use of 168 kJ of energy?

(c) Is more energy absorbed or released during the formation of Cl_3PO gas from PCl_3 and O_2 gas?

released

(d) What is the ΔH value for the decomposition of OF_2 gas into its elements?

−44 kJ/mol

(e) How much energy is required to decompose 1 mol of copper(II) hydroxide?

5. Does the following potential energy diagram represent an endothermic or an exothermic reaction? What is ΔH for this reaction?

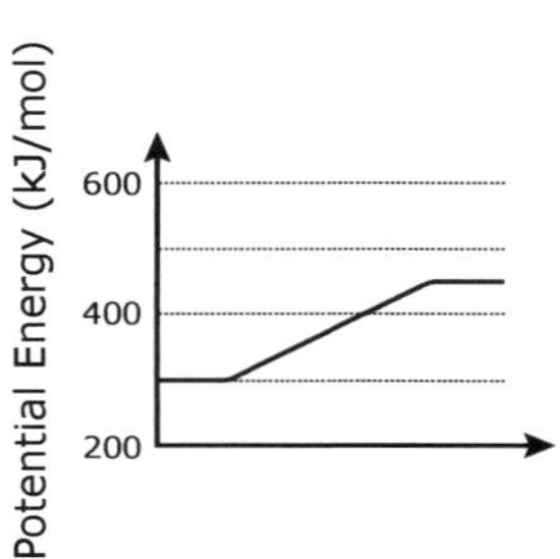

endothermic 150 kJ/mol

6. What is ΔH for this reaction?

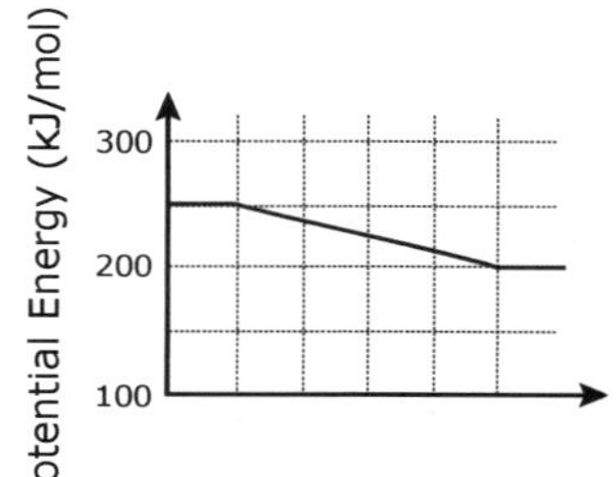

−50 kJ/mol

4.5 Enthalpy

Warm Up

Examine the following series of reactions and their associated enthalpy changes.

$CH_4(g) + 2\,O_2(g) \rightarrow CO_2(g) + 2\,H_2O(l)$ $\Delta H^\circ_{combustion} = -891$ kJ/mol

$C(s) + O_2(g) \rightarrow CO_2(g)$ $\Delta H^\circ_f = -394$ kJ/mol

$H_2(g) + \frac{1}{2}\,O_2(g) \rightarrow H_2O(l)$ $\Delta H^\circ_f = -286$ kJ/mol

Using the principles developed in Section 4.4, rearrange the reactions and combine them to give this overall reaction.

Rx 1:

Rx 2:

Rx 3:

$C(s) + 2\,H_2(g) \rightarrow CH_4(g)$

Determine the enthalpy change associated with the overall reaction.

Internal Energy, State Functions, and Conventions of Thermochemistry

Chemical energy is one of our most important energy sources. It can be converted into the heat, mechanical, and electrical energy we all use to operate a myriad of devices every day. The origin of this chemical energy lies in the position and motion of atoms, molecules, and subatomic particles. The various types of energies that combine to give the total **internal energy, *E*,** of a sample of matter include the following:

- *electronic* — kinetic energy of moving electrons and most significantly, potential energy due to electron-nuclei interactions
- *rotational* — kinetic energy due to rotation of a molecule about its center of mass
- *vibrational* — kinetic energy due to vibrations of atoms within the molecule
- *translational* — kinetic energy associated with gas molecules as they move linearly from one place to another

Many physics textbooks use the symbol *U* for internal energy.

Thermodynamics is the study of energy changes and the laws governing the conversion of heat into other forms of energy. Thermodynamics is primarily concerned with *macroscopic properties,* those you can see or measure such as temperature, pressure and volume, so a detailed analysis of the of the sources of internal energy is not necessary in this discussion. The mathematical study required is better covered in a university physical chemistry course. The reaction or physical system we are studying will be called the **system** and the rest of the universe will be called the **surroundings**. Additionally, we will refer to certain quantities as *state properties or functions.*

A **state function** or *state variable* is a property that depends on the current "state" of a system. These are conditions such as its volume, temperature, pressure and composition. State functions are independent of the pathway taken to reach the state. Common state functions include internal energy and enthalpy changes. ΔE does not depend on how a change in internal energy takes place, but on the difference between the initial and final internal energy of the system. Entropy and free energy are state functions you can look forward to encountering later in your AP Chemistry career.

Functions that do depend on the pathway taken to reach the current state may be referred to as **pathway dependent functions** or *process quantities.* Conditions such as work and heat are examples.

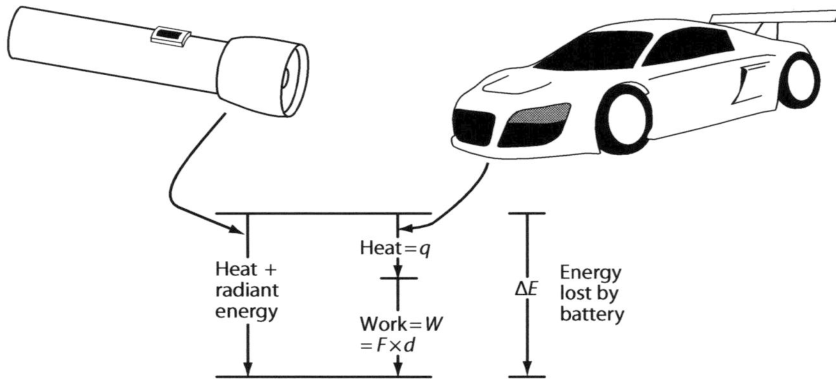

Figure 4.5.1 *A flashlight (left) and a remote control car (right) are operated using the same two D-cell batteries. The total change in internal energy is the same. However, the work done and heat and radiant energy released differ. This indicates that ΔE (internal energy equal to $q + W$) is a state function while q (heat) and W (work) are not.*

Sign conventions apply to most state functions. These are similar to those discussed for enthalpy in Section 4.4. Energy leaving or produced by the system has a negative sign. Energy entering the system from the surroundings has a positive sign. If the volume of a system decreases, ΔV will be negative. If the volume of a system increases or expands, ΔV will be positive. When work involves gases being formed or consumed in a chemical reaction, the change in the number of moles of gas, Δn, should be shown as negative if the total number of moles of gas decrease and positive if they increase.

The **first law of thermodynamics** is really as far as we'll go in thermochemistry. The first law is really just a restatement of our old friend, Antoine Lavoisier's **law of conservation of mass.**

Energy cannot be created or destroyed. It can be converted from one form to another.

$$\Delta E_{universe} = \Delta E_{system} + \Delta E_{surroundings} = 0$$

Two common methods for transferring energy between a system and its surroundings are heat, q, and work, w. The first law is sometimes expressed by defining internal energy as the sum of heat and work.

Although there are many different types of work, we will primarily discuss electrical work in our unit on electrochemistry and the work done by expanding gases. Work done by expanding gases is called, **pressure-volume work** and is equal to the product of the constant external pressure, P, exerted on the expanding gas and the change in volume, ΔV. Work can be converted to the familiar unit of energy, the joule, with the conversion factor 101.3 J equivalent to 1 litre-atmosphere.

$$\Delta E = q + W \text{ and } W = -P\Delta V$$

Sample Problem — Internal Energy, Heat, and Work Relationships

A potato cannon propels a piece of potato using the energy from a combusted fuel. The fuel performs 948 J of work on the potato and heats the cannon with 1355 J of heat. Calculate ΔE for the combustion process.

What to Think about	How to Do It
1. Determine the q and W values. 2. Assign the appropriate signs.	The cannon gets hot; therefore the reaction is exothermic. So $q = -1355$ J Work is done BY the system; therefore the reaction is exergonic. So $w = -948$ J
3. Use $\Delta E = q + W$ to determine the answer.	$\Delta E = -1355\text{ J} + (-)948\text{ J} = -2303\text{ J}$

Practice Problems — Internal Energy, Heat, and Work Relationships

1. A system absorbs 392 J of heat while the surroundings do 234 J of work on the system. What is the change in internal energy for the system?

2. A system releases 475 J of heat as it performs 524 J of work on the surroundings. Calculate ΔE for the system.

3. A system released 64 kJ of energy as its internal energy increased by 43 kJ. Did the system do work on the surroundings or was work done on the system? How much work was involved?

The ideal gas law, $PV = nRT$, can be rearranged to show that the ratio of the product of a gas sample's pressure and volume to the product of the gas sample's number of moles, n, and Kelvin temperature, is a constant. That ratio, R, only changes with the units of pressure selected. It may be 0.0821 L•atm/mol•K or 62.4 L•mmHg/mol•K for example. Multiplication of the first value by 101.3 J/L•atm gives 8.31 J/mol•K. The ideal gas law will be used extensively in the chapter on gases. It can also be used in the following derivation for pressure-volume work situations.

$$\Delta E = q - P\Delta V \text{ and since } PV = nRT \text{ then } \Delta E = q - \Delta nRT$$

When heat is absorbed or released from a chemical system and the external pressure is constant, the heat released or absorbed is equal to the enthalpy change of the process, $q_p = \Delta H$. For reactions that do not involve gases or a change in the number of moles of gas, the pressure-volume work done is zero, the $P\Delta V$ term becomes zero and $\Delta H = \Delta E$.

Sample Problem — Enthalpy vs. Internal Energy at Constant Pressure

Consider the following reaction occurring in an open container.

$CaCO_3(s) \rightarrow CaO(s) + CO_2(g) \quad \Delta H° = 571 \text{ kJ/mol}_{rxn}$

(i) How do q and ΔH compare under these conditions?
(ii) Calculate the change in internal energy.
(iii) How would ΔE and ΔH compare if both values were given to two significant figures?

What to Think About	How to Do It
1. Consider external pressure conditions. In this case, external pressure is constant and is equal to atmospheric pressure.	Under these conditions, $q_p = \Delta H$
2. $\Delta E = q + W$ where $q_p = \Delta H$ and $W = -P\Delta V = -\Delta nRT$ $\Delta E = \Delta H - \Delta nRT$ where $\Delta n = +1$ mole of gas	$\Delta E = 571 \text{ kJ/mol}_{rxn} - \left(\frac{1 \text{ mol}}{\text{mol}_{rxn}}\right)\left(\frac{0.00831 \text{ kJ}}{\text{mol K}}\right)(298 \text{ K})$ $= 571 \text{ kJ/mol}_{rxn} - 2.48 \text{ kJ/mol}_{rxn}$ $= 569 \text{ kJ/mol}_{rxn}$
3. Round the given ΔH and calculate ΔE to two significant figures.	$\Delta E = \Delta H = 570 \text{ kJ/mol}_{rxn}$ Note: There is only 2.48 kJ difference per mole of gas formed (or consumed). To two significant figures, the values are virtually the same.

Practice Problems — Enthalpy vs. Internal Energy at Constant Pressure

1. Consider the imaginary reaction: $A(s) + 2\, B_2C_3(aq) \rightarrow 4\, D(g) + 3\, EF_4(g)$
The reaction's ΔE value is measured as 442.26 kJ/mol$_{rxn}$. What is $\Delta H°$?

2. A cylinder equipped with a piston expands against an external pressure of 1.04 atm. A combusted fuel causes an expansion from 0.243 L to 1.650 L with the emission of 1.553 kJ of heat. What is ΔE for this process? Note: Be sure to include the conversion factor 101.3 J/L•atm where necessary.

3. To inflate a weather balloon you must increase its volume from 0.58 L (nearly empty for a weather balloon) to a full volume against an external pressure of 1 atm exactly. The process requires 22.632 kJ of work. What is the volume of the balloon?

Standard State Conditions

In section 4.4, we learned that enthalpy is potential energy that can be converted into heat. We also learned that any change, whether physical or chemical, will have an associated enthalpy change that can be calculated by comparing the initial and final bonding arrangement, including both intra- and intermolecular forces (IMFs) of attraction. If the overall energy released during bond formation exceeds the overall energy required for bond breaking, the enthalpy change (ΔH) will be negative. If the opposite is true, the enthalpy change will be positive. Finally, we learned that ΔH is an extensive property. Because it is expressed per mole of reaction or per mole of substance, constant values (or nearly constant values depending on the duplication of experimental conditions) for enthalpy changes may be found in tables. It is important to recognize that $\Delta H^{o}_{formation}$, abbreviated as ΔH^{o}_{f}, is really just the heat of reaction for a chemical change involving the formation of a compound from its elements in their *standard states*. In this case, *standard state* refers to the state or phase an element exists in under conditions defined, by convention, as *standard*.

> Standard state conditions are symbolized by a superscript "o" and indicate traditional "SATP" conditions of 25°C temperature, 1 atm pressure for gases, 1 mol/L concentration for aqueous species and the physical state or phase the substance exists at under these conditions.

There are a number of methods for calculating overall enthalpy changes that an AP Chemistry student should be familiar with. The three most common are the *law of Hess*, the use of tabular *heats of formation* and the use of *bond energies*.

The Law of Hess aka Hess's Law of Heat Summation

Enthalpy changes involving an overall *decrease* in potential energy are *exothermic*. The ΔH value for an exothermic change is always a *negative* value as the system is releasing energy. Changes involving an overall *increase* in potential energy are *endothermic* and the ΔH value for such a change is *positive*. Placement of the correct sign in front of ΔH values is an important accounting convention, and the signs must be applied consistently throughout all thermodynamic calculations.

As enthalpy is an *extensive property*, the *magnitude* of an enthalpy change for a chemical reaction *depends on the quantity of material* that reacts. This means if the amount of reacting material in an exothermic reaction is doubled, twice the quantity of heat will be released. Thus for the oxidation of sulphur dioxide gas:

$$SO_2(g) + \tfrac{1}{2}O_2(g) \rightarrow SO_3(g) \qquad \Delta H^{o} = -99 \text{ kJ/mol}_{rxn}$$

Doubling the reaction results in:

$$2\,SO_2(g) + O_2(g) \rightarrow 2\,SO_3(g) \qquad \Delta H^{o} = -198 \text{ kJ/mol}_{rxn}$$

A comparison of the absolute enthalpy content of the reactants and products of a reversible reaction makes it evident that the *magnitude* of ΔH for an exothermic reaction *remains the same when it is reversed*. There is merely a *sign change* and the reaction becomes endothermic. Hence if the above reaction were reversed:

$$2\,SO_3(g) \rightarrow 2\,SO_2(g) + O_2(g) \qquad \Delta H^{o} = +198 \text{ kJ/mol}_{rxn}$$

In addition to being an extensive property, enthalpy is also a *state function*. As we just learned, this means an enthalpy change is *completely independent of the pathway followed* to accomplish it. These concepts may be applied to determine the overall enthalpy change for any reaction by manipulation of a series of other reactions. The process is known as the **law of Hess** or **Hess's law of heat summation**. Simply stated:

> The *enthalpy change* of a *reaction* is expressed as the *algebraic sum* of the *enthalpy changes* of a series of other reactions that have been manipulated to produce the overall reaction.

As indicated in the Warm Up, given the following reactions and their enthalpy changes, it is possible to determine the heat of formation for methane:

$$CH_4(g) + 2\,O_2(g) \rightarrow CO_2(g) + 2\,H_2O(l) \qquad \Delta H^o_{comb} = -891 \text{ kJ/mol}_{rxn}$$

$$C(s) + O_2(g) \rightarrow CO_2(g) \qquad \Delta H^o_f = -394 \text{ kJ/mol}_{rxn}$$

$$H_2(g) + \tfrac{1}{2}\,O_2(g) \rightarrow H_2O(l) \qquad \Delta H^o_f = -286 \text{ kJ/mol}_{rxn}$$

The reaction we are attempting to come up with is:

$$C(s) + 2\,H_2(g) \rightarrow CH_4(g)$$

Begin by *looking for species that appear as reactants and products in the overall reaction*. This will provide a clue as to whether a reaction needs to be reversed or not. Second, *consider the coefficients of species that appear in the overall reaction*. This will help determine whether a reaction needs to be multiplied before the overall summation. Leaving the formation of carbon dioxide reaction as is and doubling the formation of water reaction appears to be a good start in that this will provide the reactants desired. The combustion of methane reaction will need to be reversed to provide the desired number of moles of product. Reorganization of the three equations as described with the accompanying change in their ΔH^o values results in:

$$C(s) + \cancel{O_2(g)} \rightarrow \cancel{CO_2(g)} \qquad \Delta H^o_f = -394 \text{ kJ/mol}_{rxn}$$

$$2\,H_2(g) + \cancel{O_2(g)} \rightarrow \cancel{2\,H_2O(l)} \qquad \Delta H^o_f = -572 \text{ kJ/mol}_{rxn}$$

$$\cancel{CO_2(g)} + \cancel{2\,H_2O(l)} \rightarrow CH_4(g) + \cancel{2\,O_2(g)} \qquad \Delta H^o_{rxn} = +891 \text{ kJ/mol}_{rxn}$$

$$C(s) + 2\,H_2(g) \rightarrow CH_4(g) \qquad \Delta H^o_f = -75 \text{ kJ/mol}_{rxn}$$

Sample Problem — The Law of Hess

As an alternative to burning coal, the following process, called *methanation,* can be used to produce energy from carbon monoxide, a product of coal combustion. The carbon monoxide is only one component of a mixture called "coal gas." Not only does this reaction produce energy, it also produces methane, itself a valuable component of natural gas that may be further combusted to produce energy.

$$3\,H_2(g) + CO(g) \rightarrow CH_4(g) + H_2O(g)$$

Determine the standard enthalpy change for the methanation reaction using the following series of reactions and their enthalpy changes:

$$2\,H_2(g) + O_2(g) \rightarrow 2\,H_2O(g) \qquad \Delta H^o_f = -483.6 \text{ kJ/mol}_{rxn}$$

$$2\,C(s) + O_2(g) \rightarrow 2\,CO(g) \qquad \Delta H^o_f = -221.0 \text{ kJ/mol}_{rxn}$$

$$CH_4(g) + 2\,O_2(g) \rightarrow CO_2(g) + 2\,H_2O(g) \qquad \Delta H^o_{comb} = -802.7 \text{ kJ/mol}_{rxn}$$

$$C(s) + O_2(g) \rightarrow CO_2(g) \qquad \Delta H^o_f = -393.5 \text{ kJ/mol}_{rxn}$$

Continued

What To Think About *continued*	**How To Do It**
1. Hydrogen gas only appears as a reactant in one reaction. So this reaction must be multiplied by 1.5 to give three reactant H_2 molecules.	$(2\ H_2(g) + O_2(g) \rightarrow 2\ H_2O(g)\quad -483.6\ kJ/mol_{rxn})\ x1.5$
2. To make CO a reactant requires reversal of the second reaction. It must be divided by two to give one CO_2 and the sign must be changed.	$(2\ CO(g) \rightarrow 2\ C(s) + O_2(g)\quad +221.0\ kJ/mol_{rxn})\ x\ -0.5$
3. To make methane a product, the third reaction must be reversed and the sign changed.	
4. This leaves one CO_2 to be cancelled, as it does not appear anywhere in the overall reaction. So the last reaction may remain as is.	$(CO_2(g) + 2\ H_2O(g) \rightarrow CH_4(g) + 2\ O_2(g)\quad +802.7\ kJ/mol_{rxn})\ x\ -1$
5. Changing coefficients and altering the enthalpy changes values accordingly.	$(C(s) + O_2(g) \rightarrow CO_2(g)\quad -393.5\ kJ/mol_{rxn})\ x\ 1$
6. Summing the four equations with appropriate algebraic cancelling gives the correct overall equation with the correct ΔH_{rxn} value for the equation as written.	$3\ H_2(g) + \cancel{1.5}\ O_2(g) \rightarrow \cancel{3}\ H_2O(g)\quad -725.4\ kJ/mol_{rxn}$ $1\ CO(g) \rightarrow \cancel{1\ C(s)} + \cancel{0.5\ O_2(g)}\quad +110.5$ $\cancel{CO_2(g)} + \cancel{2\ H_2O(g)} \rightarrow CH_4(g) + \cancel{2\ O_2(g)}\quad +802.7$ $\cancel{C(s)} + \cancel{O_2(g)} \rightarrow \cancel{CO_2(g)}\quad -393.5$ ============================== $3\ H_2(g) + CO(g) \rightarrow CH_4(g) + H_2O(g)$ $\Delta H_{rxn} = -205.7\ kJ/mol_{rxn}$

Practice Problems — The Law of Hess

1. The complete decomposition of NOCl gas into its elements occurs by the following reaction:

$$2\ NOCl(g) \rightarrow N_2(g) + O_2(g) + Cl_2(g)$$

Use the following two reactions and their enthalpy changes to determine the enthalpy change for the decomposition reaction.

$\frac{1}{2}\ N_2(g) + \frac{1}{2}\ O_2(g) \rightarrow NO(g)\qquad \Delta H_f = 90.3\ kJ/mol_f$

$NO(g) + \frac{1}{2}\ Cl_2(g) \rightarrow NOCl(g)\qquad \Delta H_{rxn} = -38.6\ kJ/mol_{rxn}$

Continued

Practice Problems — *Continued*

2. Polyvinyl chloride is commonly referred to as PVC. It is a polymer produced from a monomer formed by the addition of ethylene and chlorine gas. Use the following reactions and their enthalpy changes to determine the overall enthalpy change for the PVC monomer reaction:

Reaction	Enthalpy change
$H_2(g) + Cl_2(g) \rightarrow 2\,HCl(g)$	$\Delta H_f = -184.6$ kJ/mol$_{rxn}$
$C_2H_4(g) + HCl(g) \rightarrow C_2H_5Cl(l)$	$\Delta H_{rxn} = -65.0$ kJ/mol$_{rxn}$
$C_2H_3Cl(g) + H_2(g) \rightarrow C_2H_5Cl(l)$	$\Delta H_{rxn} = -138.9$ kJ/mol$_{rxn}$
$C_2H_4(g) + Cl_2(g) \rightarrow C_2H_3Cl(l) + HCl(g)$	$\Delta H_{rxn} =$ **(?)**

3. Given the following data (all species are gases):

Reaction	Enthalpy change
$2\,O_3 \rightarrow 3\,O_2$	$\Delta H_{diss} = -427$ kJ/mol$_{rxn}$
$O_2 \rightarrow 2\,O$	$\Delta H_{diss} = 495$ kJ/mol$_{rxn}$
$NO + O_3 \rightarrow NO_2 + O_2$	$\Delta H_{rxn} = -199$ kJ/mol$_{rxn}$

Calculate the enthalpy change for the following reaction: $NO + O \rightarrow NO_2$

The Use of Heats of Formation

Heats of formation reactions for each of the compounds involved in a chemical change may be rearranged, using the law of Hess to calculate the overall enthalpy change for the process. Using the heats of formation for methane, carbon dioxide, and liquid water from the Warm Up, and the previous example, we can determine the overall enthalpy change for the combustion of methane as follows:

$$CH_4(g) \rightarrow C(s) + 2\,H_2(g) \qquad \Delta H^\circ = +75\ \text{kJ/mol}_{rxn}$$

$$C(s) + O_2(g) \rightarrow CO_2(g) \qquad \Delta H^\circ_f = -394\ \text{kJ/mol}_{rxn}$$

$$2\,H_2(g) + O_2(g) \rightarrow 2\,H_2O(l) \qquad \Delta H^\circ_f = -572\ \text{kJ/mol}_{rxn}$$

$$CH_4(g) + 2\,O_2(g) \rightarrow CO_2(g) + 2\,H_2O(l) \qquad \Delta H^\circ_{comb} = -891\ \text{kJ/mol}_{rxn}$$

Close examination of this process reveals a very useful algorithm that may be used to calculate the overall enthalpy change for any reaction:

$$\Delta H^\circ_{(overall)} = \sum nH^\circ_{f(products)} - \sum nH^\circ_{f(reactants)}$$

The symbol Σ means "sum of" and n is the coefficient of each species in a balanced equation. It is critical to keep in mind that:

The H°_f for a *pure element* in its standard state is always equal to *zero*.

Observe the state of each species in a balanced equation carefully when using tabular values to complete these calculations, as the state of a substance affects its enthalpy of formation value.

The formula above can be used to calculate the overall enthalpy change for the combustion of methane as follows:

$$\Delta H^\circ_{comb} = [1 \times H_{f\,CO_2}(g) + 2 \times H_{fH_2O}(l)] - [1 \times H_{fCH_4}(g) + 2 \times H_{fO_2}(g)]$$

$$\text{thus: } \Delta H^\circ_{comb} = \left[\frac{1\ \cancel{\text{mol CO}_2}}{\text{mol}_{rxn}}\left(\frac{-394\ \text{kJ}/}{\cancel{\text{mol CO}_2}}\right) + \frac{2\ \cancel{\text{mol H}_2\text{O}}}{\text{mol}_{rxn}}\left(\frac{-286\ \text{kJ}/}{\cancel{\text{mol H}_2\text{O}}}\right)\right] -$$

$$\left[\frac{1\ \cancel{\text{mol CH}_4}}{\text{mol}_{rxn}}\left(\frac{-75\ \text{kJ}}{\cancel{\text{mol CH}_4}}\right) + \frac{2\ \cancel{\text{mol O}_2}}{\text{mol}_{rxn}}\left(\frac{0\ \text{kJ}}{\cancel{\text{mol O}_2}}\right)\right] = -891\ \text{kJ/mol}_{rxn}$$

Notice the answer is the same as that we would have produced using the law of Hess. Subtracting the heat of formation of the reactant, methane, has the same effect as reversing the equation. The heats of formation of the products are summed in both methods. Multiplication of heats of formation by the coefficient occurs in both methods as well.

Table 4.5.1 *Examples of Heats of Formation*

$NH_3(g)$	–45.9 kJ/mol	$NO(g)$	90.3 kJ/mol
$C(s)$ [diamond]	1.896	$NO_2(g)$	33.2
$N_2O_5(g)$	11.0	$C_3H_8(g)$	–105.0
$CO_2(g)$	–393.5	$PF_5(g)$	–1594.4
$C_2H_4Cl_2(g)$	–166.8	$NaHCO_3(s)$	–947.4
$C_2H_5Cl(g)$	–112.2	$Na_2SO_4(aq)$	–1387.1
$C_2H_6(g)$	–84.7	$SO_2(g)$	–296.8
$C_2H_4(g)$	52.5	$SO_3(g)$	–396.0
$HCl(g)$	–92.3	$H_2SO_4(aq)$	–907.5
$H_2S(g)$	–20.2	$H_2O(g)$	–241.8
$CH_4(g)$	–74.9	$H_2O(l)$	–285.8
$CH_3OH(g)$	–238.6	$ZnO(s)$	–348.0

Sample Problem — Heats of Formation

Given the following heats of formation, ΔH_f° of $SO_2(g)$ = –296.8 kJ/mol$_f$ and ΔH_f° of $SO_3(g)$ = –396.0 kJ/mol$_f$, what is the enthalpy change for the following reaction: $2\ SO_2(g) + O_2(g) \rightarrow 2\ SO_3(g)$?

What To Think about	How To Do It
1. Determine the ΔH_f° (heats of formation) values for each of the species involved in the reaction (with the exception of those in *elemental form* as those = 0). Note: Generally these values will be found in a *table of standard enthalpies of formation.*	ΔH_f° of $SO_2(g)$ = -296.8 kJ/mol and ΔH_f° of $SO_3(g)$ = -396.0 kJ/mol and ΔH_f° of O_2 = 0 kJ/mol (pure element)
2. Multiply products and reactants by their coefficients and subtract the sum of the products from the sum of the reactants.	$\frac{2\ \cancel{mol\ SO_3}}{mol_{rxn}}\left(\frac{-396.0\ kJ}{\cancel{mol\ SO_3}}\right) - \left[\frac{2\ \cancel{mol\ SO_2}}{mol_{rxn}}\left(\frac{-296.8\ kJ}{\cancel{mol\ SO_2}}\right) + \frac{1\ \cancel{mol\ O_2}}{mol_{rxn}}\left(\frac{0\ kJ}{\cancel{mol\ O_2}}\right)\right]$ = -198.4 kJ/mol

write on fact + lab report

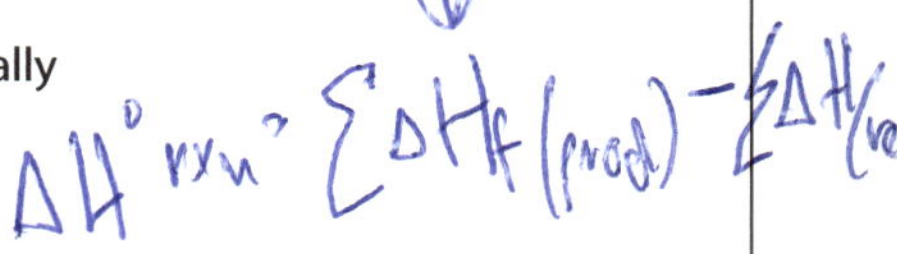

Practice Problems— Heats of Formation

Use the values in Table 4.5.1 to solve the practice problems below (values are listed alphabetically *by name* in this table):

$\Delta H^\circ_{rxn} = \Sigma \Delta H_f(prod) - \Sigma \Delta H_f(reac)$

1. Determine the enthalpy change for each of the following reactions:
   (a) $C_3H_8(g) + H_2(g) \rightarrow C_2H_6(g) + CH_4(g)$

   $= (-74.81 \text{ kJ/mol} + -84.68 \text{ kJ/mol}) - (-105 \text{ kJ/mol} + 0)$

   (b) $2\ H_2S(g) + 3\ O_2(g) \rightarrow 2\ SO_2(g) + 2\ H_2O(l)$

2. Use the following information along with the tabular data to calculate the *molar* enthalpy of ZnS(*s*).
   $2\ ZnS(s) + 3\ O_2(g) \rightarrow 2\ ZnO(s) + 2\ SO_2(g) \qquad \Delta H^\circ_f = -878.2 \text{ kJ/mol}_{rxn}$

The Use of Bond Energy

A third way to calculate enthalpy changes is to use bond energy values. Bond energy is the *energy required to break a bond.* Bond energy values are frequently presented in tables. Most AP Chemistry texts list bond energies as positive values in units of kJ/mole. Such values represent the amount of energy that must be input into the system to break the bond. To represent the value of the energy released when product bonds form, a negative sign must precede the value given in Table 4.5.2.

input of energy

Bond energy is the *enthalpy change* required to *break a given bond* in *one mole* of *gaseous molecules.* Bond energy is *always positive* and is expressed in units of kJ/mole.

The bond energy of a particular bond between two atoms, for example C-C, will vary depending on the "chemical environment" the bond is in, what other bonds are adjacent to it, and what lone pairs and bonding pairs of electrons are nearby. The bond energy for H-Cl, determined from hydrogen chloride gas, HCl, will differ from that determined within the PVC precursor, C_2H_5Cl, even when it is gasified. This means the bond energies typically reported in tables are really *average bond energies* gathered for each bond in a large variety of different compounds.

Table 4.5.2 *Average Bond Energy (KJ/mol)*

Bond	Energy	Bond	Energy	Bond	Energy	Bond	Energy
Single Bonds							
H–H	432	N–H	391	Si–H	323	S–H	347
H–F	565	N–N	160	Si–Si	226	S–S	266
H–Cl	427	N–P	209	Si–O	368	S–F	327
H–Br	363	N–O	201	Si–S	226	S–Cl	271
H–I	295	N–F	272	Si–F	565	S–Br	218
		N–Cl	200	Si–Cl	381	S–I	~170
C–H	413	N–Br	243	Si–Br	310		
C–C	347	N–I	159	Si–I	234	F–F	159
C–Si	301					F–Cl	193
C–N	305	O–H	467	P–H	320	F–Br	212
C–O	358	O–P	351	P–Si	213	F–I	263
C–P	264	O–O	204	P–P	200	Cl-Cl	243
C–S	259	O–S	265	P–F	490	Cl-Br	215
C–F	453	O–F	190	P–Cl	331	Cl-I	208
C–Cl	339	O–Cl	203	P–Br	272	Br–Br	193
C–Br	276	O–Br	234	P–I	184	Br–I	175
C–I	216	O–I	234			I–I	151
Multiple Bonds							
C=C	614	N=N	418	C≡C	839	N≡N	945
C=N	615	N=O	607	C≡N	891		
C=O	745 (799 in CO_2)	O_2	498	C≡O	1070		

When you examine a number of different average bond energies, such as those represented in this table, several patterns are noticeable. Consider the bond between hydrogen and members of the halogen family, for example. Because the highest energy bond is more difficult to break, HF behaves as a weak acid, while HCl through HI release their hydrogen ions more easily and so are strong acids.

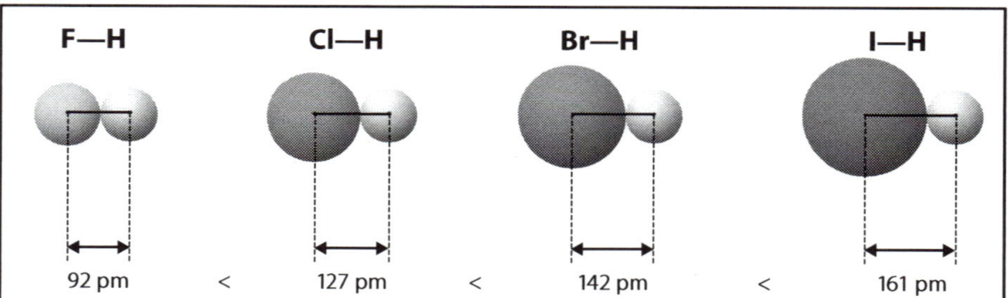

Figure 4.5.2 *Bond length increases with the atomic radius of each atom involved in the bond. Greater bond lengths result in less energetic and thus weaker bonds.*

A second pattern that is obvious is that bond energies depend not only on the elements involved in the bond, but also on whether the bond is single, double, or triple. Triple bonds are the most energetic and hence the strongest, while single bonds are the weakest and least energetic.

Bond energy and strength also relate to bond length. Triple bonds involve more electron energy-level overlap and hence are shorter. Section 6.3 contains more detail on the practical determination of bond lengths.

Because bond energies are *averages*, the answer to an enthalpy problem determined using bond energies might not be exactly the same as one calculated using heats of formation, but it will closely approximate it. Since bond energy is a state function, there is a simple algorithm available for calculating enthalpy changes using bond energies. It is similar to the one described for the calculation of enthalpy changes.

$$\Delta H_{reaction} = \sum nB.E._{(bonds\ broken)} - \sum nB.E._{(bonds\ formed)}$$

reactants products

Because the reactants and products appear in the opposite order in this equation compared to calculation of enthalpy from heats of formation students frequently make errors in the calculation of enthalpy changes using bond energies. The most common incorrect result has the correct magnitude, but the wrong sign. The easiest way to ensure you fully understand how to determine the overall bond energy change is to always remember that:

Bond *breaking requires energy* while bond *forming releases energy*!

Once the structural formulas of all species in a balanced equation are written down, the bonds that are broken and the bonds that are formed can be determined. The broken bonds are assigned *positive* bond energy values and each newly formed bond is assigned a *negative* one. Then the sum of the bond energies is calculated. For example, in the sample problem from the law of Hess,

$$CH_4(g) + 2\,O_2(g) \rightarrow CO_2(g) + 2\,H_2O(g) \qquad \Delta H^o_{comb} = -802.7\ \text{kJ/mol}_{rxn}$$

Four C-H bonds and two O=O bonds are broken while two C=O bonds and four O-H bonds are formed. Using tabular bond energy values, we would calculate:

$$\left[\frac{4\ \cancel{\text{mol C-H}}}{\text{mol}_{rxn}}\left(\frac{413\ \text{kJ}}{\cancel{\text{mol C-H}}}\right) + \frac{2\ \cancel{\text{mol O=O}}}{\text{mol}_{rxn}}\left(\frac{498\ \text{kJ}}{\cancel{\text{mol O=O}}}\right)\right] -$$

$$\left[\frac{2\ \cancel{\text{mol C=O}}}{\text{mol}_{rxn}}\left(\frac{799\ \text{kJ}}{\cancel{\text{mol C=O}}}\right) - \frac{4\ \cancel{\text{mol O-H}}}{\text{mol}_{rxn}}\left(\frac{467\ \text{kJ}}{\cancel{\text{mol O-H}}}\right)\right] = -818\ \text{kJ/mol}_{rxn}$$

While these two values are not exactly the same, they are both exothermic and are within 2% of each other. For reactions occurring in the gas state, bond energies give very close approximations to the enthalpy changes calculated with standard ΔH^o_f values.

Sample Problem — Enthalpy Changes from Average Bond Energy Values

Use Table 4.5.2 to determine the enthalpy change for the Haber process for the production of ammonia:

$$N_2(g) + 3\,H_2(g) \rightarrow 2\,NH_3(g)$$

What to Think About	How To Do It
1. Consider the bonding arrangement of the reactants and products. Structural formulas are very useful.	:N≡N: + 3 H-H ® 2 H-N̈-H (with H bonded below N)

Continued on next page

Sample Problem — *Continued*

What to Think About	How To Do It
2. Multiply the bond energies by the appropriate coefficients and apply the correct signage (+) for bonds breaking and (–) for bonds forming. Count the number of bonds carefully. Note: Should a bond remain intact, there is no need to break and reform it. Simply ignore it in the calculation.	$\frac{1\ \cancel{\text{mol N}\equiv\text{N}}}{\text{mol}_{rxn}}\left(\frac{945\ \text{kJ}}{\cancel{\text{mol}}_{\text{N}\equiv\text{N}}}\right) + \frac{3\ \cancel{\text{mol H–H}}}{\text{mol}_{rxn}}\left(\frac{432\ \text{kJ}}{\cancel{\text{mol}}_{\text{H–H}}}\right)$ $-\frac{6\ \cancel{\text{mol N–H}}}{\text{mol}_{rxn}}\left(\frac{391\ \text{kJ}}{\cancel{\text{mol}}_{\text{N–H}}}\right)$
3. Do the math!	$= -105\ \text{kJ/mol}_{rxn}$
4. It's always a good idea to consider the feasibility of your answer.	*As we are forming ammonia, an exothermic answer makes sense. The enthalpies of formation table give a* ΔH_f *as –45.9 kJ/mol of* NH_3*. The reaction forms two moles of ammonia, so our answer is close enough to be reasonable.*

Practice Problems — Enthalpy Changes from Average Bond Energy Values

Use Table 4.5.2 to produce a full *thermochemical equation* for each of the molecular representations below.

1. +  →  +

2. $H_3C–CH_2–CH_3$ (H–C–C–C–H with 8 H) + 5 O═O ⟶ 3 O═C═O + 4 H—O—H

3. $H_3C–O–H_{(g)}$ + 1½ $O{=}O_{(g)}$ ⟶ $O{=}C{=}O_{(g)}$ + H–O–H $_{(g)}$

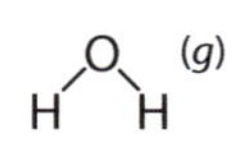

It is comforting to know that there are multiple ways to use tabular data to solve a problem in thermochemistry. But for most chemists, the real joy lies in working in the laboratory to do things such as creating the tabular data to begin with. This is the realm of calorimetry, and it will be the topic of our next section.

4.5 Review Questions

1. Complete the following table about symbols and sign conventions in the equation, $\Delta E = q + w$.

Symbol	Description	Sign	Meaning	Sign	Meaning
			System gains thermal energy		
	Work				Done by the system
ΔE		+			

2. Indicate whether each of the following is a state function or is pathway dependent:
   (a) A plane's total mileage meter

   (b) A plane's altimeter (indicates altitude)

   (c) Work

   (d) ΔH

   (e) Your monthly cell phone bill

3. Calculate the change in internal energy for a gas that absorbs 28.5 J of heat and then performs 16.4 J of work.

4. A gas expands from a volume of 1.4 L to 6.7 L against an external pressure of 1.00 atm. During this process, 565 J of heat is transferred from the surroundings to the gas.
   (a) How much work has been done?

   (b) What is the change in internal energy of the system?

5. Though we are unaware of it at rest, breathing requires work. A 70 kg man likely has an "empty" lung volume of 2210 mL.
   (a) If 50.7 J of work is required to take a single breath against a constant external atmospheric pressure of 1.00 atm, what is the man's "full" lung volume?

   (b) During exercise, the elastic lungs expand to a "full" volume of 5250 mL. How much work is required to take a single breath during exercise?

6. The following is a molecular representation of a state change occurring inside a piston-cylinder assembly against a constant external pressure of 1.05 atm.

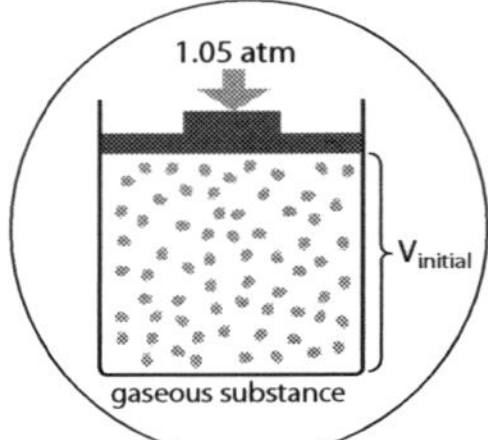

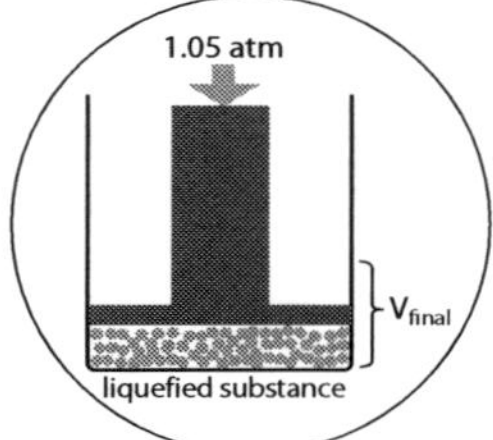

Indicate whether each of the following is (+), (–), 0 or impossible to determine.
Justify your answer in each case.
(a) w_{system}

(b) q_{system}

(c) ΔE_{system}

7. In the 1970s, scientists became concerned about the depletion of the ozone layer due to the affects of aerosol propellants such as chlorofluorocarbons. Chlorofluorocarbons are now known to absorb high-energy radiation, producing free radical chlorine atoms. These chlorine atoms have a catalytic effect on the removal of ozone from our atmosphere.

Use the following two reactions and their enthalpy changes to calculate the enthalpy change for the removal of ozone by free radical oxygen. (This is the net equation involved in ozone destruction in the atmosphere.) O atoms (free radicals) are present due to O_2 dissociation by high-energy radiation. All species are gaseous.

$O_3 + Cl \rightarrow O_2 + ClO$ $\quad \Delta H° = -126\ kJ/mol_{rxn}$

$ClO + O \rightarrow Cl + O_2$ $\quad \Delta H° = -268\ kJ/mol_{rxn}$

==================================

8. Determine the enthalpy change for the following reaction:
$CH_4(g) + 4\ Cl_2(g) \rightarrow CCl_4(l) + 4\ HCl(g)$
Using the following information:

$C(s) + 2\ H_2(g) \rightarrow CH_4(g)$ $\quad \Delta H°_f = -74.6\ kJ/mol_{rxn}$

$C(s) + 2\ Cl_2(g) \rightarrow CCl_4(g)$ $\quad \Delta H°_f = -95.7\ kJ/mol_{rxn}$

$H_2(g) + Cl_2(g) \rightarrow 2\ HCl(g)$ $\quad \Delta H°_f = -92.3\ kJ/mol_{rxn}$

9. The **Born-Haber cycle** is a hypothetical series of steps that represent the formation of an ionic compound from its constituent elements. According to the law of Hess, the enthalpy changes for each step in the series should sum to give the overall enthalpy change for the formation of the ionic compound from its elements in their standard states. The enthalpy change for the formation of an ionic compound from its ions in the gas state is called the **lattice energy** of the compound. Here is the Born-Haber cycle for cesium fluoride.

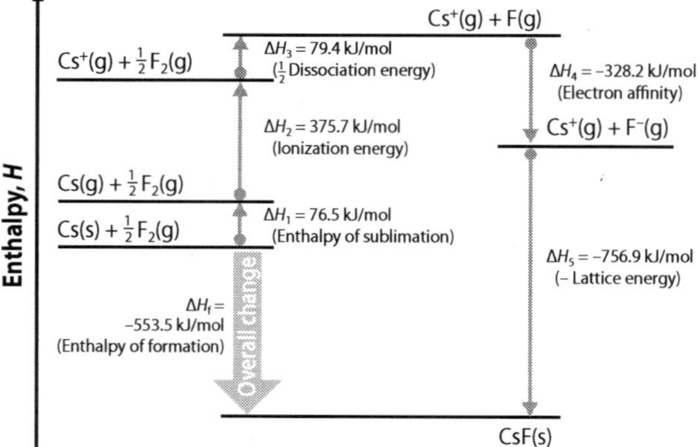

Use the Born-Haber cycle to show how five equations may be added together using the law of Hess to give the overall enthalpy of formation for cesium fluoride from the following equation: Cs(*s*) + ½ F_2(*g*) → CsF(*s*). Label each of the processes involved. Be sure to use *five steps*. The first step is done for you as an example.

Step 1:	Cs(*s*) → Cs(*g*)	ΔH_{sub} = 76.5 kJ/mol_{Cs}	sublimation of Cs
Step 2:	Cs(g) → Cs(g)	375.7 kJ/mol	ionization Cs
Step 3:	½F_2(g) → F(g)	79.4 kJ/mol	dissociation F_2
Step 4:	F(g) → F(g)	−328.2 kJ/mol	ionization F
Step 5:	Cs(g) + F(g) → CsF(s)	−756.9 kJ/mol	lattice energy
Overall Rxn:	Cs(*s*) + ½ F_2(*g*) → CsF(*s*)	ΔH_f = **?**	formation of CsF(*s*)

10. The Ostwald process for making nitric acid involves multiple steps, beginning with ammonia reacting with oxygen, forming nitrogen monoxide and water. Determine the ΔH^{o}_{rxn} for this *first step* in the Ostwald process. Begin by writing a *balanced chemical reaction*. Then use the standard enthalpy of formation values in Table 4.5.1.

11. Use the standard enthalpy of formation values in Table 4.5.1 to determine the overall enthalpy change for the reaction depicted by the following molecular representation:

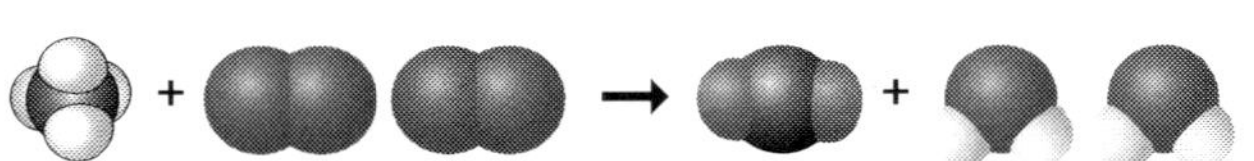

12. Consider the following *unbalanced* molecular representation of an oxidation-reduction reaction. Translate this molecular representation to a balanced formula equation. Then use the table of standard enthalpy of formation values from Table 4.5.1 to determine the overall enthalpy change for the balanced molecular equation.

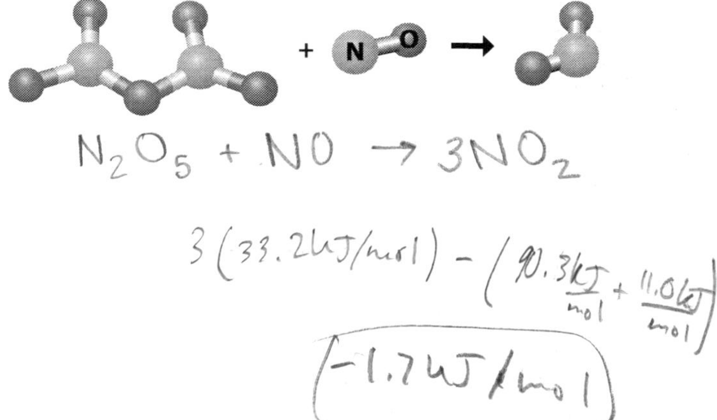

N_2O_5 + NO → $3NO_2$

3(33.2 kJ/mol) − (90.3 kJ/mol + 11.0 kJ/mol)

−1.7 kJ/mol

13. Solid baking soda (sodium bicarbonate <u>or</u> sodium hydrogen carbonate) neutralizes sulphuric acid solution spills, producing sodium sulphate, water, and carbon dioxide. Write a complete, balanced *thermochemical* equation for this process. The enthalpy values required may be found in Table 4.5.1.

$2NaHCO_3 + H_2SO_4 \rightarrow Na_2SO_4 + 2H_2O + 2CO_2$

(−1387.1 + (−285.8)(2) + (−393.5·2)) − ((−947.4·2) + (−907.5)) = 56.6 kJ/mol

14. The law of Hess Practice Problem 2 on page 214 involves steps in the production of polyvinylchloride (PVC) plastic. The addition of hydrogen chloride gas, HCl, to ethene, C_2H_4, forms the monomer, $C_2H_5Cl(l)$ which is used to make the polymer, PVC. Given the overall enthalpy change of –65.0 kJ/mol_{rxn} and a value in Table 4.5.1, determine the enthalpy of formation for the monomer, $C_2H_5Cl(l)$.

15. Chlorine gas can react in a substitution reaction with the gaseous monomer mentioned in question 14 as follows:

$C_2H_5Cl(g) + Cl_2(g) \rightarrow C_2H_4Cl_2(g) + HCl(g)$

(a) Calculate the $\Delta H°$ for the reaction above, using values from Table 4.5.2.

(H–C–C–Cl + Cl–Cl) – (H–C–C–Cl + H–Cl)

347 + 5(413) + 339 + 243 – 4(413) – 2(339)

–342 – 422 =

–103 kJ/mol

(b) Repeat the calculation done in part (a) using ΔH°_f values from Table 4.5.1.

(–166.8 kJ/mol – 92.3 kJ/mol) – (0 – 112.2 kJ/mol) =

–146.9 kJ/mol

(c) Compare the answer to part (a) with part (b). Comment on the comparison.

$\Delta H_f°$ values from table 4.5.1 are more reliable because they are precise and a's values are only averages.

16. (a) Use a highlighter or some other method to indicate the bonds that break on the reactant side and form on the product side of this reaction. Remember the note in the sample problem about enthalpy changes from average bond energy values in Table 4.5.2 — if a bond remains intact there is no need to break and reform it. Calculate the enthalpy change using the bond energy values in Table 4.5.1.

CH_2—CH_2 (bridged by O) + HCN → HOC(H)(H)—C(H)(H)—C≡N (Nitrile)

H—C≡N

(358 + 413) – (467 + 347)

–43 kJ/mol

(b) Repeat for this reaction.

$HOCH_2CH_2CN \longrightarrow$ (H)(H)C=C(H)(C≡N) + H_2O

(c) Considering bond energy is a state function, combine steps (a) and (b) into one reaction and calculate the overall enthalpy change.

17. The following shows the structural formulas for the reaction:

$$2\ CH_2CHCH_3(g) + 2\ NH_3(g) + 3\ O_2(g) \rightarrow 2\ CH_2CHCN(g) + 6\ H_2O(g)$$

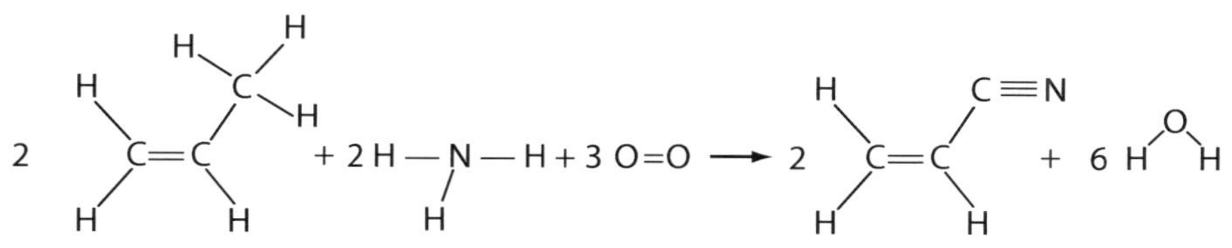

Use the bond energy in Table 4.5.2 to calculate ΔH_{rxn} for the given reaction.

4.6 Calorimetry — The Measurement of Heat Transfer

Warm Up

The apparatus shown here is used to collect data that produces the graph shown. The hot plate supplies kinetic energy to the water sample the entire time. As heat is absorbed, the temperature rises. What is that energy being used for in each labelled region on the graph? Approximately how much energy was used for each change to the water? (Region A is completed as a sample.)

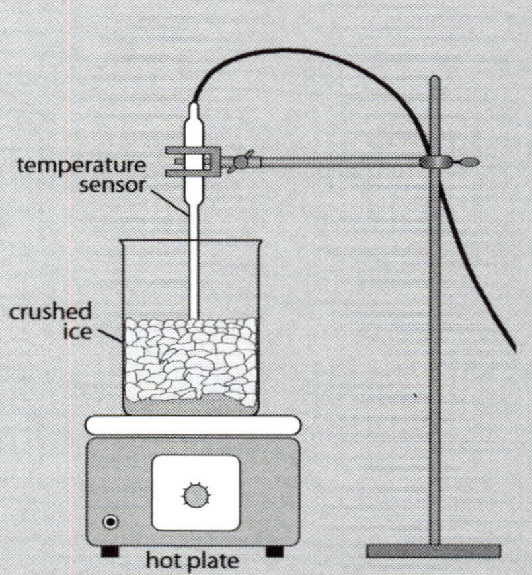

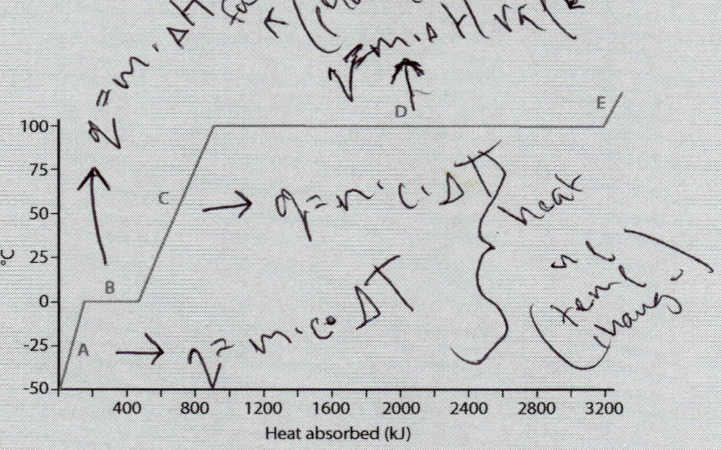

Region	Energy is used to...	Energy required
A	Heat solid water from –50 to 0°C	Approximately 180 kJ of energy
B		
C		
D		
E		

Study regions A, C, and E. What three things might cause the energy required to differ?

1.
2.
3.

Study regions B and D. What two things might cause the energy required to differ?

1.

2.

Specific Heat, Heat Capacity, Heat of Fusion, and Heat of Vaporization

Recall from section 2.1 that heat is the exchange of thermal energy between a system and its surroundings. This exchange is caused by a temperature difference and the energy always moves from a region of high temperature to a region of lower temperature.

Temperature is a measure of the average *thermal energy* in a sample of matter.

Heat is the energy *transferred* from one body to another because of a difference in temperature.

The quantity of energy required to change the temperature of a particular sample of material is the sample's **heat capacity**. It is symbolized by an upper case letter **C**. Heat capacity is generally measured in units of **J/°C**. For the most part in chemistry, it is much more useful to consider a material's **specific heat capacity**, sometimes simply referred to as **specific heat.** This is represented by a lower case letter **c**.

Specific heat capacity, *c*, is the quantity of *heat* required to raise the temperature of a *specific quantity* of a substance by *one degree celsius*.

For water, $c = 4.180$ J/g°C = 1 cal/g °C

Substance	J/g°C
Elemental Solids	
Aluminum	0.900
Beryllium	1.830
Cadmium	0.230
Copper	0.387
Germanium	0.322
Gold	0.129
Iron	0.448
Lead	0.128
Silicon	0.703
Silver	0.234
Other Solids	
Brass	0.380
Glass	0.837
Ice (–5°C)	2.090
Marble	0.860
Wood	1.700

Substance	J/g°C
Liquids	
Alcohol (ethyl)	2.400
Mercury	0.140
Water (15°C)	4.180
Gas	
Steam (100°C)	2.010

Table 4.6.1 *Specific heat capacity values for common substances*

Quick Check

Examine Table 4.6.1.

1. How do the specific heat capacities of metals compare to that of liquid water?

2. If equal masses of water and iron were exposed to the same heat source, which one would reach the temperature of 100°C first?

3. Consider equal masses of iron and water at 100°C. Which would cool to room temperature more quickly?

Regions A, C, and E of the Warm Up graph indicate that not only does the identity of a substance influence its specific heat capacity, but so does the state. Comparing regions A and C of the graph in the Warm Up, we can see that for a 50°C increase in temperature, ice required about 100 kJ but liquid water required about 200 kJ over the same temperature increment. Liquid water took two times the energy required to warm the same amount of ice. As indicated in Table 4.6.1, liquid water's specific heat capacity c = 4.18 J/g °C, while solid water, or **ice has c = 2.09 J/g°C**. Interestingly, gaseous water or **steam has c = 2.01 J/g°C,** which is close to that of ice. The high heat capacity of liquid water is responsible for the relatively constant temperatures of coastal and island cities such as Vancouver, San Francisco, Honolulu, and Shanghai.

Changes of State

Frozen water molecules vibrate but can't change places.

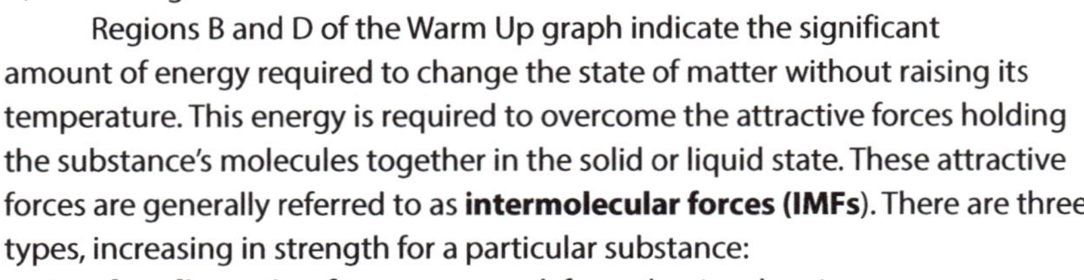

Water molecules in a liquid state slide over each other.

Water molecules in a gaseous state move randomly throughout their container.

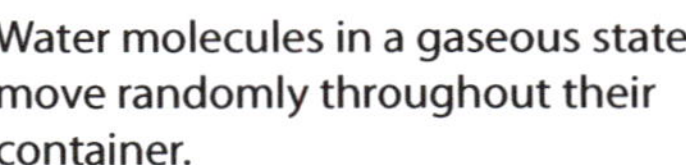

Figure 4.6.1 *The states of matter*

Regions B and D of the Warm Up graph indicate the significant amount of energy required to change the state of matter without raising its temperature. This energy is required to overcome the attractive forces holding the substance's molecules together in the solid or liquid state. These attractive forces are generally referred to as **intermolecular forces (IMFs**). There are three types, increasing in strength for a particular substance:

- **London dispersion forces** — a weak force that involves instantaneous induced poles of opposite charge on the molecules
- **dipole-dipole forces** — a slightly stronger force caused by permanent poles of opposite charge produced by differences in atoms' electronegativity at the opposite ends of bonds in a molecule
- **hydrogen bonds** — the strongest IMF is due to very strong dipoles produced by bonds where hydrogen is attached to one of the three smallest diameter, largest electronegativity elements – N, O, or F

As water melts and evaporates (or boils), its weak London dispersions forces and its strong dipole-dipole/hydrogen bonds must be overcome to allow freedom of motion as the water changes state.

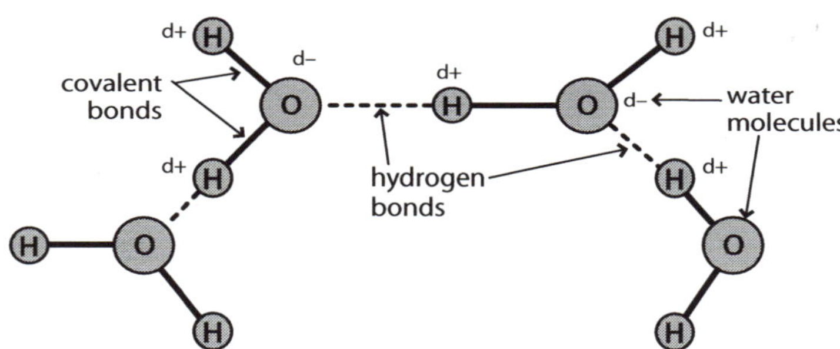

Figure 4.6.2 *Hydrogen bonds form between the slightly negative partial charges on oxygen atoms on one water molecule and the slightly positive partial charges on hydrogen atoms on another water molecule. The partial charges, indicated with a lower case delta (δ), are due to the higher electron density on the side of the covalent bond closest to the more electronegative oxygen atom and the lower electron density on the hydrogen side of the bond in the water molecule. Note the difference between intermolecular H-bonds and intramolecular covalent bonds.*

The energy required to overcome these intermolecular forces is called the **heat of fusion** or **heat of vaporization** depending on whether the substance is undergoing melting or evaporation.

The **heat of fusion** is the quantity of *heat* required to change a particular *quantity* of a pure solid *at its melting point* into a *liquid.*

$$H_{fusion} \text{ of water} = 334 \text{ J/g}$$

The **heat of vaporization** is the quantity of *heat* required to change a particular *quantity* of a pure liquid *at its boiling point* into a gas.

$$H_{vaporization} \text{ of water} = 2250 \text{ J/g}$$

Note that regions B and D in the Warm Up graph indicate the difference between H_{fusion} and H_{vap} for water. The heats of fusion and vaporization are independent of the temperature change as there is no temperature change. The temperature remains constant during a change of state. This is because all energy is being used to overcome the intermolecular forces between the particles. During cooling, heat is released as intermolecular forces are formed. The magnitude of energy needed for the change is the same, but the value of the energy is given a negative number to indicate that energy is released. The energy required for the phase change from gas to liquid is called **heat of condensation** and energy required for the phase change from liquid to solid is **the heat of solidification**. A heat change that occurs at constant temperature is referred to as **latent heat**.

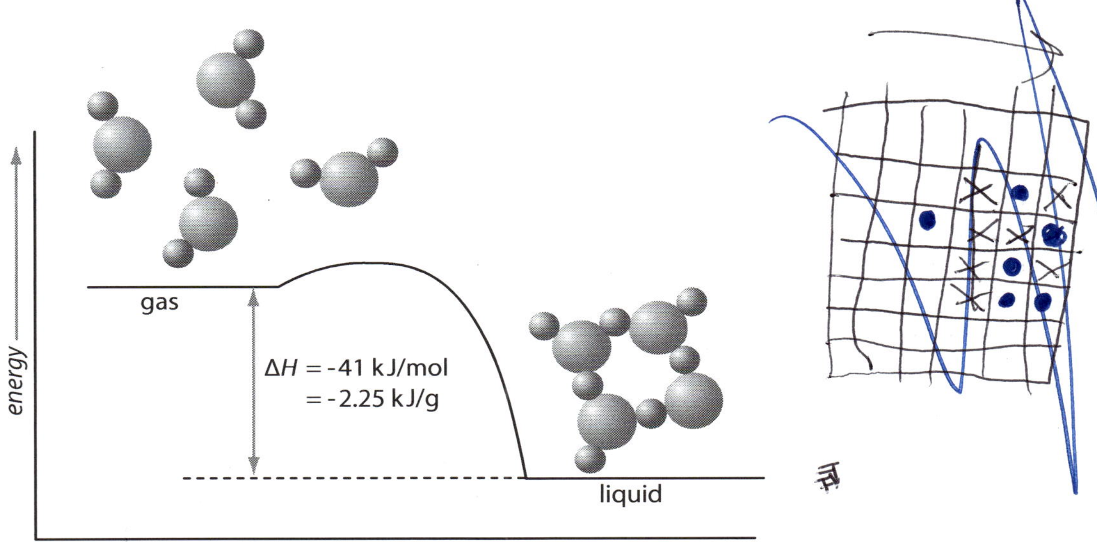

Figure 4.6.3 *Hydrogen bonds form as gaseous water condenses to become liquid. Note that $H_{vap} = -H_{cond}$ and the magnitude of the energy is the same, but the sign is reversed and the value may be expressed in units of kJ/mol or kJ/g. There will be a difference of 18.01 times when comparing the value in kJ/mol to that in kJ/g as this is the mass of one mole of water.*

The amount of heat absorbed or released during a cooling or heating process can be calculated by considering the specific heat capacity, the mass, and the temperature change. Where a state change is included, only the mass and the heat of vaporization and/or fusion need be considered. Heat is represented by q.

For a temperature change: $q = mc\Delta T$

For a state change: $q = H_{fus}m$ or $q = H_{vap}m$

For these calculations, the system is assumed to be entirely insulated from the surroundings so that no heat can enter or leave the system from or to any outside heat source or sink.

Sample Problem — Calculation of Heat Changes

Calculate the heat required to change 50.0 g of water at 25.0°C into steam at 120.0°C.

What to Think About

1. It is helpful to represent the energy changes with a sketch.
2. Apply the appropriate equations to each portion of the problem.
3. Calculate the heat required to accomplish each change. *Take care* with substitution into the equations. It is easy to confuse the *c* values for different states and the *H* values for fusion and vaporization.
4. Sum the *q* values for each portion. Take care with significant figures and units, rounding only at the end and ensuring all of the energy values have the same units before adding them together
5. Remember that when summing or subtracting the final answer is rounded to the *least precise place value*.

How To Do It

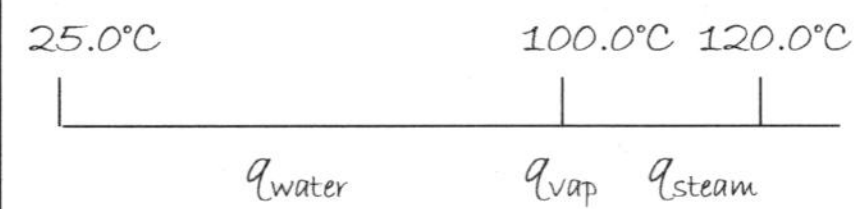

$q_{water} = mc_{water}\Delta T$

$q_{vap} = H_{vap}m$

$q_{steam} = mc_{steam}\Delta T$

$q_{water} = 50.0 \text{ g} \times \frac{4.18 \text{ J}}{\text{g°C}} \times 75.0\text{°C}$

$q_{water} = 15\,675 \text{ J}$ (3 sig figs)

$q_{vap} = \frac{2250 \text{ J}}{\text{g}} \times 50.0 \text{ g} = 112\,500 \text{ J}$ (3 sf)

$q_{steam} = 50.0 \text{ g} \times \frac{2.01 \text{ J}}{\text{g°C}} \times 20.0\text{°C} = 2010 \text{ J}$ (3 sf)

Note: All ΔT values are treated as (+).

$15\,675 \text{ J} + 112\,500 \text{ J} + 2010 \text{ J}$

$130\,185 \text{ J} = 1.30 \times 10^5 \text{ J} = 130. \text{ kJ}$

(In this case, the thousands place is the least precise.)

Practice Problems — Calculation of Heat Changes

1. Aluminum metal is commonly used to determine the temperature of different portions of a Bunsen burner flame. Calculate the heat required to completely melt a 0.325 g piece of aluminum wire beginning at a room temperature of 22.5°C. The melting point of aluminum is 660.3°C and its heat of fusion is 398 J/g. Refer to Table 4.6.1 for the specific heat capacity.

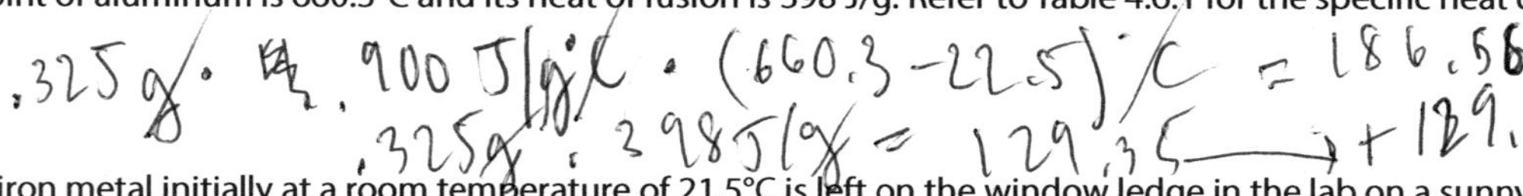

2. A piece of iron metal initially at a room temperature of 21.5°C is left on the window ledge in the lab on a sunny day. It absorbs 862.4 J of heat and warms to 32.5°C. What is the mass of the iron? See Table 4.6.1.

3. A 75.45 g sample of silicon initially at 20.5°C absorbs 1326 J of heat. What is the final temperature of the sample? See Table 4.6.1.

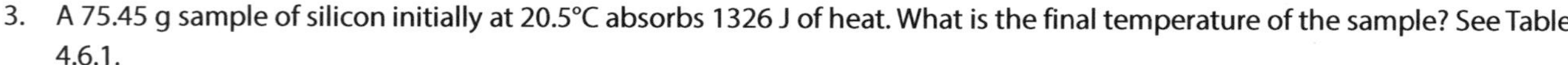

4. Calculate the heat required to change a 55.00 g ice cube at –15.0°C into steam at 125.0°C. (Hint: There should be five different *q* values in your calculation.)

The First Law of Thermodynamics – Energy is Always Conserved

Heat calculations involving physical processes with only the system and the surroundings, for example, where something hot is added to something cold, require a generalized version of the first law of thermodynamics.

> heat lost + heat gained = 0
>
> or
>
> (–) heat lost = heat gained
>
> Where *heat lost* is the *total* heat lost by the hotter substance and *heat gained* is the *total* heat gained by the colder substance.

As with the previous calculations, we are assuming the interacting systems are thermally insulated from the rest of the universe.

Sample Problem — Calculating Heat Changes in Systems Combining Hot and Cold

If 50.0 g of water at 15.0°C is added to 40.0 g of water at 85.0°C, what is the final temperature of the system?

What to Think About	How To Do It
1. A sketch along the lines of the one shown in the previous sample problem is helpful; however, the final temperature is represented by a variable such as *T*. Again, *remember* to consider all ΔT values to be positive.	15.0°C T°C 85.0°C 50.0 g q_{cold} q_{hot} 40.0 g
2. Apply the appropriate equations to each portion of the problem. Note that for simplification, we are working with the absolute values of q_{hot} and q_{cold}.	Since $q_{cold} = q_{hot}$, then $mc\Delta T_{cold} = mc\Delta T_{hot}$ and $m_{cold}c_{water}(T - 15.0)$ $= m_{hot}c_{water}(85.0 - T)$
3. Calculate the heat required to cause each change. *Take care* with substitution into the equations. In addition to different temperature values, there are different masses to keep track of.	50.0 g x 4.18 J/g°C x (T – 15.0) = 40.0 g x 4.18 J/g°C x (85.0 – T) So,
4. A bit of algebra, involving first, distribution through the brackets…then collection of like terms…and finally solving for *T*…provides an answer.	= 209T – 3135 = 14 212 – 167.2T ∴ 376.2T = 17 347
5. Notice the answer *makes sense* as it is between the two initial temperatures and closer to the cold one as the cold mass was greater.	∴ T = 17 347/376.2 = **46.1°C** Note: The significant figures in the final answer are based on the original problem rather than each step in the algebra. Sig figs apply to measurements, not algebra.

Practice Problems — Calculating Heat Changes in Systems Combining Hot and Cold

1. A 29.65 g solid gold earring at 33.5°C falls from your ear into a thermally isolated 245.0 mL cup of 65.5°C coffee. Use information from the Table 4.6.1 to determine the final temperature of the earring and the coffee when they reach the same temperature (*thermal equilibrium*). Assume the specific heat capacity and the density of the coffee is the same as those of water and that the final temperature will be between the initial temperatures.

   $M_G \cdot C_G (T_{fe} - T_{ie}) = -M_c \cdot C_c (T_{fc} - T_{ic})$

   $(29.65 g)(.129 J/g°C)(T_f - 33.5°C) = -(245.0 g)(4.18 J/g°C)(T_f - 65.5°C)$

2. A brass ball bearing with an initial temperature of 95.55°C is placed in a thermally insulated beaker containing 125.0 mL of water (assume d_{water} = 1 g/mL exactly) at 20.50°C. When the two substances reach thermal equilibrium, their final temperature is 26.55°C. What is the mass of the brass ball bearing?

3. What is the final temperature when a 348.00 g block of ice at –44.5°C is added to 95.00 g of steam at 125.5°C in an insulated system? Assume the final result will be liquid water.

Coffee Cup Calorimetry

Most people are familiar with the Calorie as it appears on the label of virtually all prepared foods we purchase in supermarkets today. The Nutrition Facts label has been required since 1994 in the United States and since 2003 in Canada.

The caloric content on these labels is in Calories (Cal) or "big C" calories. A food calorie reported on Nutrition Facts labels is actually equivalent to 1000 cal or 1 kcal.

> 1 Cal = 1000 cal = 1 kcal = 4.184 kJ
> = the energy to warm 1 g of water by 1 Celsius degree
> (or 1 Kelvin degree as the *change* is the same)

Where does the information on the caloric content of foods values come from? How is it measured? The caloric content is measured with a device called a **calorimeter**. The first calorimeter was designed and used by Antoine Lavoisier and Pierre Laplace in the early 1780s. They used the mass of ice melted by a chemical change as a measure of the amount of heat produced during the change. In laboratories everywhere, we now use the temperature change produced in a given mass of water as a measure of the amount of heat produced or absorbed during a physical or chemical change occurring in the calorimeter. If the change is exothermic, energy is released and the temperature increases; if it is endothermic, energy is absorbed from the water and the temperature decreases.

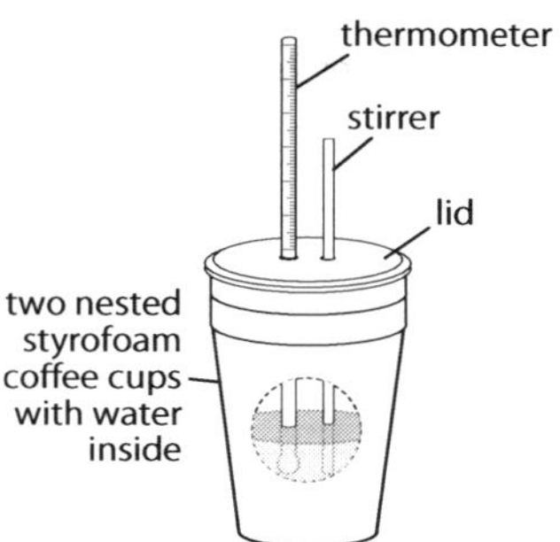

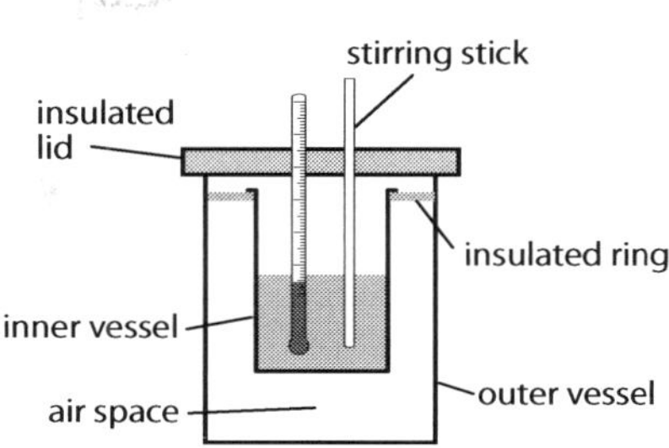

Figure 4.6.4 *Calorimeters. The nesting of two cups, one inside the other, provides reasonable insulation in a coffee cup calorimeter. A thermos with a sealed thermometer and stirrer is similar but slightly more sophisticated. A layer of air provides excellent insulation.*

The principle behind the calorimeter is once again, the law of conservation of energy, a simplified expression of the first law of thermodynamics.

heat lost + heat gained = 0

Hence, heat lost, or gained, by the physical or chemical change in the calorimeter *equals* heat gained, or lost, by the system—usually an aqueous solution—inside the calorimeter.

Simple calorimeters may be used to collect data for the situations in the practice problems in the first half of this section. Additionally, they may be used to determine heats of reaction and heats of solution.

Sample Problem — Determining the Enthalpy Change of an Aqueous Solution

A neutralization reaction between 50.0 mL of 1.00 mol/L HCl and 50.0 mL of 1.00 mol/L NaOH is performed with constant stirring at a room temperature of 20.50°C. The temperature rises to 27.13°C. Assume the solution volumes are additive and that the density and specific heat capacity of the final solution is the same as those values for water. Assume also that only a negligible amount of heat is absorbed or released from or to the surroundings. Calculate the molar enthalpy change (ΔH_{neut}) for this reaction.

What to Think About

1. Determine a balanced chemical equation for the process. As the reactants are present in "equimolar" quantities, neither is in excess, so we can assume both will be consumed completely.
2. Calculate the heat absorbed by the 100.0 mL of resulting solution. Remember to treat all temperature changes as positive values.
3. Since *heat lost = heat gained*, the heat absorbed by the solution must equal the heat released by the neutralization reaction.

How To Do It

$HCl(aq) + NaOH(aq)$ ⑧ $NaCl(aq) + H_2O(l)$

$50.0 \text{ mL} \times \frac{1.00 \text{ mol}}{1000 \text{ mL}} = 0.0500$ mol each of HCl and NaOH will be completely converted to 0.0500 mol of NaCl dissolved in water.

Since $q = mc\Delta T$,

$$q = \left(100.0 \text{ mL} \times \frac{1 \text{ g}}{\text{mL}}\right) \times \frac{4.18 \text{ J}}{°\text{C}} \times (27.13°\text{C} - 20.50°\text{C})$$

$$= 100.0 \text{ g} \times \frac{4.18 \text{ J}}{\text{g}°\text{C}} \times 6.63°\text{C}$$

$$= 2770 \text{ J}$$

Continuedon next page

Sample Problem — *Continued*

What to Think About

4. Finally, relate the heat released to the quantity of reactant neutralized. Since the reaction takes place at constant pressure, $q = \Delta H$.

5. Once the magnitude has been calculated, check the *sign*. In this case, heat was *released* from the neutralization to the solution, thus the reaction must be *exothermic* and so a *negative* sign is appropriate.

How To Do It

$q_{solution} = q_{neutralization} = 2770\ J$

$\Delta H = \frac{2770\ J}{0.0500\ mol} \times \frac{1\ kJ}{1000\ J} = 55.4\ kJ/mol$

$\Delta H_{neutralization} = -55.4\ kJ/mol$

Practice Problems — Determining the Enthalpy Change of an Aqueous Solution

1. When 500.0 mL of 2.00 mol/L $Ba(NO_3)_2$ solution at 22.50°C is combined in a coffee cup calorimeter with 500.0 mL of 2.00 mol/L Na_2SO_4 solution also at 22.50°C, a white precipitate forms and the temperature of the mixture rises to 25.60°C. Assume the calorimeter materials absorb only a negligible quantity of heat and the final solution's density and specific heat capacity are identical to those of water. Calculate the molar enthalpy of precipitation of $BaSO_4(s)$.

2. A coffee cup calorimeter contains 50.00 g of water at 20.73°C. When 2.13 g of NH_4NO_3 pellets are stirred into the water, the temperature falls to 17.41°C. Assume the heat capacity of the resulting solution is the same as that of water and that no energy is absorbed or released from or to the surroundings. Calculate the molar enthalpy of dissolution of ammonium nitrate, a chemical commonly used in the production of cold packs.

3. Given: $2\ HCl(aq) + Ba(OH)_2(aq) \rightarrow BaCl_2(aq) + 2\ H_2O(l) + 118\ kJ/mol_{rxn}$. Calculate the heat released when 300.0 mL of 0.500 mol/L hydrochloric acid is combined with 100.0 mL of 1.00 mol/L of barium hydroxide. Assume that the temperature of both solutions is initially 21.55°C. The final mixture has a mass of 400.0 g and a heat capacity the same as that of water with negligible heat "leakage" to or from the system. What is the final temperature of the mixture?

Constant Volume Calorimetry — The Bomb Calorimeter

A bomb calorimeter is more sophisticated than a coffee cup or even a thermos-type calorimeter. It is often used to determine the heat change involved in a chemical reaction, including reactions that do not occur in solution such as combustion reactions. The reaction chamber is surrounded by a metal jacket that sits inside a known mass of water at a known temperature. The prototype bomb calorimeters had extremely precise thermometers extended from inside the bomb with a sliding magnifying lens to assist in reading the temperature to the third decimal place. Modern calorimeters provide the temperature as a digital read out.

A known quantity of reacting substance is placed into the bomb and the bomb is sealed inside the calorimeter. A spark or electric current from a DC source supplies the activation energy to initiate the reaction. The maximum temperature of the system is recorded. As in the coffee cup or thermos calorimeter, it is assumed that no energy is lost or gained by the system apart from the energy produced or required by the reaction.

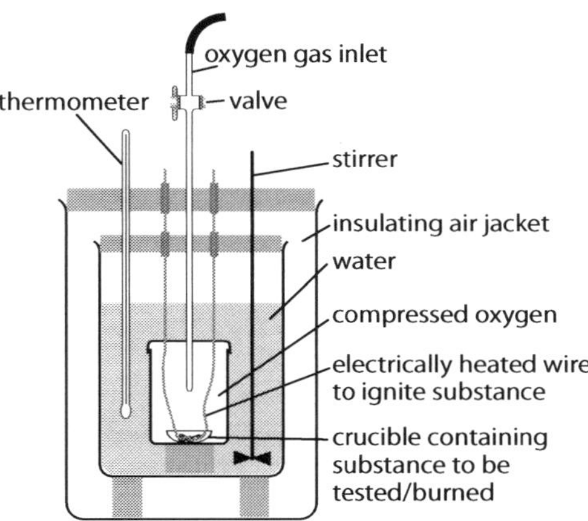

Figure 4.6.5 *A bomb calorimeter measures the heat released at constant volume, q_v or ΔE, which is extremely close to ΔH.*

Sometimes calculations involving bomb calorimeters require an overall *q* or Δ*H* value to be determined by calculating a value for the water inside the calorimeter *and* a value for the metal jacket using the specific heat capacities and the masses of each. These may be added together.

Other times, an overall *heat capacity* in units of J/°C may simply be used for the entire calorimeter and all of its components. Some references call this value a **calorimeter constant**. It indicates the number of joules the entire calorimeter must absorb or release in order to change its temperature by one Celsius (or one Kelvin since it is a *change*) degree.

Nutrition Facts

Serving Size 1 piece (219g)
Servings per container 6

Amount per serving	
Calories 520	Calories from Fat 240
	% Daily Value*
Total Fat 27g	41%
Saturated Fat 12g	61%
Cholesterol 255mg	86%
Sodium 1110mg	46%
Total Carbohydrates 29g	10%
Dietary Fiber 1g	5%
Sugars 1g	
Protein 39g	
Vitamin A 20% •	Vitamin C 4%
Calcium 15% •	Iron 25%

* Percent Daily Values are based on a 2,000 calorie diet. Your daily values may be higher or lower depending on your calorie needs:

	Calories	2,000	2,500
Total Fat	Less than	65g	80g
Saturated Fat	Less than	20g	25g
Cholesterol	Less than	300mg	300mg
Sodium	Less than	2,400mg	2,400mg
Total Carbohydrates		300g	375g
Dietary Fiber		25g	30g

Calories per gram:
Fat 9 • Carbohydrates 4 • Protein 4

Figure 4.6.6 *Nutrition Facts label for half a dozen "breakfast muffins" — not exactly a healthy way to start the day.*

Sample Problem — Calculating the Heat of a Combustion Reaction with a Bomb

Anthracene is a unique aromatic compound composed of three fused benzene rings. It is a component of coal tar and can be used to make several different anthroquinone dyes. A 5.12 g sample of anthracene, $C_{14}H_{10}$, was burned in an iron "bomb" having a mass of 1896 g. The bomb was immersed in 2.900 L of water inside a calorimeter. The initial temperature of all parts of the system was 20.80°C and the final temperature was 36.60°C. Calculate the molar heat of combustion of anthracene.

What To Think About	How To Do It
1. First find the heat absorbed by the calorimeter bomb *and* the water. Specific heat capacities of iron and water may be found in Table 4.6.1. Since water has a density of 1 g/mL, 2.900 L has a mass of 2.900 kg or 2900. g.	$q_{Fe\ Bomb} = mc_{Fe}\Delta T =$ 1896 g x $\frac{0.448\ J}{g°C}$ x (36.60°C – 20.80°C) = 13 421 J = 13.4 kJ
2. Assuming no heat loss to the surroundings, the total heat given off by the combustion must equal the sum of the heat absorbed by the water and the heat absorbed by the calorimeter jacket.	$q_{water} = mc_{water}\Delta T =$ 2900. g x $\frac{4.18\ J}{g°C}$ x (36.60°C – 20.80°C) = 191 528 J = 192 kJ
3. Since $q_{lost} = -q_{gained}$, a negative sign is required.	$q_{total} = q_{calorimeter} + q_{water}$
4. The molar heat of combustion is q/n as dictated by unit analysis.	$q_{gained\ by\ calorimeter\ +\ water} = 192 + 13.4 = 205$ kJ $q_{combustion} = q_{lost\ by\ reaction\ system} = -q_{gained}$
5. The negative value is consistent with a combustion reaction.	= –205 kJ $\frac{205\ kJ}{5.12\ g}$ x $\frac{178.0\ g}{1\ mol}$ = 7130 kJ/mol

Sample Problem — Using the Calorimeter Constant

The brand new treat Chemical Candies contains only 12.0 Calories per serving according to the Nutrition Facts label. The Chemical Candies are tested by placing one serving in a bomb calorimeter like the one in Figure 4.6.5 and burning them in $O_2(g)$. The temperature rises from 21.431°C to 27.079°C. The heat capacity of the calorimeter is 8.808 kJ/°C. What is the actual caloric content?

What To Think About	How To Do It
1. Determine the amount of energy required to increase the temperature of the calorimeter by the stated amount.	(27.079°C – 21.431°C) x $\frac{8.808\ kJ}{°C}$ = 49.75 kJ
2. Convert the energy unit from kJ to Calories where 1 Cal = 1 kcal = 4.184 kJ.	49.75 kJ x $\frac{1\ Cal}{4.184\ kJ}$ = 11.89 Cal

Practice Problems — Calculating the Heat of a Combustion Reaction

1. A 3.00 g chunk of coal, C(*s*), was burned entirely to produce $CO_2(g)$ in a copper bomb. The mass of the bomb was 2.000 kg and the mass of water in which the copper bomb was immersed was 2.778 kg. The initial temperature of the system was 21.00°C and the final temperature was 29.30°C. Calculate the heat of formation of $CO_2(g)$. See Table 4.6.1 for the specific heat capacity of copper.

2. Toluene, C_7H_8 may be tri-substituted with nitro groups, $-NO_2$, to form the explosive, trinitrotoluene or TNT. A 750.0 mg sample of toluene liquid was placed in a bomb calorimeter with excess oxygen. The heat capacity of the calorimeter was 22.53 kJ/°C. When the calorimeter was fired, the combustion of the toluene caused the temperature to increase from 23.002°C to 24.415°C. Calculate ΔH for the reaction:
$C_7H_8(l) + 9\ O_2(g) \rightarrow 7\ CO_2(g) + 4\ H_2O(l)$.

3. (a) A standard calibration reaction is used to determine the heat capacity, C, of a bomb calorimeter. The temperature increases 1.275°C because of the input of 14 580 J of energy. What is the heat capacity of the calorimeter?

   (b) Use the data in the table of heats of formation (Table 4.5.1) in section 4.5 to calculate the $\Delta H_{combustion}$ of methane, $CH_4(g)$.

   (c) A sample of 1.754 g of methane is combusted in the calorimeter calibrated in part (b). If the initial temperature of the calorimeter is 20.754°C, what final temperature should be attained?

Energy, Our Environment, and the Future

In the last three sections, we've examined the relationship between chemical reactions and energy changes. The majority of our examples have focused on the combustion of fossil fuels. Fossil fuels have many advantages as an energy source. They are convenient to use, are found in many countries in the world, and are reasonably portable to areas that need them. On the other hand, they are non-renewable and they produce pollution. Despite the problems associated with fossil fuels, we show little inclination to give them up or reduce their use any time soon.

World energy consumption by fuel

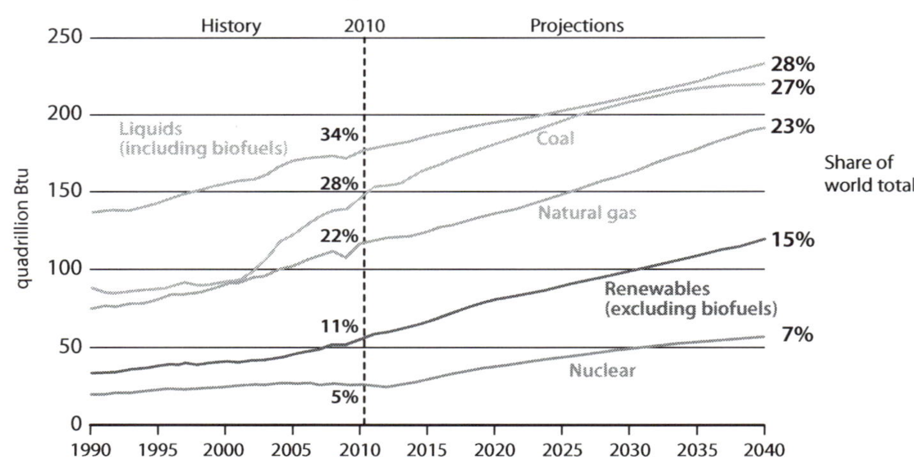

Figure 4.6.7 *Past and projected world energy consumption by fuel type*

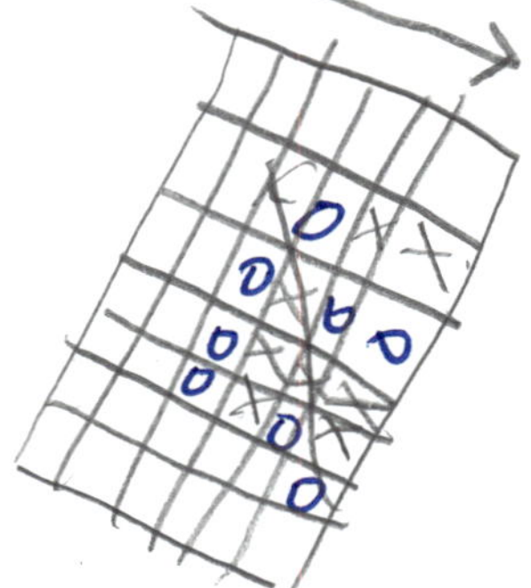

Nuclear energy has shown promise, but comes, of course, with many dangers of its own. The 2011 event in Fukushima, Japan, is only the most recent of several major nuclear accidents that have occurred in the past few decades (Figure 4.6.8). Even when nuclear reactors function successfully, there is still the problem of storage for radioactive by-products. The fallout from nuclear accidents can be long lasting and widespread.

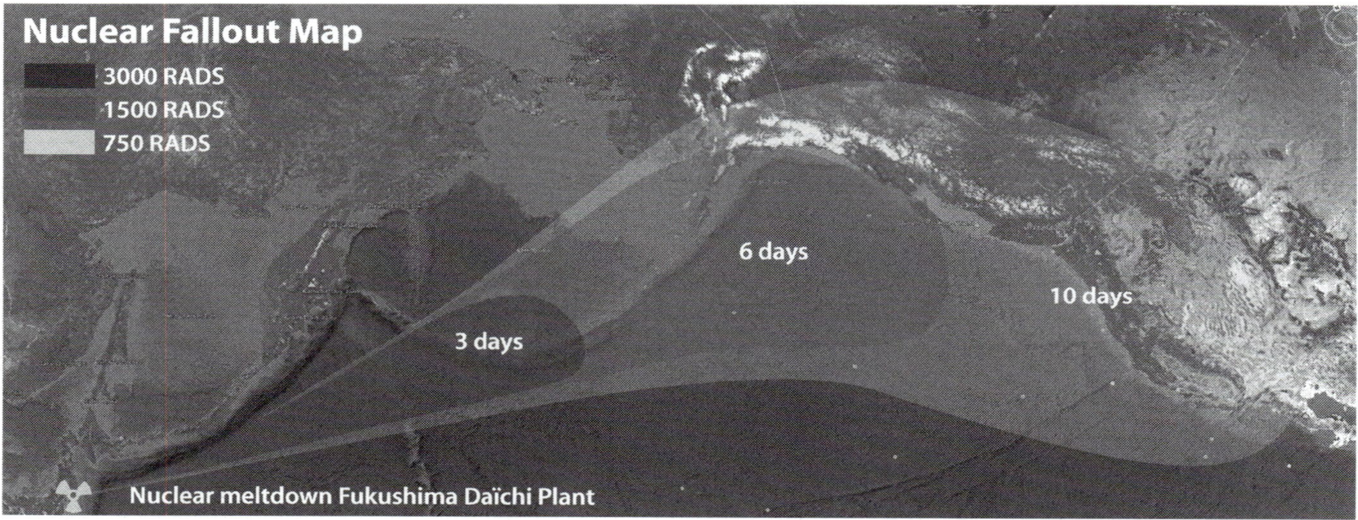

Figure 4.6.8 *Map of distribution of nuclear fallout from the Fukushima, Japan, reactor accident in March of 2011.*

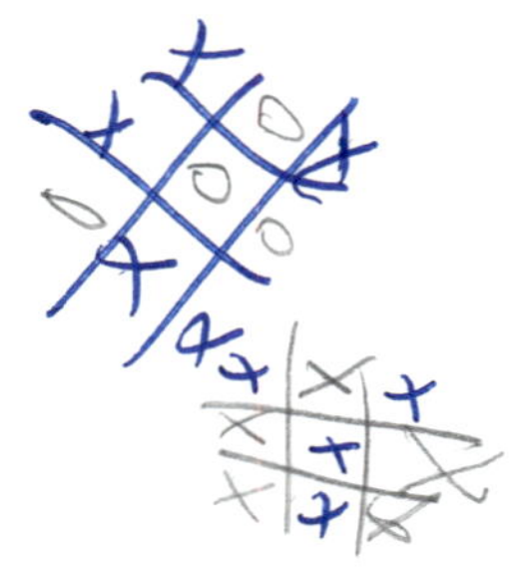

Renewable energy sources and biofuels show some of the best promise for the future. Wind power, hydro, and solar energy are some of the least polluting forms of energy production. In AP Chemistry II we will spend an entire chapter studying the application of electrochemical reactions to the production of energy in batteries and fuel cells.

As we move further into the 21st century the chemistry students of today may be responsible for changing the shape of the graph in Figure 4.6.7 completely. Maybe you will be responsible for some of the changes!

4.6 Review Questions

1. The diagram shows one mole each of the metals copper, iron, zinc, and aluminum. The quarter is included for size comparison only.

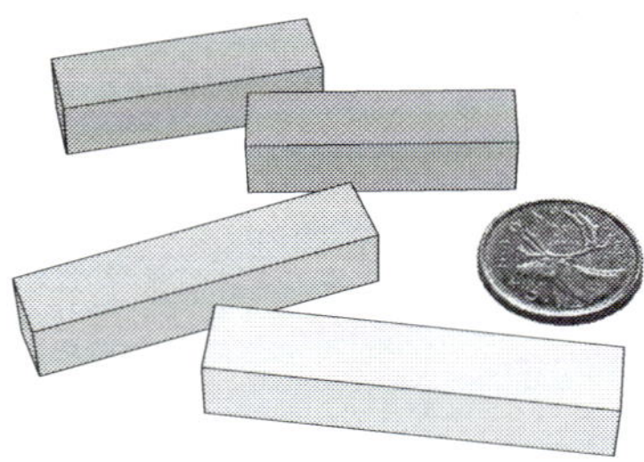

   (a) Use the pictures and a table of molar masses to rank the samples from heaviest to lightest.

   (b) Each bar is placed in boiling water for half an hour and then removed. Given the data in Table 4.6.1 and the heat capacity of zinc is 390. J/kg°C, rank the bars in order from most to least time required to cool to room temperature.

2. What mass of glass can be heated from room temperature (20.0°C) to 75.5°C if 1550 J of heat is added? See data in Table 4.6.1.

3. A restaurant worker places a 1 kg plastic jug full of water into the industrial fridge in the kitchen. At the same time, he places an empty 1 kg aluminum jug into the same fridge. One hour later one of the objects is much colder than the other. Which is colder and why?

4. In biology class, students sometimes hear of "high energy phosphate bonds." In general, how do phosphate bonds produce energy?

5. Copper can just be melted at the tip of the outer blue cone in a Bunsen burner flame where the temperature is 1085°C. How much energy is required to completely melt a 250.0 mg piece of copper wire? Assume the initial temperature of the wire was 22.5°C and the heat of fusion of copper is 205 J/g.

6. When combusted, 5.00 g of anthracite coal gives off 153 kJ of energy. What mass of coal is needed to heat a cauldron of 50.0 L water from 26.5°C until it just boils away, so that all the water vaporizes, but none of the steam is heated above 100.0°C?

7. Determine the final temperature when 145.0 g of ice at −17.5°C is placed into 335.0 g of water at 72.5°C in an insulated system. Assume everything is liquid water when the final temperature is reached.

8. A 45.05 g sample of a metal of unknown identity at 96.5°C is placed into 81.5 mL of water in an insulated container at a room temperature of 19.5°C. If the final temperature of the system is 34.5°C, what is the specific heat capacity of the metal? Use Table 4.6.1 to identify the metal.

9. A 45.0 g piece of silver metal at 15.5°C was placed into an insulated 0.345 g sample of steam at 106.0°C. The steam immediately condensed and coated the piece of silver metal with water. What is the final equilibrium temperature of the system?

10. (a) The following samples, both at 21.00°C, are mixed in a coffee cup calorimeter: 100.0 mL of 2.00 mol/L sodium hydroxide and 100.0 mL of 3.00 mol/L hydrochloric acid. After the reaction, the final solution's temperature rises to 34.40°C. Assuming no loss of heat to the surroundings and/or the calorimeter and a density and specific heat capacity for the final solution equal to those of water, calculate the molar enthalpy of neutralization for the reaction. (Hint: The acid and base are *not* in equimolar quantities.)

(b) Suppose the pr0cess in (a) were repeated with double the molarity of sodium hydroxide used.

(i) How would this affect the change in temperature (be specific)?

(ii) How would this affect the amount of heat, *q*, produced? Explain.

(iii) How would this affect the molar enthalpy of neutralization for the reaction? Explain your answer.

11. The enthalpy of dissolution of cesium hydroxide may be communicated as follows:
$CsOH(s) \rightarrow Cs^{+}(aq) + OH^{-}(aq)$ $\Delta H = -71.55$ kJ/mol. A 15.00 g sample of CsOH is dissolved in 110.0 g of water with both substances at 21.50°C. Calculate the final temperature of the solution, assuming the system is perfectly insulated and has a heat capacity equal to that of water.

12. A combustion experiment performed in a bomb calorimeter produced the following data:

heat capacity of bomb calorimeter = 9.35 kJ/°C
mass of methyl propane burned = 751 mg
initial temperature of calorimeter = 20.415°C
final temperature of calorimeter = 24.435°C

Calculate the molar enthalpy of combustion of methylpropane, which is used as lighter fluid.

13. Octane produces a tremendous amount of energy when combusted in gasoline. The following data were collected from a combustion experiment performed in a bomb calorimeter:

$\Delta H_{combustion} = -5074$ kJ/mol C_8H_{18}
heat capacity of bomb calorimeter = 10.45 kJ/°C
initial temperature of calorimeter = 21.002°C
final temperature of calorimeter = 27.014°C

Determine the mass of the sample of octane combusted in the calorimeter.

-5074 kJ/mol = m(g) · 10.45 kJ/°C · (27.014°C − 21.002°C)

-5074 kJ/mol / 62.8254 = m · 62.8254 / 62.8254

m = 80.76 g

14. (a) Use the data in the table of heats of formation (Table 4.5.1) in section 4.5 to calculate ΔH_{rxn} for the combustion of methanol, $CH_3OH(l)$.

$2CH_3OH + O_2 \rightarrow CO_2 + H_2O$

$3O_2 + 2CH_3OH \rightarrow 4H_2O + 2CO_2$

0   −238.6 · 2   −285.8 · 4   −393.5 · 2

−(−477.2) + (−1143.2 + −787) = −1453 / 2 = −726.5 kJ/mol

(b) A 525.0 mg sample of methanol was used to calibrate a calorimeter. Combustion of the sample caused the calorimeter's temperature to rise from 21.057°C to 22.425°C. What is the heat capacity of the calorimeter? (Express *C* in units of kJ/°C.)

15. (a) Before the production of unleaded gasoline, chloroethane, C_2H_5Cl, was used to produce tetraethyl lead to prevent the engine "knocking" caused by leaded gas. The reaction of ethylene, $C_2H_4(g)$, with hydrogen chloride, $HCl(g)$, produced a 12.045 g sample of chloroethane in the calorimeter mentioned in part (b) of this question. The temperature increased from 21.061°C to 22.619°C. Write a balanced chemical equation for the reaction described, including the heat term in $kJ/mol_{rxn.}$

(b) Use the data in Table 4.5.1 in section 4.5 to determine the value just calculated in part (c). Calculate the percent deviation between the experimentally determined value and the tabular one.

4.7 Calculating with Chemical Change — Stoichiometry

Warm Up

1. Write a balanced equation for the reaction between chromium metal and hydrochloric acid to form chromium(III) chloride and a reactive gas.

2. If 2 mol of chromium metal completely reacted in an excess quantity of hydrochloric acid, how many moles of hydrogen gas would be formed?

3. How many moles of hydrogen gas would form if 4 mol of chromium metal were completely reacted in excess hydrochloric acid?

Moles to Moles — Application of the Mole Ratio

In chapter 3 on the mole, stoichiometry was introduced through the quantitative relationships between the elements in a chemical compound. It is far more common to use stoichiometry to study the relationships between the various elements and compounds involved in chemical reactions. The key to doing stoichiometric calculations is an understanding of the information provided by a balanced chemical equation.

A balanced chemical equation indicates the relative amounts of the chemicals involved in the reaction. (Recall that the SI unit for amount is the mole.)

Thus for any chemical reaction, the balanced equation may be used to convert moles of reactants to moles of products or vice versa. It may also be used to convert moles of one reactant into another or of one product into another. The key to these conversions is always the *mole ratio*, which is determined from the coefficients in the balanced equation. You may find it helpful to review two-wheel conversions introduced in chapter 3 and shown in Figure 4.7.1 below.

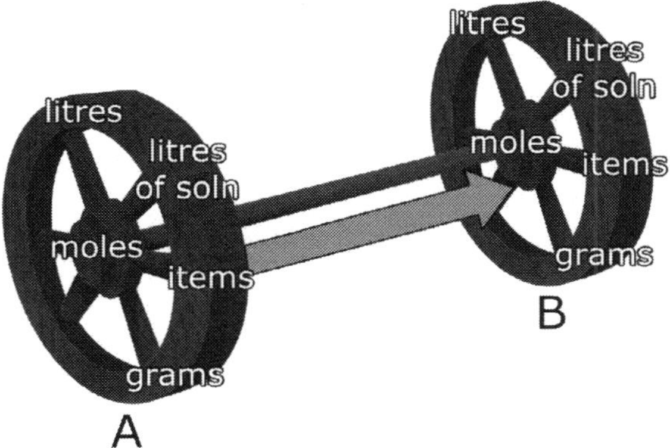

Figure 4.7.1 *The mole ratio is represented by a move across the axle in our wheel model.*

Sample Problem — Moles of One Species ←→ Moles of Another Species

A student places 7.50 mol of chromium metal in an excess of concentrated hydrochloric acid.
How many moles of hydrogen gas are formed?

What to Think about	How to Do It
1. This single replacement reaction will form the most common chloride of chromium, chromium(III). Determine the balanced chemical equation.	$2\,Cr(s) + 6\,HCl(aq) \rightarrow 2\,CrCl_3(aq) + 3\,H_2(g)$
2. As is usual with conversion factors, begin with the end in mind. You are attempting to determine the moles of hydrogen gas. As you are provided with moles of chromium metal, you must begin with this and set up a conversion factor to convert this value into moles of hydrogen gas. As the mole ratio involves whole counting numbers, the significant figures in the answer are *only determined* by the *measured value given in the question.*	$7.50\ \cancel{mol\ Cr} \times \frac{\_\_\_\ mol\ H_2(g)}{\_\_\_\ \cancel{mol\ Cr}} = \_\_\_\ mol\ H_2(g)$ $7.50\ \cancel{mol\ Cr} \times \frac{3\ mol\ H_2(g)}{2\ \cancel{mol\ Cr}} = \_\_\_\ mol\ H_2(g)$ $7.50\ \cancel{mol\ Cr} \times \frac{3\ mol\ H_2(g)}{2\ \cancel{mol\ Cr}} = 11.3\ mol\ H_2(g)$
3. Notice that as long as there is enough HCl to react with all the Cr, we don't need to concern ourselves with the HCl.	

Conversion from one species to another in a chemical reactions is accomplished by using the *mole ratio* between two species in a balanced chemical equation.

Practice Problems — Moles of One Species ←→ Moles of Another Species

Calculate the moles of the requested species given the following information. Be sure to begin with a balanced chemical equation.

1. How many moles of ammonia ($NH_3(g)$) would be formed by the combination of 15.75 mol of nitrogen gas ($N_2(g)$) with a large excess of hydrogen gas ($H_2(g)$)?

2. How many moles of water must be decomposed to form 9.45×10^{-5} mol of $O_2(g)$?

3. How many moles of calcium metal would be required to replace 1.86 mol of silver from a solution of silver nitrate?

Mass to Mass — The Molar Mass Revisited

In chapter 3, we learned to use the molar mass to convert the mass of a chemical substance to moles. We can now use the mole ratio to take such a conversion one step further. The mole ratio will allow us to convert the moles of one substance in a chemical reaction into moles of another substance. If we wish, we can then convert the moles of the new substance into its mass using an appropriate molar mass. This three-step process was introduced in chapter 3 and is shown again in Figure 4.7.2 below.

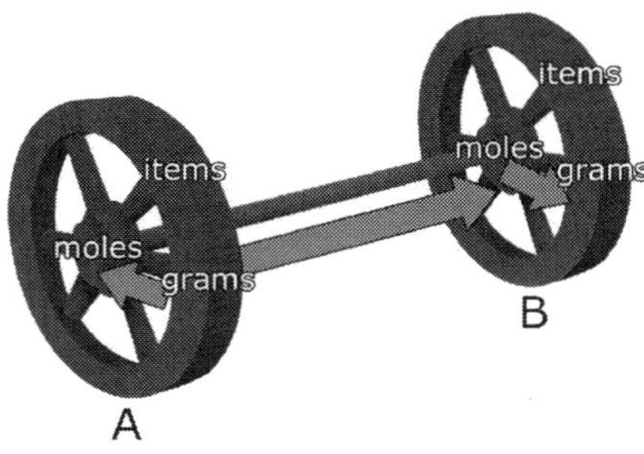

Figure 4.7.2 *Steps for converting mass of substance A to mass of substance B*

Sample Calculation: Mass of One Species ←→ Mass of Another Species

3.50 g of silver nitrate are stirred into a solution containing excess calcium chloride. How many grams of precipitate are formed?

What to think about	How to Do It
1. Write a balanced equation. The reaction is a double replacement. Nitrate compounds are always soluble hence the precipitate must be the silver chloride.	$2\ AgNO_3(aq) + CaCl_2(aq) \rightarrow 2\ AgCl(s) + Ca(NO_3)_2(aq)$
2. Begin with the given 3.50 g of $AgNO_3$. Align the conversion factors to convert • mass $AgNO_3$ to moles $AgNO_3$ • moles $AgNO_3$ to moles AgCl • moles AgCl to mass AgCl Be sure to include the formula as part of the unit.	$3.50\ g\ AgNO_3 \times \frac{mol\ AgNO_3}{\_\_\_\ g\ AgNO_3} \times \frac{mol\ AgCl}{\_\_\_\ mol\ AgNO_3} \times \frac{g\ AgCl}{\_\_\_\ mol\ AgCl} = \_\_\_\ g\ AgCl$
3. Insert the appropriate molar masses for *1 mol* of the appropriate species and the mole ratio (from the balanced chemical equation). 4. Notice the molar masses are given to one decimal place. The mole ratio is *not reduced*. Be sure to express the answer to the correct number of significant figures. Consider the mass of reactant used and the mole ratio, then ask yourself, does the answer seem reasonable?	$3.50\ g\ \cancel{AgNO_3} \times \frac{1\ \cancel{mol\ AgNO_3}}{169.9\ g\ \cancel{AgNO_3}} \times \frac{2\ \cancel{mol\ AgCl}}{2\ \cancel{mol\ AgNO_3}} \times \frac{143.4\ g\ AgCl}{1\ \cancel{mol\ AgCl}} = 2.95\ g\ AgCl$

Practice Problems — Mass of One Species ←→ Mass of Another Species

Show all work for each of the following questions. Begin with a balanced chemical equation if one is not provided. Be sure to include the formulas as part of your units in each step. Give your final answer with the correct number of significant figures.

1. The following reaction is exceptional in that a single reactant species is both oxidized and reduced:
   $2\ KClO_3(s) \rightarrow 2\ KCl(s) + 3\ O_2(g)$.
   What mass of oxygen gas would be formed by the decomposition of 45.65 g of $KClO_3$? (How should your answer compare to the mass of reactant? Does your answer make sense?)

2. This *unbalanced* equation shows one possible set of products for the reaction of aluminum and nitric acid:
   $Al(s) + HNO_3(aq) \rightarrow Al(NO_3)_3(aq) + H_2(g)$.
   Use the balanced version of this equation to determine the mass of nitric acid required to form 170 kg of hydrogen gas.

3. Hydrogen gas can be used as a reducing agent in the production of pure boron from boron trichloride. How many moles of boron would form from the reduction of 500.0 g of boron trichloride with excess hydrogen gas?

   Equation:

4. Write a balanced chemical equation for the reaction between sodium metal and water.
   How many moles of hydrogen gas would form if 2 mol of sodium reacted with excess water? What volume would this gas occupy at STP conditions?

Gases — Converting Volume to Volume

The volume-to-volume conversion is a special case that allows us to take a short cut. This is courtesy of Amedeo Avogadro, a skilled scientist who earned his bachelor's degree by the age of 16 and had a PhD at only 20 years old. Avogadro's work eventually led him to publish his hypothesis in 1811. This hypothesis states that equal volumes of gases contain equal numbers of particles under the same conditions of temperature and pressure. If this is true, it follows that equal volumes of gases contain equal numbers of moles under the same conditions.

Volumes of gases react in the *same* proportion as *moles* of gases.

Consider the equation representing the very exothermic combustion of propane gas, as shown in Figure 4.7.3.

reactants	→	products
$C_3H_8(g) + 5\ O_2(g)$	→	$3\ CO_2(g) + 4\ H_2O(g)$
1 molecule C_3H_8 + 5 molecules O_2	→	3 molecules CO_2 + 4 molecules H_2O

Figure 4.7.3 *Propane combustion*

Since molecular ratios are the same as mole ratios:

1 mol	5 mol	3 mol	4 mol

Assuming STP conditions:

22.4 L	112 L	67.2 L	not a gas at STP

Dividing through by 22.4 L gives the following volume ratios:

1 L	5 L	3 L

Notice that for calculations involving two or more gases, the mole ratio may actually be replaced by a volume ratio. This shortcut may be used only for litre-to-litre conversions as Avogadro's hypothesis is only applicable to gases.

Quick Check

Use the balanced equation in Figure 4.5.3 to determine how many litres of carbon dioxide would form from the combustion of 10 L of propane gas.

Sample Problem — Calculations Involving Gas Volume

1. How many litres of ammonia are produced when an excess of nitrogen reacts with 15 L of hydrogen gas at STP?
2. What mass of nitrogen gas is required to produce 45 L of ammonia at STP?

What to T hink about

Question 1

1. Write a balanced equation.
2. Because the first example only involves volumes, use the short cut.
   Be sure to include the formulas as part of the units.
3. Begin with the provided 15 L and insert the mole ratio as a volume ratio.
4. A quick review of the mole ratios in the balanced equation verifies that the answer makes sense.

Question 1

1. Because the second example involves both volumes and masses, do not use the shortcut.
   Again, include the formulas as part of the units.
2. As usual, begin with the given value: 45 L. Align the factors to convert volume to moles, then use the mole ratio and finish by converting to mass.
   - The first conversion factor is 1 mol/22.4 L as this is the molar volume at STP.
   - The mole ratio comes from the balanced equation.
   - The final conversion factor is the molar mass of nitrogen. Notice that nitrogen is a diatomic gas.
3. Insert appropriate numerical values and calculate an answer.
   The initial volume is very close to 2 mol at STP.
   The mole ratio predicts half that amount, or 1 mol, of nitrogen. 1 mol of diatomic nitrogen is 28.0 g.
4. Does the answer make sense?

How to Do It

$$3\,H_2(g) + N_2(g) \rightarrow 2\,NH_3(g)$$

$$15\text{ L }H_2 \times \frac{\_\_\_\_\text{ L }NH_3}{\_\_\_\_\text{ L }H_2} = \_\_\_\_\text{ L }NH_3$$

$$15\text{ L }H_2 \times \frac{2\text{ L }NH_3}{3\text{ L }H_2} = 10\text{ L }NH_3$$

$$45\text{ L }NH_3 \times \frac{\_\_\_\_\text{ mol }NH_3}{\_\_\_\_\text{ L }NH_3} \times \frac{\_\_\_\_\text{ mol }N_2}{\_\_\_\_\text{ mol }NH_3} \times \frac{\_\_\_\_\text{ g }N_2}{\_\_\_\_\text{ mol }N_2} = \_\_\_\_\text{ g }N_2$$

$$45\text{ L }NH_3 \times \frac{1\text{ mol }NH_3}{22.4\text{ L }NH_3} \times \frac{1\text{ mol }N_2}{2\text{ mol }NH_3} \times \frac{28.0\text{ g }N_2}{1\text{ mol }N_2} = 28.0\text{ g }N_2$$

Practice Problems — Calculations Involving Gas Volume

Show all work for each of the following questions. Begin with a balanced chemical equation if one is not provided. Be sure to include the formulas as part of your units in each step. Give your final answer with the correct number of significant figures.

1. The reaction, $2\ SO_2(g) + O_2(g) \rightarrow 2\ SO_3(g)$, occurs in the atmosphere when oxygen oxidizes the pollutant factory exhaust, sulphur dioxide. What volume of oxygen is required to oxidize the 2.41×10^7 L of sulphur dioxide released annually by a coal-based power plant at STP?

2. Consider the *unbalanced equation:* $NaOH(aq) + (NH_4)_2SO_4(aq) \rightarrow Na_2SO_4(aq) + H_2O(l) + NH_3(g)$. How many litres of ammonia, measured at STP, are formed by combining a solution containing 40.5 g of ammonium sulphate with a solution containing excess sodium hydroxide at STP?

3. What mass of HCl must be contained in a solution added to an excess of zinc arsenide to obtain 17.5 L of arsine (AsH_3) gas at STP?

   Equation:

Solutions — Using Molarity in Volume Conversions

One of the best ways to make two chemicals react with one another, particularly ionic compounds, is to dissolve each of them in a suitable solvent and mix the resulting solutions. The conversion factor that is specific to the stoichiometry of reactions in solution is the one that equates the amount of solute in a solution to its volume. This is the molarity. In section 3.6, you learned to calculate molarity and use it to convert between the volume of a solution and the amount of dissolved solute (moles) in that solution. Molarity can be used in combination with a mole ratio and an additional factor involving moles to perform a variety of stoichiometric conversions involving solutions.

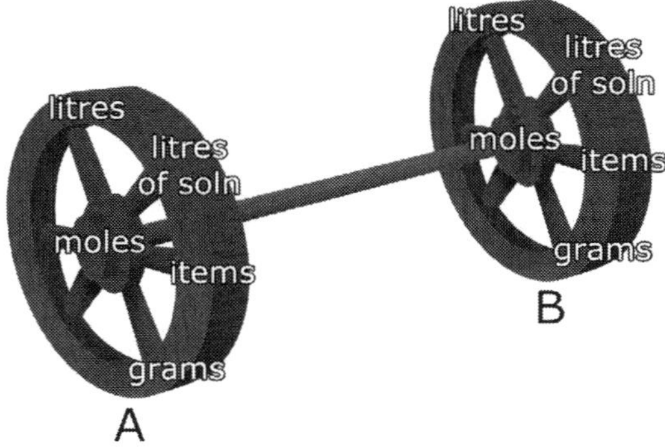

Figure 4.7.4 *This diagram illustrates the application of molar mass, molar volume, molarity, and even Avogadro's number in a variety of stoichiometric calculations.*

Quick Check

1. What is the concentration of a solution made by dissolving 117 g of sodium chloride in water to make a total volume of 1.5 L?

2. Use the molarity of the solution from question 1 to determine the mass of NaCl in 250 mL.

3. What volume of a solution of this same molarity would contain 39.0 g of sodium chloride?

Sample Problem — Calculations Involving Solution Volumes

What mass of nickel wire reacts with all the silver nitrate in 1.25 L of a 0.15 mol/L solution?

What to Think about	How to Do It
1. Write a balanced equation.	$Ni(s) + 2\,AgNO_3(aq) \rightarrow Ni(NO_3)_2(aq) + 2\,Ag(s)$
2. Begin with the end in mind. • As the answer to the problem will be in grams, a single unit, we should start the calculation with 1.25 L, also a single unit. • Remember the problem does *not* involve gas so 22.4 L/mol is not appropriate. In this case, we are dealing with 0.15 mol/1 L. • The molarity, derived from two units, will be used second, as the first *conversion factor*. • As litres will be cancelled, the molarity unit is not inverted. This is followed by the mole ratio and the molar mass.	$1.25\text{ L} \times \frac{\_\_\_\text{ mol } AgNO_3}{\_\_\_\text{ L}} \times \frac{\_\_\_\text{ mol Ni}}{\_\_\_\text{ mol } AgNO_3} \times \frac{\_\_\_\text{ g Ni}}{\_\_\_\text{ mol Ni}} = \_\_\_\text{ g Ni}$
3. Insert appropriate numerical values and calculate an answer. Notice this series converts • volume $AgNO_3$ to moles $AgNO_3$ • moles $AgNO_3$ to moles Ni • moles Ni to mass Ni As the molarity is a measured value, it limits the answer to two significant figures. The answer appears to be reasonable.	$1.25\,\cancel{\text{L}} \times \frac{0.15\,\cancel{\text{mol } AgNO_3}}{1\,\cancel{\text{L}}} \times \frac{1\,\cancel{\text{mol Ni}}}{2\,\cancel{\text{mol } AgNO_3}} \times \frac{58.7\text{ g Ni}}{1\,\cancel{\text{mol Ni}}} = 5.5\text{ g Ni}$

Practice Problems — Calculations Involving Solution Volumes

Show all work for each of the following questions. Begin with a balanced chemical equation if one is not provided. Be sure to include the formulas as part of your units in each step. Give your final answer with the correct number of significant figures.

1. The exothermic reaction $2\ K(s) + 2\ H_2O(l) \rightarrow 2\ KOH(aq) + H_2(g)$ often releases enough heat to ignite the hydrogen gas it produces. What mass of potassium metal would be required to produce 250 mL of a 0.45 mol/L solution of potassium hydroxide?

2. What volume of 0.80 mol/L sodium iodide solution would completely react with 2.4×10^{24} molecules of chlorine gas?

   Equation:

3. How many litres of carbon dioxide gas would be formed at STP if 1.5 L of 1.75 M phosphoric acid were reacted with excess potassium carbonate solution? Be cautious, as this question requires the use of both molar volume and molarity as conversion factors.

   Equation:

4.7 Activity: Stoichiometric Relationships of Hydrochloric Acid

Question

How can you measure the products of a reaction?

Background

Hydrochloric acid is the most commonly used acid in secondary school chemistry. It can be reacted with a variety of substances in several different types of chemical reactions. The products of such reactions may be separated and measured to study stoichiometric relationships in a variety of ways.

Procedure

1. Use the theoretical information provided in the "Background" above to design two different experiments to isolate and measure a product of two different reactions, each consuming 750 mL of 1.0 M HCl. You must use a single and a double replacement reaction.
   - Describe each design in point-form.
   - Provide a labelled diagram of each design.
2. Compare your designs with those of a classmate. Use your comparison to improve your designs.

Results and Discussion

1. Write a balanced chemical equation for each reaction you selected.

2. Calculate the quantity of product you would expect to measure in each experiment.

3. Exchange your answers to questions 1 and 2 with the same classmate with whom you compared experimental designs. Beginning with the classmate's answers to question 2, calculate the volume of 1.0 mol/L HCl required to form the quantity of product he or she determined for each experiment. Your classmate should perform the same calculations with your question 2 answers.

4. What answer should all students get for question 3?

4.7 Review Questions

1. Malachite is a beautiful green mineral often sculpted into jewellery. It decomposes as follows:

   $Cu(OH)_2 \cdot CuCO_3(s) \rightarrow 2\ CuO(s) + CO_2(g) + H_2O(l)$

   (a) How many moles of CuO are formed from the decomposition of 1.26 mol of malachite?

   (b) If a 1.5 kg piece of malachite is completely decomposed, how many grams of copper(II) oxide are formed?

   (c) If 706 g of copper(II) oxide are formed from the decomposition of a piece of malachite, how many litres of carbon dioxide gas would form at STP?

2. Nitromethane, a fuel occasionally used in drag racers, burns according to the reaction:

   $4\ CH_3NO_2(l) + 3\ O_2(g) \rightarrow 4\ CO_2(g) + 6\ H_2O(g) + 2\ N_2(g)$

   (a) What is the volume of nitrogen gas produced at STP if 3160 g of CH_3NO_2 is burned?

   (b) What is the mass of nitromethane burned if 955 g of nitrogen gas are produced in the exhaust of the drag racer?

   (c) What mass of water vapour is produced in the exhaust along with 3.5×10^{25} molecules of nitrogen gas?

3. What mass of zinc would completely react with 10.0 mL of 0.45 M hydrochloric acid solution?

   $Zn(s) + 2\ HCl(aq) \rightarrow ZnCl_2(aq) + H_2(g)$

4. How much energy will be required to complete the reaction of 12.2 g of sodium to produce sodium oxide?

   $4\ Na(s) + O_2(g) + 124.7\ kJ \rightarrow 2\ Na_2O(s)$

5. Potassium permanganate reacts with oxalic acid in aqueous sulphuric acid according to the equation:

   $2\ KMnO_4 + 5\ H_2C_2O_4 + 3\ H_2SO_4 \rightarrow 2\ MnSO_4 + 10\ CO_2 + 8\ H_2O + K_2SO_4$

   How many millilitres of a 0.250 M $KMnO_4$ solution are needed to react with 3.225 g of oxalic acid?

Begin the following calculations with a balanced equation.

6. The reaction of scrap aluminum with chlorine gas forms aluminum chloride. What mass of chlorine in the presence of excess aluminum is required to make 4.56 kg of aluminum chloride?

7. How many moles of sulphuric acid could neutralize 0.034 mol of potassium hydroxide solution?

8. What mass of water vapour would be formed from the complete combustion of 35.00 g of ethanol ($C_2H_5OH(l)$)?

9. Dihydrogen monosulphide gas may be prepared in a laboratory by the action of hydrochloric acid on iron(II) sulphide. How many grams of iron(II) sulphide would be needed to prepare 21.7 L of the gas at STP?

10. Carbon dioxide gas is produced in the reaction between calcium carbonate and hydrochloric acid. If 15.0 g of calcium carbonate reacted with an excess of hydrochloric acid, how many grams of carbon dioxide gas would be produced?

11. The Haber process for making ammonia gas from its elements was developed by Fritz Haber during World War I. Haber hoped to use the ammonia as fertilizer to grow food for Germany during the Allies' blockade. How many litres of hydrogen would be required to produce 40.0 L of ammonia at STP?

12. $PbI_2(s) \rightarrow Pb^{2+}(aq) + 2\,I^-(aq) \qquad \Delta H = 46.5$ kJ/mol
    How much energy would be required to dissolve 5.00 g of lead (II) iodide?

13. A piece of zinc metal was dropped into a solution of tin(IV) nitrate. If 27.5 g of tin metal was displaced, how many grams of reducing agent were used?

14. Solutions of barium nitrate and potassium sulfate were poured together. If this reaction required 6.5 mol of barium nitrate, how many grams of precipitate were formed?

15. Calcium carbonate (marble chips) is dissolved by hydrochloric acid. If 12.2 L of carbon dioxide gas forms at STP, what mass of marble chips was used?

16. When dinitrogen tetroxide decomposes into nitrogen dioxide, 56 kJ of energy is required for each mole of reactant decomposed. How much heat is absorbed if 1.25 g of product is formed?

17. A flask containing 450 mL of 0.500 M HBr was accidentally knocked to the floor. How many grams of K_2CO_3 would you need to put on the spill to completely neutralize the acid?

18. The acetic acid in a 2.5 mol/L sample of a solution of a kettle scale remover is reacted with an excess of a lead(II) nitrate solution to form a precipitate, which is then filtered and dried. The mass of the precipitate is 8.64 g. What volume of the solution was required to produce that mass?

19. How many milliliters of a 0.610 M NaOH solution are needed to completely neutralize 25.0 mL of a 0.356 M phosphoric acid solution?

20. What volume of hydrogen gas is formed at STP by the reaction of excess zinc metal with 150 mL of 0.185 mol/L hydroiodic acid?

4.8 Stoichiometry in the Real World — Excess/Limiting Amounts, Percentage Yield, and Impurities

Warm Up

Suppose you are working in an ice cream shop. A group of customers come in and they would like to order ice cream sundaes. The shop's computer page reads as follows for ice cream sundaes:

Sundae Ingredients in Stock	Number of Items	Sundae Recipe
Scoops vanilla ice cream	six scoops	one scoop vanilla ice cream
Chocolate syrup	200 mL	50 ml chocolate syrup
Super sweet red cherries	475 cherries	one cherry on top
		(Do NOT change the recipe)

1. What is the maximum number of sundaes you can make for customers?
2. What item *limits* the number of sundaes you can make?
3. How much of each of the *excess* items will still be left as sundae stock?

Excess and Limiting — Another Issue to Consider

So far, we have made several assumptions about the chemical reactions we've been studying. Given a balanced chemical equation and the quantity of one of the reactants, we've assumed:

- The reactant provided is completely pure.
- The reactant will be totally consumed in the reaction as the reaction proceeds entirely to completion.
- No alternate or side reactions will occur.
- All reactants are consumed completely in **stoichiometric quantities**, that is, in a molar ratio identical to that predicted by the balanced equation.

For example, consider the reaction between carbon monoxide and oxygen gas. Any of the following ratios may be indicated by the balanced chemical equation.

$2\,CO(g)$	+	$O_2(g)$	→	$2\,CO_2(g)$
2 molecules	:	1 molecule	:	2 molecules
2 mol	:	1 mol	:	2 mol
2 L	:	1 L	:	2 L
2(28.0 g) = 56.0g	:	32.0 g	:	2(44.0 g) = 88.0 g

Stoichiometric quantities would be present if the amounts or volumes of $CO:O_2$ reduced to 2:1. Notice the total mass of reactants consumed exactly equals the total mass of products formed. In the real world, however, this is rarely the case. It is more likely that the number of reactant particles will not be present in stoichiometric quantities. Rather one or the other reactant is likely to be **in excess**. That is, there will be more than enough of one reactant to completely react with the other.

Quick Check

Consider the following situation:

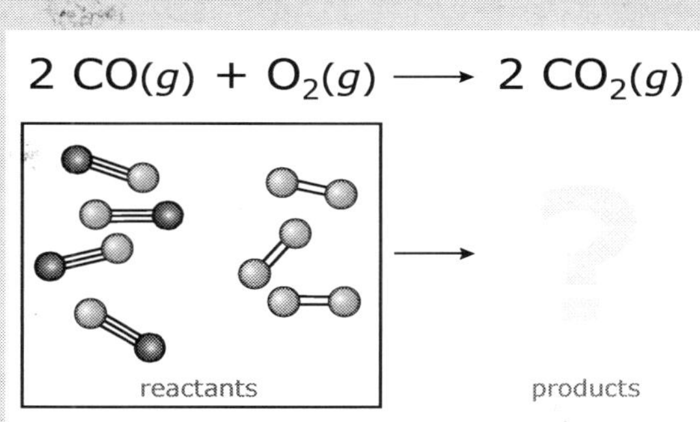

1. Which of the reactants is in excess?

2. Sketch any remaining reactants and products to show what will be present once the reaction is complete.

3. How many CO_2 particles are formed?

4. How many excess reactant particles remain?

The reactant that is totally consumed when a reaction is completed is called the **limiting reactant** (or **reagent**). This species limits the amount of product that can be formed. The reactant that remains once the limiting reactant is completely consumed is called the **excess reactant** (or **reagent**).

In section 4.7, you were always told which reactant species was in excess. In limiting and excess problems, you will be given the mass of all of the reactant species and you must determine which of these are in excess and, more importantly, which species limits the amount of product that can form. You may also have to determine how much of the excess species remains once the reaction is complete.

Sample Problem — Limiting and Excess Stoichiometry

What volume of hydrogen gas, measured at STP, is produced when 8.0 g of lithium metal is reacted with 10.0 g of water? What mass of the excess reactant remains once the reaction is completed?

What to Think about	How to Do It
1. As with any stoichiometry problem, begin by determining the balanced equation.	$2\,Li(s) + 2\,H_2O(l) \rightarrow 2\,LiOH(aq) + H_2(g)$
2. This is a single replacement reaction. Thinking of water as HOH, we replace the hydrogen with lithium and form a base.	
3. As the mole ratio of reactants is 2:2 (which reduces to 1:1), it is easy to simply compare the moles of Li:H_2O available.	
4. Begin the stoichiometric portion of the problem by determining which reactant is in excess (and which one limits the quantity of product that can be formed). In some cases, it may only be necessary to determine the moles of each reactant and compare.	$8.0\ \text{g Li} \times \frac{1\ \text{mol Li}}{6.9\ \text{g Li}} = 1.2\ \text{mol Li}$ $10.0\ \text{g } H_2O \times \frac{1\ \text{mol } H_2O}{18.0\ \text{g } H_2O} = 0.556\ \text{mol } H_2O$

Continued

Sample Problem — *Continued*

What to Think about

5. There are more than twice as many moles of lithium as there are of water. The equation shows that 1.2 mol of Li would require 1.2 mol of H_2O to completely react. Clearly there is insufficient H_2O to use up all the Li.
6. Frequently the reactants do not react in a 1:1 ratio hence each reactant must be converted completely to one product. The reactant that forms the greater quantity of product is in excess. The smaller amount of product will be the correct answer.
   Both methods (comparing moles of reactants *and* comparing the quantity of product) indicate the same species is limiting.
7. To determine the amount of excess reactant left, begin by determining the amount of excess reactant consumed.
   - Begin this calculation with the limiting reagent.
   - Apply stoichiometry to the limiting reagent to determine the amount consumed.
   - Subtract the amount used from the amount of excess present to start.
   - Notice significant figures are determined by place value as subtraction is employed in the last step.
   - Do not use the product to determine the amount consumed, as it is itself a calculated value and thus subject to error.

How to Do It

Lithium is in excess. Water is limiting.

$$8.0\ \text{g Li} \times \frac{1\ \text{mol Li}}{6.9\ \text{g Li}} \times \frac{1\ \text{mol}\ H_2}{2\ \text{mol Li}} \times \frac{22.4\ \text{L}\ H_2}{1\ \text{mol}\ H_2} = 13\ \text{L}\ H_2\ \text{gas}$$

$$10.0\ \text{g}\ H_2O \times \frac{1\ \text{mol}\ H_2O}{18.0\ \text{g}\ H_2O} \times \frac{1\ \text{mol}\ H_2}{2\ \text{mol}\ H_2O} \times \frac{22.4\ \text{L}\ H_2}{1\ \text{mol}\ H_2} = 6.22\ \text{L}\ H_2\ \text{gas}$$

The limiting reagent is the water. The lithium is in excess.
The correct amount of product is 6.22 L.

$$10.0\ \text{g}\ H_2O \times \frac{1\ \text{mol}\ H_2O}{18.0\ \text{g}\ H_2O} \times \frac{2\ \text{mol Li}}{2\ \text{mol}\ H_2O} \times \frac{6.9\ \text{g Li}}{1\ \text{mol Li}} = 3.83\ \text{g Li used up}$$

Remaining excess lithium = 8.0 – 3.83
= 4.2 g

Practice Problems — Limiting and Excess Stoichiometry

1. 25.0 g each of zinc metal and HCl dissolved in aqueous solution are reacted together. What volume of hydrogen gas, measured at STP, is formed and what mass of excess reactant is left over?

2. An acid spill containing 12.0 g of pure sulphuric acid is neutralized by 80.0 g of sodium bicarbonate (baking soda). What volume of water is formed? What mass of excess reactant is left over? (Reminder: density of water = 1.00 g/mL)

Continued

Practice Problems — *Continued*

3. When ammonia is passed over hot calcium, calcium hydride and nitrogen gas are formed. What mass of calcium hydride results when 20.0 L of ammonia measured at STP and 150 g of calcium are reacted? What quantity of excess reactant remains?

Percentage Purity — Impure Reactants

Throughout chapter 4, we've treated all of the chemicals involved in stoichiometric calculations as if they were completely pure. In reality, it is virtually impossible to obtain a chemical in a pure form. Even the purest chemicals purchased from chemical supply companies contain impurities. The purity of a chemical is commonly indicated as the percentage purity.

$$\textbf{Percentage purity} \text{ (by mass)} = \frac{\text{mass of pure chemical}}{\text{mass of impure sample}} \times 100\%$$

There are several types of stoichiometric calculations involving impurities. The most common begin with an impure reactant. The more difficult type gives a quantity of product and requires the use of this value to determine the percentage purity of a reactant.

Quick Check

1. Determine the percentage purity of the following:
   (a) A 4.5 g piece of calcium contains only 3.8 g of pure calcium metal.

   (b) Pure phosphorus makes up 17.5 g of a sample of white phosphorus weighing 20.0 g.

2. What mass of pure potassium is contained in a 0.90 g piece of 90.0% pure potassium?

Sample Problems — Percentage Purity

1. What mass of sodium hydride can be formed from the combination of 15.0 g of 80.0% pure sodium with excess hydrogen gas?
2. What is the percentage purity of a 7.5 g sample of sodium metal that formed 7.0 g of sodium hydride when reacted with an excess of hydrogen gas?

What to Think about	How to Do It
Question 1	
1. As with any stoichiometry problem, begin by determining the balanced equation. There are two elements forming one product so this is a synthesis reaction. Remember that hydrogen is a diatomic element.	$2\,Na(s) + H_2(g) \rightarrow 2\,NaH(s)$
2. Before beginning the stoichiometric portion of the problem, determine the mass of *pure* sodium available to react.	$15.0\text{ g Na} \times \frac{80}{100} = 12.0\text{ g pure Na}$
3. Now simply perform the stoichiometric conversions in the usual way. Note that the entire calculation may be done in one combined line of conversions. All measured values (including the percentage) indicate an answer with three significant figures.	Therefore $12.0\text{ g Na} \times \frac{1\text{ mol Na}}{23.0\text{ g Na}} \times \frac{2\text{ mol NaH}}{2\text{ mol Na}} \times \frac{24\text{ g NaH}}{1\text{ mol NaH}}$ or... $15.0\text{ g impure Na} \times \frac{80.0\text{ g pure Na}}{100\text{ g impure Na}} \times \frac{1\text{ mol Na}}{23.0\text{ g Na}} \times \frac{2\text{ mol NaH}}{2\text{ mol Na}} \times \frac{24\text{ g NaH}}{1\text{ mol NaH}} = 12.5\text{ g NaH}$
Question 2	
1. Fortunately, the balanced equation for the second problem is the same one.	$2\,Na(s) + H_2(g) \rightarrow 2\,NaH(s)$
2. Determining the percentage purity of the 7.5 g sample of sodium requires the mass of pure sodium in the sample. This is where stoichiometry is required. As the 7.0 g of NaH must be pure, we can use it to determine what mass of pure Na was in the reactant used to form it.	$7.0\text{ g NaH} \times \frac{1\text{ mol NaH}}{24.0\text{ g NaH}} \times \frac{2\text{ mol Na}}{2\text{ mol NaH}} \times \frac{23.0\text{ g Na}}{1\text{ mol Na}} = 6.7\text{ g pure Na}$
3. Finally, this value may be used to calculate the purity of the sodium. The final answer should be expressed to two significant figures	$\%\text{ purity} = \frac{6.7\text{ g pure Na}}{7.5\text{ g impure Na}} \times 100\% = 89\%$ The percentage purity of the sodium = 89%

Practice Problems — Percentage Purity

1. The thermite reaction is extremely exothermic, producing temperatures in excess of 2500°C. These high temperatures were used to weld iron tracks together during the early days of the railway. Thermite is a mixture of powdered aluminum and iron(III) oxide (rust) reacting as follows: $2\ Al(s) + Fe_2O_3(s) \rightarrow Al_2O_3(s) + 2\ Fe(s)$. If 2.44 g of 95% pure aluminum is reacted, how many grams of aluminum oxide can be produced?

2. How many grams of 73.0% pure iron(III) oxide are required to form 24.5 g of pure white hot iron metal in the thermite reaction? (Hint: Begin by determining the mass of *pure* oxide required.)

3. When hydrochloric acid is added to 5.73 g of contaminated calcium carbonate, 2.49 g of carbon dioxide is obtained. Write a balanced equation and find the percentage purity of the calcium carbonate.

Percentage Yield — Incomplete Reactions

Every summer, hundreds of young Canadians make money planting trees in the reforestation of British Columbia. Imagine you've joined some friends as tree planters and your group has planted 5015 Douglas fir saplings on a mountainside on Vancouver Island. Five years later, a group of forestry surveyors checking for survival find that 4655 of these saplings have taken root and are growing into healthy young trees. The percentage yield of your group's effort would be 93%.

Another of the assumptions we've been making so far is that reactions always go entirely to completion. "Completion" means that all of the limiting reactant has been converted into product, leaving only the excess reactant with none of the limiting reactant remaining at all. In real life, this is not always the case. Some reactions complete themselves only partially. As a result, much like the tree-planting example, such chemical reactions give only a partial percentage yield: less than 100% of the reactants are converted into products.

$$\textbf{Percentage yield} = \frac{\text{amount of product obtained}}{\text{amount of product expected}} \times 100\%$$

The amount of product expected is commonly referred to as the **theoretical yield**.

Sample Problem — Percentage Yield

One of the primary reasons for reforestation in British Columbia is the great loss of forests to fire each summer. The pithy cente of Douglas fir trees consists of cellulose, a starchy material made up of cross-connected molecules of glucose, $C_6H_{12}O_6$. During a small forest fire, the combustion of 8944 kg of $C_6H_{12}O_6$ molecules results in the formation of 5.75×10^6 L of carbon dioxide gas (measured at STP). What is the percentage yield?

What to Think about	How to Do It
1. Once again, in a stoichiometry problem, begin with a balanced equation. This is clearly a combustion reaction with a carbohydrate being combusted. The products are carbon dioxide and water vapour. Oxygen is a diatomic molecule.	$C_6H_{12}O_6(s) + 6\,O_2(g) \rightarrow 6\,CO_2(g) + 6\,H_2O(g)$
2. Using standard stoichiometry, convert the given mass of reactant to product. This is the volume of product formed if the reaction were to proceed 100% to completion (and the gas were measured under STP conditions). In other words, it is the *theoretical yield*. There is a metric conversion required in this problem. "Kilo" means 1000.	$8944 \text{ kg} \times \frac{1000 \text{ g } C_6H_{12}O_6}{1 \text{ kg } C_6H_{12}O_6} \times \frac{1 \text{ mol } C_6H_{12}O_6}{180.0 \text{ g } C_6H_{12}O_6} \times \frac{6 \text{ mol } CO_2}{1 \text{ mol } C_6H_{12}O_6} \times \frac{22.4 \text{ L } CO_2}{1 \text{ mol } CO_2} = 6.68 \times 10^6 \text{ L } CO_2$ The *theoretical yield* is 6.68×10^6 L CO_2.
3. Calculate the percentage yield as the quotient of the actual yield to the theoretical yield multiplied by 100%. The *entire* theoretical yield should be kept in the calculator throughout the calculation to avoid rounding errors.	Thus the percentage yield is: $\frac{5.75 \times 10^6 \text{ L}}{6.68 \times 10^6 \text{ L}} \times 100\% = 86.1\%$ yield

Practice Problems — Percentage Yield

1. A chunk of zinc metal reacts with an excess of hydrochloric acid solution. What is the percentage yield if a 7.23 g piece of zinc produces 2.16 L of hydrogen gas at STP? Begin with a balanced equation.

2. A solution containing 15.2 g of barium bromide is reacted with a solution containing excess sodium phosphate to form 9.5 g of precipitate. What is the percentage yield of the reaction? Begin with a balanced equation.

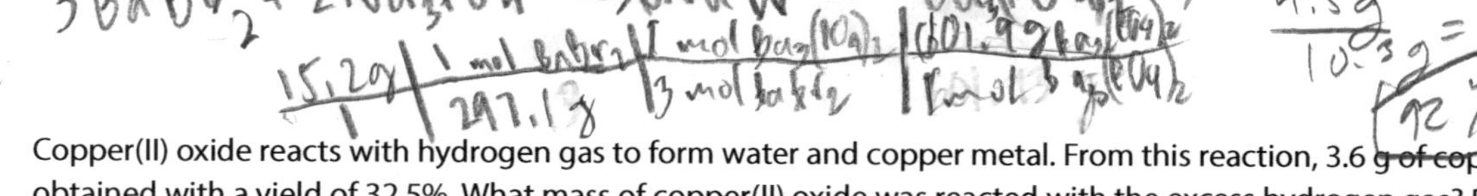

3. Copper(II) oxide reacts with hydrogen gas to form water and copper metal. From this reaction, 3.6 g of copper metal was obtained with a yield of 32.5%. What mass of copper(II) oxide was reacted with the excess hydrogen gas? Begin with a balanced equation.

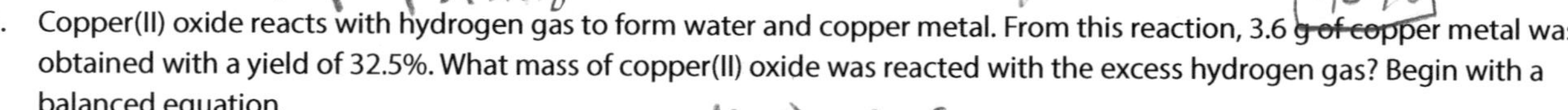

4.8 Activity: Charting and Graphing Stoichiometry

Question

What are some different ways to represent stoichiometric data?

Background

A student performs a single replacement reaction between pure magnesium metal and hydrochloric acid under two different conditions. The quantities involved are measured and recorded in tabular and graphic forms.

The reactions are performed in 250.0 mL of HCl(*aq*). The magnesium is weighed before and after the reactions are completed. The reactions are allowed to proceed for the same period of time in both trials. In both cases, once the reaction is completed, the volume of gas is measured under STP conditions.

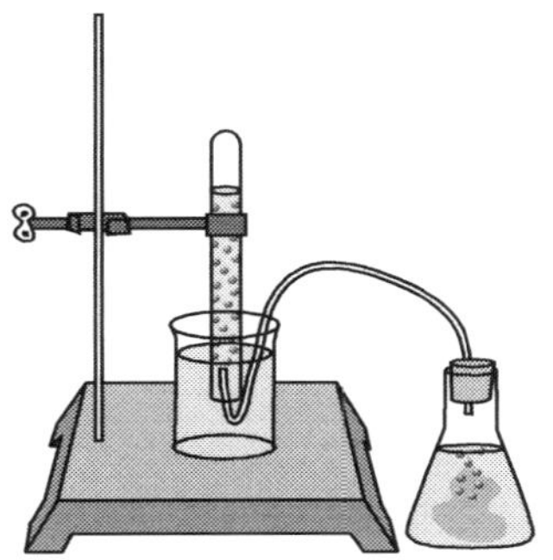

Measured Items	Very Hot	Very Cold
Initial mass of Mg(*s*)	1.00 g	1.00 g
Final mass of Mg(*s*)	0.00 g	0.75 g
Volume of $H_2(g)$	? mL	? mL
Volume of HCl(*aq*)	250.0 mL	250.0 mL
Initial Concentration of HCl(*aq*)	1.00 mol/L	1.00 mol/L

Procedure

1. Complete the following tables for the reaction under very hot and very cold conditions. Include signs in the "change in number of moles row" to indicate an increase or decrease in the number of moles.

Very Hot: $Mg(s) + 2\,HCl(aq) \rightarrow MgCl_2(aq) + H_2(g)$

Reaction species	Mg(*s*)	HCl(*aq*)	$MgCl_2(aq)$	$H_2(g)$
Initial number of moles				
Change in number of moles				
Final number of moles				

Very Cold: $Mg(s) + 2\,HCl(aq) \rightarrow MgCl_2(aq) + H_2(g)$

Reaction species	Mg(*s*)	HCl(*aq*)	$MgCl_2(aq)$	$H_2(g)$
Initial number of moles				
Change in number of moles				
Final number of moles				

Results and Discussion

1. What is the limiting reagent in the reaction under both conditions?

2. What conditions are required to complete the reaction?

3. What volume of hydrogen gas (measured at STP) is formed under very hot conditions? Under very cold conditions?

4. What is the percentage yield under very cold conditions?

5. What is the final concentration of magnesium chloride solution under very hot conditions? Under very cold conditions?

6. Using the graph "paper" below, sketch a graph to show the change in the number of moles of each species as the reaction proceeds under very hot and very cold conditions. Think of the *x*-axis as similar to that in the potential energy diagrams in section 4.3. Compare your graphs with those of a classmate.

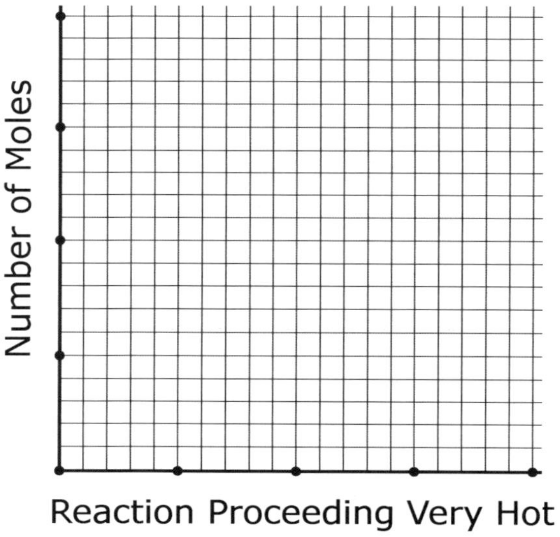

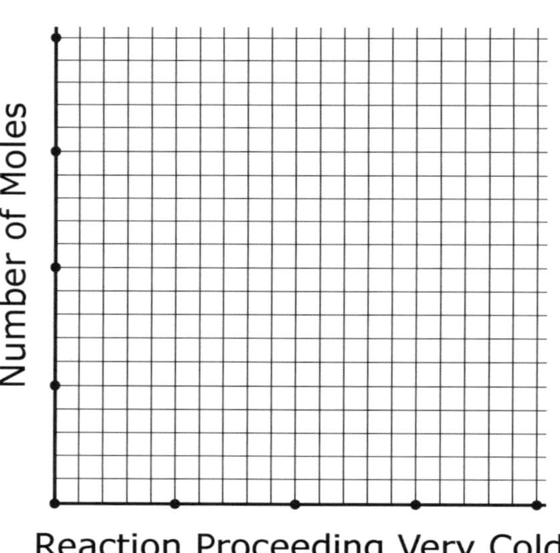

4.8 Review Questions

1. Do all reactions between two chemicals result in a complete reaction in such a way that all the reactants are consumed and turn in to products? Explain.

2. What do we call the chemicals that remain unreacted following a chemical change?

3. What is the percentage yield of a reaction?

4. Are all reactants in a chemical reaction completely pure? How might this affect a stoichiometry calculation?

5. A saturated solution of lithium fluoride, which is sometimes used as a rinse to prevent tooth decay, contains 0.132 g of LiF in 100.0 g of water. Calculate the percentage purity by mass of the LiF.

6. Automotive air bags inflate when solid sodium azide (NaN_3) decomposes explosively into its constituent elements. What volume of nitrogen gas is formed if 120 g of 85% pure sodium azide decomposes? Assume STP conditions.

7. Silver nitrate and aluminum chloride react with each other by exchanging anions:

   $3\ AgNO_3(aq) + AlCl_3(aq) \rightarrow Al(NO_3)_3(aq) + 3\ AgCl(s)$

   What mass of precipitate is produced when 4.22 g of silver nitrate react with 7.73 g of aluminum chloride in solution?

8. GeF_3H is synthesized in the reaction: $GeH_4 + 3\ GeF_4 \rightarrow 4\ GeF_3H$. If the reaction yield is 91.5%, how many moles of GeH_4 are needed to produce 8.00 mol of GeF_3H?

9. What is the maximum mass of sulphur trioxide gas that can be formed from the combination of 5.00 g each of S_8 solid with O_2 gas? Begin with a balanced equation.

10. In the reaction in question 9, 63.2 g of sulphur trioxide are produced using 40.0 g of oxygen and 48.0 g of sulphur. What is the percentage yield?

11. What volume of 0.105 mol/ L silver nitrate solution would be required to react completely with an excess of magnesium chloride solution to produce 8.95 g of precipitate? Assume the precipitate is only 75.0% pure, as it is still damp following filtration. Begin with a balanced equation.

12. What mass of silver could be formed if a large zinc wire is placed in a beaker containing 145.0 mL of 0.095 mol/L silver nitrate and allowed to react overnight? Assume the reaction has a 97% yield.

13. 8.92 g of indium oxide is reacted with an excess of water and forms 10.1 g of base. What is the percent yield?

14. What volume of chlorine gas could be produced under STP conditions if 39.8 g of 84.0% pure potassium chloride were reacted with an excess of fluorine gas?

15. An aqueous solution containing 46.7 g of copper(I) nitrate is placed into an aqueous solution containing 30.8 g of strontium bromide. The resulting mixture was filtered to remove the copper(I) bromide precipitate. Assuming a 100% yield:
(a) What is the mass of solid collected on the filter paper?

(b) Which reactant is in excess?

(c) How many grams of the excess reactant remains when the reaction has gone to completion?

16. A 20.0 g piece of calcium metal reacts with 18.0 mL of water over time. If 10.0 L of hydrogen gas is formed under STP conditions, what is the percentage yield of the reaction? (Recall the density of water is 1.00 g/mL.)

17. Excess silver nitrate is dissolved in a total volume of 250 mL of 0.103 mol/L calcium chloride solution. The resulting reaction produces 4.41 g of silver chloride precipitate. What was the percentage purity of the calcium chloride?

18. A sample of impure silver with a mass of 0.7294 g was dissolved in excess concentrated nitric acid according to the following *unbalanced* equation:
$Ag(s) + HNO_3(aq) \rightarrow AgNO_3(aq) + NO(g) + H_2O(l)$
Once the nitrogen monoxide gas was vented off in a fume hood, the resulting silver nitrate solution was reacted with a slight excess of hydrochloric acid to form a precipitate of silver chloride. The dried precipitate's mass was 0.3295 g. What was the percentage purity of the silver sample?

5 A Closer Look at Matter

This chapter focuses on the following AP Big Idea from the College Board:

Big Idea 1: The chemical elements are fundamental building materials of matter, and all matter can be understood in terms of arrangements of atoms. These atoms retain their identify in chemical reactions.

By the end of this chapter, you should be able to do the following:

- Describe the development of the model of the atom
- Describe the subatomic structures of atoms, ions, and isotopes, using calculations where appropriate

---

By the end of this chapter, you should know the meaning of the following key terms:

- atom
- atomic mass
- atomic number
- Bohr model
- electron
- isotope
- neutron
- particle charge
- proton
- relative atomic mass

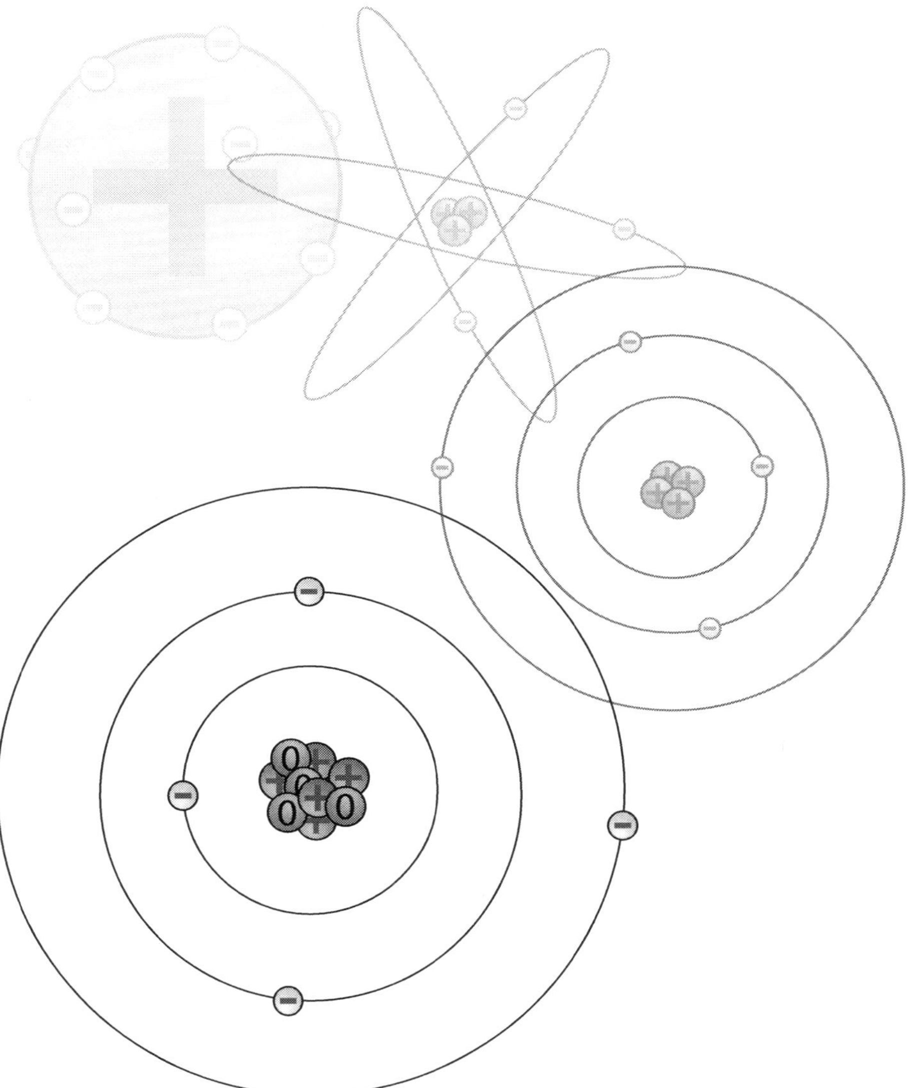

Models of the atom have gradually developed as our understanding of the composition of the atom has increased.

5.1 Early Models of the Atom — Dalton to Rutherford

Warm Up

In Science 10, you learned that an atom is the smallest part of an element that still has the properties of the element. Recall what you learned about atomic structure to answer the following questions.

1. Complete the following table about the three subatomic particles in an atom.

Subatomic Particle	Relative Charge	Relative Mass	Location in Atom
	1+		
		1 amu	
			outside nucleus

2. The two subatomic particles responsible for almost all of an atom's mass are the _______________ and the _______________.

3. Most of an atom's volume is actually _______________ _______________ (two words).

The Ancient Greeks Had It Right — for Awhile

Think about your favorite detective mystery and why you enjoyed reading it. The most interesting parts of the story were not only the ultimate answer to the mystery, but also how each clue was discovered, processed, and applied to derive that final solution.

The story of our eventual understanding of the building blocks of matter is an equally engaging read because it is like a good mystery novel!

The story begins almost 2500 years ago in ancient Greece with the philosopher Leucippos and his student Democritus. They reasoned that if a sample of solid matter such as gold was repeatedly cut into smaller and smaller pieces, the eventual result would be a particle so small it couldn't be cut into anything smaller. Democritus used the term "atomos" (Greek for "uncuttable") to refer to these smallest particles of matter. He imagined that particles of different sizes and shapes might be components of all the different types of matter.

That sounds like a promising start. However, the ancient philosophers relied largely on intuition rather than experimentation for knowledge, and soon the ideas of another philosopher replaced the idea that matter was composed of tiny particles. Aristotle proposed instead that all types of matter were actually made up of different proportions of four basic elements: earth, air, fire, and water. Unfortunately, this idea and its various incarnations were embraced for almost 2000 years in the practice of alchemy. During the next two millennia, alchemy dominated the chemical landscape (Figure 5.1.1). Many alchemists were searching for a way to change base metals into gold. Although this search was ultimately doomed to failure, some alchemists were actually serious scientists. We owe the discoveries of such useful chemical procedures as distillation, the separation of metals from ores, and the preparation of some acids to alchemy.

Figure 5.1.1 *Alchemists developed a set of symbols for the elements and linked them to the planets. For example, gold was associated with the Sun and Mars with iron.*

Science Begins and the Atom Returns

Finally, in the last half of the 1600s, the first real scientist emerged. Robert Boyle was the first person to perform and publish the results of true quantitative experiments. All of his observations convinced him that the four-element idea proposed by Aristotle was incorrect. In 1661, Boyle published the *Sceptical Chymist* in which he outlined what we now call the scientific method. He also provided an experimental definition for an element as being an "unmingled body." As this definition and Boyle's insistence on experimentation gained acceptance, more and more elements were discovered, and Aristotle's ideas about matter were eventually discarded.

Further studies over the next 140 years by such scientists as Carl Scheele, Joseph Priestley, Antoine Lavoisier, and Joseph Proust resulted in mass laws governing compound composition and chemical reactions. It was these laws that were used by the English schoolteacher John Dalton to propose a theory about matter first suggested more than 2200 years earlier. In 1808, Dalton published a book called *A New System of Chemical Philosophy* in which he presented his atomic theory. The main points of the theory are shown below.

Dalton's Atomic Theory

1. All matter is composed of extremely small particles called atoms, which cannot be broken into smaller particles, created, or destroyed.
2. The atoms of any given element are all identical to each other and different from the atoms of other elements.
3. Atoms of different elements combine in specific ratios to form compounds.
4. In a chemical reaction, atoms are separated, rearranged, and recombined to form new compounds.

Dalton's theory was a major step forward in our understanding of matter. Experimental evidence had finally led back to an idea that had made sense to some philosophers thousands of years earlier. But there were exciting revelations about the atom soon to be discovered.

Quick Check

1. Suggest a reason why Robert Boyle is often called the first true scientist.

   ____

2. Democritus and Dalton both proposed the existence of atoms. How was the development of their ideas different?

   ____

3. Which part of Dalton's atomic theory is now known to be incorrect?

   ____

Discovering the Subatomic — Thomson's Atomic Model

The relationship between matter and electric charge fascinated scientists in the 1800s. They wondered, for example, how electricity passed through matter and how it might behave in the absence of matter. Between 1859 and 1879, work done by Julius Plücker in Germany and William Crookes in England using special glass tubes soon led to one of the most important discoveries ever made about matter and the nature of the atom.

Gas Discharge Tubes and Strange Green Glows

One such device Crookes worked with consisted of a negatively charged electrical terminal (a cathode) embedded in one end of a sealed glass tube (Figure 5.1.2). About two-thirds along the length of the tube, a positive terminal (an anode) in the shape of a broad flat cross was embedded. The tube was connected to a vacuum pump. When the electric current was turned on and the air in the tube was pumped out, any air present began to glow and then change color as the tube emptied. Eventually, when all of the air was gone, the glow disappeared — almost. Close inspection in a darkened laboratory revealed a shadow of the anode cross surrounded by faint green glow at the far end of the tube opposite the cathode and a very faint glow coming from the cathode itself. Crookes concluded that something must be travelling from the cathode to the anode inside the tube even though all the air was gone.

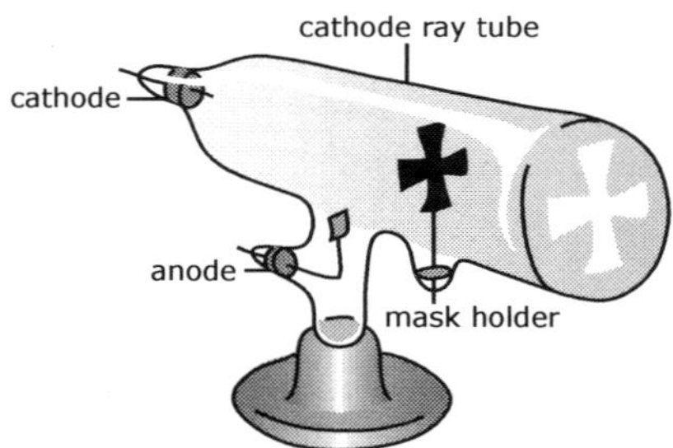

Figure 5.1.2 *Crookes' glass tube*

In Paris, Jean Baptiste Perrin discovered that a magnet placed next to the tube was able to deflect the mysterious beam, which meant that the beam was actually a stream of charged particles. Crookes confirmed this and suggested that this "cathode ray" might be composed of negatively charged particles, but no one paid much attention to that idea.

Cathode Rays and Subatomic Particles

Many researchers experimented with cathode-ray tubes, as they came to be known. However, it wasn't until the great English physicist Joseph John Thomson ("J.J." to his friends) turned his attention to these mysterious rays that a breakthrough came. In 1897, Thomson set to work to discover the nature of cathode rays. He modified the original Crookes' tube by focussing the cathode ray into a thin beam onto a fluorescent target. He then exposed the beam to an electric field in addition to a magnetic field. He found that the beam was deflected towards the positive plate in the electric field. This meant that these mysterious particles must have a negative charge (Figure 5.1.3).

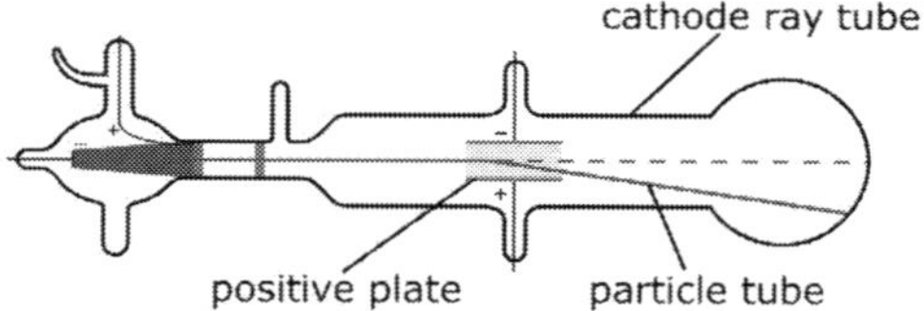

Figure 5.1.3 *The deflection of the beam of particles toward the positive magnetic plate indicated that the particles had a negative charge.*

Thomson knew that the amount of deflection a charged particle experiences in an electric field depends on the ratio of the particle's charge to its mass. The larger that ratio is (the more charge and the less mass), the greater the deflection. By carefully adjusting the currents in his modified vacuum tube, Thomson was able to calculate the charge-to-mass ratio (e/m) for cathode rays. He found that value to be 1.76×10^8 C/g (C stands for coulomb, the SI unit of charge). That was almost 2000 times greater than that of the hydrogen ion, which was the smallest charged particle known in 1897. Thomson concluded that these little negative particles were actually about 2000 times lighter than a hydrogen ion. This astounded him because it meant that he had found a particle far smaller than the smallest atom!

The Electronic Nature of the Atom

Thomson repeated the experiments many times with different metals used as the cathode and even different gases inside the tube. Each time the results were the same. This had to mean that these mysterious negative particles were present in atoms of different elements. In a speech given on April 29, 1897, to the Royal Institution, J.J. Thomson told his audience that cathode rays were actually tiny negatively charged "corpuscles" of electricity, each with an identical mass about 2000 times lighter than an atom of hydrogen. The audience wasn't yet ready to believe that bits of matter even smaller than atoms existed.

Soon, however, this revolutionary idea was accepted. This tiny "corpuscle" was identified as the **electron** and shown to be a component of every atom. In 1906, Thomson was awarded the Nobel Prize for his work on the conduction of electricity through gases in which he discovered the negative charges that became known as electrons.

In an article in England's "Philosophical Magazine" in 1897, Thomson suggested what else might be in an atom. He reasoned that if an intact atom has no charge, then there must be something positive in an atom to balance the negative charge on the electron. He discovered that "something" within a few years.

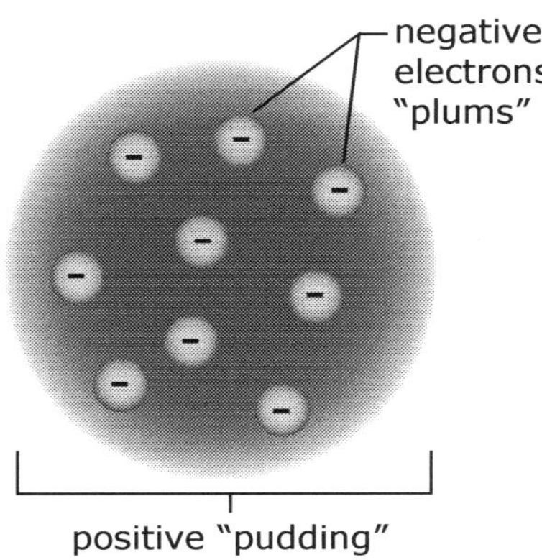

Figure 5.1.4 *Thomson's atomic model (1903)*

At this point, it's valuable to consider the significance of what Thomson discovered. First, he found that atoms were themselves built from even smaller components. Second, and arguably more important, Thomson discovered that these subatomic particles had opposite charges. This meant that the building blocks of matter are essentially electrical entities! Remember that idea, because it will be fundamental to most of the chemistry you will ever learn.

Thomson soon used hydrogen gas in a further-modified cathode-ray tube to show that positively charged particles (labelled **protons** in 1920) also existed in atoms. This led him to propose the first model of the atom since 1808. In 1903, Thomson suggested that an atom could be seen as a "spongy ball" or "plum pudding" with negative electrons distributed evenly throughout the spongy mass of the atom, much like bits of fruit in an English pudding or raisins in a muffin (Figure 5.1.4). The "plum pudding" model as it became known was soon replaced, but it was a major advance in the understanding of matter and was based on the best data available at the time.

Quick Check

1. The electron's charge was determined in 1909 by the American physicist Robert Millikan to be 1.602×10^{-19} C. Use the e/m ratio for the electron (1.76×10^{8} C/g) to calculate the electron's mass in grams.
   Hint: To determine the mass in grams, begin with the provided value of charge in coulombs and use the e/m ratio as a conversion factor. As the required answer is in grams, the e/m ratio will need to be inverted to allow the coulombs to cancel, providing an answer in grams.

2. What evidence led Crookes to conclude that the unknown ray in his vacuum tube
   (a) originated at the cathode?

   ____

   (b) was a beam of charged particles?

   ____

   (c) may be a beam of negatively charged particles?

   ____

Continued

Quick Check (*Continued*)

3. Identify the two most important components of Thomson's atomic theory.

   (a) ______________________________

   (b) ______________________________

Rutherford Changes Things

In 1895, young Ernest Rutherford, working on his father's farm in New Zealand, received the news that he'd won a scholarship to study at the University of Cambridge with J.J. Thomson at the prestigious Cavendish Laboratory. Rutherford arrived at Cambridge in time to work with Thomson during the discovery of negative electric charges. Not surprisingly, therefore, Rutherford fully believed in the "plum pudding" model of the atom.

After training with Thomson, Rutherford went to McGill University in Montreal where he devoted much of his time to studying the nature of the emissions associated with the newly discovered phenomenon of radioactivity. Rutherford's work at McGill would soon give him all the tools he needed to test Thomson's atomic model. Using samples of radioactive elements such as radium provided by Marie and Pierre Curie, Ernest Rutherford and Frederic Soddy discovered three types of emissions associated with radioactivity. They labeled these emissions as alpha particles, beta particles, and gamma rays. Their nature and properties are summarized in Table 5.1.1.

Table 5.5.1 *Characteristics of Radioactive Emissions*

Emission	Nature of Emission	Penetrating Ability	Emission Speed
Alpha (**α**) particles	helium nuclei	penetrates a few cm of air but stopped by a thin sheet of aluminum foil	~ 16 000 km/s
Beta (**β**) particles	electrons	penetrates a few mm of aluminum but stopped by a thin sheet of lead	~ 200 000 km/s
Gamma (**γ**) rays	high energy waves	penetrates at least 30 cm of lead or 2 km of air	300 000 km/s (speed of light)

By 1909, Rutherford had returned to England and joined the University of Manchester. Working with colleagues Hans Geiger and Ernest Marsden, Rutherford decided to use alpha particles as a type of "probe" to test the makeup of the atom. The experiment involved aiming alpha particles emitted from a radioactive source at very thin (1/2000 mm) sheets of gold foil, and then observing where those alpha particles struck a fluorescent screen after passing through the atoms in the foil.

Recall that Rutherford had been a student of J.J. Thomson and firmly believed that the plum pudding model accurately represented the structure of an atom. Based on that belief, Rutherford fully expected that nothing in Thomson's "spongy" atom was capable of significantly altering the path of alpha particles traveling at 16 000 km/s. All the alpha particles should, therefore, pass through the gold foil without deviating from their original path. If any deflection did occur, it would be minimal at best.

The vast majority of alpha particles behaved exactly as predicted and passed right through the gold foil without deviating (Figure 5.1.5). But (and this is a huge "but") a few particles deviated through large angles and a very few (about 1 in 20 000) didn't go through the foil at all, but rather bounced back! Rutherford wrote in his journal that "it was quite the most incredible event that has ever happened to me in my life. It was almost as incredible as if you had fired a 15-inch shell at a piece of tissue-paper and it came back and hit you." Rutherford was referring to the fact that nothing in Thomson's atomic model was capable of knocking an alpha particle far off its course, let alone turning it around. Clearly, the model of the atom proposed by Thomson needed a major revision and Rutherford was able to do just that.

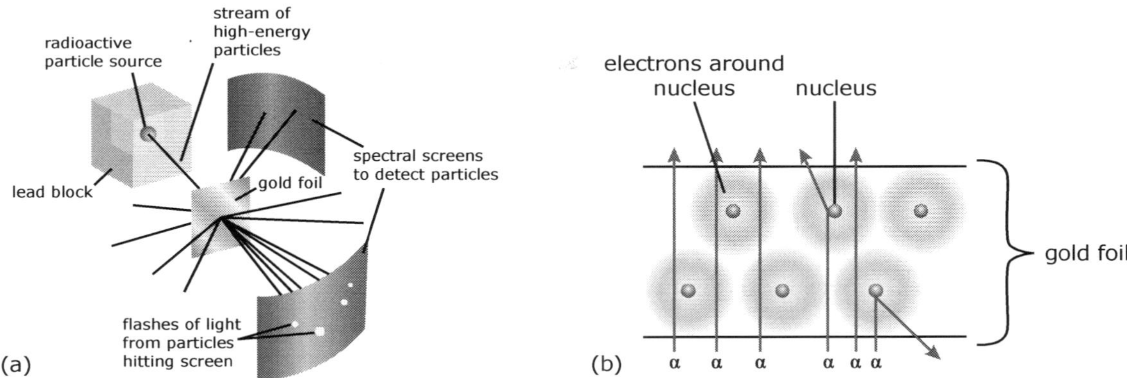

Figure 5.1.5 *(a) Rutherford's gold foil experiment; (b) Rutherford's atomic model explaining the results of the experiment*

Rutherford's Model of the Atom

Rutherford explained the results by suggesting that virtually all the mass of an atom was concentrated in a very tiny, dense, positive structure at the atom's centre he called the **nucleus**. Surrounding this nucleus was a cloud of negatively charged electrons that accounted for all of atom's volume but virtually none of its mass. Rutherford calculated that the nucleus was so small compared to the volume occupied by the surrounding electrons that the vast majority of an atom was actually empty space! Although Rutherford's model for the atom resembled a tiny planetary system with electrons orbiting a nucleus much like planets orbit the sun, Rutherford himself wrote, "The atom has often been likened to a solar system where the sun corresponds to the nucleus and the planets to the electrons....The analogy, however, must not be pressed too far."

Rutherford was responsible for perhaps the most significant contribution ever made to our understanding of atomic structure, and he received the Nobel Prize in chemistry in 1908. Shortly after discovering the nucleus, Rutherford realized that his model explained the charged nature of the atom, but couldn't account for all of its mass. He believed that a neutral particle must also exist in the nucleus that added mass but no charge to the atom. More than 20 years later, James Chadwick discovered that particle, the **neutron**, just as Rutherford had predicted.

Several significant changes to Rutherford's atomic model were still needed to explain electron behaviour. However, as Rutherford theorized, the atom is an entity whose tiny positive nucleus accounts for 99.97% of its mass but only about one trillionth of its volume! The negative electrons move rapidly within the available atomic volume held by the attraction of the nucleus. Table 5.1.2 is a simplified summary of the composition of the atom as we view it today.

Table 5.1.2 *The Composition of the Atom*

Subatomic Particle	Relative Charge	Relative Mass	Absolute Mass	Location in Atom
Proton (p^+)	1+	1 amu	1.673×10^{-24} g	inside nucleus
Neutron (n^0)	0	1	1.675×10^{-24} g	inside nucleus
Electron (e^-)	1–	0	9.109×10^{-28} g	outside nucleus

Quick Check

1. Why did Rutherford believe the nucleus was so small compared to the size of the atom itself?

 ____

2. Why did Rutherford believe that the nucleus had a positive charge?

 ____

3. To what parts of the gold foil experiment was Rutherford referring when used the following analogies:

 (a) a 15-inch shell ______________________________

 (b) a piece of tissue paper ______________________________

4. Experiments show that the diameter of the nucleus of an atom is about 10^{-14} m and the diameter of an atom itself is about 10^{-10} m. If the diameter of the nucleus was actually 2.0 cm (about the width of your thumb), determine the diameter of the entire atom.

Atomic Number, Mass Number, and Neutron Number

We can use the above table to discuss three important numbers associated with every element. The **atomic number (Z)** of an element equals the number of protons and the positive charge on the nucleus of each of its atoms. All of the atoms of a given element have the same atomic number, and each element's atomic number is different from that of any other element. For example, there are six protons in the nucleus of every carbon atom so Z = 6 for carbon. For nitrogen, Z = 7; for oxygen, Z = 8, and so on. This illustrates an extremely important point to remember: It is the number of protons that determines the identity of an atom. While the number of neutrons may vary in atoms of the same element, the number of protons always remains the same.

The presence of neutrons in the nucleus also contributes mass to an atom. The **mass number (A)** for each atom equals the sum of the number of protons and neutrons in the nucleus. A proton and a neutron each contribute one unit to an atom's mass number. For example, an atom of nitrogen with 7 protons and 7 neutrons has a mass number of 14, and an aluminum atom with 13 protons and 14 neutrons has a mass number of 27. Any particular atom can be represented using a notation that includes the element's symbol, mass number, and atomic number as shown in Figure 5.1.6.

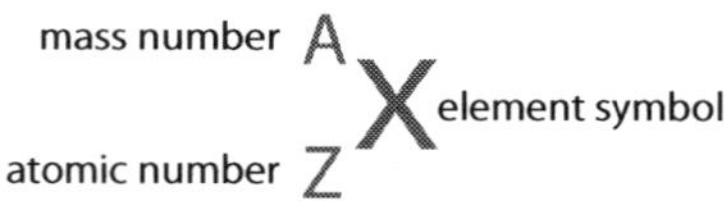

Figure 5.1.6 *Notation for showing the mass number and the atomic number of the atom of an element*

Using this notation, we can see that the **neutron number (N)** can easily be calculated by the following: N (neutron number) = A (mass number) – Z (atomic number). For example,

$^{14}_{7}\mathbf{N}$ represents a nitrogen atom with 7 neutrons (read as "nitrogen-14")

$^{19}_{9}\mathbf{F}$ represents a fluorine atom with 10 neutrons (read as "fluorine-19")

An atom's mass is measured relative to an atomic standard. The modern standard is a carbon-12 atom whose mass is defined as exactly 12 atomic mass units. Therefore, one **atomic mass unit (amu)** is defined as exactly 1/12 the mass of a carbon-12 atom. **Atomic mass** is the average mass of an element's atoms.

Chemical changes never involve change to the nucleus but often involve electrons being added to or removed from neutral atoms that form ions. An **ion** is an electrically charged atom or group of atoms. For every electron an atom gains, it also gains that amount of excess negative charge and becomes a negative ion or **anion**. Each electron lost by an atom leaves that amount of excess positive charge on the resulting positive ion or **cation**. We can use the notation in Figure 5.1.6 to represent ions as well as neutral atoms. For example:

$^{24}_{12}\mathbf{Mg}^{2+}$ shows a magnesium cation with 12 protons, 12 neutrons, and 10 electrons

$^{31}\mathbf{P}^{3-}_{15}$ shows a phosphide anion with protons, 16 neutrons, and 18 electrons

Sample Problem — Atomic Number, Mass Number, and Neutron Number

1. Determine the number of protons, neutrons, and electrons present in a 4+ ion of Pb-207.
2. Write the symbol for this cation using the notation described above.

What to Think about	How to Do It
Question 1 1. A 4+ cation has 4 fewer electrons than protons. The atomic number of Pb is 82. Therefore there are 82 protons present, but only 78 electrons because of the 4+ charge. 2. The number of protons = the atomic number The neutron number is determined by subtracting the atomic number from the mass number.	The number of neutrons is given by: 207 − 82 = 125 neutrons. The correct notation is: $^{207}_{82}\mathrm{Pb}^{4+}$

Practice Problems — Atomic Number, Mass Number, and Neutron Number

1. Determine the number of protons, neutrons and electrons present in each of the following:
   (a) $^{40}_{20}\mathrm{Ca}^{2+}$ (b) $^{128}_{52}\mathrm{Te}^{2-}$ (c) $^{52}_{24}\mathrm{Cr}^{3+}$

2. Write atomic notation for neutral atoms of the following:

   (a) bromine-79 (b) gold-197 (c) thorium-232

3. Complete the following table for atoms and ions:

Notation	Atomic Number	Mass Number	Number of Protons	Number of Neutrons	Number of Electrons
$^{95}_{42}\mathrm{Mo}$					
		79	34		36
	47	109			46
$^{232}_{90}\mathrm{Th}^{4+}$					
			83	126	83

Isotopes and Mass Spectrometry

Although all the nuclei of the atoms of a particular element have the same atomic number, they may not have the same atomic mass. Isotopes are different forms of the same element with different numbers of neutrons and therefore different mass values. For example, 98.89% of naturally occurring carbon atoms have 6 neutrons (carbon-12), 1.11% have 7 neutrons (carbon-13) and fewer than 0.01% have 8 neutrons (carbon-14).

Remember that the chemical behaviour of a particular element is determined primarily by the number of electrons. The atomic number of any neutral element equals the number of electrons surrounding the nuclei of that atom, so all of the isotopes of a particular element have almost identical chemical properties.

The number of naturally occurring isotopes of an element and their relative masses and abundances may be determined by a mass spectrometer, an instrument based on the same principles employed by J.J. Thomson to discover the electron (Figure 5.1.7).

Mass spectrometry uses the fact that charged particles moving through a magnetic field are deflected from their original path based on their charge-to-mass (e/m) ratio. The greater the ratio, the more deflection occurs. Consider the example of a beam of ionized neon (Ne^{1+}) containing the isotopes neon-20, neon-21, and neon-22. The beam enters the magnetic field chamber of a mass spectrometer, and the three isotopes separate on the basis of their e/m ratios. A detector in the spectrometer records the separations, the percent abundance, and the mass of each isotope. The mass number for neon that appears on the periodic table is the weighted average of those naturally occurring isotopes. The sample problem below shows how the calculation is done.

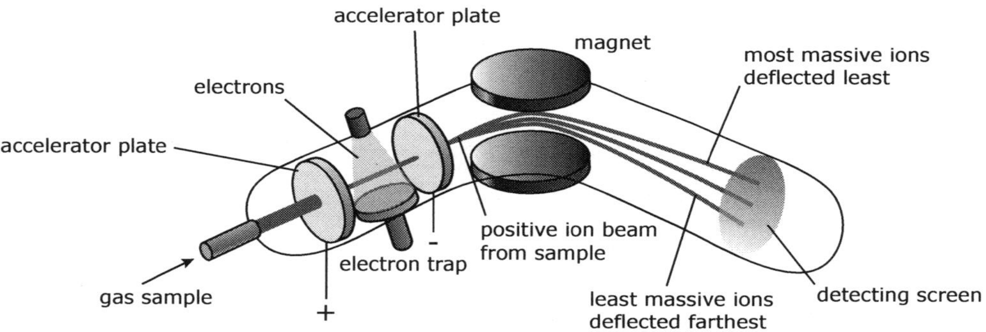

Figure 5.1.7 *Mass spectrometer*

Sample Problem — Calculating Atomic Mass

1. Use mass spectrometry data below to calculate the atomic mass of neon.

Isotope	Mass of Atom in amu (relative to ^{12}C = 12.0000)	Percent Abundance in Nature
neon-20	19.9924	90.48
neon-21	20.9938	0.27
neon-22	21.9914	9.25

What to Think about

1. The calculated atomic mass is the weighted average of the masses of each isotope.
   The sum of the three (mass) × (% abundance) products will therefore represent the atomic mass of neon.

How to Do It

(mass Ne-20) (% abundance) + (mass Ne-21) (% abundance) + (mass Ne-22) (% abundance)

(19.9924 amu) (90.48/100) + (20.9938 amu) (0.27/100) + (21.9914 amu) (9.25/100) = 20.18 amu

Sample Problem — Calculating Isotope Percent Abundance

1. Boron has two naturally occurring isotopes. Calculate the percent abundances of boron-10 and boron-11 using the following data:

Atomic mass of boron	10.81 amu
Isotopic mass of boron-10	10.0129 amu
Isotopic mass of boron-11	11.0093 amu

What to Think about

1. The weighted averages of the isotopes yield the atomic mass of 10.81 amu.
   The sum of the fractional abundances must be 1. So if x = abundance of boron-10, then the abundance of boron-11 must be $1 - x$.
   Use the method shown in the previous sample problem.
2. Solve for (x) and ($1 - x$) and then express those fractions as percentages to answer the question.

How to Do It

$(x)(10.0129 \text{ amu}) + (1 - x)(11.0093 \text{ amu}) = 10.81 \text{ amu}$

$11.0093x - 10.0129x = 11.0093 - 10.81$

$0.9964x = 0.1993$

$x = 0.2000$ and $1 - x = 0.8000$

Therefore % abundance boron-10 = 20.00%

and % abundance boron-11 = 80.00%

Practice Problems — Using Mass Spectrometry Data

1. Use the mass spectrometry data below to calculate the atomic mass of gallium.

Isotope	Mass of Atom in amu (relative to ^{12}C = 12.0000)	Percent Abundance in Nature
gallium-69	68.9256	60.11
gallium-71	70.9247	39.89

2. The following neon ions enter the magnetic field chamber of a mass spectrometer. Arrange them in order from the isotope that will be deflected most to the isotope deflected least.

$^{22}_{10}Ne^{1+}$ $^{21}_{10}Ne^{1+}$ $^{20}_{10}Ne^{1+}$

Most Deflection ⟶ Least Deflection		

3. Chlorine has two naturally occurring isotopes. Calculate the percent abundances of chlorine-35 and chlorine-37 using the following data:

Atomic mass of chlorine	35.453 amu
Isotopic mass of chlorine-35	34.9689 amu
Isotopic mass of chlorine-37	36.9659 amu

5.1 Activity: Linking the Giants

Question

What were the major scientific achievements of the scientists who contributed to our understanding of the atom?

Procedure

1. Consider the following researchers:

Robert Boyle	Julius Plücker	James Chadwick
Carl Scheele	Jean Baptiste Perrin	Frederick Soddy
Joseph Priestley	William Crookes	Ernest Marsden
Joseph Proust	J.J. Thomson	Hans Geiger
Antoine Lavoisier	Marie and Pierre Curie	Robert Millikan
John Dalton	Ernest Rutherford	

   Construct an "Atomic Theory Timeline" diagram and include all of the names given above including dates and which discovery each individual made that contributed (directly or indirectly) to our understanding of the atom.

2. Write a point-form biography of any one scientist listed above focusing on all of his or her major scientific achievements.

3. Exchange you biography with a classmate or present your biography to the class.

Results and Discussion

1. In looking at your timeline and the discoveries of the different scientists, what can you conclude about the development of scientific knowledge?

2. Why did you choose the scientist whose biography you wrote?

5.1 Review Questions

1. Briefly describe the structure of the atom as proposed by each of the following:
   (a) John Dalton

   (b) J.J. Thomson

   (c) Ernest Rutherford

2. What evidence led J.J. Thomson to propose that the mysterious negative particles he was studying were smaller than atoms?

3. How did the discovery of radioactivity contribute to Ernest Rutherford's atomic model?

4. Why was Rutherford so surprised by the results of his gold foil experiment?

5. Complete the following table for neutral atoms.

Notation	Name	Atomic Number	Mass Number	Number of Protons	Number of Neutrons	Number of Electrons
					77	54
			210	84		
	neptunium-237					
		97			150	
			257			100

6. Write the notation for the following neutral atoms.

(a) An atom with 78 protons and 117 neutrons	
(b) An atom with a mass of 237 having 90 electrons	
(c) An atom with 69 electrons and 100 neutrons	

7. Write the notation for the following ions.

(a) A 3+ cation with 80 electrons and 127 neutrons	
(b) A 1– anion with 54 electrons and 78 neutrons	
(c) An ion with 66 electrons, 69 protons and 100 neutrons	

8. Use the following mass spectrometry data to calculate the atomic mass of magnesium.

Isotope	Mass of Atom in amu (relative to $^{12}C = 12.0000$)	Percent Abundance in Nature
magnesium-24	23.9850	78.99
magnesium-25	24.9858	10.00
magnesium-26	25.9826	11.01

9. An atom's volume is mostly empty space containing a cloud of negative electrons surrounding a very tiny positive nucleus. Therefore "solid matter" as we know it is really an illusion. Suggest a reason why all matter doesn't simply collapse.

10. Silver has two naturally occurring isotopes. Calculate the percent abundances of silver-107 and silver-109 using the following data:

Atomic mass of silver	107.87 amu
Isotopic mass of silver-107	106.9051 amu
Isotopic mass of silver-109	108.9045 amu

5.2 Quantum Theory and the Bohr Model of the Atom

Warm Up

1. (a) List three properties of waves such as water waves or visible light.

   ______

   (b) What would you expect to happen when two water waves moving in opposite directions met each other?

   ______

2. (a) List three properties of solid objects or particles such as the marbles in a bag.

   ______

   (b) What would you expect to happen when two marbles moving in opposite directions met each other?

   ______

3. Are any of your answers to question 1 identical to question 2? (Stay tuned…)

   ______

Waves Behaving like Particles? Well Hit Me with a Planck!

A serious challenge to Rutherford's atomic model arose almost immediately. A very secure prediction of the physics available at the end of the 1800s was that accelerating charges should radiate energy. Because orbiting electrons are accelerating charges, electrons in atoms should lose energy. That prediction was catastrophic for Rutherford's model. It meant that all atoms, and so also all matter, should collapse in a fraction of a second as their electrons lost energy and spiraled into the nucleus! Obviously, a significant piece of the atomic puzzle was missing and even Rutherford himself was ready to abandon his view of the atom. Yet, his conclusions and his nuclear model were correct. The real problem was that the physics of the day needed to be re-written to explain the behaviour of electrons in atoms.

To begin to understand how the solution came about, we must consider the work of German physicist Max Planck. In 1900, this conservative professor began nothing short of a revolution in physics. He proposed that energy, long considered to be strictly a wave phenomenon, could be shown to behave like particles in the form of very tiny, discreet energy packets or bundles he called quanta (plural for quantum). Planck called this the quantum theory and arrived at his conclusions (reluctantly) by studying the energy radiated from heated solids. Planck developed the following equation for the energy associated with each packet or quantum:

$$\boldsymbol{E = hv}$$

where $\boldsymbol{E}$ = energy, $\boldsymbol{v}$ = frequency, $\boldsymbol{h}$ = a very tiny proportionality constant ($h = 6.626 \times 10^{-34}$ J·s) called Planck's constant. According to Planck, energy could only be absorbed or emitted in whole numbers of quanta, that is, one quantum of energy ($E = hv$), two quanta ($E = 2hv$), three quanta ($E = 3hv$) and so on, but nowhere in between. Think of each energy quantum as a glass marble in a bag of identical marbles (Figure 5.2.1). In the same way that you could only ever add or remove a specific amount of glass from the bag in the form of a whole number of marbles, so too could amounts of energy only be absorbed or emitted in the form of whole numbers of quanta.

Figure 5.2.1 *Quanta of energy are like marbles in bag. The marbles can only be removed as whole units.*

At the end of the 1800s, the behaviour of waves and the behaviour of particles were seen as very different and mutually exclusive. Waves were disturbances that moved through space, could pass through and interfere with each other, and could have any value within a range. Particles were objects with definite boundaries that bounced off each other when they collided and could only exist in certain whole-number quantities. A firm experimental and mathematical foundation supported the idea that waves were fundamentally different from particles. To now suggest that waves could behave like particles was almost sacrilegious! Planck himself wrote about his work: "By nature, I am peacefully inclined and reject all doubtful adventures. …However, a theoretical interpretation had to be found at any cost.…I was ready to sacrifice every one of my previous convictions about physical laws."

Planck's theory wasn't taken very seriously at first. But in 1905, a 26-year-old clerk in a Swiss patent office named Albert Einstein wrote five papers that changed the scientific world forever. One of those papers used the quantum theory to explain a phenomenon involving light called the "photoelectric effect" that had baffled physicists until then. According to Einstein, the only way to make sense of the photoelectric effect was to consider light as being composed of tiny discreet packets of energy. (These were later called "photons" by American chemist Gilbert Lewis.) Einstein's paper was the first practical application of the quantum theory and as a result, the theory soon began to gain widespread acceptance. In 1921, Einstein was awarded the Nobel Prize in physics for his explanation of the photoelectric effect.

Quick Check

1. Briefly state what it means for something to be a "quantized."

   ____

2. Give three common examples of things considered to be "quantized."

   ____

   ____

3. According to Planck, could an amount of energy equal to $2.5hv$ be absorbed or emitted by an object? Explain.

   ____

   ____

The Bohr Model

One of the scientists who paid particular attention to the work of Planck and Einstein was a young Danish physicist named Niels Bohr. As a young grad student, Bohr had met Ernest Rutherford at the Cavendish Laboratory in Cambridge and then worked with Rutherford at the University of Manchester. Bohr believed in the nuclear atomic model and started to see a way to "save" it using the quantum theory. If energy was indeed quantized and so could be seen to have only certain values and not others, perhaps the energies associated with electrons orbiting the nucleus had similar restrictions.

Bohr was working on this idea at Rutherford's laboratory in Manchester in 1912. In the middle of his experiments and calculations, he returned to Copenhagen to get married. He was so excited about his work that he managed to convince his new bride to cancel their honeymoon and return to England with him. Soon thereafter, Niels Bohr completed one of the most brilliant papers on atomic structure ever written. In doing so, he managed to rescue Rutherford's nuclear model of the atom.

Scientific theories are carefully constructed on a firm foundation of data gathered from a multitude of meticulously documented, rigorously controlled, and perpetually repeatable experiments. Bohr's theory was no exception. In section 5.1, we discussed the conduction of charges through gases in glass discharge tubes. Those experiments in the later years of the 1800s not only led to Thomson's discovery of the electron, but also provided Bohr with valuable data for his ideas about the nature of those electrons in atoms.

Quantum Theory Rescues the Nuclear Model

Bohr knew that when high voltage was applied across the electrodes of a sealed glass tube containing a gas such as hydrogen, the gas was heated and emitted light. As part of his investigations, Bohr looked at this light through a spectroscope. A spectroscope is a device similar to a prism, which separates the light into its component wavelengths. When Bohr viewed the light from the heated hydrogen through the spectroscope, he saw only a series of coloured lines against a black background, rather than a continuous rainbow of colour. For hydrogen, the same pattern of four coloured lines was always seen: a red, blue-green, blue, and violet line (Figure 5.2.3). For each gaseous element used, a bright-line pattern unique to that element called a **bright-line spectrum** always appeared (much like a bar code on a modern grocery item).

The phenomenon had mystified scientists. None could explain why only certain colours of light, each corresponding to specific wavelength, frequency, and energy, were emitted by the heated gases — until Bohr. Bohr realized that by applying quantum principles to the behaviour of hydrogen's lone electron, he could not only account for the existence of the bright-line spectrum, but also save Rutherford's nuclear model of the atom.

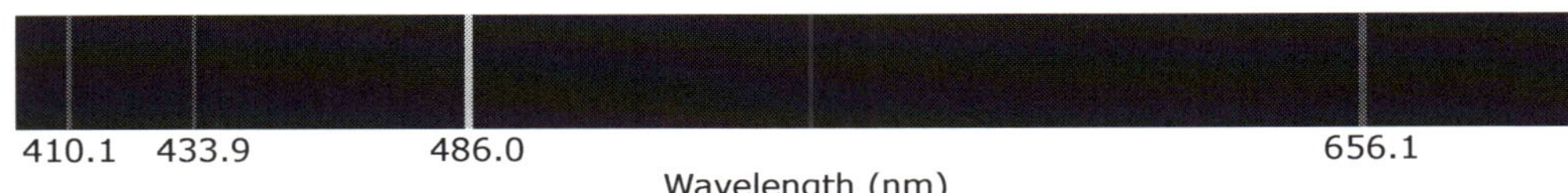

Figure 5.2.2 *Hydrogen's bright-line spectrum*

Bohr's Postulates

Bohr's postulates for hydrogen are summarized below:

1. The hydrogen atom had only certain **allowed energy levels** or **stationary states.** Each of these states corresponded to a circular electron orbit of a fixed size. The larger the allowed orbit, the greater the energy associated with it. No other orbits existed in the atom. Each allowed energy state was given an integer number "n" that Bohr called a **quantum number** with allowed values that ranged from 1 to ∞ (i.e., n could equal 1, 2, 3…etc). The lowest energy (smallest) orbit corresponded to the lowest allowed energy state called the **ground state** and was designated as $n = 1$. The larger orbits of greater energy were designated as $n = 2$, $n = 3$, $n = 4$, etc. and were said to be **excited states.**

2. As long as an electron moved in an allowed orbit or stationary state, the electron (and therefore the atom) did not radiate or absorb energy.

3. The electron could only move from one allowed orbit to another if it absorbed or emitted an amount of energy exactly equal to the energy difference between the two orbits, ΔE. This meant that the hydrogen atom could only change from one stationary energy state to another.

Bohr's Postulates — Another Look

Postulate 1 employed Planck's theory by quantizing the energies allowed for the hydrogen atom (and thus the electron). Because only certain-sized orbits were allowed, the atom was restricted to existing in only certain energy states and not others. Think of the electron as a ball on a staircase. Just as the ball can only rest on any particular stair and so have only certain amounts of potential energy and not others, so too is the electron restricted to only specific energies.

Postulate 2 meant that the nuclear model of the atom proposed by Rutherford would not collapse as predicted. Although the postulate violated the laws of classical physics, Bohr insisted that it must be true, even though he didn't know why.

Postulates 1 and 3 explained the origin and nature of hydrogen's bright-line spectrum. An atomic spectrum could not be continuous (i.e., a complete rainbow of colours) because an atom's energy states could only be certain values and not others. When a sample of hydrogen gas is heated in a discharge tube, the electrons in the hydrogen atoms absorb sufficient amounts of energy to "jump" to larger orbits. (In any one hydrogen atom, only one electron is involved, but in a sample of the gas, the electrons of many hydrogen atoms are undergoing many transitions). Once in a higher energy orbit, any electron could then return to a lower energy orbit by emitting a specific amount of energy corresponding exactly to the difference between the higher and lower energy orbits (Figure 5.2.3). If the frequency of that emitted energy corresponds to any part of the visible spectrum, then a bright line of that specific colour would be seen. Four of hydrogen's electron transitions emitted energy in the visible spectrum.

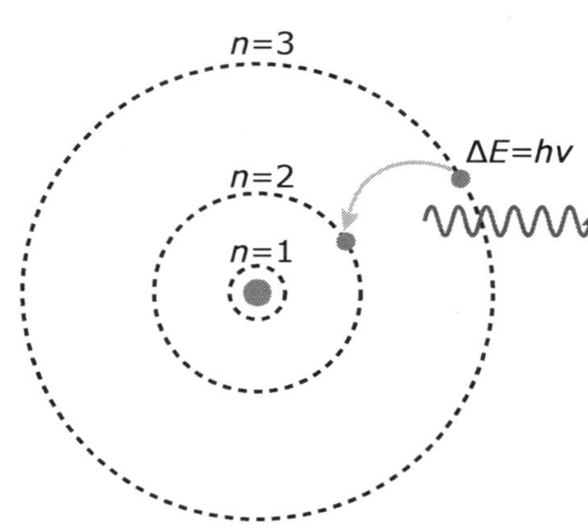

Figure 5.2.3 *When the electron moves to an inner energy level, it emits energy.*

If an excited electron emits energy and drops to $n = 2$ from a higher energy orbit, the wavelength of the emitted energy corresponds to a particular colour of visible light. If an electron drops from $n = 3$ to $n = 2$, the energy difference between the two orbits (and therefore the energy emitted) corresponds to that of red light. Hence the red line appears in the emission spectrum. The blue-green line results from an electron transition from $n = 4$ to $n = 2$, the blue line from an electron transition from $n = 5$ to $n = 2$, and the violet line from an electron transition from $n = 6$ to $n = 2$. This series of four bright lines in the visible spectrum is called the Balmer series, named after the Swiss schoolteacher who first derived a mathematical relationship between the lines in hydrogen's visible emission spectrum (Figure 5.2.4).

Bohr's model of the hydrogen atom was successful in explaining the mystery of bright line spectra. His calculations and predictions worked for hydrogen and he even calculated the radius of the orbit for hydrogen's electron in its ground state. In 1922, Niels Bohr was awarded the Nobel Prize in physics.

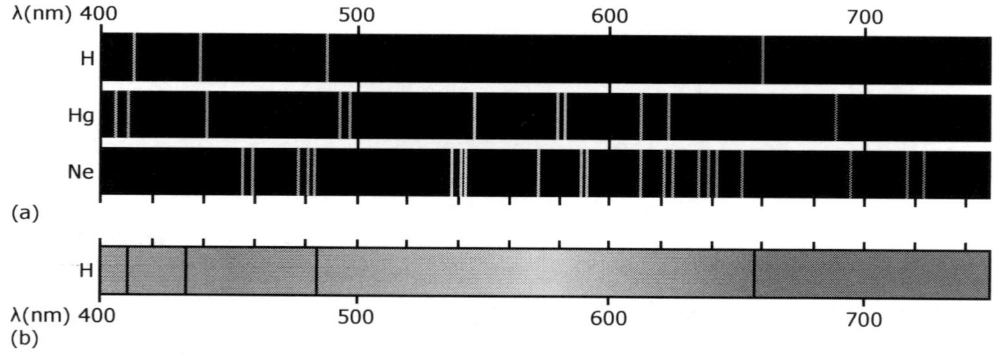

Figure 5.2.4 *(a) The emission spectra of hydrogen, mercury, and neon; (b) The absorption spectrum of hydrogen*

The Emission Spectrum of Hydrogen — Two Views

The diagram on the left in Figure 5.2.5 shows the circular orbits Bohr envisioned for the hydrogen electron and the transitions associated with the Lyman, Balmer, and Paschen emission spectra. The diagram on the right shows that the energy *differences* between various stationary states (n) decrease as the energies of those states increase. The arrows pointing down represent electrons falling to lower energy states and thus emitting energy. Electrons absorbing energy could be indicated by arrows pointing up and would represent absorption spectra.

Any electron transitions from an excited state down to $n = 1$ result in the emission of energy in the ultraviolet region of the electromagnetic spectrum (the Lyman series). Any transitions from excited states down to the third and fourth orbits result in energies in the infrared region being emitted (the Paschen and Brackett series respectively).

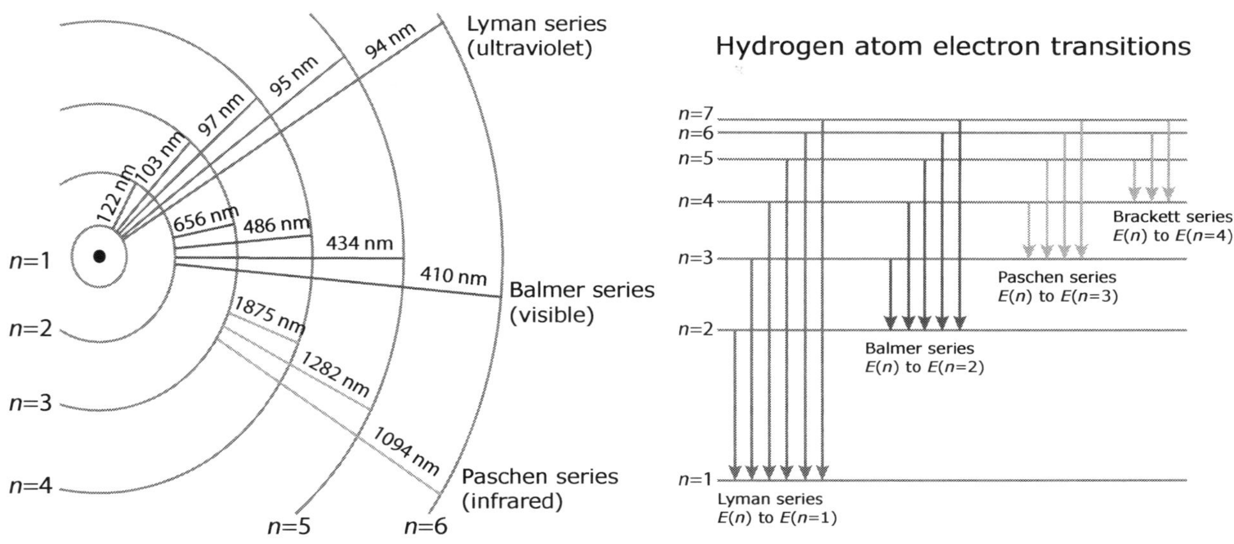

Figure 5.2.5 *The Lyman, Balmer, and Paschen emission series for hydrogen*

Quick Check

1. Describe the appearance of hydrogen's "bright-line" spectrum.

 ____

2. Briefly indicate how electrons generate each visible line in hydrogen's emission spectrum.

 ____

 ____

3. Which electron transitions in the emission spectrum generate lines in the UV region of the electromagnetic spectrum?

 ____

Using Some Simple Equations

In 1885, a Swiss schoolteacher named Johann Balmer found an equation that was able to determine the wavelengths of the lines in the visible portion of hydrogen's emission spectrum. Three years later, the Swedish physicist Johannes Rydberg derived an equation that could be used to calculate the wavelengths of all of hydrogen's spectral lines. This is worth mentioning because if a mathematical relationship exists for a natural phenomenon, it usually means there's a theoretical foundation waiting to be discovered. Both Balmer's and Rydberg's equations were based on data, rather than theory. Neither equation had any physical meaning in terms of atomic structure, but both worked.

The physical meaning was supplied by Niels Bohr. Bohr derived an equation for the energy associated with the electron in each allowed orbit. He correctly predicted the visible, ultraviolet, and infrared spectral lines in hydrogen's emission spectrum by calculating the energy differences between those stationary states.

Although a rigorous mathematical treatment of this material is not intended here, we will present two equations that are quite straightforward. The first equation gives the change in energy ΔE

(energy of photon released) when an electron initially in a higher energy orbit (with a higher quantum number n_h) drops to a lower energy orbit (and so with a lower quantum number n_l).

$$\Delta E = b\left(1/n_l^2 - 1/n_h^2\right)$$

where b is a constant with value of 2.18×10^{-18} J.

The second equation arises from the fact that, according to Planck's equation, the energy of this photon, $\Delta E = h\nu$. Because $\nu = c/\lambda$, we can replace ΔE with hc/λ. Now dividing both sides of the equation by hc yields:

$$1/\lambda = b/hc\left(1/n_l^2 - 1/n_h^2\right)$$

This equation allows us to solve for the wavelength λ of the spectral line we would observe when the electron lost energy as it made the above transition.

The combination of the constants, b/hc, is itself a constant. Remembering that Planck's constant, $h = 6.626 \times 10^{-34}$J·s and that the speed of light, $c = 3.00 \times 10^8$m/s, we can combine these three constants to give $b/hc = 1.097\ 30 \times 10^7\ \text{m}^{-1}$. Let's use this to calculate the wavelength of the spectral line we would see when hydrogen's electron made the transition from $n = 4$ down to $n = 2$.

Sample Problem — Calculating the Wavelength of Emission Spectral Lines

Calculate the wavelength λ (in nm) of the spectral line seen in hydrogen's emission spectrum when hydrogen's electron falls from the fourth allowed orbit ($n = 4$) to the second allowed orbit ($n = 2$).

What to Think about	How to Do It
1. Consider the equation: $1/\lambda = (1.097\ 30 \times 10^7\ \text{m}^{-1})\left(1/n_l^2 - 1/n_h^2\right)$ The values of n_l and n_h are given in the question: $n = 4$ and $n = 2$.	$1/\lambda = (1.097\ 30 \times 10^7\ \text{m}^{-1})\left(1/n_l^2 - 1/n_h^2\right)$ $= (1.097\ 30 \times 10^7\ \text{m}^{-1})\left(1/2^2 - 1/4^2\right)$ $= (1.097\ 30 \times 10^7\ \text{m}^{-1})(0.1875)$ $= 2.0574 \times 10^6\ \text{m}^{-1}$
2. Convert this to nanometers. This value corresponds exactly to the green line seen in hydrogen's emission spectrum.	$\lambda = \dfrac{1}{2.0574 \times 10^6\ \text{m}^{-1}} = 4.8604 \times 10^{-7}\ \text{m}$ $4.860 \times 10^{-7}\ \text{m} \times \dfrac{1.0 \times 10^9\ \text{nm}}{\text{m}} = 486.04\ \text{nm}$

Practice Problem

1. Use equation $\Delta E = b\left(1/n_l^2 - 1/n_h^2\right)$ and the value for b given above to calculate the energy released when an excited hydrogen electron drops from the fourth allowed orbit ($n = 4$) to the second allowed orbit ($n = 2$).

5.2 Activity: The Art of Emission Spectra

When the light emitted by vapourized and then thermally or electrically excited elements is viewed through a spectroscope, a unique line spectrum is observed for each element. In this activity, you will reproduce the emission spectra for lithium, cadmium, sodium, and strontium by colouring in the most visible spectral lines on diagrams representing those spectra.

Materials

- centimetre ruler
- various colours of felt pens or coloured pencils, including: blue, red, yellow and black

Procedure

1. Using felt pens or coloured pencils, draw vertical lines of the appropriate colour at each of the indicated wavelengths on the spectral diagrams for the elements listed below.
2. Once all the colours are drawn, use a black felt pen or coloured pencil to shade in all of the remaining space on each diagram. Be careful not to blacken out any of the coloured vertical lines.
3. After completing the diagrams, look up the emission spectrum of any other element of your choosing and draw that spectrum on the blank diagram below. You will discover that some atomic spectra include many lines while others contain only a few. Some suggestions are helium, mercury, potassium, or calcium.

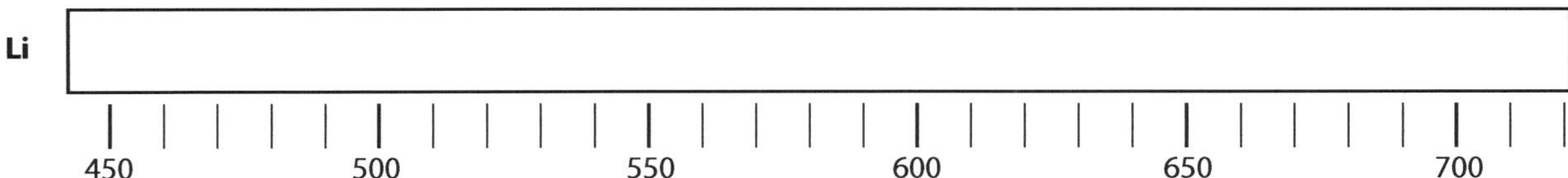

Lithium: 4 coloured lines — one blue at ~460 nm, one blue at ~496 nm, one yellow at ~610 nm, and one red at ~670 nm

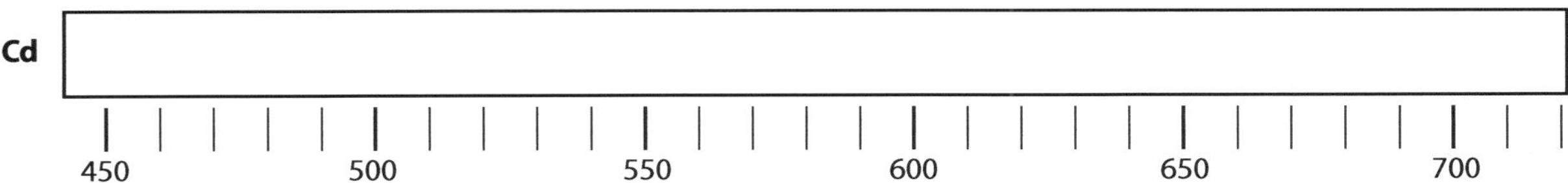

Cadmium: 5 coloured lines — three blue at ~467 nm, ~470 nm, and ~508 nm, one yellow at ~609 nm, and one red at ~642 nm

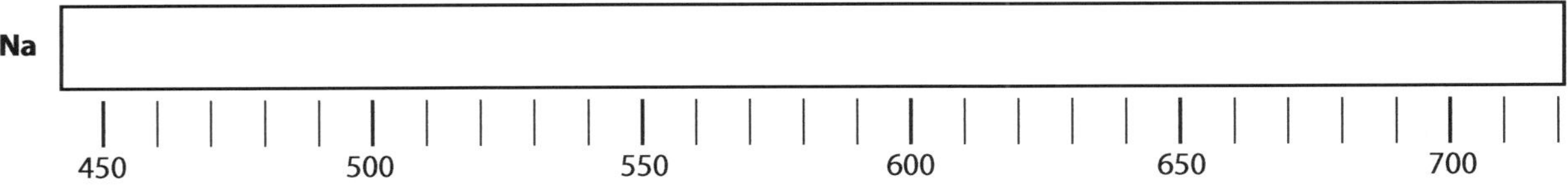

Sodium: 2 bright yellow lines close together at ~590 nm

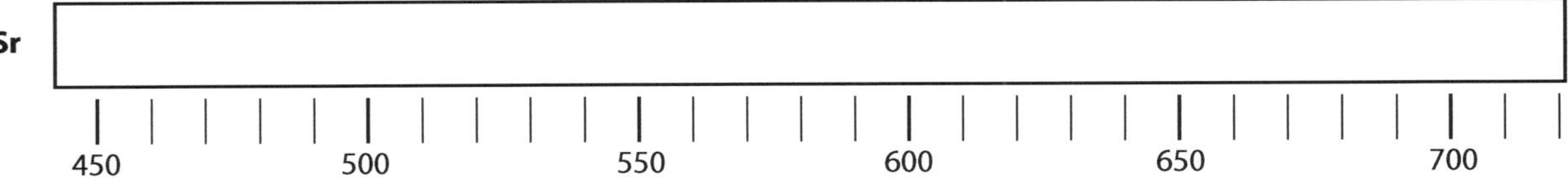

Strontium: 7 coloured lines — 4 blue at ~460 nm, ~482 nm, ~488 nm, and ~495 nm, and three red at ~670 nm, ~686 nm, and ~715 nm.

Emission Spectrum of Your Choice

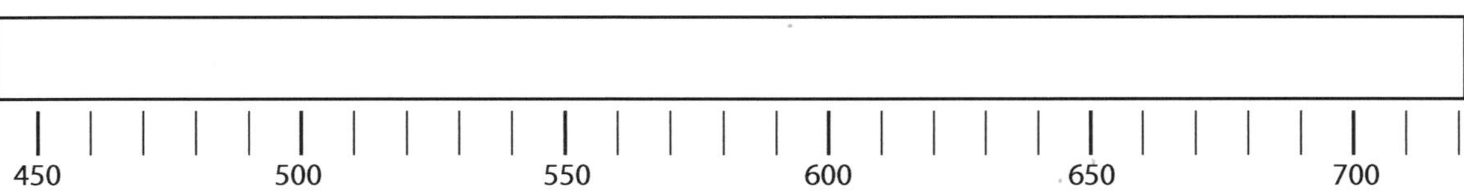

Results and Discussion

1. When we view the light emitted by heated or electrically excited vapour with the naked eye, we don't see the separate bright lines you've drawn above. Rather we see a single colour resulting from the combination all of those individual bright lines. Many cities use sodium vapour lamps for street lighting. Can you predict what colour of light those lamps emit?

2. The principle involving the emission of light resulting from excited electrons is the foundation of many modern conveniences and tools in our society from fluorescent lighting to lasers. Find out what the letters in the word "laser" stand for and find out at least 10 applications of lasers in our society.

5.2 Review Questions

1. Explain the serious problem initially associated with Rutherford's atomic model.

   It couldn't explain why the electrons stay in orbit around the nucleus

2. State Planck's quantum theory in your own words.

   one packet of light carries one unit: a quantum of energy

3. Why was this theory not accepted by most physicists at first?

4. What finally convinced the scientific community that Planck's theory was credible?

5. Explain how the work of Planck and Einstein contributed to Bohr's theory about electron behaviour.

6. State how Bohr's theory "saved" Rutherford's nuclear atomic model.

7. Briefly explain why hydrogen's visible emission spectrum does not resemble a continuous spectrum or rainbow

   because each energy level is distinct, and different distances away from each other, not in a continuous spectrum

8. Describe what you would expect to see if hydrogen's visible emission and absorption spectra were superimposed upon each other.

All the colors mixed together, so black or brown or a really small rainbow

9. Explain why, when hydrogen's electron transitions occur from excited states down to $n = 1$ or to $n = 3$, no visible spectral lines are observed.

because when that happens, infrared and ultraviolet light are emitted, which humans can't see

10. Calculate the energy released when an excited hydrogen electron returns from $n = 5$ to $n = 2$.

$c = \lambda \nu$

$\nu = c/\lambda$

$\nu = \frac{3.00 \times 10^8 \text{ m}}{\text{s}} \Big| \frac{1}{.434 \times 10^{-9} \text{ m}}$

$\nu = .069 \text{ s}^{-1}$

$E = h\nu$

$E = 6.626 \times 10^{-34} \text{ J}\cdot\text{s} \Big| \frac{.069}{\text{s}}$

$E = 4.58 \times 10^{-35} \text{ J}$

11. Calculate the wavelength of the spectral line seen when the electron transition described in 10 above occurs, and use the wavelength to identify the colour of this line.

5.3 Beyond Bohr — The Quantum Mechanical Model of the Atom

Warm Up

1. How did Max Planck and Albert Einstein contribute to the development of Niels Bohr's atomic theory?

2. State the main points of Bohr's atomic theory in your own words.

Particles Behaving Like Waves

Niels Bohr's theory firmly established the concept of fixed atomic energy levels. Although there were a few fine details of hydrogen's line spectrum that the theory couldn't account for, his model of the hydrogen atom appeared very promising. Unfortunately, when Bohr's theory was applied to the line spectra of atoms having more than one electron, it didn't work at all. All attempts to modify the theory to make it work were unsuccessful. It soon became clear that the atomic puzzle hadn't yet been solved.

Bohr assumed that an atom had only certain allowable energy levels in order to account for hydrogen's observed line spectrum. However, that assumption was not rooted in any physical theory. In other words, Bohr knew the energy levels had to be there, but not *why* they had to be there. It appeared that a new theory containing some bold ideas about the atom might be needed.

That new theory was eventually called quantum mechanics, and it had its beginnings in 1923 with the ideas of a young French aristocrat. Louis de Broglie had originally earned a degree in history and was trying to decide on a subject for his doctoral thesis in physics. He had just learned that a professor in Missouri named Arthur Compton had proven the existence of the light quanta (later called photons) proposed by Albert Einstein. A fascinating idea occurred to de Broglie: If waves behaved like particles, could it also be possible for particles to have wave properties? By proposing that matter was wavelike, de Broglie was also suggesting a reason, or theoretical foundation, for an electron's fixed energy levels. To understand this reason, we must briefly discuss some aspects of wave behaviour.

Wave Behaviour

Consider a string of length L under tension fixed at both ends, such as a guitar string (Figure 5.3.1). When the string is plucked, it begins to oscillate as a wave. As it oscillates, only certain frequencies (and therefore wavelengths) are possible if the wave is to be maintained. This stable or "standing" wave must have a wavelength (λ) such that a whole number (n) of half-wavelengths ($\lambda/2$) fit within the length L of the string. Any fractional amount of half-wavelengths will cause the wave to break down by a process known as destructive interference. Thus a stable wave can only exist if integral numbers of half-wavelengths exist within the length L of the string. That is:

$L = 1(\lambda/2)$, $L = 2(\lambda/2)$, $L = 3(\lambda/2)$, $L = 4(\lambda/2)$, $L = 5(\lambda/2)$,...etc, or if:

$L = n(\lambda/2)$, where n is a whole number: 1, 2, 3, 4,...etc.

Any situation where n is not a whole number, such as 3.3, will result in the wave breaking down. This means that there is a quantum restriction equal to $\lambda/2$ on the maintenance of the wave. Unless 1, 2, 3, 4 or any whole number of quanta (half-wavelengths) exists in the length of the string, no wave can be maintained.

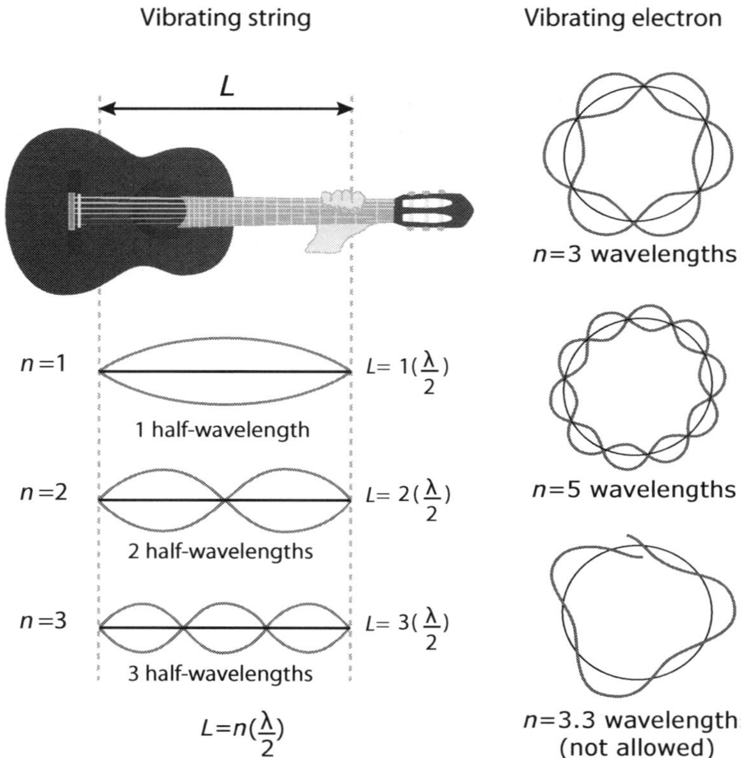

Figure 5.3.1 *Both for a guitar string and an electron, only certain wavelengths allow a standing wave to be maintained.*

Now imagine bending this string around and closing it into a circle representing an electron orbit. De Broglie considered what the requirements would be for a stable orbit if electrons did exhibit wave motion. He proposed that the only stable electron orbits were those whose size, and corresponding energy, allowed for standing electron waves to be maintained. Orbits of any other size would cause the electron wave to break down. Look again at Figure 5.3.1:

A condition for maintenance of a standing wave within a string of length *L* is a whole number *n* of half-wavelengths.	A condition for maintenance of a stable electron orbit: a circular standing electron wave.

An important consequence of prescribing a wave nature to the electron is that it suggests a *reason* for the electron's quantized energy states proposed by Bohr: The only allowed orbits ($n = 1, 2, 3$, etc.) for electrons are those whose size (and therefore energy) allows for a standing electron wave to be maintained.

De Broglie's Equation

In his Ph.D. thesis, De Broglie derived an equation to calculate the wavelength of a particle. He did so by combining two now-famous equations, one proposed by Albert Einstein and the other by Max Planck.

According to Einstein: $E = mc^2$ where *E* is energy, *m* is mass, and *c* is the speed of light
According to Planck: $E = hv$ where *E* is energy, *v* is frequency, and *h* is Planck's constant

Note also that because $c = \lambda v$, then $v = c/\lambda$
Therefore: $mc^2 = hc/\lambda$

De Broglie knew that any particle having a mass could never reach the speed of light, so he replaced the value c with v to represent the velocity of a particle. This gave:

$$mv^2 = hv/\lambda$$

Cancelling common terms yielded $mv = h/\lambda$ and so $h = mv\lambda$
Re-written as: $\boldsymbol{\lambda = h/mv}$

This is de Broglie's equation and it is significant for several reasons:

- First, it tells us that any moving particle, whether it's an electron or a baseball, has a wavelength that we can calculate.
- Second, it shows us that a particle's wavelength is inversely proportional to its mass: as the mass of a particle decreases, its wavelength increases and vice versa.
- Third (and perhaps most important), because the value of Planck's constant is so very small (6.626×10^{-34} J·s), virtually any particle big enough for us to see has a wavelength so incredibly small that it can't even be measured. However, particles with a mass as small as an electron have wavelengths that are very significant.

Calculating Wavelengths

We can demonstrate this by calculating the de Broglie wavelength for two particles, one we are familiar with and another we are not. A 100 mph (160 km/h) major league fastball and a hydrogen electron each have a wavelength (Figure 5.3.2). The baseball has a mass of 0.120 kg and a velocity of 44.4 m/s. It thus has a wavelength λ given by:

$$\lambda = \frac{6.626 \times 10^{-34}\ \text{J} \cdot \text{s}}{(0.120\ \text{kg})(44.4\ \text{m/s})} = 1.24 \times 10^{-34}\ \text{m}$$

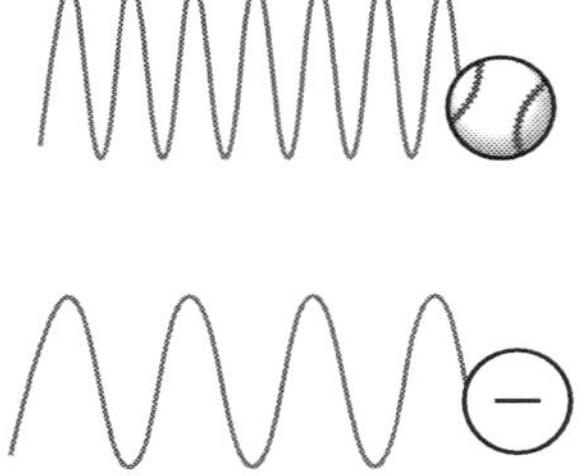

Figure 5.3.2 *All moving particles, large (a baseball) or tiny (an electron), have a wavelength that can be calculated.*

To put this wavelength into perspective, consider that a hydrogen atom has a diameter of approximately 2.4×10^{-10} m. That means the baseball's wavelength is not only far smaller than the baseball, it's also about 10^{24} times smaller than the smallest atom! Of course, no instrument can measure anything that small, and this result tells us that a baseball's particle nature is virtually all there is. That makes sense to us because "large" objects that we can see and that our frame of reference, personal experience, and common sense tell us are particles behave precisely the way we expect them to — like particles. Such objects don't pass through each other or create diffraction or interference patterns, and they certainly don't cancel themselves out. So obviously, to concern ourselves with a wave nature that is so insignificant would be ridiculous.

Now let's calculate the de Broglie wavelength for a much more elusive particle such as hydrogen's electron. The electron has a mass of 9.11×10^{-31} kg and an estimated velocity of approximately 0.7% the speed of light, which works out to 2.2×10^6 m/s. De Broglie's equation therefore yields:

$$\lambda = \frac{6.626 \times 10^{-34}\ \text{J} \cdot \text{s}}{(9.11 \times 10^{-31}\ \text{kg})(2.2 \times 10^6\ \text{m/s})} = 3.3 \times 10^{-10}\ \text{m}$$

Although this is certainly a small wavelength, it is 1.5 times larger than the hydrogen atom itself and therefore represents a significant aspect of the electron's nature. Imagine yourself shrinking down and entering hydrogen's nucleus. Looking out from that nucleus at the electron, you might see a wave rather than a particle!

Particle-Wave Duality

If the wave nature of electrons is so prominent, should we expect them to behave as other waves do? Should they produce diffraction patterns, be able to pass through each other, interfere with each other, and even cancel themselves out? As bizarre as it sounds, the answer is yes!

The answer sounds bizarre because we have no experience with particles or waves on the scale of the atomic or subatomic. In that world, where masses and distances are so small, neither particles nor waves behave the way we expect them to. In fact, the distinction between particles and waves doesn't even exist in that tiny realm. In the macroscopic world of large objects, we have either particles or waves, but in the quantum world, they are the same thing!

Many in the scientific community, including Niels Bohr, were initially skeptical about particles also being waves. Then, in 1927, Clinton Davisson and Lester Germer working at Bell Labs in the United States confirmed that electrons did indeed behave like waves. A beam of electrons directed at a nickel crystal generated a diffraction pattern similar to that produced by electromagnetic waves such as X-rays. This proved de Broglie's hypothesis and brought the theory of dual-nature full circle. Not only did waves behave like particles, but particles behaved like waves. Particle-wave duality set the stage for a very strange proposal soon to come about the nature of electrons.

In 1929, Louis de Broglie won the Nobel Prize in physics. The Swedish physicist who introduced him at the ceremony in Stockholm said, "When quite young, you threw yourself into the controversy raging around the most profound problem in physics. You had the boldness to assert, without the support of any known fact, that matter had not only a corpuscular nature, but also a wave nature. Experiment came later and established the correctness of your view."

Quick Check

1. What important concept concerning atomic structure was Bohr's theory responsible for?

   ____

2. Why did Bohr's atomic model need to be replaced?

   ____

3. If particles have a wave nature, why can't we detect that behaviour in the "big" macroscopic world?

   ____

   ____

Sample Problem — Using de Broglie's Equation

Use de Broglie's equation to calculate the wavelength of an M4 carbine rifle bullet having a mass of 4.1 g travelling at 884 m/s.

What to Think about	How to Do It
1. Remember that you should expect this wavelength to be very small given the relatively large mass of the rifle bullet.	
2. Use de Broglie's equation: *h/mv* Write the units for joules as kgm²/s².	$\lambda = \frac{h}{mv}$
3. Express all quantities in scientific notation and pay attention to significant figures in your final answer.	$= \frac{6.626 \times 10^{-34}\ \text{kg}\cdot\text{m}^2/\text{s}^2}{(0.0041\ \text{kg})(884\ \text{m/s})} = 1.8 \times 10^{-34}\ \text{m}$

Practice Problems — Using de Broglie's Equation

1. Calculate the de Broglie wavelength of an α-particle having a mass of 6.64×10^{-27} kg travelling at 16 000 km/s.

2. Calculate how small the mass of a particle travelling at 16 000 km/s would have to be to have a wavelength equal to that of green light, approximately 486 nm. (Remember to change km/s to m/s and nm to m. Note that the mass you calculate will be in kg.)

3. Andy Roddick holds the record for the fastest tennis serve at 240 km/h. Calculate the de Broglie wavelength of a tennis ball with mass of 56 g travelling at 240 km/h.

Heisenberg, Schrödinger, and Orbitals

As mentioned earlier, not everyone was comfortable with the idea that electrons could be both a particle and a wave. Around 1925, two competing mathematical theories existed that attempted to explain and predict electron behaviour. Werner Heisenberg, a young German physicist, developed "matrix mechanics," which involved complicated and difficult equations. It treated the electron as a pure particle with quantum behaviour.

An Austrian physicist named Erwin Schrödinger rejected the idea of an electron as a particle. He decided to view the electron mathematically as a pure wave to eliminate some of the strange quantum aspects of electron behaviour. In his "wave mechanical" description of the electron, Schrödinger used an equation to describe the electron as a "wave function." The math was easier than the matrix approach, and the wave equation was popular with many physicists.

Each of the two scientists believed that his interpretation was correct, yet neither seemed able to sufficiently predict the mysterious comings and goings of electrons. Within a year, it became clear that matrix and wave mechanics were actually different ways of getting to the same answers. Soon Heisenberg and Schrödinger became crucial contributors as quantum mechanics was eventually united into one theory.

Figure 5.3.3 *Erwin Schrodinger*

Heisenberg's Principle

In June of 1925, while teaching at the University of Gottingen, Heisenberg suffered a severe hay fever attack and took a leave of absence to an isolated island in the North Sea. During his stay, he focussed on the problem of electron measurement. After much thought, he came up with one of the most important principles of modern physics. Heisenberg identified a fundamental uncertainty associated with measuring any particles. He called it the uncertainty principle. In the form of a simple equation, the principle stated that it was impossible to know exactly both where any particle was located and where it was going at the same time. Furthermore, the more certain you became of one measurement, the less certain you were of the other.

Much like de Broglie's hypothesis, the equation for the Heisenberg uncertainty principle appeared quite straightforward, but the ramifications were enormous! The principle can be written this way:

$$(m\Delta v)(\Delta x) \geq h/2\pi$$

Figure 5.3.4 *Werner Heisenberg*

where m = mass of a particle, Δv = uncertainty in velocity of a particle, Δx = uncertainty in the position or location of a particle, and h = Planck's constant. Think of the symbol Δ as representing the "plus or minus value" or the "spread of results" in the velocity and location.

The equation shows that the uncertainty in where a particle of constant mass is going (Δv) multiplied by the uncertainty in where a particle is located (Δx) is greater than or equal to a very tiny constant ($h/2\pi$). This means that the two values are inversely related.

The equation tells us that as we become more certain about an object's position Δx decreases. As Δx decreases, the uncertainty in where the object is going, $\mathbf{\Delta}v$, increases and vice versa. This certainly isn't our experience in the world of large objects. For objects big enough to see, such as cars and baseballs, it's easy at any point in time to say both where they are and where they're going. If it wasn't, then the world of large moving objects would be a very dangerous place to live! But the world at the atomic scale is much less cooperative.

Once again, a similarity to de Broglie becomes evident as we see an inverse relationship involving Planck's constant. And once again, the fact that the constant is so incredibly small means that the uncertainty principle only matters on an atomic scale.

Seeing and Measuring

The key to understanding this principle at the atomic level is to ask ourselves how we "see" anything. To locate any particle of matter, whether it's a baseball or an electron, we must somehow illuminate it. We see things, whether they are big or small, because light energy in the form of photons bounces off those objects, is collected and eventually interpreted by our brain or by instruments.

For example, suppose we were given a flashlight and told to locate a baseball thrown into a dark room. No problem; we simply turn on the flashlight and immediately know where the ball is and where it's going. Of course the countless photons striking the baseball have no measurable effect on it because of the ball's large mass. But what if we used an atomic bomb to supply the energy to illuminate the baseball? Obviously that amount of energy would blow the ball (and the room and building) away so that nothing meaningful concerning its position or motion could be known.

"Seeing" an electron also requires that some form of illuminating radiation bounce off of the electron, and there lies the problem. Because the mass of an electron is so unimaginably small, even the energy of one photon striking the electron is more than enough to blow it away in much the same way that the bomb would blow away the baseball. Stated another way, for quantum systems, the very act of measuring something causes a significant change in what we're measuring. This applies to any measuring method we know. So if Heisenberg was right, then finding electrons and predicting their behaviour with certainty isn't only difficult, it's impossible!

Schrödinger's Equation

The obvious question is how can we then describe electrons in atoms at all? The answer comes in the form of a compromise from Schrödinger's wave equation. The equation is complicated and we needn't worry about solving it here, but what it tells us about electrons is important. Schrödinger represented the electron as a wave function he called ψ (Greek letter psi).

The wave function is obtained by solving the equation using the allowed energy states associated with electrons in atoms. Its square, ψ^2, gives the probability of finding those electrons within a region of space around the nucleus. The regions in which there is the highest probability of finding electrons are called atomic orbitals**.** So **atomic orbitals** represent those regions in three-dimensional space around a nucleus where electrons with a particular energy are most likely to be found. We can view an orbital as a probability volume or a "charge cloud" representing a 3D picture of where we will probably encounter electrons around the atom's nucleus. For different allowed energy states, different numbers and types of orbitals exist. We will discuss these in the next section.

So it seems that probability is woven into the fabric of matter at its most basic level and many scientists, including Albert Einstein, resisted this idea. One of Einstein's most famous statements regarding his objection to the uncertainty principle was, "God does not throw dice."

Note the difference between Bohr's electron orbit and an electron orbital. No evidence exists that electrons follow a particular path around the nucleus, and Bohr's atomic model of a negative particle in a specific orbit has been abandoned. Rather, quantum mechanics describes electron behaviour using the mathematics of waves to determine the probability of finding an electron around the nucleus. This is an orbital.

Werner Heisenberg was awarded the Nobel Prize in 1932 and Erwin Schrödinger received the honor the following year for their contributions to quantum mechanics.

At this point, it's valuable to summarize the three important aspects of the quantum mechanical view of the atom.

1. The energies of electrons in atoms are quantized because of their wave nature. This relates to the idea that only certain allowed energy states associated with standing electron waves can exist.

2. The Heisenberg uncertainty principle states that it is impossible to simultaneously state both where an electron is and where it's going.

3. Atomic orbitals are those regions in 3D space around a nucleus where electrons with a particular energy are most likely to be found.

Quick Check

1. How did Heisenberg and Schrödinger see the electron differently?

   ____

2. According to quantum mechanics, how can "throwing dice" apply to describing electron behaviour?

   ____

   ____

3. Contrast Bohr's electron orbit with the quantum mechanical electron orbital.

   ____

   ____

5.3 Activity: Uncle Werner says, "Consider This"

Question

Why must the Heisenberg uncertainty principle be considered when discussing quantum systems?

Procedure

Consider the following two scenarios and answer the questions below each one.

Scenario 1

Student A and student B are each given identical laboratory thermometers. They are asked to measure the temperature of the water in a large heated swimming pool as accurately as possible. The water temperature is approximately 35°C. Each thermometer reads 25°C before the measurement.

Student A lowers the thermometer bulb into the water in the pool. She waits for the reading to stabilize and then records the temperature.

Student B places 5 mL of pool water into an insulated test tube and then places the thermometer in the test tube. He waits for the reading to stabilize and then records the temperature.

Which reading will more accurately reflect the water temperature in the pool and why?

Scenario 2

Student A and student B are each blindfolded, given a hockey stick, and placed in identical airplane hangars. Somewhere in the hangar where student A is standing is a school bus. Somewhere in the hangar where student B is standing is a small balloon floating at eye level. The students are told to find the object in their hangar by swinging their hockey stick as fast as they can until they hit that object. As soon as they find it, they must stop at the place where they encounter the object.

Which student's final position will more accurately reflect the final location of the object they are looking for and why?

Results and Discussion

1. Use the above scenarios and your answers to the questions to make a general statement about why the Heisenberg uncertainty principle cannot be ignored when discussing quantum systems.

5.3 Review Questions

1. How were the Bohr and de Broglie pictures of the electron different?

2. How did de Broglie's hypothesis suggest a reason for the allowed energy states of electrons in atoms?

3. Why can wave-nature be ignored when describing the behaviour of macroscopic particles?

4. Why must wave nature be considered when describing the behaviour of particles as small as electrons?

5. Complete the following statements:
   (a) As a particle's mass increases, its wave nature ________________ (increases or deceases).

   (b) As a particle's mass decreases, its wave nature ________________ (increases or decreases).

6. How can de Broglie's theory be seen as the opposite of Planck's quantum theory?

7. What do the two theories of Max Planck and Louis de Broglie, taken together, mean about the existence of pure particles or pure waves?

8. Suggest a reason why we can ignore Heisenberg's uncertainty principle when locating macroscopic objects such as cars and baseballs.

9. Assume a particle is travelling at 1% the speed of light (which is approximately 3 000 000 m/s). Calculate the mass of this particle if its wavelength is approximately equal to that of gamma radiation at 1.0×10^{-12} m.

10. State a major contribution that the following scientists made to our understanding of the atom by writing one sentence for each:

    (a) Niels Bohr

    (b) Louis de Broglie

    (c) Erwin Schrödinger

    (d) Werner Heisenberg

5.4 Applying Quantum Mechanics to Electrons in Atoms

Warm Up

1. What part of Bohr's theory remains as part of the quantum mechanical view of the atom?

   ____

2. Quantum mechanics replaces the concept of an electron orbit with an orbital. What is an electron orbital?

   ____

3. The laws of probability are a necessary part of describing electron behaviour. Why?

   ____

Starting with Hydrogen — One on One

In this section, we will apply the quantum mechanical model of the atom to describing electrons in the atoms of the elements. We will begin with hydrogen and then use that information to expand our discussion to include multi-electron atoms.

In section 5.3, the analogy of a guitar string helped to explain the requirement of standing waves for the allowed energy states of electrons in atoms. If we solve Schrödinger's wave equation for the allowed energy states for hydrogen, we see that each energy state results in different numbers and types of orbitals. The equation shows us that the higher the energy, the greater the number and types of orbitals present.

Quantum Numbers

In an atom, these three-dimensional electron waves or orbitals are more complicated than a standing wave on a guitar string. To describe them, quantum mechanics employs the use of special numbers called **quantum numbers** Each quantum number specifies something different about the orbitals and electrons. We will discuss these numbers as we investigate the orbitals associated with each of allowed energy states for hydrogen.

The Principal Quantum Number (*n*)

The first quantum number is called the **principal quantum number** (*n*). It indicates the relative size of the atomic orbital.

We have already been introduced to this number because it also represents the allowed energy states for the electron. We know that the value of *n* can be a positive integer (1, 2, 3, and so on).

When hydrogen's electron is in the lowest allowed energy state or ground state, then $n = 1$. Schrödinger's equation shows us where an electron possessing that amount of energy will most likely be found. When we represent this pictorially, we see an electron "probability density diagram" resembling a spherical cloud. The cloud is what you might see if you could take many snapshots of the hydrogen electron around the nucleus and then superimpose all of them onto one picture. At the centre of this cloud is the hydrogen nucleus. The cloud's density is not uniform throughout, but is greater near the nucleus and decreases as we move away. This tells us that the probability of locating the electron is higher closer to the nucleus and lower further away from the nucleus.

As we move out from the nucleus, we find that hydrogen's electron in its ground state is likely to spend most of its time a slight distance from the nucleus, rather than at the nucleus itself. This is called the "radial probability." It's interesting to note that the electron's distance from the nucleus to the region of highest probability corresponds exactly to the orbit for this electron that Bohr calculated. Remember, however, that Bohr assumed the electron followed a circular path and would always be found at that distance from the nucleus. Quantum mechanics describes this as the most probable distance from the nucleus for the electron.

When we enclose the cloud in a volume representing about a 90% probability of finding the electron, we call this the 1s orbital. The number "1" represents the principal quantum number, telling us the size of the orbital, and the letter "s" refers to the type or "shape" of the orbital. Figure 5.4.1(a) shows an artistic representation of what a spherical 1s orbital might look like if viewed from the outside. Figure 5.4.1(b) is a cross-sectional view showing radial probability (indicated by greater dot density a slight distance from nucleus).

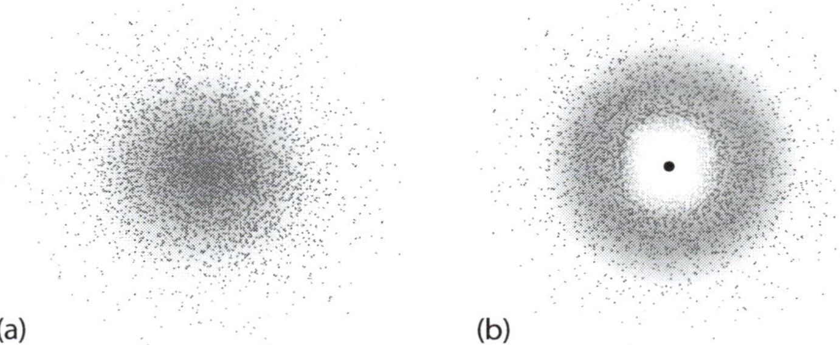

Figure 5.4.1 *(a) A view of a spherical 1s orbital from the outside; (b) A cross-sectional view of a spherical 1s orbital*

The Second Quantum Number (ℓ)

The second quantum number is called the **angular momentum quantum number** (ℓ). It is related to the shape of an atomic orbital.

The different values of ℓ at each energy level represent the number of orbital shapes or sublevels that exist in that energy level. That number equals the energy level itself. So for $n = 1$, there is only one orbital type or shape, namely the s orbital.

Each new energy level has one new orbital shape in addition to those existing in the previous level. So if hydrogen's electron is "excited" and absorbs enough energy to reach the second allowed energy state, then $n = 2$ and two orbital shapes or sublevels exist. There is an s orbital with a shape identical to the 1s, except larger, called the 2s orbital. This means that the electron with this greater amount of energy will spend more of its time farther from the nucleus. There is also a new shape: a p orbital. As $n = 2$, we call it a 2p orbital and it resembles a dumbbell or long balloon pinched in the middle (where the nucleus is located).

The Third Quantum Number (m_ℓ)

The third quantum number, called the **magnetic quantum number** (m_ℓ) tells us the orientation in space of a given atomic orbital.

The number of possible different orientations in space for any orbital shape also represents the number of individual orbitals of that particular shape or sublevel.

Only a single s orbital exists in any given energy level because a spherical cloud can only have one orientation in 3D space. However, this new p sublevel includes three separate orbitals, each with a different spatial orientation. If we consider a 3D set of Cartesian coordinates, one is oriented along an imaginary *x*-axis (with the nucleus at the origin) called a $2p_x$ orbital. The other two are oriented along the *y*- and *z*-axes and are called the $2p_y$ and $2p_z$ orbitals respectively. Each of these 2p orbitals is identical in energy to the others. For hydrogen, they are also identical in energy to the 2s orbital. Chemists call orbitals of equal energy "degenerate" orbitals.

In Figure 5.4.2, note that the lobes of each p orbital in the first three diagrams disappear at the origin where the nucleus is located. This means that the amplitude of the electron wave at the nucleus is zero. A wave amplitude of zero is called a node, and it tells us that there is a zero probability of locating the electron here. In the far left diagram in Figure 5.4.2, all three 2p orbitals are shown together. Once again, the nucleus is at the centre or origin.

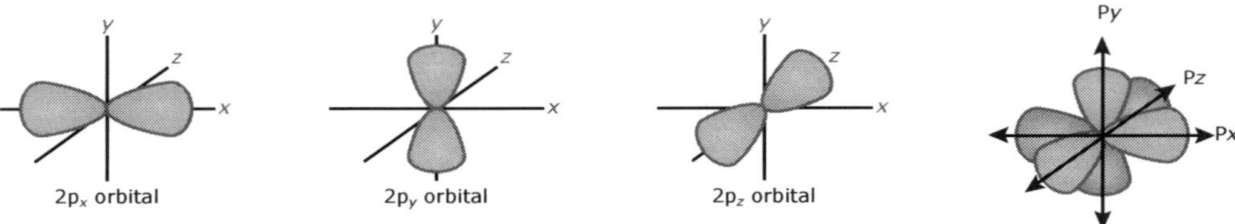

Figure 5.4.2 *The p orbitals are each shown individually in the first three diagrams. The last diagram shows them all together.*

We noted earlier that the number of different sublevels in any energy level equals the value of *n*. We also see here that a total of four orbitals exists in the second energy level. So the value n^2 tells us the number of orbitals existing in the nth energy level. In this case, there are $2^2 = 4$ orbitals: one 2s and three 2p orbitals.

The three quantum numbers, taken together, will always specify a particular atomic orbital because they tell us all we need to know about that orbital: its size, shape, and orientation in space.

If hydrogen's electron absorbs enough energy to reach the third allowed energy state, then $n = 3$ and three different orbital shapes or sublevels exist. As expected, we see one spherical 3s orbital and three dumbbell-shaped 3p orbitals. But we also discover a third sublevel whose orbitals have a more complicated shape. This is called the 3d sublevel and it contains five different orbitals, each with a different spatial orientation. Orbitals in a given sublevel are equal in energy to each other, and in hydrogen's case, are also equal in energy to all of the other orbitals in the energy level. This means that in a given energy level, hydrogen's electron has an equal likelihood of occupying any of them.

Although the d orbitals are shown in Figure 5.4.3, you may not be required to remember either their shapes or their names. You should, however, know that there are five of them.

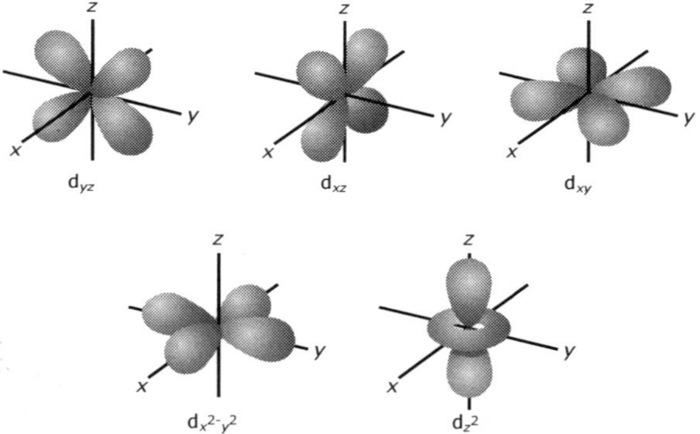

Figure 5.4.3 *The d orbitals*

Notice that as $n = 3$, there are three sublevels: 3s, 3p, and 3d. Also, there are a total of nine orbitals: one 3s orbital, three 3p orbitals, and five 3d orbitals corresponding to 3^2.

Finally, let's elevate hydrogen's electron to the fourth energy level, where $n = 4$. A higher energy level means that the electron will spend more of its time farther from the nucleus than when it possesses energy equal to $n = 1, 2$, or 3. Therefore, the orbitals or "charge clouds" are larger.

In the fourth energy level, we see the expected 4s, three 4p, and five 4d orbitals. As well, because $n = 4$, we also see a fourth shape called the 4f sublevel. Each higher energy level introduces another sublevel with a greater number (by two) of more complicated orbitals than the previous ones, and so there are seven 4f orbitals, each with a more complicated shape than the d orbitals. You should remember the number of f orbitals as well. The fourth energy level results in $4^2 = 16$ orbitals: one 4s, three 4p, five 4d, and seven 4f orbitals, all of which are equal in energy in the case of hydrogen.

Let's summarize what we have learned about energy levels and orbitals using a table and a diagram. Table 5.4.1 shows the sublevels and orbitals for the first four energy levels. Figure 5.4.4 is the energy diagram for hydrogen showing the sublevels and orbitals present from $n = 1$ through $n = 4$. Each circle represents an orbital. Note that all the sublevels are of equal energy in each allowed energy state.

Table 5.4.1 *Sublevels and orbitals for the first four energy levels*

Principal Quantum Number or Energy Level (n)	Number of Orbital Shapes or Sublevels per Energy Level (n)	Total Number of Orbitals per Energy Level (n^2)
1	**1** – 1s sublevel	**1** – the 1s orbital
2	**2** – 2s sublevel 2p sublevel	**4** – one 2s orbital three 2p orbitals
3	**3** – 3s sublevel 3p sublevel 3d sublevel	**9** – one 3s orbital three 3p orbitals five 3d orbitals
4	**4** – 4s sublevel 4p sublevel 4d sublevel 4f sublevel	**16** – one 4s orbital three 4p orbitals five 4d orbitals seven 4f orbitals

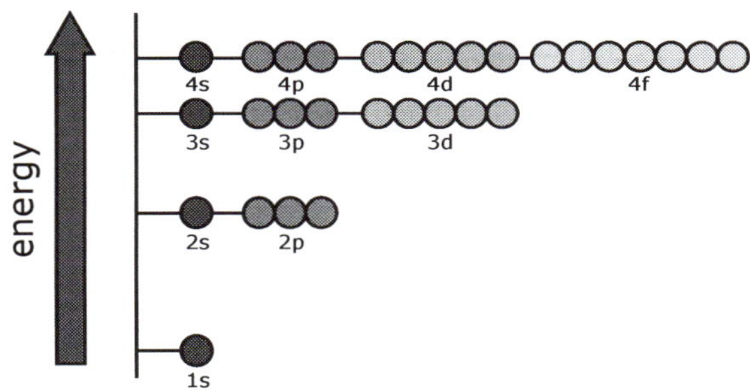

Figure 5.4.4 *Energy diagram for hydrogen. Each circle represents an orbital*

Quick Check

1. State what each of the three quantum numbers described above tells us about atomic orbitals.

2. (a) What is the difference between a 1s and a 2s orbital?

   (b) What is the difference between a $2p_x$ orbital and a $2p_y$ orbital?

3. How many different orbitals are available to an excited hydrogen electron in the fourth energy level?

The Orbitals of Multi-Electron Atoms

Hydrogen is the simplest atom with one proton in the nucleus surrounded by one electron in a 1s orbital in its ground state. There are no electron-electron interactions, and in any excited state, all of the atomic orbitals available to that single electron are of equal energy.

We might expect a different situation, however, for multi-electron atoms. Electrons are charged particle-waves. It seems reasonable to conclude that they will affect each other when two or more of them occupy the same region of space around an atom's nucleus — and they do.

To describe those electrons in multi-electron atoms, we must introduce several additional considerations.

Experiments have shown that the single electron in hydrogen generates a tiny magnetic field as if the electron were a spinning charge. Also, in any sample of hydrogen, analyzing the many atoms present shows two opposing magnetic fields. This tells us that in half of the atoms, the electrons seem to spin in one direction and, in the remainder of the atoms, in the other direction. An electron's spin is as fundamental a part of its nature as its charge.

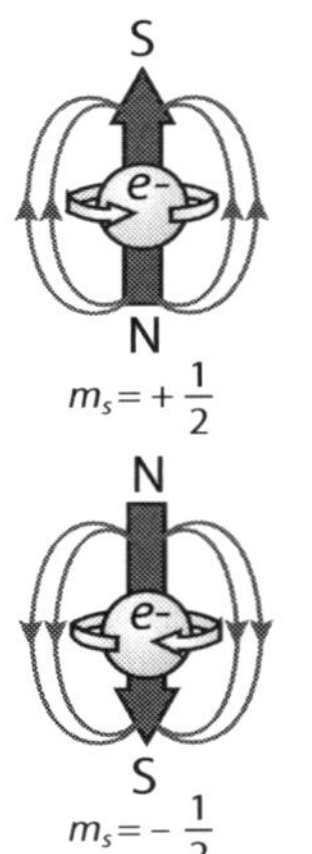

Figure 5.4.5 *The spin quantum number (m_s) identifies which possible spin an electron has.*

The fourth quantum number is called the **spin quantum number** (m_s). It tells us the two possible electron spins, either +½ or –½.

The Pauli Exclusion Principle

We already know that we can identify any orbital in an atom by the use of the first three quantum numbers, but we must use all four quantum numbers mentioned to specify any electron in an atom.

This is based on the fact that any atomic orbital can hold a maximum of two electrons. When two electrons are in the same orbital, their spins must be opposite. Originally proposed in 1925 by the Austrian physicist Wolfgang Pauli, this can be viewed as the first rule governing electrons in multi-electron atoms.

1. The **Pauli exclusion principle**: No two electrons in the same atom can be described by the same set of four quantum numbers.

If two electrons are in the same atomic orbital, they therefore have the same first three quantum numbers. Because they then must have opposite spins, their fourth quantum numbers are different.

We noted earlier that the total number of orbitals existing in any level n equals n^2.

If two electrons can occupy each orbital, the maximum number of electrons that can exist in any energy level n is given by $2n^2$.

A further consideration for multi-electron atoms is the effect of electron-electron repulsions on the relative energies of the sublevels in a given energy level. For hydrogen, where no repulsive forces exist, all of the sublevels in any energy level have identical energies. This is not the case for atoms of other elements. Although the same types of orbitals exist in multi-electron atoms, their relative energies are different. Repulsive forces cause a sublevel with a greater number of orbitals to have a greater energy. Therefore the order of sublevel energies is:

s < p < d < f.

Consider Figure 5.4.6. Compare this energy diagram for a multi-electron atom with Figure 5.4.4 for hydrogen. Note that in several cases energies get closer together as *n* increases. In these cases, repulsive forces are such that some sublevels containing smaller orbitals actually have higher energies than some larger orbitals. For example, observe the relative energy of the 3d compared to the 4s sublevel.

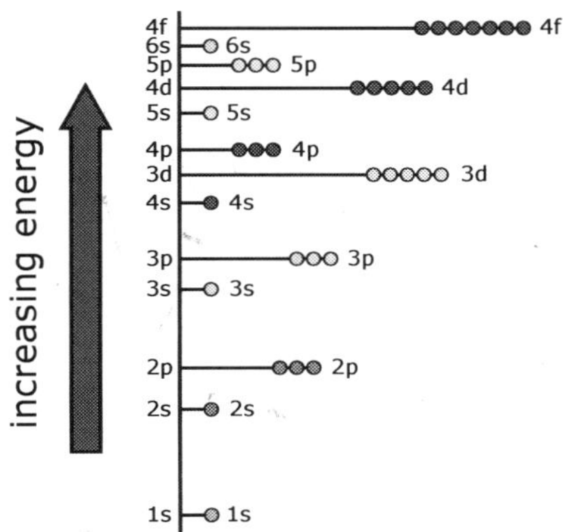

Figure 5.4.6 *Energy diagram for multi-electron atoms*

Quick Check

1. What does the fourth quantum number tell us about electrons?

2. Why can't two electrons in the same atom have the same four quantum numbers?

3. What is the maximum number of electrons that can exist in the energy levels *n* = 1 through *n* = 4?

Electron Configurations and Orbital Diagrams

We are now in a position to organize electrons into orbitals for the atoms of the elements. Understanding this organization will prove to be a powerful tool as we discuss the periodic table and bonding in the next chapter. In beginnning this process, we introduce the second rule associated with describing electrons in multi-electron atoms.

2. The **Aufbau principle**: When filling orbitals, the lowest energy orbitals available are always filled first. ("Aufbau" means a building or a construction in German.)

The order for filling orbitals is given above in Figure 5.4.6, showing sublevel energies. We start at the lowest energy orbitals and move up.

Let's begin with hydrogen. In its lowest energy or ground state, hydrogen's electron exists in the 1s orbital. We can represent this in two ways:

1. We can use a shorthand notation called an **electron configuration,** which is written in the format $n\ell^{\#}$ showing the energy level, sublevel, and number of electrons respectively. Hydrogen's electron configuration is therefore written as: $1s^1$. Read as "one s one," this tells us that hydrogen's one electron resides in the 1s orbital in its ground state.

2. We can construct an **orbital diagram**, which depicts electrons and their spin using arrows facing up and down. The arrows are placed inside boxes or over lines representing individual orbitals in sublevels. Hydrogen's orbital diagram is shown as:

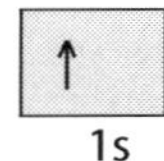

The configuration for the next element, helium, is $1s^2$. This is read "one s two" rather than "one s squared." Following the Pauli exclusion principle, the orbital diagram shows the two electrons with opposite spins in the now full 1s orbital:

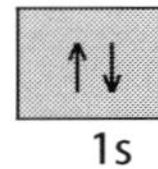

To indicate increasing sublevel energy, the boxes can be written vertically or also left to right to save space on a page. Let's continue below by moving past helium to the elements in period 2 of the periodic table using horizontally written orbital diagrams. Note that period 2 corresponds to the second energy level, $n = 2$. Following the Aufbau principle:

	Electron Configuration	**Orbital Diagram** INCREASING ENERGY				
		1s	**2s**	**2p**		
lithium	$1s^2 2s^1$	↑↓	↑			
beryllium	$1s^2 2s^2$	↑↓	↑↓			
For the 2p sublevel:						
boron	$1s^2 2s^2 2p^1$	↑↓	↑↓	↑		

Note that the sum of the superscript numbers equals the total number of electrons present. We must now use the third rule governing orbitals in multi-electron atoms:

3. **Hund's rule:** When orbitals of equal energy are being filled, the most stable configuration is the one with the maximum number of unpaired electrons with the same spin.

So carbon and nitrogen's orbital diagrams are:

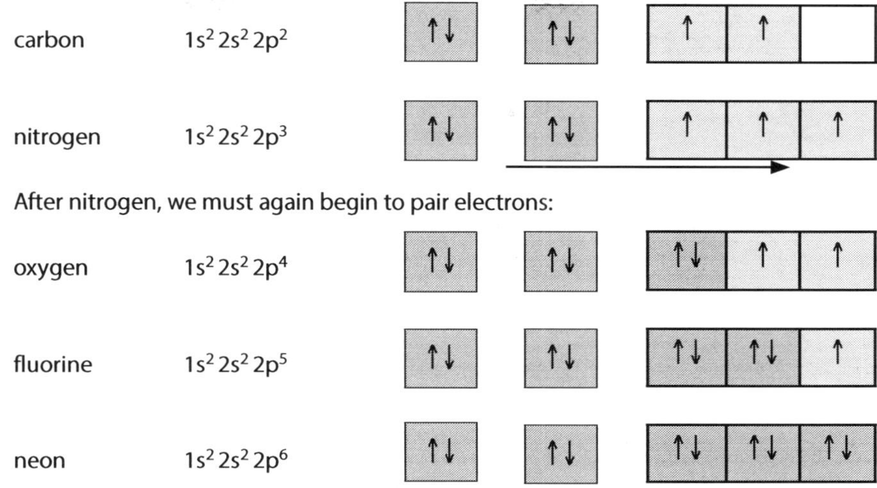

After nitrogen, we must again begin to pair electrons:

oxygen $1s^2 2s^2 2p^4$

fluorine $1s^2 2s^2 2p^5$

neon $1s^2 2s^2 2p^6$

After a noble gas, a new period begins in the periodic table and so too, a new energy level. As we begin period 3, let's represent the elements up to scandium in Table 5.4.2 using electron configurations only. We can condense electron configurations using **core notation**, in which the configuration of the previous noble gas is represented by that noble gas symbol in square brackets as shown in the table. Outer electrons are indicated in **bold** type.

Table 5.4.2 *Electron Configurations of Period 3 Elements up to Scandium*

Element	Full Electron Configuration	Core Notation
sodium	$1s^2 2s^2 2p^6$ **$3s^1$**	[Ne] **$3s^1$**
magnesium	$1s^2 2s^2 2p^6$ **$3s^2$**	[Ne] **$3s^2$**
aluminum	$1s^2 2s^2 2p^6$ **$3s^2 3p^1$**	[Ne] **$3s^2 3p^1$**
silicon	$1s^2 2s^2 2p^6$ **$3s^2 3p^2$**	[Ne] **$3s^2 3p^2$**
phosphorus	$1s^2 2s^2 2p^6$ **$3s^2 3p^3$**	[Ne] **$3s^2 3p^3$**
sulphur	$1s^2 2s^2 2p^6$ **$3s^2 3p^4$**	[Ne] **$3s^2 3p^4$**
chlorine	$1s^2 2s^2 2p^6$ **$3s^2 3p^5$**	[Ne] **$3s^2 3p^5$**
argon	$1s^2 2s^2 2p^6$ **$3s^2 3p^6$**	[Ne] **$3s^2 3p^6$**
potassium	$1s^2 2s^2 2p^6 3s^2 3p^6$ **$4s^1$**	[Ar] **$4s^1$**
calcium	$1s^2 2s^2 2p^6 3s^2 3p^6$ **$4s^2$**	[Ar] **$4s^2$**
scandium	$1s^2 2s^2 2p^6 3s^2 3p^6$ **$4s^2 3d^1$**	[Ar] **$4s^2 3d^1$**

Notice in the table that, as we move from argon to potassium, the 4s sublevel starts to fill before the 3d sublevel. After the 4s sublevel, the 3d sublevel starts to fill, reaching the first transition metal, scandium. Although the 3d sublevel fills after the 4s sublevel, the 3d sublevel still contains electrons that spend most of their time nearer the nucleus and so is inside the 4s sublevel. Some periodic tables indicate the electron configurations in order of sublevel size and so will show scandium's configuration as [Ar] $3d^1 4s^2$.

Figure 5.4.7 is a simple way of remembering the order for filling sublevels. We begin at the top with the 1s and fill that sublevel. After reaching the end of each arrow, we then start at the top of the next arrow below it. When using this diagram, you must remember how many electrons each sublevel can hold.

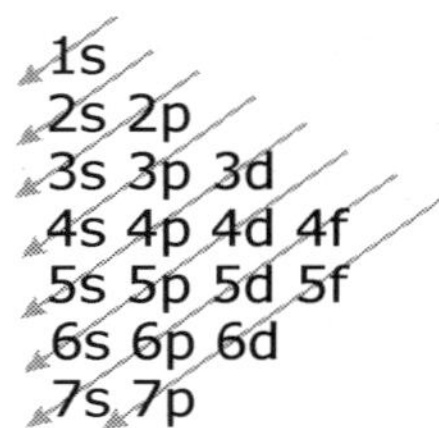

Figure 5.4.7 *This diagram indicates the order for filling sublevels.*

Sample Problem — Drawing an Orbital Diagram

Draw the orbital diagram and write the full electron configuration and the core notation for an atom of cobalt in its ground state.

What to Think about

1. Cobalt's atomic number is 27 and so the orbital diagram must account for 27 electrons. Cobalt is a transition metal in period 4 in the periodic table. We should expect the highest energy electrons to be in the 3d subshell.
2. Remember how many electrons are placed in each subshell as you fill the orbitals and employ Hund's rule as necessary.
3. Sketch the diagonal diagram to help you remember the order that subshells fill.
4. Represent each electron in an orbital using an arrow as in the notation described above.

How to Do It

Orbital diagram for cobalt:

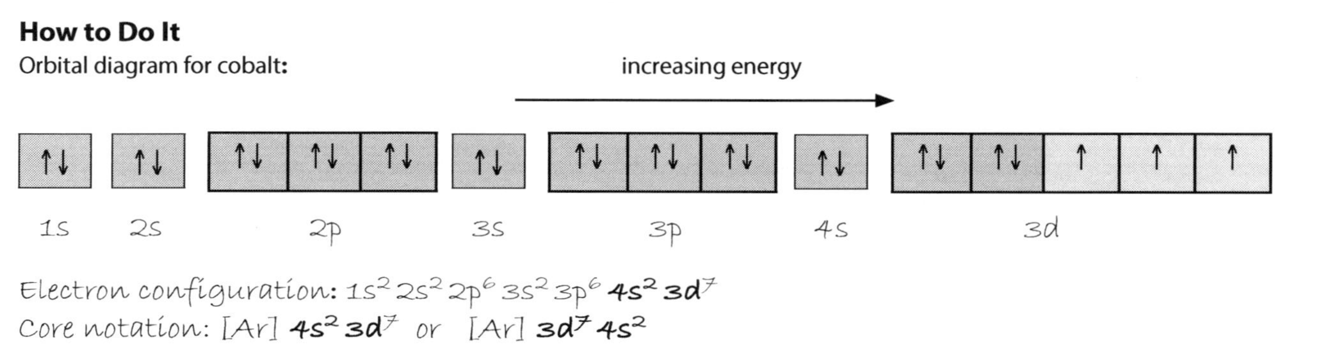

Electron configuration: $1s^2 2s^2 2p^6 3s^2 3p^6$ **$4s^2 3d^7$**

Core notation: [Ar] **$4s^2 3d^7$** or [Ar] **$3d^7 4s^2$**

Practice Problem — Drawing an Orbital Diagram

1. Write the full electron configuration and draw the orbital diagram for an atom of titanium in its ground state.

Ions and Other Charged Topics

Recall that a cation has fewer electrons than the original neutral atom and an anion has more. This means that the electron configurations for ions will be different than those for neutral atoms.

The process is easily shown using examples. To write the electron configuration for the S^{2-} anion, we simply need to add two more electrons to the last unfilled sublevel. Thus the configuration: $1s^2\,2s^2\,2p^6\,3s^2\,3\mathbf{p^4}$ for the S atom becomes: $1s^2\,2s^2\,2p^6\,3s^2\,3\mathbf{p^6}$ for the S^{2-} anion. Notice that the sulphide anion now has the same electron configuration as the nearest noble gas argon. The sulphide ion is therefore considered to be **isoelectronic** with argon because the two species have the same number and configuration of electrons.

To write cation configurations, electrons are always removed *from the outermost orbitals with the highest energy first*. Therefore, it is sometimes worthwhile to first write the neutral atom's configuration in core notation with the final orbitals listed from smallest to largest, rather than in the order the orbitals fill. Then remove the appropriate electrons from the outer orbitals first.

For example, if asked to write the configuration for the Sn^{4+} ion, first write the configuration for a neutral Sn atom as [Kr] $4d^{10}$ $\mathbf{5s^2}$ $\mathbf{5p^2}$ rather than writing [Kr] $\mathbf{5s^2}$ $4d^{10}$ $\mathbf{5p^2}$.

Now remove the four *outermost* electrons to give the configuration for Sn^{4+}: [Kr] $4d^{10}$. This avoids the error of removing two 4d electrons to give [Kr] $\mathbf{5s^2}$ $4d^8$. Note that an Sn^{2+} ion would form by losing the two 5p electrons, as they are at higher energy than the 5s.

As a final note, there are several exceptions to the orbital filling order discussed here. The elements Cr, Cu, Mo, Ag, and Au are examples of such exceptions. Your teacher may choose to discuss these and others and the possible reasons.

We shouldn't be surprised that irregularities exist. We have already seen ample evidence that the quantum world is full of surprises!

5.4 Activity: A Post-it® Periodic Table

Question

Can we organize a series of Post-it® notes on a standard periodic table to represent the order that orbitals are filled according the Aufbau principle?

Materials

- a small pad of each of four different colors of Post-it® or other sticky notes
- transparent tape

Procedure

Refer to the diagonal diagram in Figure 5.4.7 showing the order for filling sublevels.

1. Obtain a pad of small Post-it® or other sticky notes. Choose a separate color for each of the four shapes, s, p, d, and f, and write the symbol for each of the 19 sublevels (1s, 2s, 2p, etc....) on a separate note.

2. Place the notes from left to right on a flat surface in the correct order that each sublevel fills.

3. Obtain a copy of the periodic table from your teacher. Number each horizontal period of the table, beginning with 1 for the top period containing H and He, down to 7 for Fr.

4. Now "read" the periods left-to-right like words on a page, moving down at the end of each.
   Trim the bottom portion of each Post-it® note to fit, and stick the appropriate sublevel symbol onto each section of each period as you read it.

Results and Discussion

1. Once you're finished, confirm the correct location of each Post-it® note sublevel symbol with your teacher. Then place transparent tape over each to permanently attach it to the periodic table. Save this completed table for the discussion coming up in the next chapter.

5.4 Review Questions

1. If hydrogen's electron exists in a spherical orbital, why doesn't this mean that the electron moves around the nucleus in a circle?

   Because the sphere is only the shape of where the e^- are on average. Also, the e^- moves in waves instead.

2. What is the difference between a 1s orbital and a 2s orbital? What does that difference indicate about an electron possessing energy equal to $n = 2$ as compared to $n = 1$?

   2s is larger and has more energy, which means e^- in $n=2$ has more energy.

3. Describe the two differences between a $2p_x$ orbital and a $3p_y$ orbital.

4. The lobes of a p orbital disappear at the nucleus. What does this tell us about electrons in p orbitals?

5. You may have heard in previous science classes that the maximum numbers of electrons that can exist in the first four energy levels are 2, 8, 8, and 18 respectively. Do you agree with those numbers and if not, what should they be?

6. The electron configuration for phosphorus, written in core notation, is [Ne] $3s^2 3p^3$. What two things does Hund's rule tell us about the three electrons in the 3p sublevel?

   - what orbital they are in
   - how many e^- there are

7. Use the periodic table to complete the following table:

Atom or Ion	Full Electron Configuration	Core Notation
Ge	$1s^2 2s^2 2p^6 3s^2 3p^6 4s^2 3d^{10} 4p^2$	[Ar] $4s^2 3d^{10} 4p^2$
Zn^{2+}	$1s^2 2s^2 2p^6 3s^2 3p^6 4s^2 3d^8$	[Ar] $4s^2 3d^8$
Sr	$1s^2 2s^2 2p^6 3s^2 3p^6 4s^2 3d^{10} 4p^6 5s^2$	[Kr] $5s^2$
Br^-	$1s^2 2s^2 2p^6 3s^2 3p^6 4s^2 3d^{10} 4p^6$	[Ar] $4s^2 3d^{10} 4p^6$
Sn	$1s^2 2s^2 2p^6 3s^2 3p^6 4s^2 3d^{10} 4p^6 5s^2 4d^{10} 5p^2$	[Kr] $5s^2 4d^{10} 5p^2$
In^{3+}	$1s^2 2s^2 2p^6 3s^2 3p^6 4s^2 3d^{10} 4p^6 5s^2 4d^8$	[Kr] $5s^2 4d^8$

8. (a) Use the periodic table to identify the neutral atoms having the following electron configurations:

Electron Configuration	Element Name
[Ne] $3\mathbf{s}^2$	
[Ar] $4s^2 3\mathbf{d}^5$	
[Kr] $5s^2 4d^{10} 5\mathbf{p}^3$	
[Xe] $6s^2 4\mathbf{f}^7$	

(b) Notice where each of these elements is located on the periodic table. Look at the highest energy sublevel being filled (**bold type**) in each of the atoms in the table, and identify the four different sections of the periodic table associated with each of these four sublevels.

9. Consider the following six stable ions: N^{3-}, O^{2-}, F^-, Na^+, Mg^{2+}, and Al^{3+}.
(a) How many electrons are present in each ion?

10 e^-

(b) Write a single electron configuration representing all of the ions.

$1s^2 2s^2 2p^6$

(c) Which neutral atom possesses this electron configuration? What does this suggest about a possible reason for some ion formation?

Ne, ions lose/gain e^- to become stable

10. (a) Complete the following table for some elements in two families of the periodic table.

Alkali Metals	Core Notation	# Outer Electrons	Halogens	Core Notation	# Outer Electrons
lithium	[He] $2s^1$	1	fluorine	[He] $2s^2 2p^5$	7
sodium	[Ne] $3s^1$	1	chlorine	[Ne] $3s^2 3p^5$	7
potassium	[Ar] $4s^1$	1	bromine	[Ar] $4s^2 3d^{10} 4p^5$	17
rubidium	[Kr] $5s^1$	1	iodine	[Kr] $5s^2 4d^{10} 5p^5$	17

(b) Consider the numbers of outer electrons present and suggest a reason why elements belonging to the same chemical family demonstrate similar chemical behaviour.

The same chemical family have very similar if not exactly the same # of outer e^-

(c) What change occurs in the atoms as we move down each chemical family?

They have more total e^-

11. (a) On a separate sheet of paper, draw an orbital diagram for an atom of iron with sublevel energy increasing vertically. Arrange equal energy orbitals in each sublevel horizontally.

$1s^2$ $2s^2$ $2p^6$ $3s^2$ $3p^6$ $4s^2$

(b) Use a highlighter to label the electrons that would be lost when the Fe^{3+} cation forms.

6 Relationships and Patterns in Chemistry

This chapter focuses on the following AP Big Ideas from the College Board:

Big Idea 1: The chemical elements are fundamental building materials of matter, and all matter can be understood in terms of arrangements of atoms. These atoms retain their identify in chemical reactions.
Big Idea 2: Chemical and physical properties of materials can be explained by the structure and the arrangement of atoms, ions, or molecules and the forces between them.

By the end of this chapter, you should be able to do the following:

- Describe the development of the modern periodic table
- Draw conclusions about the similarities and trends in the properties of elements, with reference to the periodic table
- Justify chemical and physical properties in terms of electron population
- Demonstrate knowledge of various types of chemical bonding
- Apply understanding of bonding to create formulae and Lewis structures

---

By the end of this chapter you should know the meaning of the following **key terms**:

- alkali metals
- alkaline earth metals
- atomic radius
- covalent bonding
- electrical conductivity
- electron dot diagram
- halogens
- ionic bonding
- ionization energy
- Lewis structure
- melting point
- metal
- metalloid
- mole
- noble gases
- non-metal
- polarity
- transition metals
- valence electrons

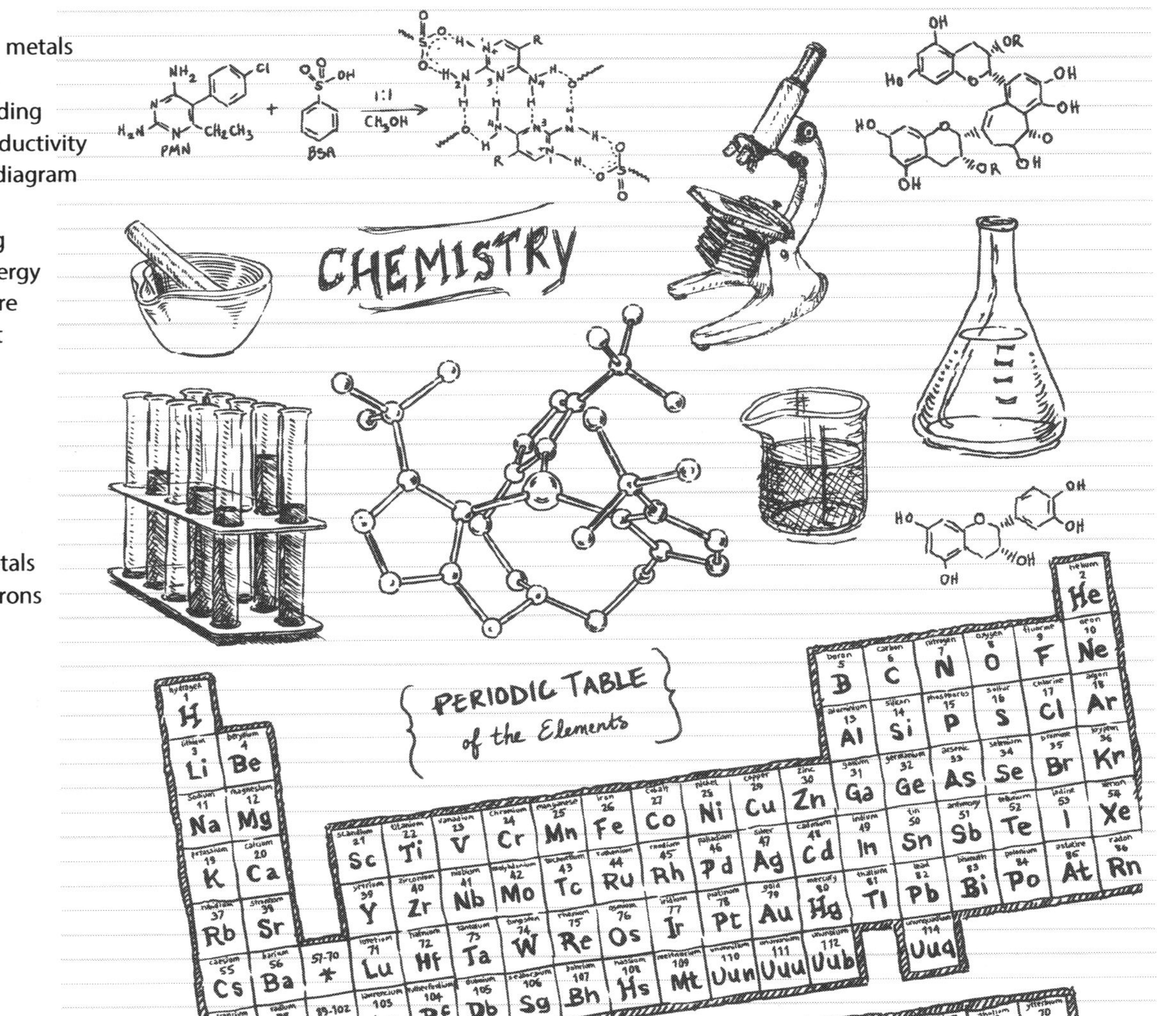

6.1 The Development of the Periodic Table

Warm Up

1. Can you suggest the meaning of the word "periodic" in the term "periodic table"?

2. On what basis are the elements arranged in the modern periodic table?

3. What is true about chemical elements that appear in the same vertical column in the table?

Discovering an Elemental Order

Science in general and chemistry in particular exist because our human species has always had an insatiable desire to make sense of the world around us. We have relentlessly sought to explain nature's phenomena, to solve her mysteries, and to discover her order and logic by deciphering the events and objects we encounter.

One of the most important and successful examples of such efforts is the development of the periodic table of the elements. This single document is arguably more valuable to chemists, and perhaps even society itself, than any piece of equipment, wonder drug, or process ever invented.

The periodic table had its beginnings in the early part of the 1800s. By 1817, 52 elements had been discovered. Although some had been known since ancient times, many new elements were being discovered using the energy available from the electric battery invented by Volta in 1800. Researchers saw the need to organize those elements and the enormous amount of information gathered about them into some kind of meaningful form. German scientist Johann Dobereiner noticed similarities within several groups of three elements such as chlorine, bromine, and iodine, which he called "triads." These similarities gave chemists some evidence that an organizational scheme was at least possible.

In 1857, English chemist William Odling proposed that the elements could be divided into groups based on their chemical and physical properties. Many of those groups actually resemble the vertical columns in the periodic table today.

In 1862, French geologist Alexandre-Emile de Chancourtois arranged the elements by increasing atomic mass. He noted that elements with similar properties seemed to occur at regular intervals. He devised a spiral graph with the elements arranged onto a cylinder such that similar elements lined up vertically. When his paper was published, however, it was largely ignored by chemists. Unfortunately, de Chancourtois had left out the graph, which made the paper hard to understand. As well, he had written the paper from a geologist's rather than from a chemist's perspective.

In 1864, English chemist John Newlands noticed that similar properties seemed to repeat every eighth element in much the same way that the notes of a musical scale repeat every eighth tone. Newlands called this the "law of octaves" and it resulted in several similar elements being grouped together, but with limited success.

The Periodic Law

The most successful organization of the elements was arrived at independently and almost at the same time by the German chemist Julius Lothar Meyer and the Russian chemist Dmitri Ivanovich Mendeleev. The chemical community, however, ultimately awarded Mendeleev the majority of the credit.

In a paper submitted to the Russian Chemical Society in March 1869, Mendeleev arranged the elements into a **periodic table** and proposed the **periodic law**, which can be stated as follows:

If elements are arranged in order of increasing atomic mass, a pattern can be seen in which similar properties recur on a regular or *periodic* basis.

Notice that this is called a "law" rather than a "theory." Theories attempt to explain *why* relationships or phenomena exist, whereas laws simply identify *that* they exist. We will see if we can supply the "why" by the end of this section.

Dmitri Mendeleev received most of the credit for several reasons. First, Mendeleev's work was published a year before Meyer's. Second, Mendeleev chose to concentrate on the chemical properties of the elements, while Meyer focused mainly on physical properties. Third, and most importantly, Mendeleev chose to leave several blank spaces in his table where he predicted as-yet-undiscovered elements with specific properties would eventually be placed. Because he had arranged similar elements vertically in his table, the location of those blank spaces effectively identified the properties that those elements would have upon being discovered. When the elements were eventually discovered, the predictions turned out to be extremely accurate.

A version of Mendeleev's table, published in 1872 and showing 65 elements is shown in Figure 6.1.1.

Reiben	Gruppo I. — R^2O	Gruppo II. — RO	Gruppo III. — R^2O^3	Gruppo IV. RH^4 RO^2	Gruppo V. RH^3 R^2O^3	Gruppo VI. RH^3 RO^3	Gruppo VII. RH R^2O^7	Gruppo VIII. — RO^4
1	Il = 1							
2	Li = 7	Be = 9,4	B = 11	C = 12	N = 14	O = 16	F = 19	
3	Na = 23	Mg = 24	Al = 27,8	Si = 28	P = 31	S = 32	Cl = 35,5	
4	K = 39	Ca = 40	– = 44	Ti = 48	V = 51	Cr = 52	Mn = 55	Fo = 56, Co=59, Ni = 59, Cu=63.
5	(Cu = 63)	Zn = 65	– = 68	– = 72	As = 75	So = 78	Br = 80	
6	Rb = 86	Sr = 87	?Yt = 88	Zr = 90	Nb = 94	Mo = 96	– = 100	Ru = 104, Rh=104, Pd = 106, Ag=108.
7	(Au = 199)	Cd = 112	In = 113	Sn = 118	Sb = 122	To = 125	J = 127	
8	Cs = 133	Bs = 137	?Di = 138	?Ce = 140	—	—	—	— — — —
9	(—)	—	—	—	—	—	—	
10	—	—	?Er = 178	?La = 180	Ta = 182	W = 184	—	Os = 195, Ir=197, Pt = 198, Au=199.
11	(Ag = 108)	Hg = 200	Tl = 204	Pb = 207	Bi = 208	—	—	
12	—	—	—	Th = 231	—	U = 240	—	— — — —

Figure 6.1.1 *The blank spaces marked with lines for elements with atomic masses 44, 68, 72, and 100 represent Mendeleev's belief that those elements would eventually be discovered and fit in the spaces. The symbols at the top of the columns (e.g., R^2O and RH^2) are molecular formulas written in the style of the 1800s. The letter "R" represents any element in the family and the formulas represent the probable hydrogen and oxygen compounds.*

An example of the accuracy of one of Mendeleev's predictions (and thus support for his periodic table) can be seen in Table 6.1.1. The table displays the properties predicted in 1871 for the element with atomic mass 72, compared to the actual properties for that element, called germanium, which was discovered in 1886.

Table 6.1.1 *Predicted and Observed Properties of Germanium*

Properties of Germanium	Predicted Properties in 1871	Observed Properties in 1886
Atomic mass	72	72.3
Density	5.5 g/cm^3	5.47 g/cm^3
Melting point	very high	960°C
Specific heat	0.31 J/g °C	0.31 J/g °C
Oxide formula	RO_2	GeO_2
Oxide density	4.7 g/cm^3	4.70 g/cm^3
Chloride formula	RCl_4	$GeCl_4$

Using the oxide formulas that he had proposed as a guide, Mendeleev also corrected the atomic masses of the elements beryllium, indium, and uranium.

Because of its obvious usefulness, Mendeleev's periodic table gained widespread acceptance among chemists. We should remember that the periodic table was constructed prior to any discoveries about the inner structure of the atom. The similarities of various elements were eventually explained based on the quantum mechanical description of their electron arrangements, but the table identified those regularities more than 50 years before they were understood!

Quick Check

1. Who was the first person to arrange the chemical elements into groups?

   ____

2. How did Newland's analogy to music apply to elemental properties?

   ____

3. How did blank spaces in Mendeleev's periodic table help it eventually gain acceptance?

   ____

   ____

The Modern Periodic Table — By the Numbers

Since its creation, the periodic table has undergone several changes. Many new elements have been discovered or synthesized since 1872, but the most significant modification occurred in 1913. Data gathered by the young British chemist Henry Moseley, combined with the discovery of isotopes, resulted in the elements of the periodic table being re-ordered according to their *atomic numbers* rather than their atomic masses.

If elements are arranged in order of increasing atomic number, a pattern can be seen in which similar properties recur on a regular or periodic basis.

The Modern Periodic Table

With the inclusion of element 117 in April 2010, the periodic table includes 118 elements, 92 of which occur naturally. Each element is assigned its own box in the table containing that element's one- or two-letter symbol, atomic number and sometimes, but not always, atomic mass. The boxes are arranged in order of increasing atomic number beginning at the top left with hydrogen and proceeding horizontally left-to-right. Because elements 113 to 118 have not yet been assigned permanent names, their temporary names simply reflect their atomic numbers. Figure 6.1.2 shows a simplified periodic table.

The horizontal rows in the periodic table are called **periods** and these are numbered beginning at the top from 1 down to 7. Each vertical column is called a **family** or **group** and these are labeled using one of two schemes. Many chemists prefer an older system, which assigns each column a number from 1 to 8 combined with either the letter A or B.

A newer system adopted by the international governing body of chemistry called IUPAC (International Union of Pure and Applied Chemistry) simply numbers each group from 1 through 18 and uses no letters. For ease of reference, we will use the IUPAC numbering system.

Because each element is a member of both a horizontal period and a vertical group, its position on the table can be specified in much the same way as a geographic location on a map can be identified using lines of longitude and latitude.

The two most important things to know about the periodic table are:

1. Elements in the same chemical family have similar chemical properties because they have similar outer electron configurations. (This is among the most important of all chemical concepts.)
2. As we move down a chemical family or across a period, there are regular changes in these properties called periodic trends. (These will be discussed in detail in the next section.)

Groups 1 and 2 on the left, and 13 through 18 on the right contain the **representative** or **main group elements**. Groups 3 through 12 are the **transition elements.** Within the transition elements are two horizontal series collectively called the **inner transition elements**. The first series, known as the **lanthanides**, fits between elements 56 and 72 in the 6th period and the second series, called the **actinides**, fits between elements 88 and 104 in the 7th period.

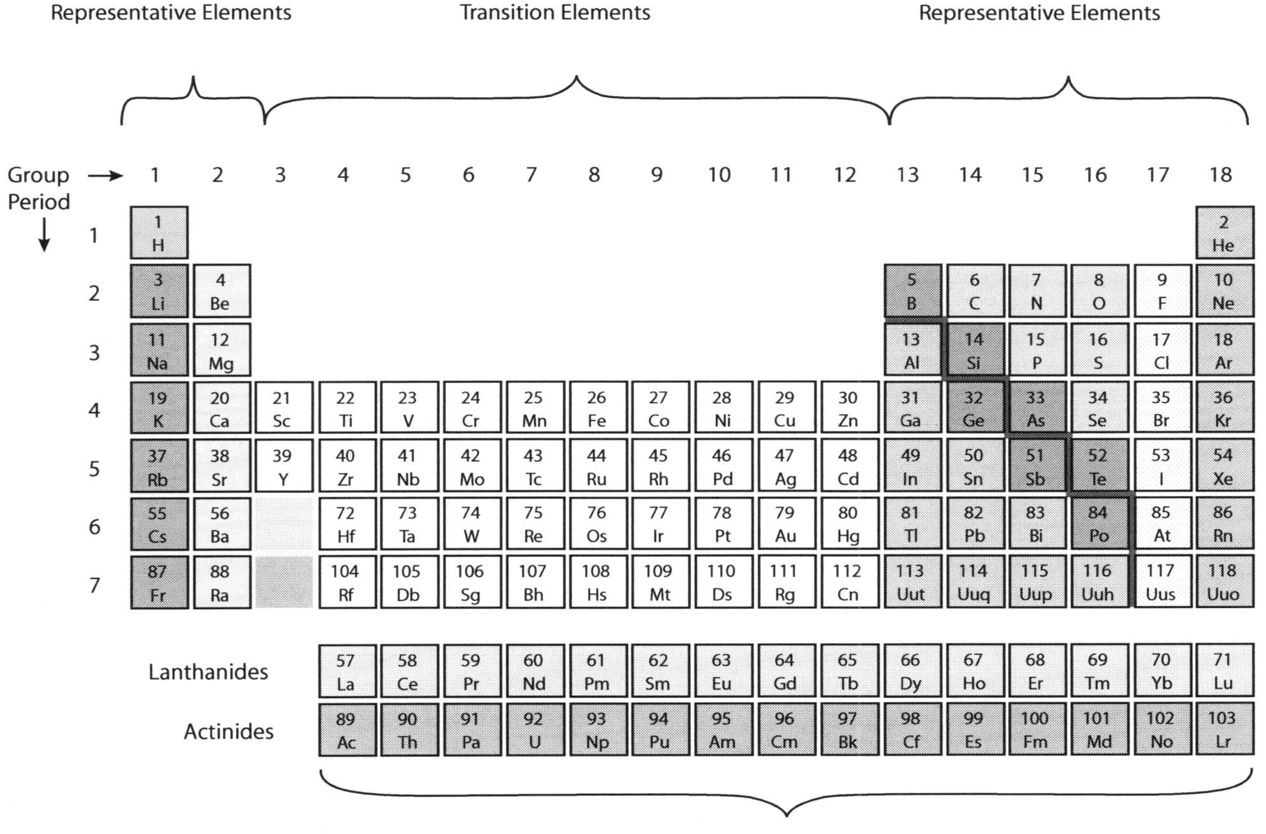

Figure 6.1.2 *This periodic table shows only the element's symbols and their atomic numbers.*

Consider the periodic table in Figure 6.1.2. The first distinction among the elements relating to their properties that we will discuss is their classification as metals, non-metals, or metalloids. The "staircase" line descending from group 13 down to group 16 separates metals on the left side from non-metals on the right.

About three-quarters of the elements are metals, including some main group elements and all of the transition and inner transition elements. Properties of **metals** include:

- solids at room temperature, except for mercury, which is a liquid
- generally shiny or lustrous when freshly cut or polished
- good conductors of heat and electricity
- generally malleable, which means they can be rolled or hammered into thin sheets
- generally ductile, which means they can be rolled or stretched into wires
- generally flexible as thin sheets or wires
- during chemical changes, tending to give up electrons relatively easily to form cations

The **non-metals** are located in the upper right portion of the table. Properties of non-metals include:

- usually gases or brittle solids at room temperature, except for liquid bromine
- solid non-metals ranging in appearance from dull or lustrous and translucent to opaque
- poor conductors of heat and electricity
- during chemical changes, tending to gain electrons from metals to form anions or share electrons with other non-metals.

Along the staircase line are several **metalloids** (also called **semi-metals**), including the elements boron, silicon, germanium, arsenic, antimony, tellurium, and polonium. These solid elements are semiconductors, which mean they are poor electrical conductors at room temperature, but become better conductors at higher temperatures. This is opposite to how metal conductivity varies with temperature. Metals become less conductive as temperature increases.

As we move right-to-left across a period and down a chemical family, the elements become more metallic. These changes involve both physical and chemical properties, and those and other trends will be discussed in the next section.

Quick Check

1. Fill in the missing spaces in the table below:

Element Name	Element Symbol	Group Number	Period Number	Metal/Non-metal/ metalloid
	Si			
osmium				
		6	4	
	Mt			
antimony				metalloid
		17	5	

2. (a) Rearrange the following alphabetical list in order of least metallic to most metallic.
aluminum, cesium, chromium, fluorine, gallium, oxygen, sulphur, zirconium

____

(b) Based on your answer to (a) above, which of the eight elements would you expect to have the:

- greatest tendency to gain an electron? ____________________
- greatest tendency to lose an electron? ____________________

A Closer Look at the Periodic Table

It is the number and type of outermost electrons that are primarily responsible for an atom's chemistry. The members of a chemical family have similar numbers and types of outermost electrons. The outermost electrons that participate in chemical bonding are known as **valence electrons**. We will be discussing chemical bonding in more detail in a later section. For now, this section will introduce some families in the periodic table and the corresponding electron arrangements that will influence the bonding behaviour of their elements.

Group 1 — The Alkali Metals

Alkali metals are located on the far left side of the periodic table. This group includes lithium, sodium, potassium, rubidium, cesium, and the rare and radioactive francium. Alkali metals are all soft, silvery solids and the most reactive of all metals. The name of the group is based on the fact that the oxide compounds of the alkali metals dissolve in water to produce strongly basic solutions. They all corrode rapidly in air to a dull gray appearance, react vigorously with water to produce hydrogen gas, and readily form compounds with non-metals.

Alkali metal atoms have one valence electron in the s sublevel with the general electron configuration [noble gas]ns^1 where "*n*" represents the outer energy level. In their chemical reactions, they readily lose that outer electron to form 1+ cations and so assume the electron configuration of the previous noble gas. Notice in Table 6.1.2 that each of the alkali metals has the same number and type of valence electrons. Note also, that as we move down the group and the value of "*n*" increases, the outermost electron spends most of the time farther and farther from the nucleus so the atoms become larger.

Table 6.1.2 *Alkali Metal Electron Configurations*

Alkali Metal	Core Notation Configuration
Li	[He] 2**s**^{1}
Na	[Ne] 3**s**^{1}
K	[Ar] 4**s**^{1}
Rb	[Kr] 5**s**^{1}
Cs	[Xe] 6**s**^{1}
Fr	[Rn] 7**s**^{1}

Group 2 — The Alkaline Earth Metals

The **alkaline earth metals** are also silver-coloured reactive metals. Although they are not as reactive as the alkali metals, they readily form compounds with non-metals. Their oxides are also alkaline but unlike alkali compounds, some group 2 compounds have a low solubility in water. They have two valence electrons and have the general electron configuration [noble gas]ns^2. They will readily form 2+ cations by losing those two valence electrons and so will achieve the identical electron configuration of the nearest noble gas. Chemists call this becoming **isoelectronic** with the noble gas.

Group 17 — The Halogens

The family of **halogens** contains the most reactive elements and is the only one in which all three states of matter are represented. At room temperature, fluorine and chlorine are gases, bromine is a liquid, and iodine and the very rare and radioactive astatine are solids.

The elemental halogens exist as diatomic molecules and readily form compounds with metals, and also hydrogen, carbon, and other non-metals. The halogens possess seven valence electrons with two electrons in the outer s sublevel and five electrons in the p sublevel. They therefore have the general ns^2np^5 outer electron configuration. In their reactions with metals, halogens will typically gain a single electron forming 1– anions and acquiring a noble gas electron configuration. When they react with non-metals, they will often share valence electrons.

Group 18 — The Noble Gases

As the name suggests, the family of **noble gases** is generally unreactive, although compounds of argon, krypton, xenon, and radon have been prepared.

All of the noble gases, except helium, have filled s and p sublevels. As the s and p sublevels are an atom's outermost orbitals, atoms of neon down to radon have eight electrons in their outer charge clouds with the ns^2np^6 configuration. They are said to possess "stable octets." This particularly stable electron configuration explains the low reactivity of the noble gases. It also explains the electron configuration achieved by many cations and anions. For example, consider Table 6.1.3, showing elements from four different families. Note that the stable ion of each element has the same electron configuration as the noble gas nearest to it in the periodic table.

Table 6.1.3 *Electron Configurations of Noble Gases and Nearby Elements*

Element	Electron Configuration for Atom	Nearest Noble Gas	Symbol and Electron Configuration for Stable Ion	
oxygen	$[He]2s^22p^4$	neon	O^{2-}	$[He]2s^22p^6$
calcium	$[Ar]4s^2$	argon	Ca^{2+}	$[Ne]3s^23p^6$
arsenic	$[Ar]4s^23d^{10}4p^3$	krypton	As^{3-}	$[Ar]4s^23d^{10}4p^6$
cesium	$[Xe]6s^1$	xenon	Cs^+	$[Kr]5s^24d^{10}5p^6$

Transition Elements

The **transition elements** include groups 3 through 12 in the periodic table. All are metals and most are hard solids with high melting and boiling points. An explanation of their chemical behaviour is beyond the scope of this course, but it differs from the representative elements. For example, the transition elements show similarities within a given period as well as within a group. In addition, many transition elements form cations with multiple charges and those cations often form complex ions. A number of transition metal compounds have distinct and recognizable colours. The differences occur mainly because the last electrons added for transition metals are placed in inner d orbitals. Electrons in these orbitals are usually closer to the nucleus than in the outer s or p orbitals filled for the representative elements.

Quick Check

1. Identify the family number and name to which each of the following properties best apply:

Property	Family Number	Family Name
(a) reactive non-metals possessing seven valence electrons		
(b) reactive solids that form 2+ cations during reactions		
(c) invisible gases that are almost totally unreactive		
(d) soft, very reactive silvery solids with one valence electron		

2. Elements in the same family demonstrate similar chemical behaviour. Consider the following chemical formulas: $LiBr$, K_2O, Sr_3N_2, AlF_3, CaO, H_2S. Write chemical formulas for:

   (a) sodium iodide ____________________ (d) rubidium sulphide ____________________

   (b) barium sulphide ____________________ (e) magnesium phosphide ____________________

   (c) gallium chloride ____________________ (f) hydrogen selenide ____________________

3. Which two families contain the most reactive elements? Can you suggest a possible reason for this given their location on the periodic table?

   ____

   ____

A Quantum Mechanical View of the Periodic Table

Let us look a little more closely at the organization of the periodic table from a quantum mechanics perspective. First we'll look at three different aspects of the elements in the periodic table.

(1) Consider Figure 6.1.3 showing the chemical families separated into the four main blocks of the table. Notice that each block corresponds to one of the four different electron sublevels. Notice also that the number of columns or families in each block exactly matches the number of electrons that occupy that sublevel. (This diagram also includes both the older and newer numbering schemes employed for the chemical families.)

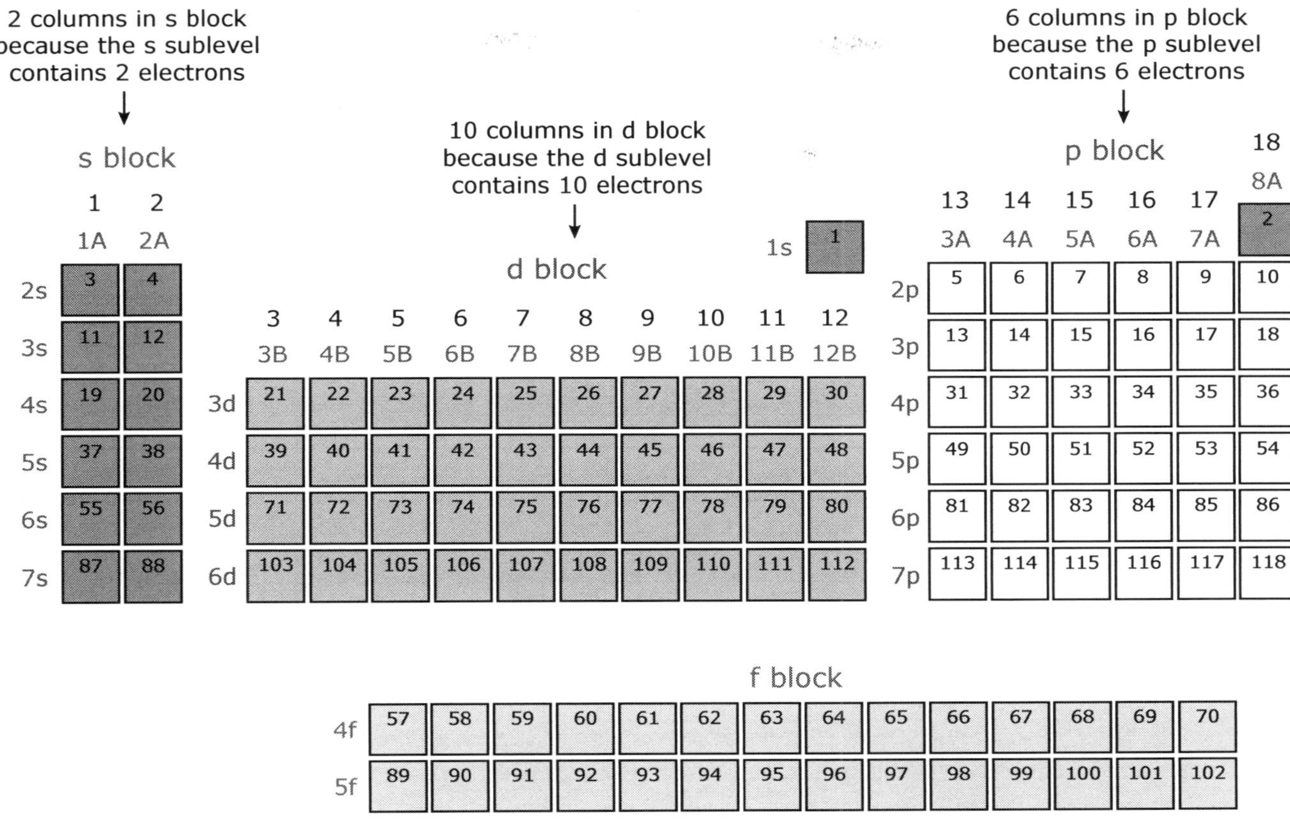

Figure 6.1.3 *The periodic table separated into its four main blocks*

Table 6.1.4 *Order of Filling Sublevels*

1s	→		
2s	→		2p
3s	→		3p
4s	→	3d →	4p
5s	→	4d →	5p
6s →	4f →	5d →	6p
7s →	5f →	6d →	7p

(2) Consider in Figure 6.1.3 the sublevels associated with each of the chemical periods in the table. Notice that as we "read" the sublevels from left to right like the words on a page, we follow exactly the order of filling sublevels specified by the Aufbau principle and summarized by the diagonal diagram in the previous chapter. That order is shown again in Table 6.1.4.

Note also that as we reach each noble gas at the end of a period, we move down and begin a new period. Each new period number specifies the value of the next energy level as we start filling the s orbital for elements on the left side of that period. Thus every new period represents a larger charge cloud or electron "shell" in which electrons spend most of their time farther from the nucleus.

(3) Finally, consider Figure 6.1.4, showing the extended form of the periodic table with the f block lanthanides and actinides inserted after barium and radium respectively. Note the consistent order and the obvious connection of electron configuration to element location in the periodic table.

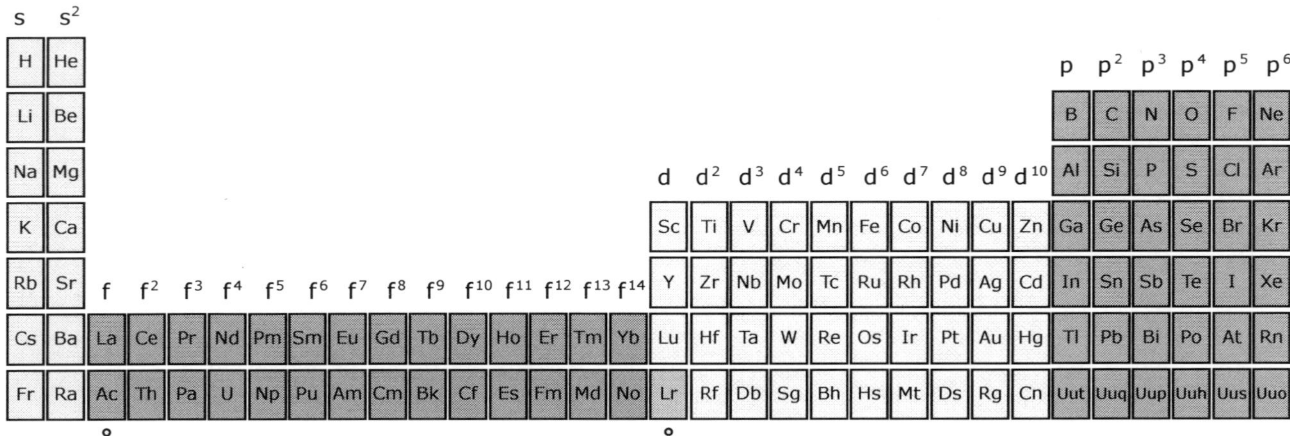

Figure 6.1.4 *Periodic table showing pattern of electron configuration*

Chemists, like all scientists, don't really believe in coincidences. We have discussed that the structure of the periodic table is based firmly on experimentation. The organization of the periods and chemical families results from and summarizes an enormous amount of empirical data gathered about the elements. It is truly amazing that this arrangement of the elements in the periodic table was essentially in place *before* the development of the quantum mechanical model of the atom! The fact that the electron configurations of the elements specified by quantum mechanics exactly matches their organization in the periodic table is one of the greatest successes in the history of science.

Far from being a coincidence, the exact correlation exists precisely because quantum mechanics provides the theoretical foundation for the experimentally derived periodic table. Stated another way, the quantum mechanical view of the atom is the "why" behind the "what" stated in the periodic law. Of course, it can also be said that the structure of the periodic table is arguably the best piece of supporting evidence for the quantum mechanical model of the atom.

Perhaps John Newlands wasn't far off the mark when he used a musical analogy in referring to elemental properties. Think of the millions of chemical reactions happening around us as symphonies played out by the instruments we call the chemical elements in nature's orchestral arrangement that is the periodic table.

6.1 Activity: The Elements of PowerPoint®

Question

How much information about an element can you present in a 10-minute presentation using Power Point® or another computer slide presentation software?

Procedure

1. Choose any one of the naturally occurring elements in the periodic table. Confirm the selection with your teacher to avoid duplicate selections among class members.
2. Using any and all resources available online or in print, produce a PowerPoint® presentation no longer than 10 minutes that includes as much information about your element as you can discover. Make sure to include the following: symbol, atomic number and mass, location on the periodic table, electron configuration, melting point, boiling point, common compounds, and uses. The presentation can include any videos showing reactions or compounds or any interesting properties of the element.

Results and Discussion

1. Be prepared to answer questions from your classmates and your teacher for a few minutes after your presentation.

6.1 Review Questions

1. What is the most important thing to know about the periodic table?

2. What significant modification to the periodic table occurred just before World War I?

3. Why do elements in the same chemical family have similar chemical properties?

4. (a) Where are the most metallic elements located on the periodic table?

   (b) Where are the most non-metallic elements located on the periodic table?

5. Consider the properties listed for eight different elements. Match each element on the left to its property on the right by writing the element's chemical symbol next to its property.

Element	Properties	Symbol
(a) chlorine	found in carbohydrates and an elemental gas in 21% of the atmosphere	
(b) silver	soft conductor that reacts explosively with water producing H_2 gas	
(c) neon	less than 30 g of this solid radioactive nonconductor exists on Earth	
(d) cesium	waxy yellow solid non-metal found in match heads, fertilizers, and detergents	
(e) oxygen	blue-gray metalloid used extensively in the computer industry	
(f) phosphorus	very reactive green gas used in the trenches in World War I	
(g) silicon	shiny solid that is the best conductor of heat and electricity	
(h) astatine	invisible unreactive gas used in lasers and some electric street signs	

6. Six different elemental properties are listed below corresponding to family numbers 1, 2, 6, 14, 17, and 18 in the periodic table. Write the appropriate family number next to each of the properties listed below. Each family number may be used only once.

Element Properties	Family Number
unreactive gas used in electric street signs and comprising 0.93% of the atmosphere	
shiny multivalent solid, good conductor, forms coloured compounds	
soft silvery solid, good conductor, reacts vigorously with water	
gray-white metalloid predicted by Mendeleev and discovered in 1886	
reactive metal present in bones and teeth possessing two valence electrons	
yellow-green gaseous non-metal and the most reactive of all the elements	

7. State four properties of elements classified as metals.

8. State four properties of elements classified as non-metals.

9. State a general rule for predicting the ion charges of many of the representative or main group elements.

10. Use your answer to question 8 above and write the formulas for the stable ions of the following:

(a) Be ______________________ (e) Ga ______________________

(b) Te ______________________ (f) Se ______________________

(c) Cs ______________________ (g) In ______________________

(d) Ra ______________________

11. Identify three properties of the elements belonging to each of the following chemical families:
(a) alkali metals

(b) alkaline earth metals

(c) halogens

(d) noble gases

12. Complete the following table by writing in the missing electron configurations. Highlight the outermost electrons in your answers. (Completed answers show outermost electrons in bold type.)

Group 2	Core Notation	Group 17	Core Notation	Group 18	Core Notation
Be		F	[He]$\mathbf{2s^2\,2p^5}$	He	
Mg		Cl		Ne	
Ca	[Ar]$\mathbf{4s^2}$	Br		Ar	
Sr		I		Kr	[Ar]$\mathbf{4s^2}$ $3d^{10}$ $\mathbf{4p^6}$
Ba	[Xe]$\mathbf{6s^2}$	At	[Xe] $\mathbf{6s^2}$ $4f^{14}5d^{10}$ $\mathbf{6\,p^5}$	Xe	
Ra				Rn	[Xe]$\mathbf{6s^2}$ $4f^{14}5d^{10}$ $\mathbf{6p^6}$

6.2 Periodic Trends — Regular Changes in Elemental Properties

Warm Up

1. What attractive force is responsible for holding the cloud of electrons in place in atoms?

   ____

2. What effect would a strengthening of that force have on the sizes of atoms?

   ____

3. What might cause a strengthening of that force?

   ____

4. What might contribute to a weakening of that force?

   ____

Periodic Trends

All of the chemical and physical behaviour of the elements is really a result of their electron configurations. In the last section, we discussed how similar outer-electron configurations explained the similar properties of elements within the chemical families of the periodic table. We will now concentrate on a second key concept associated with the organization of the elements in the table.

> As we move across a period or down a chemical family, there are regular changes in elemental properties.

These consistent and predictable changes in elemental properties are known as **periodic trends.** Identifying and explaining them can be a great benefit when describing chemical interactions between atoms.

Periodic Trends in Atomic Size

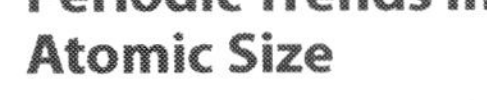

In the quantum mechanical model, the outer boundaries of an atom depend on the size of a charge cloud in which electrons spend approximately 90% of their time. This means that the sizes of individual atoms cannot be determined in the same way as we might, for example, measure the size of objects such as marbles or grapefruits. In these cases, the object's boundaries are hard and definite, unlike those of atoms.

However, we can estimate the sizes of atoms based on how close they get to one another when bonds form between them. This can be done by measuring the distance between the nuclei of identical adjacent atoms in an element sample and dividing that distance by two.

The two common definitions of atomic size stem from the classification of elements into metals and non-metals. Non-metal elements commonly occur as diatomic molecules. For these elements, atomic size is defined as the **covalent radius**, which represents one half the distance between the two identical nuclei in the molecule.

Although the nature of bonding between metal atoms is beyond the scope of this course, the process of estimating their atomic size is very similar to that for non-metals. Metal atoms pack together in the solid state to form a crystal lattice much like ions in a salt. In a sample of a metal element, half the distance between the identical nuclei of adjacent metal atoms in the crystal is defined as the **metallic radius**.

Both of the above techniques for estimating atomic size involve determining half the bond length between identical atoms in element samples as shown in Figure 6.2.1.

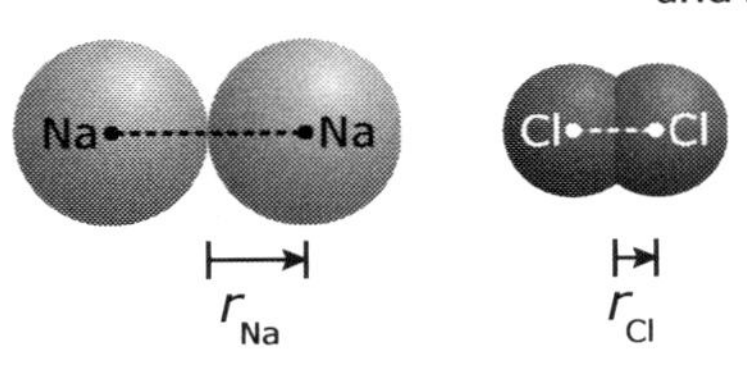

Figure 6.2.1 *Estimating atomic size involves determining bond length.*

Factors Influencing Atomic and Ionic Size

Let's consider for a moment what might influence the size of an atom. Because an atom's volume is really the result of a cloud of electrons, this question is really the same as asking: What affects the size of an atom's electron cloud? Seen from that perspective, it makes sense that two opposing factors influence atomic size:

1. The number of energy levels present. As the number of energy levels (n) increases, the probability that outer electrons will spend more time further from the nucleus increases and so the atoms become larger.
2. The amount of nuclear charge "felt" or "seen" by the outer electrons. As this effective nuclear charge increases, the outer electron cloud is pulled closer to the nucleus and the atom becomes smaller. Chemists use the symbol "Z_{eff}" to refer to the effective nuclear charge.

Of these two opposing factors, the one that predominates as we move across a period or down a chemical family will most influence how the sizes of those atoms change.

Consider Figure 6.2.2, showing the relative atomic radii of the elements. The **atomic radius** of an atom is the distance from the nucleus to the boundary of the surrounding cloud of electrons. The actual sizes range from the smallest, helium, at 31 pm to the largest, cesium, at 270 pm. How those sizes change across periods and down families shows a clear pattern.

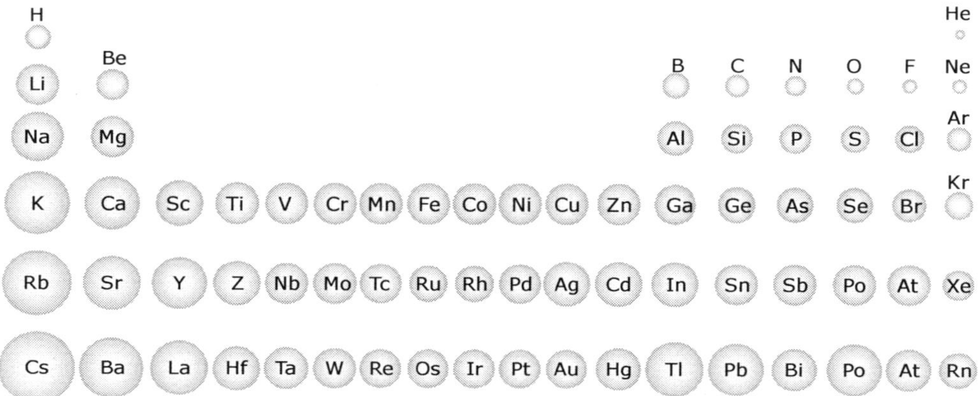

Figure 6.2.2 *Periodic table showing atomic radii*

Two definite periodic trends are evident:

As we move down a family or group, the sizes of the atoms generally increase.
As we move across a period, the sizes of the atoms generally decrease.

As we move down a chemical family and the value of *n* increases for each new element, a new inner electron level is added between the nucleus and the atom's outer electron cloud. Even though the positive charge on the nucleus is increasing, each additional inner level of electrons *effectively shields* the outer cloud from the attractive force of that nucleus, and the electron cloud increases in size. The additional inner electron clouds also repel each other, which further contributes to the increasing size of atoms in the group as we move lower in the table. This clearly shows that as the number of energy levels present in the atom increases, the size of the atom also increases.

As we move left-to-right across a period, the electrons are being added to the same outer level. This means that the level of shielding by the inner electrons remains the same. It also means that the added electrons are *ineffective at shielding each other* from the increasing positive charge on the nucleus. The result is that Z_{eff} on those outer electrons increases and the charge cloud is pulled closer and closer to the nucleus so the size of the atom decreases.

Consider Figure 6.2.3, which shows the periodic changes in atomic radii as we move from period 1 through period 6. The alkali metals are the largest members of each period and then the radii generally decrease to a minimum at the noble gases. Down each family, the atomic radii generally increase.

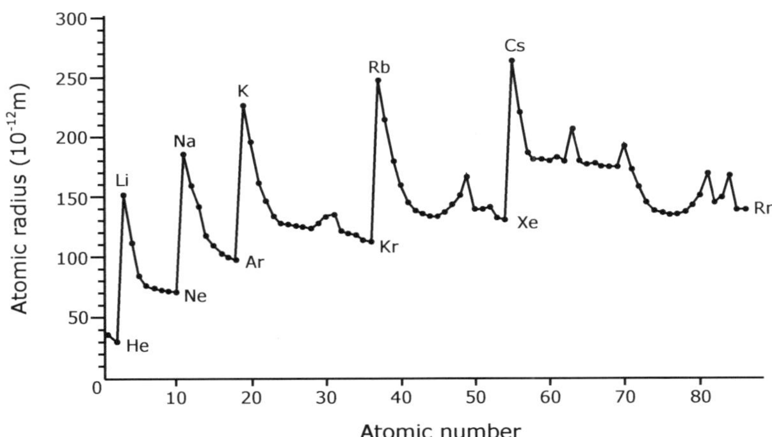

Figure 6.2.3 *Periodic changes in atomic radii as we move from period 1 through period 6*

There are exceptions to the general trends stated above and they can be explained by considering the electron configurations of the atoms and the electron sublevels being filled in each case. For example, as we move across period 4, we start filling the 4th energy level at potassium and the atomic sizes shrink as expected for the first two elements. But when we arrive at the transition elements and begin filling the 3d sublevel, the sizes remain relatively constant as we move across to zinc.

To understand this, remember that $n = 3$ electrons spend most of their time *closer to the nucleus* than those electrons in the $n = 4$ charge cloud. We would therefore expect electrons in the 3d sublevel to be capable of shielding the outer 4s electrons from the increasing nuclear charge as we move across the period. This would reduce Z_{eff}. Consider the elements vanadium and zinc. The electron configuration for V is $[Ar]3d^34s^2$ and the electron configuration for Zn is $[Ar]3d^{10}4s^2$. Even though zinc has a nucleus with 7 more protons than vanadium, the extra shielding provided by zinc's 10 electrons in the 3d sublevel is such that zinc's atomic radius is equal to vanadium's!

This shows how effective inner electrons can be at shielding outer electrons from the "pull" of an increasingly positive nucleus and significantly influence atomic size. A number of other examples can be found throughout the periodic table.

Quick Check

1. Which of the two opposing factors that influence atomic size predominates as we move across a chemical period? What is the general result?

   more nuclear charge v. more energy levels, and the general result is the atomic size increases.

2. Which of the two opposing factors that influence atomic size predominates as we move down a chemical family? What is the general result?

   same factors and trend as #1

3. In general, is "effective shielding" most evident going across a period or down a family? How can you tell?

   down a family, because even with the addition of p^+, the addition of sheilding e^- results in the same Z_{eff}

Forces Affecting Ion Size

The same forces that influence the sizes of atoms also influence the sizes of ions and in the same way. Let's consider these forces and rank the following species in order of size from largest to smallest: Al^{3+} , F^-, Mg^{2+}, N^{3-}, Na^+, Ne, O^{2-}.

Note that all of the ions have 10 electrons and are therefore isoelectronic with neon. Since each species has the same number of electrons, we can assume that the amount of shielding is also the same for each. This means that the attractive force from each nucleus is the only factor influencing the size of each species. The greater the number of protons present, the stronger the attractive force on the electron cloud and therefore the smaller the atom or ion. This tells us that ranking the species in order of atomic number (positive charge on the nucleus) will also represent the order of decreasing size. Therefore, the answer is:

$$N^{3-} > O^{2-} > F^- > Ne > Na^+ > Mg^{2+} > Al^{3+}$$

Periodic Trends in Ionization Energy

Ionization energy (*IE*) is defined as the minimum energy required to remove an electron from a gaseous atom or ion. The term is often used to mean the "first" ionization energy (IE_1) whereby a neutral atom becomes a 1^+ cation according to the following equation:

$$\text{atom } (g) \ + \ IE_1 \ \rightarrow \ \text{ion}^+ (g) \ + \ e^-$$

Ionization energy tells us how strongly an atom holds onto its outermost electrons. This is an important property because an element with a low IE_1 will be more likely to lose electrons and form cations during chemical changes. A high IE_1 might signal an element's tendency to gain electrons and form anions or perhaps not forms ions at all.

We might expect that a large atom, whose outer electrons are held less tightly, would have a lower IE_1 than a smaller atom whose outer electrons are held much more strongly. Said another way, as atomic size decreases, ionization energy should increase. This is, in fact, the general trend, as shown in Figure 6.2.4.

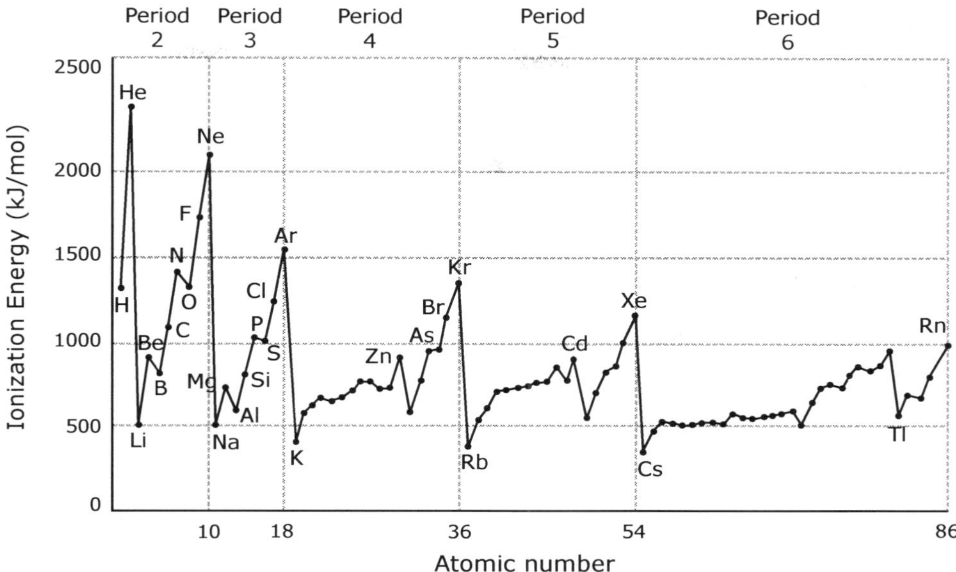

Figure 6.2.4 *As atomic size decreases, ionization energy increases.*

We can see that the lowest IE_1 values are associated with the largest atoms, which are located in the lower left corner of the periodic table. Conversely, the highest IE_1 numbers correspond to the smallest atoms, located in the upper right portion of the table.

At the beginning of each period, the largest atoms are the alkali metals, which have the lowest ionization energies. As we progress across the period and the sizes of the atoms decrease, we see a corresponding general increase in ionization energy until we reach the maximum value at each noble gas. At the beginning of the next period, the dramatic drop in ionization energy reflects the significant increase in size of that next alkali metal. As we move down a chemical family, the increase in atomic size results in a general decrease in ionization energy. The periodic trends are clearly evident up to the end of the 6th period.

The diagram shows that lower ionization energies are associated with elements nearer the left side of the periodic table, namely the metals. This tells us that metals generally tend to lose electrons when they are involved in chemical reactions. Non-metals, on the other hand, with relatively high ionization energies, have a tendency to gain or even share electrons rather than lose them. Of course, noble gases do neither of the above.

Exceptions to Ionization Energy Trends — One Example

As with atomic radii, there are several exceptions to the general trends in ionization energy, which we can explain by analyzing electron configurations. One example of this occurs with nitrogen and oxygen. Even though oxygen is a smaller atom than nitrogen, oxygen has a lower first ionization energy. Nitrogen has a single electron in each of its three 2p orbitals and a half-filled p sublevel that is quite stable. Oxygen, however, has a pair of electrons in one of its 2p orbitals (Figure 6.2.5). The increased electron-electron repulsion associated with that pairing makes it easier for oxygen to lose one of those electrons when first ionized.

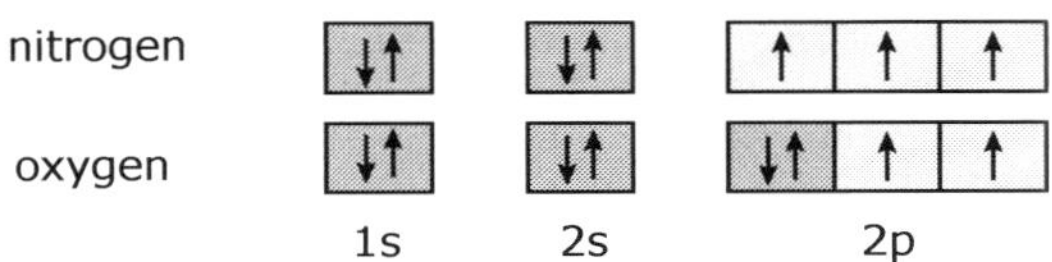

Figure 6.2.5 *Electron configurations in nitrogen and oxygen*

This reminds us that the repulsive forces between electrons, as well as the attractive forces affecting them from the nucleus, have a role to play in determining properties such as size and ionization energy.

Studying ionization energies allows us to do more than predict which elements might tend to lose or gain electrons during chemical changes. Investigating ionization energies also helps us identify which electrons are likely to be associated with those changes.

As we might expect, after removing one electron from an atom, further ionization energies increase. This occurs because each successive electron removed is being separated from an increasingly positive ion. However, those increases are *not regular*. Whenever the last outer or valence electron is removed, the next ionization requires significantly more energy because inner or "core electrons" are now involved. This can be seen using beryllium as an example. The atom has two valence electrons and the electron configuration is $1s^2 2s^2$. Table 6.2.1 shows the first three ionization energies for beryllium.

Table 6.2.1 *First Three Ionization Energies of Beryllium*

Species	Electron Configuration	Ionization Energy (kJ/mol)
Be^o	$1s^2 2s^2$	$IE_1 = 900$
Be^{1+}	$1s^2 2s^1$	$IE_2 = 1\,756$
Be^{2+}	$1s^2$	$IE_3 = 14\,860$

After the second (and last valence) electron is removed, the dramatic increase in energy required to remove the third electron reflects the fact that it is an inner or "core" electron. This shows us that core electrons are bound much more tightly to the nucleus, and thus do not take part in chemical reactions. This holds true for all of the elements in the periodic table.

Sample Problem – Trends in Ionization Energy

Using only the periodic table, rank each of the following alphabetical lists of elements in order of increasing first ionization energies.

(a) argon chlorine phosphorus sodium silicon
(b) antimony arsenic bismuth nitrogen phosphorus

What to Think about	How to Do It
1. Ionization energy increases left-to-right across a period and moving up a chemical group.	
2. The elements listed in (a) are members of period 3. List the elements in the order they appear from left-to-right in period 3.	Na < Si < P < Cl < Ar
3. The elements listed in (b) belong to group 15 of the periodic table. List the elements in the order they appear from bottom-to-top in group 15.	Bi < Sb < As < P < N

Practice Problems — Trends in Ionization Energy

1. Using only the periodic table, rank the following alphabetical list of elements in order of decreasing first ionization energy.

   aluminum argon cesium magnesium rubidium silicon sodium sulphur

   4 1 7 4 6 3 5 2   1: most IE 7: least

2. Using the periodic table, write the correct number in the space after each statement below:

   Members of this chemical family have the highest IE_1 in their period. 1

   Members of this chemical family have the lowest IE_1 in their period. 7

   Members of this chemical period have the highest IE_1 in their family. 18

   Members of this chemical period have the lowest IE_1 in their family. 1

3. The nature of the 2s sublevel is such that 2s electrons have a higher probability of being found closer to the nucleus than electrons in the 2p sublevel. Consider this and the following electron configurations:

   beryllium: $1s^2 2s^2$ boron: $1s^2 2s^2 2p^1$

   Suggest a reason why boron's first ionization energy is less than beryllium's, even though boron is a smaller atom.

   Boron is an exception because it has 1e⁻ in a higher energy level, making it farther away from the nucleus resulting in a lower force

An Introduction to Electronegativity

Our discussions so far have focused on the electron configurations, properties, and periodic trends associated with *individual atoms* of the elements. This has been directed towards an eventual understanding of how these atoms behave when they form chemical bonds.

Chemical bonding begins when the valence electrons in a region of space between two atoms are attracted by or "shared" between the adjacent nuclei. Each nucleus exerts an influence on those electrons, which ultimately determine the nature of the resulting bond.

To begin to describe this effect and the nature of the resulting bonds, let's look at an elemental property associated with bonded atoms. It is one of the most important properties in chemical bonding.

Electronegativity is defined as the relative ability of a bonded atom to attract shared electrons to itself. Atoms with relatively high electronegativities (EN) tend to pull bonded electrons closer to their nuclei. Atoms with lower EN values have their bonded electrons pulled further away. As we'll see in section 6.3, this will dictate not only the nature of the chemical bonds that form, but also the properties of the compounds containing those bonds.

We might expect that smaller atoms would have higher EN values since their nuclei would be closer to bonded electrons than the nuclei of larger atoms. We might also expect that larger atoms would therefore tend to have lower EN values. This is indeed the case, and because atomic size shows periodic trends, we shouldn't be surprised that electronegativity does as well. In fact, the general trends in electronegativity are similar to those seen in ionization energy.

We can see a clear resemblance to the trends in ionization energy, namely that EN increases going across a period and increases moving up a group (Figure 6.2.6). (The noble gases don't have EN values because they don't generally form chemical bonds.)

Increasing EN →

H 2.1																	He
Li 1.0	Be 1.5											B 2.0	C 2.5	N 3.0	O 3.5	F 4.0	Ne
Na 0.9	Mg 1.2											Al 1.5	Si 1.8	P 2.1	S 2.5	Cl 3.0	Ar
K 0.8	Ca 1.0	Sc 1.3	Ti 1.5	V 1.6	Cr 1.6	Mn 1.5	Fe 1.8	Co 1.8	Ni 1.8	Cu 1.9	Zn 1.6	Ga 1.6	Ge 1.8	As 2.0	Se 2.4	Br 2.8	Kr
Rb 0.8	Sr 1.0	Y 1.3	Zr 1.4	Nb 1.6	Mo 1.8	Tc	Ru 2.2	Rh 2.2	Pd 2.2	Ag 1.9	Cd 1.7	In 1.7	Sn 1.8	Sb 1.9	Te 2.1	I 2.5	Xe
Cs 0.7	Ba 0.9	La 1.1	Hf 1.3	Ta 1.5	W 1.7	Re 1.9	Os 2.2	Ir 2.2	Pt 2.2	Au 2.4	Hg 1.9	Tl 1.8	Pb 1.8	Bi 1.9	Po 2.0	At 2.2	Rn
Fr 0.7	Ra 0.9	Ac 1.1															

↑ Increasing EN

Ce 1.1	Pr 1,1	Nd 1.2	Pm	Sm 1.2	Eu 1.2	Gd 1.1	Tb 1.2	Dy 1.2	Ho 1.2	Er 1.2	Tm 1.2	Yb 1.1	Lu 1.2
Th 1.3	Pa 1.5	U 1.7											

Figure 6.2.6 *Periodic table showing trends in electronegativity*

The electronegativity values are numbers ranging from a low of 0.7 for cesium to 4.0 for fluorine (Figure 6.2.7). The values were determined by the great American chemist Linus Pauling.

For our purposes, we will only be interested in the relative magnitudes of the numbers.

The trends indicate that metal atoms, which are large with low ionization energies, also have relatively low EN values. Smaller non-metal atoms tend to have higher ionization energies and electronegativities. The consequences of these properties with respect to chemical bonding are coming up in the next section, so stay tuned!

Electronegativity vs. Atomic Number

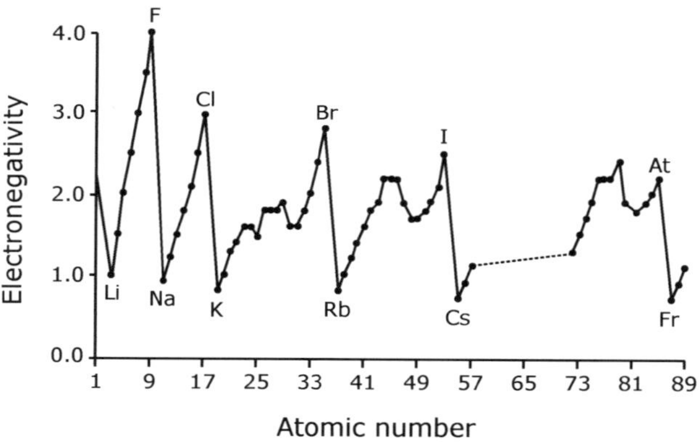

Figure 6.2.7 *Graph showing electronegativity values*

6.2 Activity: A Summary Diagram of Periodic Trends

Question

How can we summarize the three periodic trends discussed in this section using one periodic table?

Materials

Periodic table, a ruler or straight edge

Procedure

1. Consider each of the three periodic trends listed below and complete the following table by writing in either the word "increases" or "decreases" for each of the properties listed in the spaces available.

	Moving Across a Period	Moving Up a Chemical Family
Atomic Size		
Ionization Energy		
Electronegativity		

2. Print a full page version of the periodic table of the elements from whatever website you wish.

3. Using a ruler, draw three parallel vertical arrows facing up on the left margin of the periodic table. Draw three parallel horizontal arrows facing to the right across the top of the table.

4. Label each of the three arrows on the left and across the top with the terms: "Atomic Size," "Ionization Energy," and "Electronegativity." Next to each term, write the appropriate words from the table that you filled in above.

5. Using a ruler, draw a long diagonal arrow beginning at the bottom left corner of the table and extending and pointing to the top right corner. Along the top side of that arrow, write in how each of the three terms listed above changes as you move from the bottom left corner of the periodic table to the top right corner. Save this table because we will refer to it in Section 6.3.

6.2 Review Questions

1. What is meant by the term "periodic trends"?

2. Why is it difficult to measure the sizes of individual atoms?

3. Two of the elemental properties discussed in this section show similar trends when moving across a period and up a chemical family. Identify these and the trend observed.

   Ionization Energy and Electronegativity, which both decreased as you move down, and increase as you move across.

4. One of the three properties discussed shows periodic trends when moving across a period or up a family opposite to the other two properties. Identify this property and the trend observed.

   Atomic size/radius: the trend is it increases as you move down and decreases as you move across

5. Briefly explain why fluorine is a smaller atom than lithium. Consider which factor is predominating across a period.

   Fluorine is a smaller atom than lithium because they have the same amount of energy levels but Fs nuclear charge is higher

6. Where are the largest atoms located on the periodic table? Where are the smallest atoms located on the periodic table?

   largest: bottom left
   smallest: top right

7. The attraction of electrons to the nucleus and repulsion of the electrons between each other both influence the size of an atom or ion. Use this to complete the following statements.
   (a) A cation will always be ___larger___ (smaller or larger) than its parent neutral atom because of ___decreased___ (increased or decreased) attraction of the outer electrons for the nucleus and ___increased___ (increased or decreased) repulsion of the electrons for each other.
   (b) An anion will always be ___smaller___ (smaller or larger) than its parent neutral atom because of ___increased___ (increased or decreased) attraction of the outer electrons for the nucleus and ___decreased___ (increased or decreased) repulsion of the electrons for each other.

8. What role do inner or core electrons play in determining atomic size and ionization energy?

9. Complete the following table by filling in the words "lower left" or "upper right" in the appropriate spaces.

Where on Periodic Table Elements Show:	
Largest atomic radii	low R
Smallest atomic radii	top L
Lowest ionization energy	Low L
Highest ionization energy	top R
Lowest electronegativity	low L
Highest electronegativity	top R

10. Consider the first two ionization energies for lithium:

IE_1 = 519 kJ/mol IE_2 = 7 285 kJ/mol

Explain why lithium's second ionization energy is more than 10 times its first.

Because Li's first e^- to remove is on the 2nd energy level, then the 2nd e^- to move is on the 1st energy level which is much closer to the nucleus, resulting in a stronger Fatt.

11. Elements with low ionization energies tend to have relatively low electronegativities. What might this indicate about how they will behave when reacting with high *IE* and EN elements?

They could lose their val e^- to the high EN elements

12. Elements with high ionization energies tend to have relatively high electronegativities. What might this indicate about how they will behave when reacting with low *IE* and EN elements?

They could take the lower EN's val e^-

13. What do you think might occur if two non-metal atoms, each with high EN and *IE* values reacted together? (Hint: Will either have a tendency to give away electrons?)

The e^- will stay in the middle of the two! a covalent bond (the e^- is shared)

14. Write the electron configuration for nickel and zinc. Use these to explain why an atom of zinc is larger than an atom of nickel.

Ni: $1s^2 2s^2 2p^6 3s^2 3p^6 4s^2 3d^8$

Zn: $1s^2 2s^2 2p^6 3s^2 3p^6 4s^2 3d^{10}$

An atom of Zn is larger than an atom of Ni because it's d-orbital is all the way full, which means it has 2 'more' val e^- but it also has two more p^+, which means they have the same Zeff but Zn is larger because it has more p^+.

6.3 Spectroscopy: The Interaction of Matter and Electromagnetic Radiation

Warm Up

What is a photon?

What is the electromagnetic spectrum?

The Interaction of Light and Matter

Light is a form of electromagnetic radiation. The electromagnetic spectrum consists of a continuum of energies of different wavelengths. Visible light is a very small portion of this continuum. It includes wavelengths ranging from 380 to 750 nm. Light can be emitted in the form of a wave from a source or absorbed by various forms of matter. For example, plants appear green because all visible portions of white light except for the green wavelengths are absorbed by a magnesium complex in their chlorophyll.

At the atomic level, light energy is released or emitted when "excited" electrons fall to a lower potential energy state. Light that is emitted when an electron falls from a higher energy level to a lower energy level is called a *photon*. The energy of a photon is quantized, meaning that photons that exhibit a certain frequency of light have a fixed amount of energy. The energy associated with photons is always conserved according to the equation dealt with in Section 5.2.

$\Delta E = hv$ where v is frequency and h is Planck's constant, 6.626×10^{-34} Js

Electromagnetic waves oscillate in space and time, rising and falling as they move from point to point. Although wavelength and frequency vary across the electromagnetic spectrum, the speed of this radiation is fixed. The universal wave equation, relating frequency and wavelength also appeared in Section 5.2.

$c = \lambda v$ where λ is wavelength and c is the speed of light, 3.00×10^{8} m/s

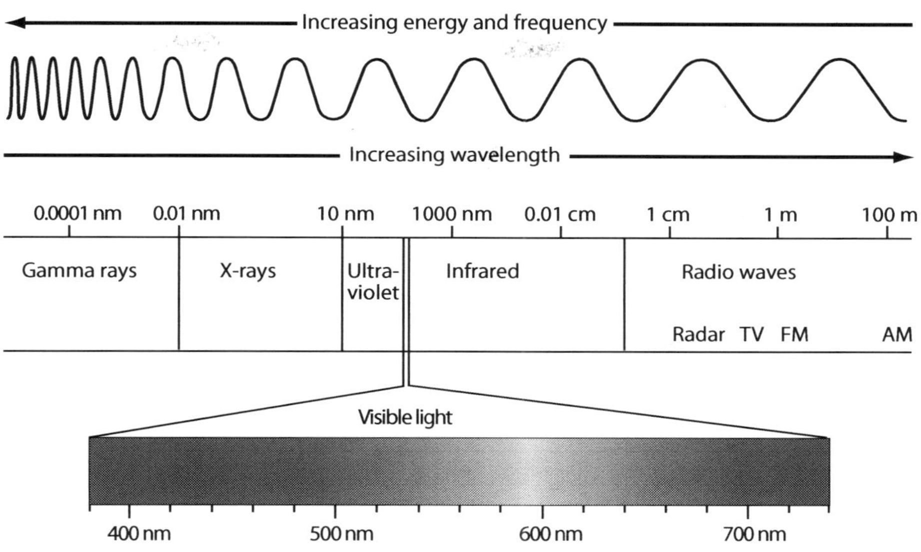

Figure 6.3.1 *The electromagnetic spectrum*

Quick Check

1. Microwaves are electromagnetic waves with a relatively long wavelength and low frequency. When a plate of spaghetti is warmed in a microwave, a photon with a wavelength of 12.2 cm is emitted.

   (a) At what frequency is this wave oscillating?

   (b) What is the transition energy of this wave?

   (c) What is the primary molecule being excited to higher rotational energies in the food being warmed in a microwave oven?

Spectroscopy

Various regions of the electromagnetic spectrum may be used to help us probe matter with the assistance of a variety of different instruments in a process called **spectroscopy** We will look at the following types of spectroscopy below:

- nuclear magnetic resonance
- infrared spectroscopy
- ultraviolet and visible-light spectroscopy
- X-rays: photoelectron spectroscopy

Nuclear Magnetic Resonance

The longest waves in the electromagnetic spectrum are called **radio waves**. The wavelengths of such waves vary from just below a metre to infinity. As can be seen by applying the equation above, wavelength (λ) and frequency (v) are reciprocally related. Since these waves have such long wavelengths, they oscillate at very low frequencies, from hundreds of megahertz down to tens of kilohertz. Superimposed on the pattern of these waves is a field of electromagnetic push-pull forces that is relatively low in energy. When radio frequency irradiation interacts with matter, there is no effect on electrons as their orbitals are separated by more energy than a radio wave can deliver. Radio waves cannot impact the position of the nucleus of an atom or the bonds in a molecule either. The matter continues to vibrate and rotate unchanged. Radio waves can, however, cause a change in **nuclear spin**. Nuclear spin is caused by the angular momentum of neutrons and protons and is analogous to electron spin as discussed in Section 5.5. The combination of spin and charge of the nucleus creates a **magnetic moment.** This means that a "nuclear magnet" behaves like a quantum mechanical compass needle that may align either up or down with an applied magnetic field. By placing the nuclei of a sample in a magnetic field and supplying just enough radio frequency energy to reorient the spins, each time a spin flips we observe a **nuclear magnetic resonance (NMR)**. The internal magnetic fields within a molecule differ at each chemically distinct site.

> Each *signal (peak)* or *group of signals* in an *NMR spectrum* is due to the *nuclear spin change* of a *hydrogen atom* in a *distinct environment within a molecule.*

An NMR spectrum can help reveal the structure of a molecule, by showing the bonding pattern. This is commonly used in the identification of organic compounds. For example, in organic compounds, NMR indicates whether a molecule contains carbon atoms that have one, two, or three hydrogen atoms attached, whether the molecule contains double or triple bonds or exists as a *cis* or *trans* isomer (see Section 8.1). Nuclear magnetic resonance imaging can even produce visual images of the human brain.

Analytical work typically involves connecting an NMR spectrometer to a computerized bank of spectra of millions of different compounds. The unknown compound can thus be compared with the spectra of millions of known standards.
The analytical chemist can then quickly and accurately identify a sample.

The recognition of functional groups and other compound characteristics following the observation of an NMR spectrum is far beyond what is required in a course such as AP Chemistry. However, spectroscopy is interesting and it is important to be aware that many different types of spectroscopy exist and may be used to help us understand more about the structure and function of various types of matter.

Quick Check

1. How do the two possible spin states of the proton in a hydrogen atom differ?

2. What causes different "signals" (distinct lines) to appear on an NMR spectrum?

3. Why would a methane molecule, CH_4, only have one distinct line on its NMR spectrum?

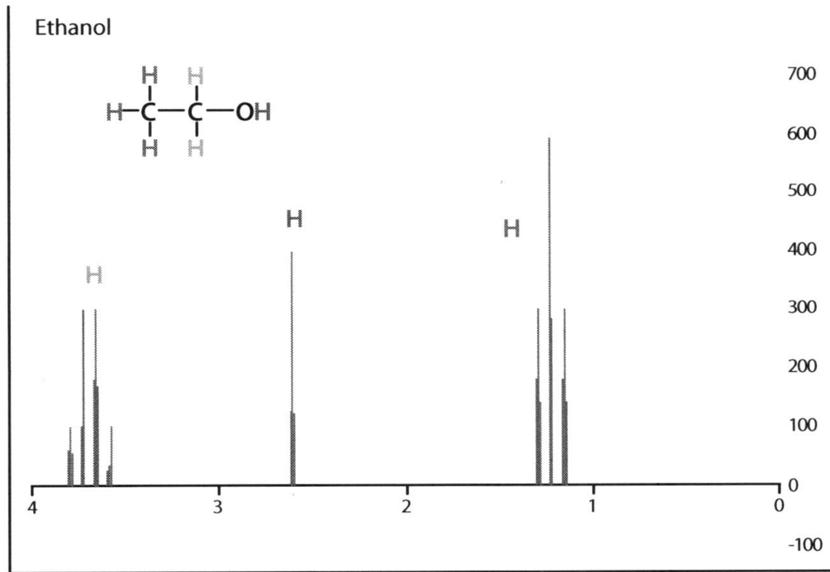

Figure 6.3.2 *^1H NMR spectrum (1-dimensional) of ethanol plotted as signal intensity vs. chemical shift. There are three different types of H atoms in ethanol regarding NMR. The hydrogen (H) on the –OH group is not coupling with the other H atoms and appears as a singlet, but the CH_3– and the –CH_2 hydrogens are coupling with each other, resulting in a triplet and quartet respectively.*

Infrared Spectroscopy

Infrared (IR) radiation has a lower energy and a longer wavelength than visible light. $E = hv$ indicates the direct relationship between energy (E) and frequency (v). The relatively short wavelengths (between 1 μm and 1 mm) of infrared radiation mean more compressed and rapidly oscillating waves have a higher frequency (from $3 \times 10^{11}\ s^{-1}$ to $3 \times 10^{14}\ s^{-1}$) and a higher energy than radio waves. The electric force accompanying an infrared wave pushes and pulls the nuclei within a molecule.

The *absorbance of an infrared photon* causes increased forces of attraction between nuclei and electrons and increased forces of repulsion between nuclei. This leads to *bonds stretching, compressing, and bending (vibrating)* in the infrared range of frequencies. Bonds experiencing these forces are undergoing *resonance*.

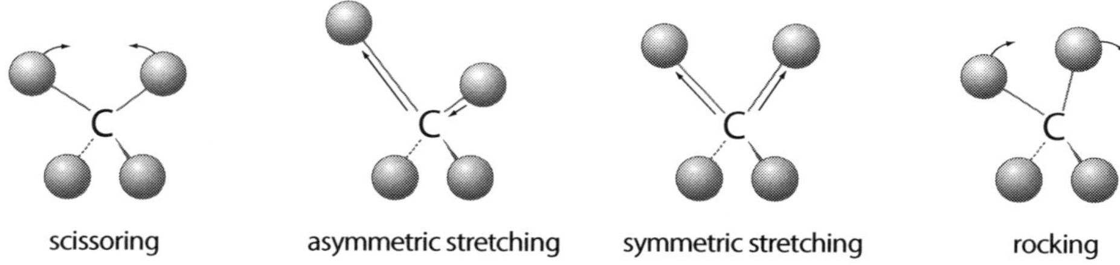

Figure 6.3.3 *All molecules routinely undergo the motions shown above. However, the absorbance of IR radiation excites a molecule from one quantum state to another, causing it to vibrate faster and more energetically than before.*

Nuclei attached to bonds may be likened to masses attached to springs. Strong bonds are like stiff springs and vibrate more rapidly. Heavy nuclei are like heavy masses and vibrate more slowly. The spring-bond analogy has limitations in that because they are quantized, molecular bonds can only vibrate with discrete energies levels. There are distinct vibrational levels just as there are distinct electronic energy levels and distinct spin levels.

In IR spectroscopy, the energy of infrared photons can equate to the difference between two allowed levels of vibration, exciting a molecule from one allowed state of vibration to another. In a molecule, each bond has its own unique difference in energy corresponding to the strength and elasticity of its vibration. This means that a bond between two particular atoms (e.g., C= O) will vibrate at nearly the same frequency in any molecule in which it is found. Consequently a vibrational spectrum is just a series of bands, each resulting from a different functional group or portion of the molecule. The spectrum as a whole is like a fingerprint for the molecule.

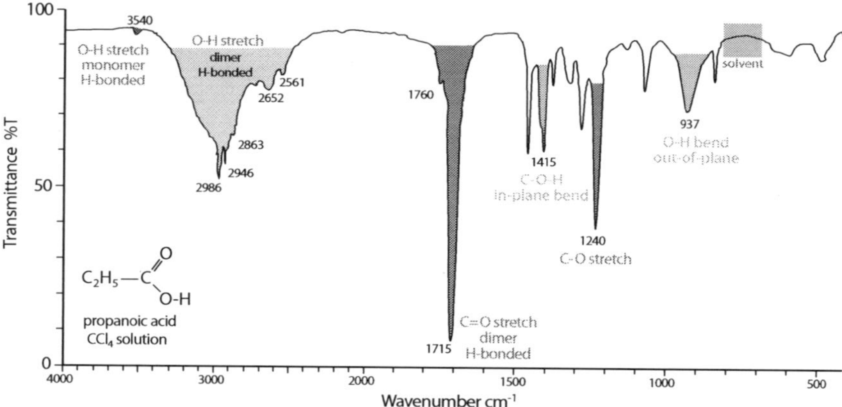

Figure 6.3.4 *Most IR spectra show the percentage of infrared radiation transmitted, rather than the percentage absorbed by different portions of the molecule. The "wavenumber" is simply a measure of the number of cycles per unit distance (in this case cm). It is analogous to a measure of frequency and hence, energy. As wavenumber decreases, so do frequency and energy, while wavelength increases.*

Even in different molecules, the *frequency of vibration of a particular functional group or structural feature* generally falls *within a narrow range* and hence can be used to *verify the presence of that group.*

Table 6.3.1 *Most Common IR Frequencies and Bond Stretches*

IR Frequency	Bond and Functional Group
3500–3200	O–H stretch in phenols
3400–3250	N–H stretch in amines, amides
3300–2500	O–H stretch in carboxylic acids
3330–3270	–C≡C–H (alkyne H)
3100–3000	=C–H stretch (alkene H)
3000–2850	-C– stretch (alkane H)
2830–2695	C–H stretch in aldehydes
2260–2210	C≡N stretch (nitrile)
2260–2100	–C≡C– stretch in alkynes
1760–1665	C=O stretch carbonyls (general)
1760–1690	C=O stretch in carboxylic acids
1750–1735	C=O stretch in esters
1740–1720	C=O stretch in aldehydes
1715	C=O stretch in ketones
1680–1640	–C=C– stretch in alkenes

Most functional groups absorb infrared light with a frequency above 1500 cm^{-1}. The region with frequencies below this primarily shows stretches between the *parent chain* atoms of the molecule and is of less use. Bizarrely this region is sometimes called the *finger print region*. It is largely ignored. As IR samples are dissolved in solvents that will themselves, absorb infrared radiation, a solvent spectrum is generally run for comparison.

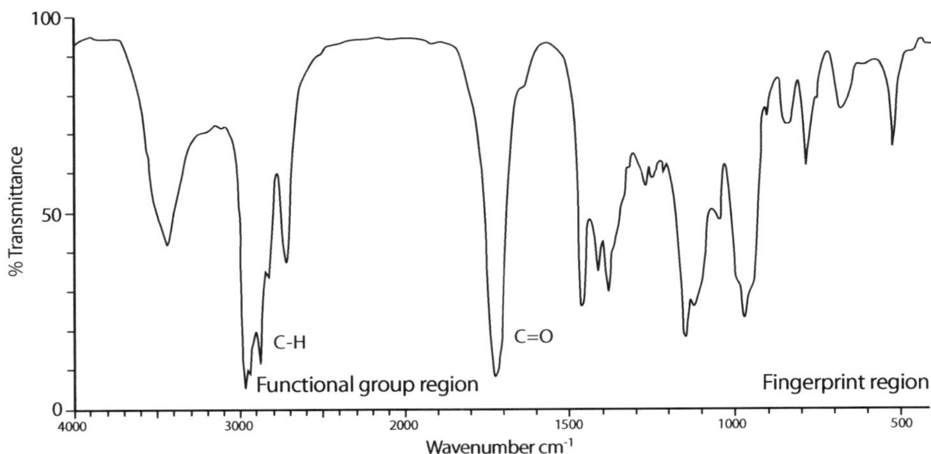

Figure 6.3.5 *A carbonyl group is extremely useful in elucidating the identity of an organic molecule. Though it generally absorbs in the region of 1660 to 1760 cm^{-1}, the exact position varies depending on whether it is part of a ketone, an ester, a carboxylic acid or an aldehyde group (see Section 9.2).*

Quick Check

1. What group might be indicated by the farthest left band in the IR spectrum in Figure 6.3.5?

2. Rank the following N to N bonds in order of increasing vibrational frequency:
   N-N, N=N, N≡N.
   Which will absorb infrared photons with the longest wavelength?

Ultraviolet and Visible-Light Spectroscopy

Visible and ultraviolet (UV) radiation are *above* infrared in terms of energy and below in terms of wavelength. Infrared radiation whose photon energies are *below* the red region of visible light gives way to visible red light at wavelengths between 800 and 700 nm. This is the region of the electromagnetic spectrum within which human beings perceive colour. The visible light portion of the spectrum extends from above 700 to just below 400 nm. The sum of all of these wavelengths makes up so-called **white light**. Wavelengths below 400 extending down to around 10 nm are associated with EMR (electromagnetic radiation) having energy above that of the violet portion of the visible range. For that reason, this portion of the spectrum is called **ultraviolet.** It is also the region within which photons may affect the most weakly held electrons, the so-called *valence electrons*. They may be excited out of their energy levels, and chemical bonding may be affected. The behaviour of these valence electrons is to a large extent governed by **Coulomb's law**.

$$F = \frac{kQ_1Q_2}{r^2}$$

This relationship between the force (F) on two charged objects, the charges (Q_1 and Q_2), and the distance between them (r) was determined in 1785 by French physicist Charles-Augustin de Coulomb. The law is sometimes referred to as the *inverse square law* for obvious reasons, and it resembles Newton's law of universal gravitation. The law shows that as the charge on one or both objects, such as a nucleus and an electron, increases, so does the force of attraction. It also shows that as the distance between an electron and the nucleus increases, the force of attraction decreases. This law can, and *should* (particularly in an AP course) be used to explain most of the atomic and ionic trends in the periodic table. This is a wonderful time to return to Section 6.2 and review those trends through the application of Coulomb's law.

The valence electrons have the greatest r value and are screened most effectively from the charge on the nucleus. The reduced charge experienced by the valence electrons is sometimes referred to as Z_{eff} or the **effective nuclear charge**. Z represents the atomic number, which is, effectively, the number of protons.

$$Z_{eff} = Z - \textit{number of screening electrons}$$

The screening electrons are all those found in energy levels below that of the valence shell. This equation indicates that the effective nuclear charge is essentially constant moving up or down a family in the periodic table. However, it definitely increases moving across a period. The reduction in the nuclear charge *felt* by a valence electron is often referred to as the **shielding effect**. This effect was mentioned in Section 6.2. While any explanation of nuclear and ionic trends such as ionization energy and radius should certainly be centred on Coulomb's law, an explanation of Z_{eff} and the shielding effect are definitely appropriate.

UV/Vis spectroscopy involves absorption of light by the valence electrons. Valence electrons occupy orbitals far from the nucleus and high in energy. Consideration of Coulomb's law and the shielding effect tells us that these electrons are attracted by an attenuated and distant nuclear charge. Consequently they are the easiest electrons to disturb. They may be ionized and, under milder excitation, may be promoted to higher levels of energy (moved from their **ground state** to an **excited state**). Transition metal ions may experience movement of electrons between *d* orbitals of different energy levels. Such movement may be accompanied by the absorbance or release of visible light of specific wavelengths (*d* orbital splitting, or *non-degenerate d* orbitals, is a topic beyond the level of an AP Chemistry course; however, your teacher may encourage you to investigate this topic further). As a consequence, compounds containing transition metal ions with partially filled *d* orbitals will exhibit colour and hence are most suitable for study with visible spectroscopy. In organic molecules, valence electrons may be excited from a *bonding* orbital to an *antibonding* orbital (see Section 6.7 on molecular orbital theory). Such excitations are not associated with colour, but rather with ultraviolet (UV) light. Finally in a lanthanide series or rare-earth containing compound, valence electrons may transition between non-degenerate *f* orbitals. Splitting of *f* orbitals leads to electron transitions associated with coloured light much like those that occur in solutions containing transition metal ions.

Ultraviolet–Visible Light Summary

- Solutions of transition metal ions produce colour due to *d* orbital electron excitation and return to ground state. (The colour of such solutions is due to the region of the spectrum they absorb in. This is in turn affected by the presence of other species such an anions or bonded ligands.)
- Organic compounds (and frequently the solvents they are dissolved in) absorb UV and visible light as they promote electrons from bonding to antibonding molecular orbitals.
- Compounds containing rare earth elements (elements from the lanthanide series – 4f) absorb UV and visible light due to f orbital excitation. (The region of the spectrum in which absorption occurs is impacted in a similar way to that of the transition metal ions.)

There is no sharp cut off between species affected by visible and invisible EMR, or colourless and coloured. The important point is that energy in this region of the electromagnetic spectrum can promote valence electrons. Moving a valence electron from an occupied to an unoccupied orbital may impact a molecule's size, shape, bond strength, polarity, paramagnetism, or colour, at least until the electron returns to its ground state. UV/Vis spectroscopy is most commonly used in *quantitative* rather than qualitative analysis of solutions, although solids and gases may also be studied. The application of the Beer-Lambert law for quantitative analysis of solutions will be discussed further in Section 6.4.

Sometimes, a valence electron may be completely removed resulting in the creation of an ion. This process is called **photoionization** — ionization caused by a photon. Such an ionization caused by light is also called the **photoelectric effect**. Most molecules require UV radiation with wavelengths below 200 nm to produce such an effect.

Quick Check

Examine the UV/Vis spectrum shown here. (a) and (b) represent two different samples of the *same* compound in aqueous solution.

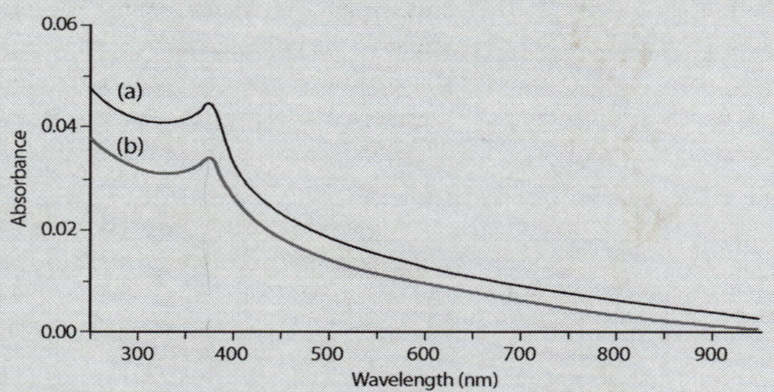

Figure 6.3.6

1. Which sample absorbed more light?

   a

2. Which sample transmitted more light?

   b

3. How does sample (a) differ from sample (b)?

   a could have a higher concentration if they are the same substance

4. At what wavelength is maximum absorbance occurring?

   375 nm

X-Rays: Photoelectron Spectroscopy

Core electrons (those below the valence shell) are considerably more difficult to remove from their atom. Consideration of Z_{eff} and Coulomb's law indicates that core electrons are attracted to a poorly shielded, more positively charged nucleus, and because they exist in an orbital that is lower in energy, their average distance from the nucleus is considerably less than that of the valence electrons. Each of these factors tells us that core electrons are much more difficult to remove. The removal of core electrons requires the significant energy of an X-ray photon with wavelengths below 10 nm all the way down to less than 0.01 nm.

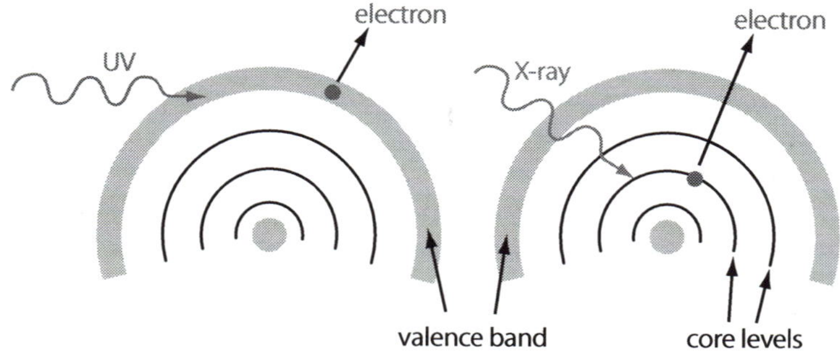

Figure 6.3.7 *UV and visible radiation have sufficient energy to remove valence electrons only, while X-rays may remove core electrons as well.*

Photoelectron spectroscopy (PES) was formerly known as *X-ray electron spectroscopy* or *XES*. It involves the use of a device that focuses a monochromatic beam of X-rays at a solid sample. Random atoms in the sample may then release electrons from any energy level in the atom. Emitted electrons are collected by a lens and passed through an electron energy analyzer to a detector. A computer then visualizes the electrons in the form of a photoelectron spectrum.

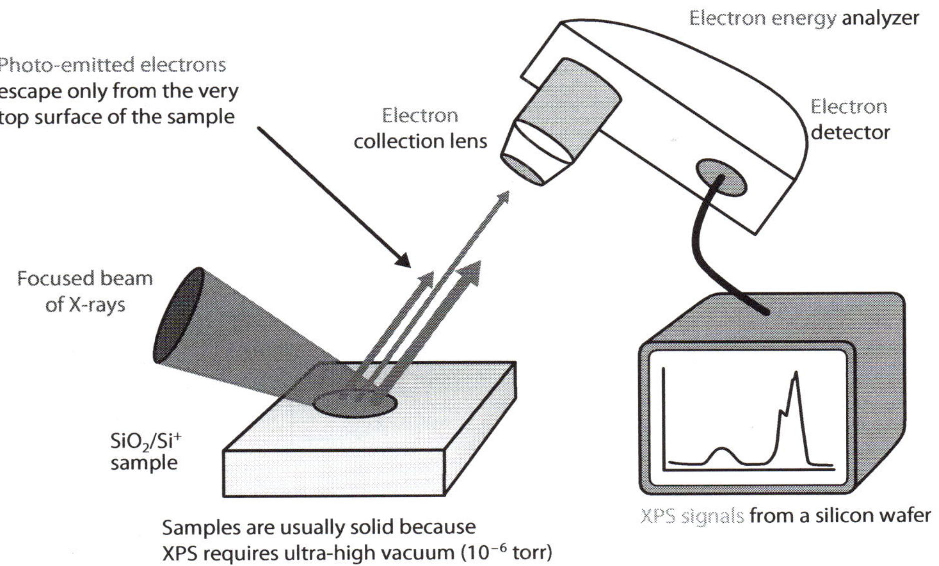

Figure 6.3.8 *Schematic diagram of the PES process*

The kinetic energy (KE) of the emitted electrons is measured by the electron energy analyzer. The energy of the X-Ray photon is simply calculated as *hv*. This means the energy required to remove an electron from an inner energy level of an atom is simply the difference between these two values.

$$E = hv - KE$$

This process is virtually identical to the one used to determine the first ionization energy of an atom except that very high energy UV or X-ray photons are required to emit core electrons. (It should be noted that occasionally the vacant orbital produced by an ejected electron may be filled by an electron *falling* from a higher energy orbital. The energy from such a fall may cause the emission of another X-ray photon or could be absorbed to cause the emission of a second electron. These are called Auger transitions and require a more complex calculation.)

A computer visualizes the data from a PES instrument as a series of peaks in a spectrum plotting the intensity of the signal on the *y*-axis against the energy needed to eject an electron, *E*, on the *x*-axis. Some PES spectra show energy increasing on the *x*-axis; however, the most common convention (and the one that is being used in sample AP assessments) is to show energy *decreasing* from left to right. Inspection of the sample NMR and IR spectra shown earlier in this section indicates that they follow the same convention. The height of each peak in a PES spectrum is directly proportional to the number of electrons of equivalent energy. The energy units found in PES spectra are MJ/mol and less commonly eV/mol. Because actual PES spectra contain extraneous peaks referred to as "noise" that are not useful to us, we will study *simulated* PES spectra.

The following simulated photoelectron spectra of elements one through five in the periodic table have been adjusted to allow direct comparison of the peak heights. This would be the case if all the spectra were produced using equivalent sample sizes.

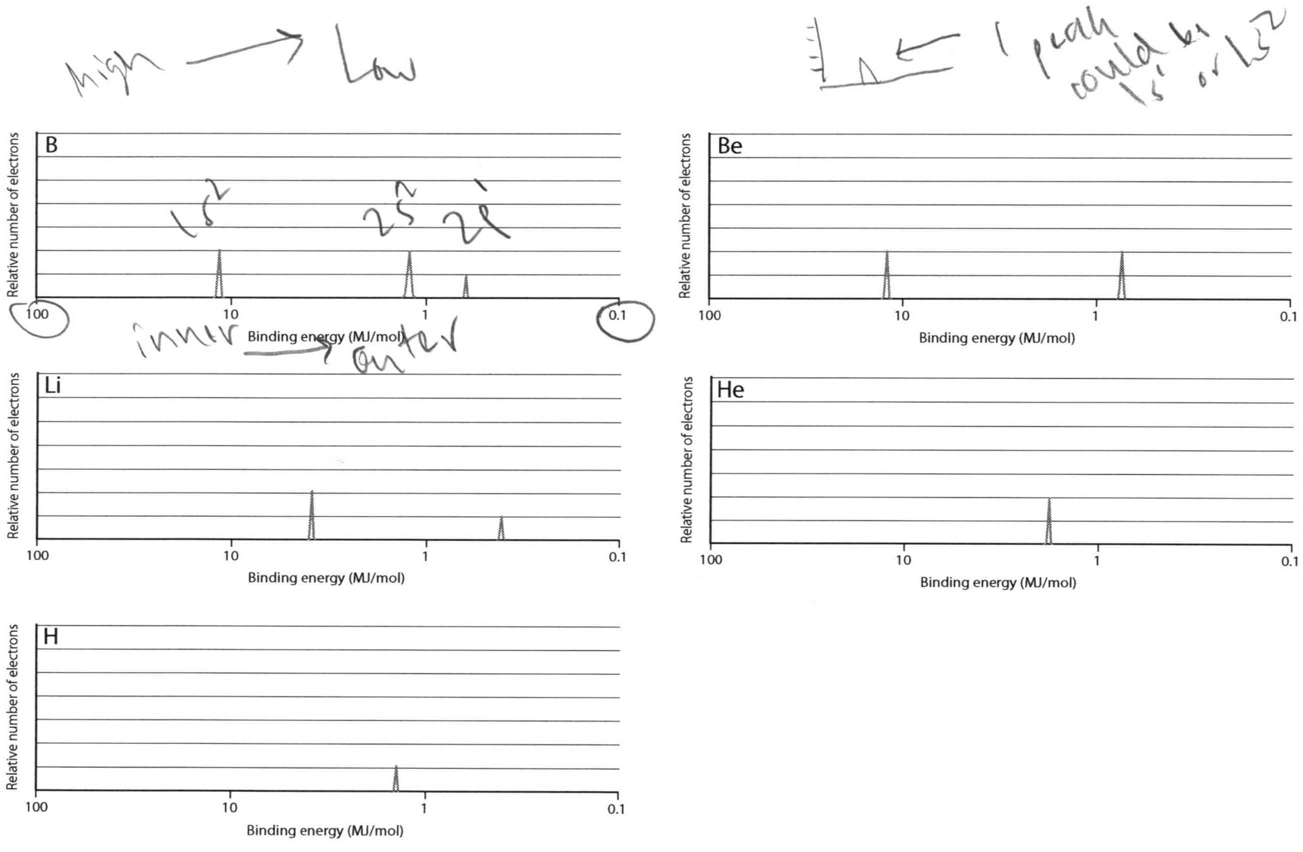

Figure 6.3.9 *Simulated photoelectron spectra of elements 1 through 5*

The number of peaks in a PES spectrum may be used to determine the number of orbitals existing in an element. The smallest peaks represent s orbitals. Full p orbitals are three times the height of a full s orbital. A full d orbital is five times the height of a full s. The highest energy peaks appear farther left and represent electrons in orbitals that are closer to the nucleus.

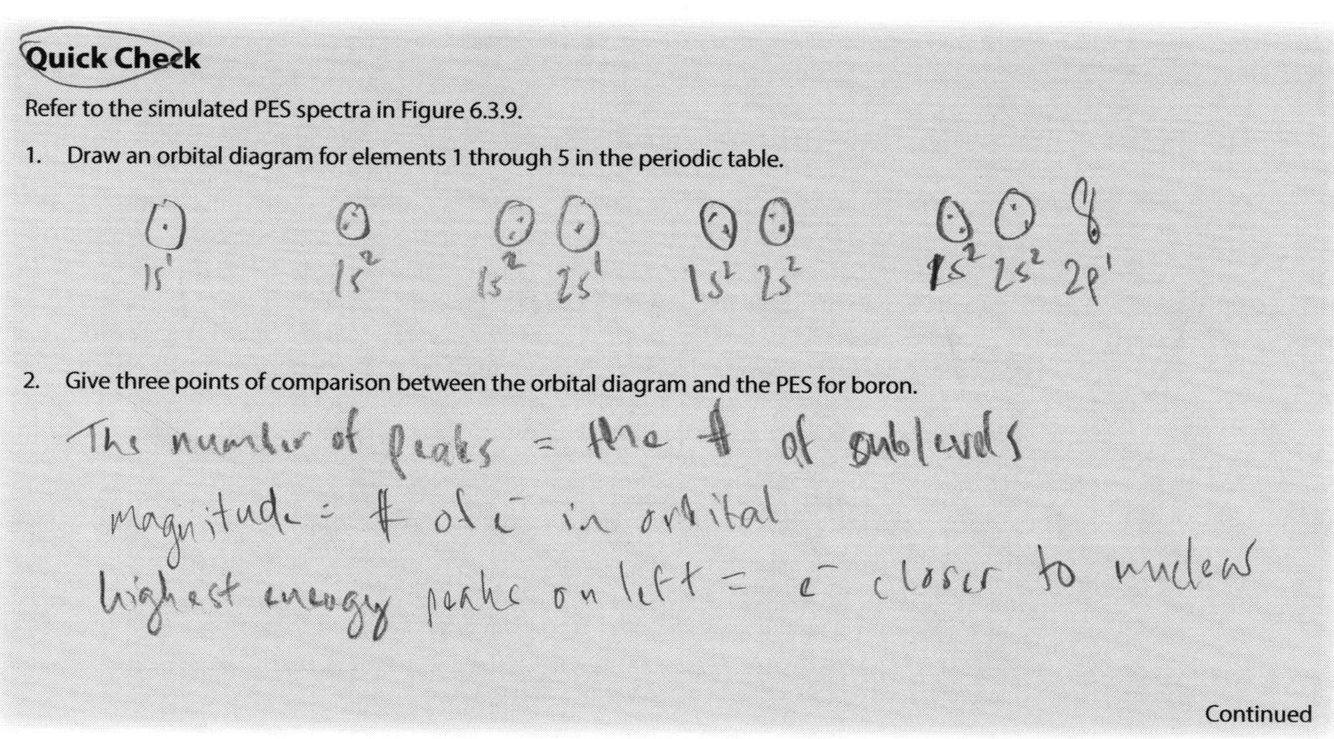

Quick Check

Refer to the simulated PES spectra in Figure 6.3.9.

1. Draw an orbital diagram for elements 1 through 5 in the periodic table.

2. Give three points of comparison between the orbital diagram and the PES for boron.

Continued

Quick Check — *Continued*

Refer to the simulated PES spectra in Figure 6.3.9.

3. Compare and explain the position of the first peak for each of the elements 1 to 5.

4. Compare and explain the heights of the final peak (farthest right) for each of the elements 1 to 5.

Sample Problem — The PES Spectrum

What element is represented by the following PES spectrum? Note that the *x*-axis is not shown to scale.

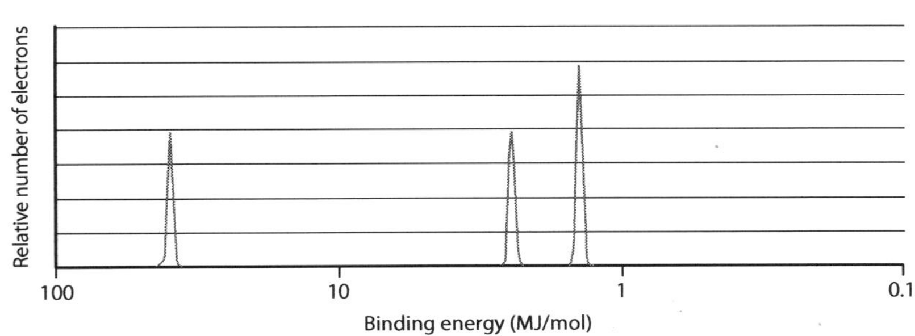

What to Think About	How to Do It
1. Count the peaks, keeping in mind that each peak represents an orbital.	There are three peaks in total.
2. Assume the highest energy peak (farthest to the left) represents the orbital closest to the nucleus.	The innermost peak must represent the 1s orbital. It follows that the other two represent the 2s and the 2p orbitals.
3. Use the relative heights of the peaks to determine the number of electrons in each orbital.	The 1s and 2s orbitals are full. However, the 2p is only 1.5 times as high as the s orbitals, and hence must contain only three electrons.
4. Use this information to discern the electron configuration and hence the identity of the element.	$1s^22s^22p^3$ represents atomic number 7 or nitrogen.

Practice Problems—The PES Spectrum

1. Identify the element represented by each PES spectrum below.

(a)

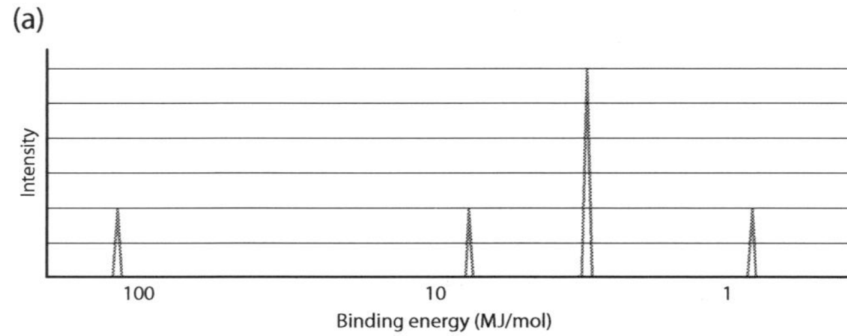

$1s^2 2s^2 2p^6 3s^2$

Mg

(b)

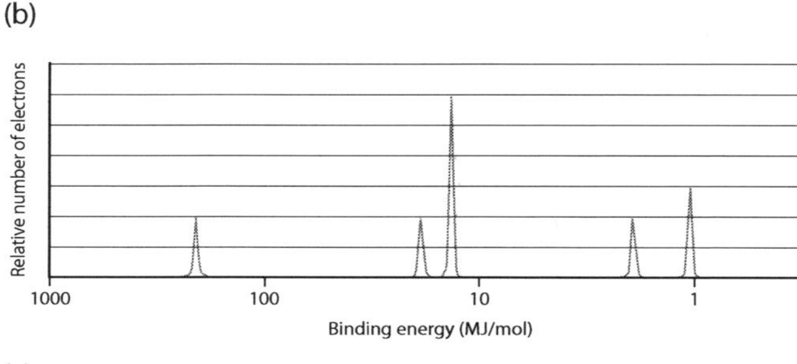

$1s^2 2s^2 2p^6 3s^2 3p^3$

P

(c)

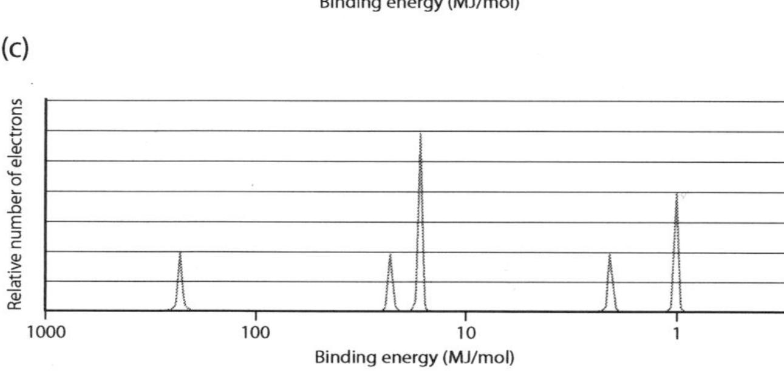

$1s^2 2s^2 2p^6 3s^2 3p^4$

S

2. Use the following axes to sketch the PES spectrum you would expect for the element potassium. Pay attention to the relative heights and positions of each of the peaks. Exact values for binding energies are not required.

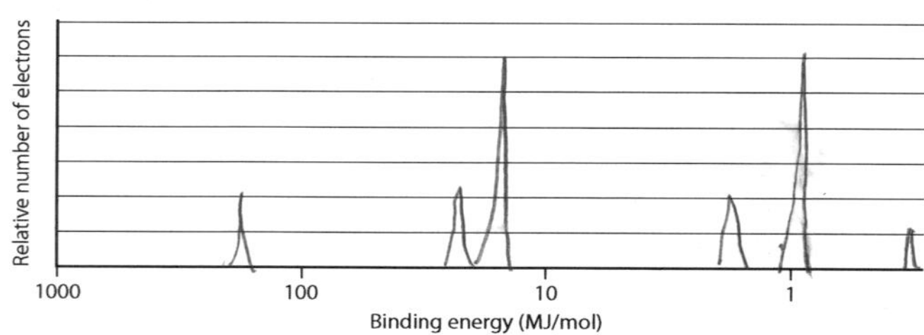

Examination of each of the spectra provided thus far indicates that the energy required to remove the innermost electrons varies significantly from element to element. The trend shows that as the atomic number increases, so does the binding energy. The following spectra moving from element number 6 to 8 to 10 across period 2 illustrates this trend for all three peaks in each element.

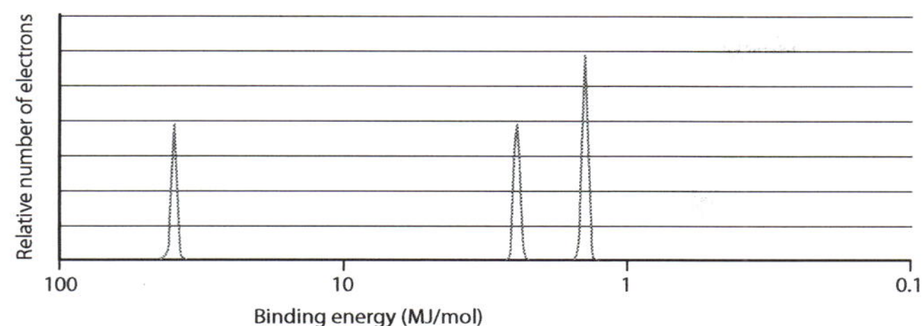

Figure 6.3.10 *PES spectra for neon, oxygen and carbon.*

The principal explanation for the increased energy required to remove the innermost electrons is the increased effective nuclear charge, Z_{eff}, as we move to the right across a period. Note this is not only true for the *1s* orbital electrons, but also holds true for the *2s* and the *2p* orbitals.

Quick Check

1. Practice Problems 1(a), (b), and (c) on page 366 represent Mg, P, and S respectively. Reexamine your answer to Practice Problem 2. Make any changes you now think necessary for your spectrum.

2. Examine Figure 6.3.10. Use the *Q* values in Coulomb's law to explain why the energy associated with the first peak is larger in neon and smaller in oxygen. Do the same for the third peak referring to both the *Q* and *r* values.

3. Examine Figure 6.3.9 again. Why are the first and second peaks the same height for all three elements while the third peak heights vary?

PES Summary

- The number of peaks = the number of orbitals (s, p, d, or f)
- The magnitude (height) of a peak is directly related to the number of electrons in the orbital the peak represents. The ratio of heights of peaks representing full *s:p:d:f* orbitals is 1:3:5:7. A full orbital is twice the height of a half full.
- The highest energy peaks appear farther *left* on the *x*-axis and represent electrons that are *closer* to the nucleus of an atom.

6.3 Review Questions

1. Complete the following table:

Region of EM Spectrum	Spectroscopic Technique	Photons Used To
Radio Waves	NMR (nuclear magnetic resonance)	Measure energy changes causing nuclear spin to study molecular structure.
Infrared		
UV/Visible		
X-rays		

2. The first ionization energies for selected elements from the second period of the periodic table are as follows:

Atom	Li-3	Be-4	C-6	N-7	F-9	Ne-10
1st IE (kJ/mol)	520	899	1086	1302	1681	2081

Use Coulomb's law to explain the trend in ionization energies in terms of the relative location of the electrons and the charge of the nucleus.

as you move across a period, the Zeff increases, which means each atom has a higher + higher attraction on its valence e^-

3. (a) Calculate the photon frequencies in 1/s for each of the following regions of the electromagnetic spectrum.
   (b) What range of the spectrum does each energy correspond to?
   (c) What type of spectroscopy might it be useful for?

Wavelength Range	(a) Frequency (1/s)	(b) Range	(c) Spectroscopy
700 nm to 400 nm			
400 nm to 10 nm			
10 to 0.01 nm			

4. Note the IE's for the 1*s* electron of the following second row elements:

Element	Li	Be	B	C	N	O	F
kJ/mol	4820	10 600	18 300	27 000	38 600	51 100	66 600

A substance is bombarded with X-rays having a wavelength of 1 nm. A photoelectron is ejected from the substance. Its energy is 69,500 kJ/mol. Which of the elements listed above must be in the sample?

5. What element does each PES spectrum below represent?

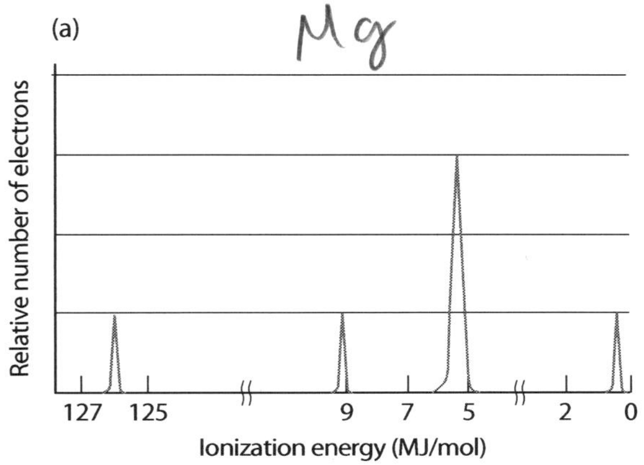

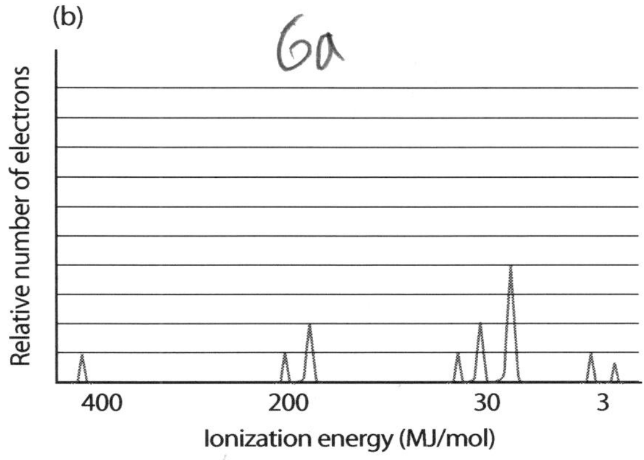

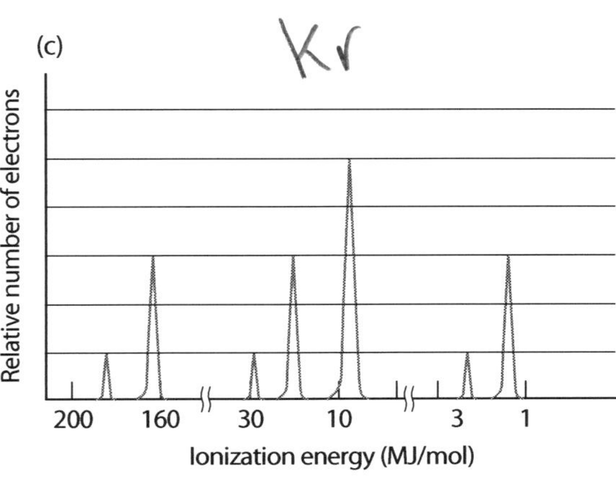

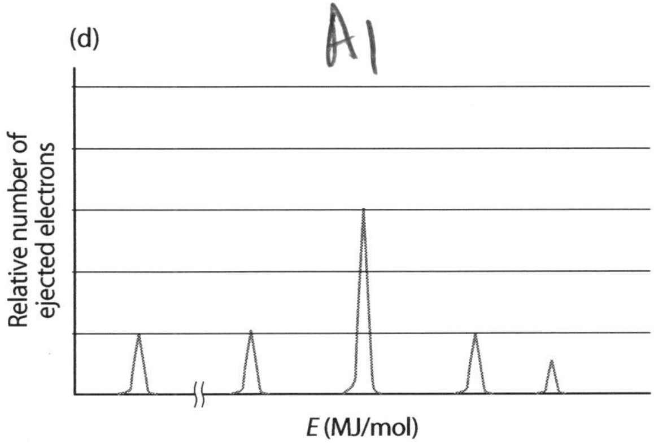

6. (a) Identify the element whose PES spectrum is shown.

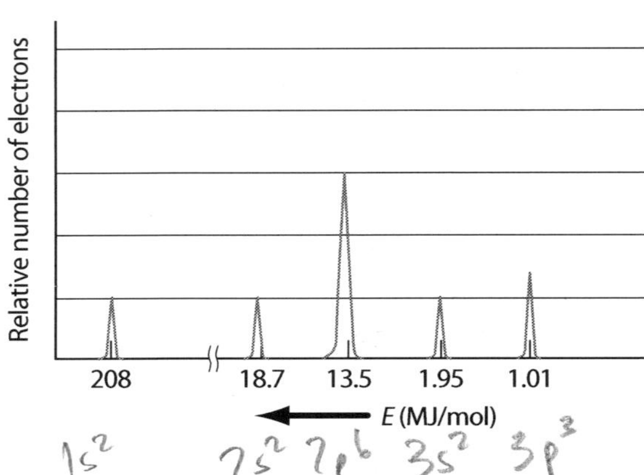

(b) Draw the Bohr diagram for this element.

(c) Sketch the PES spectrum for the atom having 8 fewer protons than this atom. Label the axes clearly and show the approximate energies.

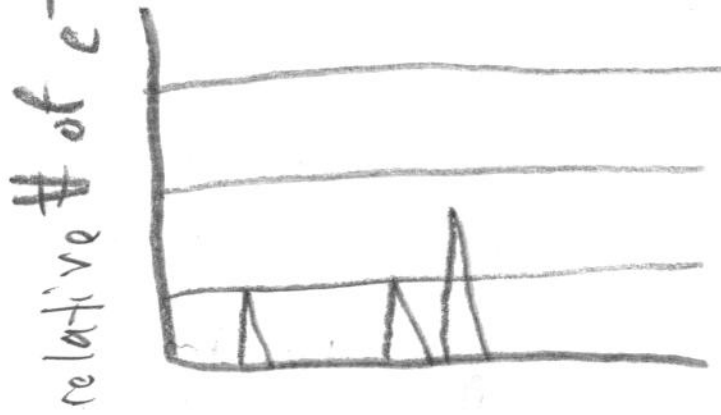

(d) If photons of wavelength 1.25×10^{-8} m bombarded the original element, which, if any, of the electrons could be emitted?

6.4 Describing Chemical Bonding

Warm Up

1. What term do we give to an atom's outer electrons that take part in chemical bonding?

 ____

2. Define electronegativity.

 ____

3. In which region of the periodic table are elements located that tend to
 (a) lose outer electrons most easily during chemical changes?

 ____

 (b) gain outer electrons most easily during chemical changes?

 ____

An Introduction to Chemical Bonding

All matter is composed of atoms, and those individual atoms are far too small to see. From that, it seems reasonable to conclude that matter must be made up of large numbers of atoms connected or bonded together. In this section, we will investigate the nature of the bonds between atoms and how those bonds determine important properties in compounds.

Atoms are electrical species with a negative cloud of electrons surrounding and attracted to a positive nucleus. As you have learned, the electrostatic forces of attraction and repulsion within atoms influence properties such as atomic size, ionization energy, and electronegativity. Those same forces and properties also play a role whenever atoms bond together.

When two atoms approach each other, all of the electrostatic interactions associated with equally and oppositely charged particles occur. The negative electron clouds of the atoms exert repulsive forces on each other, as do the positive nuclei of each atom. This repulsion slows the approaching atoms and converts some of their kinetic energy to potential energy. In addition, each nucleus also begins to attract the approaching atom's outer electron cloud. These attractive forces are most intense in the region of space where the electron clouds "overlap" between the adjacent nuclei. If the attractive forces between the atoms are stronger than the repulsive forces, the two atoms together are in a state of lower energy than when they were apart. Thus, a chemical bond forms between them.

Types of Chemical Bonds

The events described above apply to the formation of all chemical bonds. But recall that we have classified elements as metals and non-metals based on a number of physical and chemical properties that correlate to different positions on the periodic table. These properties and the three possible ways that these two varieties of elements can combine give rise to three different *types* of chemical bonds, which are listed in Table 6.4.1. In this course, we will cover ionic and covalent bonds.

Table 6.4.1 *Types of Chemical Bonds*

Atoms Involved in Chemical Bond	Type of Chemical Bond
1. metal bonded to non-metal	ionic bond
2. non-metal bonded to non-metal	covalent bond
3. metal bonded to metal	metallic bond

Table 6.4.1 is a simplified summary of chemical bonds because the bonds between atoms in most chemical compounds have varying proportions of both ionic and covalent characteristics. We will begin with clear examples of each type of bond to introduce the concepts involved.

Ionic Bonds

Ionic bonds form between two atoms with large differences in their ionization energies and electronegativities. Recall from Section 6.2 that such combinations typically occur when relatively large metal atoms located on the far left side of the periodic table in groups 1 or 2 combine with smaller non-metal atoms on the far right side of the table belonging to groups 16 or 17.

Look again at the table of electronegativities introduced in section 6.2 (Figure 6.2.6). Imagine a "collision," for example, between an alkali metal atom such as sodium and a halogen atom such as chlorine. These elements are located at opposite ends of the 3rd period of the periodic table and therefore exhibit significant differences in size, ionization energy, and electronegativity.

Compared to an atom of sodium, a chlorine atom is smaller with a higher ionization energy and electronegativity. As a result, when the outer electron clouds of these two atoms encounter each other, sodium's lone valence electron will be closer to chlorine's nucleus than to its own. It will therefore feel a stronger attraction from chlorine's nucleus than from its own. In fact, because the difference in the electronegativities of these two elements is *greater than 1.7*, the probability of finding sodium's outer electron near chlorine's nucleus is so great that the sodium atom can be considered to *transfer* that valence electron to the chlorine atom. Electronegativity difference is often abbreviated as **ΔEN**.

The large sodium atom, having lost the only electron in its 3rd energy level, is now a much smaller positively charged sodium cation (Na^+). The relatively small chlorine atom, having gained an extra electron, becomes a larger negatively charged chloride anion (Cl^-). These two oppositely charged ions are now bound together by an electrostatic attraction called an **ionic bond**.

> An **ionic bond** is the electrostatic attractive force between the oppositely charged ions produced when a metal atom transfers one or more electrons to a non-metal atom.

The electron transfer from sodium to chlorine and the resulting ionic bond is shown in Figure 6.4.1. These diagrams are **Bohr model** diagrams, showing the number of electrons in the shells surrounding the nuclei of the atoms and ions.

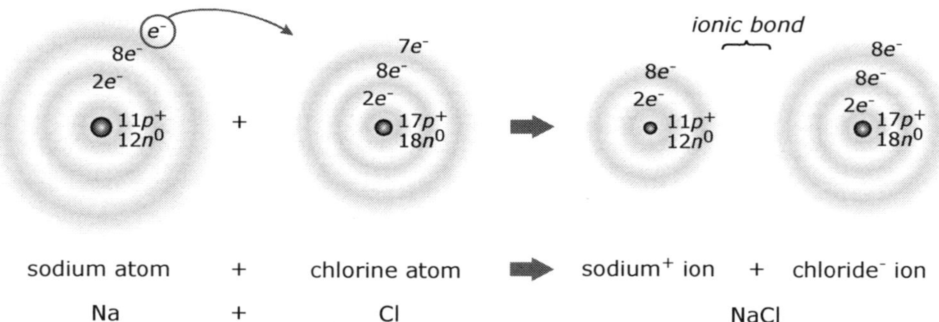

Figure 6.4.1 *An electron transfers from sodium atom to a chlorine atom, resulting in the formation of an ionic bond between the ions.*

The Ionic Crystal Lattice

Obviously, when any macroscopic sample of chlorine gas and sodium metal react together, countless atoms will transfer electrons to form countless oppositely charged ions. These oppositely charged species being produced in close proximity are drawn together into an ordered, solid, three-dimensional array of cations and anions called a **crystal lattice** (Figure 6.4.2). The smallest whole number cation-to-anion ratio in this structure represents the chemical formula for the ionic compound, in this case, NaCl.

Figure 6.4.2 *NaCl crystal lattice*

The vast number of interionic forces present in a crystal lattice locks all of the ions into place. This helps explain why all ionic compounds are solids with high melting temperatures (e.g., sodium chloride melts at 801°C.)

Ionic compounds form a number of different crystal structures depending on the relative sizes and ratios of their ions. Those ratios in turn depend on the charges on the ions in the compound.

Recall from section 6.1 that the representative elements in groups 1, 2, 13, 15, 16, and 17 of the periodic table tend to form stable ions by losing or gaining sufficient electrons to become isoelectronic with the nearest noble gas. This results in the common ion charges shown in Table 6.4.2 for those groups.

Table 6.4.2 *Common Ion Charges in Groups 1, 2, 13, 15, 16, and 17*

Group Number	1	2	13	15	16	17
Most Common Ion Charge	1+	2+	3+	3-	2–	1–

We can think of ionic bond formation as a case of *extremely unequal electron sharing*. Both metal and non-metal nuclei attract the valence electrons between them when their atoms meet. However, the non-metal pulls those electrons so close to its own nucleus that it effectively captures the metal's valence electrons and forms the metal cation and non-metal anion. An accurate analogy might be a grossly mismatched tug-of-war, except that in this case, the smallest competitor wins.

Several important points should be mentioned when summarizing ionic bonding:

1. Ionic compounds form between metals and non-metals whose ΔEN exceed 1.7. They typically form when metals from groups 1 or 2 react with non-metals from groups 16 or 17 of the periodic table.
2. During the formation of an ionic bond, metal atoms will transfer one or more valence electrons to the more electronegative non-metal atoms. This occurs because of the metal's relatively low ionization energies and electronegativities. In the process, metal cations and non-metal anions form and are attracted to each other by ionic bonds.
3. Ionic compounds form structures known as crystal lattices. The vast number of attractive forces present in such lattices account for the high melting temperatures of ionic compounds.
4. The formulas for ionic compounds represent the smallest whole number ratios of cations-to-anions that are electrically neutral.

Quick Check

1. What event occurs when atoms of metals and non-metals react to become cations and anions?

2. Identify the three types of chemical bonds based on the different elements involved.

3. Which chemical families in the periodic table are typically associated with ionic bond formation?

Sample Problem — Ionic Bond Formation

Write formulas for the compounds formed when the following elements combine and justify that the bonds present are ionic by determining the ΔEN in each case.

(a) Ca and Br (b) Al and O (c) Be and O (d) Rb and N (e) Ba and Cl

What to Think about	How to Do It
1. Write the element symbols with their charges and criss-cross the numbers. 2. Reduce formulas to smallest whole number ratios 3. Determine ΔEN values using the table above. Values above 1.7 represent ionic bonds.	(a) Ca^{2+} Br^{1-} → $CaBr_2$ ΔEN = 1.8 (ionic bond) (b) Al^{3+} O^{2-} → Al_2O_3 ΔEN = 2.0 (ionic bond) (c) Be^{2+} O^{2-} → BeO ΔEN = 2.0 (ionic bond) (d) Rb^{1+} N^{3-} → Rb_3N ΔEN = 2.2 (ionic bond) (e) Ba^{2+} Cl^{1-} → $BaCl_2$ ΔEN = 2.1 (ionic bond)

Practice Problems — Ionic Compounds

1. Write formulas for the ionic compounds formed when the following elements combine:

   (a) Ba and Br

   (b) Be and O

   (c) Sr and N

   (d) Mg and Cl

   (e) Fr and F

2. Justify that the bonds in the following compounds are ionic by calculating the ΔEN values for each.

   (a) RbF

   (b) $RaCl_2$

   (c) KBr

   (d) Na_2O

3. Write formulas for the ionic compounds formed when the following elements combine. Using the ΔEN values, arrange the compounds in order of the increasing ionic character of the bonds in each compound.

   (a) Na and N (b) Sr and Br (c) Li and Cl (d) Cs and F (e) Rb and O

Covalent Bonds

Now let's look at the formation of a bond between two atoms of the same non-metal element, such as hydrogen (Figure 6.4.3). Obviously, the electronegativities of these or any two identical atoms would be the same.

As mentioned above, bond formation begins with atoms "colliding." As the two hydrogen atoms approach each other, their kinetic energy increases as each electron cloud is attracted to the other's approaching positive nucleus. The two atoms continue moving together until the repulsive forces of the two negative electron clouds and the two positive nuclei slow the atoms and convert their kinetic energy into potential energy.

As the atoms get close to each other, their electron clouds may overlap enough to cause attractive forces to exceed repulsive ones. The two valence electrons will move into the region of space between the adjacent nuclei because this is where they experience the most attractive force from those two centres of positive charge. The two atoms will settle into a position next to each other with the pair of valence electrons in a cloud of negative charge between the two nuclei. As the electron clouds of each hydrogen atom overlap, the two valence electrons experience the maximum attractive force between the two adjacent nuclei. This force of attraction of a pair of valence electrons between two adjacent nuclei constitutes a single **covalent bond**. In our example, the result of this covalent bond is a molecule of hydrogen, H_2

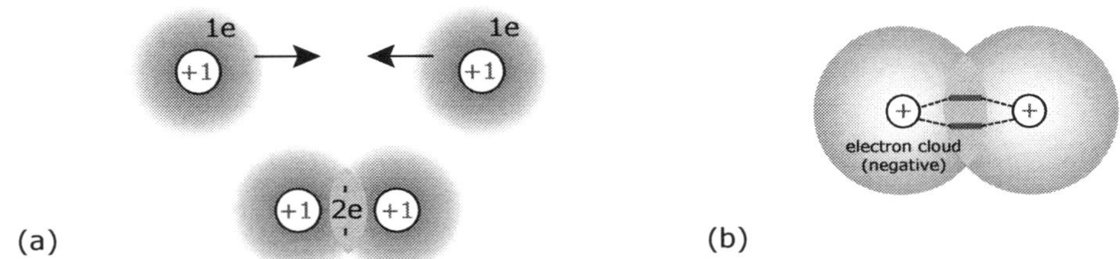

Figure 6.4.3 *(a) Two hydrogen atoms collide and two valence electrons move into the space between the nuclei. (b) The valence electrons experience a force of attraction from the two nuclei. This attraction holds the two atoms together to form* H_2.

Because this bond has formed between two atoms of hydrogen, the electronegativity difference associated with the atoms in the bond must be zero. This tells us that, on average, the pair of bonded electrons will spend the majority of their time equidistant between the two hydrogen nuclei. Stated another way, this means that the density of the electron charge cloud is greatest in the region of space halfway between the two adjacent nuclei. This is true whenever two atoms of the same element form covalent bonds. The "equal sharing" of valence electrons is sometimes referred to as a "pure covalent" or non-polar covalent bond.

Although both ionic and covalent bond formation involves only valence electrons, there are several important differences between the two events:

1. Covalent bonds typically form between two non-metal atoms rather than between metal atoms and non-metal atoms.
2. Because no electron transfer occurs and no ions form, all of the species prior to and following covalent bond formation between two atoms are electrically neutral.
3. The force of attraction in a covalent bond is between a pair of electrons and two adjacent positive nuclei, rather than between a cation and an anion as in an ionic bond. Electrons in covalent bonds are *always associated into pairs*.
4. Covalent compounds often exist as independent molecules rather than large crystal structures.

Polar Covalent Bonds

Table 6.4.3 *Relationship of ΔEN and Bond Designation*

ΔEN	Bond Designation
0	non-polar covalent
< 0.4	mostly covalent
0.4 – 1.7	polar covalent
> 1.7	ionic

We have discussed above the two extreme cases of bonding: complete electron transfer and completely equal electron sharing. Between these extremes are covalent bonds involving *unequal* electron sharing.

When atoms with different electronegativities form covalent bonds, those ΔEN values may be minimal or significant. If ΔEN is less than 0.4, the bonding electrons between the two atoms spend no more of their time nearer one nucleus than the other. Such bonds are designated as being mostly covalent because ΔEN appears to be insignificant. Another way to characterize this is to say that these bonds have very little "ionic character."

However, as ΔEN increases beyond 0.4, the pair of bonding electrons will be drawn closer and closer to the nucleus of the atom with the higher electronegativity. This unequal distribution of electron density will give that end of the bond a partially negative "pole" and the other a partially positive "pole." A bond "dipole" is said to exist and the bond itself is known as a **polar covalent bond**.

As the ΔEN increases and the bonds become more and more polar, we could say that the amount of ionic character in those bonds increases (Table 6.4.3).

Let's look at an example of a polar covalent bond. When a hydrogen atom having an electronegativity of 2.1 bonds to a chlorine atom with an electronegativity of 3.0, the ΔEN = 0.9. The electron density will be concentrated near chlorine giving that end of the bond a partial negative charge and leaving the hydrogen end with a partial positive charge. The bond dipole is said to be in the direction of chlorine and we can designate this polar covalent bond in several ways. Two are shown in Figure 6.4.4. The lower case Greek deltas (δ) indicate that there are slight or *partial* charges associated with each end of the HCl molecule. Note also that more electron density is associated with chlorine. Another depiction of this polar covalent bond simply shows the hydrogen chloride bond as a straight line between the element symbols. Beneath this is an arrow facing in the direction of the highest electron density or the negative end of the bond dipole.

Figure 6.4.4 *Polar covalent bond depictions. The bond dipole is in the direction of the chlorine.*

Atoms That Form More Than One Bond

So far we have considered the formation of only one bond per atom in two different molecules, namely H_2 and HCl. Notice that hydrogen and chlorine each require a single electron to become isoelectronic with their nearest noble gas. In hydrogen's case, one more electron will complete its first energy level. When chlorine acquires another electron it achieves a stable octet in its valence shell.

In each example, the sharing of a pair of valence electrons, whether equal or not, gives each atom in the bond the benefit of that extra electron in its valence shell. The bond also allows both atoms to have *all of their valence electrons paired,* which is a very stable configuration from a quantum mechanical perspective.

Of course, non-metals sometimes require more than one electron to achieve a stable outer electron shell and have all of their valence electrons paired. Consider several non-metals in groups 14, 15, and 16. To achieve a stable octet containing four electron pairs in each of their valence shells, carbon requires four electrons, nitrogen needs three, and oxygen needs two.

This tells us that the number of electrons required by an atom to achieve the stable outer electron configuration of the nearest noble gas also represents the number of covalent bonds that the atom must form.

We can use Table 6.4.4 to predict formulas for compounds formed between elements in these families. For example, when phosphorus and chlorine react together, phosphorus requires three electrons to complete its octet, while chlorine requires only one.

Table 6.4.4 *Electrons Needed to Achieve a Stable Octet for Non-metals*

Periodic Table Group Number	14	15	16	17
Electrons Needed to Achieve Stable Octet	4	3	2	1

The element with the lower electronegativity, in this case phosphorus, normally requires the most electrons and is written first in a chemical formula. Place the number of electrons it requires above its symbol on the right (similar to a charge without the sign). Then do the same for chlorine as follows: P^3 Cl^1 Now criss-cross those numbers to give the formula: PCl_3.

The process is similar to writing ionic formulas except no charges exist and you don't always reduce the formula to the smallest ratio of atoms. This is because a covalent formula does not represent a ratio. Rather, it tells us the actual number of atoms that exist in the molecule. Assume at this point, however, that you *can* reduce covalent formulas unless told otherwise by your teacher.

There are also numerous examples where more than one pair of electrons is shared between the same two atoms. Two pairs of shared valence electrons results in a double covalent bond and three pairs will produce a triple covalent bond. We will discuss multiple bonds in detail in the next section. For now, we will only mention that as the number of electron pairs shared between two adjacent nuclei increases, so does the strength of the covalent bond.

Sample Problem — Covalent Bond Formation

Predict the formulas for the compounds formed when the following elements combine and determine whether the bonds present are non-polar covalent or polar covalent.

(a) N and F (b) C and H (c) Si and N (d) C and S (e) O and O

What to Think about	How to Do It
1. Determine how many electrons each atom requires to complete its valence shell and write that number above the symbol. 2. Criss-cross those numbers and reduce ratios if possible (for now). 3. Determine the ΔEN for each and classify the bonds present.	(a) $N^3 F^1 \rightarrow NF_3$ $\Delta EN = 1.0$ (polar covalent) (b) $C^4 H^1 \rightarrow CH_4$ $\Delta EN = 0.4$ (polar covalent) (c) $Si^4 N^3 \rightarrow Si_3N_4$ $\Delta EN = 1.2$ (polar covalent) (d) $C^4 S^2 \rightarrow CS_2$ $\Delta EN = 0$ (non-polar covalent) (e) $O^2 O^2 \rightarrow O_2$ $\Delta EN = 0$ (non-polar covalent)

Practice Problems — Comparing Types of Chemical Bonds

1. Consider the ΔEN values and pair up the elements Al, Cl, N, and Na to write the formula for the types of compounds identified below. Justify each choice by showing the appropriate ΔEN value next to each formula.
   (a) A compound with an ionic bond

   (b) A compound with a polar covalent bond

   (c) A compound with a non-polar covalent bond

2. Calculate the ΔEN values for the bonds in the following compounds. Then arrange the compounds in order from those containing bonds in which the electrons are shared most equally to those in which the electrons are shared most unequally.
   (a) H_2O (b) PCl_3 (c) CI_4 (d) SiO_2 (e) AlN

3. Complete the following table:

Elements Present	Formula	ΔEN Value	Nature of Bonds	Atom Possessing Greater Electron Density
C and S				
B and Cl				
Al and O				
N and I				
Ca and F				

The Strength of Ionic vs. Covalent Bonds

Remember that ionic compounds are solids at room temperature and have high melting points. This results from the vast number of interionic forces locking all of the ions together in place in the crystal lattice. As mentioned earlier, the common ionic compound NaCl melts at 801°C.

Covalent compounds, however, usually exist as individual molecules and in any of the three states of matter: solid, liquid, or gas. We shouldn't conclude from this, however, that covalent bonds are any weaker than ionic bonds. Consider, for example, the molecule methane, CH_4, the main component of natural gas.

Although the melting point of methane (–182°C) is very low compared to sodium chloride, this physical property does not reflect the strength of the C – H bonds in methane or indicate that the bonds are weak compared to those in NaCl.

This is because no chemical bonds are broken when methane or any molecular covalent compound melts. Instead, weak intermolecular forces *between* the molecules are overcome. The result is that molecules are separated *from each other* rather than breaking the bonds between the atoms within those molecules.

The energy required to separate the bonded carbon and hydrogen atoms within the molecules from each other is far more than that required to simply pull the molecules apart. In the final section of this chapter, we will discuss the different forces that hold molecules together. Although some of those forces are stronger than others, *none are as strong as chemical bonds*.

Compelling evidence of the strength of covalent bonds can be seen by studying compounds called **network covalent solids**. Rather than consisting of individual molecules, these substances are held together by covalent bonds that extend throughout the entire sample. In the same way that melting an ionic solid requires overcoming all of the attractive forces between the oppositely charged ions in the crystal lattice, melting a network covalent solid involves breaking all of the covalent bonds within what is effectively a giant molecule literally as big as the sample.

Consider quartz, for example, which is a network covalent solid having the formula SiO_2 (Figure 6.4.5). The fact that no separate molecules exist in a quartz crystal means that the melting point is very high: 1550°C. The melting point does reflect the strength of the bonds in the compound. It shows us that covalent bonds can be as strong as ionic bonds.

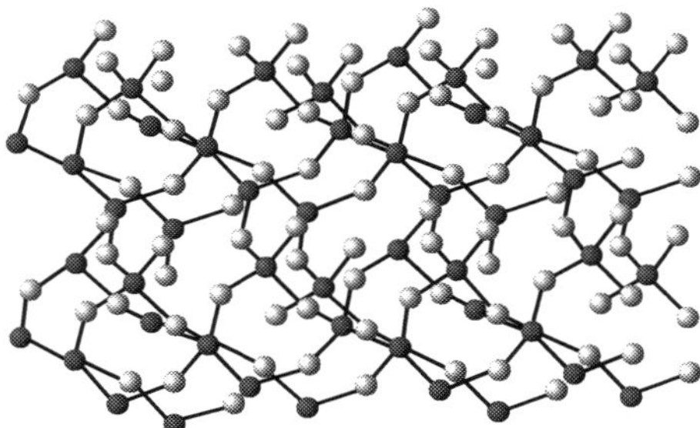

Figure 6.4.5 *A quartz crystal*

6.4 Activity: The Colours of Chemical Bonds

Question

Can one primary colour blending into another be used to depict the transition from pure covalent bonding to ionic bonding?

Materials

Either blue, green, and yellow coloured pencils or blue, green, and yellow watercolour paint and brushes.

Procedure

1. Use the three grids below, (A), (B), and (C). In each of the blank spaces, write the correct formula for the compound resulting from the combination of the two elements that intersect at that space. Remember to write the least electronegative atom symbol first.

2. Consult the electronegativity table given earlier (Figure 6.2.6). Determine the electronegativity difference for each pair of elements to determine the type of bonds present in those compounds. Then shade in the spaces around each formula according to these directions: Shade in the spaces around the compounds containing ionic bonds yellow, covalent bonds blue and polar covalent bonds green.

(A)

	Li	**Be**	**B**	**C**	**N**	**O**	**F**
F							

(B)

	Na	**Mg**	**Al**	**Si**	**P**	**S**	**Cl**
Cl							

(C)

	K	**Ca**	**Ga**	**Ge**	**As**	**Se**	**Br**
Br							

Results and Discussion

1. Does every metal-non-metal combination result in an ionic bond?

6.4 Review Questions

1. (a) For a chemical bond to form between two atoms, how must the energy associated with the bonded atoms compare to the energy when the atoms are apart?

they are at a higher energy state when they're apart

(b) What does this tell us about the attractive forces compared to the repulsive forces between them?

They have to be equal when a bond exists

2. What is an ionic crystal lattice and how does it explain the high melting points of ionic compounds?

3. Use your answer to question 2 to explain why formulas for ionic compounds do not represent neutral independent molecules of those compounds.

4. Identify the attractive forces associated with
(a) ionic bonds

ionic

(b) covalent bonds

covalent

5. (a) Identify two similarities between ionic and covalent bonds.

- both cause e to move
- both can be soluble

(b) Identify two differences between ionic and covalent bonds.

6. Complete the following table by writing in the formulas of the compounds formed from the pairs of elements. Determine the ΔEN value for each and then classify the bonds as non-polar covalent, polar covalent, or ionic.

Elements	Compound Formula	ΔEN Value	Nature of Bonds Present
(a) rubidium and oxygen	Rb_2O	2.7	ionic
(b) strontium and bromine	$SrBr_2$	1.8	ionic
(c) carbon and sulphur	CS_2	0	covalent
(d) silicon and chlorine	$SiCl_4$	1.2	covalent

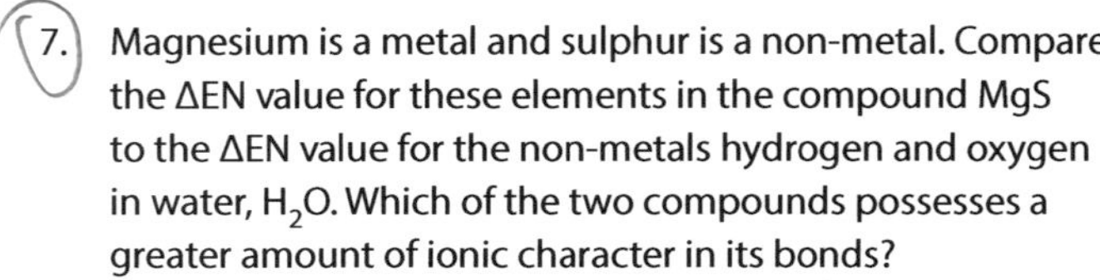

7. Magnesium is a metal and sulphur is a non-metal. Compare the ΔEN value for these elements in the compound MgS to the ΔEN value for the non-metals hydrogen and oxygen in water, H_2O. Which of the two compounds possesses a greater amount of ionic character in its bonds?

MgS ΔEN = 1.3
H_2O ΔEN = 1.4
Water has more Ionic character b/c a higher ΔEN

8. Glucose is a covalent compound with the molecular formula $C_6H_{12}O_6$. This and many other covalent formulas aren't reduced to the smallest whole-number ratios of atoms in the compound. Why not?

9. Many covalent compounds have much lower melting points than ionic compounds. Why does this not mean that covalent bonds are weaker than ionic bonds?

Because some molecules with covalent bonds also have IMF and to melt the only attraction forces that have to be overcome are the IMFs, which are significantly weaker

10. Diamond is a form of pure carbon containing only covalent bonds. It is the hardest substance known and has a melting point of about 3550°C. What name do we give to this type of covalent substance? Suggest a reason for its very high melting point.

network covalent
it has a very high melting point because it only has covalent bonds, which are the strongest type of bond

11. Consider the nature of the covalent bonds present in HCl and in N_2. Which substance would you expect to have the higher melting point? Give a reason for your answer.

H-Cl should have a higher melting point because it is polar covalent while N_2 is non-polar.

6.5 Lewis Structure Diagrams

Warm Up

1. Why do elements in the same chemical family display similar chemical behaviour?

   ____

2. How can you determine the number of valence electrons in each of the representative or main group elements?

   ____

3. Define the term "stable octet."

   ____

Depicting Atoms, Ions, and Molecules in Two Dimensions

As you learned earlier, an atom's valence electrons are the outermost electrons. These are the electrons involved in chemical bonding. This means that, in chemical behaviour, the valence electrons of an atom are really the only electrons that matter.

In 1916, the American chemist Gilbert N. Lewis devised a system of representing the atoms of the elements based on the number of valence electrons they possess. This notation system uses each element symbol to represent the nucleus and all of the inner electrons of an atom (Lewis called this the "kernel" of an atom). It then surrounds that symbol with a series of dots representing that atom's valence electrons. These **electron dot diagrams** are called **Lewis structures**.

The notation is a simple and useful way to represent atoms and serves as a foundation to help us understand and predict chemical behaviours and compound structures without the need for sophisticated bonding theories. Our discussion of Lewis structures and diagrams will be confined to the representative or main group elements in the periodic table, that is, groups 1, 2, 13, 14, 15, 16, 17, and 18.

We will begin by discussing Lewis structures for individual atoms and ions, and then expand that discussion to include Lewis diagrams for molecular compounds and polyatomic ions.

Lewis Structures for Atoms

To write a Lewis structure for an atom, you need only determine the number of an atom's valence electrons. Recall from our discussion of the periodic table that this process is straightforward for the main group elements. For any period, beginning at the alkali metals, we see that atoms of this family have one valence electron. As we move across the period, each main group family has atoms with one additional valence electron up to the stable octet of four electron pairs present in each noble gas (except helium) (Table 6.5.1).

Table 6.5.1 *Valence Electrons in Main Group Atoms*

Main Group Number	1	2	13	14	15	16	17	18
Valence Electrons	1	2	3	4	5	6	7	8
Valence Electron Configuration	ns^1	ns^2	$ns^2 np^1$	$ns^2 np^2$	$ns^2 np^3$	$ns^2 np^4$	$ns^2 np^5$	$ns^2 np^6$

To draw Lewis structures for the atoms, follow these steps:

1. Write the element symbol.
2. For hydrogen place a single dot next to the symbol. For helium place a pair of dots.
3. For 2nd period elements and beyond: for each valence electron present, place one dot around that symbol at one of the four positions of the compass: west, east, north, or south.
4. If more than four valence electrons are present, begin pairing the dots only after the four compass positions are filled.

The relative placement of the paired and unpaired dots isn't as important as how many of each is present. Figure 6.5.1 shows the Lewis structures for the main group elements of the first three periods.

Group Number	1	2	13	14	15	16	17	18
	H·							He:
	Li·	·Be·	·B·	·C·	·N:	·O:	·F:	:Ne:
	Na·	·Mg·	·Al·	·Si·	·P:	·S:	·Cl:	:Ar:

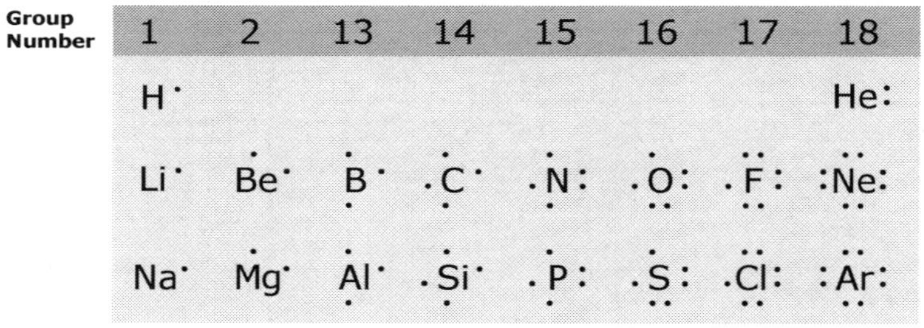

Figure 6.5.1 *Lewis structures for main group elements of the first three periods*

As you view Figure 6.5.1, consider the following important points:

1. As each element in a family has the same number of valence electrons, the Lewis structure for those elements has the same number of dots.
2. For the metals, the *total number of dots* represents the number of electrons that each atom loses when forming a cation.
3. In a correctly drawn Lewis structure for a non-metal, the number of *unpaired* dots shown represents either the number of electrons that atom *must gain* when forming an anion, or the number the electrons the atom *must share* to complete its octet when forming covalent bonds.

Lewis Structures for Monatomic Ions

From points 2 and 3 above, we can see that writing Lewis structures for monatomic ions is straightforward.

For the metals in groups 1, 2, and 13, the Lewis structure for their *stable ions* does not include any dots. The element symbol is usually enclosed in square brackets with the cation's charge written outside the brackets on the upper right. The magnitude of that positive charge simply equals the number of dots (which represent electrons) that were removed from the neutral atom's Lewis structure. Remember that because the number of protons in the nucleus has not changed, a loss of any number of electrons will result in that amount of positive charge on the cation.

For the non-metals in groups 15, 16, and 17, the Lewis structures for their anions all include four pairs of dots surrounding the element symbol enclosed in square brackets with the appropriate negative charge written outside the brackets on the upper right. The magnitude of the negative charge written outside the brackets equals the number of *unpaired* dots that were originally present in the parent atom's Lewis structure. This also equals how many electrons were required to generate the four pairs resulting in a stable octet.

The Lewis structures are shown for the sodium and chloride ions in Figure 6.5.2. Note that the chlorine atom originally had one unpaired dot. This required one electron for four pairs resulting in the charge of 1− on the anion. The sodium has had its one dot removed to form a 1+ cation.

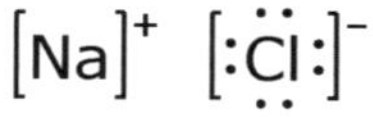

$[Na]^+ \quad [:\ddot{\underset{..}{Cl}}:]^-$

Figure 6.5.2 *Lewis structures for sodium ions and chloride ions*

Quick Check

1. What do the "dots" in a Lewis structure for an atom or an ion represent?

   val e⁻

2. What do the total number of dots present in the Lewis structures for the metals in groups 1, 2, and 13 tell us about the cations these atoms will form during a chemical change?

   what charge the cation will have: +1, +2, +3

3. The Lewis structures for nitrogen, phosphorus, and antimony include one pair of dots and three unpaired dots. How many electrons do these atoms require to form a stable octet?

   3

Sample Problem — Drawing Lewis Structures

Draw the Lewis structures for the representative elements belonging to period 4 of the periodic table.

What to Think about	How to Do It
1. Elements in the same chemical family have the same number of valence electrons. 2. Those electrons are represented by placing dots around each element symbol. 3. Consider Figure 6.4.1. Begin at group 1 and give potassium 1 valence electron. Continue to the right placing the same number of dots around each symbol in the same way that the dots appear for the other members of each group.	**Group Number** 1: K· 2: Ca· 13: Ga· 14: ·Ge· 15: ·As: 16: ·Se: 17: :Br: 18: :Kr:

Practice Problems — Building Lewis Structures

1. Write the Lewis structures for the main group elements in period 5 of the periodic table.

   Rb· Sr: In: Sn: Sb: Te: I: Xe:

2. Write the Lewis structures for the following atoms and ions.

   (a) Ba (b) Al^{3+} (c) Bi (d) I^- (e) Te

   Ba· [Al]$^{+3}$ Bi [:I:]$^{-1}$ Te

3. Convert the following atomic symbols to the Lewis structures for the ions of those elements:

   (a) Ca (b) Se (c) Ga (d) As

   [Ca]$^{+1}$ [:Se:]$^{-2}$ [Ga]$^{3+}$ [:As:]$^{-3}$

Lewis Structures for Molecules

Each of the pages in this book is a flat surface and any diagrams or images that you see on these pages can only be two-dimensional representations of the real three-dimensional world. Of course, the ionic and molecular compounds that make up that world are also three-dimensional. Understanding their shapes is a very important part of explaining and predicting their behaviour.

Recall that ionic compounds normally exist as ordered, three-dimensional arrays of cations and anions called crystal lattices. The arrangement of ions in these crystals maximizes the attractions between the oppositely charged ions within the lattices and minimizes the repulsions between ions with the same charges. The diagram of an NaCl crystal lattice in section 6.3 helped with visualizing such a structure.

When molecules form, their three-dimensional shapes are also governed by the attractive and repulsive forces that exist within them. The first step toward visualizing the three-dimensional shape of a molecule is to convert its molecular formula into a two-dimensional Lewis structure.

$$:\ddot{\underset{..}{Cl}}-\ddot{\underset{..}{Cl}}:$$

Figure 6.5.3 *Lewis structure of Cl_2*

One of the simplest examples of a Lewis structure is a diatomic halogen molecule such as Cl_2 (Figure 6.5.3). The single line between the atoms represents one pair of shared electrons. The other pairs of electrons are referred to as non-bonding or **lone pairs** of electrons. Note that all 14 of the valence electrons possessed by the 2 chlorine atoms are accounted for in the Lewis structure. Note also that each chlorine atom now has the benefit of an extra valence electron and thus has a stable octet.

As with any new procedure, learning to draw Lewis diagrams for molecules is easier if you follow a series of steps. Let's begin with a simple example: the Lewis structure for a molecule of nitrogen trichloride, NCl_3.

Step 1: Determine the total number of valence electrons in the molecule.

A correctly drawn Lewis structure must account for all of the valence electrons present. In this case, nitrogen has five valence electrons and each chlorine atom has seven. Therefore the total number of valence electrons is given by: $5 + (3 \times 7) = 26$.

Note that this is an even number, which will be true for all of the examples you will see. There are a few cases where odd numbers of electrons exist, but the vast majority of molecules (and polyatomic ions) possess even numbers of valence electrons. All bonding electrons exist in pairs.

Step 2: Construct the "skeleton" of the molecule using lines to indicate single covalent bonds between the atoms.

To generate the most likely skeleton of the molecule, the following set of guidelines will be of great help. The guidelines are based on numerous empirical observations and hold true for the vast majority of molecules. They also correspond to what we would expect given the electron configurations and electronegativities of the atoms involved. They may seem difficult to remember at first, but you won't need to use all of them for every molecule you draw. As with any new skill, the steps will become more familiar with practice.

Guidelines for Generating Molecule "Skeletons"

1. If the general formula for the compound is of the form "AX_n," then the central atom "A" will be the one with the lower group number, which also usually corresponds to the lower electronegativity. Obviously, if only two atoms exist in the molecule, then no central atom exists.
2. Hydrogen atoms form only one bond and so do not achieve an octet of electrons.
3. Fluorine atoms always form only one bond, and the other halogen atoms *usually* form only one bond. Exceptions to this occur if those halogens are central atoms and are bonded to other smaller halogens or to oxygen.
4. (a) Oxygen atoms normally form two bonds and don't often bond to each other in compounds with other elements. (An exception to this is hydrogen peroxide.)
   (b) Nitrogen atoms normally form three bonds.
   (c) Carbon atoms normally form four bonds.
5. Avoid creating rings or cyclic structures when you draw skeletons.

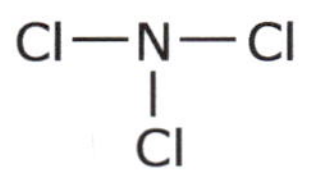

Figure 6.5.4 *Molecular skeleton for NCl_3*

Using the above rules, we see that a central atom exists and that nitrogen is most likely that central atom. We can therefore sketch the molecular skeleton for NCl_3 shown in Figure 6.5.4. The relative orientation of each chlorine atom around the nitrogen atom isn't that important because Lewis structures do not depict shape or 3-D geometry. All the matters at this stage is that nitrogen is in the centre and each chlorine atom is a peripheral or surrounding atom.

Step 3: Subtract the number of valence electrons used to construct the skeleton from the total number of valence electrons available from step 1 to determine the number of valence electrons remaining.

Consider that each line drawn in the skeleton represents a pair of bonding valence electrons, so, in this case, the number of valence electrons remaining is:

$26 - (3 \times 2) = 20.$

Step 4: Assume that all of the atoms in the molecule obey the octet rule (except hydrogen). Determine the number of additional valence electrons required (beyond those already present as a result of the bonds drawn) to give all of those atoms the required eight valence electrons.

In this case, because each peripheral chlorine atom has one bond and is therefore associated with two valence electrons, each chlorine atom needs six more electrons to complete its octet. The central nitrogen has three bonds and so has the benefit of six valence electrons. This means that the nitrogen atom needs only two more valence electrons to complete its octet. The calculation to determine the total number of required valence electrons is: $(3 \times 6) + 2 = 20$

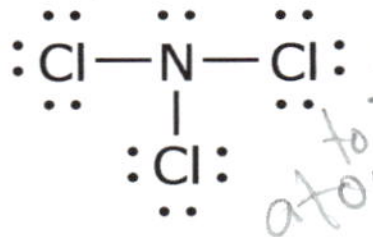

Figure 6.5.5 *Lewis structure for NCl_3*

Step 5: Compare the number of valence electrons available (from step 3) to the number of valence electrons needed to complete the octets of the atoms (from step 4). If those two numbers match, pair up the electrons. Beginning with the peripheral atoms and ending with the central atom, place those electron pairs where they're needed to satisfy the octets. In this case, the two numbers do indeed match and so the resulting Lewis structure is shown in Figure 6.5.5. If the numbers don't match, there is a procedure we'll discuss later.

At this point, consider the following:

Criteria Governing the Octet Rule in a Lewis Structure

(a) A peripheral or surrounding atom must not violate the octet rule in a Lewis structure. If an atom does violate the octet rule, then it must be a central atom in the molecule. This doesn't apply to hydrogen, which is associated with only two electrons in molecules.

(b) ***Exception (i)*** Atoms belonging to the second period in the periodic table will not have expanded octets in Lewis structures. An expanded octet (more than eight valence electrons) is only possible for elements belonging to the 3rd period or higher because only those atoms have access to d orbital electrons. These electrons are unavailable below the third energy level.

Exception (ii) The atoms Be, B, and Al will often have incomplete octets such that only two or three pairs of valence electrons will be associated with these central atoms in Lewis structures for molecules.

Step 6: If the numbers in step 5 above agree, then as a final step, check that the total number of valence electrons represented in the diagram matches the total number of valence electrons you began with in step 1.

In this example, the number of valence electrons in the diagram matches the number in the molecule.

Quick Check

1. Suggest a reason why the elements Be, B, and Al are not able to achieve a valence octet when they form covalent compounds.
   because they each have less than 4 val e⁻

2. Hydrogen sulphide, H_2S, is a poisonous, foul-smelling, and flammable gas. Why is the molecular skeleton "S – H – H" incorrect for this molecule?
   b/c Hs can't bond together because they only need 1 e⁻ for a full octect

3. Determine the total number of valence electrons present in each of the following molecules:
   (a) H_2Se 8 (b) CCl_4 32 (c) NF_3 26 (d) PCl_5 40 (e) SF_6 48

Sample Problem — Drawing a Lewis Structure for a Molecule

Draw the Lewis structure for a molecule of water, H_2O.

What to Think about	How to Do It
1. Each hydrogen atom will form one bond and the oxygen will form two. The oxygen must therefore be the central atom even though it has a higher electronegativity than hydrogen. Oxygen has six valence electrons and hydrogen has one.	
2. Use the steps listed above:	
Step 1: Determine the total number of valence electrons in the molecule.	$6 + (2 \times 1) = 8$ valence electrons present in molecule
Step 2: Construct the "skeleton" of the molecule.	H – O – H
Step 3: Determine the number of valence electrons remaining.	Electrons available: 8 Electrons used in skeleton: 4 Electrons remaining: $8 - 4 = 4$
Step 4: Assume that all of the atoms in the molecule obey the octet rule (except hydrogen).	Electrons required to complete oxygen's octet: 4
Step 5: Compare the number of valence electrons available to the number of valence electrons needed to complete the octets of the atoms. Pair up remaining electrons and place them where needed to satisfy oxygen's octet.	
Step 6: Available electrons match electrons in the diagram. Note that in the final structure, oxygen is associated with two bonding pairs and two non-bonding (or lone pairs).	H—Ö—H (with a lone pair above and below O)

Practice Problems – Drawing Lewis Structures for Molecules

1. Construct the Lewis structure for a molecule of carbon tetrachloride, CCl_4.

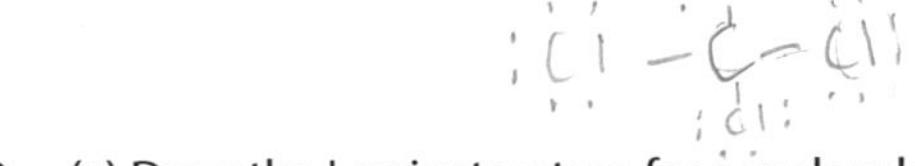

2. (a) Draw the Lewis structure for a molecule of ammonia, NH_3.

   (b) When you're finished drawing the structure, determine how many bonding pairs and how many lone pairs of electrons are associated with the central atom.

3. (a) Draw the Lewis structure for a molecule of boron trichloride, BCl_3.

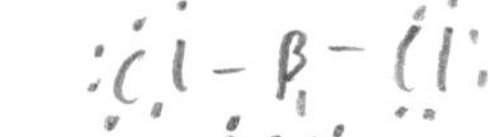

   (b) Consider the central atom in your structure. Does it possess a stable octet of eight electrons?

Drawing Lewis Structures for Molecules Containing Multiple Bonds

We have seen that one pair of valence electrons shared between two adjacent nuclei constitutes a single covalent bond. There are also many cases where the covalent bonds between two atoms involve more than one pair of shared electrons. These are known as **multiple bonds**. If two pairs of electrons are shared between the same two atoms, the bond is called a double bond and if three pairs exist, the bond is a triple bond.

As you might expect, as multiple bonds involve more attractive forces between two atoms than single bonds do, multiple bonds are stronger. Bond strengths are usually measured by the amount of energy required to break a mole of those bonds and are thus represented by the unit kJ/mol. The greater attraction between the atoms in a multiple bond also draws those bonded atoms closer together, which means that multiple bonds are also shorter than single bonds. Table 6.5.2 compares some single and multiple bond strengths and lengths.

Table 6.5.2 *Single and Multiple Bond Strengths and Lengths*

Bond	Bond Energy (kJ/mol)	Bond Length (pm)
C – C	347	154
C = C	614	134
C ≡ C	839	120
N – N	160	145
N = N	418	125
N ≡ N	941	110
C – O	358	143
C = O	799	123
C ≡ O	1072	113

Let's follow the steps outlined above to draw the Lewis structure for a molecule that contains double bonds, such as carbon dioxide, CO_2.

Step 1: The total number of valence electrons is given by: $4 + (2 \times 6) = 16$

Step 2: Carbon has the lower group number and electronegativity, and oxygen doesn't usually bond to itself in compounds with other elements. Therefore the following skeleton is likely:

O – C – O

Step 3: As four electrons were used to construct the above skeleton, 12 of the original 16 electrons remain to complete each atom's octet.

Step 4: Each of the oxygens in the skeleton requires six electrons and the carbon atom requires four electrons to complete their valence shells. This gives a total of:

$(2 \times 6) + 4 = 16$ electrons.

Step 5: Notice that 16 electrons are required but only 12 electrons are available to complete the octets of the atoms. We are therefore lacking four electrons. This means that we must return to step 2 and re-draw the molecular skeleton such that we incorporate one *multiple bond* for each pair of electrons that we lack to complete the octets._

Because we are four electrons short, we can consider either of the following modified skeletons:

skeleton 1: **O = C = O** or skeleton 2: **O ≡ C – O**

Although both skeletons above show carbon forming a total of 4 bonds, as oxygen normally forms two bonds, we would choose skeleton 1, showing each oxygen atom participating in a double bond as being the most likely skeleton. Note also the symmetry associated with this choice as opposed to skeleton 2. Molecules will often possess a high degree of symmetry and that also makes this choice more likely: **O = C = O**

Now we again return to following the steps:

Step 3: Each line in the skeleton represents a pair of shared electrons, so each double bond indicates two electron pairs or four electrons. Therefore eight electrons have been used in constructing the skeleton, so the number of electrons remaining is given by: $16 - (2 \times 4) = 8$

Step 4: The two oxygen atoms each need four more electrons to complete their octets, but the carbon atom now has the benefit of eight valence electrons and so requires no more. This means that only eight electrons are needed to complete the octets of the atoms in the skeleton.

Step 5: As the number of electrons we need now matches the number available, we pair up those electrons to give the Lewis structure for carbon dioxide. Figure 6.5.6 shows two possible ways of representing that structure.

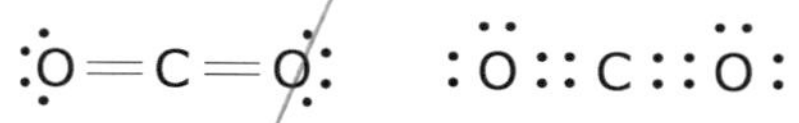

:Ö=C=Ö: :Ö::C::Ö:

Figure 6.5.6 *Lewis structures for CO_2*

As a final step we see that all 16 valence electrons have been accounted for in the Lewis structure. The construction of this molecule can be understood by considering how the valence electrons present in each individual atom are reorganized as the two double bonds form:

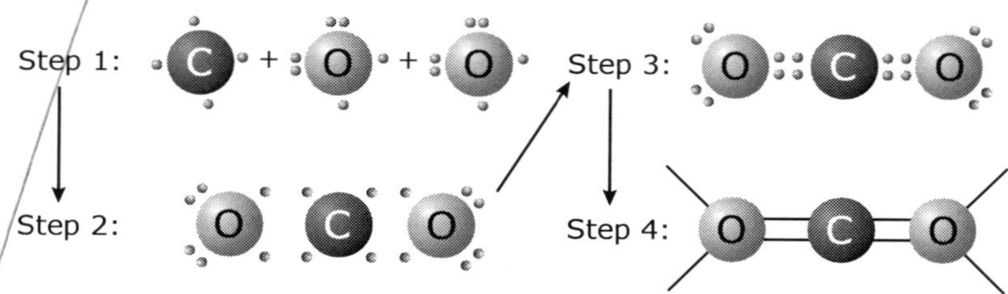

Figure 6.5.7 *Constructing the molecule from the Lewis structures*

Drawing Lewis Structures Containing Atoms With Expanded Octets

Sometimes we discover that fewer electrons are available than needed to complete the octets of the atoms in a molecule. At other times, we might encounter situations where more electrons are available than needed. This normally results in **expanded octets** associated with the central atom in a Lewis structure. Remember that an expanded octet is only possible for an atom if d orbital electrons are available. That is only possible for elements belonging to period 4 or higher in the periodic table.

Let's investigate this by drawing the Lewis structure for one of the few compounds involving noble gases, namely XeF_4. To do this, we follow the steps below:

F
|
F —Xe — F
|
F

Figure 6.5.8 *Molecular skeleton for XeF4*

Step 1: Total number of valence electrons $= 8 + (4 \times 7) = 36$

Step 2: Molecular skeleton: See Figure 6.5.8.

Step 3: Electrons used in skeleton: $4 \times 2 = 8$
Electrons remaining: $36 - 8 = 28$

Step 4: Electrons required to complete octets: $4 \times 6 = 24$

Note that xenon needs no electrons but each fluorine atom needs six electrons to complete its octet.

Step 5: We have 28 electrons available but only need 24. At this point, we first place the 24 electrons where they're needed in pairs around each peripheral fluorine atom. We then place the remaining two pairs of electrons around the central xenon. The orientation of the lone pairs on the central atom is not important. Simply placing two pairs at any two locations available on xenon is all that matters. Note that xenon has an "expanded octet" of 12 valence electrons.

:F:
|
:F—Xe—F:
|
:F:

Figure 6.5.9 *Lewis structure for XeF_4*

Step 6: All 36 valence electrons are accounted for in the Lewis structure (Figure 6.5.9).

Sample Problem — Drawing a Lewis Structure Containing a Multiple Bond

Draw the Lewis structure for a molecule of hydrogen cyanide, HCN.

What to Think about	How to Do It
1. Calculate the total valence electrons present in the molecule.	Total of 10 valence electrons available
2. Determine the most likely molecular skeleton.	H – C – N
3. Determine electrons used in skeleton and those remaining.	4 electrons used to construct the skeleton, 6 electrons remaining.
4. Determine electrons needed to complete octets.	The carbon needs 4 more electrons and the nitrogen needs 6 to complete their respective octets.
5. Compare the number of valence electrons available to the number of valence electrons needed to complete the octets of the atoms.	Only 6 electrons are left: 4 electrons short
6. The original skeleton must be changed to incorporate multiple bonds.	
7. Hydrogen only forms one bond and so cannot be the central atom. The two extra bonds must be added between the nitrogen and carbon atoms in the form of a triple bond. Of the remaining two atoms, carbon has the lower group number and electronegativity. Carbon is therefore the most likely central atom. Carbon normally forms four bonds and nitrogen forms three.	H – C ≡ N
8. We see that 8 valence electrons (4 × 2) have been used in this new skeleton, leaving only 2 of the original 10. Pair up those final 2 electrons and place them on nitrogen. As carbon's octet is now satisfied and nitrogen only needs 2 more electrons, the number of available electrons matches the number required.	H—C≡N:
9. A final check shows us that all 10 valence electrons are accounted for.	

Practice Problems – Lewis Structures Containing Multiple Bonds and Expanded Octets

1. Formaldehyde is used as a disinfectant, an embalming agent, and as a component in many organic synthesis reactions. Draw the Lewis structure for a molecule of formaldehyde, CH_2O. (Hint: Carbon is the central atom.)

   H-C-Ö:
   |
   H

2. Carbon monoxide is an invisible, odorless, and toxic gas that renders hemoglobin unable to transport oxygen to body tissues. Draw the Lewis structure for a molecule of CO.

   :C≡O: 4 + 6 = 10, −2, 8

3. Bromine trifluoride is a very reactive and toxic liquid that explodes on contact with water and organic compounds. Draw the Lewis structure for a molecule of BrF_3.

   F – Br – F, | F   7 + 3 (7) = 28, −6, 22

Drawing Lewis Structures for Polyatomic Ions

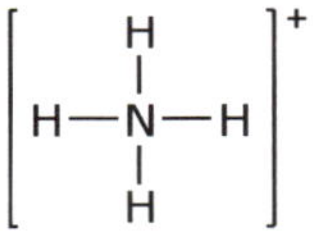

Many polyatomic ions contain non-metal atoms bonded covalently to each other. To draw a Lewis diagram for a polyatomic ion, we follow the same steps discussed above but must be careful to count the correct number of valence electrons present when we begin. Remember that the magnitude of the charge on a cation equals the number of valence electrons *removed* from the original neutral species. The amount of negative charge on an anion represents the number of electrons *added*.

Consider the ammonium cation, NH_4^+. The positive charge tells us that one valence electron has been removed from the total number of valence electrons possessed by the five neutral atoms. To begin this Lewis structure, we therefore count a total of $5 + (4 \times 1) - 1 = 8$ valence electrons. Following the above steps, we eventually arrive at the Lewis structure in in Figure 6.5.10. We normally enclose Lewis structures for both monatomic and polyatomic ions in square brackets, as shown.

Figure 6.5.10 *Lewis structure for the ammonium cation, NH_4^+*

The Curious Case of Resonance

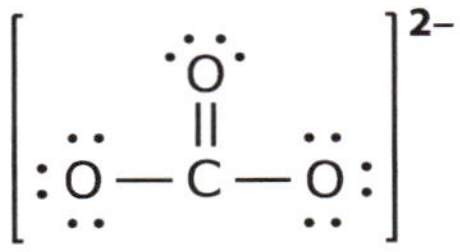

When a molecule or ion contains double bonds next to single bonds, there are often several different and equally correct Lewis structures that we can draw. Consider the case of the carbonate anion, CO_3^{2-}. This ion has a total of: $4 + (3 \times 6) + 2 = 24$ valence electrons. (Note the extra two electrons due to the charge.)

Following the steps learned earlier, we realize that we are short two electrons when completing the octets of all the atoms. We therefore incorporate one double bond into the skeleton. The final Lewis structure therefore becomes the one shown in Figure 6.5.11.

Figure 6.5.11 *Lewis structure for the carbonate anion, CO_3^{2-}*

If this represented the actual structure, we would expect that the two single carbon – oxygen bonds would prove to be longer and weaker than the double bond. Experimental data indicates, however, that all three bonds are equal in strength and length. They appear to be stronger than a single C – O bond, but weaker than a double bond. They are also slightly shorter than a single bond, but slightly longer than a double bond. It is as if the two electrons in the multiple bond have been shared equally or "averaged" between the central carbon and each of the three oxygen atoms.

Chemists call these electrons "delocalized" because they're not associated with any one pair of bonded atoms, but are rather "spread out" equally between all three pairs. Lewis structures cannot properly show delocalized electrons. They represent this phenomenon by depicting the double bond in each of the possible locations in a series of diagrams and connecting each diagram with a set of double arrows. The diagrams are called **resonance structures**. It must be emphasized, however, that the pair of electrons *does not* move around between pairs of atoms as the diagrams might suggest. The three diagrams in Figure 6.5.12 are simply the only way to depict delocalized bonding electrons using Lewis structures. The phenomenon of resonance is evident in an important organic compound called benzene.

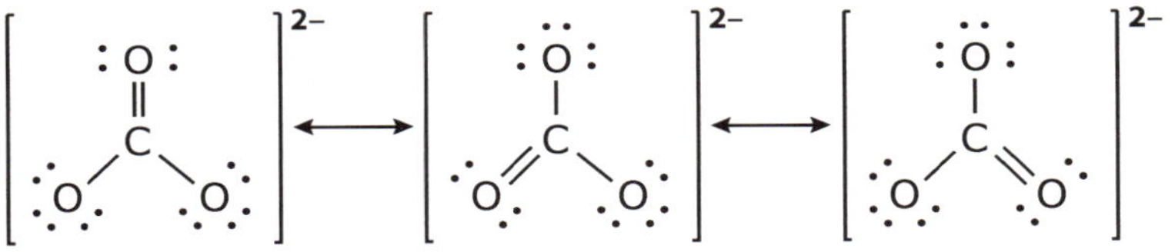

Figure 6.5.12 *Resonance structures for a carbonate ion*

Lewis Structures for Molecules with More than One Central Atom

Molecules and ions can be much more complicated than we have discussed above. Lewis structures are not often used to depict such species, but we can still employ the process when several central atoms exist in relatively simple molecules and ions. In these examples, you will be given the basic skeleton and can then proceed with the remaining steps to generate the correct Lewis structure.

Consider a simple organic acid called formic acid whose formula is CH_2O_2 (or HCOOH). Recall that carbon, oxygen, and hydrogen normally form four bonds, two bonds, and one bond respectively. In Figure 6.5.13, note that both a carbon atom and an oxygen atom are between other atoms in different locations in the structure.

You should now be able to complete the diagram following the remaining steps. The final Lewis structure you arrive at should be the one shown in Figure 6.5.14. You will encounter many such molecules when discussing organic chemistry.

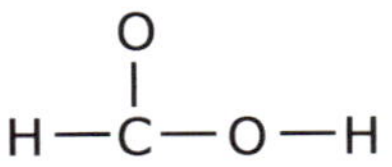

Figure 6.5.13 *Skeleton for formic acid, CH_2O_2 (or HCOOH)*

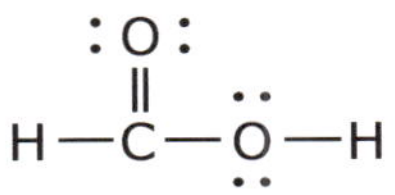

Figure 6.5.14 *Lewis structure for formic acid, CH_2O_2 (or HCOOH)*

6.5 Activity: Making the Leap to Three Dimensions

Question

How can we use Lewis structures to predict the three-dimensional shapes of molecules or polyatomic ions?

Materials

modelling clay

Popsicle® sticks or wooden splints

Procedure

1. Consider the Lewis structures discussed in this section: NCl_3, H_2O, CO_2, NH_4^+, XeF_4, and CO_3^{2-}. Review each as you fill in the following table. The first one is done for you.

1. Chemical Formula	2. Number of Atoms Bonded to Central Atom	3. Number of Lone Pairs on Central Atom	4. Sum of Columns 2 and 3
NCl_3	3	1	3 + 1 = 4
H_2O			
CO_2			
NH_4^+			
XeF_4			
CO_3^{2-}			

2. Obtain some modeling clay and wooden splints or Popsicle® sticks. Using the clay, make a small sphere about the size of a lemon. This will represent the central atom in each of the above species.

   In any chemical species, each pair of bonding or lone pair of electrons represents regions of negative charge. It follows, then, that when these are attached to a central atom in a molecule or polyatomic ion, they will attempt to minimize the repulsive forces between them. They accomplish this by assuming positions in three-dimensional space around the central atom such that they are as far away from each other as possible, while still remaining bonded to that central atom.

3. To represent this, consider each molecule and ion listed above. Look at the total number in column 4 for each species and select that number of sticks. Now insert them into the clay such that they are all as far away from each other as possible in three-dimensional space.

Continued

4. Sketch the shapes that you construct for each species in the appropriate space in the table below.

Chemical Formula	Sketch of 3-D Shape
NCl_3	
H_2O	
CO_2	
NH_4^+	
XeF_4	
CO_3^{2-}	

5. Are all of the shapes different? If not, which ones look similar? How do the numbers in column 4 compare for those shapes that might look similar?

6.5 Review Questions

1. Consider the following list of elements. Place each in the appropriate column in the table below depending on whether it obeys the octet rule, likely has an incomplete octet, or could potentially have an expanded octet in a Lewis structure.

   H, Be, B, C, N, O, F, Al, Si, P, S, Cl

Incomplete Valence Octet	Valence Octet	Expanded Valence Octet

2. Helium and neon are in the same chemical family but yet have different numbers of dots in their Lewis structures. What is the reason for this? Explain why neither element ever forms chemical compounds.

3. Consider the following pairs of elements in the table below. If each pair was part of a molecule or polyatomic ion, which of the two would most likely be the central atom and which would be the peripheral or surrounding atom? Place each element of each pair in the appropriate column in the table.

4. The molecule tetrafluoroethene is a building block of the synthetic material known as Teflon®. Tetrafluoroethene has the formula C_2F_4. Consider the following molecular skeletons for this molecule. Complete the Lewis structure for the most likely skeleton.

```
F           F      F           F
 \         //       \         /
  C ─── C            C ═══ C
 /         \        /         \
F           F      F           F

F           C
 \         /
  C ═══ F
 /         \
F           F
```

5. Draw Lewis structures for each of the following molecules in the space provided.

   OF_2

   H_2S

Element Pair	Probable Central Atom	Probable Peripheral Atom
(a) phosphorus and chlorine		
(b) nitrogen and oxygen		
(c) carbon and sulphur		
(d) nitrogen and hydrogen		
(e) oxygen and fluorine		

PCl_3

CCl_2F_2

6. Draw Lewis structures for each of the polyatomic ions in the space provided.

OH^-

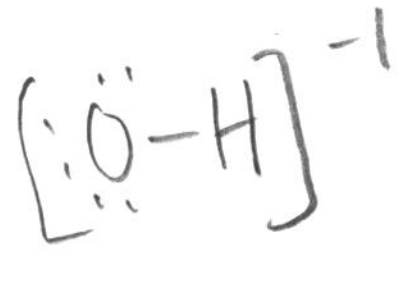

AlH_4^-

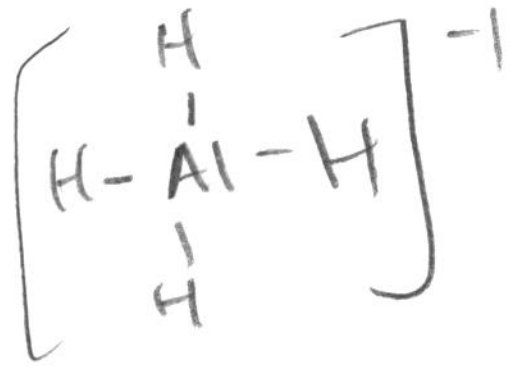

CN^-

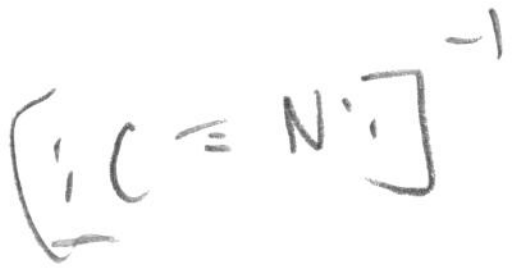

7. Draw Lewis structures for each of the following. Each central atom in the molecules or ions has an expanded octet.

SF_6

PCl_5

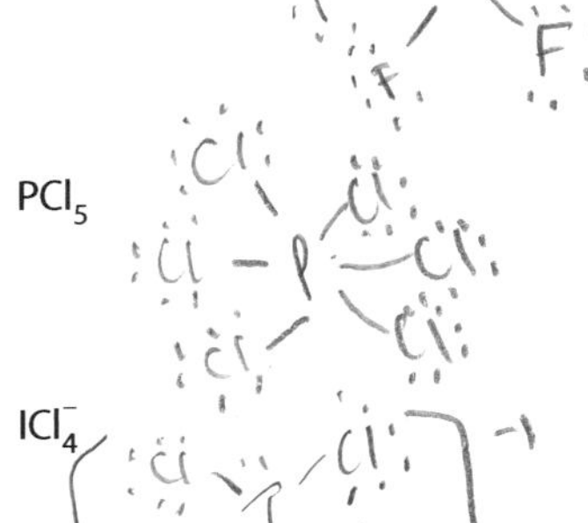

ICl_4^-

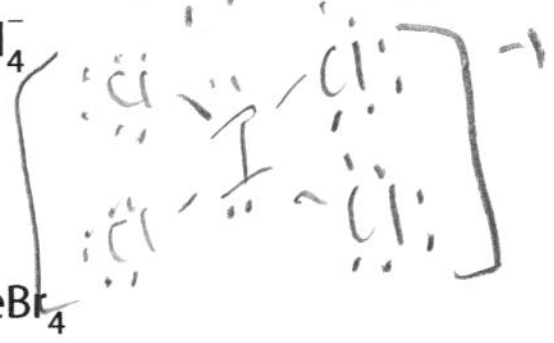

$SeBr_4$

8. Draw Lewis structures for each of the following containing multiple bonds.

CS_2

SCO (C is central)

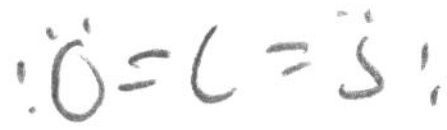

O_3 (Draw two resonance structures)

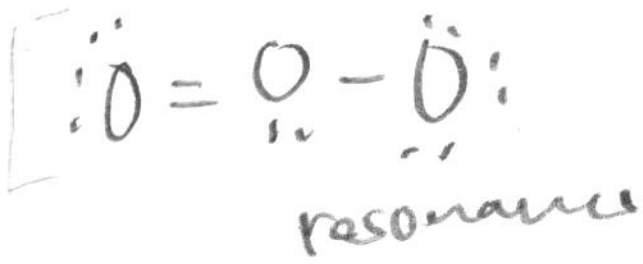

NO_3^- (Draw three resonance structures)

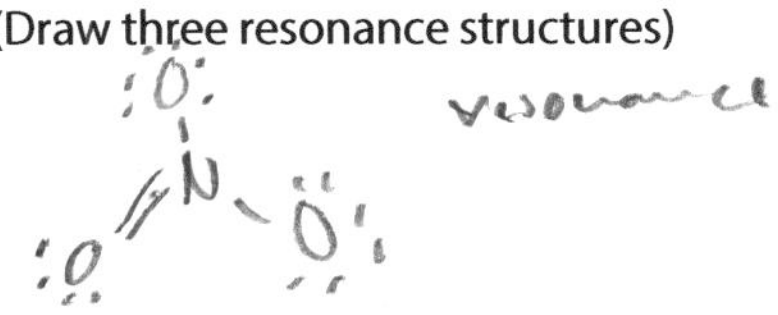

9. Convert the following molecular skeletons into complete Lewis structures.

H — C — C — H

H — O — O — H

```
H     H
|     |
C --- C
|     |
H     H
```

```
      H
      |
H --- C --- O --- H
      |
      H
```

6.6 The Shape and Behaviour of Molecules

Warm Up

1. What does an element's electronegativity tell us?

____

2. Use your answer to question 1 to define the term "polar covalent bond."

____

3. If a substance contains polar *molecules*, how might that affect its melting and boiling points?

____

Converting Lewis Structures into Three Dimensions — VSEPR Theory

Drawing Lewis structures serves an important purpose beyond indicating connectivity of atoms in molecules and polyatomic ions. The two-dimensional collections of symbols, lines, and dots often allow us to deduce the three-dimensional shapes of the chemical species they represent. Determining the shapes of those chemical species is an essential part of understanding and predicting their physical and chemical behaviour.

The process of inferring a three-dimensional shape from a Lewis structure is based on a very simple premise: Valence electrons represent regions of negative charge that repel each other.

> Any group of valence electrons associated with a central atom will tend to orient themselves in three-dimensional space around that atom so as to minimize the repulsion between them. Examples of such groups of valence electrons include a lone pair, bonding pair, or multiple pairs involved in a double or triple bond.

In short, while remaining attached to the central atom, these groups of electrons will position themselves as far away from each other as possible. This is the fundamental principle behind the **valence shell electron pair repulsion (VSEPR) theory,** which chemists use whenever they convert Lewis structures into molecular shapes.

Let's imagine a central atom in three-dimensional space and apply the above principle to distribute two, three, four, five, and six electron groups around that centre. When we do, we discover that a different spatial arrangement results for each number of electron groups. Each arrangement minimizes the repulsive forces between the groups by occupying the maximum amount of space around the central atom.

We can show these five arrangements using balloons attached together to represent the electron groups. Just as the balloons will fill up all the available space around their centre of attachment, so too will electron groups fill up the available space around a central atom (Figure 6.6.1).

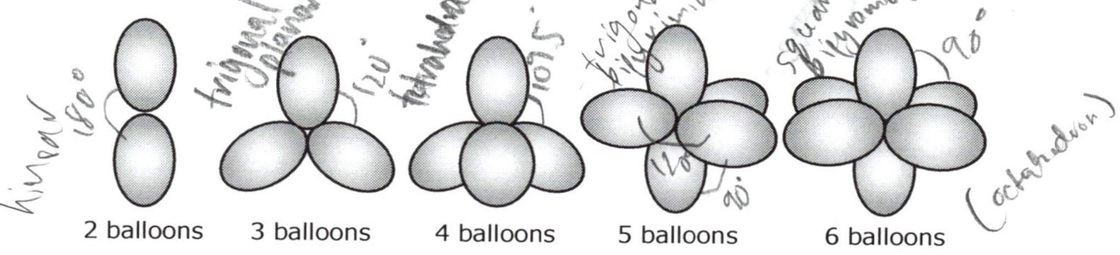

Figure 6.6.1 *Balloons in different arrangements around a central attachment*

If the electron groups are *bonding electrons*, then the peripheral atoms they bind to the central atom adopt that same arrangement and produce a *molecular shape.*

Several experimental tools exist that allow us to determine molecular geometry. X-ray crystallography as well as neutron and electron diffraction are employed for compounds in the solid

phase. For molecules in the gaseous phase, gas electron diffraction is used.

Electron groups and their repulsive effects ultimately determine where and how the nuclei of the atoms in a molecule or polyatomic ion arrange themselves in three-dimensional space. And it's the resulting *shapes of those species* that we really care about.

We will consider each of the five electron group arrangements separately. Let's begin by assuming that each electron group is a bonding group connecting the central atom (with single or multiple bonds) to the peripheral atoms. We'll then expand our discussion to include lone-pair electron groups on the central atom. As a general notation, the central atom is "**A**," a peripheral or surrounding atom is "**X**," and a lone-pair of electrons on the central atom is "**E**."

Two-Bonding Electron Groups: AX_2

X—A—X

Figure 6.6.2 *The shape of two-bonding electron groups is linear.*

When two groups of bonding electrons connect the central atom to two peripheral atoms, the notation "$\mathbf{AX_2}$" applies. The surrounding atoms are as far as possible from each other on opposite sides of the central atom. The shape is *linear* with the X–A–X bond angle being 180° (Figure 6.6.2).

The shape is the same whether the two-bonding groups are the shared electrons in two single bonds, two double bonds, or a single and a triple bond. For example, consider the following three molecules. Note that all are AX_2 molecules with the same linear shape and that any lone-pairs attached to the surrounding atoms do not affect their orientation around the central atom.

:C̤̈l—Be—C̤̈l:

Ö=C=Ö

H—C≡N:

Figure 6.6.3 *AX_2 molecules have the same linear shape whether the shared electrons form two single bonds, two double bonds, or a single and a triple bond.*

Three-Electron Groups: AX_3 and AX_2E

When three groups of electrons orient around a central atom, two shapes are possible. If all the electron groups are bonding, then an $\mathbf{AX_3}$ arrangement gives rise to a *trigonal planar* (or flat triangle) molecule with X–A–X bond angles of 120°. The bonding electron group interactions are called "*bond-pair – bond-pair*" (BP-BP) interactions.

If one of the three electron groups is a lone-pair rather than a bonding pair, we use the notation $\mathbf{AX_2E}$. The molecule that we see is *bent* or *angular* with the lone-pair occupying one of the three corners of the triangle. As lone-pair electrons are attracted to only one atomic nucleus, they are held less tightly than bonding electron groups. Their electron clouds therefore occupy more space and exert more repulsive force on bonding electron groups than those groups exert on each other. These more intense "*lone-pair – bond-pair*" (LP-BP) interactions force the bonded atoms closer together in an AX_2E molecule and so reduce the X–A–X bond angle to less than 120°.

Similar to lone-pairs, we would also expect that larger peripheral atoms would exert *more repulsive forces* than smaller ones, and thus affect bond angles in a molecule. In Table 6.6.1, a solid triangle represents an atom or lone electron pair projecting out of the page, while a dashed line means the atom or lone-pair goes into the page.

Table 6.6.1 *Shapes of Three-Electron Groups: AX_3 and AX_2E*

AX_mE_n Notation	Molecular Shape	Sample Lewis Structure
X—A(X)(X) AX_3	trigonal planar	:F: — B — :F: :F: boron trifluoride
E—A(X)(X) AX_2E	bent or angular	:Ö—S̈=Ö: sulphur dioxide (1of 2 resonance structures)

Four-Electron Groups: AX_4, AX_3E, and AX_2E_2

Four electron groups will occupy the four corners of a regular tetrahedron and may result in three different molecular shapes. If all the electron groups are bonding, then the molecule is labeled as **AX_4** and adopts a tetrahedral (four-sided or four-faced) shape with each of the X–A–X bond angles at 109.5°. An example of this is methane gas, CH_4.

If one of the four electron groups is non-bonding, the molecule is considered **AX_3E** and the lone-pair occupies one of the four corners of the tetrahedron. The molecule we see is called a trigonal pyramid. Once again, the more intense LP-BP interactions will push the bonded atoms closer together than they would be in an AX_4 molecule. Evidence of this is seen in an AX_3E molecule such as ammonia in which the H–N–H bond angles are only 107° rather than 109.5°.

When two of the four groups of electrons are lone-pairs, the designation **AX_2E_2** applies. Two of the four corners will be occupied by the two bonded atoms and the remaining two corners by the lone-pairs. The molecule will be an angular shape similar to AX_2E, although the X–A–X bond angle will be smaller. In such an arrangement, not only will each of the two lone-pairs force the bonded atoms closer together via LP-BP interactions, but they will also exert a repulsive force on each other called a *lone-pair – lone-pair* (LP-LP) interaction. This is the most intense of the electron group repulsive interactions. The combined result of the additional repulsive forces is an even smaller X–A–X bond angle. In water, for example, the H–O–H bond angle is found to be only 104.5°. Table 6.6.2 below shows the molecular shapes of four-electron groups.

Table 6.6.2 *Shapes of Four-Electron Groups: AX_4, AX_3E, and AX_2E_2*

AX_mE_n Notation	Molecular Shape	Sample Lewis Structure
AX_4	tetrahedral	methane
AX_3E	trigonal pyramidal	ammonia
AX_2E_2	bent or angular	water

Five-Electron Groups: AX_5, AX_4E, AX_3E_2, and AX_2E_3

If more than four electron groups surround a central atom, that atom will have an expanded octet so it must belong to period 3 or higher in the periodic table. Expanded octets are only possible if d orbitals are available and none exist below the third energy level.

When five electron groups are present, two distinct sets of positions are occupied by those groups. One set of three positions lies in a trigonal plane, and the electron groups are referred to as *equatorial groups*. A second set of two positions places each group of electrons above and below the trigonal plane. These are called *axial groups*. The equatorial electron groups are separated by 120° bond angles, and the axial and equatorial groups are separated by 90°. Once again, LP-BP and LP-LP interactions play a role in reducing X–A–X bond angles as the number of lone-pairs attached to the central atom increases. Table 6.6.3 shows the molecular shapes of five-electron group systems.

Table 6.6.3 *Shapes of Five-Electron Groups: AX_5, AX_4E, AX_3E_2, and AX_2E_3*

AX_mE_n Notation	Molecular Shape	Sample Lewis Structure
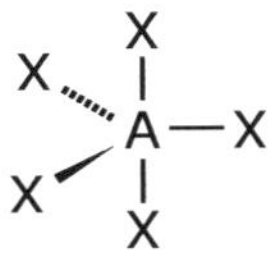 AX_5	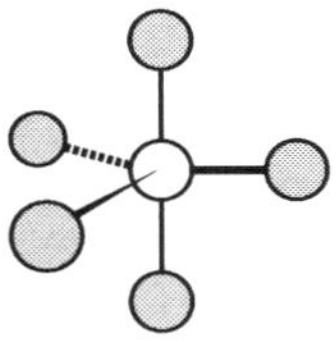 trigonal bipyramidal	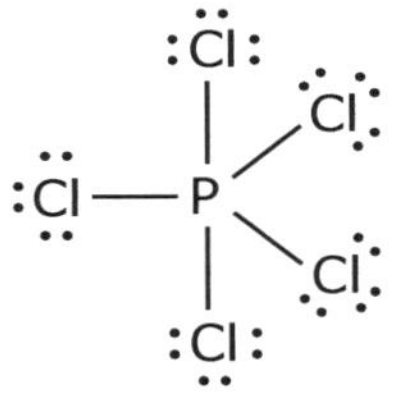 phosphorus pentachloride
 AX_4E	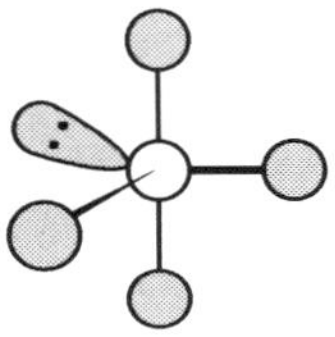 seesaw	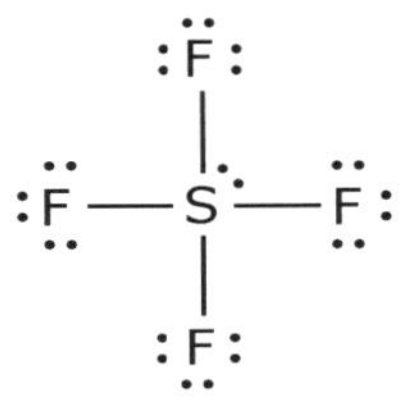 sulphur tetrafluoride
 AX_3E_2	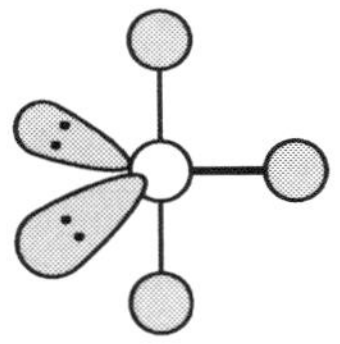 T-Shaped	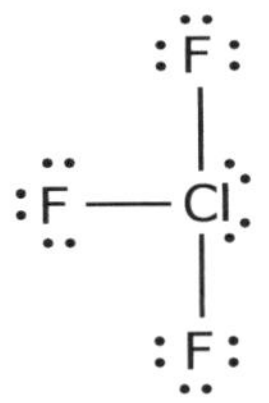 chlorine trifluoride
 AX_2E_3	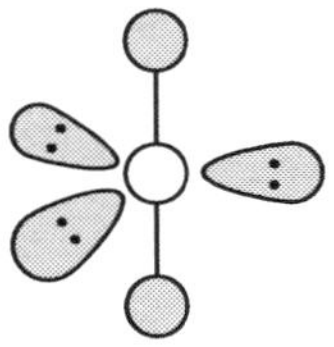 linear	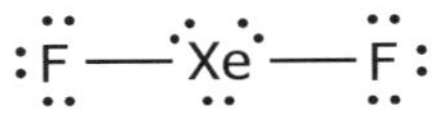 xenon difluoride

Six-Electron Groups: AX_6, AX_5E, and AX_4E_2

The final major electron group arrangement has six electron groups around the central atom. Unlike the five-electron group system, all six vertices are equivalent and point towards the corners of an octahedron as shown in Table 6.6.4.

If all of the electron groups are bonding, then the molecule is labeled as **AX_6**. The shape adopted by the molecule is octahedral (eight-faced) and all of the X–A–X bond angles are 90°.

When one of the six-electron groups is a non-bonding pair, it doesn't matter which of the six locations that lone-pair occupies around the central atom because all locations are identical. The molecule is classified as **AX_5E** and the molecular shape is square pyramidal. The lone pair is directed downward at the bottom centre of the four-based pyramid as Table 6.6.4 shows.

If two of the six-electron groups are lone-pairs, there are two orientations available in an octahedral shape. They could lie adjacent to each other with a separation of 90°, or lie opposite each other separated by 180°. As the diagram shows below, the two lone-pairs will always be as far away from each other as possible and separated by 180°. This minimizes the significant LP-LP repulsive interaction between them.

Table 6.6.4 *Shapes of Six-Electron Groups: AX_6, AX_5E, and AX_4E_2*

AX_mE_n Notation	Molecular Shape	Sample Lewis Structure
AX_6	octahedral	sulphur hexafluoride
AX_5E	square pyramidal	bromine pentafluoride
AX_4E_2	square planar	tetrachloroiodate ion

Quick Check

1. What is the fundamental principle associated with VSEPR Theory?
peripheral atoms stay as far away from each other as possible

2. Consider the electron group interactions: LP-BP, BP-BP, and LP-LP. Arrange these in order from least intense to most intense.
LP-LP → LP-BP → BP-BP

3. Although methane, ammonia, and water each have four electron groups associated with the central atom, the bond angles between the atoms in each molecule are 109.5°, 107°, and 104.5° respectively. Explain why.
because there are more and more lone pairs, which have slightly less repulsive forces than BP, decreasing the ∠ slightly

Molecular Formulas to Molecular Shapes

We are now in a position to combine the information from this and the previous section to predict molecular shapes starting with a molecular formula. The steps will guide you through this process:

Step 1: Beginning with the formula, determine the Lewis structure using the steps outlined in Section 6.4.

Step 2: Consider the central atom in the completed Lewis structure. Note the number of bonded atoms and lone pairs associated with that atom.

Step 3: Assign an AX_mE_n notation to the molecule or polyatomic ion. (Note any bond angles affected by the presence of one or more lone pairs.)

Step 4: Refer to the appropriate electron group arrangement category given in the tables above to determine the shape of the molecule.

(You're done!)

Sample Problem – Deducing a Molecular Shape

Determine the shape of the molecule tellurium tetrachloride, $TeCl_4$

What to Think about	How to Do It
1. Refer to the steps listed in section 6.4 to determine the Lewis structure for the molecule. 2. Tellurium has the lower electronegativity and so is the central atom. All of the chlorine atoms will therefore obey the octet rule and form only one bond. Note that tellurium is a member of the 5th period in the periodic table and is therefore capable of having an expanded octet. 3. There are five electron groups around the central atom. Four are bonding groups and one is a lone-pair of electrons. The molecule is therefore classified as AX_4E. An AX_4E molecule will have a "seesaw" shape.	:Cl: — Te — :Cl: (Lewis structure: Te bonded to four Cl atoms, each Cl with three lone pairs; one lone pair on Te)

Practice Problems

1. Complete the following table for each of the chemical species.

Lewis Structure	AX_mE_n Notation	Molecular Shape (Name and Diagram)
(a) [Lewis structure of SOF_4: S double-bonded to O and single-bonded to four F]	SOF_4 AX_5	trigonal bipyramid
(b) [Lewis structure of XeF_4: Xe bonded to four F with two lone pairs]	XeF_4 AX_4E_2	square planar

2. Complete the following table for each of the chemical species.

Chemical Formula	Lewis Structure	AX_mE_n Notation	Molecular Shape (Name and Diagram)
(a) CCl_4		AX_4	tetrahedral
(b) PF_3		AX_3E	trigonal pyramidal
(c) SCl_2		AX_2E_2	bent

no to 396

From Polar Bonds to Polar Molecules

Recall the concept of electronegativity and the table of electronegativity values, which you saw in section 6.2 (Figure 6.6.4).

Increasing EN →

H 2.1																	He
Li 1.0	Be 1.5											B 2.0	C 2.5	N 3.0	O 3.5	F 4.0	Ne
Na 0.9	Mg 1.2											Al 1.5	Si 1.8	P 2.1	S 2.5	Cl 3.0	Ar
K 0.8	Ca 1.0	Sc 1.3	Ti 1.5	V 1.6	Cr 1.6	Mn 1.5	Fe 1.8	Co 1.8	Ni 1.8	Cu 1.9	Zn 1.6	Ga 1.6	Ge 1.8	As 2.0	Se 2.4	Br 2.8	Kr
Rb 0.8	Sr 1.0	Y 1.3	Zr 1.4	Nb 1.6	Mo 1.8	Tc	Ru 2.2	Rh 2.2	Pd 2.2	Ag 1.9	Cd 1.7	In 1.7	Sn 1.8	Sb 1.9	Te 2.1	I 2.5	Xe
Cs 0.7	Ba 0.9	La 1.1	Hf 1.3	Ta 1.5	W 1.7	Re 1.9	Os 2.2	Ir 2.2	Pt 2.2	Au 2.4	Hg 1.9	Tl 1.8	Pb 1.8	Bi 1.9	Po 2.0	At 2.2	Rn
Fr 0.7	Ra 0.9	Ac 1.1															
			Ce 1.1	Pr 1.1	Nd 1.2	Pm	Sm 1.2	Eu 1.2	Gd 1.1	Tb 1.2	Dy 1.2	Ho 1.2	Er 1.2	Tm 1.2	Yb 1.1	Lu 1.2	
			Th 1.3	Pa 1.5	U 1.7												

↑ Increasing EN

Figure 6.6.4 *Periodic table showing electronegativity values*

As stated at the beginning of this section, an essential part of understanding and predicting the chemical and physical properties of substances is determining the shapes of their molecules. Among the most *significant consequences* of molecular shape is the *polarity of molecules*.

Molecular polarity not only affects physical properties such as melting point, boiling point, and solubility, but also influences a substance's chemical reactivity in both synthetic and biological processes.

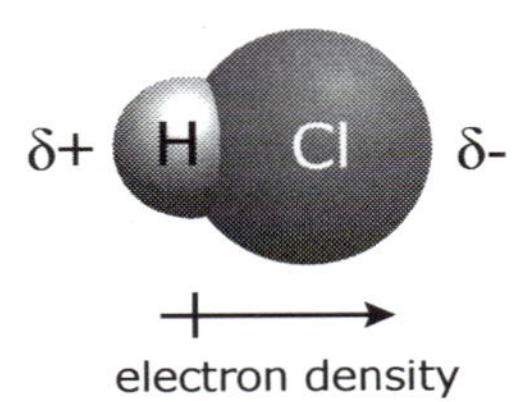

Figure 6.6.5 *HCl is a diatomic molecule containing a polar bond.*

Recall that a chemical bond is considered to be polar if electron-sharing in the bond is unequal enough due to the electronegativity differences of the atoms involved. If a diatomic molecule contains a polar bond, then the *molecule itself* must also be polar, as in a compound such as HCl (Figure 6.6.5).

However, if a molecule contains *more than two atoms*, the shape of the molecule as well as the polarity of its bonds will play a role in determining if the entire molecule will be polar. Stated another way, if the bonds within the molecule are polar, the molecule itself may or may not be, depending on its shape. Let's consider an example of each.

In carbon dioxide, each of the two C==O double bonds is quite polar because the two atoms have a $\Delta EN = 1.0$. However, because the molecule itself is AX_2 and therefore linear, each of those identical bond dipoles is pointing in a direction exactly opposite to the other because of the 180° O – C – O bond angle. This means that the molecular shape is such that the bond dipoles *effectively cancel each other out* resulting in a non-polar molecule. You can compare this to two evenly matched tug-of-war teams pulling in opposite directions on a rope — neither team wins because they are equally strong.

In water, just as in CO_2, a central atom is bonded between two identical peripheral atoms and each of those two bonds has a significant and identical dipole. However, because H_2O qualifies as an AX_2E_2 molecule, it is bent or V-shaped. This means that the molecular shape is such that the bond dipoles point in the same general direction and so reinforce each other. This results in a polar molecule.

Chemists can detect and measure a molecule's polarity in an electric field. They assign a magnitude to that polarity expressed as a "dipole moment." Water is very polar and has a significant dipole moment, but the dipole moment of non-polar carbon dioxide is zero. As Figure 6.6.6 shows, the water molecule has a net dipole, while the carbon dioxide molecule does not. The importance of the polarity of water molecules cannot be overstated as we will soon see.

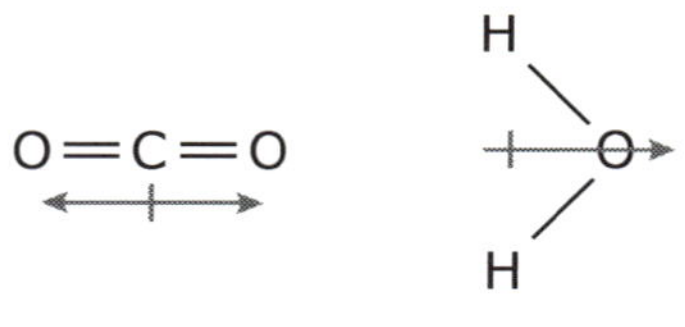

O=C=O

non-polar

H–O–H

polar

Figure 6.6.6 *The V-shape of a water molecule results in a significant dipole moment.*

In the above example, two *different molecular shapes* were the reason that bond dipoles in one molecule cancelled out, but didn't cancel in another molecule. There is also a possibility that two molecules having the *same shape* and containing polar bonds could be either polar or non-polar. We can use two AX_4 molecules to demonstrate this.

In Figure 6.6.7, carbon tetrachloride on the left is a symmetric molecule with four chlorines situated at the corners of a tetrahedron. Each C – Cl bond is polar in the direction of chlorine because carbon and chlorine have electronegativities of 2.5 and 3.0 respectively. The four bond dipoles, however, cancel out as they point in opposite directions in the symmetric molecule and so the molecule itself is non-polar. Carbon tetrachloride is a liquid used as a solvent for other non-polar substances. As you will soon see, one non-polar substance will usually mix well with another.

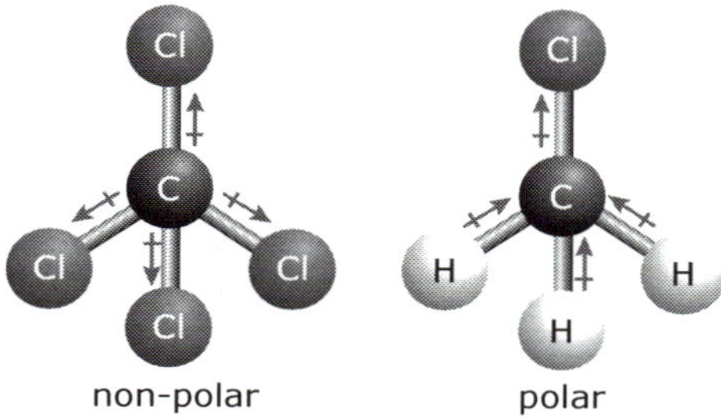

Figure 6.6.7 *Two molecules having the same shape can have different polarities. Carbon tetrachloride, on the left, is non-polar; chloromethane, on the right, is polar.*

The molecule on the right in Figure 6.6.7 is called chloromethane. All of its bond dipoles point in the same general direction. Each C – H bond is polar towards the carbon due to carbon's higher EN value (2.5 vs. 2.1), and the C – Cl bond polarity points in a similar direction towards chlorine. Now, as was the case with water above, the bond dipoles reinforce each other and so the entire molecule is polar.

In this example, molecular composition rather than molecular shape determined whether a molecule was polar or non-polar. In all cases, however, the key question is the same.

Does the molecule contain polar bonds and, if so, do the bond dipoles cancel each other or not?

If bond dipoles exist but cancel each other, then the molecule is non-polar. If bond dipoles don't cancel or if they reinforce each other, then the molecule is polar. Answering this question often involves attempting to visualize and even manipulate a three-dimensional shape based on a diagram drawn on a flat page. Although that might seem difficult at first, it will become easier with practice. Remembering the simple guidelines below will also help.

Guidelines for Determining If a Molecule Is Non-polar or Polar

1. When the peripheral atoms in a molecule are identical and arranged symmetrically around a central atom, any bond dipoles that exist will cancel out and the molecule will be non-polar.
2. When the molecule is asymmetric (not symmetric) either due to its shape or its composition, any bond dipoles that exist will usually not cancel out and the molecule will be polar.

If you review all the shapes listed in the tables given earlier, you will notice that several shapes have the peripheral atoms arranged *symmetrically* around the central atom. "Symmetrical" means balanced or evenly arranged.

In most cases, symmetrical molecules are AX_m molecules in which no lone pairs exist on the central atom. All such molecules containing identical peripheral atoms will be non-polar, regardless of the bond dipoles that exist.

Can you discover any shapes where lone pairs *do exist* on the central atoms that include symmetrically arranged peripheral atoms? If so, then those molecules will also prove to be non-polar as long as the peripheral atoms are all the same.

Sample Problem

Consider the Lewis structure shown here for the compound chlorine trifluoride:
Determine the shape of the molecule and if the molecule is polar.

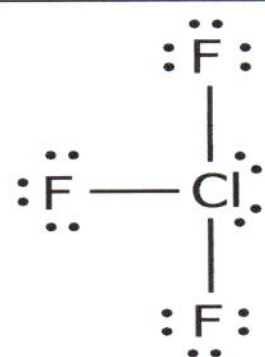

What to Think about

1. To determine if the bonds are polar, find the ΔEN from the electronegativity table.
   The bonds are therefore polar in the direction of fluorine.
2. To determine if the molecule is polar, assign an AX_mE_n label and find the molecular shape.
   The molecule has an AX_3E_2 designation and so adopts a "T-shaped" structure.
3. Considering the molecular shape, decide if the molecule is symmetric or asymmetric and therefore either polar or non-polar.
   The bond dipoles therefore do not cancel and so the molecule is polar.

How to Do It

$\Delta EN = 4.0 - 3.0 = 1.0$

F
Cl — F
F

electron density

Practice Problems

1. Complete the following table by listing the AX_mE_n notations and their shapes in the appropriate columns for all the symmetric and asymmetric molecules that you can find. Assume that all the peripheral atoms in the molecules are the same. The first entries are done for you.

***Symmetric* Molecules**		***Asymmetric* Molecules**	
AX_mE_n Notation	**Shape of Molecule**	**AX_mE_n Notation**	**Shape of Molecule**
AX_2	linear	AX_2E	bent or angular

2. Complete the following table.

Lewis Structure	AX_mE_n Notation	Molecular Shape (Name and Diagram)	Polar Molecule? (Yes / No)
(a) $H_2C{=}\ddot{O}:$ (H–C(–H)=O)	AX_3	trigonal planar	yes
(b) $H{-}\ddot{N}{-}H$ with H below N	AX_3E_1	trigonal pyramid	yes
(c) PCl_5 (P bonded to five :Cl:)	AX_5	trigonal bipyramidal	no

Intermolecular Forces

We have seen that opposite charges are ultimately responsible for all chemical bonds. Electron-deficient positive ions are attracted to electron-abundant negative ions in ionic bonds. Pairs of negative electrons are attracted to adjacent positive nuclei in covalent bonds.

The chemical bonds within molecules are called **intramolecular** forces. ("Intra" means "within.") Attractive forces between molecules and between ions and molecules are called **intermolecular forces.**

Intermolecular forces are as dependent on electrostatic attraction as intramolecular forces are. However, because they typically involve smaller charges and/or greater distances between the chemical species, they aren't as strong as chemical bonds. Yet these forces are so important that without them, life itself could never exist on this tiny "blue marble" in space we call Earth.

Our final discussion of this chapter will focus on the various types of intermolecular forces that exist. We will begin with the forces that act between neutral molecules, and then consider a force that acts between molecules and ions. Let's start where our previous discussion ended by revisiting polar molecules.

Dipole-Dipole Forces — Attractions Between Polar Molecules

Within any substance containing polar molecules, each molecule has a positive and a negative pole — a **molecular dipole**. Because of these partial charges, the molecules in the liquid and solid phases will naturally orient themselves so that the positive pole of one molecule will be next to and attract the negative pole of an adjacent molecule. This force of attraction is called a **dipole-dipole force**. This network of dipole-dipole forces will result in higher melting and boiling points because more energy will be required to overcome the attractions between the molecules.

The more polar those molecules are, the stronger the dipole-dipole forces. Figure 6.6.8 shows two depictions of polar HCl molecules with the dipole-dipole force acting between them.

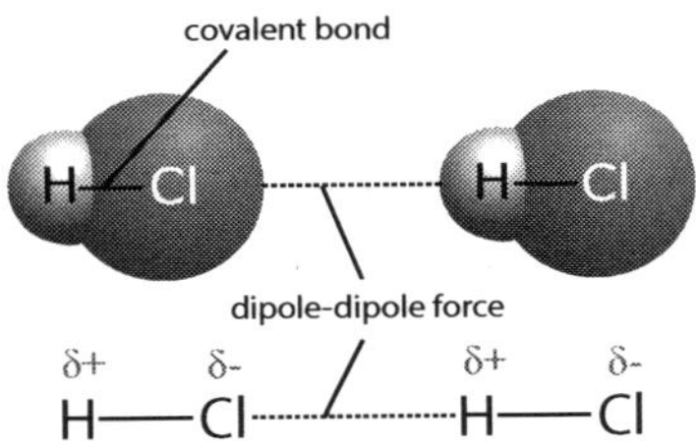

Figure 6.6.8 *One way to show dipole-dipole forces is to draw the actual molecule shapes (top diagram). Another way is to use the element symbols only (bottom diagram).*

Hydrogen Bonds — Special Dipole-Dipole Forces

A much stronger example of a dipole-dipole force exists between polar molecules that contain a hydrogen atom bonded to either nitrogen, oxygen, or fluorine. The atoms of these 2nd period elements are each small, highly electronegative, and have lone electron pairs. All of these properties are significant.

The H – **N**, H – **O**, and H – **F** bonds in each of these molecules will be *very polar* due to hydrogen's low electronegativity resulting in a large ΔEN. This means that a significant amount of electron density will be removed from hydrogen, leaving it with a large partial positive charge. This will also leave its nucleus almost unshielded because hydrogen has no core electrons. The other end of the molecule will gain that electron density and thus acquire a large partial negative charge.

The partially positive hydrogen in one molecule will then be attracted to the lone electron pair of the partially negative atom of another molecule. That attractive force will be particularly strong not only because of the extremely polar bonds within the molecules, but also because *all of the atoms involved are small.* This allows the tiny electropositive hydrogen to get very close to the lone pairs on the partially negative nitrogen, oxygen, or fluorine atoms of the other molecules. This intense intermolecular force is known as a **hydrogen bond**.

It is not an exaggeration to state that hydrogen bonds make life on Earth possible. For example, consider that most of our Earth and most of our bodies are composed of water. Water molecules have a relatively low mass and the vast majority of substances composed of such molecules have very low boiling points, even if those molecules are polar. Look at Figure 6.6.9 showing the boiling points of the binary (two element) hydrides of groups 14 to 17 of the periodic table.

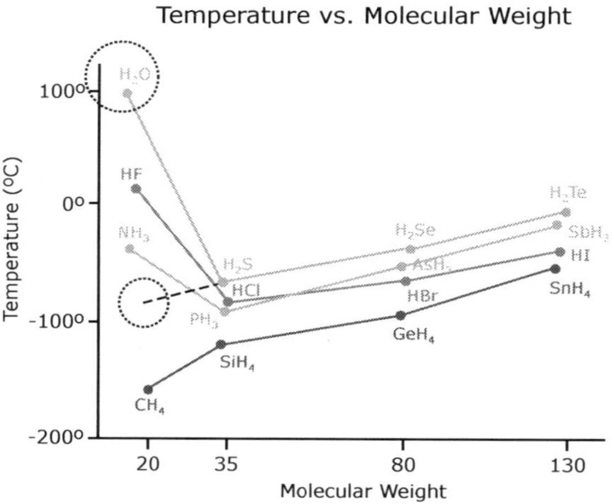

Figure 6.6.9 *Boiling points of binary hydrides of groups 14 to 17*

The group 14 hydrides are all symmetric AX_4 molecules and non-polar, so we would expect those substances (SnH_4, GeH_4, SiH_4, and CH_4) to have low boiling points, and they do. Note that the boiling points of these compounds decrease with decreasing molar mass. The binary hydrides of the remaining groups, however, are asymmetric polar molecules. Their dipole-dipole forces contribute to higher boiling points than seen in group 14.

Something very interesting occurs, however, with the lightest hydrides in groups 15, 16, and 17. Look at how the boiling points change for hydrides as we move up each group. Consider the group 16 binary hydrides for example: H_2Te, H_2Se, H_2S, and finally H_2O (water). As the mass of each polar AX_2E_2 molecule decreases, the boiling point drops, but not consistently. After H_2S, if the trend were consistent, we would expect water to have a boiling point of approximately –90°C (see dashed line in Figure 6.6.9). The fact that the actual boiling point is almost 200°C higher than that is clear evidence of the strength of the hydrogen bonds in water (Figure 6.6.10a). Life as we know it would be very unlikely if water became a gas at –90°C! Even the fact that ice floats is due to hydrogen bonding. That characteristic of water is of great importance to aquatic life during cold temperatures.

The significance of hydrogen bonds is further demonstrated by the fact that the three-dimensional structure of many proteins and even the base-pairing in the double helix of DNA molecules depend on the existence of these essential forces. These are hydrogen bonds involving an oxygen or nitrogen atom (Figure 6.6.10b).

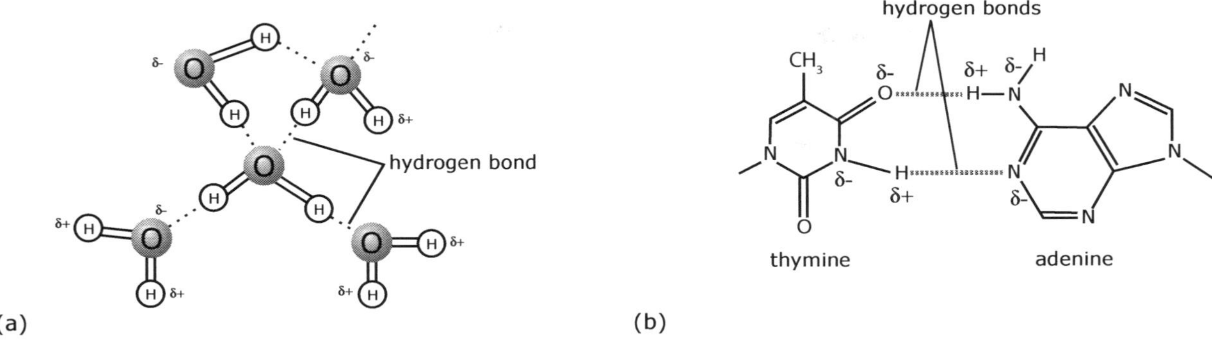

Figure 6.6.10 *(a) Hydrogen bonds in water; (b) Hydrogen bonds in DNA base-pairing*

Dispersion (London) Forces — A Growing Attraction

For a molecular substance to exist as a liquid or solid, the molecules must be close together. This means some kind of intermolecular attractive force must exist between those molecules.

So far, we have discussed two of these intermolecular forces. Dipole-dipole forces and hydrogen bonds act to cause polar molecules to "stick" together and maintain a molecular substance in the liquid or solid state of matter.

However, we might expect that substances composed of non-polar molecules might never exist as liquids or solids since they have no particular reason to attract each other. That is definitely not the case. Many molecular substances composed of non-polar molecules exist as liquids or even solids at room temperatures. Those that don't can usually be condensed or solidified under the right conditions. The obvious question would be: What intermolecular force would cause non-polar molecules to attract each other?

The explanation of this force relies on the quantum mechanical description of the atom and the force itself is named for the physicist, Fritz London, who used quantum mechanics to explain the basis of the attraction. We'll use a non-polar molecule as an example.

Consider a sample of chlorine gas, Cl_2. As the $\Delta EN = 0$, the molecules are non-polar and the electron density in the negative cloud surrounding this diatomic molecule is evenly distributed. This means that *on average*, the electrons will spend no more of their time nearer one chlorine nucleus than the other, and so the probability distribution is even throughout the orbital cloud.

However, at any instant, there is a *possibility* that there may be more electron density on one side of the molecule than the other, resulting in an instantaneous molecular dipole. This dipole will have little effect on any other Cl_2 molecules that are far away. But if those molecules are in close proximity, even a short-lived dipole in one molecule will distort or polarize the electron cloud of a neighbouring molecule. This happens because the negative pole of the instantaneous dipole will repel electron density in the nearby electron cloud to the opposite side of that molecule. As well, the positive pole will pull electron density to the near side of another neighbouring molecule. Each induced dipole results in an intermolecular attraction between the newly polarized molecules and induces more dipoles in surrounding molecules. As a result, the dipoles *disperse* throughout the sample, causing the molecules to attract each other. These intermolecular forces of attraction are called **dispersion forces** or **London dispersion forces**.

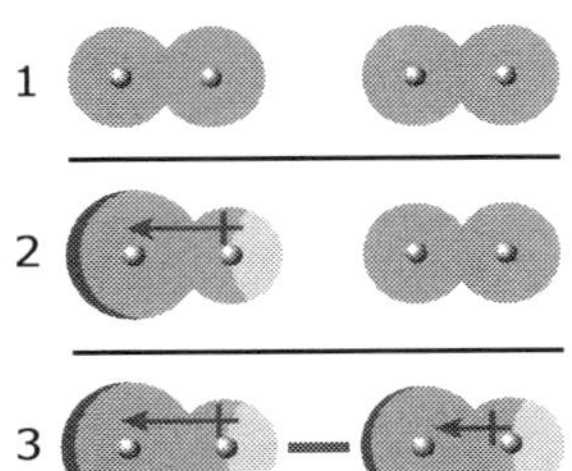

Figure 6.6.11 *An instantaneous dipole in the non-polar molecule on the left (2) induces a dipole in its neighbouring molecule on the right (3).*

Figure 6.6.11 shows an instantaneous dipole in the non-polar molecule on the left inducing a dipole in the neighbouring molecule on the right. The dispersion force then exists between the two molecules.

Although London forces are the *only* forces acting between non-polar molecules, they exist between the particles of *all* substances. Except in the case of strong hydrogen bonds, they may be the dominant intermolecular force even for polar molecules.

The strength of dispersion forces will increase as the size of the molecules involved increases. This is because large electron clouds are more loosely held than smaller clouds. Thus they are more easily deformed or polarized by a nearby dipole than compact tightly held clouds are.

Even molecular shape can play a role in dispersion forces. Molecules with more surface area have electron clouds that are spread out and so are more easily distorted by neighboring dipoles.

Consider the melting and boiling points of diatomic halogens of group 17. The higher temperatures required for these phase changes as we descend the group is evidence of the increasing strength of the London forces between the molecules.

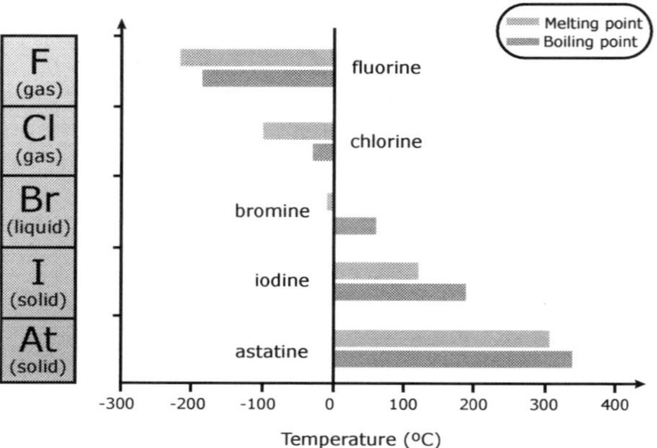

Figure 6.6.12 *Melting and boiling points of diatomic halogens of group 17*

Ion-Dipole Forces — Surround and Separate

We will conclude our discussion of intermolecular forces by focusing on an important interaction that occurs when an ionic compound dissolves in water.

The ionic bonds holding a crystal lattice together are strong. However, when the surface of that lattice is in contact with water, each ion on that surface will attract the oppositely charged end of polar water molecules near them. That attraction between an ion and a polar molecule is called an **ion-dipole force.** These attractive forces soon overcome those between the ions themselves, so the crystal structure begins to break down. As the ions move away from the lattice surface, they immediately become surrounded or enclosed in what chemists call a **hydration shell.**

At the centre of one type of hydration shell, the negative oxygen ends of water molecules orient themselves next to and surround a cation. At the centre of another shell, an anion is engulfed by water molecules oriented with their positive hydrogens next to the ion's negative charge. Figure 6.6.13 shows the ion-dipole forces acting between water and Na^+ and Cl^- ions in an aqueous solution. Ion-dipole forces are the primary force responsible for the solubility of ionic compounds in water and aqueous solutions of some ionic compounds are almost as necessary for life as water itself.

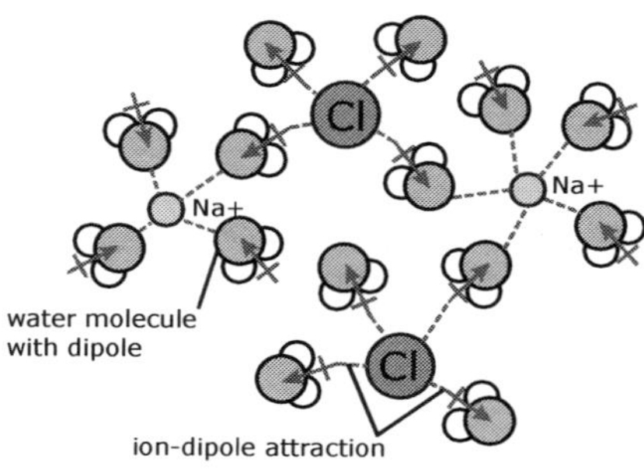

Figure 6.6.13 *Ion-dipole forces between water molecules and Na^+ and Cl^- ions in an aqueous solution*

Valence Bond Theory — The Hybridization of Atomic Orbitals and the Concept of Formal Charge

G.N. Lewis's dot structures provide useful models of the arrangement of atoms in covalent molecules. By evaluating the total number of valence electrons in a molecule and the formal charge on the atoms, Lewis structures provide a way to represent whether covalent molecules contain single or multiple bonds. The repulsion that occurs between bonding and/or non-bonding pairs of electrons can be used to predict molecular shape. This is the VSEPR theory. Consideration of the electronegativity of atoms within a molecule's Lewis structure provides a way to deduce whether a molecular dipole exists. The strength of the intermolecular forces (IMFs) in molecules is determined by a combination of London dispersion forces and dipole forces. Intermolecular forces influence all of the physical and chemical characteristics of these molecules.

There are some limitations and over simplifications associated with the Lewis structure model of covalent molecules. For example, we know that electrons are not accurately represented as pairs of dots in a region of space between two atoms that produce a bond. The quantum mechanical model explains that electrons actually exhibit particle-wave duality in atoms and that they are located in orbitals. The quantum mechanical model may be reviewed in Sections 5.2 to 5.4 and 6.1 and 6.2.

Valence bond theory describes the location of bonding and non-bonding, lone electrons in quantum-mechanical orbitals, created by overlap of the standard s, p, d, and f orbitals we learned about earlier in Chapters 5 and 6. **Hybridization** is a mathematical process in which these standard atomic orbitals are combined to form new atomic orbitals called **hybrid orbitals**. Hybrid orbitals are located on individual atoms, but their shapes and energies differ from those of standard atomic orbitals. Hybrid orbitals are more stable than standard atomic orbitals. They *minimize* the energy of the molecule by *maximizing* the orbital overlap in a bond. The mathematical equations involved in hybridization are very complex; however, the following statements help describe it.

- The sum of the number of standard atomic orbitals is equal to the number of hybrid orbitals formed.
- The combinations of standard atomic orbitals determine the number and energies of the hybrid orbitals formed.
- The type of hybridization that occurs is the one with the lowest overall potential energy.
- We can use the electron geometry determined by the VSEPR theory to predict the type of hybridization.

sp^3 Hybridization

This is the most common type of hybridization as it is found in molecules whose central atom is surrounded by a stable octet. Methane, CH_4 is a classic example of sp^3 hybridization. Each hydrogen has one valence electron existing in a 1s orbital, while carbon has four valence electrons, two existing in a 2s orbital, and two in two lobes of a 2p orbital. Carbon's orbital diagram would convert as shown in Figure 6.6.14 (notice the 1s electrons are not affected).

C $1s^22s^22p^2$

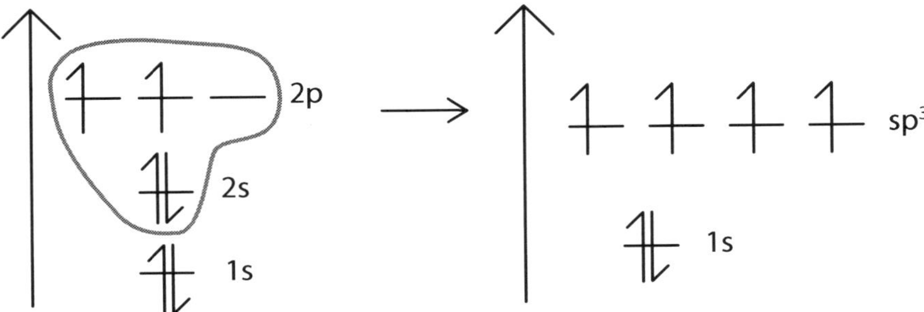

Figure 6.6.14 *Conversion of carbon's orbital diagram*

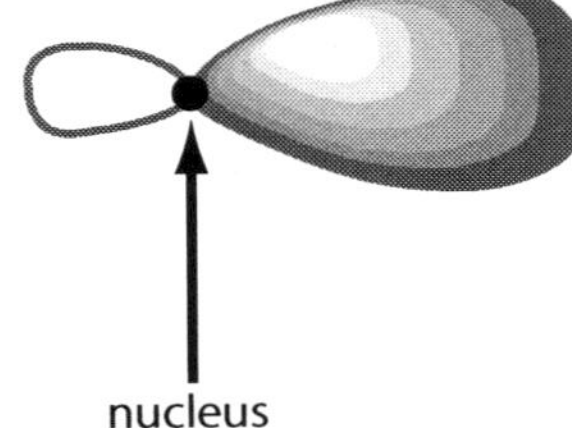

Figure 6.6.15 *An sp^3 hybrid orbital*

The s and p orbitals combine to form four *identical* bonding orbitals, designated sp^3. Each of these can share their electron with one hydrogen atom. This is called sp^3 hybridization. *One* spherical s orbital and *three* figure-8-shaped p orbitals (one p_x, one p_y and one p_z) combine to form *four* identical sp^3 hybrid orbitals. An sp^3 hybrid orbital resembles a p orbital with an enlarged end (Figure 6.6.15).

There are *four* of these that overlap about a central point to make a methane molecule, CH_4 (or any AX_4 species). This is typical of a *tetrahedral* arrangement with all bond angles approximately 109.5° (Figure 6.6.16).

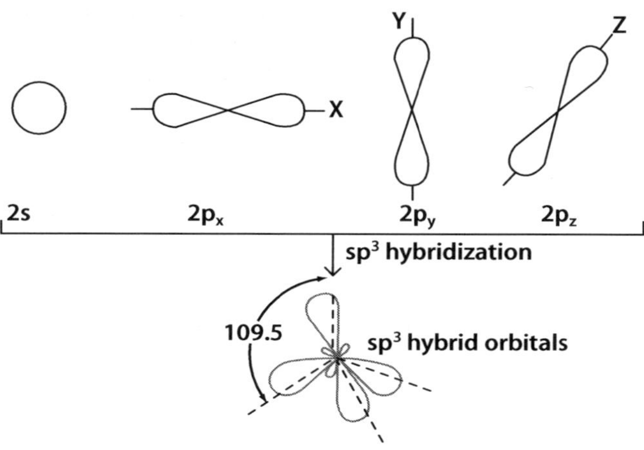

Figure 6.6.16 *A methane molecule*

- Hybridized orbitals can hold lone pairs or bonding pairs.
- The region in space occupied by a pair of bonding or lone electrons, regions of high electron density, is a "domain".
- Lone electrons exert greater repulsive forces than bonding electrons.

Sample Problem — Deducing Molecular Shape and Hybridization

Determine the shape and the hybridization for a molecule of water.

What to Think About	How To Do It
1. Refer to the steps listed in Section 6.5 to determine the Lewis structure for the molecule.	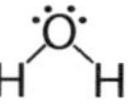
2. Determine the number of electron "domains" around the central oxygen atom.	The four electron domains are arranged in a tetrahedron. Two of the domains contain lone pairs of electrons. **Four sp^3 hybrid orbitals are** oriented in a tetrahedral array. Two of the sp^3 orbitals are occupied by bonding electron pairs and two are occupied by non-bonding electron pairs leading to an **angular** or **bent** (**V-shaped**) arrangement.
3. Four electron domains will be most likely to exist as four sp^3 hybrid orbitals.	Due to the large interelectron repulsion of the lone-paired electrons, the usual 109.5° bond angle found in a tetrahedron will be reduced and closer to 104.5° between the hydrogen atoms. 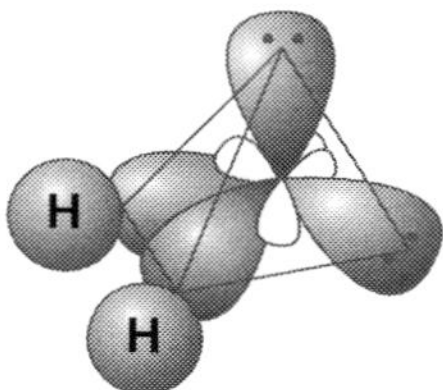

sp^3d and sp^3d^2 Hybridization

Elements in the third row of the periodic table (or below) are able to form bonding arrangements involving *expanded octets*. In third period elements such as phosphorus, sulphur, and chlorine, the 3d orbitals are so close in energy to the 3s and 3p orbitals that the hybridization of one s, three p, and one d orbital results in a *trigonal bipyramid* geometry. Sp^3d hybridization is particularly common for molecules whose central atoms have five valence electrons.

Elements with six, seven, or eight valence electrons can accommodate an expanded octet to produce up to six bonds. The formation of sp^3d^2 hybrid orbitals in an *octahedral* (or *square bipyramid*) array can be accomplished by the hybridizing of one s, three p, and two d orbitals. (See Figure 6.6.17)

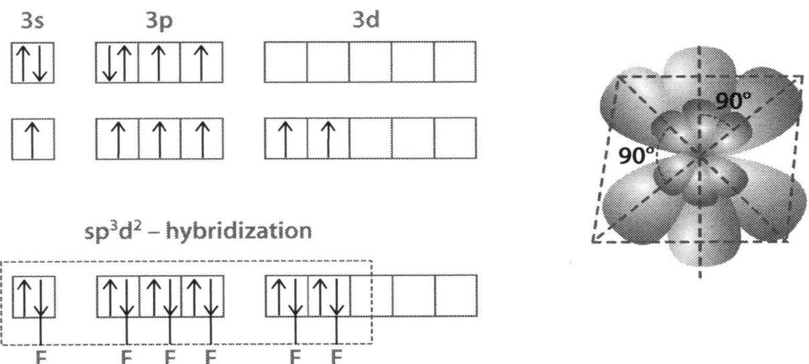

Figure 6.6.17 *As shown, sp^3d^2 hybridization creates six degenerate orbitals in an octahedral array. Six single bonds all 90° apart extend from a central atom as in sulphur hexafluoride, SF_6, for example.*

Note: While the use of electron geometry to predict hybridization is largely successful, there are cases where it fails. H_2S for example is predicted to have tetrahedral *electron* geometry and a bent shape with about a bond angle of about 104°. In fact, the bond angle is closer to 90°, indicating that this molecule is largely unhybridized. Recently, complex computer-based calculations indicate that the sp^3d and sp^3d^2 hybrids are the most difficult to accurately predict. For this reason, these two types of hybridization are not being assessed on the AP Chemistry examination at the moment.

Sigma (σ) and Pi (π) Bonding

A sigma (σ) bond occurs when two atomic orbitals combine to form a covalent bond that lies along an axis connecting the nuclei of the two atoms. The simplest example of a sigma bond would be the overlap of two 1s orbitals in the formation of diatomic hydrogen, H_2. Sigma bonds are also formed by the overlap of two hybridized orbitals. In double bond formation, there is overlap between two hybridized orbitals, called a sigma bond overlap, and the overlap of two unhybridized p orbitals, which is called a pi (π) bond overlap. A double bond consists of one sigma and one pi bond overlap.

A pi bond occurs due to p_y or p_z orbital overlap in a sausage-shaped region above and below (in the case of p_y overlap) or in front and behind (in the case of p_z overlap) the nuclei of bonded atoms (Figure 6.6.18).

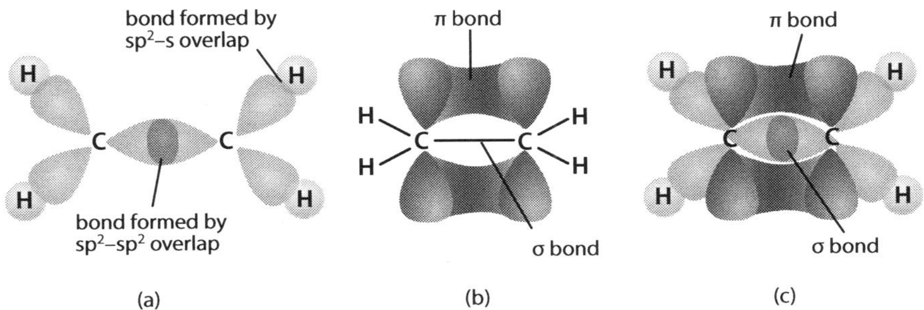

Figure 6.6.18 *(a) shows overlap of p_x hybridized orbitals along an axis between the carbon atoms to form a σ bond; (b) shows overlap of p_y orbitals above and below an axis between the carbon atoms to form a π bond; (c) shows double-bonded C_2H_4 with one σ and one π bond between the two carbon atoms in the molecule.*

sp and sp^2 Hybridization

Double and triple bonds are commonly associated with carbon atoms and always consist of one sigma (σ) and one or two pi (π) bonds. In terms of hybridization, the entire region of orbital overlap is considered one hybrid orbital, even though it may be a double or triple bond. For this reason, multiple bonds are often associated with sp or sp^2 hybridization.

In the determination of molecular shape and/or hybridization, it is important to think of a double or triple covalent bond as occupying one domain only.

Other examples of compounds that exhibit sp and sp^2 hybridization are those with beryllium or boron (see Section 6.5 for exceptions to Lewis structures) as these may form stable compounds with less than an octet of electrons around their central atoms.

Sample Problem — Deducing Molecular Shape, Hybridization, and Presence of Sigma (σ) and Pi (π) Bonds

Determine the shape and hybridization for a molecule of methanal, CH_2O. Determine the number of sigma and pi bonds in the molecule. The common name for methanal is formaldehyde.

What To Think About	How To Do It
1. Refer to the steps listed in Section 6.4 to determine the Lewis structure for the molecule.	H, H – C = O: (Lewis structure: two H atoms bonded to C, C double-bonded to O with two lone pairs)
2. Determine the number of electron "domains" existing around the central atom (the double bond is one domain).	There are a total of 12 valence electrons with carbon occupying the central position in the molecule. This means a double bond is needed between the carbon and the oxygen atoms.
3. The total number of orbitals is conserved.	There are **three** electron domains. This indicates three hybrid orbitals. The orbitals should be **sp^2 hybridized**.
4. Maximize the inter-domain distance to predict the shape of the molecule and the bond angles.	The molecule should have 120.5° bond angles and should be **trigonal planar**.
5. All single bonds are σ and all multiple bonds consist of first σ and then π bonds.	There should be 3 **σ** bonds (between C and each H and C and O) and 1 π bond (between C and O).

Practice Problems—Deducing Molecular Shape, Hybridization, and Presence of Sigma (σ) and Pi (π) Bonds

1. Draw Lewis structures for each of the following species.

   a) CH_4 b) H_3O^+ c) OF_2 d) HCN e) SF_6 f) SOF_4

   F—O—F   14+6=20−4=16

   H−C≡N: 1+4+5=10−8=2

2. State the shape and the central atom hybridization for each of the structures.

   c. bent   d. linear

3. Label each molecule as polar or non-polar.

   c. polar   d. polar

Table 6.6.5 *Summary Table Including Hybridization, Bond Type, and Shape*

Hybridization	# Of Bonds	# Lone Pairs	Molecular Shape		Bond Angle	Example
sp	2	0		Linear	180°	CO_2
sp^2	3	0		Trigonal planar	120°	SO_3
sp^2	2	1		Angular	< 120°	SO_2
sp^3	4	0		Tetrahedral	109.5°	CH_4
sp^3	3	1		Trigonal pyramidal	< 109.5°	NH_3
sp^3	2	2		Bent (angular)	< 109.5°	H_2O
sp^3d	5	0		Trigonal bipyramidal	120°, 90°	PCl_5
sp^3d	4	1		Seesaw or irregular tetrahedron	< 120°, < 90°	SF_4
sp^3d	3	2		T-shaped	< 90°	CF_3
sp^3d	2	3		Linear	180°	XeF_2
sp^3d^2	6	0		Octahedron	90°	SF_8
sp^3d^2	5	1		Square pyramidal	< 90°	IF_5
sp^3d^2	4	2		Square planar	90°	XeF_4

Formal Charge

Formal charge is an entirely fictitious charge that is used to defend the most probable Lewis structure of a molecule when several different Lewis structure arrangements are possible. The formal charge on an atom in a molecule is the charge each atom would have *if all bonding electrons were shared equally between the bonded atoms*. There are a couple of ways to calculate the formal charge of each atom.

formal charge of an atom = the number of valence electrons – [the number of lone electrons + the number of bonding electron pairs]

This method for calculating formal charge can be simplified if the Lewis structure is drawn using lines for each bonding pair of electrons. In that case:

formal charge = valence electrons – (dots + lines)

While not particularly scientific sounding, this is a very easy way to calculate formal charge. Formal charges are generally shown next to each atom in a structure with a *circle* drawn around the charge.

It is important to remember that formal charges are *not* actual charges. They do *not* produce electronegativity or polarity in a molecule. They simply assist us in determining which is the most likely structure from among a selection of Lewis structures. The following general rules apply to formal charges.

1. The *sum* of all formal charges in a *neutral molecule* is equal to *zero.*
2. The *sum* of all formal charges in an *ion* is equal to the *ion's charge.*
3. *Small* or *zero* formal charges on atoms are preferred.*
4. For structures with atoms with a non-zero formal charge, the preferred structure will be the one with a negative charge on the more electronegative element.

* *Statement 3 has been questioned by bonding theorists lately — in fact a structure that satisfies the octet rule may be more likely than one in which formal charges are minimized. For the AP exam, it is a good idea for a student to indicate awareness that the predictive power of formal charge is limited.*

Sample Problem — Deduction of a Preferred Structure Using Formal Charge

Hydrocyanic acid is produced by bubbling gaseous hydrogen cyanide through water to produce an aqueous solution. Draw two possible structures for the molecule with a triple bond between the C and the N and assign formal charges to all atoms. Which structure is preferred based on minimizing formal charge?

What to Think About	How to Do It
1. Refer to the steps listed in Section 6.5 to determine the Lewis structure for the molecule. 2. If there is more than one possible resonance structure or isomer, repeat the steps and produce any alternate structures. Note: there are several resonance structures possible, but the question limits us to the two involving a triple C-N bond.	There are a total of 10 valence electrons. The structure may be drawn with the carbon in the centre or the nitrogen. Either way, the C-N bond must be triple (as indicated in the question) and the H bond single. Possible structures include: H-C≡N: and H-N≡C:
3. Calculate formal charges using the formula: valence electrons – (dots + dashes) for each atom in the first structure.	H: 1 – (0 + 1) = 0 C: 4 – (0 + 4) = 0 N: 5 – (2 + 3) = 0
4. Repeat for the second structure.	H: 1 – (0 + 1) = 0 N: 5 – (0 + 4) = +1 C: 4 – (2 + 3) = -1
5. Place the "charges" on the appropriate atoms in a circle.	(0) (0) (0) H-C≡N̈ and H-N≡C̈ (0) (+1) (-1)
6. Predict the preferred structure.	The first structure (with the central carbon) is preferred.

Practice Problems—Assigning and Using Formal Charges

1. Assign formal charges to each atom in each of the following two structures for CO_2. Predict which structure is favoured.

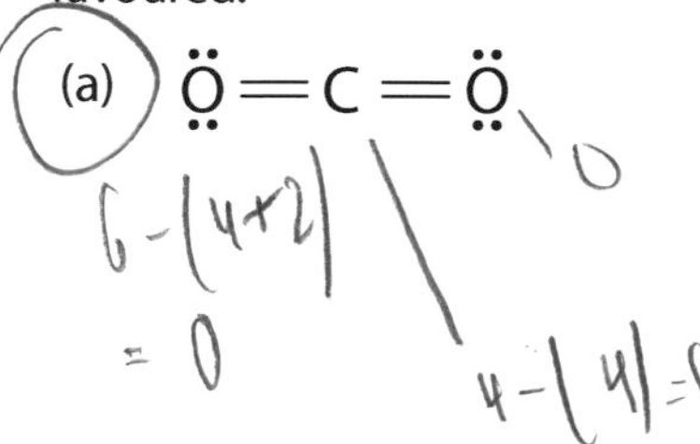

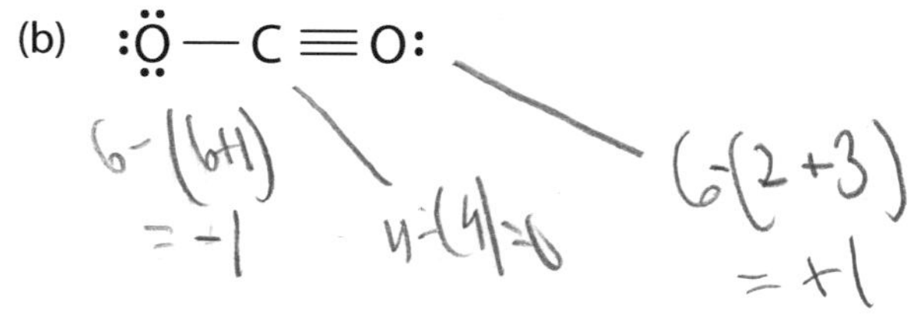

2. Assign formal charges to each atom in each of the following six structures for SCO. Predict which structure is favoured. Which is least likely to form?

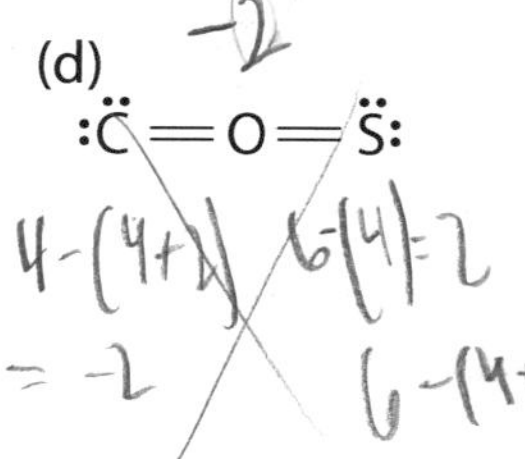

(b) :Ö — C ≡ S:

(c) :O ≡ C — S̤̈:

(d) :C̈ = O = S̈:

(e) :C̤̈ — O ≡ S:

(f) :C ≡ O — S̤̈:

3. Draw two structures for SO_3, one with an expanded octet and one without. You do not need to show resonance structures for the non-expanded form. Use formal charges to predict which structure is favoured. Check the Internet to see whether you can find any information indicating that the other structure might, in fact, be favoured.

6.6 Activity: Modeling the AX_mE_n Molecules

Question

How can building the various AX_mE_n shapes help us to determine molecular polarities?

Materials

- modelling clay
- Popsicle® sticks or wooden splints
- small spherical balloons

(Note: A good quality molecular model kit can be used in place of the above items.)

Procedure

1. Using the modelling clay, make a small sphere about the size of a lemon as you may have done in the activity at the end of section 6.4. This sphere will represent the central atom (**A**) for each AX_mE_n category you construct.
2. You will need a total of nine sticks. Trim three of the sticks to a length of about 4 cm. Blow up three small spherical balloons until they are about 12 cm long and tie the ends. Tape the tied ends of the balloons to the ends of shortened sticks. The regular sticks will represent bonded electron groups attached to peripheral atoms (**X**). The balloons taped to the trimmed sticks will represent lone-pair electrons (**E**).
3. The modelling clay, sticks, and balloons will allow you to construct each of the AX_mE_n molecules discussed in this section and listed in the table below. After you build one, simply take the structure apart to build the next.

Build each of the shapes listed in the table below, but before you take each apart, look at each structure and ask yourself the following question: If each of the bonds in these molecules were polar and all of the peripheral atoms were the same, would the *molecule* be polar or non-polar?

Complete the following table below as you construct each shape:

AX_mE_n Notation	Sample Molecule	Name of Shape	Polar Molecule? Yes/No
AX_2	CO_2		
AX_3	BF_3		
AX_2E	SO_2		
AX_4	CH_4		
AX_3E	NH_3		
AX_2E_2	H_2O		
AX_5	PCl_5		
AX_4E	SF_4		
AX_3E_2	BrF_3		
AX_2E_3	XeF_2		
AX_6	SF_6		
AX_5E	BrF_5		
AX_4E_2	XeF_4		

Results and Discussion

1. Note that an electronegativity value is not listed for xenon in the table shown earlier in this section. In spite of this, you are still able to determine if the two molecules above containing Xe as the central atom are polar or not. Why?

6.6 Review Questions

1. (a) What do the letters: V S E P, and R in the term "VSEPR theory" stand for?

   (b) What does the theory allow us to do?

2. Why do non-bonding or lone-pair electrons attached to a central atom occupy more space than bonding electron pairs?

3. Consider the following Lewis structures. Would you expect these molecules to have the same shape or a different shape? Explain.

```
 ..         ..                H
:F — B — F:                   |
 ..    |    ..            H — C = O:
      :F:                        ..
       ..
```

4. For each pair of columns, draw lines to connect the AX_mE_n notation on the left to the correct shape listed on the right. (The first one is done for you.)

AX_mE_n Notation	Molecular Shape	AX_mE_n Notation	Molecular Shape
AX_3	angular	AX_4E	T-shaped
AX_2E_3	trigonal bipyramidal	AX_2E	octahedral
AX_4	trigonal pyramidal	AX_3E_2	square pyramidal
AX_3E	trigonal planar	AX_6	square planar
AX_2E_2	tetrahedral	AX_5E	angular
AX_5	linear	AX_4E_2	seesaw

5. Consider the Lewis structures for methane and ammonia.

   (a) Which molecule will have the smaller X–A–X bond angle and why?

```
     H             ..
     |         H — N — H
H — C — H          |
     |             H
     H
```

   (b) Identify the main intermolecular force acting between the molecules of methane and between the molecules of ammonia in pure samples of each compound.

6. Assume that all of the peripheral atoms are the same for each AX_mE_n category listed below and complete the following table. (Note that two different bond angles exist in an AX_5 molecule.)

AX_mE_n Category	AX_2	AX_3	AX_4	AX_5		AX_2E_3	AX_6	AX_4E_2
X–A–X Bond Angle	180°	120°	109.5°	90°	120°	180°	90°	90°

7. Consider the following group 17 binary hydrides: HI, HBr, HCl, and HF. Which should have the highest boiling point and why?

HF because Fluorine is the smallest of the 4 so the F_{att} are higher, resulting in a higher boiling point.

8. The industrial production of ammonia, NH_3, from H_2 and N_2 is called the Haber process, named for Fritz Haber, the German chemist who developed it just before World War I. During the process, in a gaseous mixture of all three substances, NH_3 must be separated from H_2 and N_2. This is done by cooling the gaseous mixture so as to condense only the NH_3. This leaves the elemental nitrogen and hydrogen as gases to be recycled and produce more ammonia. Why does only the ammonia liquefy upon cooling, but not the H_2 or N_2?

The ammonia liquifies upon cooling because it has a higher melting point (which means it will return to a solid first when cooling) b/c it has polar bonds which are harder to break than the non-polar bonds of H_2 + N_2.

9. Identify two examples of how hydrogen bonding between molecules makes life on Earth possible.

10. Iodine is a non-polar diatomic molecule, yet its molecules have enough attraction for each other that the element exists as a solid at room temperature. Identify the attractive force and explain why it is strong enough to keep the molecules of I_2 attached to each other even at room temperature.

induced-dip to induced-dip: it is strong enough if enough I_2's are attached to each other, creating a lot of LDF

11. Ionic compounds such as NaCl have very high melting points because a great deal of energy is required to overcome the many attractive forces between the oppositely charged ions in an ionic crystal lattice. NaCl melts at 801°C, yet its ions will readily separate from each other at room temperature when the solid is added to water. Explain this by discussing the predominant force that allows an ionic compound to dissolve in water.

12. Complete the following table:

Lewis Structure	AX_mE_n Notation	Shape of Molecule (Name and Diagram)	Type of Intermolecular Force Acting Between Molecules
(a) 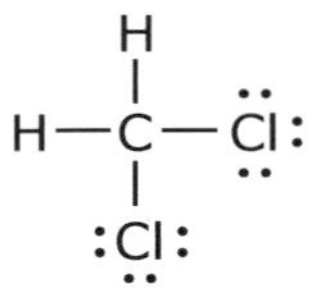 H_2CCl_2 Lewis structure (H—C—Cl with H above, Cl below; lone pairs on each Cl) dichloromethane			
(b) 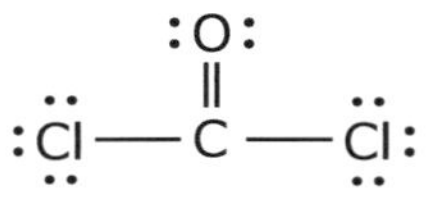 $COCl_2$ Lewis structure (O=C double bond, Cl—C—Cl; lone pairs on O and each Cl) phosgene			
(c) 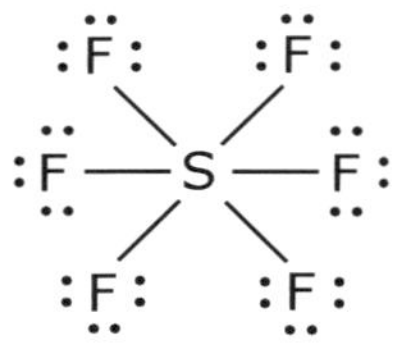 SF_6 Lewis structure (six F bonded to S; lone pairs on each F) sulphur hexafluoride			
(d) 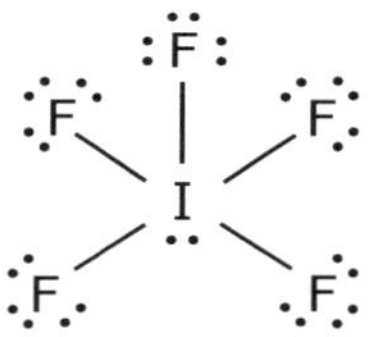 IF_5 Lewis structure (five F bonded to I, one lone pair on I; lone pairs on each F) iodine pentafluoride			

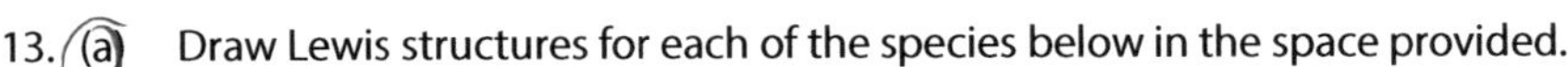

13. (a) Draw Lewis structures for each of the species below in the space provided.

(b) State the shape and the central atom hybridization for each.

1: sp^3 bent 2: sp^3d^2 square pyramid 3: square planar 4: trigonal planar 5: octahedral 6: square planar

(c) Consider the polarity of the bonds in each molecule and then determine whether there is a molecular dipole.

1: np 2: p 3: np 4: p 5: p 6: p

(d) Indicate the number of sigma and/or pi bonds in each molecule or ion.

1: 2s, 2: 5s 3: 4s 4: 3s 5: 6s 6: 4s s = sigma p = pi

(e) Assign formal charges to each atom in each of the species.

1 SCl_2

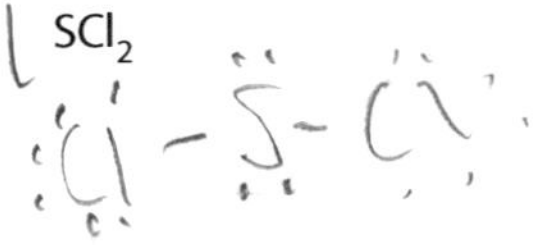

$2(7) + 6 = 20 - 4 = 16$

S: $6 - (4+2) = 0$

Cl: $7 - (6+1) = 0$

2 TeF_5^-

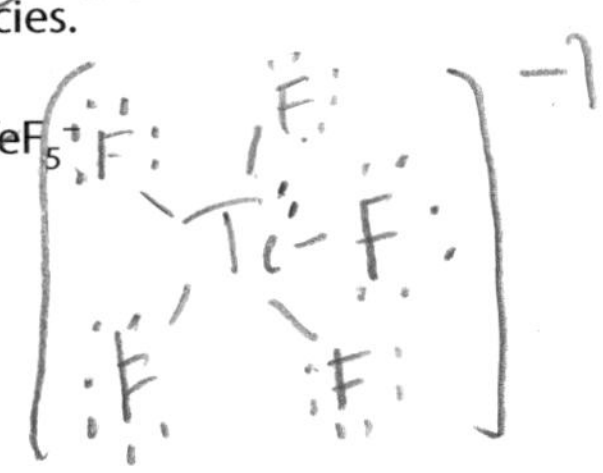

$6 + 5(7) = 41 + 1 = 42 - 10 = 32$

Te: $6 - (5+2) = -1$

F: $7 - (1+6) = 0$

3 XeF_4

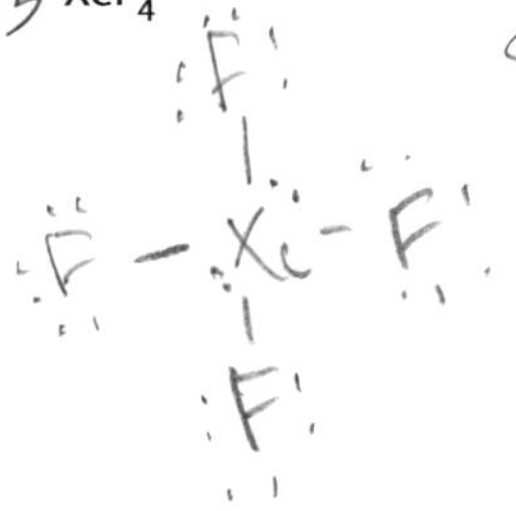

$8 + 4(7) = 36 - 8 = 28$

Xe: $8 - (4+4) = 0$

F: $7 - (6+1) = 0$

4 CO_3^{-2}

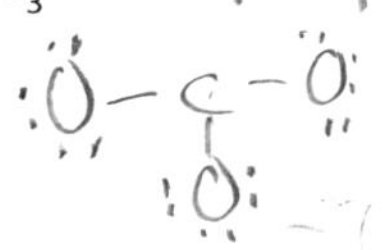

$4 + 3(6) = 22 + 2 = 24 - 6 = 18$

C: $4 - (3+0) = 1$

O: $6 - (6+1) = -1$

5 IOF_5

$7 + 6 + 5(7) = 48 - 12 = 36$

I: $7 - (6+0) = 1$

O: $6 - (6+1) = -1$

F: $7 - (6+1) = 0$

6 IF_4^+

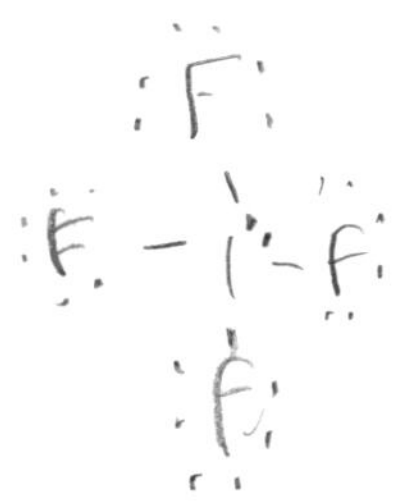

$7 + 4(7) = 35 - 1 = 34 - 8 = 26$

I: $7 - (4+2) = 1$

F: $7 - (6+1) = 0$

6.7 Molecular Orbital Theory

Warm Up

1. What advantages does the valence bond (hybridization) theory have over the Lewis dot (VSEPR) theory as a way of describing covalent chemical bonds?

2. Can you think of some limitations of the valence bond theory?

Advantages of the Valance Bond Theory and Hybridization

The VSEPR theory and Lewis structures provide a simple method for predicting molecular shapes and molecular polarity. VSEPR theory does not explain *why* bonds exist between atoms or why resonance structures, which are drawn with one single and one double bond, actually have identical bonds that are the same length. The concept of hybridization and the development of valence bond theory extended Lewis's idea of covalent bonds to the realm of atomic orbitals predicted by quantum mechanics.

According to the valence bond theory, two atoms that form a covalent bond come close enough together that their partially filled outermost atomic orbitals overlap. A stable molecule is formed when the nuclei of the two atoms are separated by a distance at which the repulsions between the nuclei are balanced by the attractions between the nucleus of one of the atoms and the bonding electrons of the other atom. This optimum distance between two bonded nuclei in any covalent bond occurs at the lowest potential energy state of the system as two atoms approach one another. Figure 6.7.1 shows the change in potential energy versus the distance between two hydrogen atoms involved in the formation of a diatomic H_2 molecule.

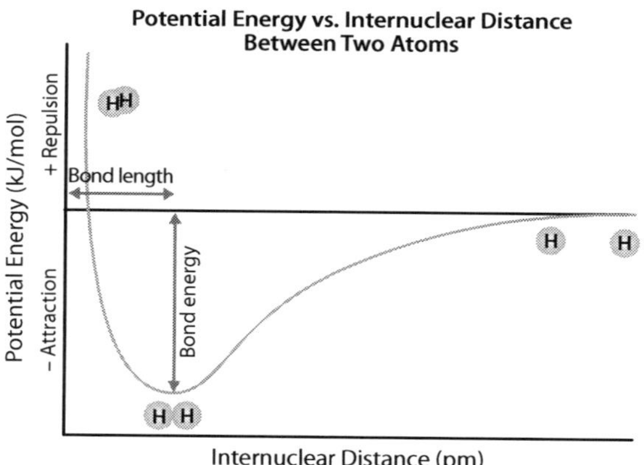

Figure 6.7.1 *The relationship between potential energy and distance in the formation of a diatomic H_2 molecule.*

If you examine this graph from the *right* to the *left*, you will notice that when two atoms are far enough apart, there is virtually *no change* in their potential energy as they neither attract nor repel one another. However, as they get closer together, the overlap between their 1s orbitals increases, the potential energy of the system begins to decrease, and this leads to increased bond stability. Should the atoms approach one another even more, a sudden increase in energy would occur, as the repulsive forces between the nuclei would suddenly exceed the attractive forces between the nuclei and the bonding electrons. Notice that the point at which attractive and repulsive forces are perfectly balanced is the point where the system's potential energy reaches a minimum and hence the molecule is most stable. This point may be used to determine both *bond energy* and *bond length*.

According to the Lewis theory, a covalent bond forms when atoms share their outer shell electrons. In valence bond theory, the valence atomic orbital of one atom merges with that of another to form a new **hybrid bonding orbital** that shares a region of space (also called a **domain**) in which two electrons of opposite spin may exist, forming a covalent bond. It is important to recall that hybrid orbitals may also contain non-bonding electrons or lone pairs.

Limitations of the Valence Bond Theory

The molecular orbital (MO) model enhances our ability to predict molecular structures. Other theories do not adequately apply to molecules with unpaired electrons or molecules with an odd numbers of electrons. Molecular orbital theory accurately predicts *bond energy, bond length, bond order,* and *paramagnetism* or *diamagnetism* in a molecule. MOT also offers a better explanation for the spectral data obtained when electrons move between energy levels in molecules and ions.

Molecular orbitals are formed from the atomic orbitals of the atoms in a molecule. The number of molecular orbitals is *conserved*. This means that two atomic orbitals combine to form two molecular orbitals. Molecular orbitals, like atomic orbitals, may hold a maximum of two electrons, each with opposite spins. This is consistent with the Pauli exclusion principle as described in section 5.4 of this book.

Given a pair of molecular orbitals the first orbital will always have a lower potential energy and hence be more stable. The first orbital is designated a bonding orbital. The second orbital of the pair will have a higher potential energy and be unstable. It is called an antibonding orbital. Antibonding orbitals are specified with an asterisk (Figure 6.7.2). As in valence bond theory, molecular orbitals formed through the overlap of orbitals along the *x*-axis, for example overlapping s or p_x atomic orbitals, form sigma (σ) bonding or sigma* (σ*) antibonding molecular orbitals while overlap of p_y or p_z orbitals form pi (π) bonding or pi* (π*) antibonding molecular orbitals (Figure 6.7.3). Note that, σ* is generally read as "sigma star." In keeping with the particle-wave duality exhibited by electrons, we can see that a σ bonding molecular orbital is the result of *constructive* addition of atomic orbitals with increased electron density between the nuclei. *Destructive* orbital addition results in a node with minimal electron density between the nuclei in a σ* antibonding molecular orbital.

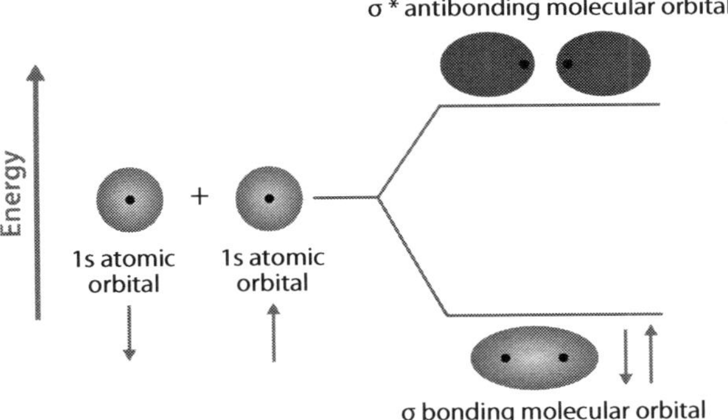

Figure 6.7.2 *Bonding and antibonding molecular orbitals: Two s atomic orbitals overlap to form two molecular orbitals. The lower energy, more stable orbital is called a "bonding" orbital. The higher energy, unstable orbital is called an "antibonding" orbital and is designated with an asterisk, *.*

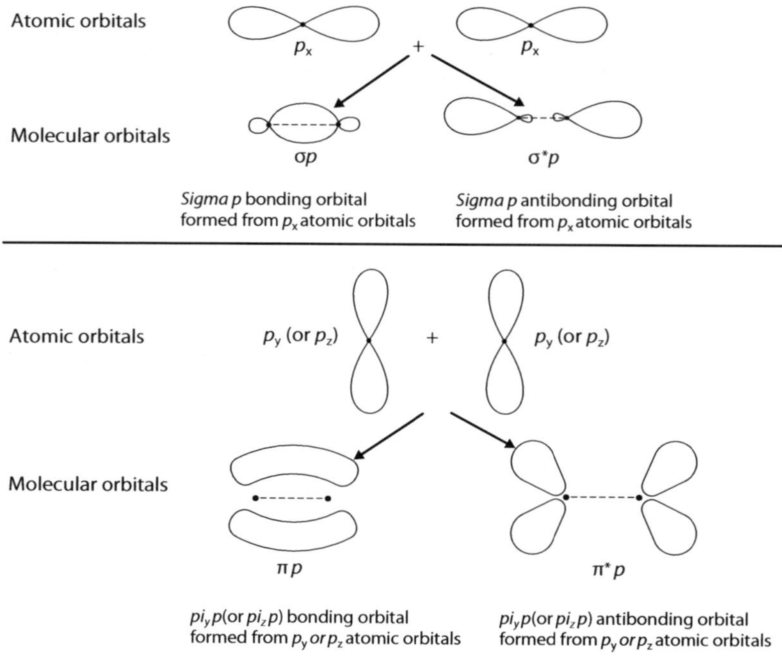

Figure 6.7.3 *Atomic orbital overlap that describes a molecular orbital: Two p_x atomic orbitals combine to form two σp orbitals, one bonding and one antibonding. The p_y and p_z atomic orbitals combine to form π bonding and antibonding orbitals. The bonding orbitals have a lower potential energy and more stability than antibonding orbitals. Antibonding orbitals are always designated with * (pronounced "star").*

The Molecular Orbital Diagram

A molecular orbital diagram provides information about bond order, bond length, bond energy, and magnetic behaviour. It is drawn in a similar fashion to an atomic orbital diagram (see section 5.4), although it is usually shown between the atomic orbital diagrams that combine to produce it. The diagrams are generally presented vertically. It is important to keep the Aufbau principle (see section 5.4) in mind as molecular orbitals, like atomic orbitals, are filled in order from lowest to highest potential energy. For simplicity, we will stick to diatomic species in the examples presented in this book. Hydrogen is a simple *homonuclear* species. Its molecular orbital diagram is depicted by the combination of two monoatomic hydrogen atoms, as shown in Figure 6.7.4.

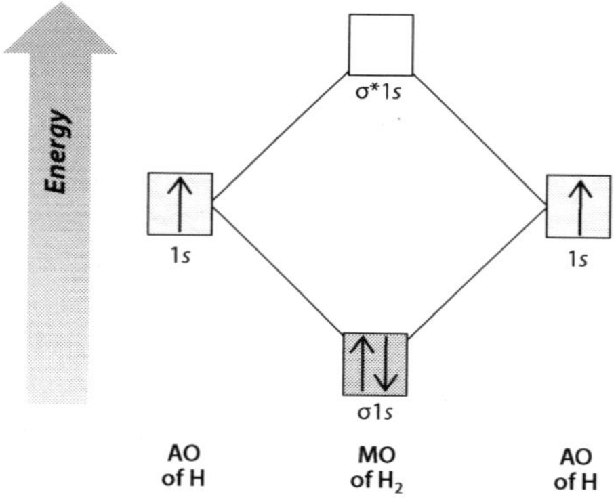

Figure 6.7.4 *Molecular orbital diagram of diatomic hydrogen*

$$\text{bond order} = \frac{\text{number of bonding } e^- - \text{number of antibonding } e^-}{2}$$

The calculated *bond order* is analogous to the *number of bonds* between atoms.

The bond order for a hydrogen molecule is (2 – 0)/2 = 1. A bond order of 1 indicates the bond is a single bond. A bond order of 2 would indicate a double bond and 3, a triple bond. Quadruple bonds do not occur. A bond order of zero, would indicate an impossible bond. Bonds form when there are more bonding electrons than non-bonding electrons. This is an indication of stability.

Fractional bond orders are indicative of **resonance** (see section 6.4). In a benzene ring, C_6H_6, the bond order between any pair of carbon atoms is 1.5, indicating that each bond between two carbon atoms consists of *delocalized electrons* shared over the entire six-sided ring. When the bond lengths are measured, all six bonds have the same length. Benzene rings are often drawn with alternating double and single bonds (Figure 6.7.5). If the bonds were actually alternating single and double bonds, the bonds' lengths would be different. In fact, the bonds' lengths are equal and, as the bond order of 1.5 indicates, the bond length is proportional to that of one and a half carbon-carbon single bonds.

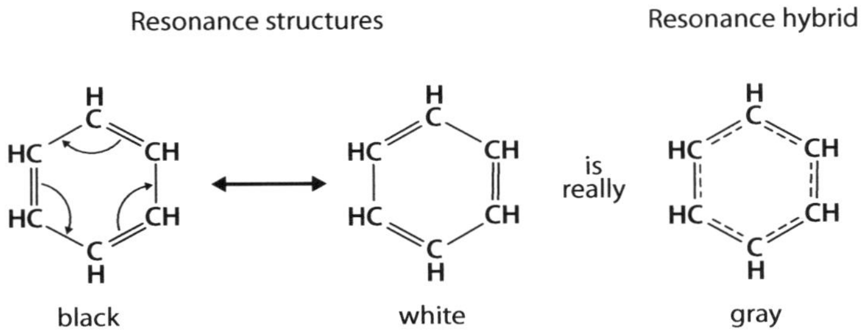

Resonance structures | Resonance hybrid

black ⟷ white is really gray

Figure 6.7.5 *Carbon-carbon bonding in the benzene ring*

Bond order is directly proportional to *bond energy.*
and
Bond order is *inversely* proportional to *bond length.*

Triple bonds are shorter, due to more orbital overlap, and are higher in energy and stronger than double bonds, which are, in turn, shorter and stronger than single bonds.

Filling Order for Molecular Orbitals

Molecular orbitals follow the same rules as atomic orbitals as they fill with electrons. **Hund's rule** (see section 5.4) states that electrons fill orbitals in an energy sublevel individually before they pair up. The **Aufbau principle** states that the lower energy orbitals will fill first. The tricky part is, which orbitals are lowest in energy and is the pattern always the same? As is often the case in science, rules can have exceptions. Molecular orbitals fill as you might expect (σ before π) with the exception of three homonuclear diatomic elements. These elements are B_2, C_2, and N_2. In the case of these three elements, their small atomic radius leads to 2s and 2p orbital interactions such that the σ2s orbital has a *lower* potential energy and the σ2p has a *higher* potential energy leading to an irregular filling order. The filling order for diatomic boron to diatomic neon is depicted in Figure 6.7.6. The irregularity occurs only in the just-mentioned three elements. They are included here merely for the sake of interest. *The AP exam does not expect students to memorize these irregularities in filling order, so please don't waste grey matter doing so.

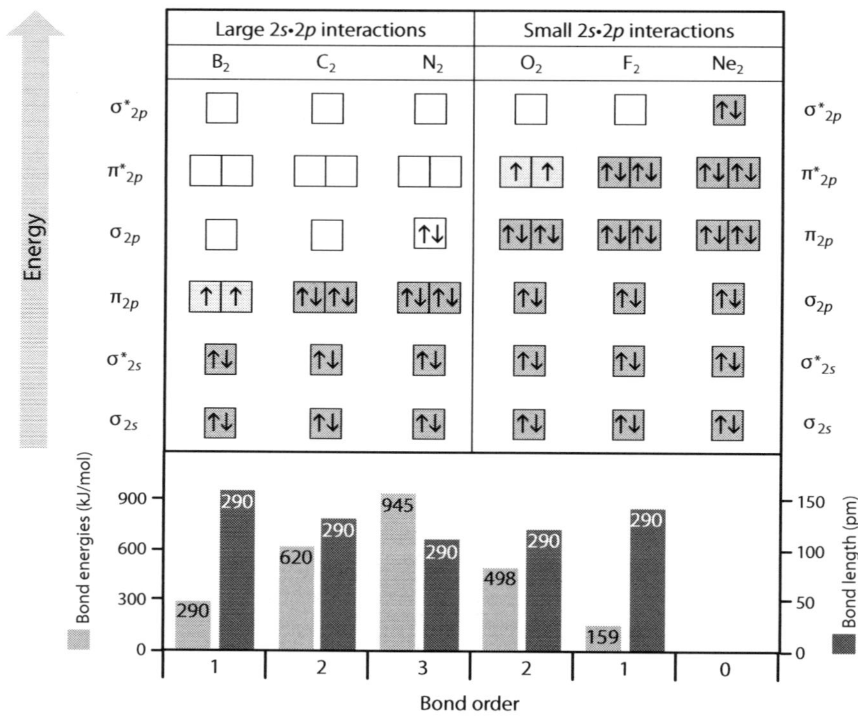

Figure 6.7.6 *Filling order of diatomic elements: Interactions between electrons in the small diameter diatomic elements B_2, C_2 and N_2 explains the differences in the filling order of these molecules.*

Sample Problem — Drawing and Interpreting a Molecular Orbital Diagram

Draw a molecular orbital diagram for the Li_2 molecule. What is its bond order? What does this indicate about the bonding and the stability of the molecule?

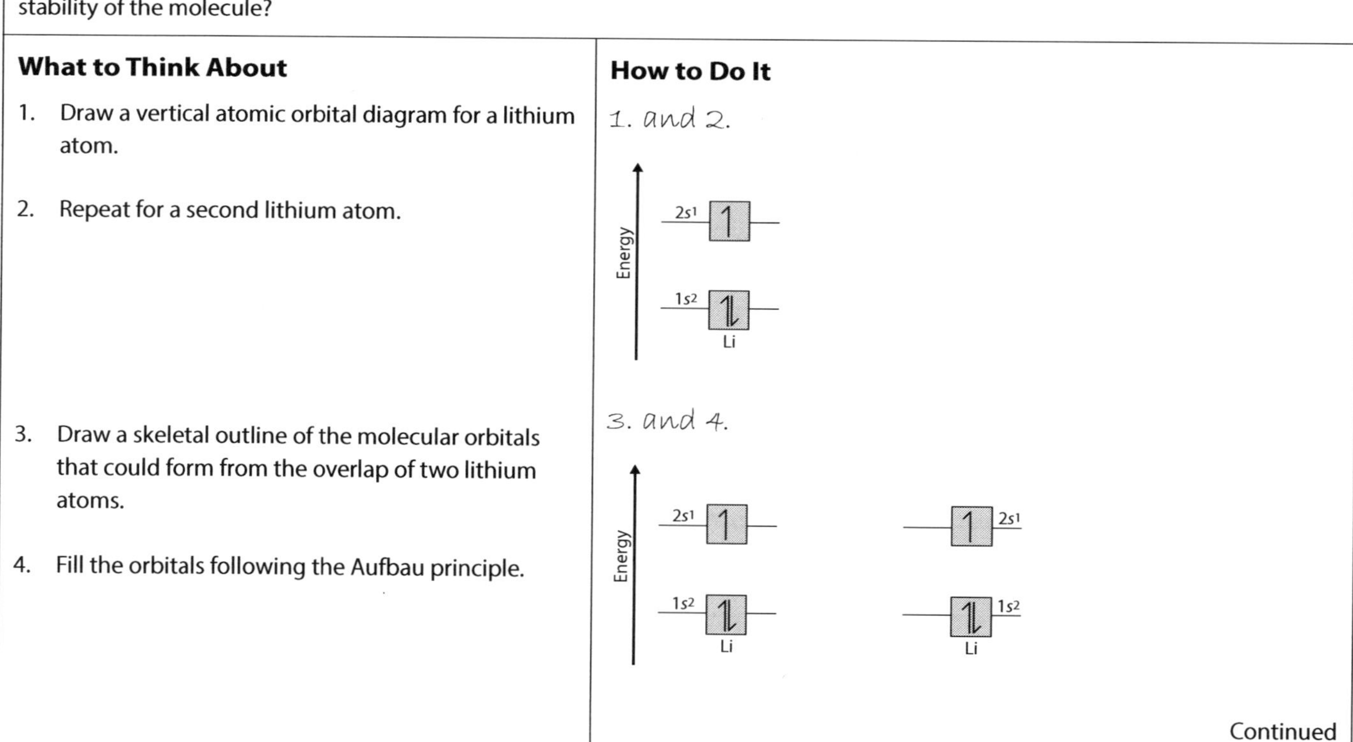

Sample Problem — Continued

What to Think About

5. Calculate the bond order and comment on its meaning.

How to Do It

5. Bond Order

$\frac{4 - 2}{2} = 1$

The molecule contains a single bond and is stable.

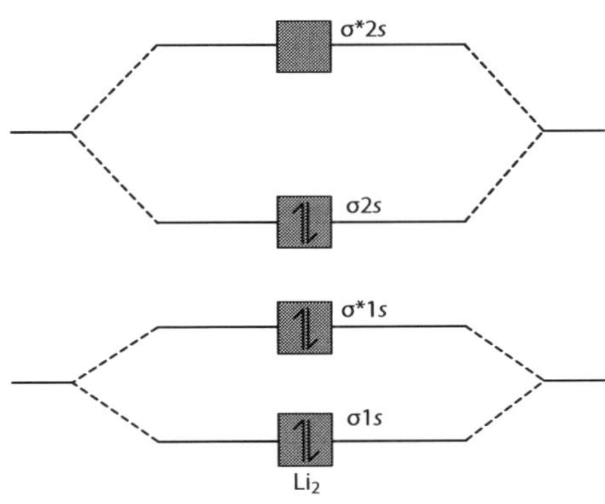

Practice Problems — Drawing Molecular Orbital Diagrams and Calculating Bond Order

Draw the molecular orbital diagram for the following molecules and determine the bond order of the covalent bond in each. Note that heteronuclear diatomic molecules involving atoms adjacent to one another in the periodic table contain atoms that are so similar their molecular orbital diagrams are drawn in the same way as those for homonuclear diatomic molecules.

1. Be_2

2. CO

3. NO

Molecular Orbital Diagrams for Larger Molecules and Ions

Molecular orbital diagrams for larger molecules and ions often do not include the core electrons. This is because the cores of such molecules contain equal numbers of bonding and antibonding electrons and so the effects of these electrons cancel out.

Sample Problem — Drawing and Interpreting a Larger Molecular Orbital Diagram

Draw a molecular orbital diagram for a fluorine molecule, F_2. What is its bond order? What does this indicate regarding the type of bond in fluorine?

What To Think About	How To Do It
1. Draw an orbital diagram for fluorine.	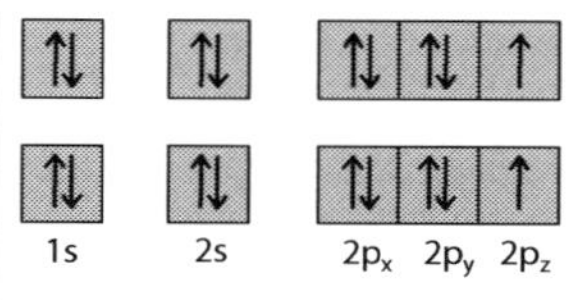
2. Draw a vertical version of two fluorine atoms with empty molecular orbitals in between. ore electrons (n=1) need not be shown.	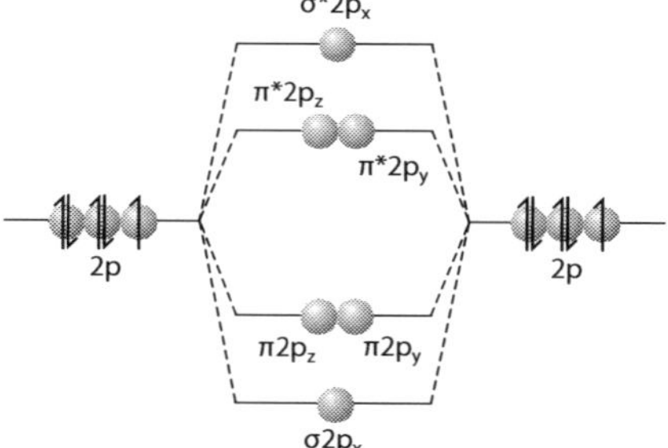 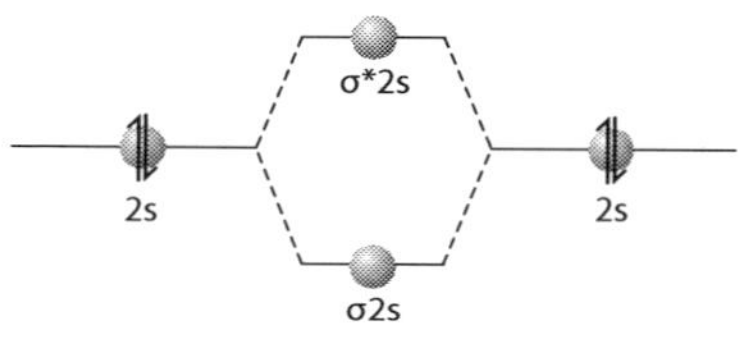
3. Sum the atomic electrons to determine the number of molecular electrons to be placed in the diagram.	7 + 7 = 14 valence electrons in total to be placed in the molecular orbitals in the diagram
4. Place these electrons into the molecular orbitals.	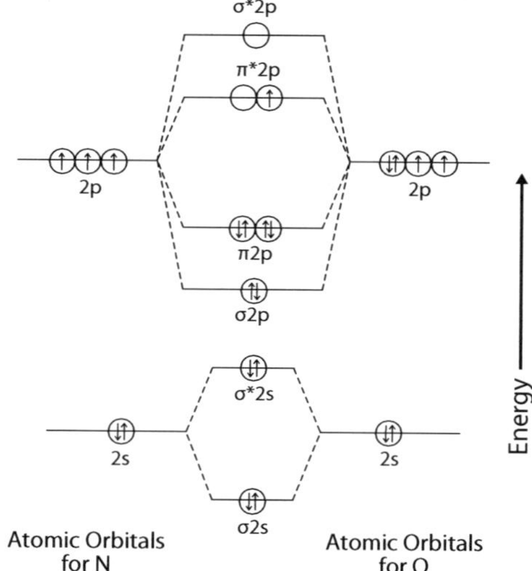
5. Calculate the bond order and describe the resulting bond.	Bond order = $\frac{8-6}{2}$ = 1 thus the bond is **single** and the molecule is stable.

Molecular orbital diagrams for ions are drawn in the same way as uncharged molecules except that electrons are added or removed from the molecular orbitals to account for the ion's charge.

Quick Check

1. Draw a Lewis diagram of the ions NO^- and NO^+.

2. Draw MO diagrams of the ions NO^- and NO^+.

3. Calculate the bond order for the uncharged molecule and each of the ions. Compare types of bond, their strengths and their lengths for the two ions.

4. How do the bonds predicted by the Lewis structures compare to those predicted by MO theory?

Paramagnetism

One of the first problems that surfaced with the valence bond theory was its inability to properly predict paramagnetism. Substances that are paramagnetic are attracted to a magnetic field. Substances that are not paramagnetic are diamagnetic. Diamagnetic substances are weakly repelled by a magnetic field.

Paramagnetic substances are attracted to a magnetic field due to the presence of *unpaired* electrons in their electronic configuration.

Quick Check

1. Draw a Lewis structure for O_2 gas.

2. Draw a molecular orbital diagram for O_2 gas.

3. Which of the species in the Practice Problems on page 405 are diamagnetic? What about the ions in the Quick Check on page 407?

Molecular Models: A Summary

In sections 6.3 through 6.6, we have examined a variety of models that describe the bonding that occurs in covalent molecules. Lewis structures provide a foundation for understanding covalent bonds. VSEPR and valence bond theory explain how electrons in hybridized orbitals repel one another to produce different molecular geometries. Molecular orbital theory provides more insight into the stability of covalent bonds. The behaviour of coordination compounds containing partially filled d-orbital electrons require yet another bonding theory called crystal field theory in which the normally degenerate d orbitals split into different energies depending on the spatial orientation of these orbitals. Movement of electrons between these different energy d orbitals manifests a variety of beautiful colours in coordination compounds. It is important to remember that all of these descriptions of the bonding in molecules and ions are models. No model is perfect, but each has something to contribute to our understanding of chemical bonding.

6.7 Review Questions

1. Compare and contrast molecular and atomic orbitals.

2. Compare and contrast bonding and antibonding molecular orbitals.

3. Use the following MO diagram of Li_2 to sketch the Li_2^+ and the Li_2^- ions. Calculate the bond order of all three species. Compare the stability, bond strength, bond length, and magnetic properties of each of the species.

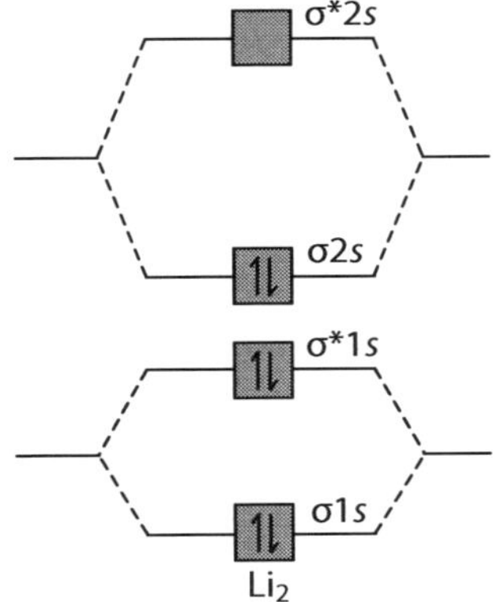

4. Give two species, one uncharged, and one anion that could have the following electron configuration (determined from an MO diagram):
$(\sigma 3s)^2(\sigma 3s^*)^2(\sigma 3p)^2(\pi 3p)^4(\pi 3p^*)^4$

5. (a) What compound is represented by the following MO diagram?

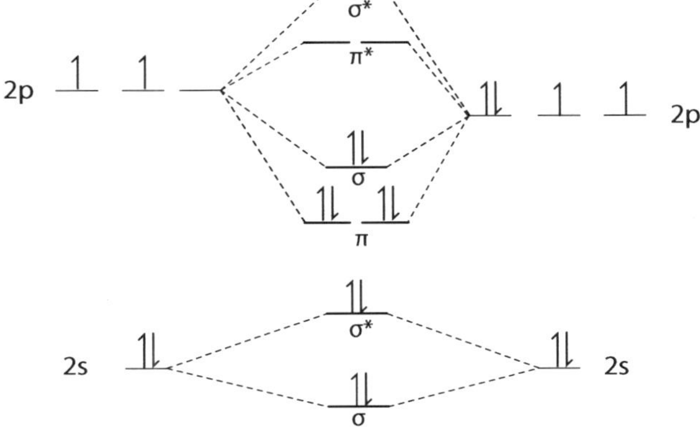

(b) Calculate the bond order of this compound. What does this suggest about the bonding in the compound? Why are the π2p orbitals being filled before the σ2p orbital?

6. The portion of the atmosphere that lies approximately 100 km above Earth's surface is called the ionosphere. In addition to the two principal gases, N_2 and O_2, found in air, there is a significant amount of NO gas along with ions of all three species present at this altitude.

(a) Use MOT to compare the bond orders of the (+1) cations of these three gases to their uncharged molecules.

(b) How does ionization affect the magnetic behaviour of each of these species?

7. Use the following outline to diagram the species C_2, C_2^-, and C_2^+. Determine the bond orders of each and indicate whether they are stable.

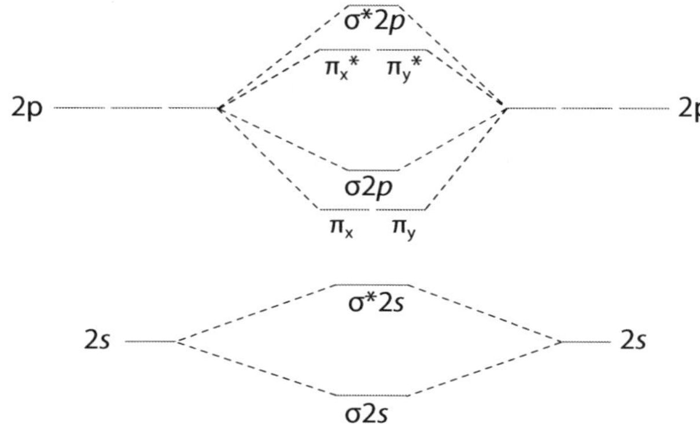

8. Use MOT and calculate bond order to predict whether each of the following molecules or ions exists in a relatively stable form.

(a) H_2^{2-}

(b) Ar_2

(c) He_2^{2+}

(d) F_2^{2-}

7 Solution Chemistry

This chapter focuses on the following AP Big Ideas from the College Board:

Big Idea 2: Chemical and physical properties of materials can be explained by the structure and the arrangement of atoms, ions, or molecules and the forces between them.
Big Idea 3: Changes in matter involve the rearrangement and/or reorganization of atoms and/or the transfer of electrons.

By the end of this chapter, you should be able to do the following:

- Distinguish between a solution and a pure substance
- Predict the relative solubility of a solute in a solvent, based on its polarity
- Relate ion formation to electrical conductivity in aqueous solutions
- Calculate the concentration of ions in solution

By the end of this chapter you should know the meaning of these **key terms**:

- acid-base neutralization
- dissociation equation
- electrical conductivity
- ion charge
- ionization equation
- molarity
- molar solution
- mole
- non-polar
- polar
- solute
- solution
- solvent

The interactions of solutes and solvents create solutions with a wide range of useful properties.

7.1 The Nature of Solutions

Warm Up

Below is a list of common substances. Classify each as a pure substance or mixture by placing a checkmark in the appropriate column:

	Pure Substance	Mixture
Car exhaust		
Tap water		
Carbon dioxide		
Freshly squeezed orange juice		
Stainless steel		
Tea		
Diamond		
Cigarette smoke		

Solutions

In the Warm Up above, most of the substances are mixtures. In chapter 2, you learned to classify matter as a pure substance or mixture. Pure substances are either elements or compounds. You can write a chemical formula for a pure substance. A mixture contains two or more components mixed in a variety of proportions. The components can be separated by physical means. There are many types of mixtures: suspensions, colloids, and mechanical mixtures. In this chapter, we will be looking more closely at a specific type of mixture: a solution.

A **solution** is a homogeneous mixture that exists in one phase. It has a uniform composition throughout the sample on a macroscopic level and retains some of the properties of its components. For example, a sample of ocean water is a mixture of water, salts, and other dissolved substances. It looks the same throughout and has some properties of its components such as a salty taste.

A solution is made up of a solute and a solvent. The **solute** is the substance that is dissolved in the solvent. The **solvent** is the substance that dissolves one or more solutes in a solution. More than one type of solute can be dissolved in the solvent. In a solution of salt water, the salts are the solutes and the water is the solvent. Typically the solvent is the substance in the mixture in the greatest quantity, and the solute is the component in the solution in the lesser quantity.

For some solutions, the components can be mixed in any proportion to give a homogeneous mixture. In this case, we say that the components are **miscible**. This means they are soluble in any proportion. For example, we can mix water and alcohol in any proportion to form a solution. Alcohol and water are miscible. When we mix corn oil and water together, they do not mix in any proportion. We say that vegetable oil and water are **immiscible** (Figure 7.1.1).

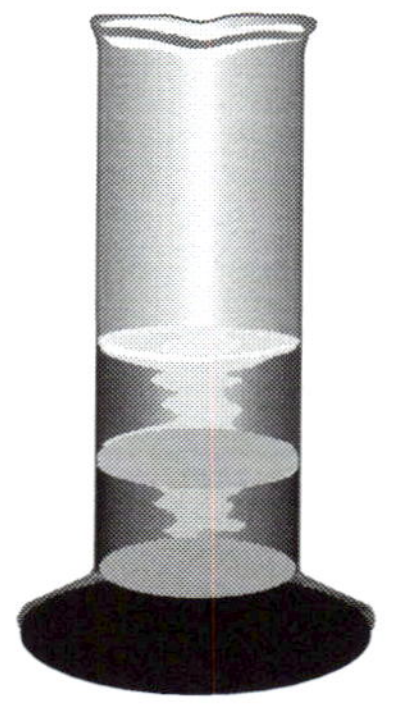

Figure 7.1.1 *Immiscible liquids do not mix. The liquids are corn oil (above) and water (below)..*

A solution can exist in any of the three phases: solid, liquid, or gas. The table below summarizes examples of solutions:

State of Solute	State of Solvent	State of Solution	Example
gas	gas	gas	air
gas	liquid	liquid	carbonated water
gas	solid	solid	hydrogen in palladium
liquid	liquid	liquid	alcohol in water
liquid	solid	solid	mercury in silver amalgam
solid	liquid	liquid	sugar in water
solid	solid	solid	alloys such as brass, a solution of copper and zinc

Quick Check

In the warm up activity, you classified the substances as pure substances or mixtures. For the substances that you classified as mixtures, list the ones that are solutions.

____

Water: The Most Common Solvent

Many chemical reactions occur in solutions. If the solvent is water, we call it an **aqueous** solution. Important reactions happening in your body and many reactions used in your everyday life are aqueous reactions.

A solute that dissolves in a solvent is said to be **soluble.** For example, NaCl is soluble in water.

The **solubility** of a substance is the maximum amount of solute that will dissolve in a given amount of solvent at a particular temperature.

There are many units of solubility including:

- molarity (M): moles of solute/litres of solution
- grams of solute/mL of solution
- grams of solute/100 g water
- ppm: parts per million

When the solubility is given as a molarity, we call it the **molar solubility**.

Sample Problem — Converting Between Units of Solubility

The solubility of $CaSO_4$ is 1.1 g/L at 25°C. Calculate its molar solubility.

What to Think about	How to Do It
1. We need to convert between mass and moles of solute. To do this, use the molar mass of $CaSO_4$.	The molar mass of $CaSO_4$ is 136.1 g/mol.
2. The molar solubility is measured using units mol/L or M.	$M = \frac{1.1\ \cancel{g}}{1\ L} \times \frac{1\ mol}{136.1\ \cancel{g}} = 8.1 \times 10^{-3}\ M$ The molar solubility is 8.1×10^{-3} M.

Practice Problems — Converting Between Units of Solubility

1. The molar solubility of $SrCO_3$ is 2.4×10^{-5} M at 25°C. What is its solubility in g/L?

2. The solubility of Ag_3AsO_4 is 1.4×10^{-6} M at 25°C. What is its solubility in g/mL?

3. If 500 mL of a saturated solution of AgCl contains 9.3×10^{-4} g AgCl, what is its molar solubility?

4. The solubility of $Cu(IO_3)_2$ is 2.6×10^{-3} M at 25°C. What mass of dissolved solute is present in 250 mL of solution?

Determining Whether or Not a Solute will Dissolve in Water

Recall that a salt is an ionic compound made up of a cation and anion. Substances that do not dissolve in a given solvent are **insoluble**. For example, carbon is insoluble in water.

Some salts dissolve better in water than others. To predict the solubility of some salts, we can use a solubility table like Table 7.1.1. As you examine this table, note the following:

- The word "soluble" means that more than 0.1 mol of solute will dissolve in 1.0 L of solution at 25°C.
- "Low solubility" means that less than 0.1 mol of solute will dissolve in 1.0 L of solution at 25°C. This does not mean that this substance is insoluble; just that very little can dissolve.
- The alkali ions are listed individually at the top of the table in the first row. Farther down the table, they are simply referred to as "alkali ions."

Table 7.1.1 *Solubility of Common Compounds in Water*

Note: *In this table, soluble means* > 0.1 mol/L at 25°C.

Negative Ions (Anions)	Positive Ions (Cations)	Solubility of Compounds
All	Alkali ions: Li^+, Na^+, K^+, Rb^+, Cs^+, Fr^+	Soluble
All	Hydrogen ion: H^+	Soluble
All	Ammonium ion: NH_4^+	Soluble
Nitrate: NO_3^-	All	Soluble
Chloride: Cl^- Or Bromide: Br^- Or Iodide: I^-	All others	Soluble
	Ag^+, Pb^{2+}, Cu^+	Low solubility
Sulphate: SO_4^{2-}	All others	Soluble
	Ag^+, Ca^{2+}, Sr^{2+}, Ba^{2+}, Pb^{2+}	Low solubility
Sulphide: S^{2-}	Alkali ions, H^+, NH_4^+, Be^{2+}, Mg^{2+}, Ca^{2+}, Sr^{2+}, Ba^{2+}	Soluble
	All others	Low solubility
Hydroxide: OH^-	Alkali ions, H^+, NH_4^+, Sr^{2+}	Soluble
	All others	Low solubility
Phosphate: PO_4^{3-} Or Carbonate: CO_3^{2-} Or Sulphite: SO_3^{2-}	Alkali ions, H^+, NH_4^+	Soluble
	All others	Low solubility

also means insoluble (<0.1 mol/L)

Quick Check

1. What is an anion? A cation?
an anion is a − charged ion, cation is +
2. Salts containing which cations are always soluble? first group metals
3. Salts containing which anion are always soluble? NO_3^-
4. Salts containing which anions have a low solubility most often? S^{2-}, OH^-, PO_4^{3-}, CO_3^{2-}, SO_3^{2-}

Sample Problem — Predicting the Relative Solubility of Salts in Water

According to the solubility table (Table 7.1.1), is AgCl soluble in water, or does it have a low solubility?

What to Think about	How to Do It
1. Identify the anion in the salt.	The anion is chloride: Cl^-
2. On the table, find the anion, then read across from that anion and find the cation in the salt.	The cation is Ag^+
3. If it is soluble, then the salt has a solubility greater than 0.1 M. If it has a low solubility, then its solubility is less than 0.1 M.	AgCl has a low solubility in water.

Practice Problems — Predicting the Relative Solubility of Salts in Water

For the following salts, use the solubility table (Table 7.1.1) to predict whether they are soluble (S), or have a low solubility (LS):

1. NaCl	S	6. zinc sulphite	LS
2. $CaCO_3$	LS	7. ammonium hydroxide	S
3. $CuCl_2$	S	8. cesium phosphate	S
4. $Al_2(SO_4)_3$	S	9. copper(I) chloride	LS
5. BaS	LS	10. chromium(III) nitrate	S

Saturated and Unsaturated Solutions

A solution is **unsaturated** when the solute is completely dissolved in the solvent. Consider making a solution of NaCl in water. At the beginning, you add a small amount of NaCl to the water, and the NaCl completely dissolves. The solution is unsaturated. As you add more NaCl, it continues to dissolve. At a certain point, as you add NaCl, no more will dissolve. A **saturated** solution is one in which no more solid will dissolve. For the solution to be saturated, there must be undissolved solid in the solution. Some solutions can be **supersaturated**. In these solutions, there is more dissolved solute than there would normally be. Supersaturated solutions are very unstable. They can be made by preparing a more concentrated solution at a higher temperature, then slowly cooling the solution (Figure 7.1.1).

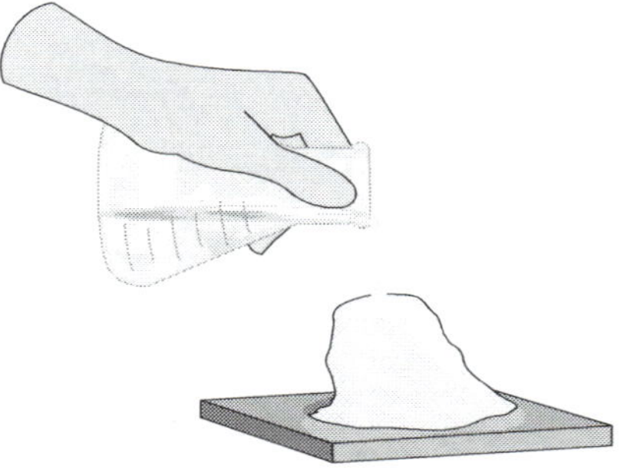

Figure 7.1.1 *As the supersaturated solution of sodium acetate trihydrate is slowly poured onto a plate, it immediately crystallizes as the solid solute reforms*

7.1 Activity: Change in Solubility with Temperature

Question

How does the solubility of different salts change with temperature?

Background

You have probably observed that you can dissolve more salt in hot water than in cold water because the solubility of a substance changes with temperature. The solubility of some salts in water as a function of temperature is shown in the graph below. Each line on the graph represents a different salt.

From the graph, you can see that different salts have very different solubilities in water. For example, at 100°C, the solubility of NaCl in water is 6.7 M while for AgCl it is 1.4×10^{-4} M. In the example above, AgCl has a low solubility compared to NaCl.

Procedure

1. Use this graph to answer the questions below. The graph represents the solubility of a number of different salts in water. Note the units of solubility given on the *y*-axis.

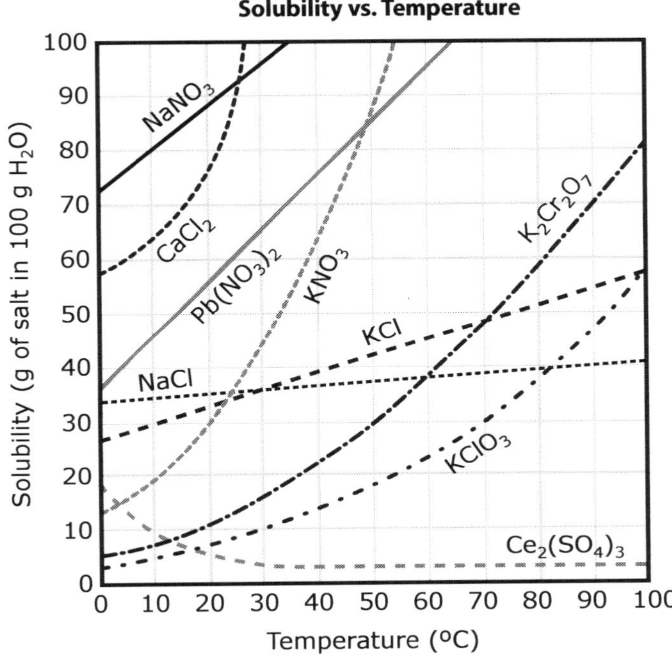

Results and Discussion

1. Which salt has the highest solubility at 5°C? At 28°C?

____

2. Does the salt with the lowest solubility at 0°C have the lowest solubility at 90°C?

____

3. Complete this sentence:
   As the temperature increases, the solubility of most salts ____________. (increases or decreases)

4. For which salt does the amount of solute dissolved decrease as temperature increase?

7.1 Review Questions

1. Define homogeneous, heterogeneous, pure substance, and mixture. Give an example for each.

2. Classify the following as a pure substance or a mixture. If it is a mixture, then state whether or not it is a solution.

   (a) distilled water

   (b) 9 carat gold

   (c) gasoline

   (d) wood

   (e) bronze

   (f) chocolate chip ice cream

   (g) coffee

   (h) coal

3. Complete the following sentences using the terms solute, solvent, miscible, and immiscible.
   A solution is composed of a __________ and __________.
   The __________ is the substance that makes up the larger part of the solution. If two components can be mixed in any proportions to make a homogeneous mixture, they are __________.

4. Give an example of two substances that are immiscible when mixed. Describe what you would see if you mixed them together.

5. When the solubility of a substance is given, what information must be specified?

6. The molar solubility of lead(II) bromide is 2.6×10^{-3} M. What is its solubility in g/ml?

7. A saturated solution contains 0.0015g CaC_2O_4 dissolved in 250 mL solution. What is the molar solubility of CaC_2O_4?

8. The molar solubility of $AgIO_3$ is 1.8×10^{-4} M. Express its solubility in g $AgIO_3$ /mL water. Assume that the volume of solvent = volume of solution.

9. What does the term aqueous mean?

10. Using Table 7.1.1, list three salts containing the sulphide anion that would have a low solubility in water at 25°C.

11. Using Table 7.1.1, list three salts containing the anion carbonate that would be soluble at 25°C.

Na_2CO_3

K_2CO_3

H_2CO_3

12. List the cations in a salt that are soluble when paired with any anion.

H^+, Li^+, Na^+, K^+, Rb^+, Cs^+, Fr^+

13. Classify each of the following compounds as soluble or low solubility according to Table 7.1.1.

(a) H_2SO_4 S

(b) MgS S

(c) $(NH_4)_2SO_3$ S

(d) RbOH S

(e) $PbSO_4$ LS

(f) $CuBr_2$ S

(g) $Zn(NO_3)_2$ S

(h) $FeSO_4$ S

14. A student dissolves 0.53g of $LiCH_3COO$ in water at 25°C to make 100 mL of solution. Is the solution formed saturated or unsaturated? Justify your answer with calculations and by referring to Table 7.1.1.

$$\frac{.53g}{100mL} \cdot \frac{1000mL}{1L} \cdot \frac{1mol}{65.99g} =$$

.08 mol/L

unsaturated because table says < .1 mol/L for unsaturated

7.2 What Dissolves and What Doesn't — "Like Dissolves Like"

Warm Up

In chapter 6, you learned that chemical bonds *between atoms* in a molecule can be classified as ionic, polar covalent, and nonpolar covalent. These are intramolecular forces. However, there are also attractive forces *between molecules* that are called intermolecular forces. For each of the following substances, list all of the intermolecular forces present.

Substance	Intermolecular Forces Present
Example: H_2O	hydrogen bonding, dipole-dipole, dispersion forces
I_2	
HF	
PCl_3	
CH_3CH_2OH	

Like Dissolves Like

Many people take vitamins to supplement their diet. Two commonly used vitamins are vitamins A and C. Vitamin A plays an important role in maintaining vision, bone growth, and a properly functioning immune system. The most common form of vitamin A is called retinol and is found in foods from animals. Your body can store vitamin A because it is fat-soluble. This vitamin is not soluble in water so it is called "hydrophobic," which means "water hating."

Vitamin C, called ascorbic acid, is also important for your immune system and is a powerful anti-oxidant. Because your body cannot store vitamin C in your fat cells, you must get an adequate amount from your daily diet. A deficiency of vitamin C leads to a disease called scurvy. Historically, sailors on long sea voyages would get scurvy because they didn't have fresh fruit to eat. The link between scurvy and vitamin C was not made until 1932. However, sailors were treated for scurvy earlier than this with citrus fruits. Britain's Royal Navy used limes to prevent scurvy, so British sailors were called "limeys." Vitamin C is water-soluble so it is called "hydrophilic," which means "water loving."

In this section we will explore why certain substances dissolve in a particular solvent. Why does vitamin C dissolve in water but not in fat? The answer lies in the structure and intermolecular forces present in the vitamins, fat, and water.

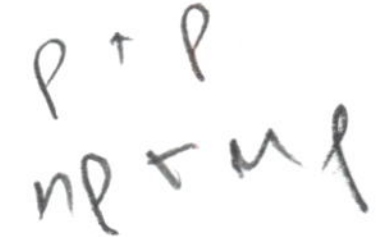

"Like dissolves like" means that a solute will dissolve in a solvent if both contain similar types of intermolecular forces and these forces are of similar magnitude.

There are three important criteria for a substance to dissolve:

1. The particles in the solute must be separated from each other to go into the solvent. The attraction between solute particles must be overcome or replaced.
2. The particles in the solvent must be separated from each other to allow space for the solute particles. The attraction between solvent particles must be overcome or replaced.
3. The solute and solvent particles must interact with each other.

An Ionic Solute in a Polar Sovent: NaCl(*s*) in water

- The solute is held together by the attraction of the positive Na+ ions to the negative Cl^- ions (Figure 7.2.1). For this solute to dissolve, the attraction between these two ions must be overcome.

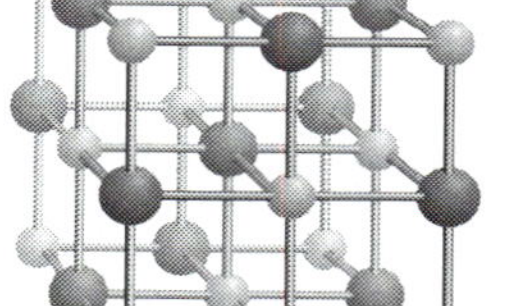

Figure 7.2.1 *NaCl crystal*

- The water molecules in the solvent are attracted to each other by hydrogen bonding. Each water molecule has a positive end and a negative end. The molecules line up and hydrogen bonds form between water molecules.

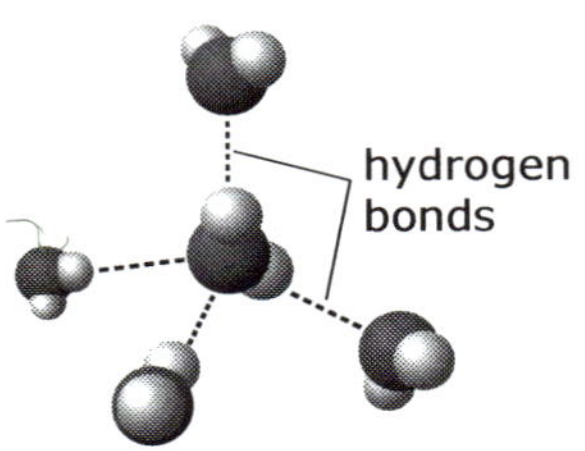

Figure 7.2.2 *Hydrogen bonding in water*

- As water molecules bump into the solid solute, the negative dipoles on the oxygen atoms are attracted to the positive ions in the solute. Likewise, the positive dipoles on the hydrogen atoms are attracted to the negative ions in the solute. Both ions become hydrated, which means they are surrounded by water molecules. The water molecules' attraction for each other and the attraction of the ions for each other are now replaced by the water molecules' attraction for each ion. Notice how the water molecules align themselves around each ion (Figure 7.2.3).

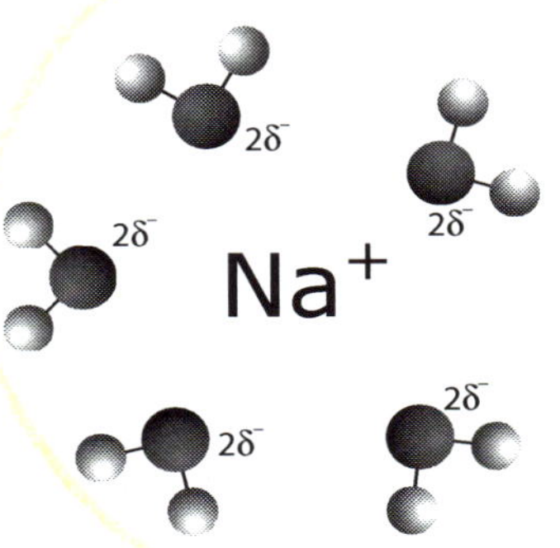

Negative dipoles on the oxygen atoms are attracted to the positive sodium ions.

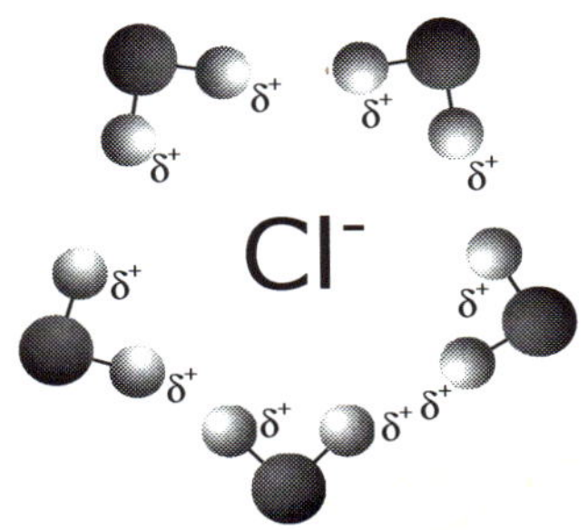

Positive dipoles on the hydrogren atoms are attracted to the negative chloride ions.

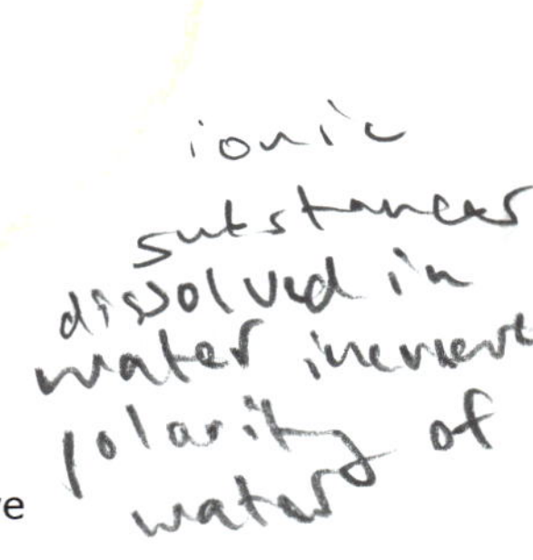

Figure 7.2.3 *Water molecules surround the ions from NaCl.*

The strong attraction of water molecules for each ion is called the **ion-dipole force.** This force is similar in size and type to the ionic attractions in the solute and the hydrogen bonds in the solvent.

Not all ionic salts are soluble in water. The detailed explanation of why salts such as AgCl are *not* able to dissolve well in water is beyond the scope of this course. Simply put, the attraction of the Ag^+ ion to the Cl^- ion is too large for the ion-dipole forces to overcome.

Quick Check

1. What is "like" between NaCl and H_2O? Why do they interact as they do?

____

____

2. Explain why water molecules will not surround I_2 molecules? What forces must be overcome between each water molecule?

____

3. Would you expect NaCl to dissolve in oil, which is a non-polar solvent? Explain.

____

4. Predict whether NaCl would dissolve in NH_3 liquid. Draw a diagram to show the forces acting within the solute, the solvent, and the resulting mixture.

____

A Polar Solute in a Polar Solvent: Ethanol in Water

- Ethanol contains an oxygen atom bonded to a hydrogen atom on the end of a hydrocarbon chain (Figure 7.2.4). In an ionic compound, the –OH group is called hydroxide and helps us identify the substance as a base. In an organic molecule such as ethanol, the –OH group is called a hydroxyl group and is associated with an alcohol. The –OH group at the end of the alcohol is polar and forms hydrogen bonds with nearby ethanol molecules. The hydrocarbon chain acts as a non-polar section, but in ethanol it is quite small.

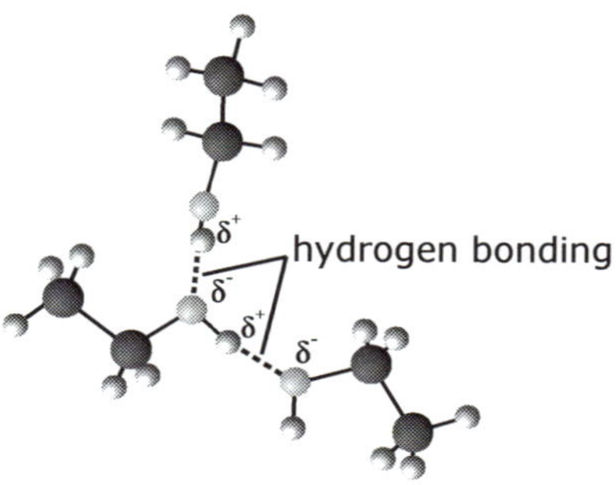

Figure 7.2.4 *Hydrogen bonding in ethanol,* C_2H_5OH

- Water is polar. Water molecules are strongly attracted to each other by hydrogen bonds.
- When ethanol and water are combined, the hydrogen bonding between water and ethanol molecules is similar in strength to the hydrogen bonds in the ethanol solute and water solvent individually. Therefore, water and ethanol are miscible.

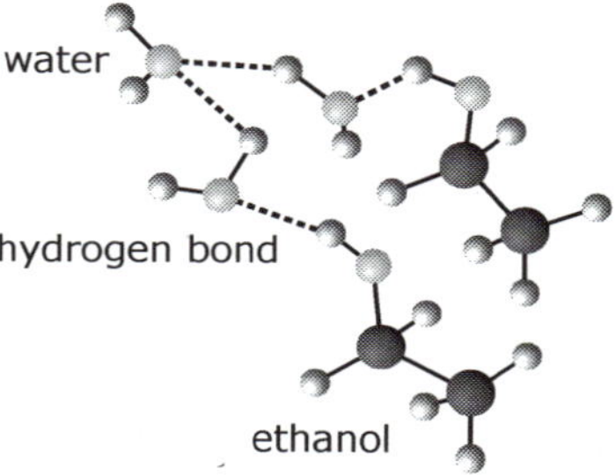

Figure 7.2.5 *Ethanol-water hydrogen bonding*

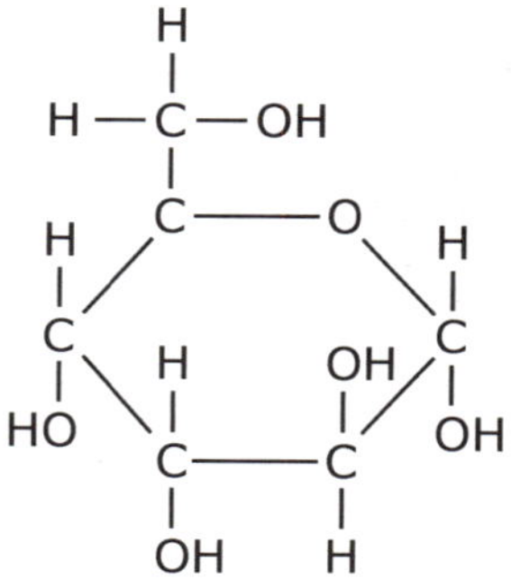

Figure 7.2.6 *Glucose molecule*

As the hydrocarbon chain part of an alcohol gets larger, the molecule becomes more non-polar. The hydrogen bonds between the larger alcohols are much weaker so the water molecules are not as attracted to the alcohol molecule. It becomes more difficult for the larger hydrocarbon chain on the alcohol to fit between water molecules. For this reason, butanol and pentanol are only partially soluble in water, and larger alcohols are almost insoluble in water.

Similarly, other organic compounds containing an –OH group are soluble in water. As you know, sugar is highly soluble in water. In fact, sugar has a higher solubility in water than NaCl does.

Each sugar molecule has five –OH groups on it (Figure 7.2.6). Each is available to make hydrogen bonds with water. Generally speaking, the more –OH groups on a hydrocarbon, the more soluble it will be in water.

Formaldehyde in Chloroform

- Formaldehyde is a polar covalent compound. Molecules of formaldehyde are attracted to each other through **dipole-dipole forces**. In this type of force, the positive pole of one molecule is next to and attracts the negative pole of an adjacent molecule. In formaldehyde, the negative dipole on the oxygen atom in one molecule is attracted to the positive dipole on the carbon atom in the other molecule as shown by the dotted lines in Figure 7.2.7.

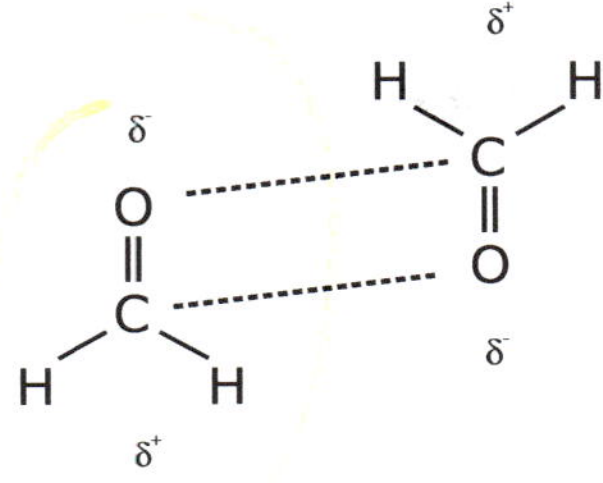

Figure 7.2.7 *Dipole-dipole attraction between formaldehyde molecules*

- Chloroform is also a polar covalent compound containing dipole-dipole forces (Figure 7.2.8).

Figure 7.2.8 *Dipole-dipole attraction between chloroform molecules. The arrows point from positive to negative.*

- Formaldehyde is soluble in chloroform because the dipole-dipole interaction between formaldehyde and chloroform molecules in the solution is similar in strength to the dipole-dipole interactions in the solute and solvent individually.

Ionic and polar covalent solutes dissolve in polar covalent solvents.

Quick Check

1. Will ammonia dissolve in water? Explain.
   yes, b/c its polar + water is polar
2. Is ethanol soluble in hexane, C_6H_{14}? Explain.
   No, b/c hexane isn't p
3. Which is more soluble in water: C_2H_6 or CH_3OH? Explain.
   polar and C_2H_6 isn't
4. Octanol has the formula $C_8H_{17}OH$. Explain why octanol does not dissolve in water.
   not very polar b/c LDF cancel dipole

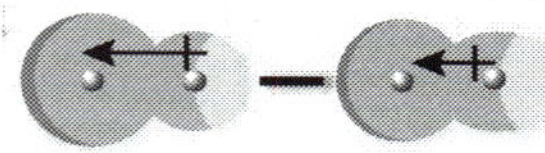

Figure 7.2.9 *Momentary dipoles or dispersion forces between I_2 molecules*

A Non-polar Solute in a Non-polar Solvent: Iodine in Carbon Tetrachloride

- Iodine, I_2, is a non-polar substance. The only interactions between I_2 molecules are very weak **London dispersion forces**. These forces occur when electrons on the atom of one molecule repel the nearby electrons on the atom of the other molecule. This creates a momentary and very weak positive dipole on the second molecule and the two molecules are weakly attracted to each other (Figure 7.2.9).

- Carbon tetrachloride, CCl_4, is also non-polar and interactions between molecules are limited to dispersion forces only.

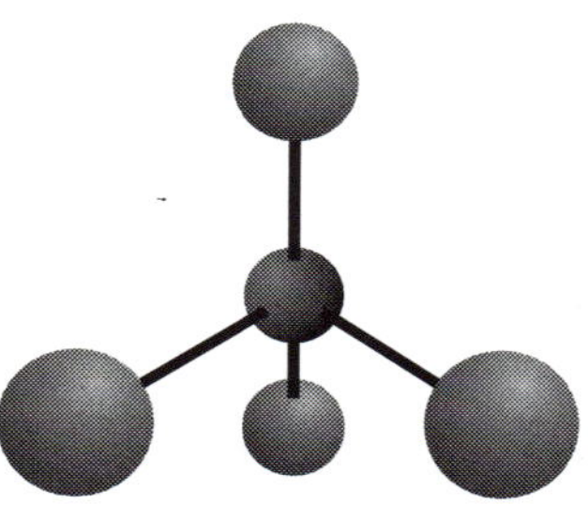

Figure 7.2.10 *Carbon tetrachloride*

- The dispersion forces acting between a molecule of I_2 and a molecule of CCl_4 are similar to the dispersion forces in each solute and solvent.

Non-polar covalent solutes are only soluble in non-polar solvents.

Quick Check

1. Paint thinner is a non-polar covalent solvent. Is iodine soluble in paint thinner? Explain.

   yes, because iodine is np

2. Mothballs are made of naphthalene, $C_{10}H_8$. Will a mothball dissolve better in water or paint thinner? Explain.

   paint thinner, b/c they are both np

3. A student places 10 mL of water and 10 mL of CCl_4 into a beaker. Solid iodine is added to the beaker. Explain what you would see and sketch a diagram of it.

   no dissociation, maybe slight

4. Why can a molecule of CCl_4 not come between water molecules?

   b/c the attractive force from CCl_4 aren't stronger than water's attractive force to itself

Fat and Water Soluble Vitamins

At the beginning of this section, you learned about the importance of vitamins A and C and their solubility in fat. The fat in your body is made up of non-polar molecules weakly attracted to each other by dispersion forces. By looking at the structure of vitamin A, you can see that it is a long hydrocarbon chain with a polar end on it (Figure 7.2.11). The length of the long hydrocarbon chain makes it essentially non-polar despite the presence of the hydroxyl group, so the forces between the vitamin A molecules are only weak dispersion forces. The fat molecules can dissolve with the vitamin A molecules because the dispersion forces in the fat and vitamin A molecules before they are mixed are replaced by the dispersion forces between the fat and vitamin A molecules in the resulting mixture.

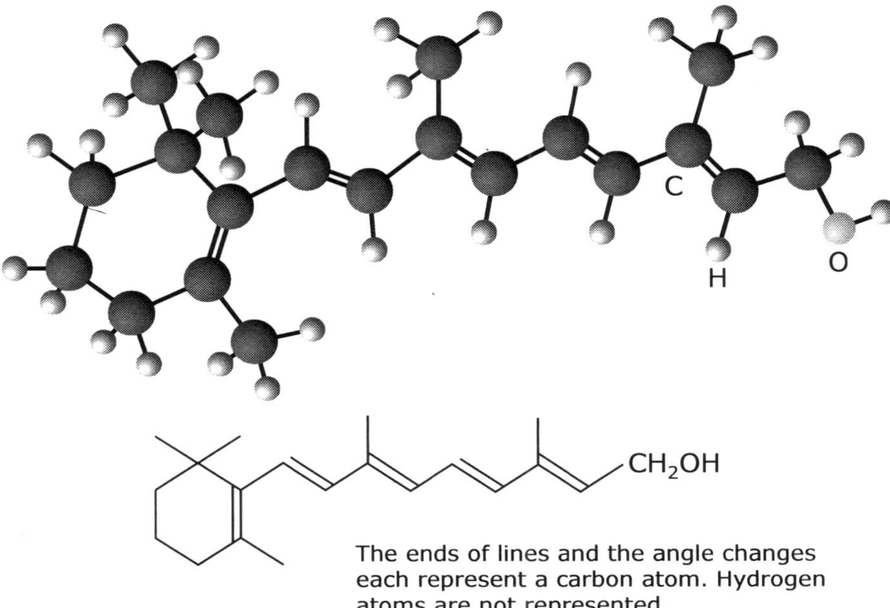

CH_2OH

The ends of lines and the angle changes each represent a carbon atom. Hydrogen atoms are not represented.

Figure 7.2.11 *Vitamin A*

Vitamin A is not water-soluble because the non-polar vitamin A molecules cannot get between the water molecules. The water molecules are attracted to each other through hydrogen bonds. This attraction cannot be overcome with a non-polar molecule. Vitamin C, however, contains many –OH groups, which makes it polar (Figure 7.2.12). The attraction between water molecules can be overcome by the attraction of water molecules for vitamin C molecules.

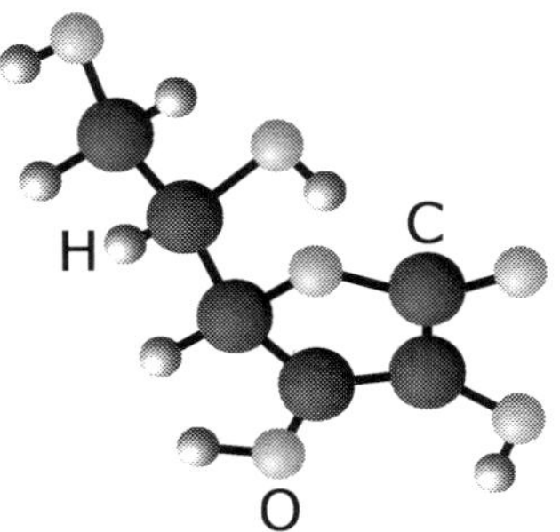

Figure 7.2.12 *Vitamin C*

Soaps

Soaps are an application of the like-dissolves-like principle. They are formulated to use organic molecules that contain positive and negative ions. Each negative ion has a long hydrocarbon "tail" that is non-polar and a "head" that is polar (Figure 7.2.13).

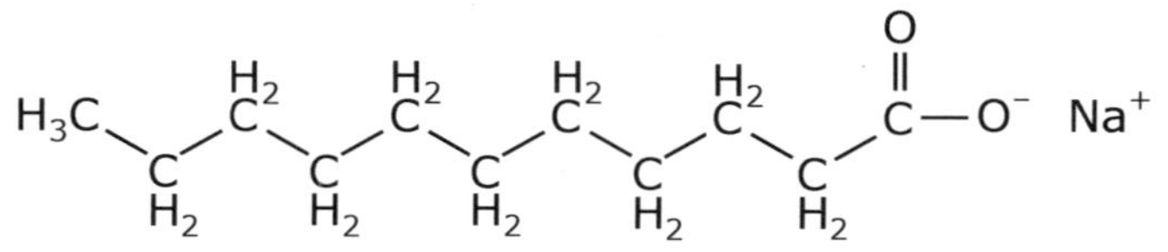

$H_3C-CH_2-CH_2-CH_2-CH_2-CH_2-CH_2-CH_2-CH_2-CH_2-C(=O)-O^-\ Na^+$

non-polar hydrocarbon tail   polar head

Figure 7.2.13 *A soap ion showing the non-polar "tail" and the polar "head"*

A molecule like this acts as an emulsifying agent, which allows immiscible liquids to become suspended in each other. The head is typically a $-COO^-$ group attached to a long chain made up of carbon and hydrogen. The $-COO^-$ group is polar and carries a negative charge. It interacts with the water molecules via ion-dipole forces and hydrogen bonding. The tail section is largely non-polar and will dissolve other non-polar grease and oil particles.

The soap molecules clump together with the hydrophilic heads pointing out, and the hydrophobic tails pointing in. These clumps are called "micelles" (Figure 7.2.14). The micelles trap the oil and grease in the centre. When you rinse off with water, the hydrophilic outside of the micelle rinses out with the water, taking the hydrophobic greasy centre with it.

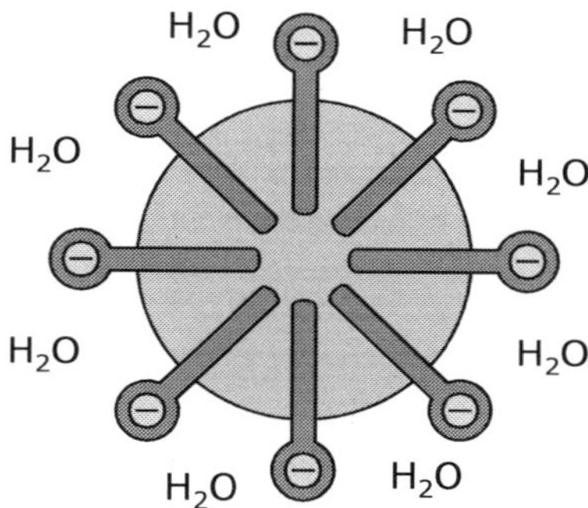

Figure 7.2.14 *A micelle*

7.2 Activity: Determining the Bond Type of a Solute

Question

What type of intramolecular bonds are present in an unknown solute?

Background

Stains on clothing may be thought of as a solute. In order to clean out a stain, it must be dissolved by a solvent. The type of solvent that successfully dissolves the stain identifies the type of stain on the clothing. Remember that "like dissolves like."

Procedure

1. A dry cleaner observes that a stain on a piece of clothing dissolves in water but not in tetrachloroethene. Look at the diagram of the structure of tetrachloroethene and answer the questions below.

```
Cl       Cl
  \     /
   C = C
  /     \
Cl       Cl
```

Tetrachloroethene

Results and Discussion

1. What types of intermolecular forces exist in water? In tetrachloroethene?
2. State the two possible bond types or intramolecular bonds present in the solute.
3. Explain why the stain did not dissolve in tetrachloroethene.
4. Explain why you cannot narrow down the solute bond type to just one type.
5. Compare your answers to those of another group. How do they compare?

7.2 Review Questions

1. Explain the phrase "like dissolves like" in your own words.

polar solutes dissolve in polar solvents, same w/ np

2. Is ethanol hydrophilic or hydrophobic? Explain using a diagram.

Hyrophilic b/c it's polar b/c of its OH bond

3. Is $Br_2(l)$ more soluble in $CS_2(l)$ or $NH_3(l)$? Explain.

CS_2 b/c Br_2 is np and so is CS_2

4. Explain why NH_3 is very soluble in water, but NCl_3 is not.

b/c NH_3 is p and NCl_3 is np, and water is p

5. When I_2 is added to water, it does not dissolve. However, if I_2 is added to an aqueous solution of KI, it will dissolve. Use the following reaction, and your understanding of intermolecular forces to explain the above observations.
$I_2(s) + I^-(aq) \rightarrow I_3^-(aq)$

The dipole in KI is strong enough to induce a dipole in I_2 and make it dissolve, but water's attraction isn't that strong.

6. Which is more soluble in water? Explain.
(a) C_4H_{10} or C_3H_6OH

polar

(b) $MgCl_2$ or toluene (C_7H_8)

polar

7. Glycerin is a common solvent and is found in many skin care products. A student mixed 10 mL of water, 10 mL of glycerin and 10 mL of carbon tetrachloride together. A small amount of $CuCl_2$ was added to the mixture. Explain what you would see.

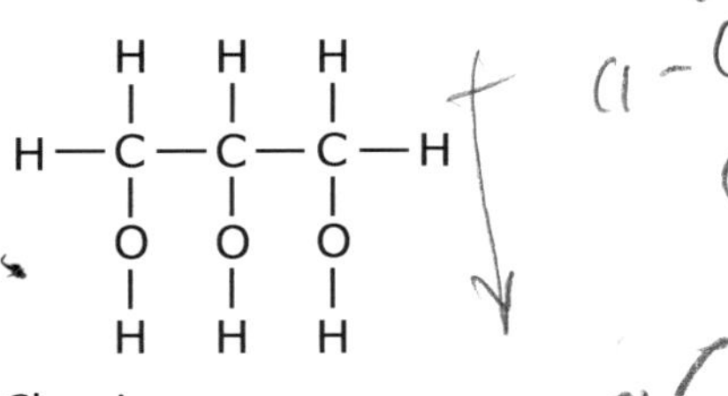

Glycerin

because glycerin and $CuCl_2$ have dipoles they would dissolve but a np CCl_4 wouldn't

8. Ethylene glycol is commonly used as antifreeze. Underline the solvent in which it would be most soluble in each pair below.

Ethylene glycol

(a) water or paint thinner (a non-polar covalent solvent)

(b) ammonia or carbon tetrachloride

(c) hexene (C_6H_{12}) or glycerin (a polar covalent solvent)

9. List the intermolecular forces present between the following solutes and solvents:

(a) CsCl in H_2O

H-bonding, ion-dip

(b) CH_3OH in glycerin

H-bond, dip-dip

(c) N_2 in C_8H_{18}

LDF

(d) acetone in ammonia

dip-dip

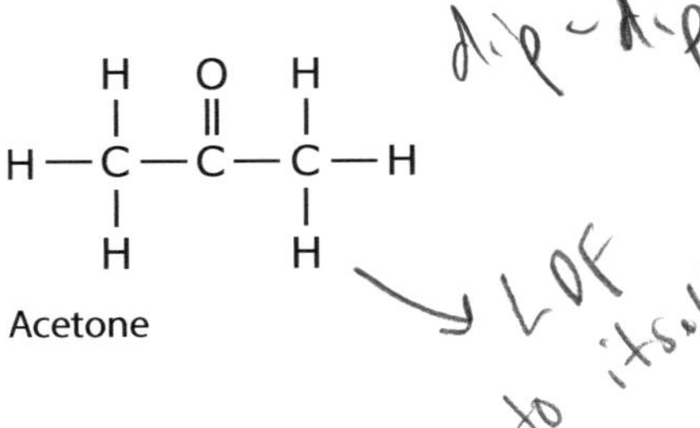

Acetone

LDF to itself

7.3 Dissociation Equations and Solution Conductivity

Warm Up

If you are a coffee drinker, you have experienced the effects of dilution and concentration. Assume you were making yourself a cup of coffee.

1. Describe how you would make a strong cup of coffee. Think about the amounts of water and coffee required.

   ____

2. If you wanted to dilute the coffee in your cup, what would you do?

   ____

3. When you dilute the coffee, have you changed the amount of caffeine present in the cup? Explain.

   ____

Diluting Solutions

In Chapter 3 and in section 7.1, you learned that a solution's concentration can be represented by molarity. The **molarity** of a solution is a measure of the amount of solute in moles in a given volume of solution. When we add water to a solution, the concentration decreases. We say the solution is diluted. The opposite of diluted is concentrated. To make a solution more concentrated, we could evaporate or remove some of the solvent from the solution. We could also add more solute to the solution. The symbol [ ] around a formula indicates molar concentration and is measured in mol/L. For example, in the sample problem below, the question asks "What is the new [HCl]?" This means "What is the new molar concentration of HCl?"

Sample Problem — Dilution Calculation

A 15.0 mL sample of 3.0 M HCl was diluted by adding 10.0 mL of water. What is the new [HCl] ?

What to Think about	How to Do It
1. We have increased the volume of the final solution by adding water. The amount or moles of HCl has not changed.	$\text{mol HCl} = \frac{3.0 \text{ mol HCl}}{1 \cancel{\text{L HCl}}} \times 0.015 \cancel{\text{L HCl}}$ $= 0.045 \text{ mol HCl}$
2. The final volume of solution is 0.0250 L. Use this amount to calculate the new molar concentration.	$15.0 \text{ mL} + 10.0 \text{ mL} = 25.0 \text{ mL} = 0.0250 \text{ L}$ $[\text{HCl}] = \frac{0.045 \text{ mol HCl}}{0.0250 \text{ L solution}}$ $= \frac{1.8 \text{ mol HCl}}{1 \text{ L}}$
3. This answer makes sense because the final concentration is less than the original concentration.	$= 1.8 \text{ M}$
This two-step calculation is usually shown as one longer calculation. Notice that the units of L HCl cancel.	$[\text{HCl}] = \frac{3.0 \text{ mol HCl}}{1 \cancel{\text{L HCl}}} \times \frac{0.0150 \cancel{\text{L HCl}}}{0.0250 \text{ L solution}}$ $= \frac{1.8 \text{ mol HCl}}{1 \text{ L}}$ $= 1.8 \text{ M}$

Practice Problems — Dilution Calculations

1. A 50.0 mL sample of 0.100 M NaOH was diluted by adding 30.0 mL of water. What was the resulting [NaOH]?

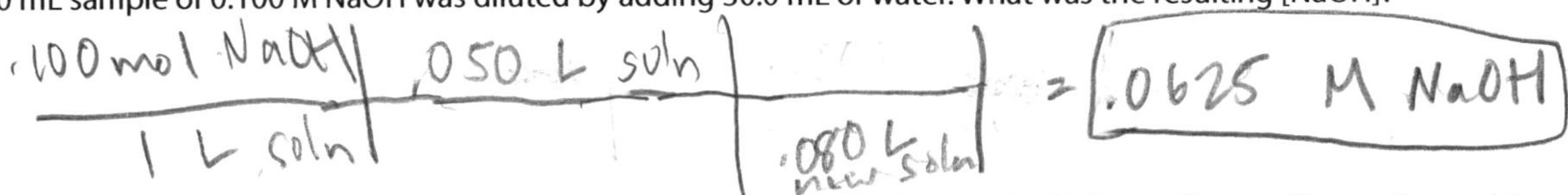

2. A 35.0 mL sample of 1.5 M H_2SO_4 was diluted to 50.0 mL. What was the final $[H_2SO_4]$? (Note: The wording in this problem is different. What is the final volume?)

3. A student dissolved 0.25 g of calcium nitrate in 100.0 mL water. A 50.0 mL sample of this solution was diluted to 75.0 mL. What was the final concentration?

4. Calculate the concentration that results when 18.0 mL of 0.40 M K_2CrO_4 is added to 20.0 mL of water.

Ions in Solution

Most people are familiar with what happens when table salt is added to water; the salt dissolves. To understand how this happens, we must look at the interactions between the ions in the solid table salt and the water molecules.

In the solid NaCl sample, positively charged Na^+ ions are attracted to negatively charged Cl^- ions. They are arranged in a crystal lattice as shown in Figure 7.3.1. Water molecules are polar. A negative pole exists on the oxygen atom, and a positive pole exists on the hydrogen atoms. The oxygen atoms of the water molecules are attracted to the sodium ions in the solid. In the same way, the hydrogen atoms of the water are attracted to the chloride ions in the solid. The solid dissolves as the water molecules separate the ions from the solid NaCl structure. **Solvation** is the process of solvent molecules surrounding solute particles. When the solvent is water, it can also be called **hydration**.

We can write an equation called a **dissociation equation** to represent the process of the positive and negative ions in the salt being separated by the solvent. An **ionization equation** is an equation that represents the breaking apart of a solute into ions. It is similar to a dissociation equation. When acid molecules break apart into ions, we describe the extent of ionization by using the term

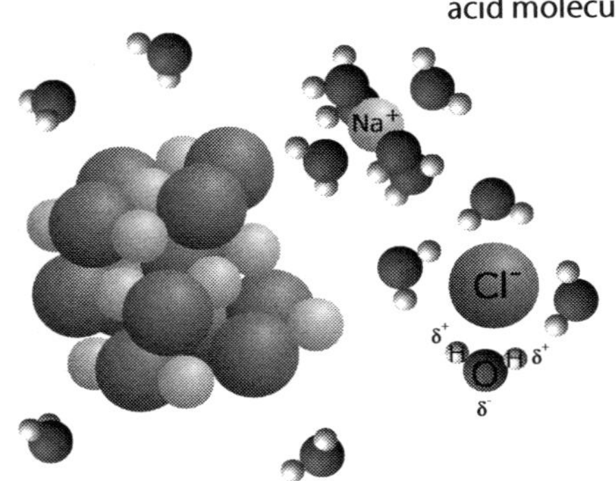

Figure 7.3.1 *NaCl dissolving in water*

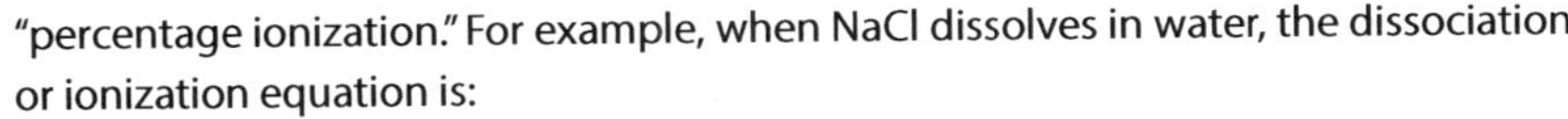

"percentage ionization." For example, when NaCl dissolves in water, the dissociation or ionization equation is:

$$NaCl(aq) \rightarrow Na^+(aq) + Cl^-(aq)$$

If the salt were $CaCl_2$ instead, the dissociation equation would be:

$$CaCl_2(aq) \rightarrow Ca^{2+}(aq) + 2\ Cl^-(aq)$$

Notice in the balanced equation that two chloride ions are produced for every one calcium ion. It is important to balance these equations properly for both *mass* or *number of atoms* and *charge*.

Quick Check

Write balanced dissociation equations for each salt when it is dissolved in water.

1. $Al(NO_3)_3$
2. $(NH_4)_2SO_4$
3. potassium chromate
4. zinc phosphate

Calculating Concentration

From the dissociation equations, you can see that the mole ratios represent the relative amounts of ions in solution. If we know the concentration of the solution, we can then calculate the concentration of each individual ion present as well.

Consider a 1.0 M solution of NaCl. According to the dissociation equation, when 1 mol of NaCl dissolves, it produces 1 mol of Na^+ ions and 1 mol of Cl^- ions. So in 1.0 M NaCl: $[Na^+]$ = 1.0 M and $[Cl^-]$ = 1.0 M

$$NaCl(aq) \rightarrow Na^+(aq) + Cl^-(aq)$$

$NaCl(aq)$	$Na^+(aq)$	$Cl^-(aq)$
1.0 M	1.0 M	1.0 M

If instead we had a 1.0 M solution of $CaCl_2$, according to the dissociation equation: $[Ca^{2+}]$ = 1.0 M but $[Cl^-]$ = 2.0 M

$$CaCl_2(aq) \rightarrow Ca^{2+}(aq) + 2\,Cl^-(aq)$$

$CaCl_2(aq)$	$Ca^{2+}(aq)$	$2\,Cl^-(aq)$
1.0 M	1.0 M	2(1.0 M) = 2.0 M

Quick Check

Calculate the concentration of all ions in each of the following. Begin by writing the balanced dissociation equation for each.

1. 3.0 M $Zn(NO_3)_2$
2. 0.50 M Na_2CO_3
3. 1.5 M ammonium oxalate
4. 3.2×10^{-3} M calcium phosphate

Dissociation and Dilution

Another example of dilution is when two solutions are mixed together. The resulting solution has a larger volume than the original solutions. The following sample problem combines an understanding of dissociation and dilution concepts.

Sample Problem — Dilution Calculation for Mixed Solutions

A 15.0 mL sample of 3.0 M HCl was added to 10.0 mL of 2.0 M $CaCl_2$. Calculate the concentration of each ion in solution. Assume no reaction occurs.

What to Think about	How to Do It
1. Calculate the concentration in mol/L.	$[HCl] = \frac{3.0 \text{ mol HCl}}{1 \text{ L HCl}} \times \frac{0.0150 \text{ L HCl}}{0.0250 \text{ L solution}}$ $= \frac{1.8 \text{ mol HCl}}{1 \text{ L}}$ $= 1.8$ M
2. Each solution was diluted when mixed, so first calculate the new concentration of each solution.	Final volume of solution: $15.0 + 10.0 = 25.0$ mL
3. Next, each solution contains ions so we write dissociation equations for each salt.	$[CaCl_2] = \frac{2.0 \text{ mol } CaCl_2}{1 \text{ L } CaCl_2} \times \frac{0.0100 \text{ L } CaCl_2}{0.0250 \text{ L solution}}$ $= 0.80$ M $CaCl_2$
4. Under each dissociation equation, use the mole ratio to calculate the concentration of each ion.	$HCl(aq) \rightarrow H^+(aq) + Cl^-(aq)$ 1.8 M 1.8 M 1.8 M
5. Notice that there are chloride ions from both original solutions, so we add their concentrations together.	$CaCl_2(aq) \rightarrow Ca^{2+}(aq) + 2\,Cl^-(aq)$ 0.80 M 0.80 M $2(0.80 \text{ M}) = 1.6$ M $[H^+] = 1.8$ M $[Cl^-] = 1.8 \text{ M} + 1.6 \text{ M} = 3.4$ M $[Ca^{2+}] = 0.80$ M

Practice Problems — Calculating the Concentrations of Ions in Solution

Calculate the concentration of each ion in the following solutions. Assume no reactions occur.

1. A 35.0 mL sample of 0.20 M HNO_3 was added to 75.0 mL of 0.15 M $Al(NO_3)_3$.

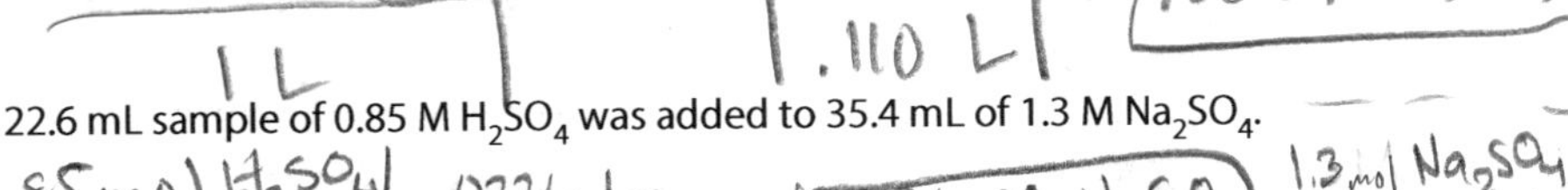

2. A 22.6 mL sample of 0.85 M H_2SO_4 was added to 35.4 mL of 1.3 M Na_2SO_4.

3. A 50.0 mL sample of 0.10 M potassium phosphate was added to 40.0 mL of 0.20 M potassium oxalate.

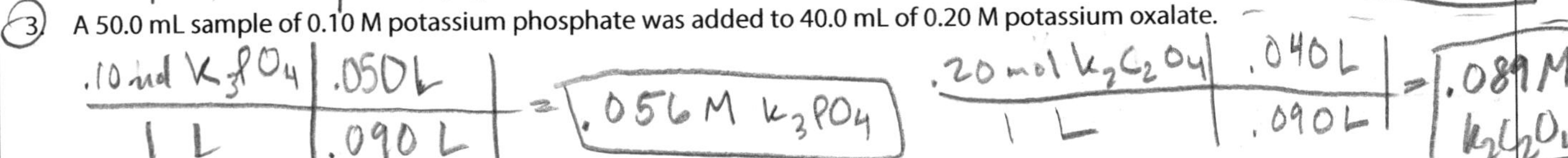

4. A 100.0 mL sample of 2.3×10^{-3} M ammonium phosphate was added to 40.0 mL of 4.5×10^{-2} M ammonium sulphide.

Electrical Conductivity of Solutions

Have you ever been in an outdoor swimming pool during an electrical storm? Is a swimming pool a safe place to be in this case? When electric charge is carried through a solution, we say that the solution conducts electricity. An **electrolyte** is a substance that dissolves in solution to produce ions. A strong electrolyte completely dissociates in solution, while a **weak electrolyte** only partially dissociates. Substances that do no dissociate at all are called **non-electrolytes**.

Electric charge is carried through a solution by the movement of ions. The charged ions must be free to move in the solution. The positive ions will move toward the negative electrode, and the negative ions will move toward the positive electrode. The movement of these ions completes the electrical circuit. The more ions present, the greater the conductivity.

A light bulb apparatus is a simple piece of equipment used to test for electrical conductivity (Figure 7.3.2). Your teacher may demonstrate this to you. The light bulb is plugged in, and the electrodes are placed into the solution. The brighter the bulb glows, the stronger the electrolyte is.

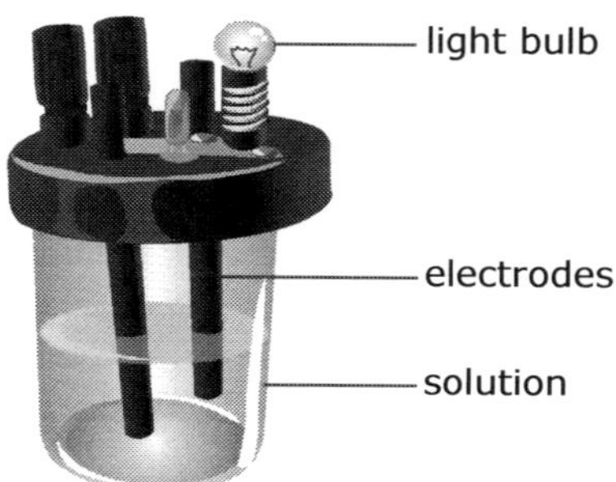

Figure 7.3.2 *Apparatus for testing for electrical conductivity*

In a nonelectrolyte, there are no ions to carry the electric charge across the space so no electricity flows. The space between the electrodes acts as an open switch in a circuit. Most covalent or molecular substances are nonelectrolytes. There are a few exceptions noted below.

Ionic solutions made by dissolving an ionic substance in water are electrolytes. An ionic solid that has a low solubility in water will only produce a few ions and so will not conduct electricity well. A melted liquid of an ionic salt will also conduct electricity; however an ionic solid will not. In a solid, the ions are locked in place and cannot move to carry electric charge.

Electrical Conductivity of Acids and Bases

Acids and bases conduct electricity as well. The formulas of most acids contain only nonmetals. They do not appear to be ionic. However, acids act by releasing an H^+ ion. Some acids will dissociate completely to form ionic solutions. We call these **strong acids**. Other acids contain molecules that remain mostly intact, but a few molecules of these acids will dissociate into ions. These are called **weak acids** because they do not form many ions. Water is another example of a molecular or covalent compound that dissociates to a small extent as follows:

$$H_2O(l) \rightarrow H^+(aq) + OH^-(aq)$$

The concentration of H^+ and OH^- ions in water is only 1.0×10^{-7} M each so water is a poor electrical conductor. Organic acids are compounds containing carbon, hydrogen, and oxygen. They contain the carboxyl group so their formulas end in –COOH. These substances are not ionic, but a few of the molecules in a sample will release the H^+ ion from this group. You should be familiar with vinegar, which is acetic acid, CH_3COOH. It dissociates as follows:

$$CH_3COOH(aq) \rightarrow CH_3COO^-(aq) + H^+(aq)$$

In a solution of vinegar, there will be only a few ions of H^+ and CH_3COO^- present to carry electrical charge. Therefore vinegar is a weak electrolyte. Table 7.3.1 summarizes some common acids and bases and their relative ability to dissociate into ions.

Table 7.3.1 *Ability of Common Acids and Bases to Dissociate*

Substance	Classification	Extent of Dissociation
HCl, HBr, HI, HNO_3, H_2SO_4, $HClO_4$	strong acid	dissociate 100%
NaOH, KOH, $Ca(OH)_2$	strong base	dissociate 100%
CH_3COOH, C_6H_5COOH	weak acid	very little
NH_3	weak base	very little

Quick Check

1. How can you tell from a substance's formula if it is ionic or molecular? Give two examples of an ionic compound.

____

____

2. Sugar has the formula $C_{12}H_{22}O_{11}$. Will a sugar solution conduct electricity? Explain.

____

____

3. Explain why a 1.0 M solution of HCl will be a stronger electrolyte than a 1.0 M solution of CH_3COOH.

____

____

Key Points about Electrical Conductivity of Solutions

Here are the key points to remember about electrical conductivity of solutions:

- Electric current is carried through a solution by ions. The more ions there are, the higher the electrical conductivity.
- Soluble salts will dissolve in water to make many ions and consequently a solution with high conductivity. Salts with low solubility will form a solution with few ions and therefore their solutions will have low electrical conductivity.
- Covalent compounds do not form ions so do not conduct electricity in solution. Exceptions are some acids and bases.
- Strong acids and bases ionize completely in solution.
- Weak acids and bases ionize very little in solution.

One of the most important applications of electrical conductivity of solutions is happening in your body right now. Your brain sends messages to the cells in your body by sending electrical impulses down your nerve cells. The electrical signal is carried along the nerve cell by concentration differences of Na^+ and K^+ ions both inside and outside the cell. The electrical signal must move through the solutions in your tissues. For example, if you do not have enough sodium and potassium ions present, you may experience muscle cramps. Many chemical reactions in your body rely on the fact that ions in solutions conduct electricity.

So, do you stay in the swimming pool during an electrical storm, or do you get out? Since there are salts dissolved in the pool water, it will conduct electricity. You need to get out!

7.3 Activity: Investigating Electrical Conductivity

Question

Which types of solutions are good electrical conductors?

Background

In order for a solution to conduct electricity, it must contain mobile ions. The more ions there are in solution, the stronger the electrolyte.

Procedure

1. A student has a light bulb conductivity apparatus and 100.0 mL of each of the following solutions in a beaker:
   - 1 • 4.0 M $C_{12}H_{22}O_{11}$
   - 2 • 1.0 M NaCl
   - 3 • 0.8 M Na_2CO_3
   - 4 • 2.0 M CH_3COOH
   - 5 • 3.0 M C_2H_5OH (ethanol, an alcohol)
   - 6 • 0.8 M HCl
   - 7 • 2.0 M NH_3

   Make a sketch of each solution containing a conductivity apparatus. Label each beaker's contents. ~~Use a coloured pencil to show the relative brightness of the light bulb in each.~~

2. ~~Compare your answers to those of another group. Did you agree?~~

Results and Discussion

1. Which solutions were ionic? Covalent?

   I: 2, 3, 6 C: 1, 4, 5, 7

2. For each ionic solution, write a dissociation equation for the solute, and calculate the concentration of each ion present.

   $NaCl(aq) \rightarrow Na^+(aq) + Cl^-(aq)$ — 1 M, 1 M, 1 M

   $Na_2CO_3(aq) \rightarrow 2Na^+(aq) + CO_3^{2-}(aq)$ — .8 M, 1.6 M, .8 M

   $HCl(aq) \rightarrow H^+(aq) + Cl^-(aq)$ — .8 M, .8 M, .8 M

3. Calculate the total ion concentration of each ionic solution by adding all of the ion concentrations together. Write this value under its corresponding diagram.

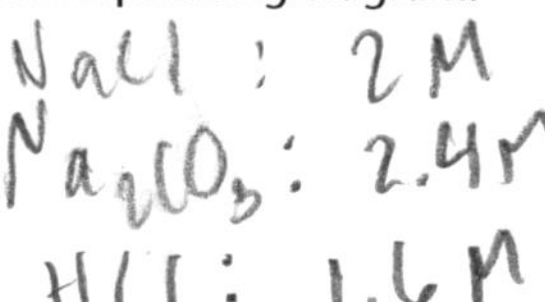

   NaCl : 2 M
   Na_2CO_3 : 2.4 M
   HCl : 1.6 M

4. Rank the solutions in order from strongest electrolyte to weakest electrolyte. List the nonelectrolytes last. Use an equal sign (=) for solutions that are about equally conductive.

   strongest Na_2CO_3 → NaCl → HCl
   all others: none

5. Summarize the rules for determining if a solute will make a solution that is a good electrical conductor.

   good conductor if it dissociates in water

7.3 Review Questions

1. Calculate the concentration of the following solutions when:
   (a) 175 mL of 0.55 M HCl is added to 25 mL of water

   (b) 45.0 mL of 0.035 M $Na_2Cr_2O_7$ is diluted to 100.0 mL

   (c) a 100.0 mL sample of 2.0 M NaOH is evaporated until the resulting volume of solution is 75.0 mL

2. Hydrochloric acid can be purchased as a 6.0 M solution. What volume of this stock solution must be used to prepare 250.0 mL of 2.5 M HCl?

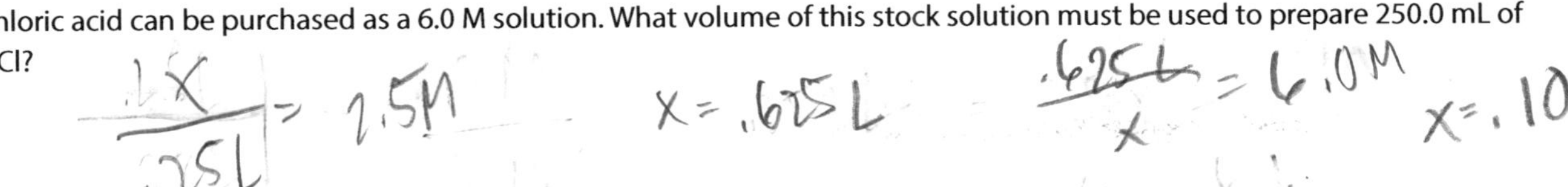

3. Explain how the terms "solvation" and "hydration" are different.

4. Explain why the cation in a solute will be attracted to a solvent water molecule.

5. The solute KI is dissolved in water. Sketch a diagram showing the ions present in this solute surrounded by water molecules. Assume six water molecules surround each ion. Be sure to draw the water molecules aligned appropriately around the ion with respect to dipoles.

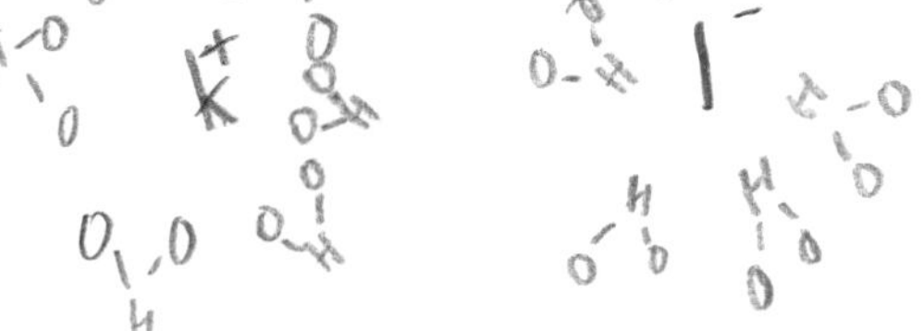

6. Write balanced dissociation equations to represent the dissolving of the following solutes in water:
   (a) $FeCl_3$
   (b) $MnHPO_4$
   (c) $Zn(SCN)_2$
   (d) $Al_2(Cr_2O_7)_3$
   (e) silver oxalate
   (f) iron(III) sulphite
   (g) chromium(II) chromate
   (h) ammonium hydrogen oxalate

7. A student adds 250.0 mL of 0.60M HCl to 300.0 mL of 1.0 M HCl. What is the final [HCl]?

8. Calculate the concentration of each ion in the following:
(a) 0.20 M $CuCl_2$

(b) 1.5 M $Li_2C_2O_4$

(c) 6.0 M nitric acid

(d) 1.4×10^{-3} M magnesium permanganate

(e) the resulting solution when 18.5 mL of 0.25 M $Al(NO_3)_3$ is mixed with 22.4 mL of 0.50 M $Cu(NO_3)_2$

9. A solution is made by dissolving some solid $(NH_4)_2CrO_4$ in water. If the $[NH_4^+] = 0.60$ M, what is the $[CrO_4^{2-}]$?

10. Sketch a light bulb apparatus in a solution of KNO_3. Show which ions move to the positive and negative electrodes. Is this solution a good electrolyte? Explain. electrolyte = strong acid

− ← K^+ NO_3^- → +

it's a good electrolyte b/c it's a strong acid and dissociates easily

11. List the acids that are strong electrolytes. Explain why they are considered strong.

12. You are given two beakers, one containing 3.0 M HNO_3 and one containing 6.0 M $C_{12}H_{22}O_{11}$. Explain how you could use a light bulb apparatus to distinguish the two solutions.

You could observe that $C_{12}H_{22}O_{11}$ is soluble but doesn't dissociate but HNO_3 does both

13. Classify the following as being good electrolytes, weak electrolytes or nonelectrolytes: strong acid or soluble
(a) 0.1 M $HClO_4$ good

(b) distilled H_2O non

(c) 1.0 M CH_3COOH weak

(d) 0.1 M $ZnSO_4$ strong

(e) $C_8H_{18}(l)$ non

(f) 6.0 M NH_3 weak

14. Consider the following statement: "If a solution has a high concentration, it will conduct electricity well." Do you agree or disagree? Explain.

7.4 An Introduction to Titrations

Warm Up

1. Balance the following neutralization equation:
   ___ $H_2SO_4(aq)$ + _2_ $NaOH(aq)$ → _2_ $H_2O(l)$ + ___ $Na_2SO_4(aq)$

2. Write the balanced equation for the reaction between aluminum hydroxide and hydrobromic acid to form aluminum bromide and water. $2Al(OH)_3 + 3HBr \rightarrow AlBr_3 + 3H_2O$

3. Complete and balance the following equation:
   $2NH_4OH(aq) + H_2SO_4(aq) \rightarrow$ H_2O + $(NH_4)_2SO_4$

4. Write the formulas for the acid and base that will react to give the salt K_2CO_3 and water.

   $2KOH + CO_2$

   5. ?

Titration

A **titration** is a quantitative analysis method used to determine the concentration of an unknown solution by reacting it with another substance of known concentration. The most common types of titrations make use of an acid-base neutralization reaction or a reduction-oxidation reaction. In this section, we will focus on acid-base titrations. In a neutralization reaction, an acid reacts with a base to form a salt and water:

$HCl(aq)$ + $NaOH(aq)$ → $NaCl(aq)$ + $H_2O(l)$
acid + base → salt + water

Solving Titration Problems

In chapter 4, you learned how to perform calculations based on balanced chemical equations. A titration problem is essentially a simple stoichiometric calculation. For any titration, the balanced chemical equation is a good starting point. In a titration, one reactant completely uses up the other reactant. By knowing the amount of one substance used in a reaction, the amount of the unknown substance is calculated by using the mole ratio from the balanced equation.

Sample Problem — Calculating the Unknown Concentration of an Acid

A student completely reacted 10.00 mL of HCl with 18.25 mL of 0.100M NaOH. Calculate the [HCl].

What to Think about	How to Do It
1. Write a balanced chemical equation for the acid-base reaction.	$HCl(aq) + NaOH(aq) \rightarrow NaCl(aq) + H_2O(l)$
2. Calculate the moles of substance that you know.	$\text{moles NaOH} = \frac{0.100 \text{ mol NaOH}}{1 \text{ L NaOH}} \times 0.01825 \text{ L NaOH}$ $= 0.001825 \text{ mol NaOH}$
3. Using the balanced equation, convert the amount of substance you know to the amount of substance you don't know.	$\text{moles HCl} = 0.001825 \text{ mol NaOH} \times \frac{1 \text{ mol HCl}}{1 \text{ mol NaOH}}$ $= 0.001825 \text{ mol HCl}$
4. Calculate the concentration by dividing the moles of HCl by litres of HCl. The same type of calculation can be used to calculate the unknown concentration of the base.	$[HCl] = \frac{0.001825 \text{ mol HCl}}{0.01000 \text{ L HCl}}$ $= 0.183 \text{ M}$

Practice Problems — Simple Titration Calculations

1. A student titrated 25.00 mL of HCl with 15.62 mL of 0.30M NaOH. Calculate the [HCl].

2. In a titration, a 10.00 mL sample of NaOH was titrated with 24.25 mL of 0.20M H_2SO_4. Calculate the [NaOH].

3. A student used 22.68 mL of 0.015M $Sr(OH)_2$ to titrate 5.00 mL of HNO_3. Calculate the $[HNO_3]$.

4. What volume of 0.50M $H_2C_2O_4$ is required to titrate 10.00 mL of 0.12M NaOH?

Practical Aspects of Titration

In a titration, there are two solutions. The solution whose concentration is known is called the **standardized solution**. The other solution is of unknown concentration.

Since titration is a quantitative method of analysis, the precision of the measuring tools used will determine how precise your final answer will be. Recording your data to the correct number of significant figures, and paying close attention to significant figures in calculations is very important in a titration. Special glassware enables accurate titration. It is important to know the names of this glassware.

- Burette (Figure 7.4.1): contains the standardized solution. The numbering on the burette allows us to measure the initial volume before the titration and final volume after the titration. Subtracting these two volumes gives us the volume of standardized solution added to the Erlenmeyer flask. Notice the scale reads from 0.00 mL at the top to 50.00 mL at the bottom.

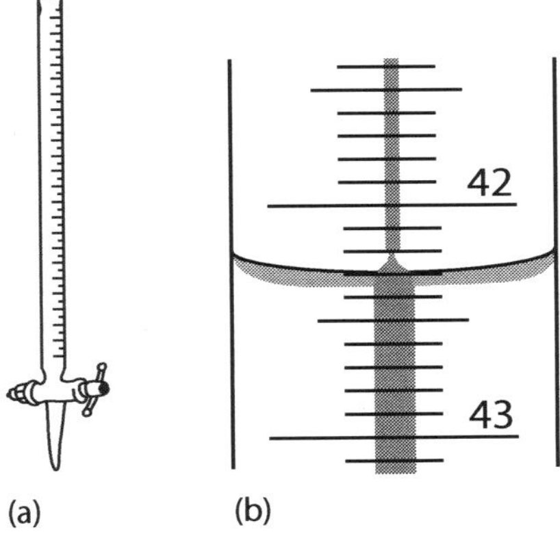

Figure 7.4.1 *(a) A burette (b) The reading on this burette is 42.30 mL.*

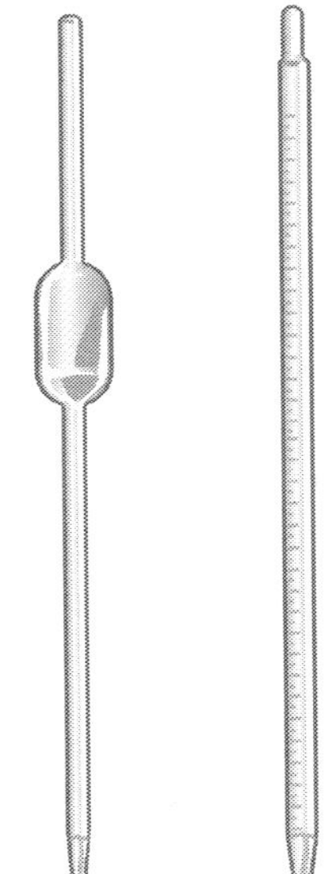

Figure 7.4.2 *Examples of pipettes*

- Pipette (Figure 7.4.2): used to measure and deliver a precise volume of the solution of unknown concentration to the Erlenmeyer flask. Pipettes come in a number of sizes: 1.00 mL, 5.00 mL, 10.00mL, 25.00 mL, etc. They may be graduated like a burette, or designed to deliver a specific volume. A pipette bulb is used to suck the solution up into the pipette. Never suction the solution by mouth.

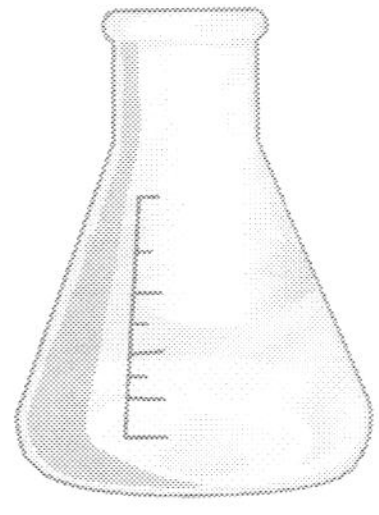

Figure 7.4.3 *An Erlenmeyer flask*

- Erlenmeyer Flask (Figure 7.4.3): contains the measured volume of solution of unknown concentration and a few drops of an indicator at the beginning of the titration. As the titration proceeds, solution from the burette is added drop by drop to the solution in the Erlenmeyer flask where the reaction takes place. The indicator changes colour when the reaction between the moles of acid and moles of base is complete.

- The **equivalence point** occurs when the moles of H^+ equal the moles of OH^-. When the indicator changes colour, the **endpoint** is reached. This is when you record the final burette reading.

When the titration apparatus is put together, it looks like Figure 7.4.4.

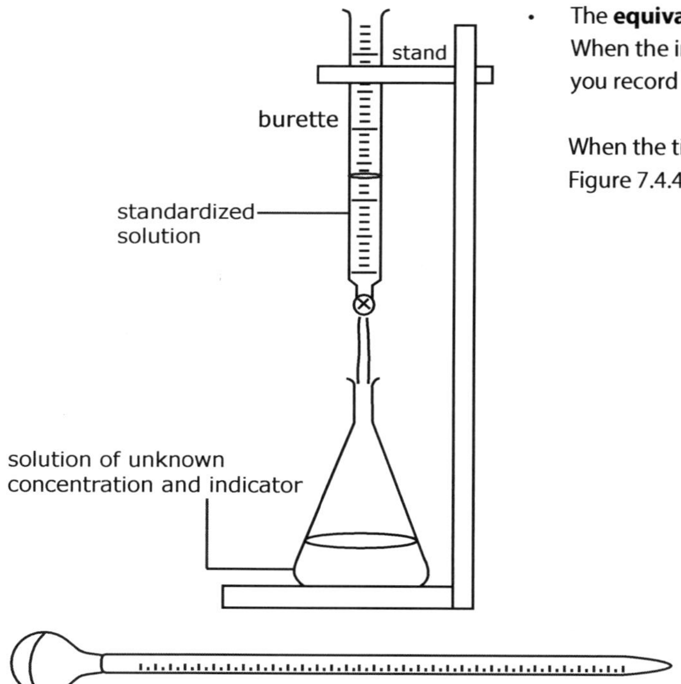

Figure 7.4.4 *A titration apparatus*

Quick Check

1. How is a pipette different from a burette?

____

2. What solution goes into the burette?

____

3. Which piece of glassware is the indicator added to?

____

4. What is "equivalent" at the equivalence point?

____

7.4 Activity: Titrating CH_3COOH with NaOH

Question
What is the unknown concentration of a sample of CH_3COOH?

Background
In Science 10 you learned about chemical indicators and how they are used to test for the presence of acids or bases. An indicator will be one colour in the presence of an acid, and a different colour in the presence of a base. One such indicator is phenolphthalein. In this activity you will see how phenolphthalein can be used to indicate when an acid has completely reacted with a base. When there is an excess of acid, the phenolphthalein will be colourless. Once the acid has been completely used up and there is an excess of base, the phenolphthalein will turn pink. This colour change occurs within one drop of NaOH being added.

Procedure
1. The steps involved in a titration of CH_3COOH using NaOH are described below. Answer the questions following each step to help you to understand what is happening at each part of the titration.
2. Discuss each step with your partner.

Results and Discussion
1. Write a balanced equation for the reaction between $CH_3COOH(aq)$ and $NaOH(aq)$.

2. Consider a solution of CH_3COOH of unknown concentration. It was titrated with a standardized solution of 0.15M NaOH. A student used a pipette to deliver 10.00 mL of CH_3COOH to the Erlenmeyer flask. A few drops of phenolphthalein were added. What would be the colour of the solution in the flask? ______________

3. The standardized 0.15 M NaOH was placed in the burette. The initial reading on the burette was 0.50 mL. A few drops of NaOH from the burette were allowed to drip into the flask. The solution in the flask did not change colour.
   Why does the solution in the flask not change colour when the NaOH is added?

   ____

4. After adding more NaOH drop by drop, the solution became pink. At this point, no more NaOH was added. The final reading on the burette was 12.30 mL.
   What volume of NaOH was added to the flask? ________________

5. When the colour of the indicator changed, the endpoint had been reached.
   Why did the colour of the solution become pink?

   ____

6. Once the titration was completed, the contents of the flask were rinsed down the drain, and the flask was rinsed out with water. To ensure that the data was accurate, a second and third titration was completed. We call these **trials**. An example of the data collected would look like the table shown below.
For each trial, complete the subtraction and calculate the volume of NaOH added. The average volume of NaOH is calculated by averaging the two trials within 0.1 mL. Fill in the table with the appropriate values.

Molarity of NaOH = 0.15 M	Trial #1	Trial #2	Trial #3
Initial burette reading (mL)	0.50	12.31	23.75
Final burette reading (mL)	12.31	23.75	35.22
Volume of NaOH added (mL)			
Average volume NaOH (mL)			

7. Using the concentration of NaOH and average volume of NaOH, calculate the moles of NaOH used in the titration.

8. Use the mole ratio from the balanced equation to calculate the moles of CH_3COOH present in the flask.

9. Calculate the molarity of the CH_3COOH by dividing the moles of CH_3COOH by the volume of CH_3COOH in the flask.

10. Compare your answer to that of another group.

7.4 Review Questions

1. Describe how you can tell from a formula if a substance is an acid or a base. Use examples.

2. Complete and balance the following acid-base neutralization equations:

   (a) $HI(aq) + LiOH(aq) \rightarrow$

   (b) $Ca(OH)_2(aq) + HNO_3(aq) \rightarrow$

   (c) $CH_3COOH(aq) + NH_4OH(aq) \rightarrow$

   (d) $H_2SO_4(aq) + KOH(aq) \rightarrow$

3. A student titrates a standardized solution of $H_2C_2O_4$ to determine the concentration of NaOH. The indicator used was phenolphthalein. Draw an apparatus used for the titration. Label all glassware and their contents. Describe what colour the solution would be in the flask at the beginning of the titration and at the end of the titration.

4. Define the terms "standardized," "equivalence point," and "endpoint."

5. A student titrated 10.00 mL HCl with 0.050 M $Sr(OH)_2$. The table below shows the data collected. Calculate the [HCl].

Molarity of $Sr(OH)_2$ = 0.050 M	**Trial #1**	**Trial #2**	**Trial #3**
Initial burette reading (mL)	0.00	16.05	32.93
Final burette reading (mL)	16.05	32.93	49.68
Volume of $Sr(OH)_2$ added (mL)			
Average volume $Sr(OH)_2$ (mL)			

6. A 25.00 mL sample of 0.20 M H_2CO_3 was titrated with 0.50 M NaOH. What volume of NaOH was required to reach the equivalence point?

7. A 10.00 mL sample of vinegar (CH_3COOH) was titrated with 18.20 mL of 0.50 M NaOH. Calculate the [CH_3COOH].

8. In order to standardize a solution of NaOH, 0.18 g of oxalic acid, $H_2C_2O_4 \cdot 2H_2O$, was dissolved to make 250.00 mL of solution. A 25.00 mL sample of this solution was titrated against 15.25 mL NaOH. Calculate the [NaOH].

9. Aspirin has the formula $C_9H_8O_4$. Only one of the H atoms is released when it acts as an acid. An aspirin tablet with a mass of 0.50 g was dissolved in water, and titrated with 18.30 mL of 0.10 M NaOH. Calculate the mass of aspirin in the tablet, and then the percent by mass of aspirin in the tablet.

10. A 250.00 mL sample of $Ca(OH)_2$ was titrated with 7.25 mL 0.10 M HCl. Calculate the mass of $Ca(OH)_2$ present in the solution.

11. A student dissolved 0.1915 g of an unknown acid HA in 10.00 mL of water. This solution was then titrated with 0.100 M NaOH. The table below shows the data collected. Calculate the molar mass of the acid HA.

Molarity of NaOH = 0.100 M	**Trial #1**	**Trial #2**	**Trial #3**
Initial burette reading (mL)	0.00	15.25	30.47
Final burette reading (mL)	15.25	30.47	45.87
Volume of NaOH added (mL)			
Average volume NaOH (mL)			

8 Gases

This chapter focuses on the following AP Big Idea from the College Board:

Big Idea 2: Chemical and physical properties of materials can be explained by the structure and the arrangement of atoms, ions, or molecules and the forces between them.

By the end of this chapter, you should be able to do the following:

- Use KMT and intermolecular forces to predict the macroscopic properties of real gases
- Use particle representations to explain the effect of changes in the macroscopic properties of gases
- Calculate temperature, pressure, volume, and moles of an ideal gas
- Analyze data for real gases to identify deviations from ideal behaviour and explain using molecular interactions

By the end of this chapter you should know the meaning of these key terms:

- *a* and *b* factors
- atmospheric pressure
- Avogadro's hypothesis
- barometer
- Boyle's law
- Charles's law
- combined gas law
- Dalton's law of partial pressures
- diffusion
- effusion
- gas
- gas laws
- Guy-Lussac's law
- ideal gas law
- kinetic molecular theory
- manometer
- mean free path
- mole fraction
- partial pressure
- root mean square velocity
- standard atmospheric pressure
- torr
- vapour pressure
- volatile

In a hot air balloon, a gas burner is used to heat air to a temperature of about 212°F (100°C). Since hot air is lighter and less dense than the cool air around the balloon, the heated air causes the whole balloon to rise.

8.1 The Gaseous State

Warm Up

glass

water

1. No matter how many dishwashers you have in your home (in my home there were three — my brother, my sister, and me), you've likely inverted a glass filled with water in the sink and noted the water didn't run out completely. Why does the water remain in the glass?

2. If you lived in Denver Colorado, often called the "mile high city" due to its elevation of 5280 ft or 1610 m, how would the height of the supported water column compare? Explain your answer.

Introducing Gases

We have occasionally used gases to illustrate some of the topics dealt with in Chemistry 1 so far this year. In this unit, we will study the behaviour of gases in detail and examine some of the most frequently encountered properties of gases. We will be discussing the kinetic molecular theory, and we will develop a number of mathematical relationships between pressure, volume, temperature, and the amount of substance present. These relationships are called **gas laws**.

Specific Properties of Gases

The word **gas** comes from *gaos*, a Dutch form of the word *chaos*. Gases were the last set of substances to be understood chemically. Until about 1750, the only gas known was the most familiar one, the air, which lies over Earth in a blanket about 80 km thick. Air is composed of 78% nitrogen and 21% oxygen, with small quantities of argon, carbon dioxide and a variety of other gases.

As you were reminded in section 2.1, most substances can exist as solids, liquids, or gases. The state in which we observe any substance depends on the temperature and pressure. The state in which a particular substance exists at a specific temperature and pressure depends on the attractive forces between particles of that substance. The state affects the physical properties of the substance.

Special Properties of Gases

- Gases, unlike solids and liquids, expand to fill any space available.
- Most gases are colourless and many are odourless.
- All gases have a very low density.
- All gases can be mixed in any proportion to form solutions.
- The volume of a gas changes dramatically with a change in pressure or temperature.
- The three properties of volume, pressure, and temperature are interrelated for a particular mass of gas.

Measurement of Gas Pressure

Pressure is the exertion of a force by one body on another. The forces exerted on your body, and everything else, by the air in the atmosphere is known as **atmospheric pressure**. There are two devices that are commonly used to measure pressure exerted by gases. One is used mainly for the measurement of atmospheric pressure. The other is used to measure the pressure of enclosed gas samples under various conditions.

The Barometer

Like all earthly matter, air is subject to the pull of gravity. Air near Earth's surface is compressed by the mass of air above it. For this reason, the pressure of the atmosphere has its maximum value at sea level. In Denver, Colorado, 1.6 km, or 1 mile, above sea level, the atmospheric pressure has decreased by 20%. Some football enthusiasts feel this is why the Denver Broncos rarely lose when playing at home in the Mile High Stadium. Above 3 km, the low pressure makes breathing uncomfortable for people not used to such altitudes. This is the reason for the breathing apparatus used by mountain climbers, pressurized cabins in commercial airplanes, and pressure control in spacecraft.

The **barometer** is used to measure atmospheric pressure (Figure 8.1.1). Designed by an Italian scientist named Evangelista Torricelli in the early 1600s, it consists of a long glass tube sealed at one end and filled with a liquid. The tube is then inverted and placed in a dish of the same liquid. This causes some of the liquid to flow out of the tube into the dish, creating a vacuum at the sealed end of the tube. Not all of the liquid flows out because the force exerted by the air — the atmospheric pressure — on the surface of the dish supports the column of liquid. The distance or height between the surface of the liquid in the tube and the surface of the liquid in the dish is a measure of the pressure exerted by the atmosphere. The height of the column depends on the liquid used and the elevation of the barometer. The most commonly used liquid in a barometer is mercury. The height of such a mercury column at sea level where the elevation is 0 m is 760 mm. This measurement, 760 mm of mercury, is defined as **standard atmospheric pressure**.

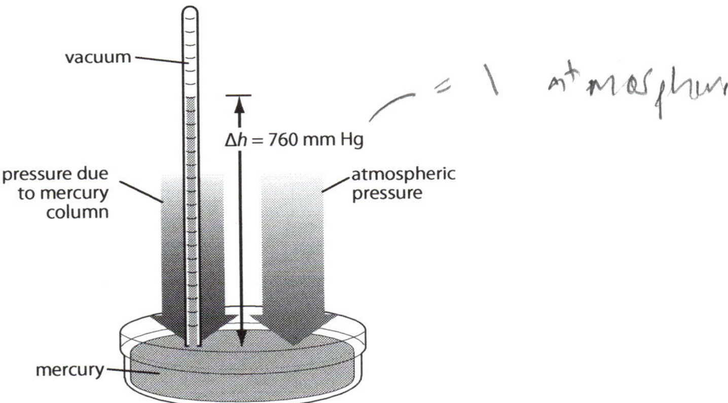

Figure 8.1.1 *A barometer measures atmospheric pressure as a reflection of the height of a column of mercury the pressure can support.*

The Manometer

The pressure exerted by a gas in a closed container can be measured using a **manometer**. The principle involved is the same as that of the barometer. A manometer consists of a U-tube partially filled with mercury. One side of the U-tube is connected to the gas container. The other side is open to a region of known pressure, most often the atmosphere. The gas in the container exerts a force on the mercury that tends to push it down. Atmospheric pressure exerts a force on the mercury at the open end of the tube. The difference between the heights of the two mercury levels is a direct measure of the difference between the two gas pressures. This pressure difference is often referred to as "delta h" or $\boldsymbol{\Delta}h$. Referring to the Figure 8.1.2, we can say that:

$$P_{gas} = (P_{atm} + P \text{ due to } \Delta h) \text{ mm Hg}$$

Knowing the atmospheric pressure as read on a barometer and the value of Δh, we can readily calculate the pressure exerted by the gas in a closed container. All pressures must be in the same units.

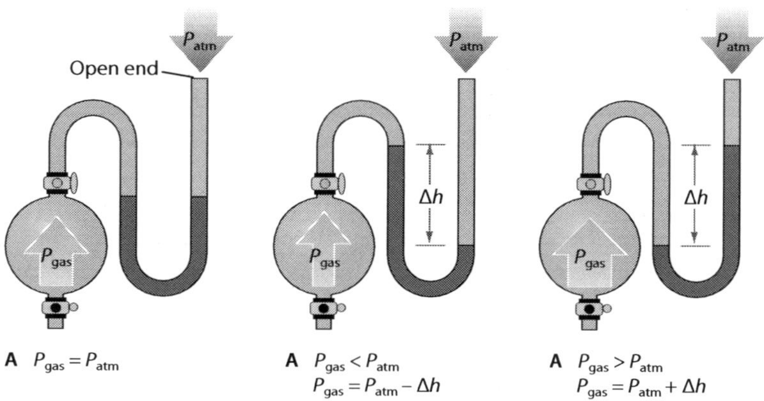

Figure 8.1.2 *Manometers measure the pressure exerted by an enclosed sample of gas. Note that Δh may be added or subtracted depending on whether the enclosed gas pressure is greater or less than atmospheric pressure.*

Sample Problem — Measuring Gas Pressure

When a container of gas is connected to a manometer, the mercury in the open end of the U-tube rises until it is 112 mm higher than the mercury in the container side. If the atmospheric pressure, measured with a barometer, is 765 mm Hg, what is the gas pressure in the container?

What to Think About	How To Do It
1. Visualize the manometer. 2. Is the contained gas pressure more or less than atmospheric pressure? 3. In this example, the enclosed gas pressure is 112 mm greater than atmospheric pressure so Δh must be *added* to the atmospheric pressure.	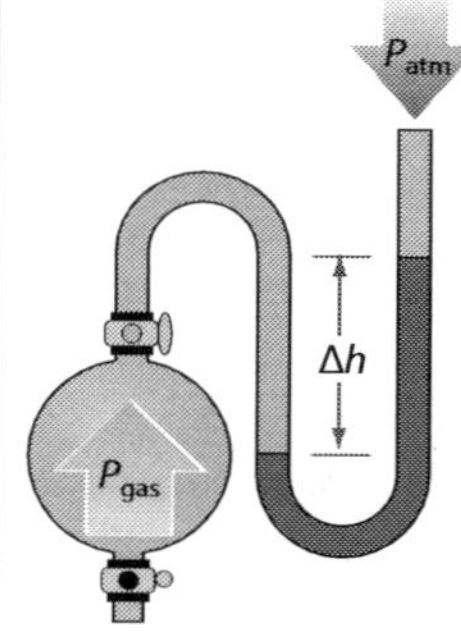 765 + 112 = 877 mm Hg

Practice Problems — Measuring Gas Pressure

1. Consider the following two measuring devices found in a chemistry laboratory. What is the pressure of the enclosed gas sample?

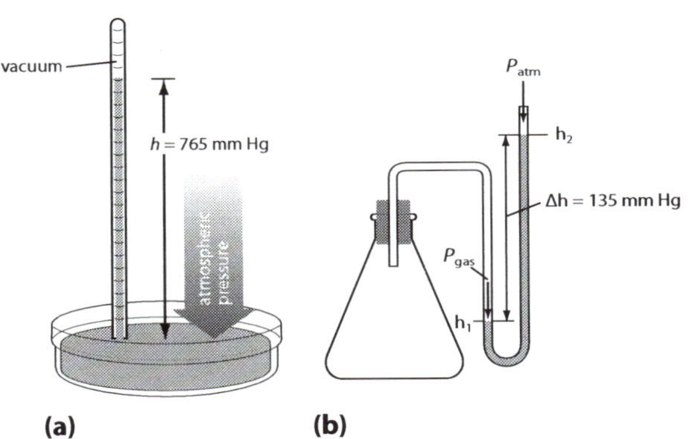

2. Assume the barometer in Practice Problem 1 supports a 72.4 cm column of mercury. Consider this second device found in the lab. What is the pressure of the sealed gas sample?

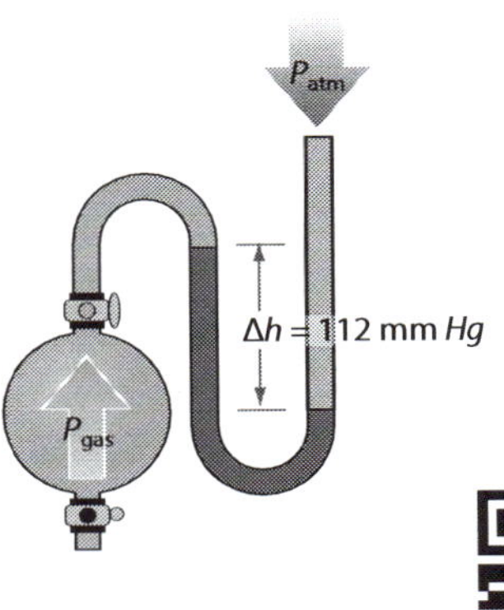

Units of Pressure Measurement

There are several different units that may be used to measure pressure. We encountered some of these at the start of the course while studying conversion factors. Pressure is defined as the force per unit area. In his work with the mercury barometer, Torricelli's use of the height of a mercury column to reflect pressure led to gas pressures being expressed in units of "mm Hg." Because mm Hg is awkward to write, this unit is often called a **torr** in honour of Torricelli. Thus standard atmospheric pressure can be expressed as 760 mm Hg or 760 torr. This equivalence has led to another unit, the atmosphere for pressure. One atmosphere (atm) equals 760 mm Hg or 760 torr. This unit is particularly useful for the measurement of very high pressures.

Another common unit of pressure is "pounds per square inch" or psi. If you remember that pressure is a force per unit area, this unit makes perfect sense. Atmospheric pressure at sea level, or standard atmospheric pressure, is nearly 15 psi. Atmospheric pressure at sea level is also very nearly one bar. This unit comes from the Greek word root *baro*, meaning pressure.

The SI unit for pressure is the pascal (Pa), named after physicist and mathematician, Blaise Pascal. The pascal is defined as a pressure of 1 newton per square meter. The pascal is really a very small unit. For example, a playing card lying flat on a table exerts about 1 pascal of pressure. As a result, it is common to use the kilopascal (kPa) instead.

To summarize, it is possible to express standard atmospheric pressure or pressure at sea level in many different ways. The equivalences between the various units of pressure are very important for use as conversion factors.

1.00 atm = 760. mm Hg = 760. torr = 14.7 psi = 101.3 kPa = 1.01 bar

Sample Problem — Using Pressure Units

The city of Denver is commonly referred to as the "Mile High City" due to its elevation in the Rocky Mountains. Assume atmospheric pressure in Denver is only 82.0% of the pressure at sea level. Calculate this pressure. Express your answer in each of the six units defined above.

What to Think About	How To Do It
1. Determine atmospheric pressure in Denver by taking 82.0% of the pressure at sea level.	$\frac{82.0}{100} \times 1.00\ \text{atm} = \mathbf{0.820\ atm}$
2. Use the equivalences in the box above to create appropriate conversion factors to convert 0.820 atm to the required units.	$0.820\ \cancel{\text{atm}} \times \frac{760.\ \text{mm Hg}}{1.00\ \cancel{\text{atm}}} = \mathbf{623\ mm\ Hg}$ $= \mathbf{623\ torr}$ $0.820\ \cancel{\text{atm}} \times \frac{14.7\ \text{psi}}{1.00\ \cancel{\text{atm}}} = \mathbf{12.1\ psi}$ $0.820\ \cancel{\text{atm}} \times \frac{101.3\ \text{kPa}}{1.00\ \cancel{\text{atm}}} = \mathbf{83.1\ kPa}$ $0.820\ \cancel{\text{atm}} \times \frac{1.01\ \text{bar}}{1.00\ \cancel{\text{atm}}} = \mathbf{0.828\ bar}$
3. Ensure that the number of significant figures is correct in each calculation.	All answers should be expressed to three significant figures.

Practice Problems — Using Pressure Units

1. Any pressure measured in a closed container is actually being measured relative to the atmospheric pressure that surrounds it. A common example is tire pressure. The total pressure in a tire is the sum of the pressure read on a tire gauge and atmospheric pressure. Bicycle tires can be inflated to a much higher pressure than automobile tires. The recommended gauge pressure for a mountain bike tire is between 40 and 60 psi. If a tire gauge indicates the pressure in a mountain bike tire is 55.0 psi, what is the overall tire pressure in units of kPa? Assume the atmospheric pressure is "standard" or 14.7 psi.

2. A closed-end manometer has all the gas removed from the U-tube before mercury is added. The result is a vacuum in the sealed end of the U-tube. This produces a device that can measure the total pressure in a closed container directly. With a closed-end manometer there is no need to add atmospheric pressure to determine the total pressure in a container. Consider closed-end manometer (a) below. Determine the total pressure in the flask once it is filled with gas in (b). Express your answer in atm.

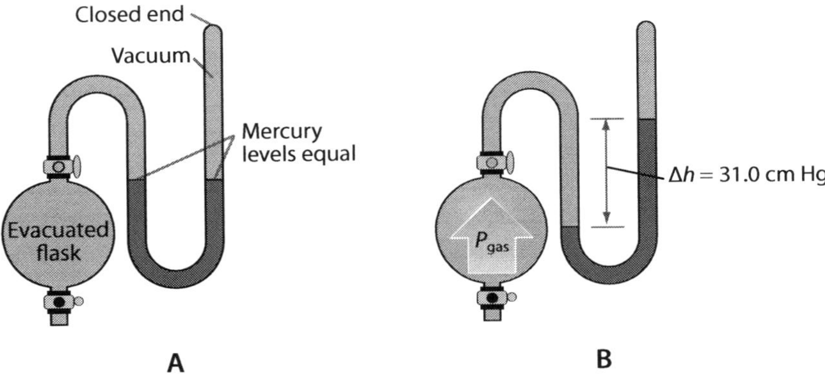

3. The pressure gauge in a full scuba tank in Cuba reads 206 bar. Convert this pressure to units of psi which are standard scuba units in North America.

8.1 Review Questions

A barometer appears as follows at sea level.

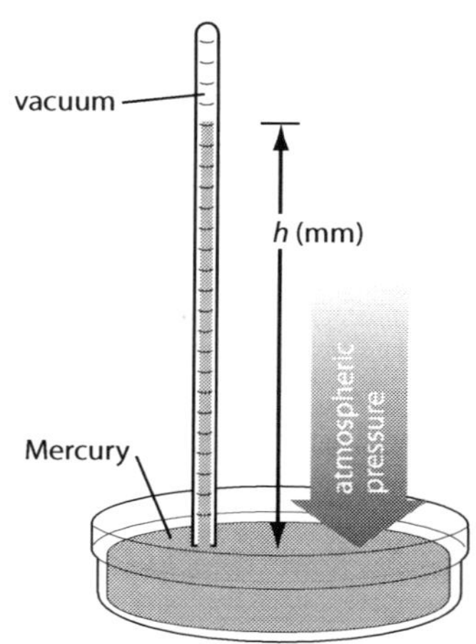

1. Imagine the barometer is placed in a hyperbaric chamber where the pressure is greatly increased. How will this affect the height of the mercury column and therefore the pressure reading? Give a clear explanation.

If the pressure is increased, then the mercury column will rise b/c the mercury will be displaced to the other side and the column will rise

2. Complete the following table. Support your answers with appropriate calculations.

mm Hg	atm	kPa
7098.4	9.34 atm	946.142 kPa
4169.1	5.49 Atm	555.696 kPa

9.34 atm | 760 mmHg / 1.0 atm = 7098.4 mm

9.34 atm | 101.3 kPa / 1.00 atm = 946.142 kPa

555.696 kPa | 1.00 atm / 101.3 kPa = 5.49 atm | 760 mmHg / 1.0 atm = 4169.1

3. Complete the following table. Be sure to show all work.

mm Hg	atm	kPa
4845.0	6.375 atm	645.789
711.23	.9358	94.8 kPa

6.375 atm | 760 mmHg / 1.0 atm = 4845 mm Hg

6.375 atm | 101.3 kPa / 1.0 atm = 645.789 kPa

94.8 kPa | 1.0 atm / 101.3 kPa = .9358 atm | 760 mmHg / 1.0 atm = 711.23

4. What is the pressure of the following gas samples attached to U-tube manometers open to an atmospheric pressure of 749.5 mmHg?

$P_{gas} = P_{atmos} + \Delta h$

(a) left arm height = 208.6 mm
Right arm height = 585.9 mm

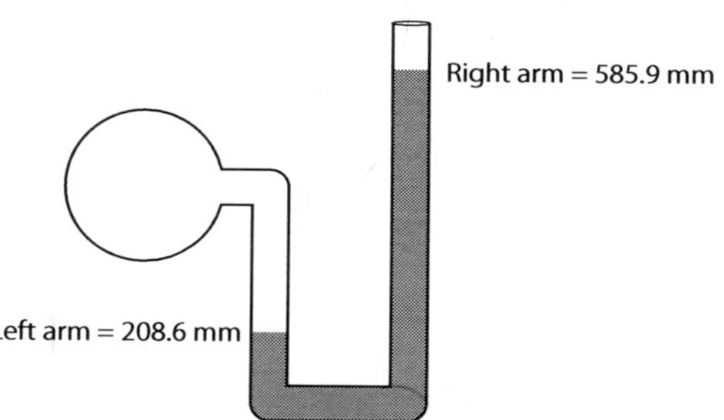

Pressure in bulb: 1126.8 mmHg

585.9 − 208.6 = 377.3 mm
+ 749.5
1126.8 mm

(b) Left arm height = 57.2 cm right arm height = 34.6 cm

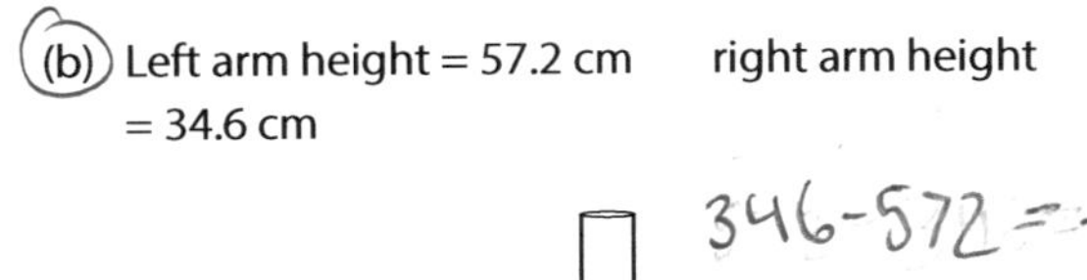

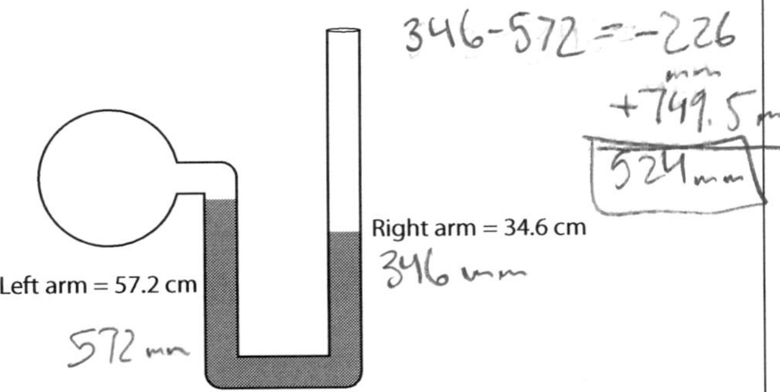

Pressure in bulb: ____________

5. Racing bicycle tires may be inflated to pressures close to double those of mountain bikes. Additionally, the tires have smooth surfaces and are much thinner than mountain bike tires so that far less surface area is in contact with the pavement. These factors combine to allow racing bikes to ride much faster than mountain bikes. The gauge pressure of a racing bike tire reads 118 psi. What is the total pressure exerted by the air in the racing bike tire? Assume the atmospheric pressure is standard 14.7 psi and express your final answer in units of torr.

6. The atmospheric pressure is 17.4 psi, h_1 is 136.5 mm, and h_2 is 199.8 mm. Calculate the pressure inside the bulb and state in units of kPa.

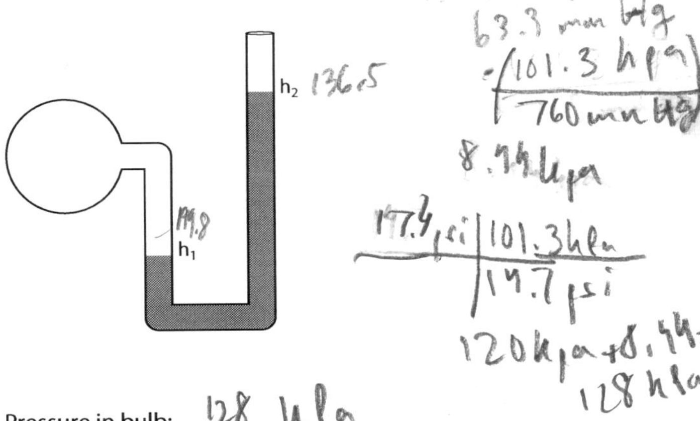

Pressure in bulb: ____________

7. The pressure in the bulb is 8.03 psi, the h_1 is 46.00 cm, and the h_2 is 16.83 cm. Calculate the atmospheric pressure and state in units of torr.

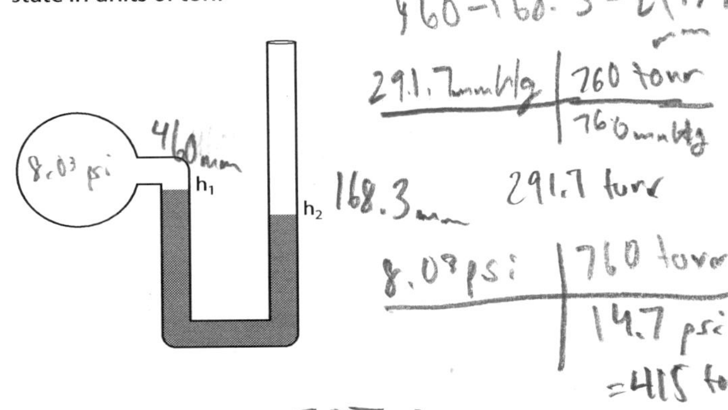

Atmospheric Pressure: ____________

8.2 The Gas Laws

Warm Up

Consider a sealed glass syringe half filled with gas as shown.

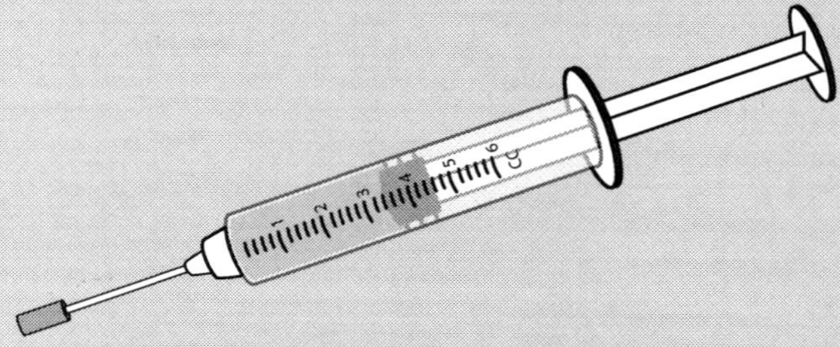

1. Predict what would happen to the volume of the gas sample under each of the following conditions. Give a reason for each of your predictions.

   (a) The syringe is placed into a hyperbaric chamber where the pressure exerted on its exterior (including the plunger) is increased.

   (b) The syringe is dropped into a beaker of boiling water.

2. Assume a nail is driven through the body of the syringe and the shaft of the plunger so the plunger cannot move. Predict what would happen to the pressure exerted by the gas inside the syringe under condition (b) above.

Boyle's Law: Pressure and Volume

Robert Boyle studied the relationship between the volume and the pressure of a sample of a gas in 1662. Boyle was already known for his book *The Skeptical Chemist* in which he refuted the Aristotle's idea that all matter was composed of earth, air, fire and water. He redefined elements as "unmingled bodies." Using a J-tube containing a trapped air sample, Boyle used the multistory entryway of his home to study the effect of altering pressure on the volume of the air. He found that increasing the pressure on a gas sample causes the volume to decrease proportionally. If the pressure is doubled, the volume is cut in half. If the pressure is tripled, the volume becomes one-third of its original value.

An alternative way to perform Boyle's experiment would be to manipulate the volume. If the volume of a container of gas were halved, the same number of gas particles would now strike the sides of the container twice as frequently, effectively doubling the pressure of the gas sample (Figure 8.2.1).

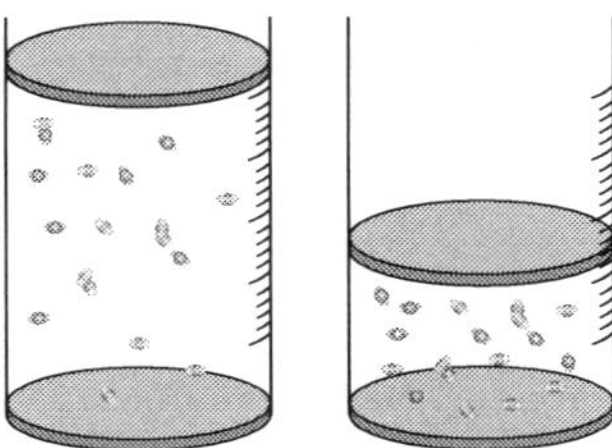

Figure 8.2.1 *Halving the volume of a gas sample results in twice as many collisions with the walls of the container. This causes the pressure to double.*

Fortunately for Boyle, the temperature of his air sample remained relatively constant since a variation in temperature would have affected his results. Boyle plotted his volume data against pressure and obtained the graph in Figure 8.2.2. Manipulation of the data resulted in a straight line being obtained when volume was plotted against the inverse of pressure:

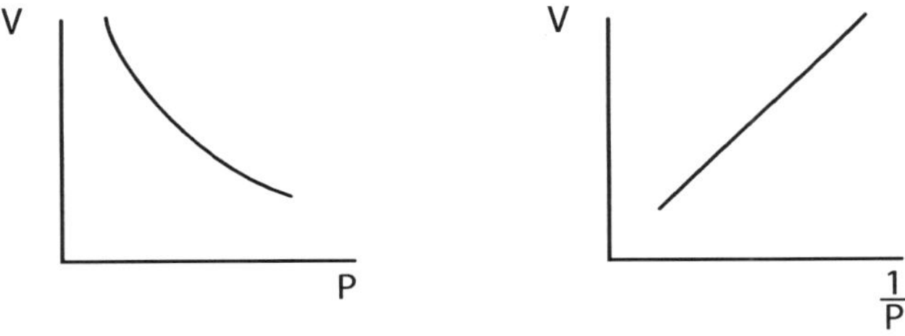

Figure 8.2.2 *A plot of volume versus pressure for a trapped sample of gas with the temperature held constant produces a hyperbola. This is typical of a reciprocal or inverse relationship. Replotting the same volumes against the reciprocal of pressure gives a direct relationship. Note that the line appears to intersect the origin.*

The result of this experiment was **Boyle's law** that states:

At constant temperature, the volume occupied by a fixed mass of gas is inversely proportional to its pressure.

Mathematically speaking, we can say that:

$$V \propto \frac{1}{P}$$

This proportionality can be changed into an equivalency by introducing a constant, k so that $y = mx + b$ becomes:

$$V = k\frac{1}{P} + 0 \text{ or } V = \frac{k}{P} \text{ or } PV = k$$

The value of the constant, k depends on the size of the sample and the temperature.

This law is commonly used to calculate the new pressure or volume after one of these variables has been changed. As Boyle's law states that the product of pressure and volume will be a constant for a fixed temperature, we can modify our mathematical relationship.

$$P_1V_1 = P_2V_2$$

Note that P_1 and V_1 represent the original pressure and volume of the gas, and P_2 and V_2 represent the pressure and volume after some change.

Sample Problem — Boyle's Law: Pressure and Volume

Zippy decides to go to Colorado for a skiing vacation. He fills his favourite red balloon with air. The volume of the balloon is 5.0 L in Vancouver at 101 kPa pressure. He takes the balloon to Steamboat Colorado where the atmospheric pressure is only 91 kPa when he arrives. If the temperature is the same in both places, what is the new volume of the balloon?

What to Think About	How to Do It
1. Since $P_1V_1 = P_2V_2$ this is really just a simple algebra problem. The tricky part is correctly identifying which conditions are initial (P_1 and V_1) and which are final (P_2 and V_2).	Initially the volume of the balloon is 5.0 L. So this is V_1. V_2 is to be determined. The initial pressure is 101 kPa, while the final pressure is 91 kPa.
2. From $P_1V_1 = P_2V_2$, algebra shows us that $V_2 = \frac{P_1V_1}{P_2}$.	So $V_2 = \frac{101 \text{ kPa} \times 5.0 \text{ L}}{91 \text{ kPa}} = $ **5.5 L**
3. It is always helpful to consider *what* sort of answer to expect and whether your answer *makes sense*.	The pressure has decreased by a factor of 101/91 or 1.1 (one and one-tenth) times. Thus it makes perfect sense that the volume has increased by one-tenth or 0.5 L.

Practice Problems — Boyle's Law: Pressure and Volume

1. While in Colorado, Zippy decides to take in a football game. At half time. he buys a bag of Cheese Curls. He finds the bag is puffed up because the air sealed inside at sea level has expanded under the lower pressure of the venue formerly known as Mile High Stadium. If 100.0 mL of air was sealed inside the bag at sea level, what volume will the air occupy at the same temperature at Mile High Stadium? Remember the pressure at Mile High Stadium is 83.1 kPa, as determined in the second practice problem in the first section. Assume the bag was so wrinkled when filled that it would not limit gas expansion.

2. Zippy feels like celebrating (the Seahawks beat the Broncos in an away game) and so he takes his red balloon up to his 24th floor hotel room. Remember the balloon's volume was 5.0 L at a pressure of 101 kPa in Vancouver. If the balloon's volume is now 5.6 L and the temperature has not changed, what is the pressure in Zippy's hotel room?

Charles's Law: Volume and Temperature

We know that air expands when heated, thereby decreasing its density. On December 1, 1783, the French scientist, Jacques Charles's was on the second balloon ever to lift a human being off the surface of Earth. Heated air with a lowered density was responsible for this amazing feat. This accomplishment so impressed King Louis XVI that Charles was given a laboratory at the Sorbonne. Charles studied the effect of temperature on the volume of gases. Not surprisingly, as temperature increased, so does volume. In fact, the relationship is a direct one (doubling the temperature doubles the volume) *as long as the temperature is in degrees Kelvin.*

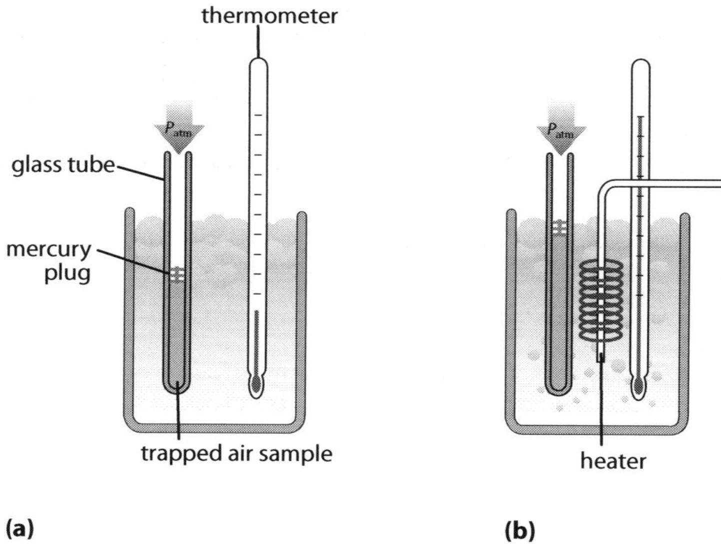

Figure 8.2.3 *Moving a trapped gas sample from an ice bath (a) to a boiling water bath (b) results in a significant increase in the volume of the sample.*

Charles originally plotted his volume data against Celsius temperatures. The result, shown in Figure 8.2.4(a) indicated that a volume of zero would occur at –273°C. At this temperature, there would be a total lack of motion of particles. Later, Lord Kelvin suggested that this represented an absolute minimum of temperature. The result of this finding was the Kelvin temperature scale in which a degree is the same size as a Celsius degree, but 0 K = –273°C. A second plot of volume against temperature in degrees Kelvin shows a straight-line relationship that is easier to work with as it passes through the origin (Figure 8.2.4(b)).

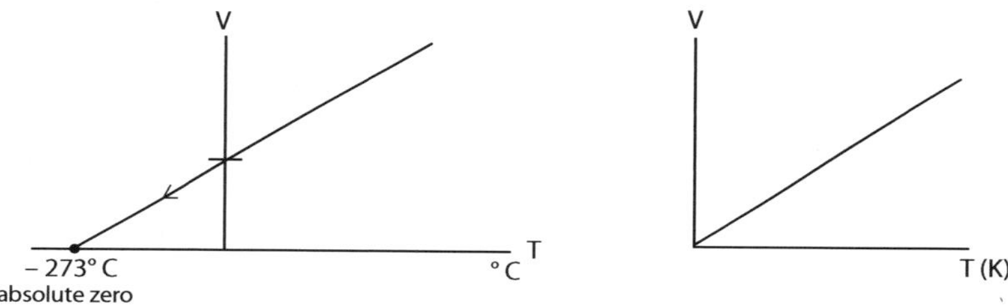

Figure 8.2.4 *Volume versus temperature produces a linear relationship with an x-intercept that represents absolute zero using both Celsius and Kelvin scales.*

The most difficult part of studying this relationship, called Charles's law is the maintenance of a constant pressure. At constant pressure, the volume of a fixed mass of any gas is directly proportional to its Kelvin temperature.

The equation for the graph plotted above shows that: $V = kT$ or $\frac{V}{T} = k$

where V is the volume of a gas at temperature T in Kelvin degrees.

Since we usually wish to relate the volume of a fixed mass of gas at two different temperatures, we rewrite the equation in a more useful form.

$$\frac{V_1}{T_1} = \frac{V_2}{T_2}$$

Much like Boyle's law, V_1 and V_2 are the initial and final volumes, and T_1 and T_2 are the initial and final Kelvin temperatures.

Sample Problem — Charles's Law: Volume and Temperature

When Zippy arrives at the football game, he forgets his red balloon in the rental car. The balloon's volume at this point is 5.5 L and the temperature is 2.0°C. While in the car, the hot sun increases the temperature of the balloon to 26.5°C. Assuming the pressure in the car remains constant, what is the balloon's new volume when Zippy returns?

What to Think About	How to Do It
1. As with Boyle's law, the key is the proper identification of variables. Charles's law has an added twist in that the temperatures must be converted to the Kelvin scale. (Your teacher may wish to convert by adding 273.15 K for a more precise temperature.) It is important to remember that the **precision** of the original temperature will determine the number of **sig figs** in the new temperature. (Review section 1.4.)	Initial conditions involve a 5.5 L balloon at 2.0°C. A quick review of section 1.4 reminds us: $2.0\text{°C} \times \frac{1\text{ K}}{1\text{°C}} + 273\text{ K} = 275.0\text{ K}$ Thus $V_1 = 5.5\text{ L}$ and $T_1 = 275.0\text{ K}$ $26.5\text{°C} \times \frac{1\text{ K}}{1\text{°C}} + 273\text{ K} = 299.5\text{ K}$
2. Charles's law states that $\frac{V_1}{T_1} = \frac{V_2}{T_2}$	Application of algebra shows that $V_2 = \frac{V_1 T_2}{T_1} = \frac{5.5\text{ L} \times 299.5\text{ K}}{275.0\text{ K}}$ $= 6.0\text{ L}$
3. As always, it is helpful to consider *what* sort of answer to expect and whether your answer *makes sense.* Notice leaving the temperatures in Celsius would have predicted an increase in volume of over 13X. Definitely not a reasonable prediction.	The Kelvin temperature has increased by a factor of 299.5/275.0 or 1.089 times. This means the new volume should be approximately 1.1 (one and one-tenth) times larger and it is!

Practice Problems — Charles's Law: Volume and Temperature

1. When he leaves for breakfast the next day, Zippy places his Cheese Curls on the windowsill in the sun. Over a period of time, the temperature of the Cheese Curls increases from 19.0°C to 34.5°C. If the volume of the bag is 121.9 mL when they are placed on the windowsill, what will the volume be after warming? (Assume the pressure remains constant.)

2. Alarmed by the increase in volume of his Cheese Curls bag, Zippy decides to place them in the mini-bar in an effort to restore the original volume. Assuming the pressure remains constant, if the volume is reduced from 128.4 mL at the windowsill temperature of 34.5°C to 115.0 mL, what is the temperature of the mini-bar?

Gay-Lussac's Law: Pressure and Temperature

Charles never did publish his work. Rumour has it he was having too much fun riding around in hot air balloons. In the early 1800s, another French scientist names Joseph Gay-Lussac repeated Charles's work and published the results. Like Charles, Gay-Lussac was a hot air balloon fanatic. In 1804, he ascended to a height of 7 km in a hydrogen-filled balloon setting an altitude record that remained unbroken for 50 years.

Gay-Lussac discovered that if a gas is contained in a vessel that cannot expand then as the Kelvin temperature is increases, the pressure increases proportionally (Figure 8.2.5).

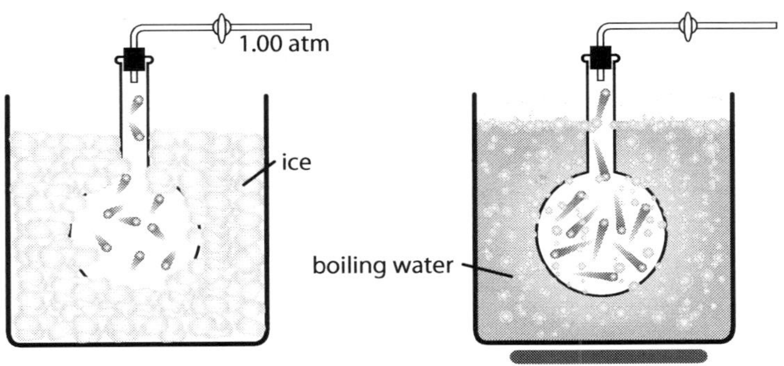

Figure 8.2.5 *The particles of gas in a sealed flask undergo a significant increase in kinetic energy and hence, velocity, when moved from an ice bath (a) to a bath of boiling water (b). The more frequent and more energetic collisions with the walls of the flask produce a significant increase in pressure.*

Gay-Lussac's measurements of pressure related to temperature resulted in the graph in Figure 8.2.6.

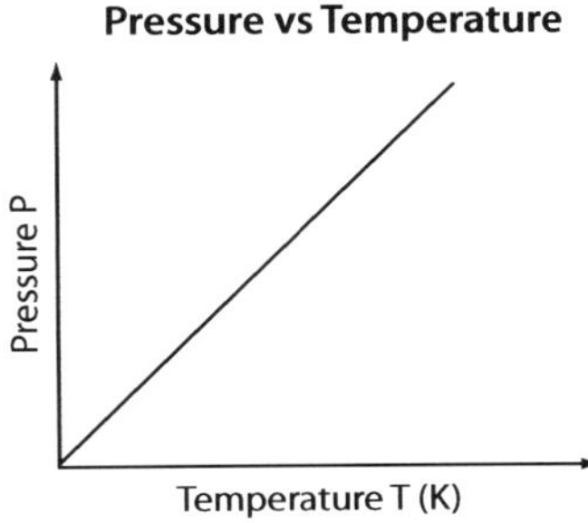

Figure 8.2.6 *A plot of pressure versus Kelvin temperature produces a direct relationship passing through the origin.*

The mathematical relationship is $P = kT + 0$ or $\frac{P}{T} = k$

At constant volume, the pressure of a fixed mass of any gas is directly proportional to its Kelvin temperature.

The most useful mathematical form of Gay-Lussac's law relates pressures at two different temperatures with the volume held constant.

$$\frac{P_1}{T_1} = \frac{P_2}{T_2}$$

where P_1 and P_2 are the initial and final pressures, and T_1 and T_2 are the initial and final Kelvin temperatures.

Sample Problem — Gay-Lussac's Law: Pressure and Temperature

On opening the cupboard that contained the mini-bar, Zippy notices a series of high-priced snacks on a shelf just above the fridge. He is particularly interested in a 255 mL vacuum packed can of Pring-Pong Potato Chips. Assume the Pring-Pong Chips were sealed at a pressure of 505 mm Hg and a temperature of 5.0°C. As Zippy is examining the can in his 19.0°C hotel room, what is the pressure inside the can now?

What to Think About	How To Do It
1. As with Charles's law, we must properly assign the variables. In addition, we must convert both temperatures into degrees Kelvin.	Initial conditions are 505 mm Hg and 5.0°C. These values are P_1 and T_1 and the temperature must be converted to degrees Kelvin. $5.0\text{°C} \times \frac{1\text{ K}}{1\text{°C}} + 273\text{ K} = 278.0\text{ K}$ The final temperature, T_2, will be $19.0\text{°C} \times \frac{1\text{ K}}{1\text{°C}} + 273 = 292.0\text{ K}$
2. Attention must be paid to the algebra. In this case, we are solving for the final pressure (or P_2).	$\frac{P_1}{T_1} = \frac{P_2}{T_2}$, hence, $P_2 = \frac{P_1T_2}{T_1}$ $= \frac{505\text{ mm Hg} \times 292.0\text{ K}}{278.0\text{ K}}$
3. Does the answer make sense or is it … *nonsense?*	= **530. mm Hg** An increased temperature should cause the pressure to increase by a factor of 292.0/278.0 or 1.05 times. This is equivalent to an increase of one-half of one-tenth of the total pressure or approximately 25 mm Hg.

Practice Problems — Gay-Lussac's Law: Pressure and Temperature

1. Returning from breakfast, Zippy finds himself hungry again. He decides to finally eat his Cheese Curls. He rather enjoys the cold Curls and decides to try the Pring-Pongs cold as well. He places the can into the mini-bar and leaves it in the 2.4°C environment until it reaches that temperature. Considering the pressure in the can was 530. mm Hg at 19.0°C, what will the pressure be once the can has equilibrated in the mini-bar?

2. Zippy decides he needs a drink to wash down the cold Pring Pongs. There are two 355 mL cans of Kookie Cola in the mini-bar. The Kookie Cola is carbonated and the refrigerated can is under 36.5 psi pressure even at 2.4°C. Zippy drinks one can and accidentally leaves the other one on the dresser. If the pressure in the can rises to 38.9 psi, what is the temperature in Zippy's hotel room at this point? Assume the solubility of the carbon dioxide is not affected by this temperature change.

The Combined Gas Law — Pressure, Volume, and Temperature

In each of the three laws discussed so far, one of the variables important to gases —pressure, volume, or temperature — was held constant. However, in real life, it is much more common that all three variables change. For example, if we consider a weather balloon which is released into the atmosphere. As its altitude increases, the temperature, volume, and pressure of the gas inside the balloon change.

Wouldn't it be great if we could calculate the new value of any one of the three variables when the other two change? The relationship that will allow us to do just that is simply a combination of Boyle's, Charles's, and Guy-Lussac's laws. This relationship is called the **combined gas law.**

$$\frac{P_1V_1}{T_1} = \frac{P_2V_2}{T_2}$$

In order to compare the results obtained in experiments involving gases at various temperatures and pressures, scientists have adopted a set of standard conditions to which such results may be readily converted. These conditions are called standard temperature and pressure. In section 3.4 you learned that one mole of any gas occupies a volume of 22.4 L under these conditions.

Standard temperature and pressure (STP) refers to a temperature of 273°K (0°C) and a pressure of 101.3 kPa (1 atm)

Normally it is not very convenient to carry out an experiment at STP since the temperature in most laboratories is well above 0°C and the atmospheric pressure is seldom exactly 101.3 kPa. However, as long as we record the temperature and pressure when we make our measurements, we can use the combined gas law equation to convert our data to these standard conditions if required.

Sample Problem — The Combined Gas Law: Pressure, Volume, and Temperature

Zippy's second day of skiing led to a big toe sprain on the rope tow at the bunny hill. Zippy is required to spend 24 hours in a Colorado hospital under observation. He passes the time creating and solving gas law problems much like this one: Once upon a time, the economy size (325 mL) can of Big Brute Aerosol Deodorant contained a propellant gas at 445 kPa and 12°C (which explained why it was so cold under the arms when applied in the morning). What volume would this propellant gas occupy if it were allowed to escape into a 101 kPa and 21°C environment?

What to Think About	How To Do It
1. As with the simple laws, we must properly assign the variables. In addition, we must convert both temperatures into degrees Kelvin.	Initial conditions are 325 mL, 445 kPa and 12°C. These values are V_1, P_1 and T_1. The temperature must be converted to degrees Kelvin. $12\text{°C} \times \frac{1\text{ K}}{1\text{°C}} + 273\text{ K} = 285\text{ K}$ The final temperature, T_2, will be $21\text{°C} \times \frac{1\text{ K}}{1\text{°C}} + 273 = 294\text{ K}$
2. Attention must be paid to the more complex algebra. In this case, we are solving for the final volume (or V_2).	Since $\frac{P_1V_1}{T_1} = \frac{P_2V_2}{T_2}$ $V_2 = \frac{P_1V_1T_2}{T_1P_2}$ $= \frac{445\text{ kPa} \times 325\text{ mL} \times 294\text{ K}}{285\text{ K} \times 101\text{ kPa}}$ $= 1477.150 = \mathbf{1480\text{ mL}}$
3. Does the answer make sense?	There is a small increase in temperature (294/285) and a large pressure decrease (445/101) both of which contribute to an increase in volume.

Practice Problems — The Combined Gas Law: Pressure, Volume, and Temperature

1. To ensure a more comfortable stay at the hospital, Zippy decided to place his rubber air mattress over the hard hospital bed. Noting a gas cylinder chained near the bed, Zippy decided to use this gas source to inflate his air mattress. If the gas cylinder had a volume of 58.0 L of oxygen contained under a pressure of 222 psi and a temperature of 12°C, what volume would the gas occupy if it were released at standard atmospheric pressure (14.7 psi) and a temperature of 22°C? If Zippy's mattress was rated for a volume of 500 L, was this a good idea?

2. While in the hospital, Dr. Bundolo decided to remove a rather bothersome plantar's wart located conveniently near Zippy's big toe. The doctor used a gaseous anesthetic to prepare Zippy for the operation. This gas, a nitrogen compound, occupies a volume of 18.0 L at a pressure of 44.4 kPa and a temperature of 125°C. What would its volume be at STP?

The Ideal Gas Law: Pressure, Volume, Temperature, and Moles

The simple gas law equations are concerned with the relationships between temperature, pressure, and volume. While these equations are very useful, they do not relate temperature, pressure, or volume to the amount of gas that is present. We know, from our study of molar volume, that the amount of gas present is related to the volume of the gas at STP through the molar volume, 22.4 L/mol. The ideal gas equation is an equation that relates the amount of a substance (remember the SI unit for *amount* is the *mole*) to pressure, volume, and temperature, so that if any three of these four parameters are know, the fourth may be readily determined.

ideal gas law: $PV = nRT$

where P = pressure of the gas
V = volume of the gas in litres
n = amount of the gas in moles
R = ideal gas constant
T = temperature of the gas in Kelvin degrees

The Ideal Gas Constant

In section 3.4, we learned of **Avogadro's hypothesis** that states that one mole of any gas occupies the same volume as long as the temperature and pressure are held constant (Figure 8.2.7).

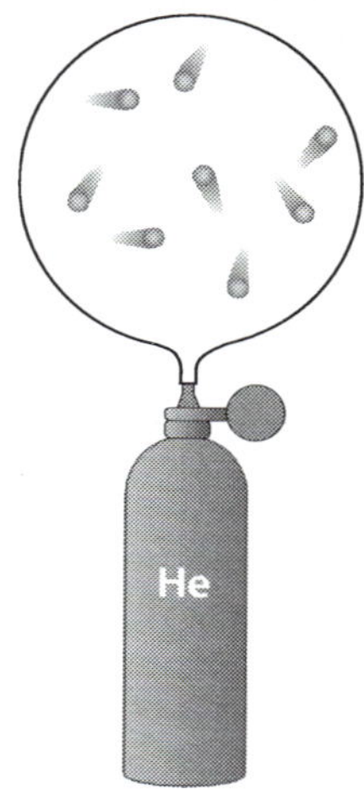

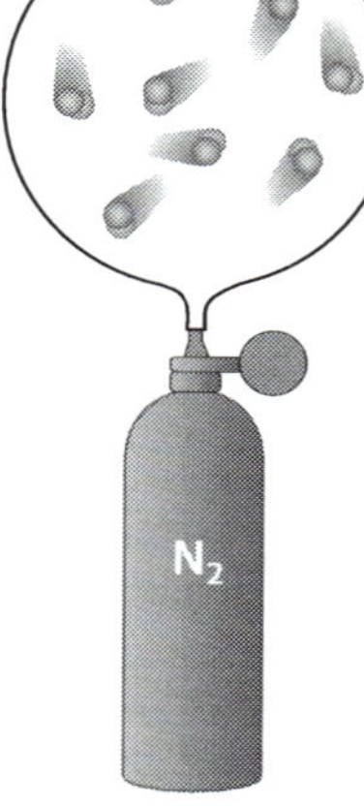

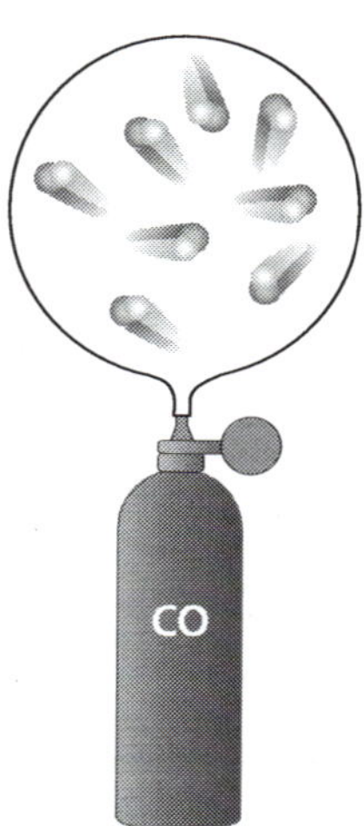

$n = 1$ mol	$n = 1$ mol	$n = 1$ mol
$P = 1$ atm (760 torr)	$P = 1$ atm (760 torr)	$P = 1$ atm (760 torr)
$T = 0°C$ 273 K)	$T = 0°C$ 273 K)	$T = 0°C$ 273 K)
$V = 22.4$ L	$V = 22.4$ L	$V = 22.4$ L
Number of gas particles $= 6.02 \times 10^{23}$	Number of gas particles $= 6.02 \times 10^{23}$	Number of gas particles $= 6.02 \times 10^{23}$
Mass = 4.003 g	Mass = 28.02 g	Mass = 28.01 g

Figure 8.2.7 *Regardless of identity, 22.4 L of gas under STP conditions will always contain the same number of gas particles – 6.02 x 10^{23} or 1 mole.*

This hypothesis is very handy as it allows us to determine the value of the ideal gas constant, *R*, by merely substituting 1 mole of gas at STP conditions into the ideal gas equation.

$$\text{Since } PV = nRT,\ R = \frac{PV}{nT} = \frac{(101.3\text{ kPa}) \times 22.4\text{ L}}{1\text{ mole} \times 273\text{ K}} = 8.31\ \frac{\text{kPa·L}}{\text{mol·K}}$$

Quick Check

Determine other values for the ideal gas constant, *R*, by substituting the following standard atmospheric pressures for *P* into the ideal gas equation. Note that the molar volume 22.4 L is rounded to three significant figures. Consequently, *R* values determined by this method are correct to only three significant figures.

Standard *P*	Substitution Work Shown	*R* Value
1 atm	$\frac{(1\text{ atm}) \times 22.4\text{ L}}{1\text{ mol} \times 273\text{ K}}$	0.0821 $\frac{\text{L·atm}}{\text{mol·K}}$
760. mm Hg	$\frac{(\qquad) \times 22.4\text{ L}}{1\text{ mol} \times 273\text{ K}}$	$\frac{\text{mm Hg·L}}{\text{mol·K}}$
14.7 psi		
101.3 kPa		

R values provided in the AP exam table of constants:

$$8.314\ \frac{\text{L·kPa}}{\text{mol·K}} = 0.08206\ \frac{\text{L·atm}}{\text{mol·K}} = 62.36\ \frac{\text{L·torr}}{\text{mol·K}}$$

R is occasionally presented in tables of constants as 8.31 J/mol·K due to the fact that a Pa is really the amount of pressure exerted by a force of 1 newton on an area of 1 m^2 and 1 L is really the same as 1 dm^3. Hence, 1 kPa × 1 L is the same as 1 newton-metre, which you may recall from physics is the same as 1 joule. This *R* value was also used briefly in section 4.5 and will be used much more frequently in AP II.

What Is an "Ideal" Gas?

Strictly speaking, the ideal gas equation should only be applied to "*ideal gases,*" that is, gases that conform to the assumptions of the kinetic molecular theory. Two of the assumptions of this theory are that the molecules of a gas possess zero volume (virtually all of the volume of any gas sample is empty space), and that there are no attractive forces between gases (gas collisions are completely elastic — particles lose no momentum following a collision). In fact, the molecules of all gases do possess some, though very little, volume and there is a small attraction between their particles.

However, provided the temperature involved is not too low and the pressure is not too high, most gases behave as if they are ideal, and the ideal gas equation gives us a correct answer to our calculations. In section 8.4, you will find an equation that takes into account the attractive forces acting between molecules and the actual volume of the molecules themselves. This equation may be used when the ideal gas equation in not applicable.

PV=nRT

Sample Problem — The Ideal Gas Law

A 1.45 L container is filled with sulphur dioxide gas at a pressure of 115.0 kPa and a temperature of 28°C.

(i) How many moles of sulphur dioxide gas are in the container?

(ii) Calculate the mass of sulphur dioxide gas in the container.

What to Think About	How To Do It
1. This is a classic substitution into $PV = nRT$ to find the missing variable calculation. 2. As the pressure is provided in units of kPa, be sure to use the appropriate R value of 8.31 kPa/mol·K.	Simply begin with $PV=nRT$ and solve for n using the appropriate values and units for R and T. $28\,°C \times \frac{1\,K}{1\,°C} + 273\,K = 301\,K$ $n = \frac{PV}{RT} = \frac{115.0\,kPa \times 1.45\,L}{8.31\,\frac{L \cdot kPa}{mol \cdot K} \times 301\,K}$
3. The second part of the problem would typically not be separated out. You would need to recognize the necessity of finding moles and then simply multiply by the molar mass.	$n = $ **0.0667 mol** $m = 0.0667\,mol \times \frac{64.1\,g\,SO_2}{1\,mol}$ $=$ **4.27 g of SO_2 gas**

Practice Problems — The Ideal Gas Law

1. Find the volume of 1.00 g of water if it were converted to the gas state at its boiling point of 100.0°C at standard atmospheric pressure.

Continued

Practice Problems — The Ideal Gas Law (continued)

2. At 30.0°C and 98.1 kPa, a 3.26 g sample of an unknown, unreactive gas has a volume of 3.00 L. What is the molar mass of the gas? Assume it is a diatomic gas and identify it. Hint: The first step is to determine the number of moles, then apply the unit g/mol for molar mass to calculate the value.

PV = nRT   n = ?   30 + 273 = 303

$\frac{PV}{RT} = n$ $\frac{98.1 \text{ kPa} \cdot 3.00 \text{ L}}{8.314 \frac{\text{L}\cdot\text{kPa}}{\text{mol}\cdot\text{K}} \cdot 303 \text{ K}} = .117$ mol

3.26 g / .117 mol = 27.86 g/mol

3. A diatomic gas has a density of 1.95 g/L at 1.50 atm and 27°C. Determine the molar mass of this gas and identify it. Hint: The density tells us that 1.00 L of the gas under the given *T* and *P* has a mass of 1.95 g. Now solve the problem as in number 2.

PV = nRT   n = ?   27 + 273 = 300

$n = \frac{PV}{RT}$ $\frac{1.50 \text{ atm} \cdot 1.00 \text{ L}}{.08206 \frac{\text{L}\cdot\text{atm}}{\text{mol}\cdot\text{K}} \cdot 300 \text{ K}} = .061$ mol

1.95 g / .061 mol = 32.0 g/mol

Derivations Using *PV* = *nRT*

PV = *nRT* may be used as the genesis of each of the simple gas laws. Of course, each of Boyle's, Charles's, Gay-Lussac's and even the combined gas law is very intuitive and can be easily figured out. However, if there is a short cut available to help verify the validity of our intuition, why not use it? Since *R* is a constant, it stands to reason that

R is the *ratio* of $\frac{PV}{nT} = \frac{PV}{nT}$ now and forever. Hence, $\frac{P_1V_1}{n_1T_1} = \frac{P_2V_2}{n_2V_2}$. Now if we

simply cancel any variables that remain constant, we can derive each of the simple gas laws in turn. Boyle's law for example involves a fixed quantity of gas, at a constant

temperature, hence *n* and *T* are constant, leaving: $\frac{P_1V_1}{\cancel{n_1T_1}} = \frac{P_2V_2}{\cancel{n_2T_2}}$ becomes $P_1V_1 = P_2V_2$.

Quick Check

Use the information in the paragraph above as a model to complete the following table.

Simple Law	Constant Variables	Derivation Shown	Final Form of Law
Charles's law	pressure & moles	$\frac{\not{P_1}V_1}{\not{n_1}T_1}=\frac{\not{P_2}V_2}{\not{n_2}V_2}$	
Gay-Lussac's law			
Combined gas law			

Molar Mass and Density: Another Ideal Gas Law Derivation

Section 3.4 discussed a simple method for converting between molar mass, molar volume, and density. These conversions work nicely for any system at STP. We can expand on this relationship for non-STP situations using the ideal gas law.

We know that molar mass $= \frac{\text{mass}}{\text{moles}} = \frac{\text{mass}}{\frac{PV}{RT}} = \frac{\text{mass}}{PV} \times \frac{RT}{V} = \frac{mRT}{P}$

Since m/V is actually density, the equation can be written as $MM = \frac{dRT}{P}$

Some folks prefer to write the equation as the "kitty cat equation."

$$\text{molecular weight} = \text{molar mass} = MW = \frac{dRT}{P}$$

The nickname comes from MeoW for molecular weight. The "dRT" is what kitty cats put on the "P" in their litter boxes — just a little something to fall back on if your derivation fails you.

Quick Check

1. Solve problems 2 and 3 from the ideal gas law Practice Problems using the "kitty cat equation." Compare your answers.

8.2 Review Problems

1. Consider the following identical containers each filled with 1 mole of helium gas. Container one is rigid and cannot expand. The piston in container two can rise or drop to allow free expansion or contraction of the gas volume.

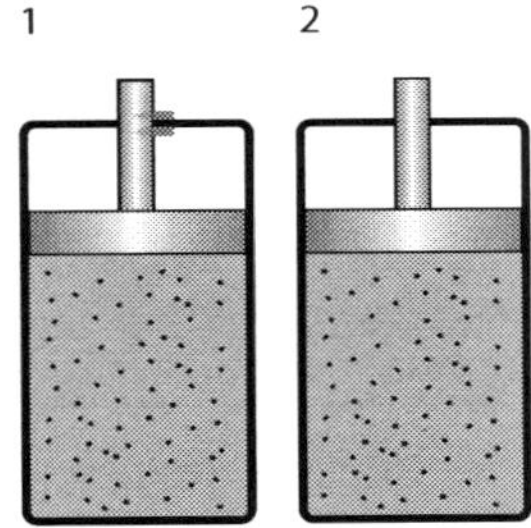

What is the effect on the (i) pressure and (ii) density of each sample if:

(a) The containers are dropped into an ice bath?

(b) Another mole of gas is injected through a rubber portion of the piston?
Be sure to support your answer with an explanation.

2. Consider the following flasks, each containing the same number of particles of the same gas at the same temperature. What simple gas law is depicted? How is the ratio of *PV*/*nT* held constant?

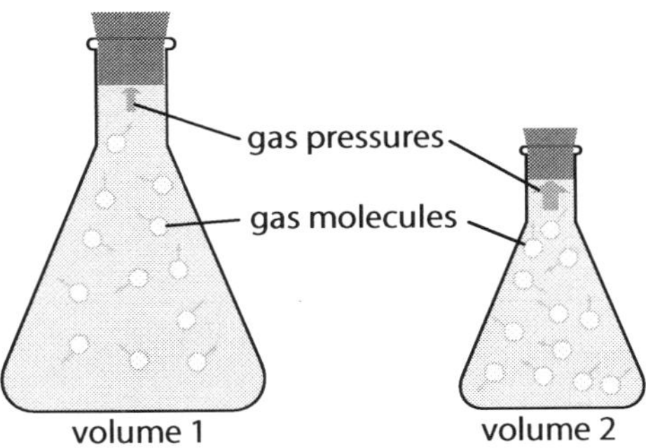

3. Consider the following flexible containers each containing the same number of particles of the same gas at the same pressure. What simple gas law is depicted? How is the ratio of *PV*/*nT* held constant?

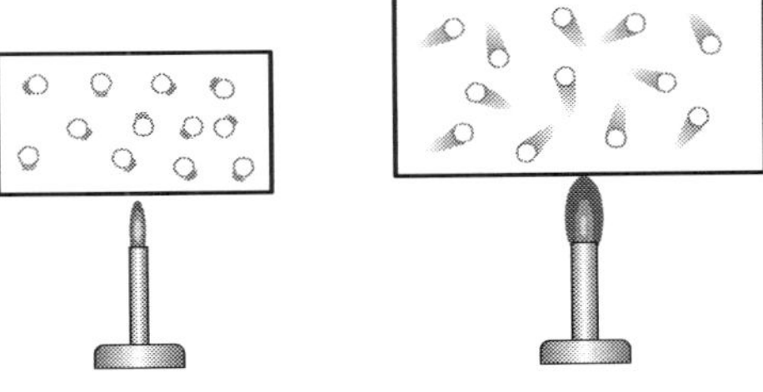

4. Consider the following container under two different conditions. From condition one to two, there are twice as many gas particles and the Kelvin temperature has been doubled. The volume remains constant. How is the ratio PV/nT maintained?

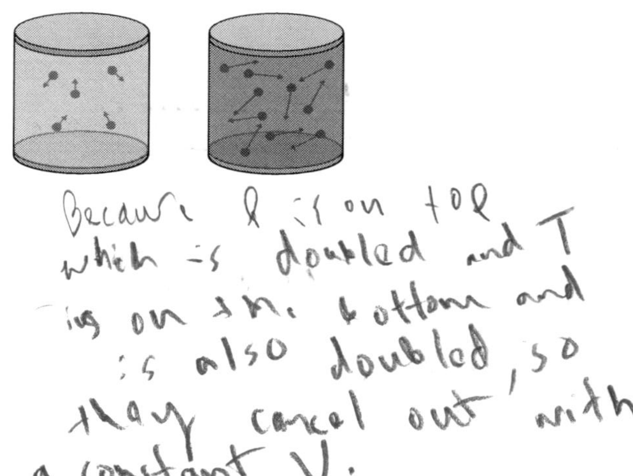

5. At 46°C, a sample of ammonia gas exerts a pressure of 4.8 atm. What is the pressure when the volume of the gas is reduced by 1/10 (0.10) of the original value when the temperature remains constant?

6. A 1.45 L sample of radon gas is kept in a sealed radiation-resistant container at 1.53 atm and 32°C. What will the pressure be if the temperature is lowered to 21.663°C?

7. A sample of polluted air is kept in a sealed container at 34.6°C and 31 psi. During winter, the temperature decreased to −15.672°C. At what temperature did the pressure in the container reach 26.75 psi?

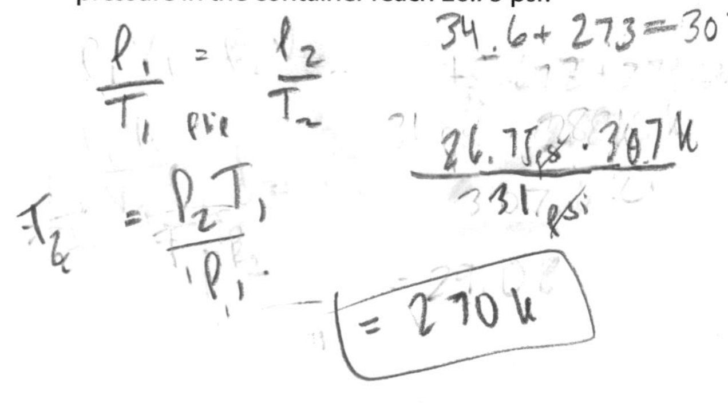

8. A sample of the gas "bozone" occupies a volume of 53.1 L at 52°C and 675 torr. What volume will this gas occupy at STP?

9. A gas lecture cylinder is labeled to deliver 52.3 L of helium gas at room pressure. Assuming room pressure is 101.3 kPa, what is the pressure of the gas inside the cylinder when it arrives from the company fully sealed? The volume of the cylinder is 1.40 L.

10. A racing tire has a pressure of 34.8 psi at 15°C. Assuming the volume remains constant during the race, what is the new tire pressure when the car crosses the finish line and the tire's temperature has increased to 91°C?

11. A standard scuba tank holds a volume of 70.0 ft^3 of air under SATP conditions (25°C and 1.00 atm). What volume would this air occupy if released under the conditions a diver experiences under 20 m of water on the northwest coast while winter diving? This diver would experience temperatures of 6.5°C and a pressure of 315 kPa.

12. Jo Bob collects a sample of gas from the exhaust pipe of his sister's car. The sample contains 1.21 x 10^{23} molecules of gas at a pressure of 775 mm Hg and a temperature of 38°C. What is the volume of the gas sample?

13. A 44.8 L sample of gas weighs 128.2 g at a temperature of 273 K and a pressure of 760.0 torr. What is the molar mass of this gas?

14. A 7.50 g sample of lithium metal is dropped into 25.0 mL of 1.5 M hydrochloric acid. What volume of hydrogen gas would be evolved once the limiting reactant has been consumed? (The reaction is performed at SATP conditions; hence the temperature is 25.0°C and the pressure is 101.3 kPa.)

$PV = nRT$

15. The propane tank by the science portable near the backfield of a typical school has a volume of 2210 L. Assuming the tank contains 3150 moles of propane gas, what is the pressure inside the tank on a nice warm day of 28°C?

$P = \frac{nRT}{V}$ $\quad 28 + 273 = 301\text{ K}$

$P = \frac{3150\text{ mol} \cdot 8.314 \frac{\text{kPa}\cdot\text{L}}{\text{mol}\cdot\text{K}} \cdot 301\text{ K}}{2210\text{ L}}$

$P = 3570\text{ kPa}$

16. Bonzo lives on the planet X, which has an atmospheric pressure of 164 kPa. A nice day on planet X has a temperature of –36°C. If Bonzo exhales 11.0 g of carbon dioxide, what is the volume of gas?

CO_2: C = 12.01, + 2.16 (sic), 44.01 g/mol

$\frac{11.0\text{ g}}{} \Big| \frac{1\text{ mol}}{44.01\text{ g}} = .250\text{ mol}$

$-36 + 273 = 237\text{ K}$

$V = \frac{nRT}{P}$

$V = \frac{.250\text{ mol} \cdot 8.314 \frac{\text{kPa}\cdot\text{L}}{\text{mol}\cdot\text{K}} \cdot 237\text{ K}}{164\text{ kPa}}$

$V = 3.00\text{ L}$

17. For an unknown gaseous *element*, 3.23 g occupy 5.60 L at 153°C and 101.3 kPa.

(a) What is the molar mass of the element?

$PV = nRT$

$n = \frac{PV}{RT} = \frac{101.3\text{ kPa} \cdot 5.60\text{ L}}{8.314 \frac{\text{kPa}\cdot\text{L}}{\text{mol}\cdot\text{K}} \cdot 426\text{ K}}$

$153 + 273 = 426\text{ K}$

$n = .160\text{ mol}$

$3.23\text{ g} / .160\text{ mol}$

20.2 g/mol

(b) How many *atoms* are contained in 3.23 g of this element?

$\frac{.160\text{ mol}}{} \Big| \frac{6.022 \times 10^{23}\text{ atoms}}{1\text{ mol}} =$

9.64×10^{22} atoms

(c) What is the identity of the mysterious unknown element?

Neon

8.3 Vapour and Partial Pressures

Warm Up

Use the box on the left to sketch a molecular representation of a sample of clean air (remember from section 8.1 that air is a roughly 80:20 parts $N_2(g)$:$O_2(g)$ mixture). Use the box on the right to do the same for a sample of moist air. This box will show what happens when the "humidity is high."

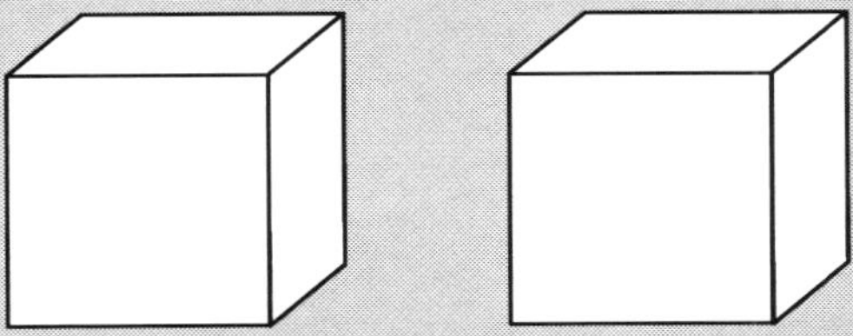

Keep Avogadro's hypothesis in mind as you do this. Equal volumes of gas should contain equal numbers of particles.

(a) Are these accurate representations of what the gas samples actually look like? Explain your answer.

(b) What percent of the pressure exerted by particles colliding with the walls of the box on the left is due to oxygen gas? How does the pressure exerted by oxygen (called the "partial pressure" of oxygen) in the box on the right compare with that in the box on the left? Explain.

(c) Why do meteorologists say the "barometer is falling" when it is about to rain?

Vapour Pressure

We know from everyday experience that puddles of water eventually evaporate after a rain even though the temperature is well below water's boiling point. At room temperature, the average kinetic energy of the water molecules is not sufficient for vaporization to take place, yet some of the molecules have enough energy to escape from the surface of the water and enter the gas phase (Figure 8.3.1). Hence, over a period of time, an entire puddle of water evaporates, even at room temperature.

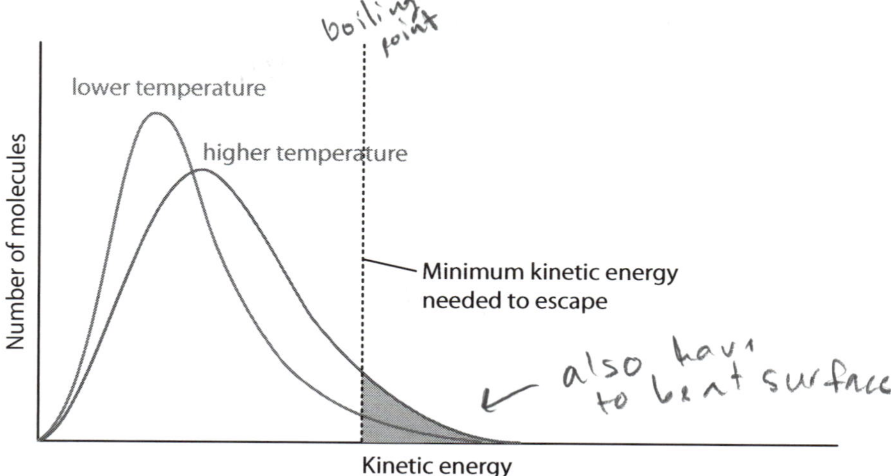

Figure 8.3.1 *There is a distribution of energies in any sample of matter. In the case of a liquid sample, some of the molecules have very little energy and some have enough to actually escape the surface of the liquid and become gaseous. The area under the curve to the right of the minimum "escape KE" represents the particles with enough energy to evaporate. The lower curve, shifted to the right, represents what would happen to the distribution at a higher temperature.*

English chemist and weather aficionado John Dalton found that even when water was placed in a sealed container, some of the liquid evaporated. This gaseous water exerted a pressure on the walls of the container. We now use the term "vapour" for the gaseous portion of a substance present above the liquid phase of that substance (Figure 8.3.2).

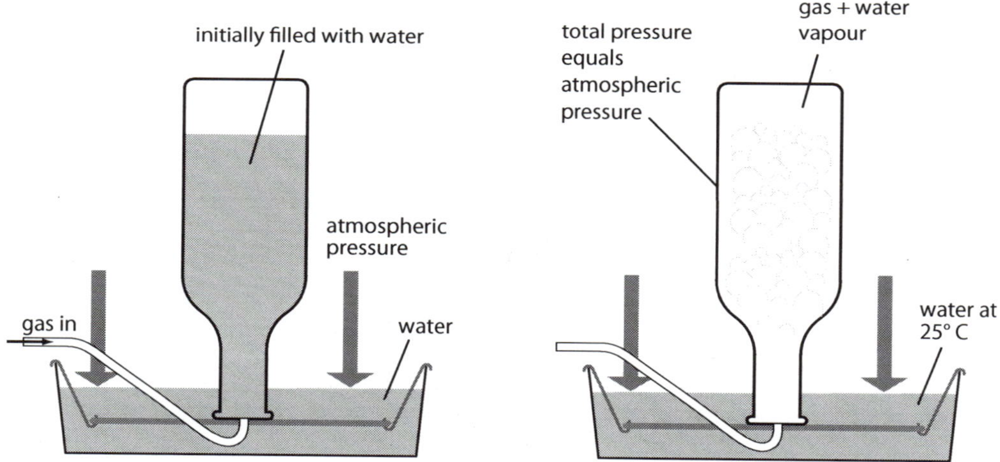

Figure 8.3.2 *Gas collected over water will contain some gaseous water due to water's vapour pressure.*

The pressure exerted by the vapour of a substance is known as the **vapour pressure** of the substance. Vapour pressure explains why we can smell some liquid substances such as nail polish remover and even some solids like black licorice.

The vapour pressure of a substance depends first, on its chemical structure and second, on the temperature of the substance. At a given temperature, there is a maximum value the vapour pressure can reach.

Vapour Pressure and Boiling Point

Every liquid possesses a vapour pressure. As shown in Table 8.3.1, the vapour pressure of a liquid, in this case water, increases with an increase in temperature. When the vapour pressure reaches atmospheric pressure, the liquid begins to boil.

Table 8.3.1 *As temperature increases, so does vapour pressure.*

Temperature (°C)	Vapour Pressure (kPa)
0	0.61
20	2.34
40	7.37
60	19.9
80	47.3
100	101.3

From this information, we arrive at a definition for the boiling point of a liquid as the temperature at which its vapour pressure equals atmospheric pressure (Figure 8.3.3).

The boiling point of a substance is the temperature at which the substance's vapour pressure reaches atmospheric pressure.

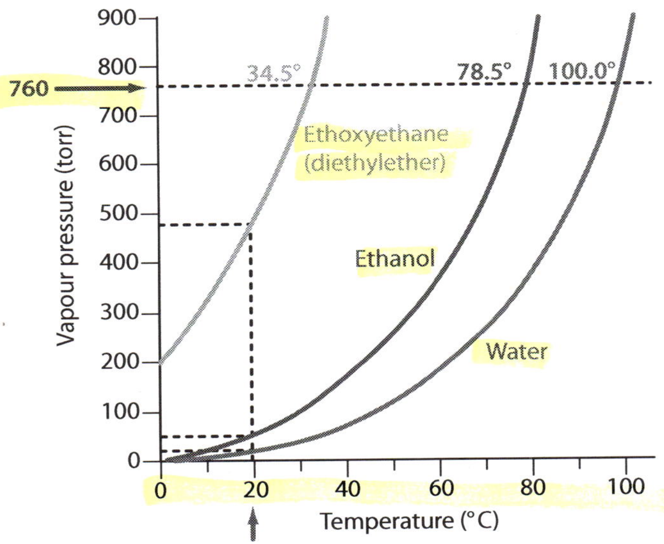

Figure 8.3.3 *The vapour pressure versus temperature graph for three different liquids. The boiling points may be read as the temperatures at which the liquids' vapour pressures reach 760 torr (or 760 mm Hg). This is atmospheric pressure at sea level. The vapour pressures can be read as the values on the y-axis at room temperature.*

Boiling and Atmospheric Pressure

It should follow from the information above that boiling points change with atmospheric pressure. As the atmospheric pressure decreases, boiling points become lower and lower. For example, the boiling point of water in Denver, Colorado, is 94°C. As a consequence, it takes longer to boil an egg at high altitudes, since the water is boiling at a lower temperature (Figure 8.3.4).

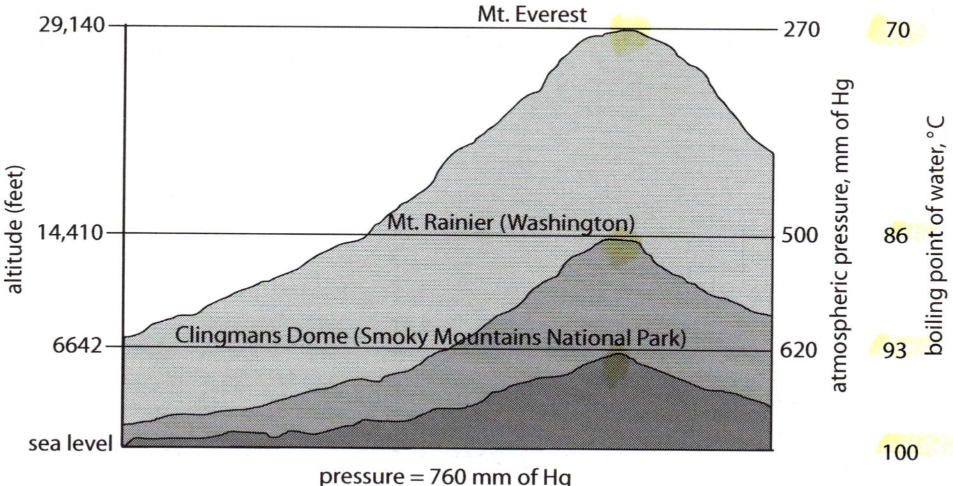

Figure 8.3.4 *The effect of altitude on atmospheric pressure and consequently on the boiling point of water. The boiling point drops 1 °C for every 300 m (or 1,000 ft) of altitude.*

Intermolecular Forces and Boiling Point

The reason different liquids have different boiling points is related to the attractive forces between the particles of different liquids. *Intermolecular forces* (*IMFs*), including *London dispersion forces, dipole-dipole forces,* and *hydrogen bonds,* were discussed in sections 6.5 and 7.2. Stronger IMFs result in fewer molecules (or atoms) having enough energy to overcome the attraction and escape into the gas phase.

Table 8.2.2 *Vapour Pressure (at 25°C) and Boiling Points for Various Liquids*

Liquid	Vapour Pressure (kPa at 25°C)	Boiling Point (°C)
Diethyl ether	57.9	34
Ethanol	5.6	78
Water	2.3	100
Mercury	0.024	357

Diethyl ether's (ethoxyethane's) bent shape gives it a slight polarity that produces dipole-dipole forces that hold its molecules together. Ethanol, like all alcohols, can hydrogen bond to its neighbours, but to a lesser extent than water can. The liquid metal, mercury, bonds to its neighbouring atoms using the "sea of electrons" bonding model that holds its atoms tightly together, making its vapour pressure very small.

Liquids that have a high vapour pressure will evaporate very readily and are said to be **volatile**.

Quick Check

1. A "bell jar" is placed over a beaker partially filled with water.

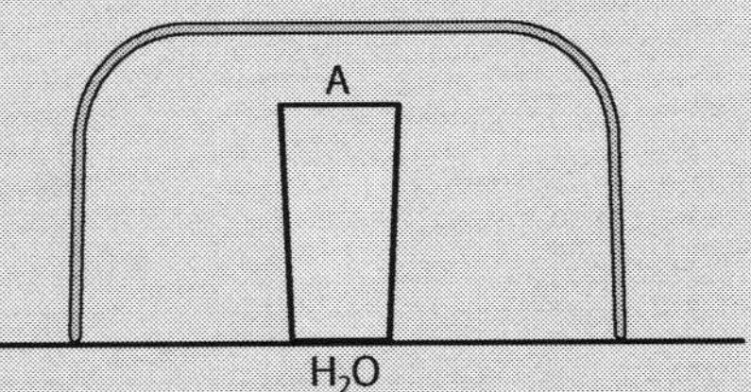

   (a) What will happen to the height of the water in the beaker over time? Explain why.

   (b) If the temperature of system is increased, how will the answer to part (a) change? Explain clearly.

   (c) If the system is transported to the top of Mount Rainier in Washington where the atmospheric pressure is only 500 mm Hg, how will the answer to part (a) change?

2. A "bell jar" is placed over the two beakers shown. Acetone is a low polarity, volatile liquid. How will the vapour pressure of the water inside the bell jar compare with the vapour pressure of the acetone after one hour has passed? Explain your answer.

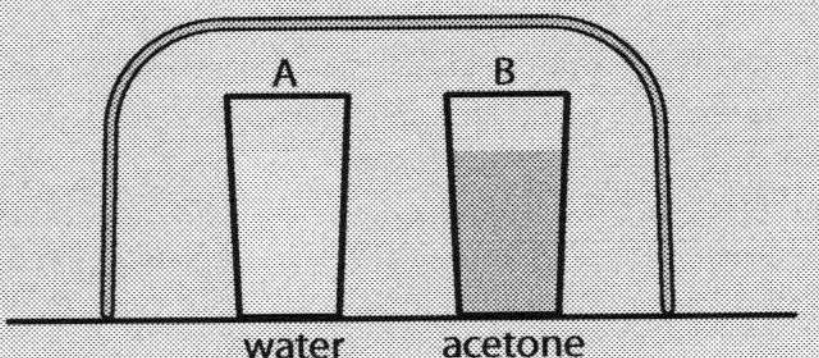

Dalton's Law of Partial Pressures

Dalton did a series of experiments in which he prepared various gases and collected them in a glass collection jar by displacing water from the jar using a pneumatic trough.

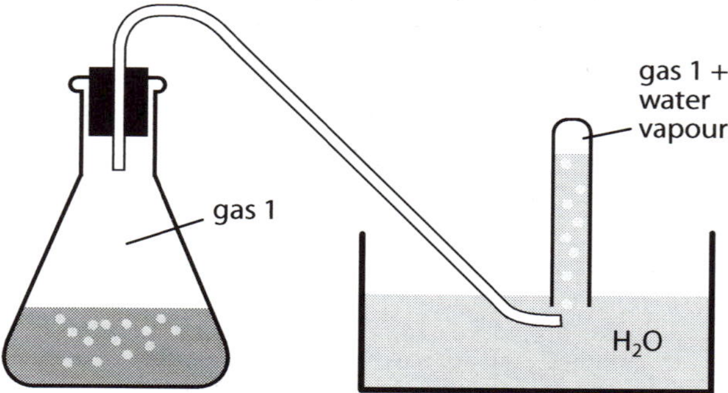

Figure 8.3.5 *Any gas collected over water is actually a mixture of the dry gas and water vapour.*

At first, Dalton assumed that by doing this, he obtained a jar full of the gas he was preparing and nothing else. Later he realized that he was wrong and that the jar must also contain a certain amount of water vapour mixed with the gas (Figure 8.3.5). Dalton realized at this point that each of these gases contributed to the total pressure in the jar. The contribution made by each gas is called its **partial pressure**. The result of these studies was **Dalton's law of partial pressures**.

The total pressure of a mixture of gases is equal to the sum of the partial pressures of the component gases (Figure 8.3.6).

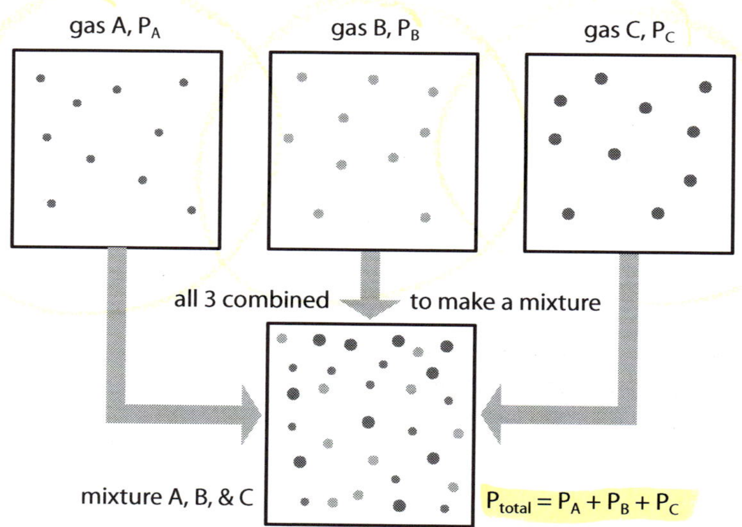

Figure 8.3.6 *When combined each individual gas continues to exert its own partial pressure producing a mixture of gases whose overall pressure is simply the sum of the individual partial pressures.*

Sample Problem — Dalton's Law of Partial Pressures

When a certain amount of nitrogen is introduced into a 1.0 L flask already containing oxygen, the pressure in the flask increases from 35 kPa to 77 kPa. Calculate the partial pressure of each gas in the final mixture.

What to Think About	How To Do It
1. Dalton's law of partial pressures says that the total pressure is the sum of the partial pressures.	The total pressure is 77 kPa and the P_{oxygen} gas was initially 35 kPa.
2. As the given pressure of 35 kPa is for oxygen, the difference must be due to the pressure of nitrogen.	The pressure of oxygen is given as the initial pressure. P_{oxygen} = **35 kPa** The pressure of the nitrogen is the remaining pressure, or $P_{nitrogen}$ = 77 – 35 = **42 kPa**

Practice Problems — Dalton's Law of Partial Pressures

1. Two gases are combined and sealed in a 2.0 L container. The 3.0 L of argon gas and 1.0 L of xenon gas each exert 1.00 atm pressure on the walls of their container.

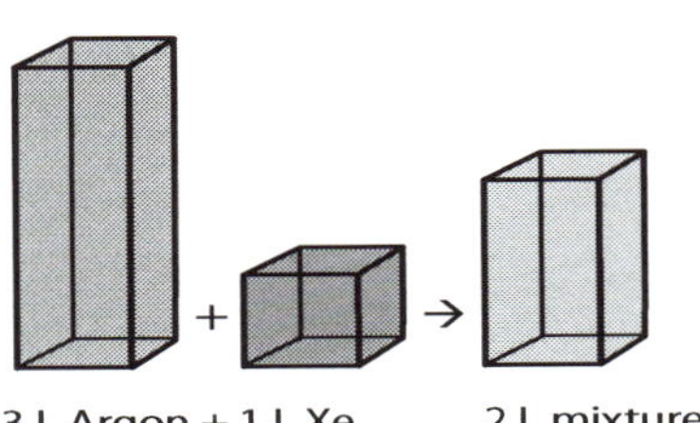

   (a) Calculate the partial pressure of each gas in the 2.0 L container.

   (b) What is the total pressure in the 2.0 L container?

2. Examine the labeled system below. Assume all three valves are opened and the gases diffuse throughout the system and equilibrate. What is the total pressure in the system?

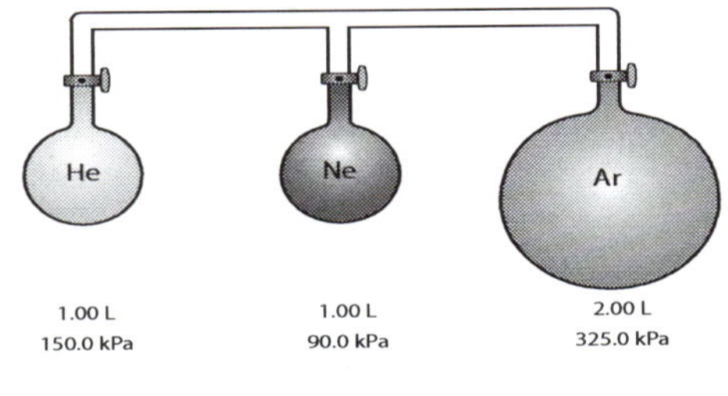

Collecting Gas Over Water: The Partial Pressure of Water Vapour

Returning to the production of gases in the laboratory, if we perform calculations involving the pressure or volume of gas formed in the lab, we must correct for the water vapour present. We do this by subtracting the vapour pressure of water from the pressure of the wet gas. The vapour pressure of water at various temperatures can be found in reference tables like Table 8.2.1 on page XX.

Sample Problem — The Partial Pressure of Water Vapour

A student performs an experiment in which she prepares hydrogen gas by reacting hydrochloric acid with zinc metal. After collecting 250.0 mL of the gas by displacement of water from a gas collection jar over a pneumatic trough, the student equilibrates the system to an atmospheric pressure of 99.2 kPa and the lab temperature of 24°C. Given that the vapour pressure of water is 2.98 kPa at 24°C, what mass of hydrogen has she collected?

What To Think About	How To Do It
1. The pressure of the *dry* hydrogen must be determined by subtracting the partial pressure of water vapour at the appropriate temperature from the total pressure in the collection jar.	$P_{total} = 99.2$ kPa and $P_{water\ vapour} = 2.98$ kPa, thus $P_{dry\ hydrogen} = 99.2 - 2.98 = 96.22$ kPa
2. As each gas expands individually to fill the entire container, the volume of the dry gas is the same as that of the container. This volume, the dry gas pressure and the temperature can be used to calculate the moles of gas present using the ideal gas law.	$PV = nRT$ and $24°C \times \frac{1\ K}{1°C} + 273\ K = 297\ K$ hence, $n = \frac{PV}{RT} = \frac{96.22\ \text{kPa} \times 0.2500\ \text{L}}{8.31\ \frac{\text{L·kPa}}{\text{mol·K}} \times 297\ \text{K}}$ $= \mathbf{0.0097}465$ mol
3. The mass of hydrogen can be determined from the moles using the molar mass of diatomic hydrogen gas.	$0.0097465\ \text{mol} \times \frac{2.0\ g\ H_2}{\text{mol}}$ $= \mathbf{0.0195\ g}$

Practice Problems — The Partial Pressure of Water Vapour

1. A 0.65 g sample of powered zinc metal reacts completely in sulphuric acid to produce zinc sulphate and hydrogen gas. The gas is collected over water as shown in the accompanying diagram. Assuming the pressure in the laboratory is 101.3 kPa and the temperature of the gas sample is 20.0°C, what is the volume of the dry H_2 gas collected?

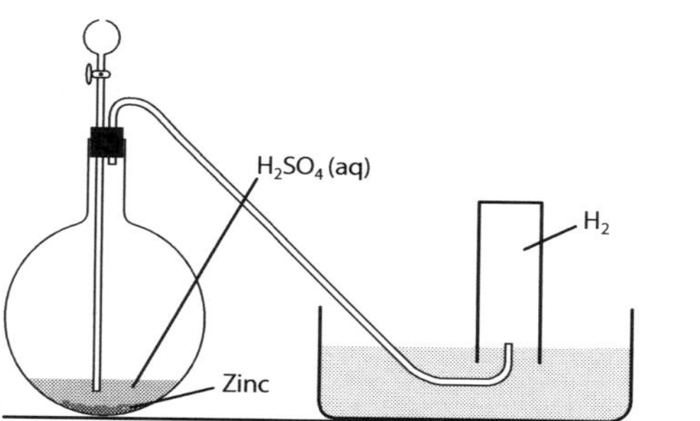

Continued

Practice Problems — Continued

2. Nitrogen gas is collected over water at 25.0°C and 14.7 psi. Given that the vapour pressure of water is 23.8 mm Hg at this temperature, what total volume of gas must be collected to obtain 4.10 g of nitrogen?

The Calculation of Partial Pressures

We can derive a general formula which will allow calculation of the partial pressure of each gas present in a mixture of gases if the total pressure and the composition of the mixture are known. From the ideal gas law:

$P_{total}V = n_{total}RT$, so we can set up the following ratio:

$$\frac{P_{one\ component}V}{P_{total}V} = \frac{n_{one\ component}RT}{n_{total}RT}$$

Now by cancelling the constant values *V*, *R*, and *T*, we obtain:

$$\frac{P_{one\ component}}{P_{total}} = \frac{n_{one\ component}}{n_{total}}$$

Finally, this can be rearranged to give a new expression for the partial pressure of any one component in a mixture of gases:

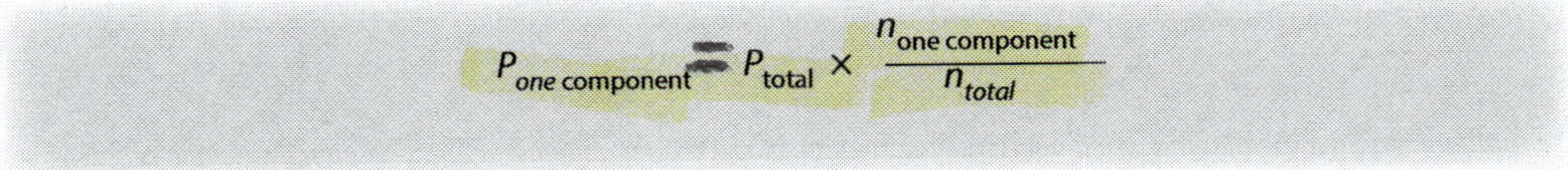

$$P_{one\ component} = P_{total} \times \frac{n_{one\ component}}{n_{total}}$$

The fraction $\frac{n_{one\ component}}{n_{total}}$ is called the **mole fraction** of the component.

We can always check our answers for the partial pressures of each gas in a mixture by adding them together once they have been calculated. The overall sum should always equal the total pressure of the mixture.

Sample Problem — Calculating Partial Pressures

A technician injects 7.50 g of liquid nitrogen into a sealed glass bulb filled with 12.0 g of neon gas. The nitrogen vaporizes and fills the container to produce a total pressure of 1.40 atm. What is the partial pressure of each of the gases in the container?

What to Think About	How To Do It
1. The mole fraction of each gas is required to calculate its partial pressure. This requires the moles of each gas.	$7.50\ \text{g}\ N_2 \times \frac{1\ \text{mol}}{28.0\ \text{g}} = 0.268\ \text{mol}$ $12.0\ \text{g}\ Ne \times \frac{1\ \text{mol}}{20.0\ \text{g}} = 0.600\ \text{mol}$ $n_{total} = 0.268 + 0.600 = 0.868\ \text{mol}$
2. The partial pressure of each gas is determined by multiplying the mole fraction of each gas by the total pressure.	$P_{nitrogen} = \frac{0.268\ \text{mol}}{0.868\ \text{mol}} \times 1.40\ \text{atm}$ $= \mathbf{0.432\ atm}$ $P_{neon} = \frac{0.600\ \text{mol}}{0.868\ \text{mol}} \times 1.40\ \text{atm}$ $= \mathbf{0.968\ atm}$
3. All figures should be carried through the entire calculation and only rounded at the end.	A quick check should show that the sum of each of the partial pressures equals the total pressure: $0.432 + 0.968 = 1.400\ \text{atm}$

Practice Problems — Calculating Partial Pressures

1. A mixture of 0.50 mol of hydrogen and 0.25 mol of oxygen in a sealed flask has a total pressure of 6.0×10^1 kPa. Calculate the partial pressure exerted by each of the two gases.

2. A mixture of gases contains 5.00×10^{23} molecules of CO_2, 6.00 g of CH_4, and 0.300 mol of NH_3. The total pressure exerted by the gases is 80.0 kPa. What is the partial pressure of each gas? Hint: First change all the quantities given into moles.

12.01 + 4(1.01) = 16.05 g/mol

5.00×10^{23} molecules × 1 mol / 6.022×10^{23} molecules = .830 mol CO_2

6.00 g × 1 mol / 16.05 g = .374 mol CH_4 + .300 mol NH_3 + .830 mol = 1.504 mol

.374 mol / 1.504 mol × 80.0 kPa = 19.9 kPa CH_4

.300 mol / 1.504 mol × 80.0 kPa = 16.0 kPa NH_3

.830 mol / 1.504 mol × 80.0 kPa = 44.1 kPa CO_2

8.3 Review Questions

1. Assume the total pressure of both gases depicted in the sealed container is 760.0 torr. What is the partial pressure of each of the component gases?

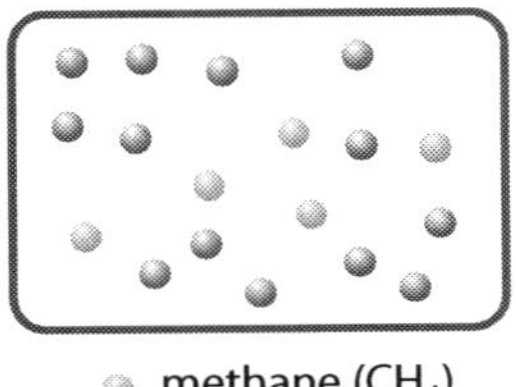

methane (CH_4)
oxygen (O_2)

2. (a) Is the vapour pressure of water at 25°C at an altitude of 3000 m in the mountains less than, equal to, or more than the vapour pressure of water at sea level at 25C? Explain your answer clearly.

   (b) The vapour pressure of a liquid, X at 25°C is equal to that of a liquid, Y at 50°C. If the sizes of molecules X and Y are essentially the same, which of the two liquids has the stronger intermolecular forces? Justify your choice.

   (c) Why does the rate of evaporation of a beaker of water inside a larger sealed container at a constant temperature decrease with time?

3. A pressure cooker is essentially a large pot with a lid that can be sealed air tight.

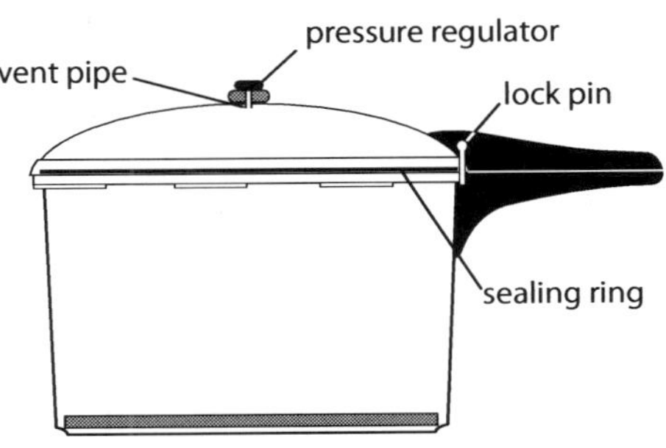

Explain how a pressure cooker is able to cook dried beans in a fraction of the time required to cook them in a normal pot.

4. A steel tank contains 40.0 g of helium, 180.0 g of oxygen, and 50.0 g of nitrogen gas. What is the partial pressure of each gas if the total pressure is 175 kPa?

5. If 2.00 g of carbon dioxide and 4.00 g of argon gas are placed into a 1.25 L container at 75°C, what is the total pressure?

6. A sealed glass bulb contains 20.0 g of oxygen, 30.0 g of nitrogen, and 40.0 g of argon gas. If the partial pressure of the oxygen gas is 66.0 kPa, what is the total pressure in the bulb?

7. Anaerobic bacteria can live without oxygen. A gas mixture designed to support such bacteria contains 3.0% hydrogen and 97.0% carbon dioxide gases by mass. If the total pressure is 1.00 atm, what is the partial pressure of each gas in the mixture?

8. The following system contains 20.0 psi each of gases A and B in the end bulbs with an evacuated bulb in the centre. Both stopcocks are opened at once. What is the new overall pressure in the system?

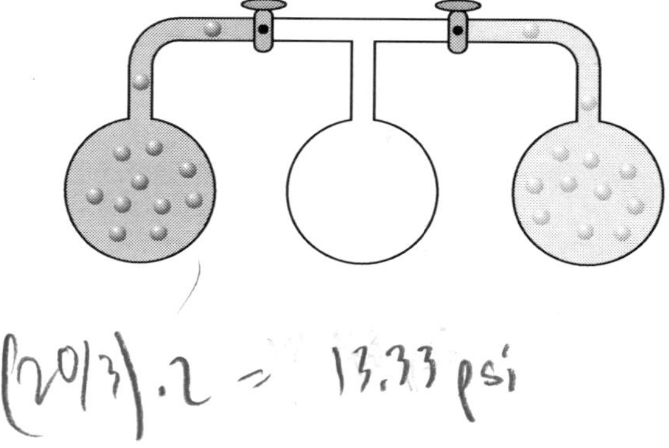

9. The following system is equilibrated with an atmospheric pressure of 1.00 atm in all parts. A thin layer of catalyst near the opened valve causes the gases to react to form ammonia. Give the partial pressures of each gas and the total pressure in the system when the reaction is complete.

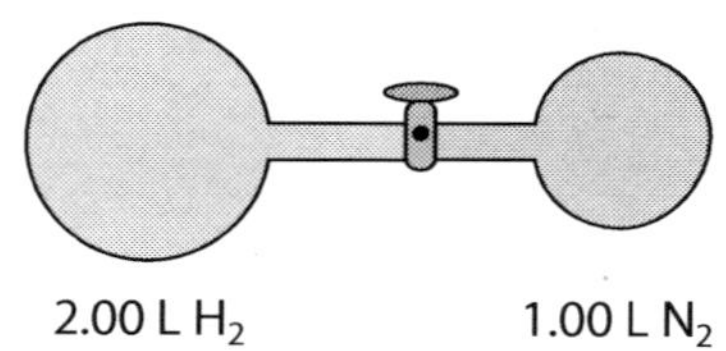

10. The penny coin was removed from circulation in Canada In February of 2014. The United States may soon do the same. The major reason for this move was the rising value of copper metal. When copper's value increased, pennies were produced as a zinc slug with a thin layer of copper plated over top. Zinc reacts readily with hydrochloric acid, while copper does not. A triangular file is used to nick the edge of a penny to expose the zinc slug below the layer of copper. The zinc reacts with the acid releasing bubbles from the nicked area until nothing remains but a thin shell of copper. If 0.948 L of hydrogen gas is collected over water at 20.0°C and a total pressure of 752 mm Hg, determine the percentage by mass of the copper in the 2.586 g penny.

11. A 239.4 mg sample of a drug designed to treat malaria was run through a series of reactions to convert all the nitrogen in the compound into $N_2(g)$. The gas collected over water at 23.8°C and a pressure of 755.5 torr had a volume of 18.66 mL. The vapour pressure of water at this temperature is 22.11 torr.

(a) Calculate the percent by mass of nitrogen in the sample.

(b) A 3.239 mg sample of the drug is combusted in air to produce 8.785 mg of $CO_2(g)$ and 2.160 mg of water vapour. Determine the percent by mass of carbon and hydrogen in the sample. Assume that any remaining element aside from the nitrogen determined in part (a) is oxygen. Determine the empirical formula.

(c) If the molar mass of the compound is 324.0 g/mol, what is the actual molecular formula of the drug?

12. Deep sea scuba divers breathe a gas mixture called heliox. Under very high pressures, the nitrogen in air enters the blood stream and causes a drunken type of state called nitrogen narcosis. The lack of nitrogen allows divers to descend to very deep depths without worrying about nitrogen toxicity. A 12.5 L scuba tank contains a helium-oxygen mixture containing 250.0 g of helium and 47.5 g of oxygen at 25°C. Calculate the partial pressure of each of the gases in the tank and determine the total pressure exerted by the heliox.

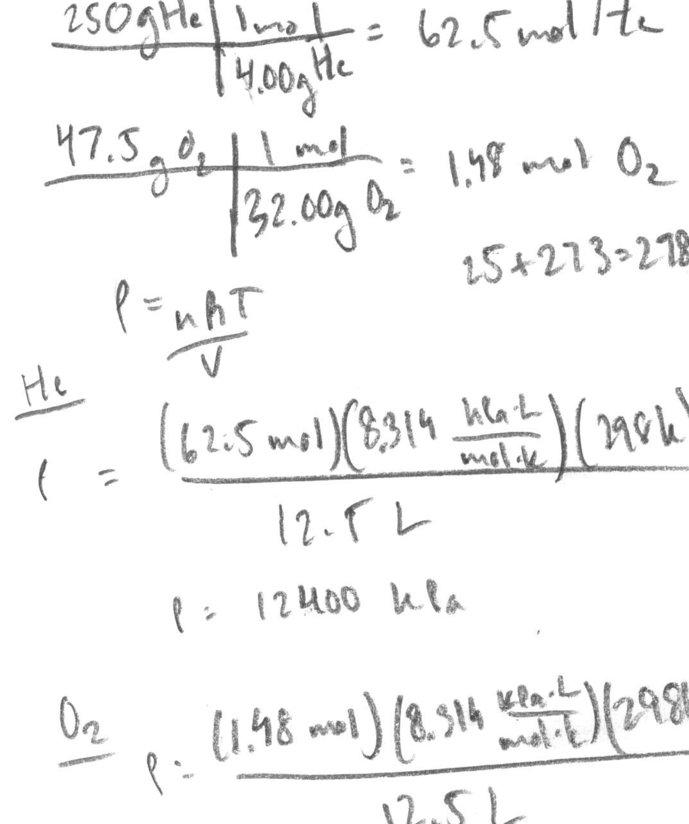

8.4 The Kinetic Molecular Theory and Real Gas Behaviour

Warm Up

Assume the box shown here has a volume of 22.4 L and exists under standard temperature and pressure (STP) conditions. Draw a molecular representation of oxygen gas filling the box. List three ways in which your drawing fails to represent the actual situation.

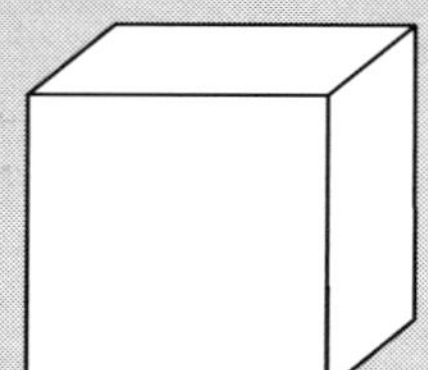

A Model for Gases — The Kinetic Molecular Theory

Your first introduction to chemistry in elementary school may have been a study of the kinetic molecular theory of matter (KMT). This theory states that matter is composed of particles such as molecules, atoms, or ions in continuous motion (Figure 8.4.1). In the solid state, the particles are close together and only vibrate. In a liquid, the particles are farther apart and move around. In a gas, the particles are much farther apart and move around freely in a random fashion. A mole of gas occupies 22.4 L, while a mole of most liquids has a volume of only 18 mL. In this section, we will take a closer look at how this theory applies to gases.

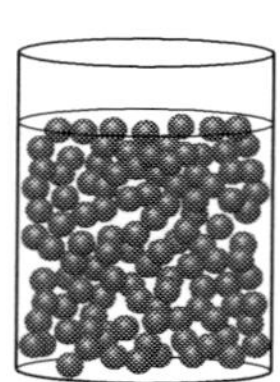

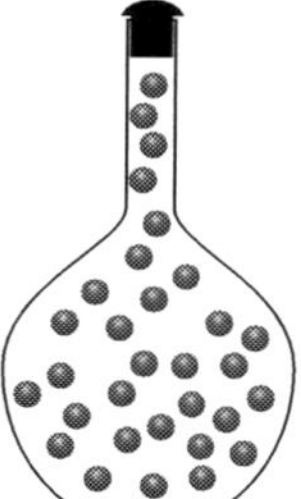

Figure 8.4.1 *The particles of a solid are packed tightly together. Liquid particles are farther apart and can move freely. A gas is virtually impossible to represent because the particles are no more than tiny points in space with less than 0.01% of the volume occupied by the actual gas molecules. There is a regular distribution of speeds for the molecules. Some are hardly moving while others have far more energy and are moving very quickly.*

When we use KMT to explain the behaviour of gases, we make a number of assumptions about the size of the molecules, the way they behave, and what does and does not occur during particle collisions. Such assumptions are included in the *postulates* of the kinetic molecular theory.

The Postulates of the Kinetic Molecular Theory

1. The volume of gas particles can be assumed to be negligible relative to the space between them.
2. Gas particles are in constant motion. Gas particles colliding with the walls of their container produce pressure.
3. Gas particles neither attract nor repel one another.
4. The average kinetic energy of a gas sample is directly proportional to the temperature of the gas in Kelvin degrees.

Molecular Size

The size of individual gas particles is so small compared to the distance between them that at room temperature and standard atmospheric pressure more that 99.99% of the volume of any gas is actually empty space. Because of all this empty space, it is easy to compress a gas so that it occupies a smaller volume just by applying an external force.

Continuous Motion of Gas Particles

Individual gas particles are in perpetual, random, straight-line motion. During the course of this motion, they frequently collide with one another and then rebound in a perfectly elastic manner. The continuous random motion of gas particles prevents them from collecting in one area and causes them to be uniformly distributed throughout any container they are placed in. This movement is called "diffusion" and is a property of all gases. Diffusion also allows gases of different types to be mixed together to form solutions of any proportion.

Kinetic Energy of Gas Particles

Kinetic energy is the energy resulting from movement. The value of the kinetic energy of an object depends on its mass and velocity. This may be expressed mathematically as kinetic energy = $\frac{1}{2}mv^2$ where *m* is the mass and *v* is the velocity.

$$KE = 1/2mv^2$$

There is a *normal distribution of energies* in any sample of matter (Figure 8.4.2).

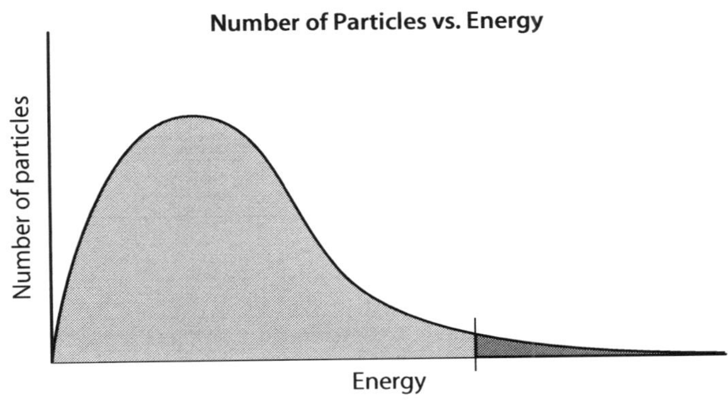

Figure 8.4.2 *Any gas sample contains a normal distribution of energies.*

At any given temperature, however, the molecules in all gases have the same *average* kinetic energy. This average kinetic energy is directly proportional to the Kelvin temperature.

$$KE = 3/2RT$$

Thus, if we have a sample of hydrogen gas and oxygen gas at the same temperature, both gases will have the same average kinetic energy. It follows that the average velocity of an oxygen molecule must be less than that of a hydrogen molecule since the mass of the oxygen is 16 times greater. The relatively high velocities of molecules of hydrogen and atoms of helium account for the fact that Earth's atmosphere contains very little of these two gases. They escaped from Earth's gravitational attraction many millions of years ago.

The Elasticity of Gas Particles

In any sample of gas, the particles are moving very quickly. Gas particles at room temperature or 25°C move at speeds in the order of 200 to 2000 m/s, which convert to 450 to 4500 miles per hour. As explained on the previous page, the speed is related to the mass of the gas particles (Figure 8.4.3).

As a result of this tremendous speed, gas particles collide with one another very frequently. One of the assumptions of the KMT is that no energy is lost during these collisions. In other words, the collisions are perfectly elastic. If this were not the case, the particles would gradually lose their kinetic energy. In fact, particles do transfer kinetic energy from one to another during collisions, but the average kinetic energy of all the particles present in a sample remains constant. Collisions between the gas particles and the walls of their container produce pressure (Figure 8.4.3).

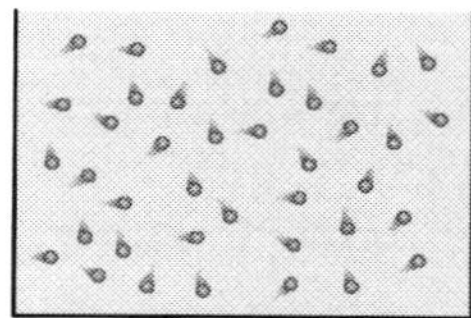

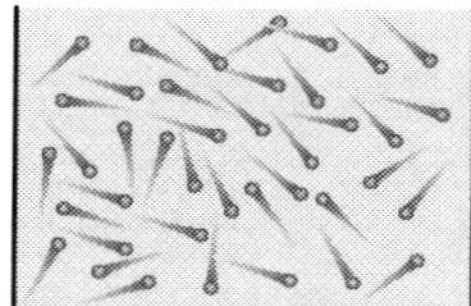

Figure 8.4.3 *The average velocity of gas particles is directly related to the Kelvin temperature of the sample. There is a normal distribution of energies in any gas sample with some particles barely moving while others move extremely quickly. Collisions between the particles are perfectly elastic and collisions with the walls of the container produce pressure. The representations above show the molecules much larger than they actually are. In reality, less than 0.01% of the volume of the container is occupied by gas particles.*

Quick Check

Use the postulates of the kinetic molecular theory to explain each of the following gas laws:

(a) Boyle's law

(b) Charles's law

(c) Gay-Lussac's law

(d) Dalton's law of partial pressures

Root Mean Square Velocity

The Kelvin temperature is a measure of the average kinetic energy (*KE*) of any sample of gas particles.

For a mole of any gas:

$$KE_{avg} = \frac{3}{2}RT \qquad \text{(I)}$$

where $R = 8.31$ J/K·mol

Also,

$$KE_{avg} = N_A(\tfrac{1}{2}m\overline{\mu}^2) \qquad \text{(II)}$$

where N_A = the number of particles in a mole (Avogadro's number)
m = the mass of the gas particle
$\overline{\mu}^2$ = average of the squares of the particle velocities

Thus, the average kinetic energy of one gas particle in a sample is equal to $\tfrac{1}{2}m\overline{\mu}^2$.

The average velocity of a gas particle is called the root mean square velocity and is written as:
$V_{rms} = \sqrt{\overline{\mu}^2}$

Rearranging equations (I) and (II) from above gives:

$$\frac{3}{2}RT = \tfrac{1}{2}m\overline{\mu}^2$$

$$\mu_{rms} = \sqrt{\frac{3RT}{M}}$$

It is necessary to insert the molar mass in kg to allow proper unit analysis. One joule is equivalent to one $\frac{\text{kg}\cdot\text{m}^2}{\text{s}^2}$. The molar mass in kg cancels, leaving the square root of m^2/s^2, which gives an appropriate unit for velocity of m/s.

Sample Problem — Root Mean Square Velocity and Average Kinetic Energy

Calculate the root mean square velocity and the kinetic energy of carbon monoxide gas at 25°C.

What To Think About

1. The root mean square velocity equals the square root of 3RT/M, where R is 8.31 J/mol·K, T is in Kelvin degrees and M is the molar mass in kg.
2. Be sure to divide *before* taking the square root.
3. Unit analysis requires the substitution of $\frac{kg \bullet m^2}{s^2}$ for J and insertion of the molar mass in kg/mol.
4. The kinetic energy is simply $3/2RT$ where $R = 8.31$ J/mol·K and the temperature is in Kelvin degrees.

How To Do It

$$\mu_{rms} = \sqrt{\frac{3RT}{M}}$$

$$\mu_{rms} = \sqrt{\frac{3(8.31\ J/mol \bullet K)(298\ \cancel{K})}{0.0028\ \cancel{kg}}}$$

$$\mu_{rms} = \sqrt{\frac{3(8.31\ \frac{\cancel{kg} \bullet m^2/s^2}{\cancel{mol \bullet K}})(298\ \cancel{K})}{0.028\ \cancel{kg/mol}}}$$

$= \mathbf{515\ m/s}$

$KE_{avg} = 3/2RT$

$= 3/2 \times 8.31\ J/mol\ \cancel{K} \times 298\ \cancel{K}$

$= \mathbf{3710\ J}$

Practice Problems — Root Mean Square Velocity & Average Kinetic Energy

1. Calculate the root mean square velocity and the average kinetic energy of atoms of Ar gas at 25°C.

2. Calculate the root mean square velocity and the average kinetic energy of ozone molecules, O_3, high in the stratosphere where the temperature is –83°C.

Range of Velocities in a Gas Sample

In a real gas, there are large numbers of collisions between gas particles. When the lid is removed from a perfume bottle, it takes some time for the odour to move through the air. This is due to collisions occurring between the perfume vapour and the oxygen and nitrogen particles that make up most of the air. The average distance a particle travels between collisions in a sample of gas is called the **mean free path**. This distance is typically very small and in the range of 60 nanometres. The many collisions result in a wide range of velocities as particles collide and exchange kinetic energy. Figures 8.4.4 and 8.4.5 illustrate the velocity distributions for various gases at STP conditions and a particular gas under changing conditions of temperature. The peak of each curve indicates the most common particle velocity.

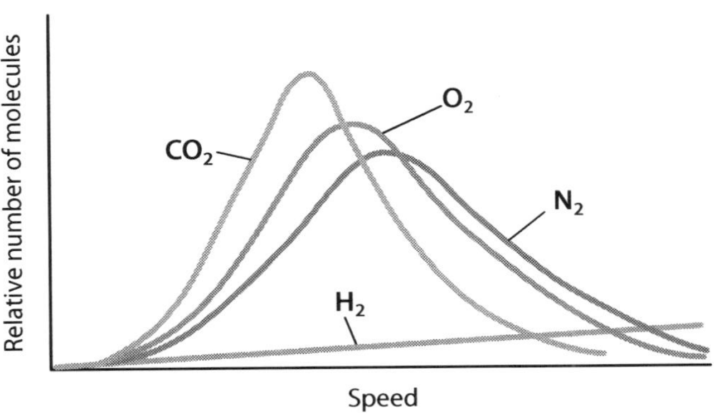

Figure 8.4.4 *The velocity distributions reflect the kinetic energy distribution for all the particles in samples of CO_2, O_2, N_2, and H_2 gas. While the average velocity of an oxygen molecule is 500 m/s, many O_2 particles have other velocities. As the mass of a particle increases, its average velocity decreases.*

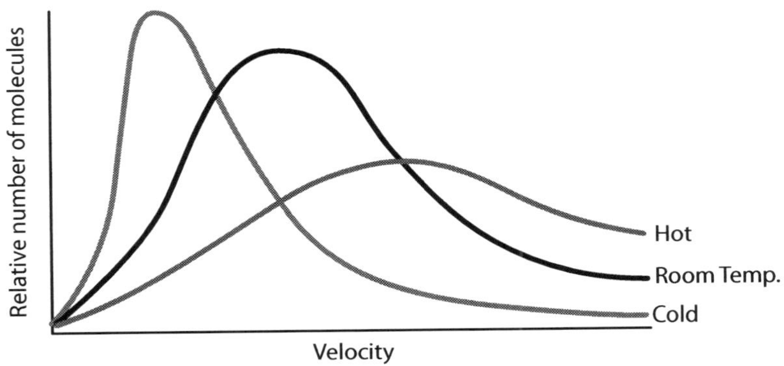

Figure 8.4.5 *Increasing the temperature of a gas sample broadens the entire distribution of velocities, causing the average velocity of a particle to increase.*

Effusion and Diffusion

Two important terms for describing gases are diffusion and effusion. The odour emitted from a perfume bottle takes several moments to permeate an entire room as the vapor bounces off oxygen and nitrogen molecules, zigzagging its way through the air in random straight-line motion. **Diffusion** is the term used to describe the mixing of one gas through another. The rate of diffusion is the rate of this mixing.

The rate of diffusion is calculated by directly relating the relative distance travelled by two types of molecules in the same period of time to their relative velocities. Both of these ratios are inversely related to the square root of the ratio of the molecules' masses.

$$\frac{\text{distance travelled by gas 1}}{\text{distance travelled by gas 2}} = \frac{V_{rms} \text{ for gas 1}}{V_{rms} \text{ for gas 2}} = \sqrt{\frac{m_2}{m_1}}$$

Effusion is the passage of a gas through a tiny orifice into an evacuated chamber. The rate of effusion measures the speed at which the gas is transferred into the chamber.

Figure 8.4.6 *Lighter gases move more quickly and effuse more rapidly than heavier ones, as predicted by the equation, $KE = 1/2mv^2$.*

Scottish chemist Thomas Graham developed Graham's law of effusion. It states the rate of effusion is inversely proportional to the square root of the mass of its particles.

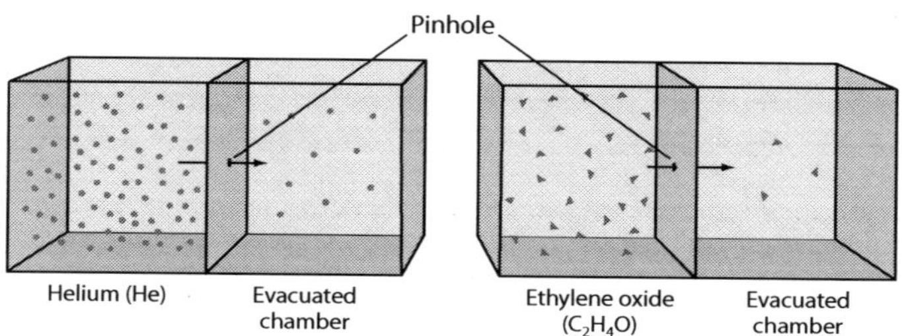

Figure 8.4.7 *The rate of effusion of a light gas such as helium is much faster than that of a more massive gas like ethylene oxide.*

Since the effusion rate for a gas depends directly on the average velocity of its particles, the rates of effusion of two gases at the same temperature may be compared by an equation similar to the one used for diffusion above.

$$\frac{\text{rate of effusion for gas 1}}{\text{rate of effusion for gas 2}} = \frac{\mu_{rms} \text{ for gas 1} \sqrt{\frac{3RT}{M_1}}}{\mu_{rms} \text{ for gas 2} \sqrt{\frac{3RT}{M_2}}} = \frac{\sqrt{M_2}}{\sqrt{M_1}}$$

Sample Problem — Graham's Law

Carbon monoxide effuses at a rate that is 2.165 times faster than that of an unknown noble gas. Calculate the molar mass of the unknown gas and determine its identity.

What to Think About

1. Graham's law of effusion is required to solve this problem.
2. Identify the lighter gas as gas 1 so the effusion rate ratio is >1. This makes the algebra a little easier.

How To Do It

$$\frac{\text{effusion rate for gas 1}}{\text{effusion rate for gas 2}} = \frac{\sqrt{\mathcal{M}_2}}{\sqrt{\mathcal{M}_1}}$$

$$\frac{\text{effusion rate for gas 1}}{\text{effusion rate for gas 2}} = \frac{\sqrt{\mathcal{M}\text{ of X}}}{\sqrt{\mathcal{M}\text{ of CO}}}$$

What to Think About

3. Substitute 2.165 for the effusion rate ratio. The molar mass of CO may be substituted as 28.0 g/mol. It is not necessary to convert the molar mass to kg as the kilo prefix will cancel in the ratio form of the equation.

How To Do It

$$2.165 = \frac{\sqrt{\mathcal{M}\text{ of X}}}{\sqrt{28.0\text{ g/mol}}}$$

$$\therefore \sqrt{\mathcal{M}\text{ of X}} = 2.165(\sqrt{28.0\text{ g/mol}})$$

$$= 11.4561\text{ g/mol}$$

What to Think About

4. Determine the identity of the noble gas by comparison of known molar masses of the noble gas family with the calculated molar mass.

How To Do It

$$\therefore \mathcal{M}\text{ of X} = 11.4561^2 = 131\text{ g/mol}$$

The molar mass matches that of **xenon gas.**

Practice Problems — Graham's Law

1. Calculate the ratio of the effusion rates of H_2 and UF_6. UF_6 is a gas used to produce fuel for nuclear reactors.

2. A popular experiment involves the determination of the distances travelled by $NH_3(g)$ and $HCl(g)$ from opposite ends of a glass tube. When the two gases, meet they form a visible white ring of NH_4Cl.

NH_3 17 g/mol $\qquad$ NH_4Cl $\qquad$ HCl 36.5 g/mol

distance

100 cm

(a) Which end of the tube will be closer to the white ring of ammonium chloride? Justify your answer with an explanation.

Continued

Practice Problems — Continued

2. (b) Calculate the ratio of the distance traveled by $NH_3(g)$ to distance traveled by $HCl(g)$.

(c) Give two factors that must be carefully controlled to ensure the expected result.

3. If the average velocity of a N_2 molecule is 475 m/s at 25°C, what is the average velocity of a He atom at 25°C?

The Effects of Volume and Intermolecular Forces on Real Gases

Measurement of the volume of one mole of most gases at STP results in a number that is *near, but seldom exactly equal to* 22.4 L. As pressure increases and temperature decreases, the volume of one mole of gas deviates even further from this value. In section 8.2 it was stated that gases behave most ideally when *pressure is low* and *temperature is high*. The reason for this is two-fold:

1. Real gases *do* have some volume, while ideal gases are assumed to have no volume and to exist as tiny points in space.
2. Real gases *exert some attractive forces* on their neighbouring particles, while ideal gases are assumed to be completely independent of the gas particles that surround them.

In 1873, Johannes van der Waals modified the ideal gas law to fit the behaviour of real gases. Van der Waals inserted two small correction factors. The first accounts for the *volume* of the gas particles themselves and the second corrects for the *IMFs* existing between gas particles. The Van der Waal's equation is really just a more complex form of the ideal gas law.

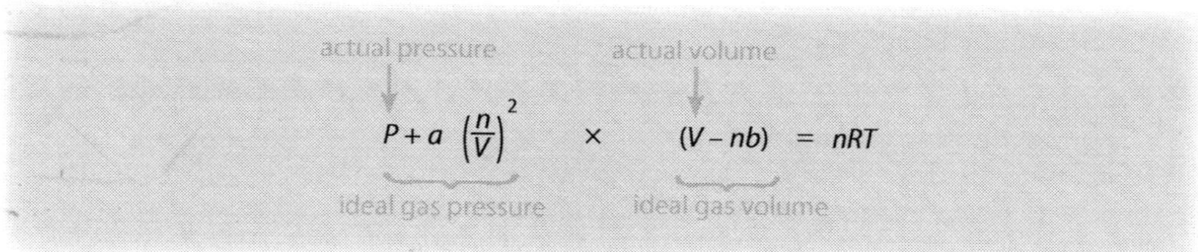

The "correction factors" include an ***a* factor** and a ***b* factor**, which account for the attractive forces and the volume that real gases demonstrate. Every gas has its own unique values for *a* and *b*. Note that the units of *a* and *b* allow proper cancellation to produce units of pressure and volume respectively when substituted into the van der Waals equation.

Table 8.4.1 *Van der Waals Constants for Common Gases*

	a atm litres^2 / mole^2	*b* litres/mole
N_2	1.39	0.0391
O_2	1.36	0.0318
CO	1.49	0.0399
CO_2	3.59	0.0427
CCl_4	20.4	0.138
HCl	3.67	0.408
H_2	0.244	0.0266
H_2O	5.64	0.0237
CH_4	2.25	0.0428
He	0.034	0.0237
Ne	0.211	0.0171
Ar	1.35	0.0322
Kr	2.32	0.0398
Xe	4.19	0.0511

The effect of IMF's and gas volume on real gas behaviour becomes quite obvious when you examine a graph of *PV/nT* versus *P* for real gases (Figure 8.4.8). Since *PV* = *nRT*, *PV/nT* should equal *R*.

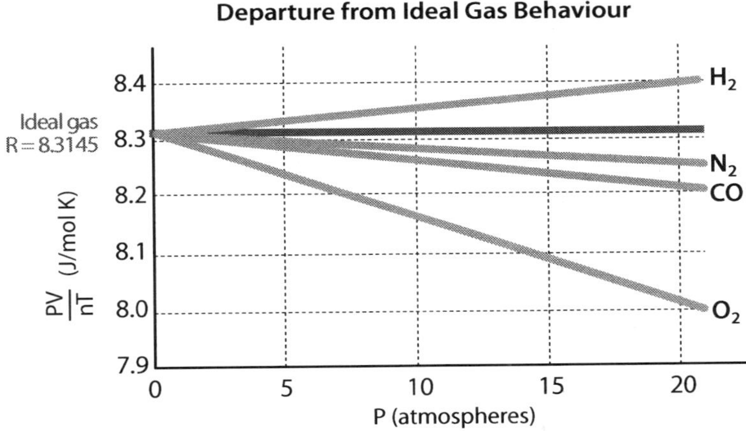

Figure 8.4.8 *As pressure increases, deviation from ideal behaviour becomes more pronounced. The deviation is most noticeable for larger gases. This makes sense as larger gases have a greater volume and exert larger London dispersion forces on each other.*

The effect is further demonstrated with examination of a graph of *PV/RT* versus *P* for one mole of a gas at three different temperatures (Figure 8.4.9). Since *PV* = *nRT*, *PV/RT* should equal 1 for one mole of gas.

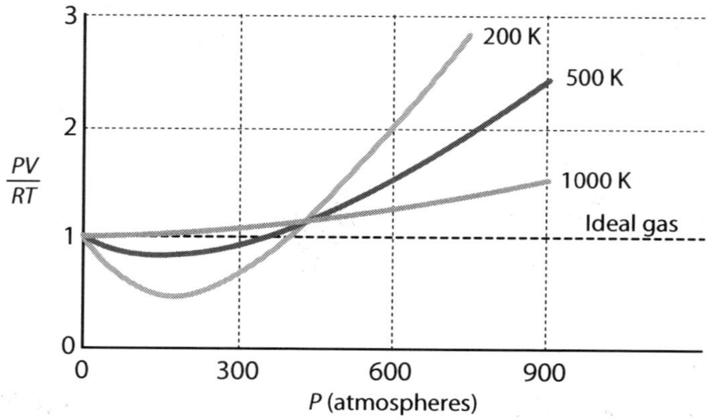

Figure 8.4.9 *As temperature decreases, deviation from ideal behaviour becomes more pronounced. Gases behave most ideally when the temperature is high.*

Examination of the data in Table 8.4.1 and the graphs in Figures 8.4.8 and 8.4.9 provides support for the statement that gases behave most ideally when pressure is low and temperature is high. Low pressure and high temperature make real gas volume and real gas attractive forces *less noticeable.*

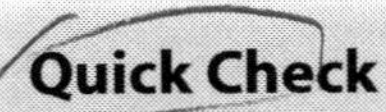

Quick Check

1. Examine the graphs in Figures 8.4.8 and 8.4.9.
   (a) Which particle deviates the most from ideal behaviour? Give two reasons for this behaviour. 

   O_2: largest molecule

   (b) What temperature provides the most ideal behaviour? Explain.

   higher temp. b/c IMFs are minimized

2. Explain the general pattern for the values of *a* and *b* moving down the noble gas family. (A simple statement of the trend is *not* an adequate answer.)

   a increases as you move down the group

   b increases as you move down
   except He → Ne

3. Explain the same pattern moving from N_2 to CO_2 to CCl_4.

   a values:
   $N_2 \rightarrow CH_4 \rightarrow CO_2$
   b values:
   $N_2 \rightarrow CO_2 \rightarrow CH_4$
   (least → greatest)

4. Explain the same pattern moving from N_2 to CO to HCl to H_2O.

   a values:
   $N_2 \rightarrow CO \rightarrow HCl \rightarrow H_2O$
   b values:
   $H_2O \rightarrow N_2 \rightarrow HCl \rightarrow CO_2$
   (least → greatest)

8.4 Review Questions

1. Calculate the average kinetic energies of Ne(*g*) and N_2(*g*) at 298 K and 596 K. What pattern is noticeable between kinetic energy and temperature?

2. Calculate the root mean square velocities of Ne(*g*) and N_2(*g*) at 298 K and 596 K. What pattern is noticeable between root mean square velocities and temperature?

3. At 25°C and 1 atmosphere pressure, which of the following gases shows the greatest deviation from ideal behaviour? The least? Give two reasons for your choice.

   CH_4 SO_2 O_2 H_2

4. Consider the van der Waals equation for real gases.
   (a) Which of the two molecules, H_2O or H_2S, has the higher value for *a* and which has the higher value for *b*? Explain.
   (b) One of the van der Waals constants can be correlated with the boiling point of a substance. Specify which constant and how it is related to the boiling point.

5. Five identical balloons are shown below. Each is filled to the same volume with the pure gases indicated at 25°C and 1.0 atmosphere pressure.

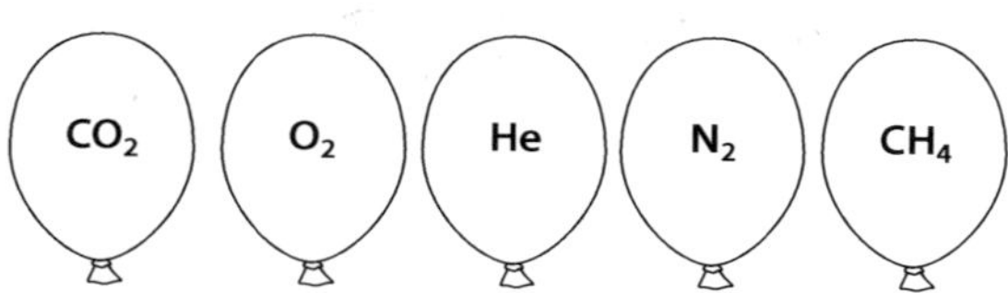

   (a) Which balloon contains the greatest mass of gas? Explain.

(b) Compare the average kinetic energies of the gas molecules in the balloons. Explain.

(c) Which balloon contains the gas that would be expected to deviate most from the behaviour of an ideal gas? Explain.

(d) Twelve hours after being filled, all the balloons have decreased in size. Predict which balloon will be the smallest. Explain your reasoning.

6. Consider a 5.0 L container of helium gas at STP. How will the following be affected by the changes given below?
   (a) kinetic energy
   (b) average velocity
   (c) frequency of collisions
   (i) The Kelvin temperature is increased by 100°C.
   (ii) The volume is halved.
   (iii) The number of moles of gas is doubled.

7. Calculate the root mean square velocity and the average kinetic energy of Br_2, Cl_2, and F_2. Which has the greatest:
   (a) velocity?
   (b) kinetic energy?
   (c) effusion rate?

8. A sample of neon effuses from a container in 38 s. The same amount of an unknown noble gas requires 77.5 s. What is the unknown gas?

9. The rate of effusion of an unknown gas is four times faster than oxygen gas. Calculate the molar mass and identify the gas.

10. A sample of helium takes 9.0 minutes to effuse into a 2.0 L evacuated container. How long would it take for a sample of oxygen gas to effuse into the same container?

11. Calculate the pressure exerted by 0.250 mol of CH_4 gas in a 0.500 L container at 25.0°C.

(a) Using the ideal gas law

$PV = nRT$ $\quad 25 + 273 = 298\text{ K}$

$P = \frac{nRT}{V}$

$P = \frac{.250\text{ mol} \cdot (0.0821\ \frac{\text{atm}\cdot\text{L}}{\text{mol}\cdot\text{K}}) \cdot (298\text{ K})}{.500\text{ L}} = 12.2\text{ atm}$

(b) Using the van der Waals equation

$\left(P + a\left(\frac{n}{V}\right)^2\right) \times (V - nb) = nRT$

$\left(P + 2.25\ \text{L}^2/\text{mol}^2 \left(\frac{.250\text{ mol}}{.500\text{ L}}\right)^2\right) \times (.500\text{ L} - .250\text{ mol} \cdot .0428\text{ L/mol}) = .250\text{ mol} \cdot .0821\ \frac{\text{atm}\cdot\text{L}}{\text{mol}\cdot\text{K}} \cdot 298\text{ K}$

$P = 11.9\text{ atm}$

(c) Explain the difference in the values.

The IMFs of CH_4 at the low T cause the P to decrease

12. (a) Repeat question 11 using a 50.0 L container.

(b) Explain the differences between the answers for the two questions.

9 Organic Chemistry

By the end of this chapter, you should be able to do the following:

- Describe characteristic features and common applications of organic chemistry
- Demonstrate knowledge of the various ways that carbon and hydrogen can combine to form a wide range of compounds
- Generate names and structures for simple organic compounds
- Differentiate the various types of bonding between carbon atoms
- Identify common functional groups
- Perform a simple organic preparation

By the end of the chapter you should know the meaning of these **key terms:**

- alcohol
- aldehyde
- alkane
- alkene
- alkyne
- amide
- amine
- aromatic
- benzene ring
- bromo-
- chloro-
- cyclic
- ester
- ether
- ethyl-
- fluoro-
- hydrocarbon
- ketone
- methyl-
- organic acid
- organic chemistry
- substituent groups

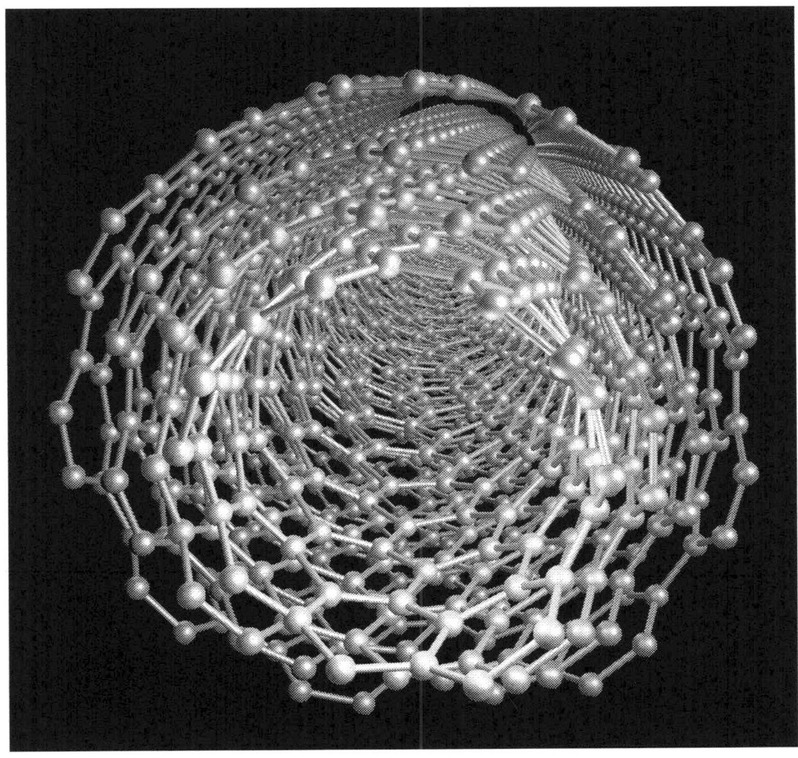

A model of a multi-walled carbon nanotube: sheets of one-atom thick carbon atoms in a hexagonal arrangement and curved into tubes. Wider tubes have narrower tubes inside them.

9.1 Simple Hydrocarbons and Isomerism

Warm Up

1. Draw the Lewis dot structure for carbon.

2. How many valence electrons does a carbon atom have? ____________

3. Classify the following compounds as ionic or covalent:

   (a) Na_2CO_3 ____________________

   (b) C_2H_6 ____________________

   (c) CO_2 ____________________

   (d) CaC_2 ____________________

   (e) C_2H_5OH ____________________

Organic Compounds

Chemical compounds can be classified as belonging to one of two very large groups: organic compounds or inorganic compounds. Organic compounds contain carbon atoms, usually bonded to other carbon atoms and hydrogen atoms. They may also contain other elements such as halogens, nitrogen, oxygen, phosphorus, and sulphur. Note that some compounds such as carbonates, carbides, and oxides of carbon contain carbon but are not classified as organic compounds. For example, in the question 3 above, C_2H_6 and C_2H_5OH are organic. The remaining compounds in question 3 are inorganic: Na_2CO_3, CO_2, and CaC_2.

Chemists have been distinguishing organic and inorganic compounds for hundreds of years. Organic compounds were called "organic" because it was believed that these compounds could only be made from living things such as plants or animals. Scientists thought that organic compounds contained a "life force" or "vitality." Friedrich Wohler proved that this belief was inaccurate in 1828 when he heated an inorganic salt, ammonium cyanate [$NH_4(NCO)$] and produced urea [$(NH_2)_2CO$], an organic compound (Figure 9.1.1). Urea is a waste product of protein metabolism and, up to that time, was thought to be produced only from living things.

$$H_4N-O-C\equiv N \xrightarrow{\text{heat}} H_2N-\underset{\underset{O}{\|}}{C}-NH_2$$

ammonium cyanate **urea**

Figure 9.1.1 *Heating ammonium cyanate produces urea.*

Once scientists learned that organic compounds could be made in the lab, a whole new branch of chemistry was born: **organic chemistry**. Even though we now know that not all organic compounds come from living organisms, we still use the word "organic" to describe many carbon compounds.

Recall that a carbon atom has four valence electrons. Because of this, carbon can share electrons with other atoms to complete its outermost electron shell. Each carbon atom can form four covalent bonds. A carbon atom may bond to other carbon atoms in a chain using single, double, or triple bonds, and carbon chains may link to form carbon rings or cages.

With so many different ways that carbon can bond, there are millions of known organic compounds. Every day, you use organic products such as foods, cosmetics, plastics, clothing fibres, pharmaceuticals, and fuels.

Sample Problem — Using Structural Formulas to Represent Organic Compounds

Butane is a fuel used in lighters. It has the formula C_4H_{10} and has four carbon atoms attached to each other in a chain with only single bonds. Draw a structural formula for butane.

What to Think about	How to Do It
1. The four carbon atoms are bonded to each other in a chain, so draw four carbon atoms attached to one another in a line.	C — C — C — C
2. Each carbon atom can form four covalent bonds. The first carbon atom has one bond to the carbon atom beside it. It can therefore bond with three hydrogen atoms.	H on top, H below; H—C—C—C—C
3. The next two carbon atoms have two other carbon atoms already covalently bonded to them. They can only bond with two hydrogen atoms each.	H H H on top, H H H below; H—C—C—C—C
4. The last carbon atom is already bonded to one other carbon atom. It can form three bonds with hydrogen. The formula shown on the right is called a structural formula.	**Structural Formula:** H H H H on top, H H H H below; H—C—C—C—C—H
5. Condense this structural formula by writing the number of hydrogen atoms bonded to each carbon.	**Condensed Structural Formula:** $CH_3 - CH_2 - CH_2 - CH_3$
6. To condense this formula even more, use a line to represent each carbon bond. Do not show the carbon or hydrogen atoms at all. Notice that the lines will not be attached in a straight line. Organic molecules are not linear. At the end of each line segment is a carbon atom not shown. Hydrogen atoms are also not shown in this formula.	**Carbon Skeleton Formula:** C/C\C/C (zigzag) becomes a zigzag line

Practice Problems—Using Structural Formulas to Represent Organic Compounds

1. Octane, a constituent of gasoline, has the molecular formula C_8H_{18}. Draw a structural formula, condensed structural formula, and carbon skeletal formula for octane. Assume that the carbons are all bonded in a single chain to each other.

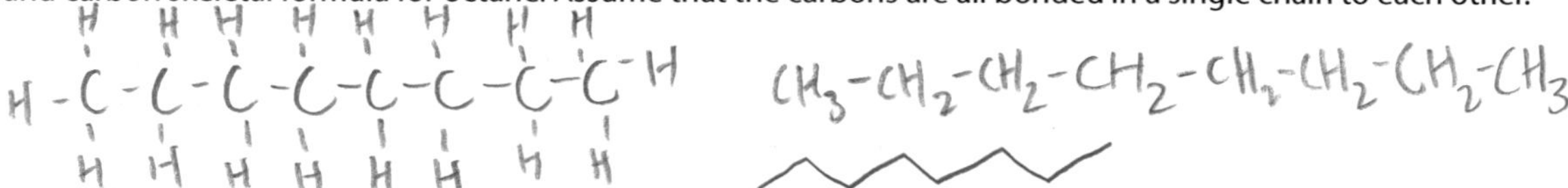

2. Draw a structural formula, condensed structural formula, and carbon skeletal formula for C_6H_{12}. Arrange the carbon atoms in a closed ring shape so that each carbon atom is bonded to two other carbon atoms.

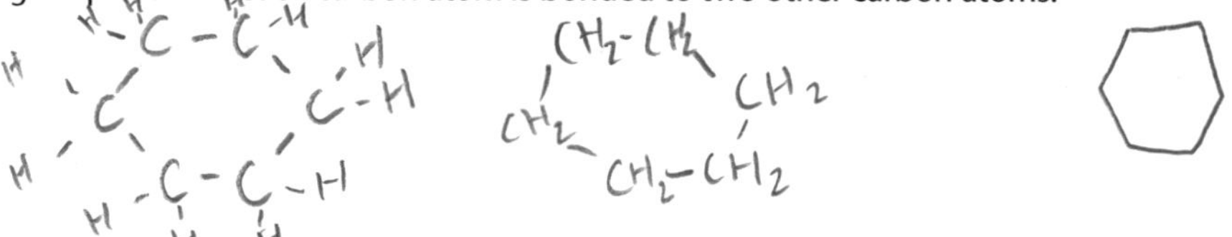

3. The carbon skeleton formula for an organic compound is shown below. Draw the structural and condensed structural formula. What is its molecular formula?

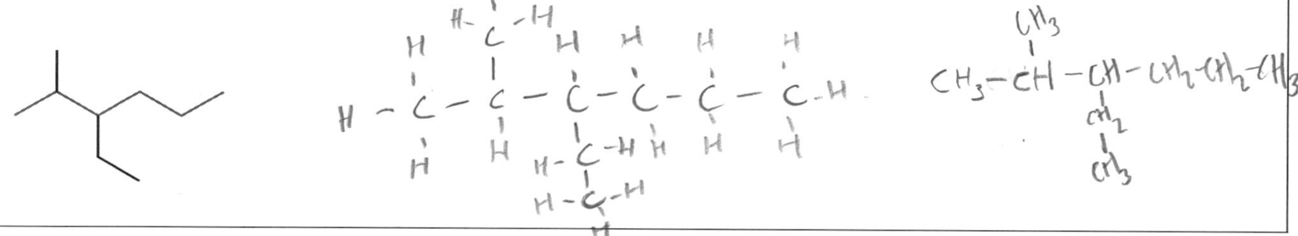

Hydrocarbons

Hydrocarbons are the simplest types of organic compounds. **Hydrocarbons** are compounds that contain only carbon and hydrogen atoms. We will examine five types of hydrocarbons: alkanes, cycloalkanes, alkenes, alkynes, and aromatic hydrocarbons.

Table 9.1.1 *Greek Prefixes*

No. of C Atoms	Prefix
1	*meth-*
2	*eth-*
3	*prop-*
4	*but-*
5	*pent-*
6	*hex-*
7	*hept-*
8	*oct-*
9	*non-*
10	*dec-*

Alkanes

Alkanes are hydrocarbons containing only single bonds. They are **saturated**, meaning that there is no room for other atoms to bond to the carbon skeleton. They have the general formula $C_nH_{(2n+2)}$. Table 9.1.2 on the next page lists the first 10 straight-chain alkanes that you need to know.

How to Name Alkanes

Notice in Table 9.1.2 that each alkane name ends in "-ane." You will need to memorize the prefixes that have been italicized in the table. The prefix indicates the number of carbon atoms bonded together in the chain. For example, hexane means six carbons bonded in a chain. *Hex* is the Greek word for six. Table 9.1.1 lists the prefixes.

Not only do carbon atoms bond together to make chains, but often branches of carbon atoms are connected to the carbon atoms of the main chain. These branches are called **substituent groups**. Rules for naming branched alkanes are on the page after Table 9.1.2.

Table 9.1.2 *10 Straight-Chain Alkanes You Need to Know*

Name	Molecular formula	Structural formula	Ball and stick model	Space filling model
methane	CH_4	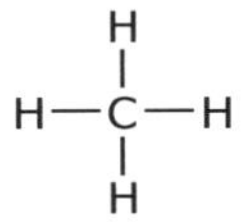 H H—C—H H	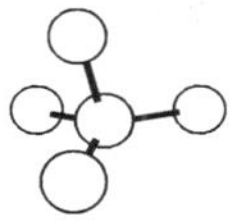	
ethane	C_2H_6	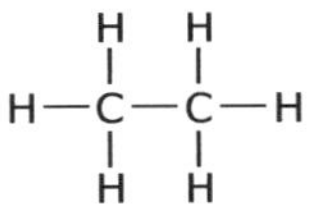 H H H—C—C—H H H	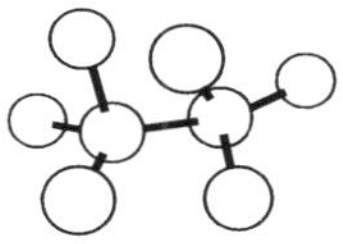	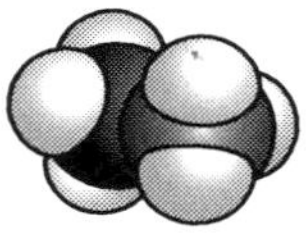
propane	C_3H_8	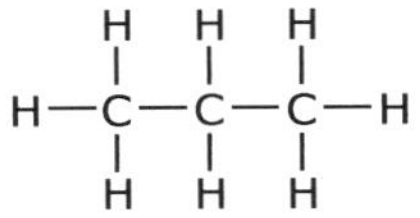 H H H H—C—C—C—H H H H	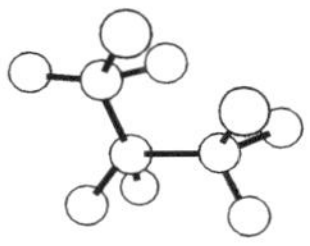	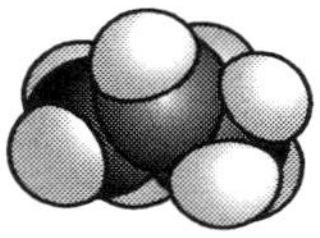
butane	C_4H_{10}	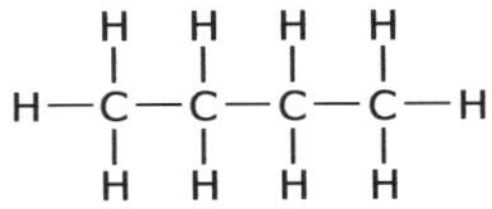 H H H H H—C—C—C—C—H H H H H	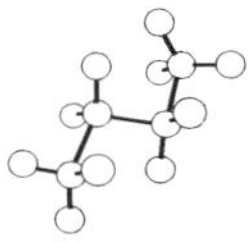	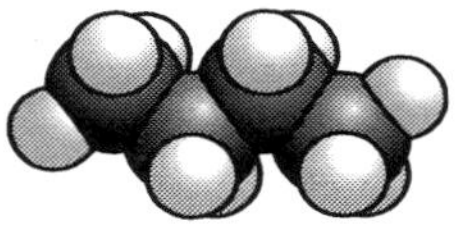
pentane	C_5H_{12}	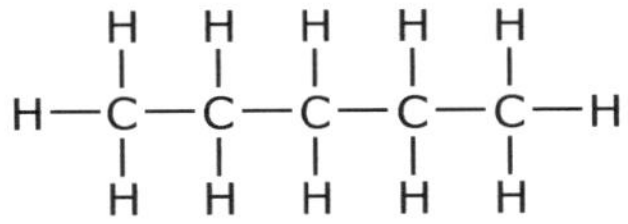 H H H H H H—C—C—C—C—C—H H H H H H	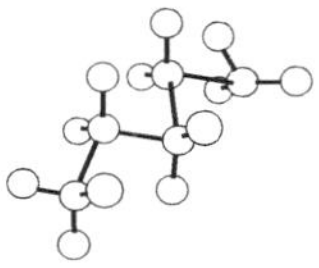	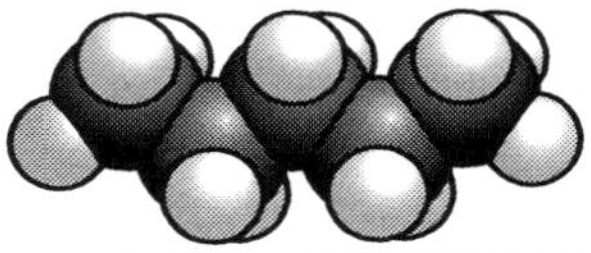
hexane	C_6H_{14}	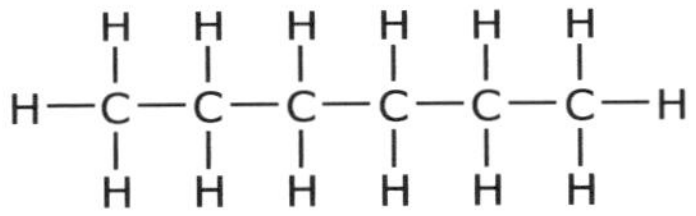 H H H H H H H—C—C—C—C—C—C—H H H H H H H	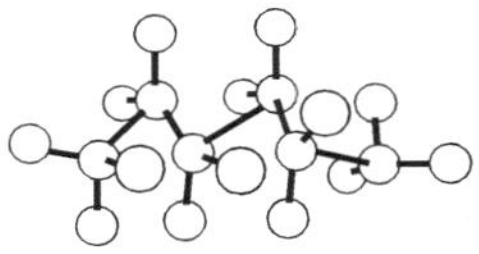	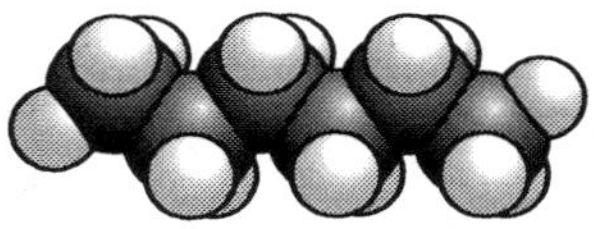
heptane	C_7H_{16}	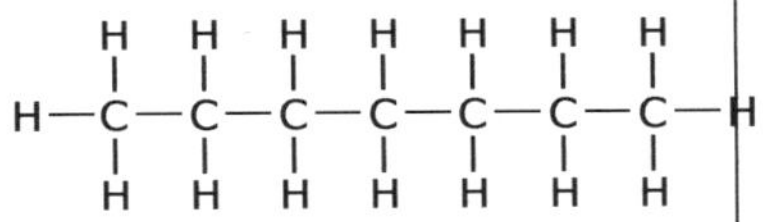 H H H H H H H H—C—C—C—C—C—C—C—H H H H H H H H	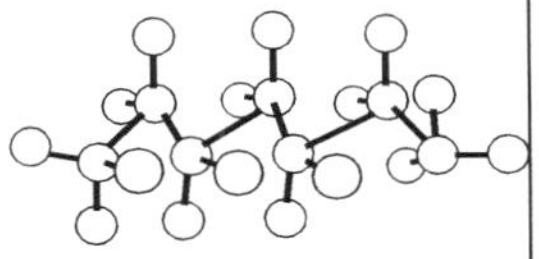	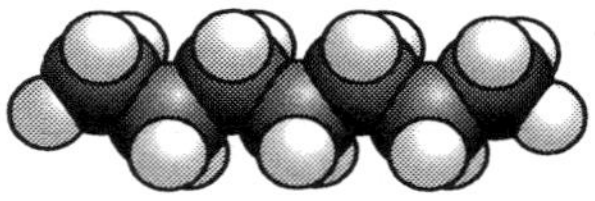
octane	C_8H_{18}	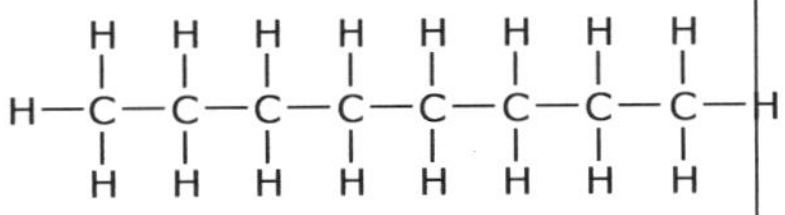 H H H H H H H H H—C—C—C—C—C—C—C—C—H H H H H H H H H	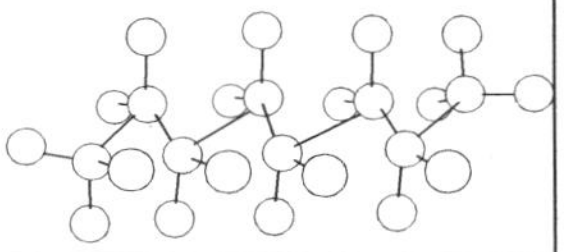	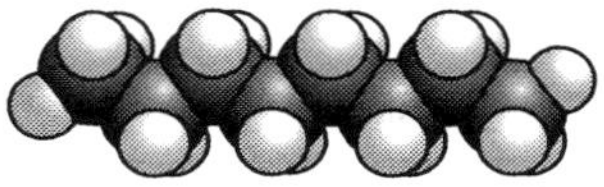
nonane	C_9H_{20}	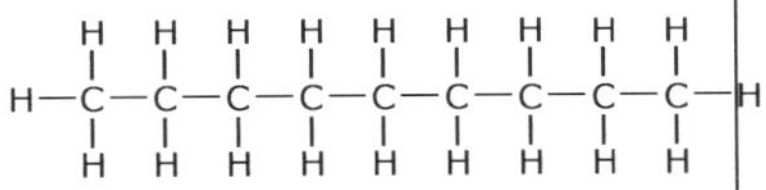 H H H H H H H H H H—C—C—C—C—C—C—C—C—C—H H H H H H H H H H	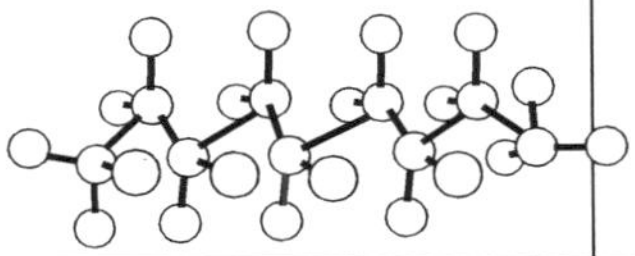	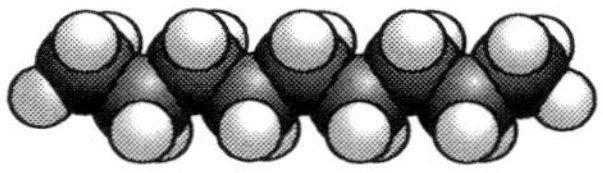
decane	$C_{10}H_{22}$	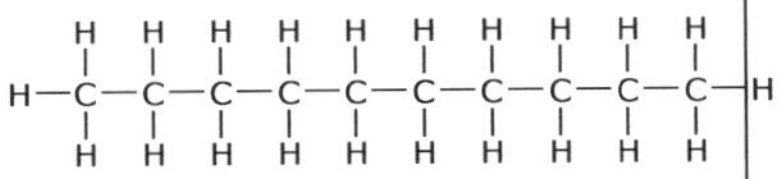 H H H H H H H H H H H—C—C—C—C—C—C—C—C—C—C—H H H H H H H H H H H	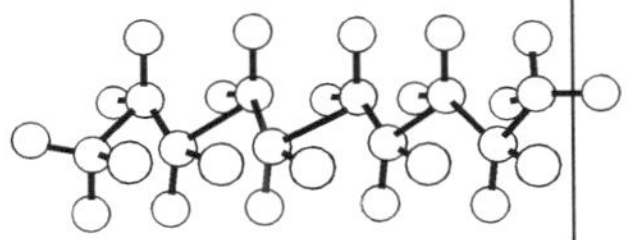	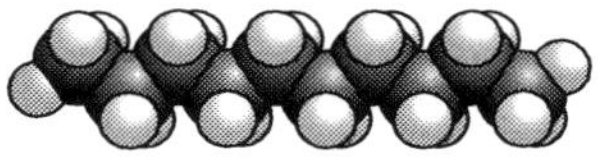

Naming Branched Alkanes

To name a branched alkane, there are a few rules:

1. Find the longest continuous chain of carbon atoms. It does not have to be in a straight line. This is the "parent" chain. State the number of carbon atoms using the appropriate prefix and the ending "ane."
2. Number the carbon atoms in the parent chain starting at the end closest to the branches. Branches are called "alkyl" groups. The carbon atom's number becomes like the "address" of the branch off the parent chain.
3. Name each branch with a prefix according to the number of carbon atoms it contains. Branch names end in "yl" instead of "ane." For example, a branch containing one carbon atom is called a **methyl** branch. If the branch contains two carbon atoms, it is called an **ethyl** branch. List the branches in alphabetical order. Then, if two, three, or four branches have the same number of carbon atoms, use the prefixes "di" (two), "tri" (three), and tetra" (four). For example, if there are two branches each with three carbons, they are called "dipropyl."
4. State the name of the alkane by first listing the "address" of each branch, then naming the branches, then naming the parent. Use commas between numbers and hyphens between a number and a branch name.

Figure 9.1.2 shows an example of a branched alkane correctly named and incorrectly named. Note that the carbon atoms in the parent chain must be numbered starting at the end closest to the branch.

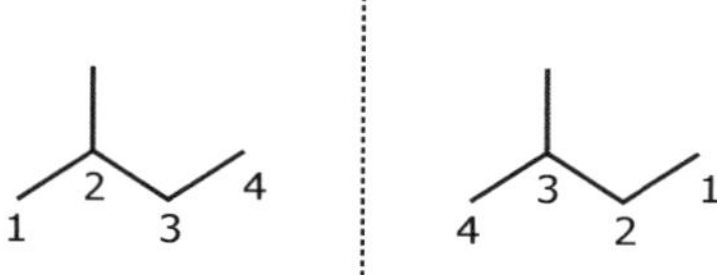

2-methyl-butane
Correct:
Branch has the lowest number.

3-methyl-butane
Incorrect

Figure 9.1.2 *Example of how to name a branched alkane*

Sample Problem — Naming Simple Alkanes

Name the simple alkane shown here.

$$CH_3-CH(CH_3)-C(CH_3)(CH_2-CH_3)-CH_2-CH_2-CH_3$$

What to Think about	How to Do It
1. The longest chain of carbon atoms is six and the prefix for six is "hex." Name the parent chain.	hexane
2. The parent chain carbons are numbered from the left, because the branches start closer to the left. The branch addresses from left to right would be 2, 3, 3. There is a methyl group attached to the second and also the third carbon atom in the parent chain.	2,3-dimethyl
3. There is an ethyl group attached to the third carbon in the parent chain.	3-ethyl
4. The name states the address then the branch names alphabetically, then the parent chain. Alphabetically, "ethyl" will be listed before "methyl." We do not consider the prefixes "di" and "tri" etc. when listing alphabetically.	3-methyl: CH_3 on carbon 3 $^{1}CH_3-{}^{2}CH-{}^{3}C-{}^{4}CH_2-{}^{5}CH_2-{}^{6}CH_3$ 2-methyl: CH_3 on carbon 2; 3-ethyl: CH_2-CH_3 on carbon 3 parent chain =hexane 3-ethyl-2, 3-dimethylhexane

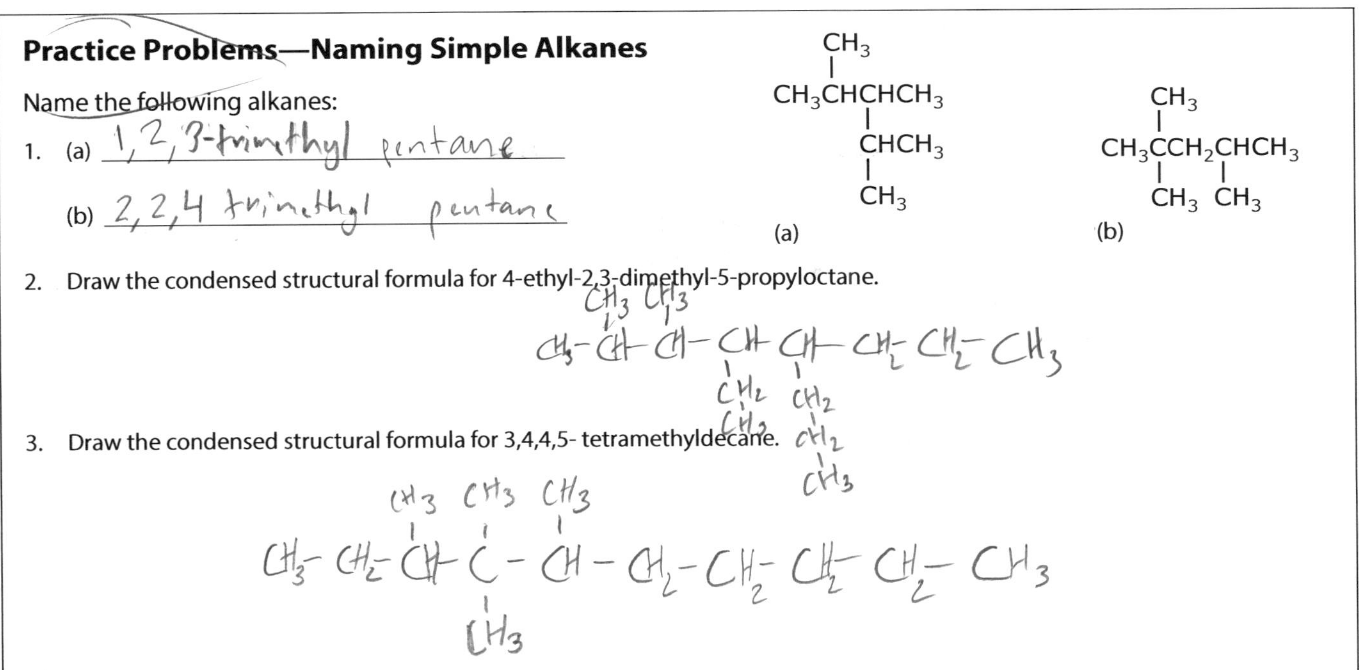

Structural Isomers

Consider Table 9.1.2 below. What do you notice about the molecular formulas of the two substances in the table? Pentane and 2-methybutane are different compounds with different chemical properties, and yet they have the same molecular formula. These are called **structural isomers**. There is one more structural isomer of C_5H_{12}. Can you figure it out? Read on to find out how.

Table 9.1.2 *Examples of structural isomers*

Name	Structural Formula	Molecular Formula
pentane	H H H H H H—C—C—C—C—C—H H H H H H	C_5H_{12}
2-methylbutane	H H—C—H H H H H—C—C—C—C—H H H H H	C_5H_{12}

You need to be methodical when drawing isomers of a compound. For example, the compound pentane has 5 carbon atoms and 12 hydrogen atoms. Let's focus on the carbon skeleton. The most obvious way to arrange five carbon atoms is in a single chain:

$CH_3 — CH_2 — CH_2 — CH_2 — CH_3$

We can also arrange four carbon atoms in a chain and have the fifth carbon atom as a methyl branch. Note that the branch cannot go on either end of the carbon chain because then it would be a part of the parent chain, giving us pentane again. We can put the methyl branch on the second carbon in the parent chain, as shown in Figure 9.1.3.

```
1      2      3       4              4      3      2       1
CH3 — CH — CH2 — CH3              CH3 — CH — CH2 — CH3
       |                                 |
       CH3                               CH3

  2 - methylbutane                  3 - methylbutane
  (Correct name)                    (Wrong name)
```

Figure 9.1.3 *2-methylbutane*

Why is there not a molecule called 3-methylbutane? It depends on numbering the carbon atoms in the parent chain. Remember to always number the carbons in the parent chain starting from the end closest to the branch. The "address" of the branches must be the lowest numbers.

Finally, we can arrange three carbon atoms in the parent chain and have two methyl branches on the second carbon, as shown in Figure 9.1.4.

```
        CH3
        |
CH3 — C — CH3
        |
        CH3
```

Figure 9.1.4 *2,2-dimethylpropane*

There are three structural isomers for C_5H_{12}. As the number of carbon atoms in a molecule increases, the number of possible isomers increases dramatically.

- C_5H_{12} has three structural isomers.
- C_6H_{14} has five structural isomers.
- C_7H_{16} has nine structural isomers.
- $C_{20}H_{42}$ has more than 300 000 structural isomers.

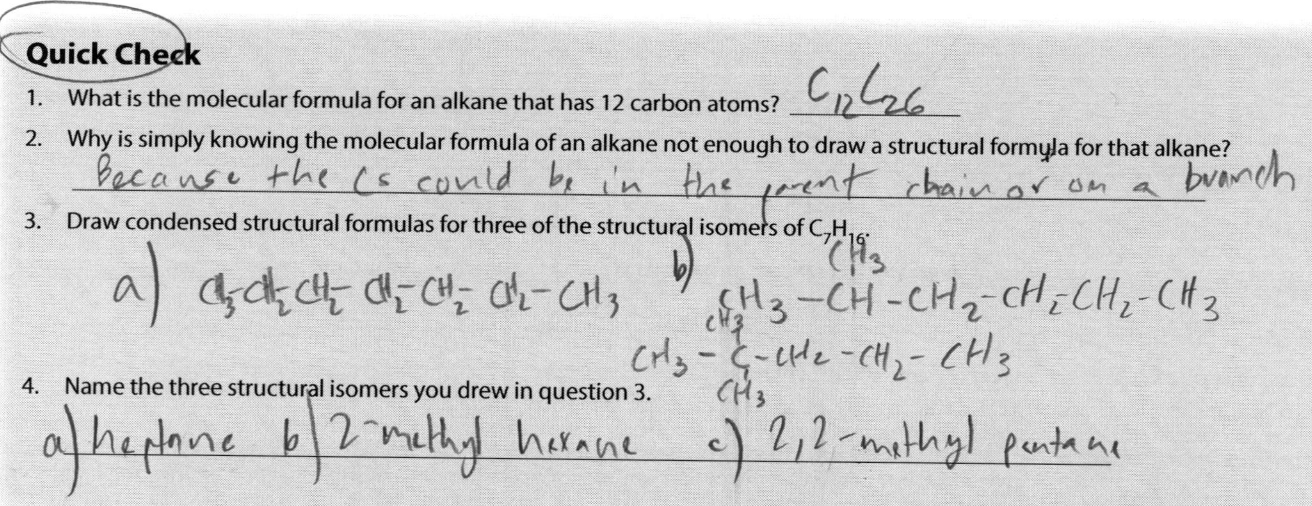

Quick Check

1. What is the molecular formula for an alkane that has 12 carbon atoms? ______
2. Why is simply knowing the molecular formula of an alkane not enough to draw a structural formula for that alkane?
3. Draw condensed structural formulas for three of the structural isomers of C_7H_{16}.
4. Name the three structural isomers you drew in question 3.

Cycloalkanes

Carbon atoms may bond to each other and form a **cyclic** structure called a ring, like the one in the diagram below. The hormones testosterone and progesterone are examples of compounds that contain ring structures.

Consider the molecule shown in Figure 9.1.4(a). This compound has the formula C_5H_{10}. Alkanes have the general formula $C_nH_{(2n+2)}$. The general formula for a cycloalkane like the one in the diagram is $C_nH_{(2n)}$. The carbon skeleton formula for this compound is shown in Figure 9.1.4(b).

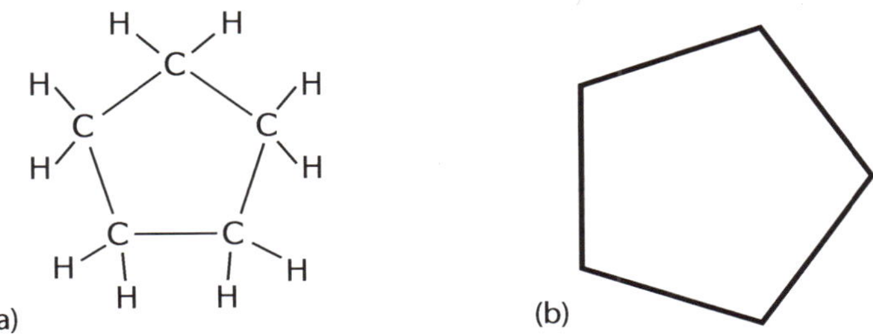

Figure 9.1.4 *(a) C_5H_{10}; (b) the carbon skeleton formula for C_5H_{10}*

When naming an alkane that contains a ring structure, the same rules apply as for a chain alkane. See Figure 9.1.5 for examples.

1. The ring that contains the greater number of carbon atoms is the parent chain. The prefix "cyclo" is placed before the parent chain name.
2. The carbon atoms in the parent ring are numbered either clockwise or counterclockwise so that the lowest numbers are used to identify the placement of the branches.
3. If the ring structure is not the longest continuous carbon chain, then it is named as a branch with the prefix "cyclo" and ends in "yl."

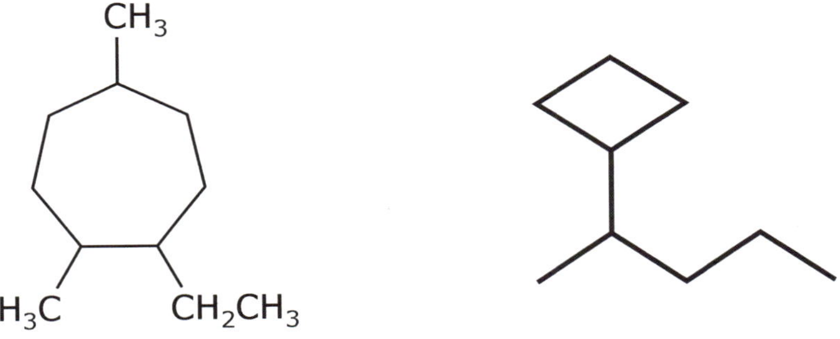

(a) 1-ethyl-2,5-dimethylcycloheptane (b) 2-cyclobutylpentane

Figure 9.1.5 *Example of alkanes that contain ring structures*

Alkenes

Alkenes are hydrocarbons containing double bonds. They are **unsaturated**. This means that the double bond is a reactive site where other atoms could attach to the carbon skeleton. They have the general formula C_nH_{2n}. As you saw above, cycloalkanes have the same general formula as alkenes. Molecules with this general formula contain either one alkane ring or one double bond.

The rules for naming alkenes are the same as for alkanes except that an alkene's parent chain name ends in "ene." See Figure 9.1.6 for an example.

- The parent chain must contain the double bond.
- The position of the double bond is indicated in the name by stating the number of the carbon atom in the parent chain that the double bond follows.
- The parent chain carbon atoms are numbered starting at the end closest to the double bond.

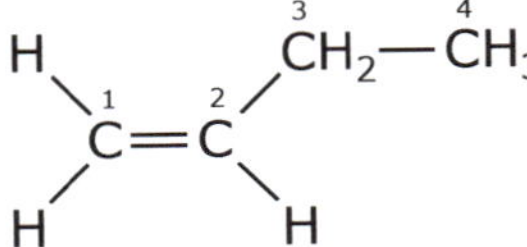

Figure 9.1.6 *An example of an alkene: 1-butene*

In some cases, the groups attached to the double-bonded carbon atoms provide for a new type of isomerism, as shown in Figure 9.1.7. **Geometric isomers** are alkenes that have the same structure, but the orientation of the groups across the double bond are different. Geometric isomers are also called ***cis-trans*** **isomers**.

For example, *cis*-2-butene has two hydrogen atoms bonded to the double-bonded carbon atoms on the same side of the double bond. Both hydrogen atoms are below the double bond. *Trans*-2-butene has the groups bonded to the double-bonded carbon atoms on opposite sides of the double bond. One hydrogen is above the double bond, and the other hydrogen is below the double bond.

cis-2-butene

trans-2-butene

Figure 9.1.7 *Examples of cis-trans isomers*

Quick Check

1. What is the molecular formula for an alkene containing one double bond and seven carbon atoms?

   C_7H_{14}

2. Draw a cycloalkane containing seven carbon atoms. What is its molecular formula?

   C_7H_{14}

3. Name the compound shown here.

   1-ethyl, 2-methyl cyclohexane

4. Draw cyclohexane and write its molecular formula. Beside it, draw the 2 geometric isomers of 2-hexene, and write their molecular formulas. Classify each molecule as saturated or unsaturated.

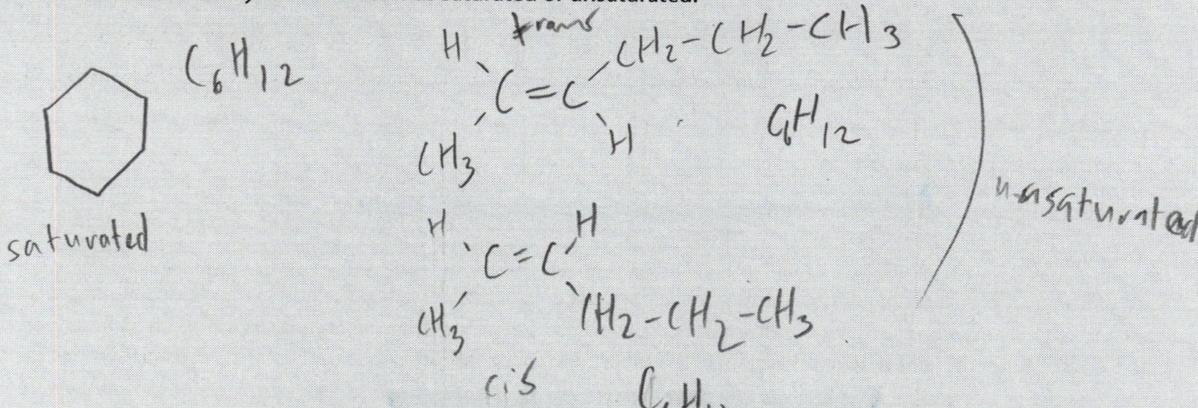

Alkynes

Alkynes are hydrocarbons containing triple bonds. They are also unsaturated. They have the general formula $C_nH_{(2n-2)}$.

The rules for naming alkynes are the same as for alkanes except the parent chain name ends in "yne." See Figure 9.1.8 for an example.

- The parent chain must contain the triple bond.
- The position of the triple bond is indicated in the name by stating the number of the carbon atom in the parent chain that the triple bond follows.
- The parent chain carbon atoms are numbered starting at the end closest to the triple bond.

Figure 9.1.8 *3-methyl-1-pentyne*

Aromatic Hydrocarbons

Benzene is a hydrocarbon with six carbon atoms in a ring. This structure is called a **benzene ring**. It has the molecular formula C_6H_6. The bonds between each carbon atom are slightly longer than a double bond, but slightly shorter than a single bond. The electrons in the benzene molecule are *delocalized*, meaning that they are spread across more than one atom. In other words, there is more than one way to draw its Lewis structure. Equivalent Lewis structures are called **resonance structures**. We can represent benzene using the resonance structure shown in Figure 9.1.9(a). It can also be represented as shown in Figure 9.1.9(b).

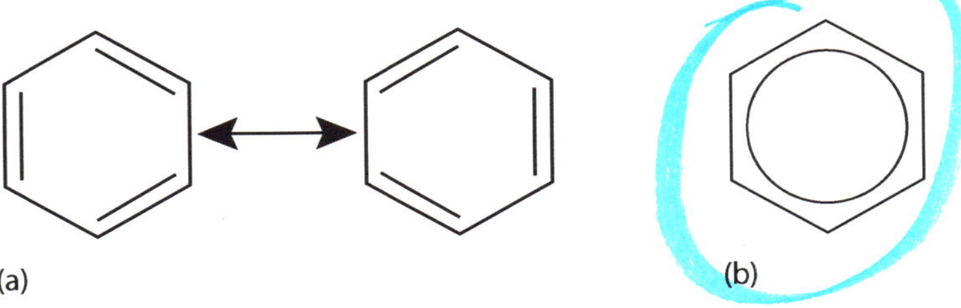

Figure 9.1.9 *Examples of resonance structures for benzene*

Aromatic hydrocarbons always contain at least one benzene ring. When one of the hydrogen atoms in a benzene ring is replaced by another atom or group, we call it a monosubstituted benzene. Monosubstituted benzenes are named by simply using the name of the substituted group as a prefix attached to "benzene."

If more than one hydrogen atom in a benzene has been replaced, we call it a polysubstituted benzene. For polysubstituted benzenes, branches are named and their "address" on the benzene ring is indicated in a similar way to that used for cycloalkanes. We label the first substituted carbon as 1 and proceed either clockwise or counterclockwise in such a way as to give the lowest combination of numbers of substituted carbons.

For benzenes where only two branches exist on the ring, the three possible 1,2-, 1,3-, and 1,4- positions can also be indicated using the prefixes "ortho," "meta," and "para" respectively. These prefixes describe how close the branches are to each other on the benzene ring (Figure 9.1.10). A benzene ring with one methyl branch is commonly called toluene. A benzene ring with two methyl branches is commonly called xylene.

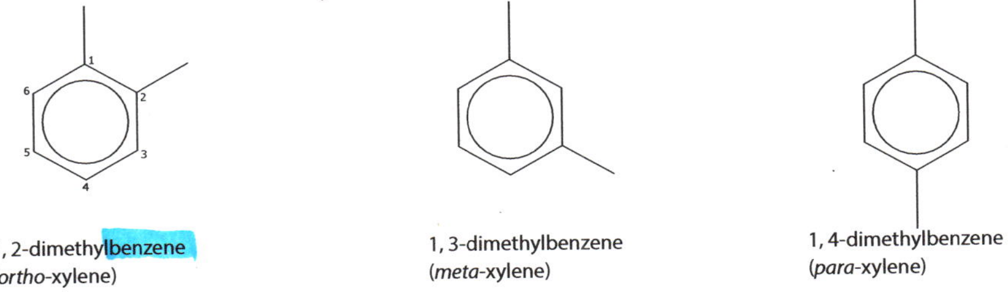

Figure 9.1.10 *Examples of prefixes used to describe the branches on a benzene ring*

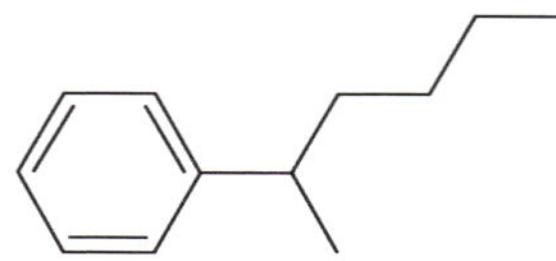

Figure 9.1.11 *2-phenylhexane*

Some organic compounds have benzene as a branch. If this is the case, the branch name is "phenyl" (Figure 9.1.11).

Figure 9.1.12 shows the structures and names of some common aromatic compounds.

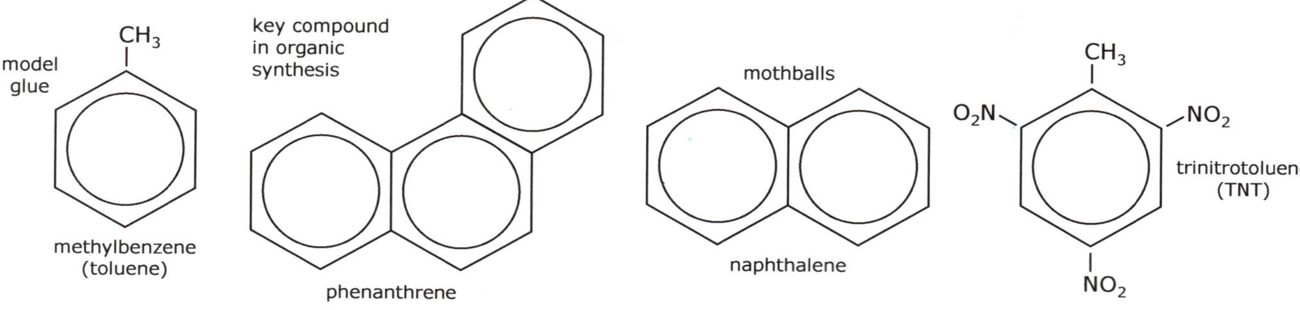

Figure 9.1.12 *Examples of common aromatic compounds*

Quick Check

1. What is the molecular formula for an alkyne containing one triple bond and 8 carbon atoms in a chain?

   C_8H_{14}

2. Do alkynes exhibit *cis* and *trans* isomerism? Explain.

   No because the triple bond holds the carbons to the same bond angle

3. Draw the condensed structural formula for 3,4-dimethyl-1-hexyne.

   $CH \equiv C - CH(CH_3) - CH(CH_3) - CH_2 - CH_3$

4. Draw the structural formula for benzene.

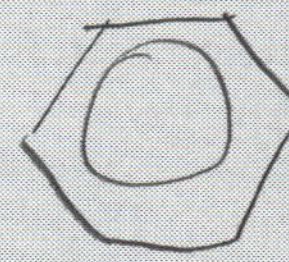

9.1 Activity: Building and Naming Structural Isomers

Question

How many structural isomers are there for hexane?

Background

Structural isomers have the same molecular formula, but are different arrangements of the same atoms. The general formula for an alkane is $C_nH_{(2n+2)}$.

Procedure

1. You will need one organic chemistry model kit to share with your partner. Working together, construct and name the structural isomers of C_6H_{14}.

Results and Discussion

1. Draw the condensed structural formula for hexane.

2. Using your model kit, build hexane.

3. Build the different structural isomers of C_6H_{14}. Draw the condensed structural formula for each isomer you build. Write the name of each isomer under its condensed structural formula.

4. How many structural isomers are there for hexane? ______________

5. Build 3-hexene. Draw the condensed structural formula for the two geometric isomers of 3-hexene, and write the name of each one under its formula.

9.1 Review Questions

1. How is a condensed structural formula different from a carbon skeleton formula? Use an example.

2. Draw carbon skeleton structural formulas for all of the isomers of the alkane with seven carbon atoms. Under each diagram, write the isomer's name.

3. What is the difference between a structural isomer and a geometric isomer? Use an example in your answer.

4. Draw 1-pentene. Does this molecule exhibit *cis-trans* isomerism? Explain.

5. Classify the following as being *cis* or *trans* isomers:

(a)

H and H on one side, CH_3 and $CH_2—CH_3$ on the other: H(CH₃)C=C(H)(CH₂—CH₃)

(b)

$CH_3—CH_2—CH_2$ and H on one carbon, H and $CH_2—CH_2—CH_3$ on the other: $CH_3—CH_2—CH_2$(H)C=C(H)$CH_2—CH_2—CH_3$

(c)

Phenyl and H on each carbon: C=C with a benzene ring on each carbon and H on each carbon

6. An important nutrient for your body is fat. Infants require a diet high in fat for brain development. Your body needs fats for energy and to dissolve certain vitamins. Fats in foods are classified as saturated, unsaturated, and polyunsaturated. Animal products contain a high level of saturated fats. What is meant by the term "saturated"?

7. (a) Unsaturated fats are generally a liquid at room temperature. What is meant by the term "unsaturated"?

(b) Which of the following are unsaturated: alkanes, alkenes, alkynes, cycloalkanes, aromatics?

8. Classify the following as alkane, alkene, alkyne, cycloalkane, or aromatic without drawing the structure. Some may have more than one classification.

(a) C_5H_{10} ____________

(b) $C_{15}H_{32}$ ____________

(c) C_9H_{16} ____________

(d) C_6H_6 ____________

9. Name the following compounds.

(a)

```
H           CH2—CH3
  \        /
   C == C
  /        \
CH3—CH2—CH2   H
```

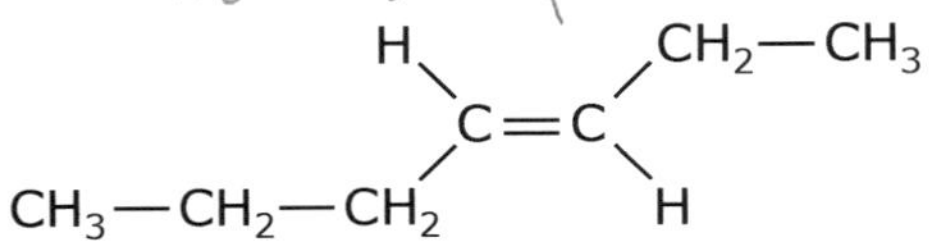

(b)

(c)

```
CH3—CH2—CH—CH2—CH3
        |
CH3—CH2—C—CH2—CH3
        |
CH3—CH2—CH—CH2—CH3
```

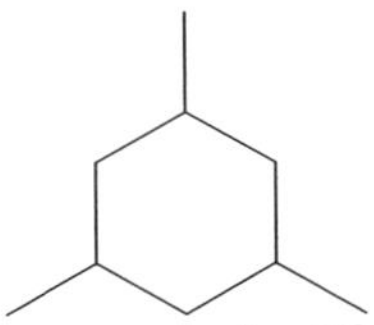

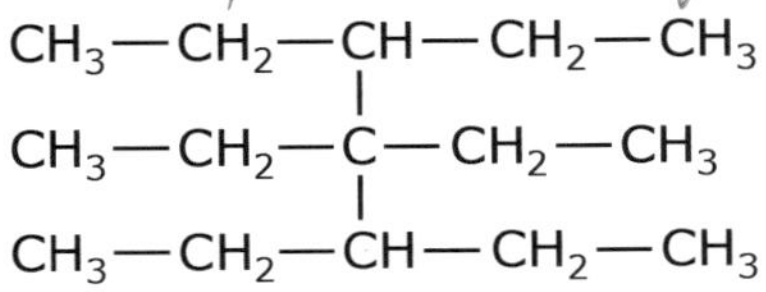

(d)

```
      CH
    /    \\
 CH2      CH
   |      |
   CH —— CH2
   |
  CH3
```

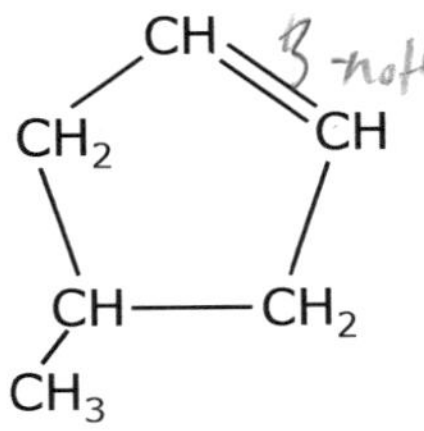

(e)

```
                 CH2—CH3
      (benzene ring)
CH3—CH2
           CH3
```

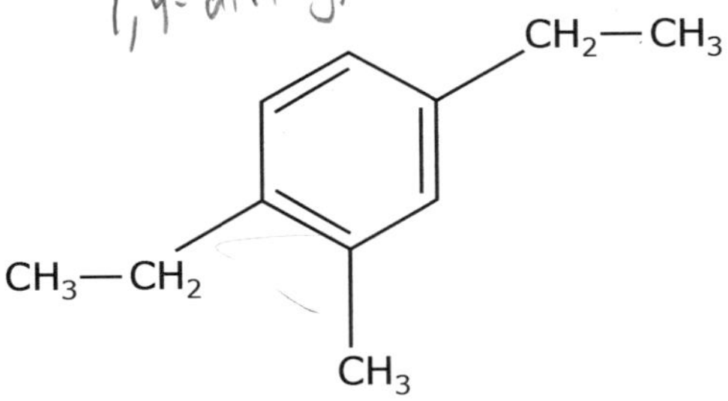

(f)

(g)

(h)

```
CH≡C—CH—CH—CH3
     |    |
CH3—CH2  CH2—CH3
```

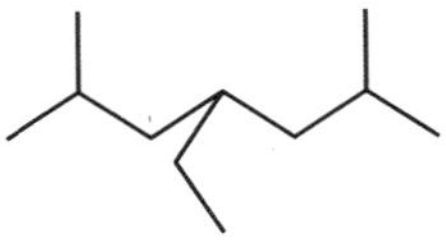

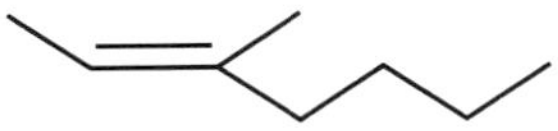

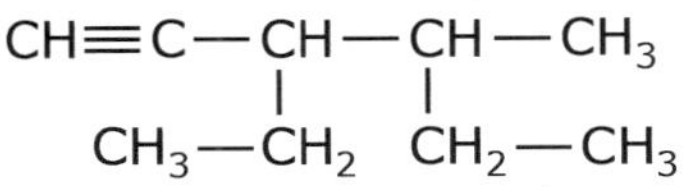

10. Draw condensed structural formulas for the following compounds.

(a) 4-ethyl-3,5-dimethylnonane

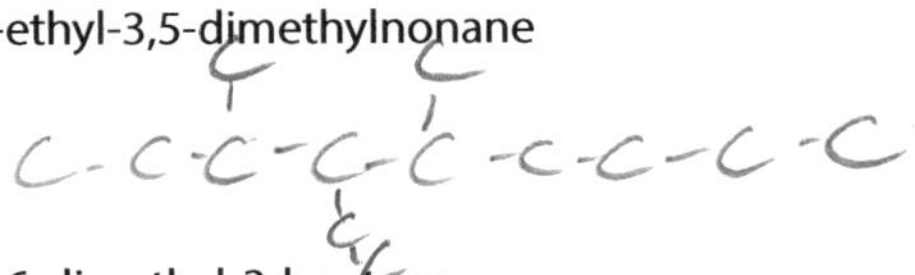

(b) 5,6-dimethyl-3-heptyne

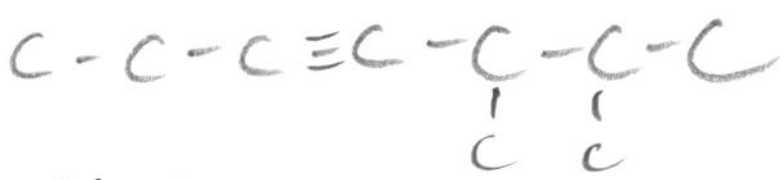

(c) *trans*-2-heptene

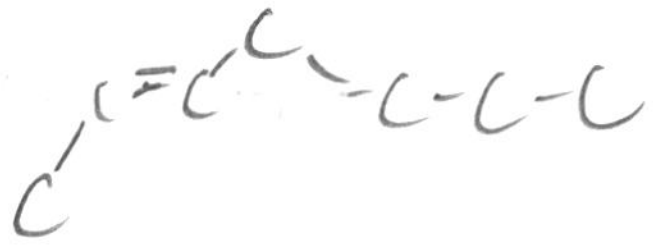

(d) 1,3-dimethyl-2-propylcycloheptane

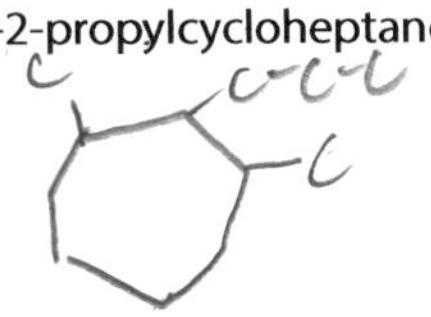

(e) 4,5,5-trimethyl-2-heptyne

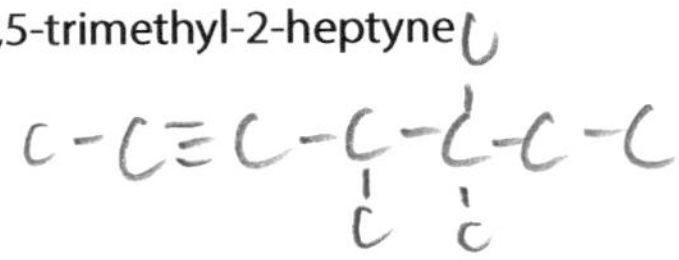

(f) ethylcyclohexane

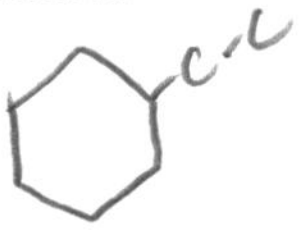

(g) 4-ethyl-3,3-dimethyloctane

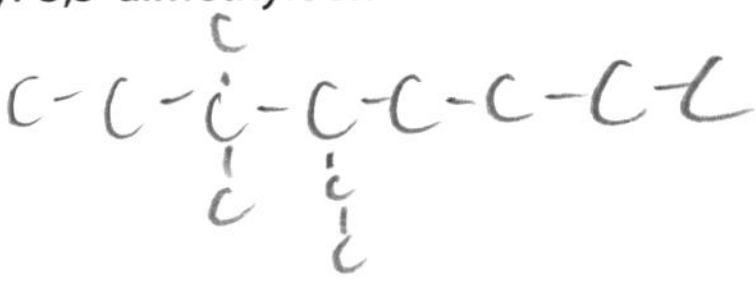

(h) 3-cyclopentyl-5,5-dimethyl-1-hexene

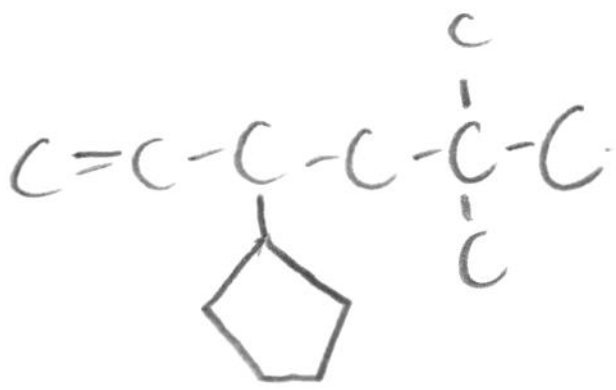

9.2 Functional Groups

Warm Up

Every day, you use products that contain organic compounds.
In the list below, place a checkmark beside each product that you have in your home.

	Product		Product
☐	vanilla flavouring	☐	fuels (gasoline, for example)
☐	nail polish remover	☐	cosmetics
☐	insecticide	☐	glue
☐	acetaminophen (Tylenol)	☐	asphalt
☐	antifreeze	☐	nylon
☐	wax	☐	Teflon
☐	plastics	☐	paint thinner

Functional Groups

Earlier in this chapter, you learned about organic compounds containing carbon and hydrogen atoms. The number of isomers possible for large hydrocarbons is enormous. Now imagine how many more isomers would be possible if we included atoms of oxygen, nitrogen, sulphur, or other elements! If you look into reference books such as the *Handbook of Chemistry and Physics*, you will see that organic compounds greatly outnumber inorganic compounds. All of the products listed in the Warm Up above contain organic compounds. You are surrounded by organic chemistry!

In section 9.1, you learned about the structures of alkenes, alkynes, and aromatic hydrocarbons, such as benzene. Groups of organic compounds like these are called functional groups. A **functional group** is an atom, group of atoms, or organization of bonds in an organic molecule that react in a characteristic manner. Organic compounds with the same functional group react in a similar manner

Functional groups are identified by the placement of certain atoms in a molecule.

Chemists use a shorthand to represent carbon and hydrogen atoms that are not part of the functional group. We use the symbol **R** to represent the hydrocarbon fragment of the organic molecule not involved in the functional group. **R'** (called "r prime") may be used for a different hydrocarbon fragment in the same molecule.

You do not need to know how to name many of these compounds. You simply need to be able to identify the functional group. Naming rules will be given for the types of organic compounds you should be able to name.

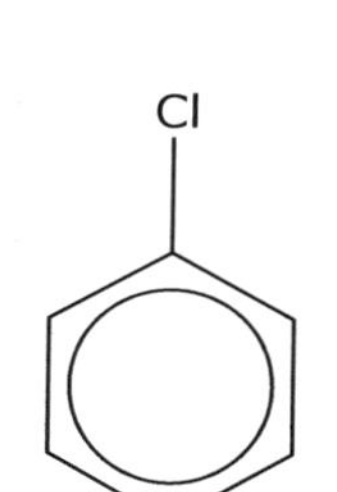

(a) chlorobenzene

(b) 2-bromo-4-chloropentane

Figure 9.2.1 *Examples of alkyl halides*

Alkyl Halides: R-X (where X = F, Cl, I, or Br)

Organic compounds containing halogens are called alkyl halides (Figure 9.2.1). They are named using the same rules you learned in section 9.1 except that the halogen atom is named as a branch group. It is treated the same way as an alkyl group was in section 9.1. The prefixes to use for each element are:

F = **fluoro** Cl = **chloro** Br = **bromo** I = **iodo**

Alcohols: R-OH

Organic compounds containing a **hydroxyl** (–OH) group attached to a carbon atom are called **alcohols**. Do not confuse a hydroxyl group with a hydroxide ion. Compounds with a hydroxide ion are bases and are ionic. Alcohols are covalent compounds that do not readily release the –OH group. Here are the rules for naming alcohols:

1. The parent chain must contain an atom attached to the –OH group. Number the carbon atoms in the parent chain such that the –OH group is given the lowest number.
2. The name of the parent chain ends with "–ol" instead of "–e."
3. Name and identify positions of the branches as usual.

Table 9.2.1 shows examples of how these rules are used. The first example, ethanol, is the alcohol consumed in alcoholic beverages. While all alcohols are toxic to humans, ethanol is somewhat less so, although large quantities consumed in a short period of time can cause death. Ethanol is also an important additive to fuels and is used as a solvent for flavourings, colourings, and pharmaceuticals.

Table 9.2.1 *Examples of how to name alcohols*

Alcohol Name	Structure
Ethanol (commonly called ethyl alcohol) • Notice that a number is not required to indicate the position of the hydroxyl group as it must be at the end of a two-carbon chain.	$CH_3—CH_2—OH$
3-methyl-1-butanol	$CH_3—CH(CH_3)—CH_2—CH_2—OH$
2-propanol (commonly called isopropanol or isopropyl alcohol) • The name "isopropyl" refers to the branch of three carbons (recall from Table 9.1.1 in section 9.1 that "prop-" means three). The branch is attached at the second carbon atom in the chain of three carbon atoms. • Isopropyl alcohol is used as a cleaner for electronics, and for sterilizing solutions.	OH H_3C CH_3

Quick Check

1. Draw full structural formulas for the following compounds:
   (a) 3,3-dichloropentane (b) *cis*-1,2-dichloroethene (c) 4,4-dimethyl-3-hexanol

2. Name the following compounds:

   (a) $CH_3—OH$ ______________________

   (b) $CH_3—CH_2—CH_2—CH_2—Br$ ______________________

3. There are two isomers of C_3H_7OH that are alcohols. One of them, 2-propanol is shown in Table 9.2.1 above. Draw the other isomer and name it.

4. Ethanol poisoning occurs when the body cannot metabolize alcohol fast enough. What kinds of products are commonly consumed that lead to ethanol poisoning?

   ____

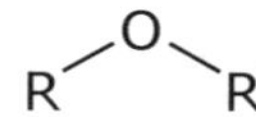

Ethers

Ethers are organic compounds in which two hydrocarbon fragments are attached by an oxygen atom. You do *not* need to know how to name ethers. Table 9.2.2 shows examples of ethers.

Table 9.2.2 *Examples of Ethers and Their Applications*

Ether Name	Application	Structure
Methoxymethane (commonly called dimethyl ether)	aerosol spray propellant	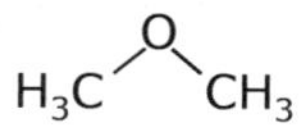 H_3C O CH_3
Ethoxyethane (commonly called diethyl ether)	early anesthetic	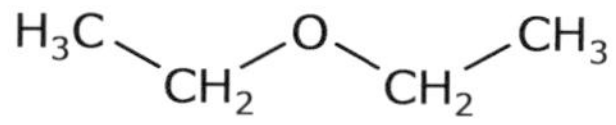 H_3C CH_2 O CH_2 CH_3
Methoxybenzene (commonly called methylphenyl ether)	anise (licorice) flavoring	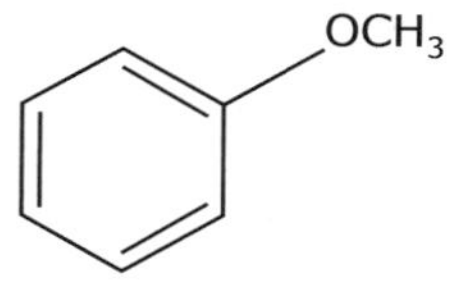 OCH_3

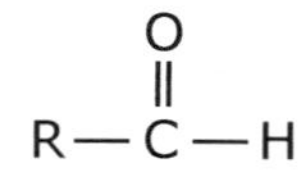

Aldehyde

An **aldehyde** is an organic compound containing a carbonyl group at the end of a carbon chain. A **carbonyl** group is a carbon atom double bonded to an oxygen atom. Aldehydes are used to produce dyes and organic acids. You may be familiar with formaldehyde, which is used as a biological preservative. Almond extract and some perfumes contain benzaldehyde. You do *not* need to know how to name aldehydes. Figure 9.2.2 shows two examples of aldehydes.

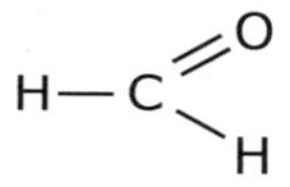

(a) methanal (commonly called formaldehyde)

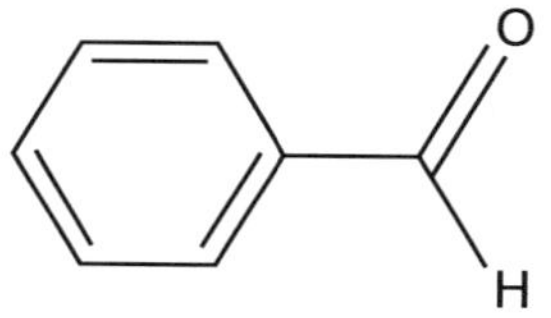

(b) benzaldehyde

Figure 9.2.2 *Examples of aldehydes*

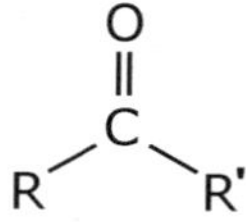

Ketone

A ketone is an organic compound also containing a carbonyl group, but unlike an aldehyde, the carbonyl group of a ketone is not at the end of the carbon chain. Nail polish remover is a ketone commonly called acetone. Ketones are used as solvents and to make polymers and pharmaceuticals. A **polymer** is a very large molecule that is produced by linking together many smaller molecules. We will explore polymers in the next section. You do *not* need to know how to name ketones. Figure 9.2.3 shows two examples of ketones.

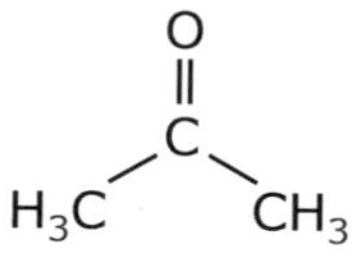

(a) propanone (commonly called acetone)

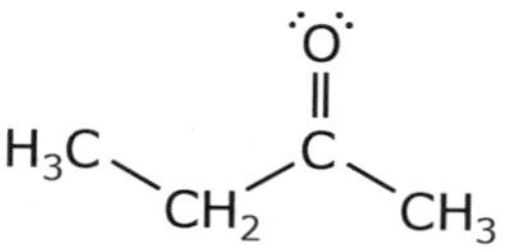

(b) 2-butanone (commonly called ethylmethylketone)

Figure 9.2.3 *Examples of ketones*

Quick Check

1. What is a carbonyl group?

   ____

2. Consider the following classes of organic compounds: alkyl halide, alcohol, ether, aldehyde and ketone. Circle the ones that contain a carbonyl group.

3. (a) Describe how an ether and a ketone are similar and how they are different.

   ____

   ____

   (b) Describe how an aldehyde and a ketone are similar and how they are different.

   ____

   ____

4. Estrogen is a steroid and the primary female sex hormone. On the diagram of estrogen below, circle and label the functional groups.

CH_3 O

HO

Carboxylic Acid

$R-C(=O)-OH$

A carboxylic acid is an organic compound containing a **carboxyl** (–COOH) group. These are sometimes called organic acids and are commonly found as food preservatives. White vinegar is a 5% solution of ethanoic acid, commonly called acetic acid. Methanoic acid (commonly called formic acid) is the compound responsible for the sting of bee or red ant bites. Carboxylic acids usually have unpleasant odours. You do not need to know how to name most carboxylic acids. (In section 9.3, you will learn how to name a carboxylic acid for a specific type of reaction.) Figure 9.2.4 shows two examples of carboxylic acids.

$CH_3-C(=O)-O-H$

(a) ethanoic acid (commonly called acetic acid)

$H-C(=O)-OH$

(b) methanoic acid (commonly called formic acid)

Figure 9.2.4 *Examples of carboxylic acids*

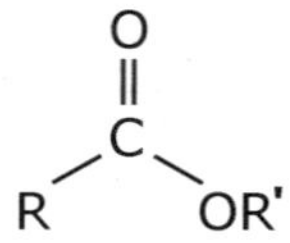

Ester

An ester is an organic compound in which a –COO– group connects two other hydrocarbon fragments. Many esters have strong fruity odors and are used in perfumes and flavorings. DNA and some plastics and explosives contain ester groups. You do *not* need to know how to name esters. Figure 9.2.5 shows two examples of esters.

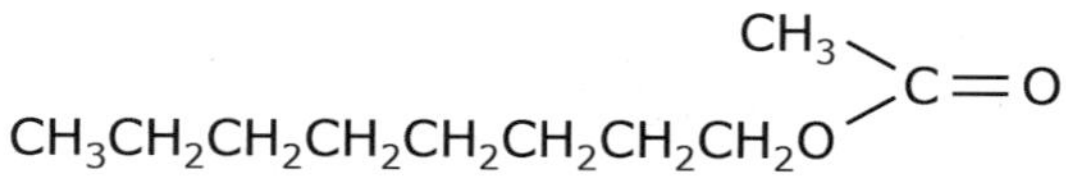

$CH_3CH_2CH_2CH_2CH_2CH_2CH_2CH_2O(CH_3)C{=}O$

(a) octyl ethanoate (orange flavouring)

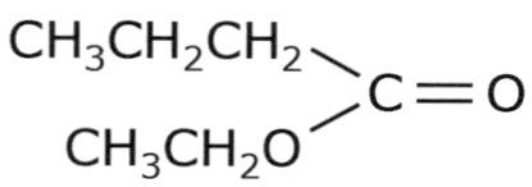

$CH_3CH_2CH_2(CH_3CH_2O)C{=}O$

(b) ethyl butanoate (pineapple flavouring)

Figure 9.2.5 *Examples of esters*

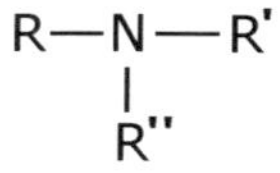

Amines: R-NH_2 or R-NH-R′ or as in the diagram to the left

Amines are organic compounds containing only single bonds and nitrogen atoms attached to a carbon atom. Amines are used to produce dyes and drugs. For example, chlorpheniramine is used as an antihistamine. Ephedrine and phenylephrine are decongestants. You do *not* need to know how to name amines. Figure 9.2.6 shows two examples of amines.

$CH_3 — NH_2$

(a) methylamine

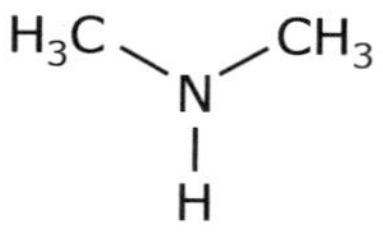

$H_3C–NH–CH_3$

(b) dimethylamine

Figure 9.2.6 *Examples of amines*

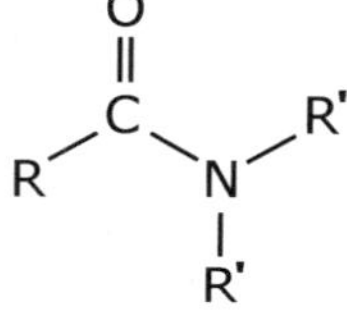

Amides

Organic compounds containing a nitrogen atom bonded to a carbonyl group are called amides. Amides are found in plastics, rubber, inks, and cosmetics. Amides are also used to make nylon and Kevlar. The pain killer acetaminophen is an amide. An amide group links amino acids together in the peptide chains that make up proteins. You do not need to know how to name amides. Figure 9.2.7 shows two examples of amides.

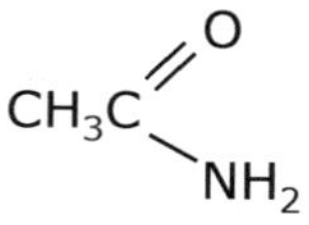

$CH_3C(=O)NH_2$

(a) ethanamide (ethylamide)

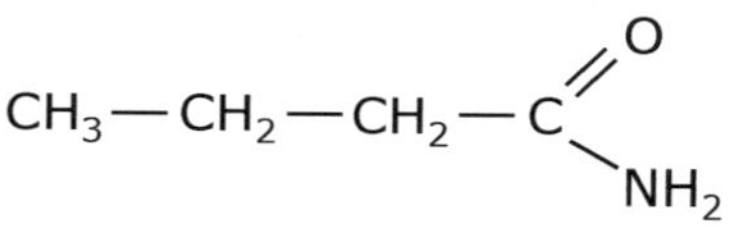

$CH_3 — CH_2 — CH_2 — C(=O)NH_2$

(b) butanamide

Figure 9.2.7 *Examples of amides*

Quick Check

1. What is a carboxyl group?

2. How are a carboxylic acid and ester similar and how are they different?

both have a carbonyl attached to an O, but carboxylic acid ends the molecule with an OH instead.

3. How are an amine and an amide similar and how are they different?

both involve N, but amines only had single bonds

4. (a) Aspirin is a common pain reliever. On the structure of aspirin shown below, circle and name the functional groups.

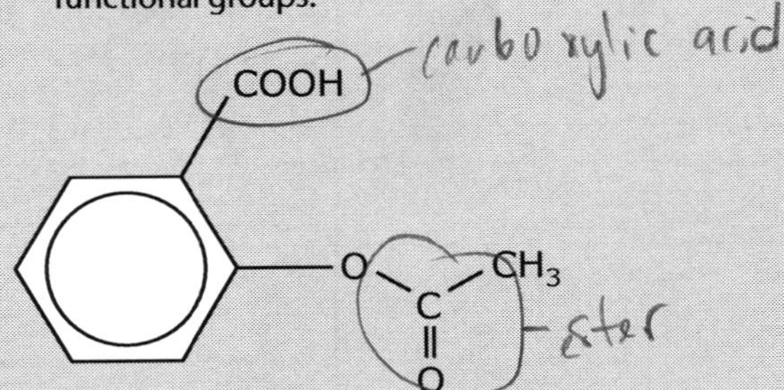

(b) Cocaine is an addictive stimulant for the central nervous system. On the structure of cocaine shown below, circle and name the functional groups.

O
O
N
CH_3O
O

ester
amine
ester

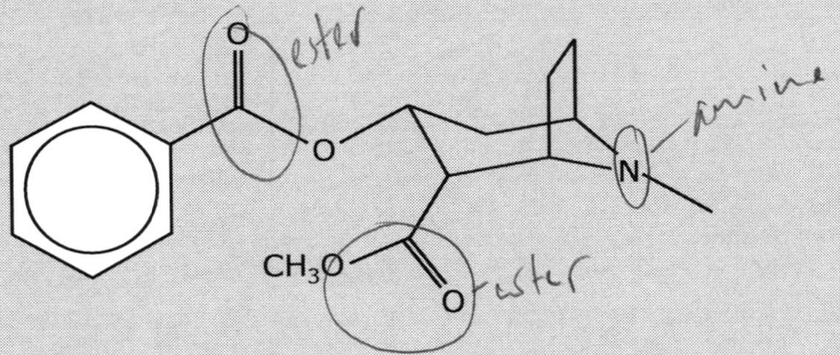

Functional Group Summary

Table 9.2.3 summarizes what you have learned about the functional groups described in this section.

Table 9.2.3 *Functional groups*

<table>
<tr><th>Functional Group</th><th>Classification of Organic Compound</th></tr>
<tr><td>H H
| |
—C=C—</td><td>alkene</td></tr>
<tr><td>—C≡C—</td><td>alkyne</td></tr>
<tr><td>H   H
\   /
C=C
/   \
H—C   C—
\\   //
C—C
/   \
H   H</td><td>aromatic hydrocarbon</td></tr>
<tr><td>X
|
—C—
|</td><td>alkyl halide</td></tr>
<tr><td>OH
|
—C—
|</td><td>alcohol</td></tr>
<tr><td>| |
—C—O—C—
| |</td><td>ether</td></tr>
<tr><td>O
||
—C—H</td><td>aldehyde</td></tr>
<tr><td>O
||
—C—</td><td>ketone</td></tr>
<tr><td>O
||
—C—OH</td><td>carboxylic acid</td></tr>
<tr><td>O
|| |
—C—O—C—
|</td><td>ester</td></tr>
<tr><td>NH_2
|
—C—
|</td><td>amine</td></tr>
<tr><td>O
||
—C—NH_2</td><td>amide</td></tr>
</table>

9.2 Activity: Recognizing Functional Groups

Question

Can you classify an organic compound according to its functional group?

Background

The reactivity of an organic compound depends largely on the presence of its functional group. You can classify organic compounds by their functional group by carefully examining which groups of atoms are present on a molecule. You should be able to recognize the following types of functional groups in the following organic compounds: alkane, alkene, alkyne, cycloalkane, aromatic, alkyl halide, alcohol, ether, amine, amide, aldehyde, ketone, carboxylic acid, and ester.

Procedure

1. Work with a partner.
2. Copy the following structure diagrams onto a piece of paper.

1. 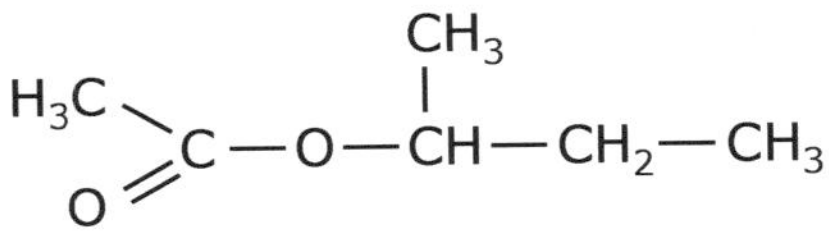 $H_3C-C(=O)-O-CH(CH_3)-CH_2-CH_3$	2. Cl, Cl, CH_3 (benzene ring) 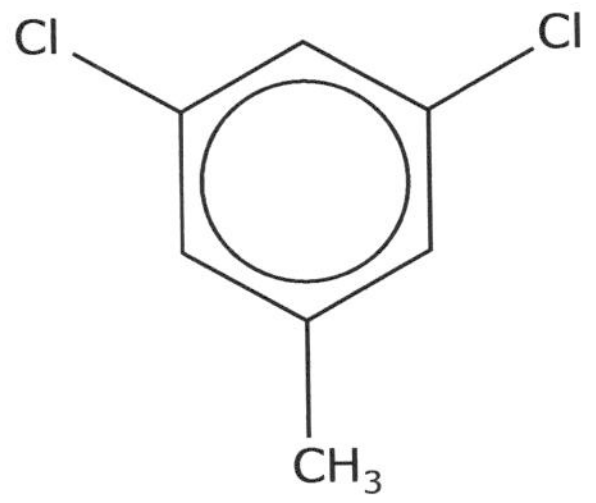
3. $HC\equiv C-CH_3$ 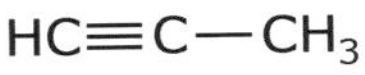	4. 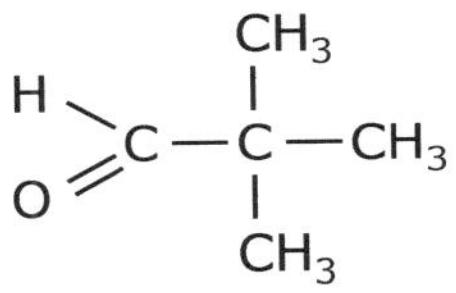 $H-C(=O)-C(CH_3)_2-CH_3$
5. 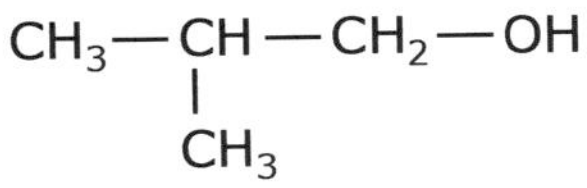 $CH_3-CH(CH_3)-CH_2-OH$	6. 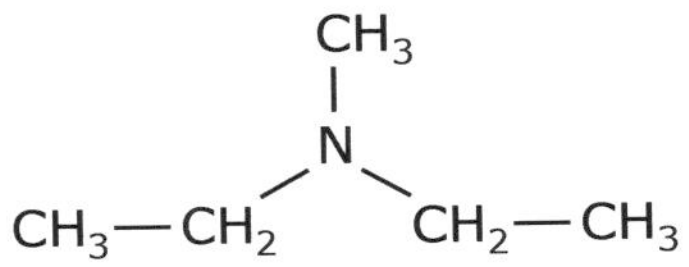 $CH_3-CH_2-N(CH_3)-CH_2-CH_3$
7. 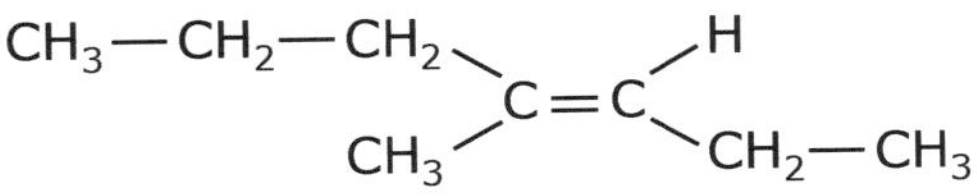 $CH_3-CH_2-CH_2(CH_3)C=C(H)CH_2-CH_3$	8. 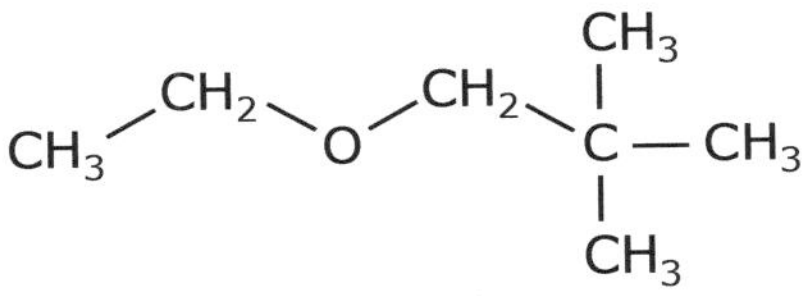 $CH_3-CH_2-O-CH_2-C(CH_3)_2-CH_3$
9. 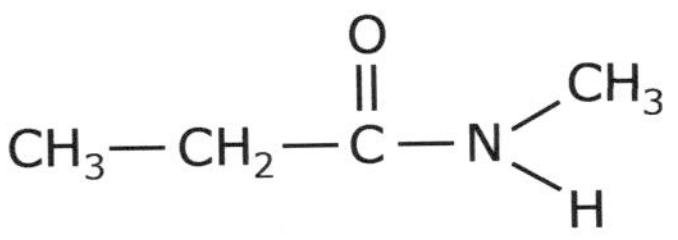 $CH_3-CH_2-C(=O)-N(CH_3)H$	10. 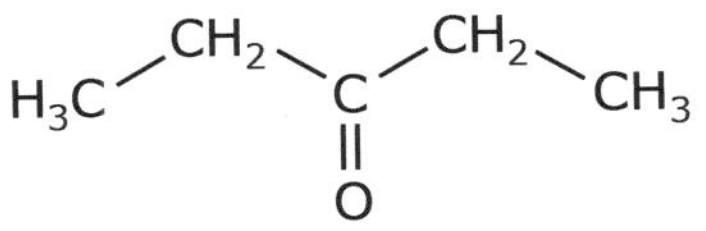 $H_3C-CH_2-C(=O)-CH_2-CH_3$

Continued on next page

3. Cut the paper into 10 squares and place each square face down on the table.

4. Take turns with your partner. Turn over one piece of paper, and state which functional groups are represented. Some examples may include more that one functional group. If your partner agrees, you get to keep that piece of paper. If your partner disagrees, place that piece of paper to the side.

Results and Discussion

1. Once you have completed all 10 squares, count how many questions you answered correctly. _______________

2. For questions where you disagreed, re-examine the question and try to come to an agreement about the functional group. If you cannot agree, ask a nearby pair of students.

3. You know how to name some of these compounds. List the names below of as many as you can and compare your answers to those of a nearby pair of students.

9.2 Review Questions

1. What elements other than carbon and hydrogen commonly appear in organic molecules?

   Oxygen, nitrogen

2. What is a functional group? Give two examples of a functional group.

3. Alkyl halides contain one or more of which family of elements?

4. Complete the following table:

Name of group	Atoms and their arrangement
hydroxyl	OH
carbonyl	C=O
carboxyl	O=C–OH

5. Name the following compounds:

(a)

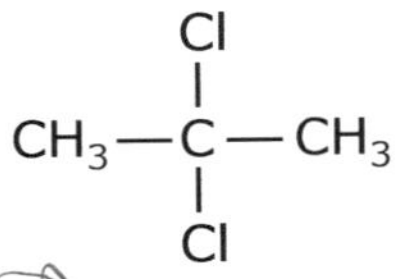

$$CH_3-\underset{Cl}{\overset{Cl}{C}}-CH_3$$

(b)

$$Br-CH-CH_2-OH$$
$$CH_3-\underset{Cl}{C}-CH_2-CH_3$$

(the CH of the first line is bonded to the C of the second line)

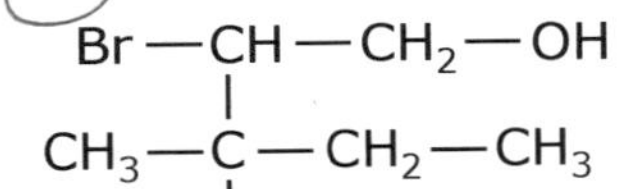

3methyl 3chloro 2-Bromo 1-pentanol

(c)

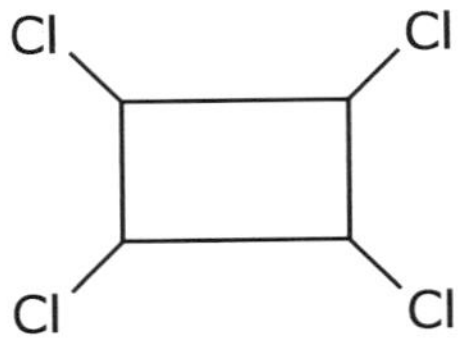

Cl Cl

Cl Cl

(d)

4-Bromo 2-hexene

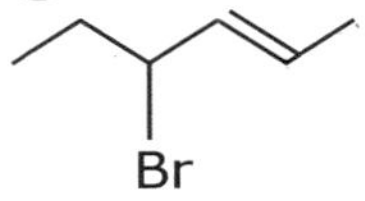

Br

(e)

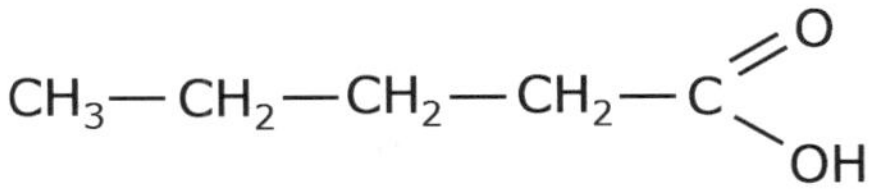

$$CH_3-CH_2-CH_2-CH_2-C(=O)OH$$

(f)

F

F F

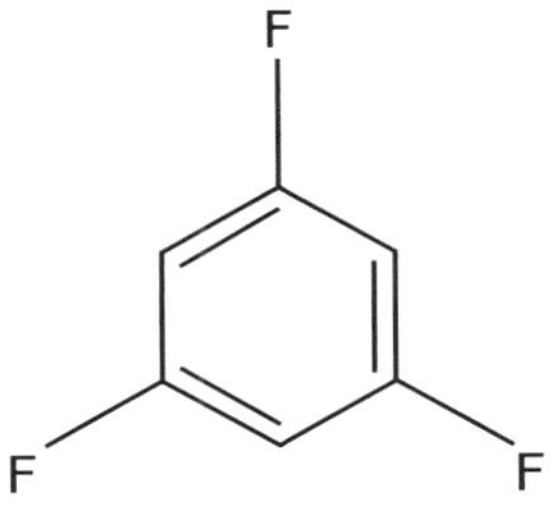

6. Draw condensed structural formulae for each compound below.

(a) cyclopentanol

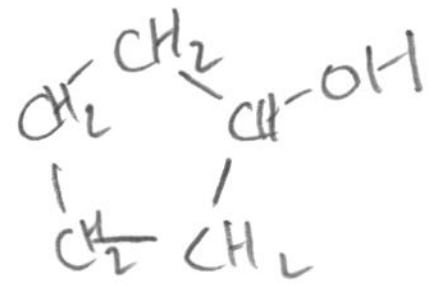

CH_2–CH_2–CH–OH, ring: CH_2 – CH_2 – CH_2

(b) 1,1-dichloroethene

(c) 2-methyl-3-pentanol

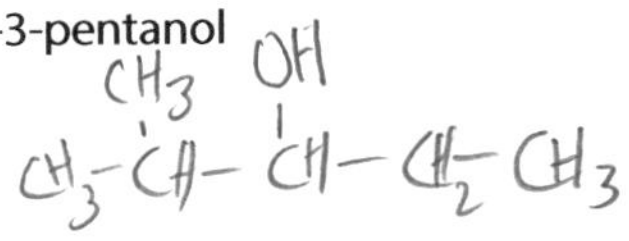

$$CH_3-\overset{CH_3}{CH}-\overset{OH}{CH}-CH_2-CH_3$$

(d) 2-chloropropane

(e) 1,1-dichloro-3,3-dimethyl-2-hexanol

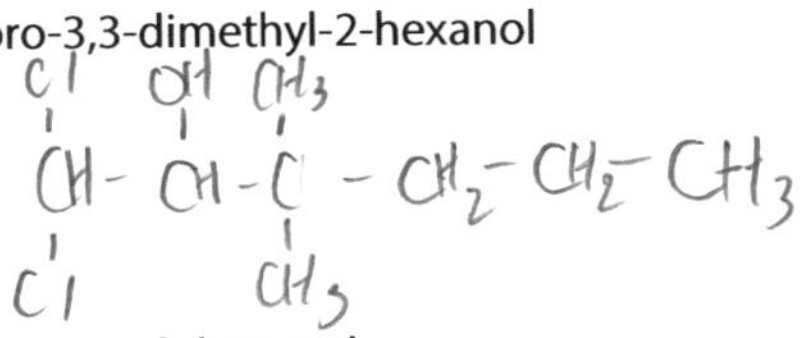

$$\underset{Cl}{\overset{Cl}{CH}}-\overset{OH}{CH}-\underset{CH_3}{\overset{CH_3}{C}}-CH_2-CH_2-CH_3$$

(f) 2,3,5-tribromocyclohexanol

7. Both organic and inorganic compounds may contain an –OH group. In an ionic compound, what is the name of the –OH group? In an organic compound?

8. Which functional groups contain only the following?
(a) single bonded oxygen atoms
(b) double bonded oxygen atoms
(c) both single and double bonded oxygen atoms

9. How is an amide different than a carboxylic acid? How are they similar?

10. For each of the following compounds named, classify the compound according to its functional group. For some compounds, more than one functional group may be used. Draw condensed structural formulas for as many of these as you can.
(a) 2,3-dichloropentane
(b) 2-decyne
(c) *trans*-3-hexene
(d) 1,2-dimethylbenzene
(e) 2-chloro-2-pentanol
(f) 3-methylbutanamide
(g) propanal
(h) pentanoic acid

11. Classify the following molecules according to their functional group.

(a) $CH_3-CH(CH_3)-CH{=}O$

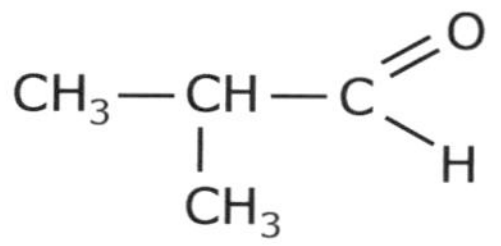

(b) $C_6H_5-C(=O)-OH$

(c) $CH_3-C(=O)-CH_2-CH_3$

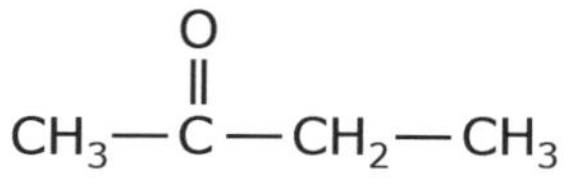

(d) CH_3-CCl_3

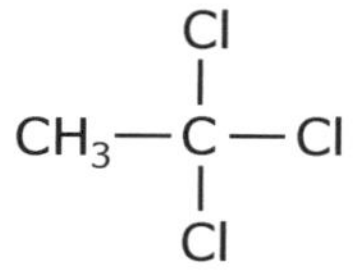

(e) $H-CH(OH)-CH(OH)-H$

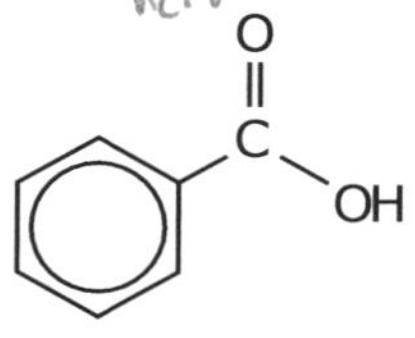

(f) $C_{17}H_{35}C(=O)-O-C_2H_5$

(g) $C_6H_{11}-NH_2$

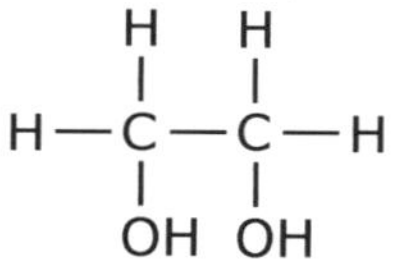

(h) $CH_3CH_2CH_2-C(=O)-N(H)-CH_3$

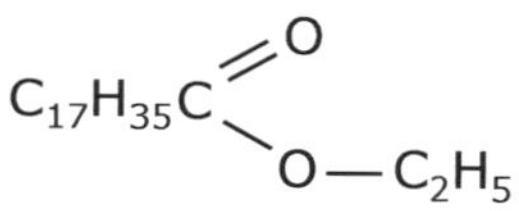

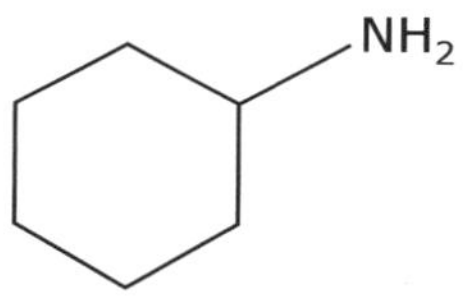

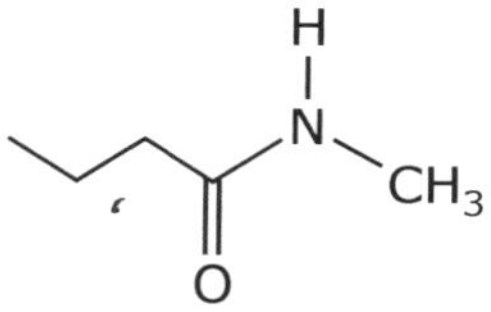

12. The following molecules are common organic compounds. For each molecule, circle and identify each functional group present. These molecules contain more than one functional group.
(a) vanillin (a food flavoring)

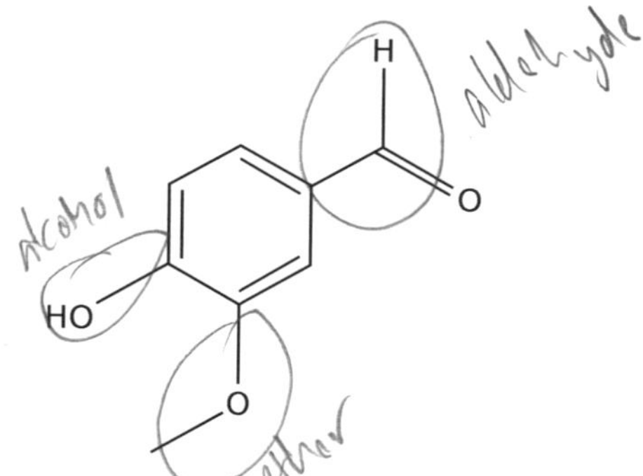

(b) morphine (a painkiller) Note that, in this diagram, the thicker black line represents a chain containing two carbon atoms coming out of the page towards you. This chain attaches the nitrogen atom to the carbon atom in the flat chain.

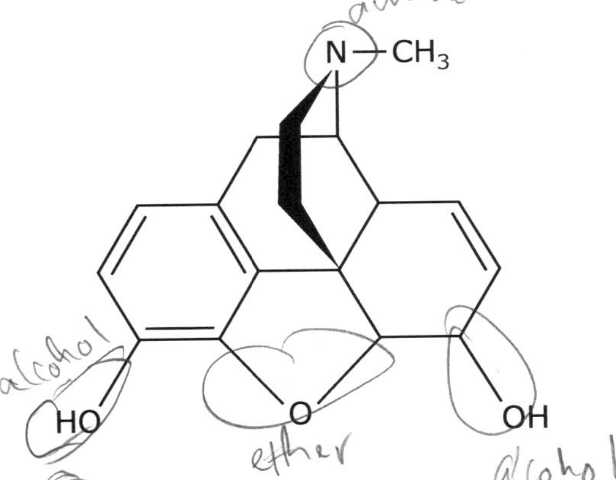

(c) ibuprofen (a painkiller)

(d) capsaicin (the molecule that makes chili peppers "hot"; used in pepper spray)

(e) penicillin G (an antibiotic)

(f) caffeine (the active ingredient in coffee that keeps chemistry students awake while studying)

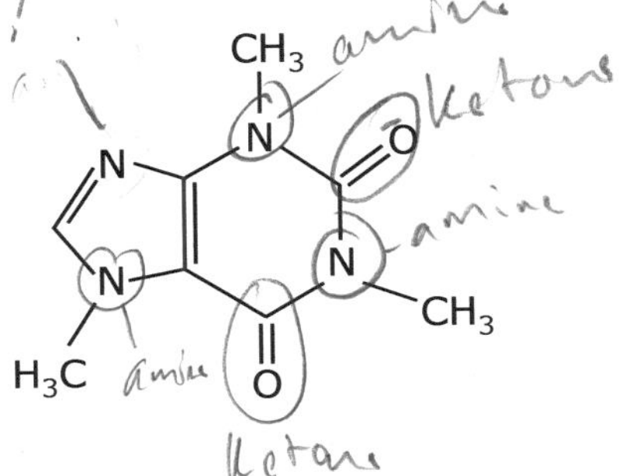

(g) theobromine (found in chocolate)

9.3 Reactions of Organic Molecules

Warm Up

1. Unsaturated fats such as those found in olive oils and avocados are healthier than saturated fats found in coconut oil and butter. What do the words "unsaturated" and "saturated" mean in terms of organic molecular structure?

   ____

2. Earlier in this book you learned about the types of chemical reactions. What are the products of the combustion of a hydrocarbon or carbohydrate?

   ____

3. The chemical reactivity of an organic compound largely depends on the type of organic compound involved. Match the functional group in the column on the left to the correct description from the column on the right. Draw lines to connect each pair.

(a) alcohol	(i) contains a carboxyl group
(b) alkyne	(ii) contains a halogen
(c) carboxylic acid	(iii) contains a hydroxyl group
(d) alkyl halide	(iv) contains a double bond between two carbon atoms
(e) alkene	(v) contains a –COOR group
(f) ester	(vi) contains a triple bond between two carbon atoms

Simple Organic Reactions

Countless organic reactions are happening in your body as you read this. In a living organism, the reactions between organic compounds are the basis for the functioning of systems such as respiration, reproduction, digestion, and circulation. The production of proteins, carbohydrates, and nucleic acids, such as DNA and RNA, involves reactions of organic molecules. Not only is organic chemistry within you, it surrounds you. An enormous variety of organic molecules exists. Many of the products we use daily are made from organic compounds such as fabrics, building materials, food products, drugs, paints, fuels, greases, perfumes, explosives, plastics, dyes, and soaps. A large number of these products are synthesized in a lab.

This chapter began by introducing the work of Friedrich Wohler. He was the first chemist to recognize that an organic compound could be produced in a lab. In this section, we will focus on some simple reactions of organic molecules that occur in nature and in the lab.

Combustion Reactions

The fuel for your car is a mixture of hydrocarbons that react with oxygen in a combustion reaction to produce energy. This is a type of oxidation reaction. It's also an exothermic reaction. Earlier, you learned that the products of hydrocarbon combustion are water and carbon dioxide. The example below shows the reaction of octane (C_8H_{18}) and oxygen.

$$2\ C_8H_{18}(l) + 25\ O_2(g) \rightarrow 16\ CO_2(g) + 18\ H_2O(g) + \text{energy}$$

octane + oxygen → carbon dioxide + water + energy

This equation represents the complete combustion of octane, which occurs when there is an excess of oxygen. The flame appears a clean blue or yellow.

Incomplete combustion may occur when there is a limited amount of oxygen. In that case, products may be carbon monoxide or carbon and water. The solid carbon is the sooty material that you see in blackened smoke. Carbon monoxide is a colourless, odorless, and very poisonous gas. Your home may have a carbon monoxide detector. It will sound an alarm if the fuels heating your home are undergoing incomplete combustion. Your car exhaust contains carbon monoxide as well. It is dangerous to run your car in an enclosed space such as a garage. Every year, people die from carbon monoxide poisoning.

Here is another example of complete and incomplete combustion, this time using methane (CH_4):

Complete combustion: $CH_4(g) + 2\,O_2(g) \rightarrow CO_2(g) + 2\,H_2O(g)$ + energy

Incomplete combustion: $CH_4(g) + O_2(g) \rightarrow C(s) + 2\,H_2O(g)$ + energy

Or $2\,CH_4(g) + 3\,O_2(g) \rightarrow 2\,CO(g) + 4\,H_2O(g)$ + energy

Quick Check

1. Some cars are powered by propane. Write the balanced chemical equation for the complete combustion of propane.
   ____
2. Find out if your home has a carbon monoxide detector. Why might a carbon monoxide detector be a good idea?
   ____
3. Write a balanced chemical equation to represent the incomplete combustion of propane.
   ____

Types of Reactions

In chapter 4, you learned about many types of reactions. Organic compounds undergo different types of reactions. In this section, we will look at some simple reactions called substitution, addition, and elimination reactions.

Substitution Reactions

In a substitution reaction, an atom or group of atoms from a reactant takes the place of an atom or group of atoms on the organic molecule. For example, methane reacts with chlorine when exposed to ultraviolet light to produce chloromethane, as shown in Figure 9.3.1.

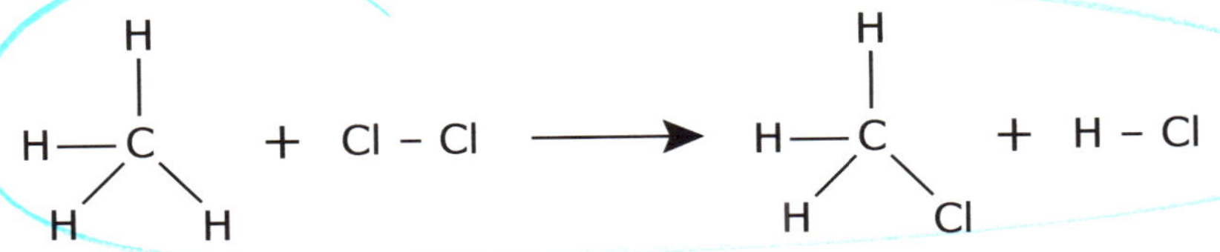

$$CH_4 + Cl{-}Cl \longrightarrow CH_3Cl + H{-}Cl$$

Figure 9.3.1 *Reaction of methane with chlorine*

One of the chlorine atoms is substituted for a hydrogen atom. Notice that the number of atoms that the central carbon atom bonds to does not change. It is bonded to four atoms in both the reactants and products. This reaction can go further with another chlorine atom replacing a hydrogen atom, which produces dichloromethane:

$$CH_3Cl + Cl_2 \rightarrow CH_2Cl_2 + HCl$$

Aromatic compounds can undergo substitution reactions many times. In the example in Figure 9.3.2, benzene reacts with chlorine to produce chlorobenzene and hydrochloric acid. Chlorobenzene will further react with Cl_2 to form dichlorobenzene (Figure 9.3.3).

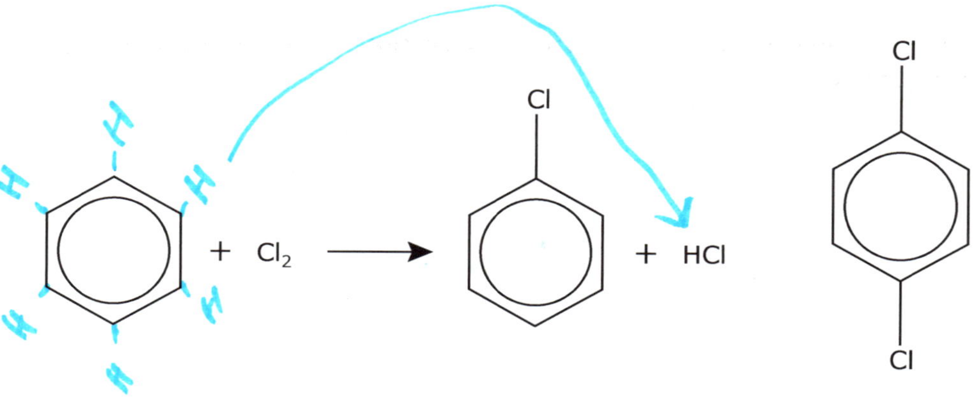

Figure 9.3.2 *Reaction of benzene with chlorine*

Figure 9.3.3 *Dichlorobenzene*

Addition Reactions

An addition reaction occurs when an unsaturated compound becomes saturated. In an addition reaction, electrons in the double or triple bond are shared with a reactant molecule. A triple bond may become a double bond or a double bond may become a single bond. It can be represented in general terms as shown in Figure 9.3.4.

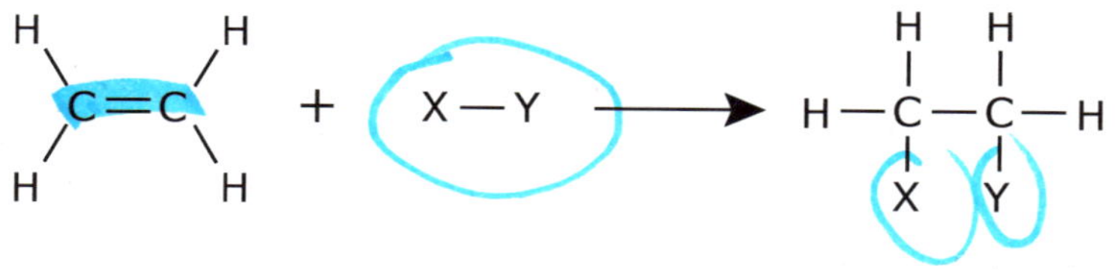

$$H_2C{=}CH_2 + X{-}Y \longrightarrow H{-}CH(X){-}CH(Y){-}H$$

Figure 9.3.4 *An addition reaction*

Halogens are particularly reactive with alkenes and alkynes. When an addition reaction occurs, a halogen atom is added to each of the carbon atoms involved in the multiple bond. This may be called a **halogenation** reaction (Figure 9.3.5). Notice that the number of atoms each carbon atom is bonded to has increased. In the reactants, each carbon atom is bonded to three other atoms. In the products, each carbon atom is bonded to four other atoms.

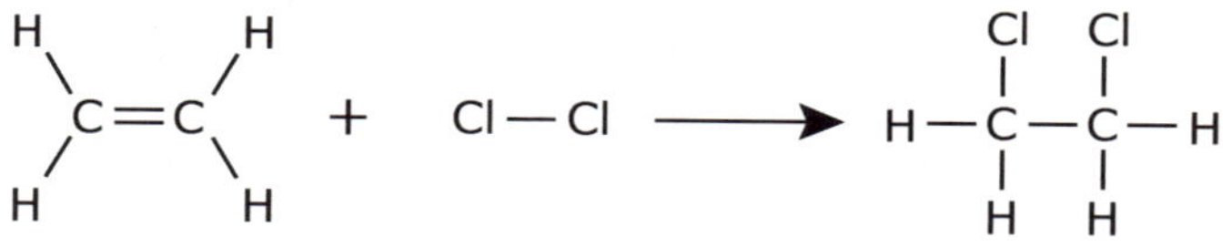

$$H_2C{=}CH_2 + Cl{-}Cl \longrightarrow H{-}CH(Cl){-}CH(Cl){-}H$$

Figure 9.3.5 *A halogenation reaction*

Ethanol is a common additive to gasoline and is produced synthetically by the addition reaction between ethene (ethylene) and water (Figure 9.3.6). The acids H_3PO_4 or H_2SO_4 act as a catalyst to speed up the rate of this reaction.

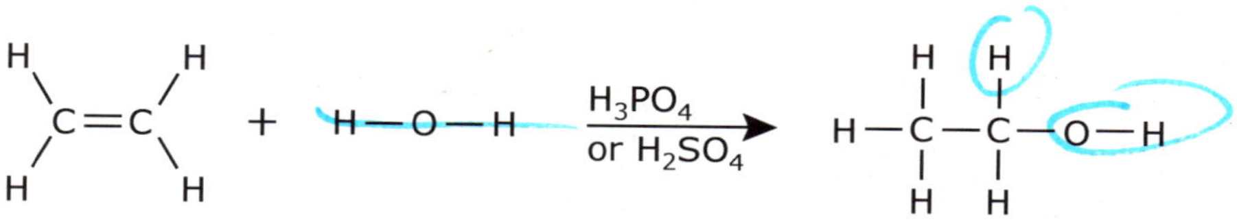

$$H_2C{=}CH_2 + H{-}O{-}H \xrightarrow[\text{or } H_2SO_4]{H_3PO_4} H{-}CH_2{-}CH_2{-}O{-}H$$

Figure 9.3.6 *Production of ethanol*

When the atoms being added to the unsaturated site are hydrogen atoms, the reaction can also be called **hydrogenation** (Figure 9.3.7).

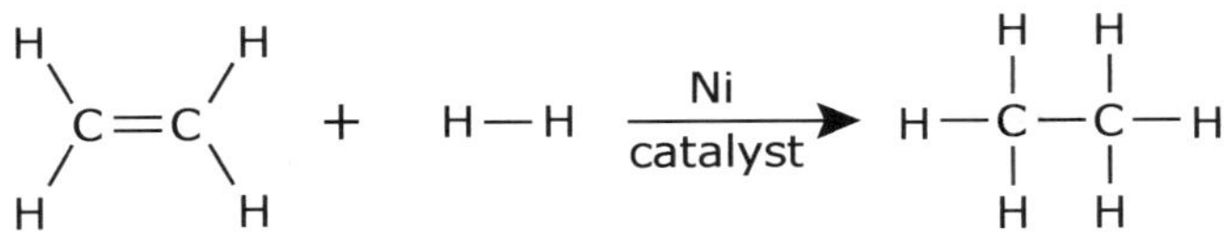

$$H_2C{=}CH_2 + H{-}H \xrightarrow[\text{catalyst}]{\text{Ni}} H{-}\underset{H}{\overset{H}{C}}{-}\underset{H}{\overset{H}{C}}{-}H$$

Figure 9.3.7 *A hydrogenation reaction*

Alkynes can also undergo addition reactions (Figure 9.3.8).

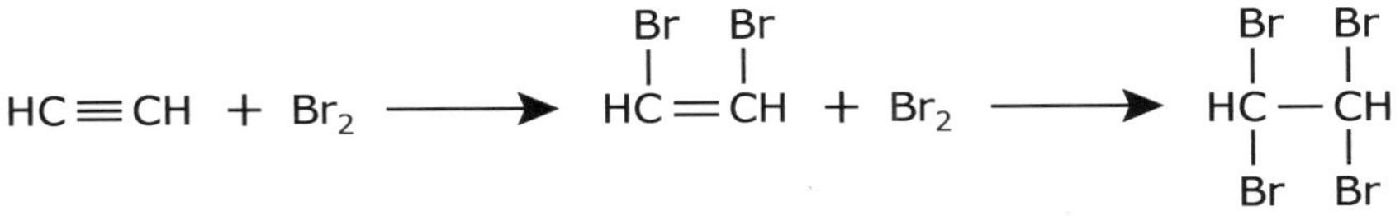

$$HC{\equiv}CH + Br_2 \longrightarrow \overset{Br}{HC}{=}\overset{Br}{CH} + Br_2 \longrightarrow \underset{Br}{\overset{Br}{HC}}{-}\underset{Br}{\overset{Br}{CH}}$$

Figure 9.3.8 *Alkyne addition reaction*

Quick Check

1. How can the number of atoms bonded to the carbon assist your classification of a reaction as addition or substitution?

   substitution has 4 atoms bonded to one C

2. Classify the following as substitution or addition reactions:

   (a) substitution

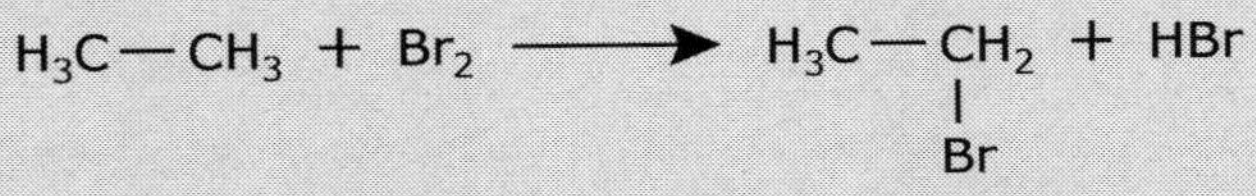

   $$H_3C{-}CH_3 + Br_2 \longrightarrow H_3C{-}\underset{Br}{CH_2} + HBr$$

   (b) addition

   $$(H_3C)HC{=}CH(CH_3) + HCl \longrightarrow H_3C{-}CH_2{-}\overset{Cl}{CH}{-}CH_3$$

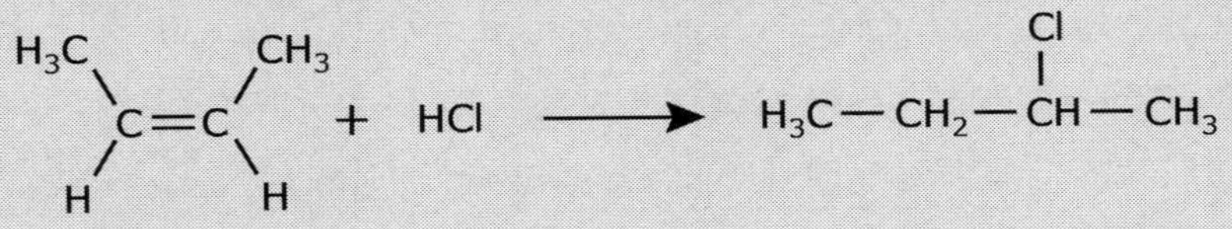

3. Using structural formulas, draw reactions showing the following. For each reaction, write the name of the reactants and products under the appropriate molecule.

   (a) formation of bromoethane

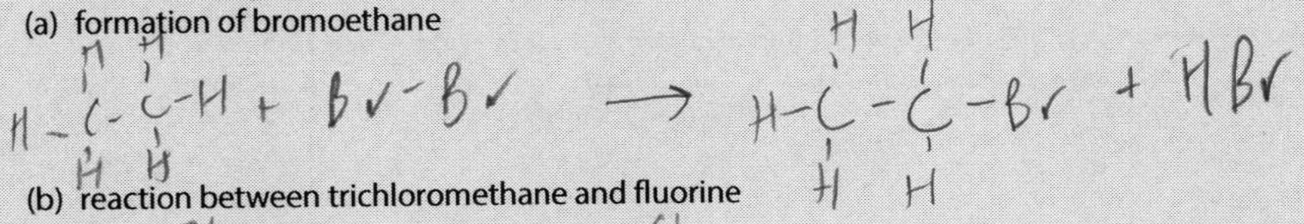

   $$H{-}\underset{H}{\overset{H}{C}}{-}\underset{H}{\overset{H}{C}}{-}H + Br{-}Br \rightarrow H{-}\underset{H}{\overset{H}{C}}{-}\underset{H}{\overset{H}{C}}{-}Br + HBr$$

   (b) reaction between trichloromethane and fluorine

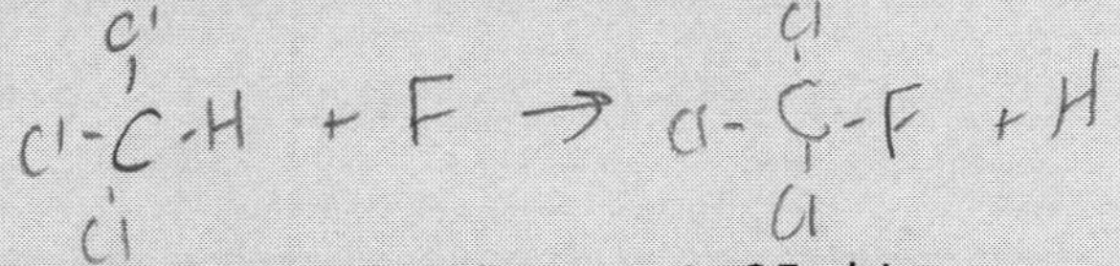

   $$Cl{-}\underset{Cl}{\overset{Cl}{C}}{-}H + F \rightarrow Cl{-}\underset{Cl}{\overset{Cl}{C}}{-}F + H$$

4. Can an alkane undergo an addition reaction? Explain.

   No because it can't become more saturated

Elimination Reactions

An elimination reaction is the opposite of an addition reaction. A small molecule such as H_2O or HX is eliminated, as shown in Figure 9.3.9.

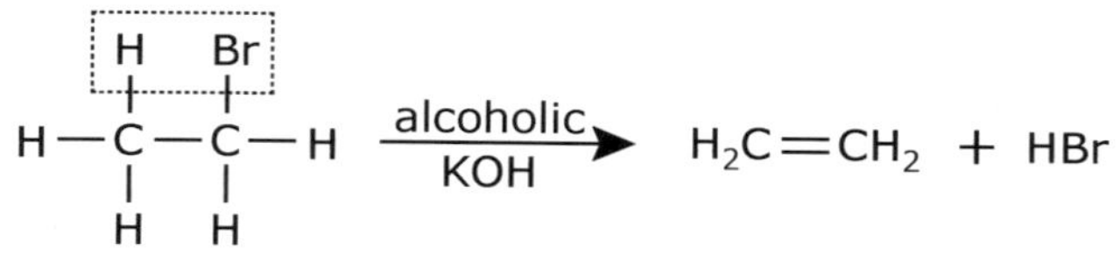

$$\mathrm{H{-}\overset{\displaystyle H}{\underset{\displaystyle H}{C}}{-}\overset{\displaystyle Br}{\underset{\displaystyle H}{C}}{-}H \xrightarrow[\text{KOH}]{\text{alcoholic}} H_2C{=}CH_2 + HBr}$$

(H and Br are eliminated)

Figure 9.3.9 *An elimination reaction*

Notice that in an elimination reaction, the number of atoms that a carbon atom is bonded to decreases. Each carbon atom in the reactant is bonded to four other atoms. In the products, each carbon atom is only bonded to three other atoms.

If water is eliminated, the reaction can also be called **dehydration** or **condensation** (Figure 9.3.10).

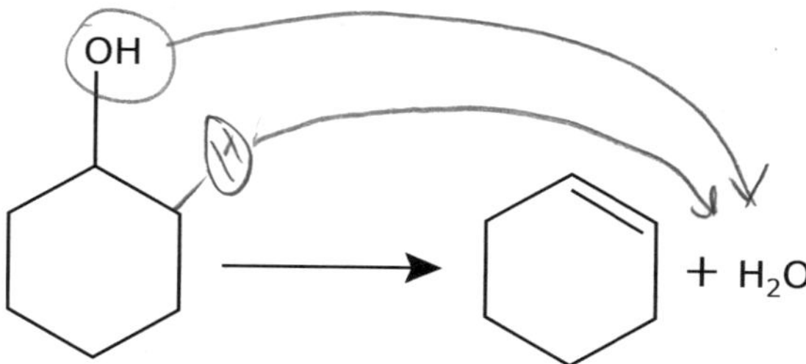

Figure 9.3.10 *Dehydration or condensation*

Esterification is the process of reacting an organic acid and an alcohol to produce an ester. Esters have a sweet, often fruity, scent. Esterification is a type of dehydration or elimination reaction.

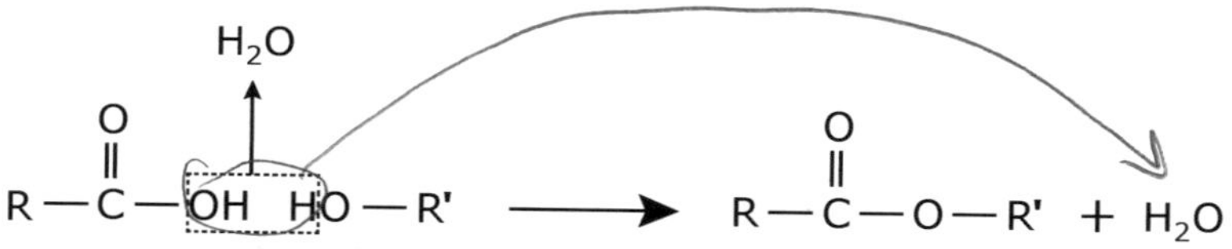

$$\mathrm{R{-}\overset{\displaystyle O}{\overset{\|}{C}}{-}OH\ \ HO{-}R' \longrightarrow R{-}\overset{\displaystyle O}{\overset{\|}{C}}{-}O{-}R' + H_2O}$$

Figure 9.3.10 *Esterification*

The –OH group on the carboxylic acid combines with the H atom from the alcohol group to make water. The name of the ester is derived from the names of the alcohol and carboxylic acid. The first part of the name of an ester comes from the alcohol. The alcohol portion of the ester is named by removing the "-ol" ending and changing it to "-yl." The name of the carboxylic acid part is changed by dropping the "-oic acid" part and adding "-oate."

An example of an ester is ethyl butanoate, which has the sweet smell of pineapple. It is produced when ethanol and butanoic acid are reacted, as shown below and in Figure 9.3.11:

butanoic acid + ethanol → ethyl butanoate + water

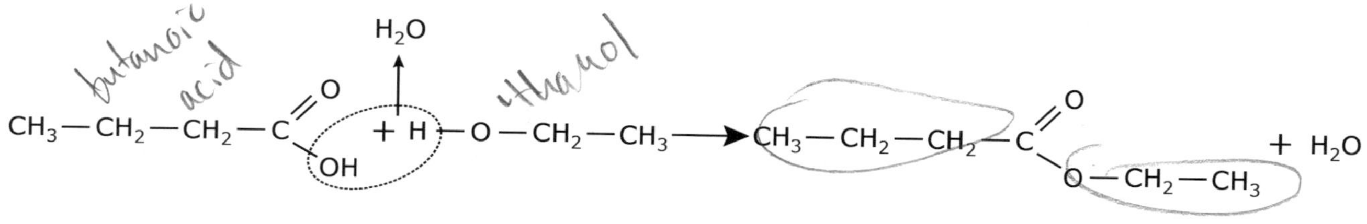

$$\mathrm{CH_3{-}CH_2{-}CH_2{-}C({=}O){-}OH + H{-}O{-}CH_2{-}CH_3 \longrightarrow CH_3{-}CH_2{-}CH_2{-}C({=}O){-}O{-}CH_2{-}CH_3 + H_2O}$$

Figure 9.3.11 *Formation of ethyl butanoate*

Animal and vegetable fats and oils are esters. The fat in Figure 9.3.12 is made from octadecanoic acid, commonly called stearic acid, and propane-1,2,3-triol, commonly called glycerol. Its real name is propane-1,2,3-triyl trioctadecanoate, but it is better known as glyceryl tristearate.

$$\begin{array}{l} CH_3(CH_2)_{16}COOCH_2 \\ \qquad\qquad\qquad\quad | \\ CH_3(CH_2)_{16}COOCH \\ \qquad\qquad\qquad\quad | \\ CH_3(CH_2)_{16}COOCH_2 \end{array}$$

Figure 9.3.12 *Glyceryl tristearate*

Saturated fats are molecules where the organic acid part of the carbon chain does not contain any double bonds. An unsaturated fat contains double bonds in the carbon parent chain of the organic acid section. Fats are an important nutrient for your body. They supply your body with energy and help in the absorption of fat-soluble vitamins. People on a Mediterranean diet, consisting of fruits, vegetables, fish, and whole grains, consume more unsaturated fats than saturated fats. This is believed to be one reason why people on this diet have healthier lives.

Sample Problem — Writing Equations for Simple Organic Reactions

Using structural diagrams, represent the reaction between methanol and ethanoic acid. Name the product, a solvent common in products like airplane glue.

What to Think about	How to Do It
1. Methanol is an alcohol, and ethanoic acid is a carboxylic acid. When these react, an ester is formed.	Methanol $CH_3 - OH$ Ethanoic acid $CH_3 - C(=O) - OH$
2. The carboxylic acid loses the –OH group, and the alcohol loses the –H atom.	$CH_3 - C(=O) - O - H + H - O - CH_3 \longrightarrow CH_3 - C(=O) - O - CH_3$ (with H_2O removed)
3. To name the ester: • methanol becomes "methyl" • ethanoic acid becomes "ethanoate"	$CH_3 - C(=O) - O - CH_3$ The ester is called methyl ethanoate.

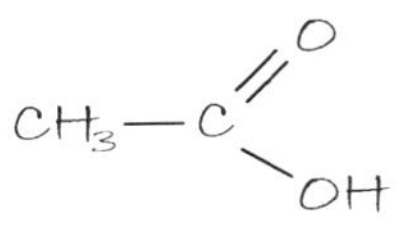

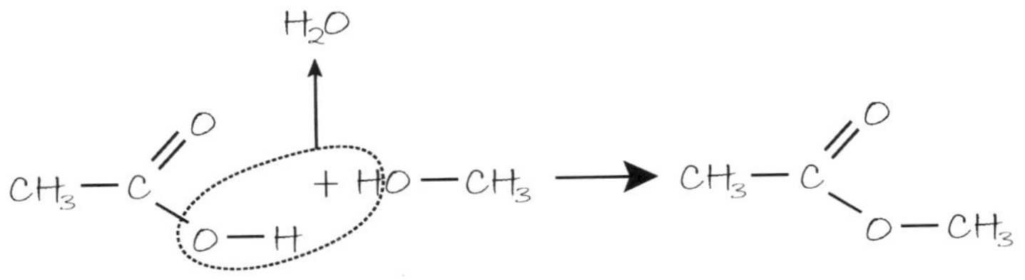

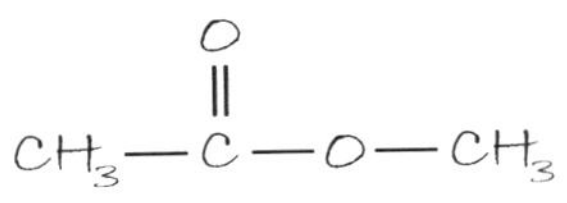

Practice Problems — Writing Equations for Simple Organic Reactions

1. Oil of wintergreen contains the ester formed when methanol and salicylic acid react. What is the name of the ester responsible for this pleasant odor?

   methyl salicylate

2. Ethyl heptanoate smells like apricots. Draw structural diagrams to represent the reaction that produces ethyl heptanoate.

   $CH_3-CH_2-CH_2-CH_2-CH_2-CH_2-\overset{O}{\overset{\|}{C}}-O-CH_2-CH_3 \leftarrow CH_3-CH_2-CH_2-CH_2-CH_2-CH_2-\overset{O}{\overset{\|}{C}}-OH + H-O-CH_2-CH_3$

3. Chlorofluorocarbons (CFCs) in the stratosphere are molecules that use up Earth's protective ozone layer. Ozone molecules at this level absorb harmful UV-B and UV- C radiation. One such CFC is called chlorodifluoromethane. Draw structural diagrams to represent how this CFC is produced. Assume that methane reacts with chlorine, and then the product reacts with excess fluorine. What type of reactions are these?

   $CH_4 + Cl_2 \rightarrow CH_3Cl + HCl$; $CH_3Cl + F_2 \rightarrow CH_2FCl + HF$

Polymerization

In chapter 3, you learned how to calculate the molar mass of a compound. The molecules that we have been discussing in this text so far have been relatively small. The chemical formulas of these molecules contain relatively few atoms. In the 1920s, a chemist named Hermann Staudinger proposed that some natural compounds such as rubber and cellulose were composed of very, very large molecules containing tens of thousands of atoms each. He called these "macromolecules." These compounds have molar masses greater than a few thousand.

The word "polymer" means "many parts." Polymers are really long molecules made by stringing together smaller parts called "monomers." The word "monomer" means "one part." A polymer might look like Figure 9.3.13. There are many types of monomers that can be linked together, so imagine how many types of polymers exist!

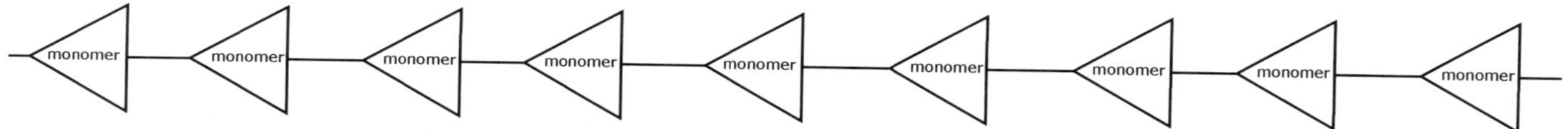

Figure 9.3.13 *A polymer model*

Polymers are found in nature and in many useful materials made synthetically. In your body, examples of polymers include DNA, starch, and proteins. Polymers we use every day include rubber, silk, plastics, nylon, Styrofoam, pharmaceuticals, Teflon, paints, and Plexiglas.

The name of a polymer depends on the monomer that it was made from. If the repeating unit is only one monomer, it is called a homopolymer (Figure 9.3.14). A copolymer contains a mixture of repeating units (Figure 9.3.15). In Figure 9.3.14, the monomer is shown on the left. When monomers are linked together to produce a polymer, the polymer is represented by showing the monomer in brackets, with the *n* representing some large number of repeat units.

$F_2C=CH_2 \xrightarrow{\text{polymerization}} [-CF_2-CH_2-]_n$

vinylidene flouride → polyvinylidene

Figure 9.3.14 *A homopolymer*

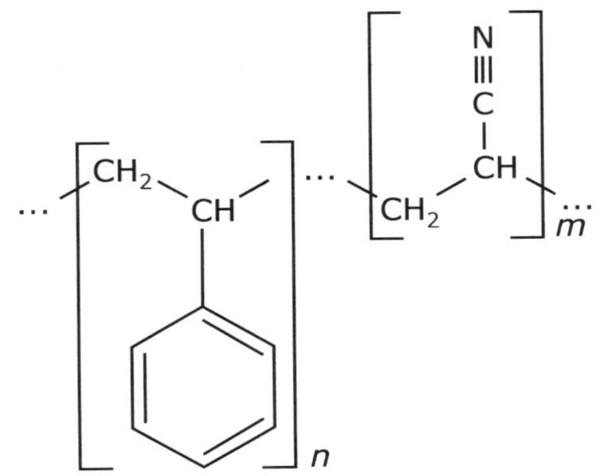

Figure 9.3.15 *A copolymer*

Addition Polymerization

You may have heard of polyethylene, one of the most common plastics. It is a polymer made up of repeating units of ethane. To make polyethylene, thousands of ethene molecules are reacted together in a huge addition reaction called "addition polymerization" (Figure 9.3.16).

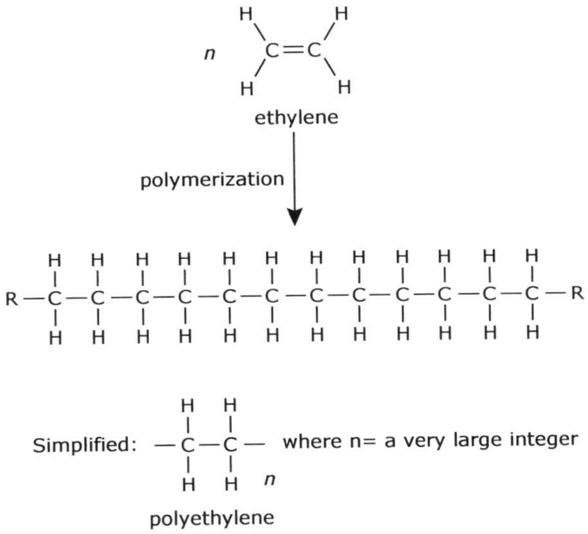

ethylene

polymerization

Simplified: where n= a very large integer

polyethylene

Figure 9.3.16 *Formation of polyethylene*

When the carbon backbone in the molecule is linear with few branches, we call it "high-density polyethylene" or HDPE. Long strands of these molecules can fit close together. If the carbon backbone of the molecule has many polyethylene branches, we call it "low-density polyethylene" or LDPE because the long chains of polymer cannot be packed tightly together. HDPE is much stronger and stiffer than LDPE, but LDPE is less expensive to make (Figure 9.3.17). Products made of HDPE include milk jugs, plastic garbage cans, shampoo bottles, and water pipes. LDPE products include plastic films, food wrap, and garbage bags.

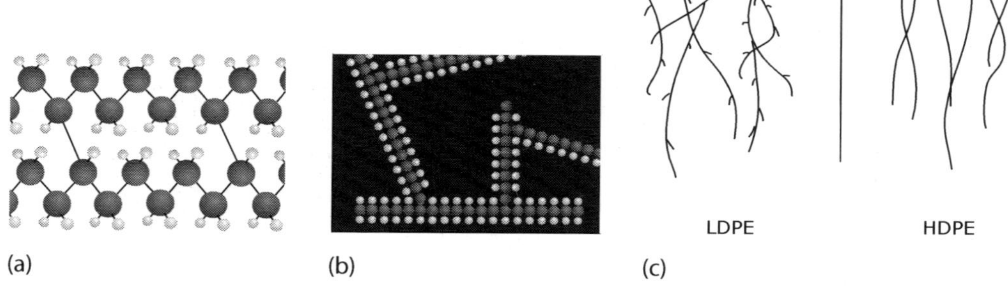

Figure 9.3.17 *(a) High-density polyethylene; (b) Low-density polyethylene; (c) LDPE and HDPE fibres*

Polyethylene macromolecules have molecular weights in the hundreds of thousands. Ultra-high molecular weight polyethylenes (UHMWPEs) are used in bulletproof vests and artificial joints and have molecular weights in the millions!

Polyethylene is called a thermoplastic because it can be melted and molded into other shapes. Because of this property, many of these plastics can be recycled. Polyethylene does not biodegrade, so it contributes to the problem of putting these plastics in landfills.

Other Examples of Polymers

Addition reactions are one common way to produce many different polymers. Other polymers made by addition reactions include those shown in Table 9.3.1.

Table 9.3.1 *Examples of Polymers Formed by Addition Reactions*

Name	Formula	Monomer	Applications
Polypropylene (PP) different grades	$-[CH_2\text{-}CH(CH_3)]_n-$	propylene $CH_2{=}CHCH_3$	Indoor/outdoor carpeting, plastic bottles, upholstery
Poly(vinyl chloride) (PVC)	$-(CH_2\text{-}CHCl)_n-$	vinyl chloride $CH_2{=}CHCl$	Pipes, siding, flooring
Polystyrene (PS)	$-[CH_2\text{-}CH(C_6H_5)]_n-$	styrene $CH_2{=}CHC_6H_5$	Insulation, furniture, packing materials
Polytetrafluoroethylene (PTFE, Teflon)	$-(CF_2\text{-}CF_2)_n-$	tetrafluoroethylene $CF_2{=}CF_2$	Non-stick surfaces on cooking utensils, lining in engines, electrical insulation
Polychloroprene (cis + trans) (Neoprene)	$-[CH_2\text{-}CH{=}CCl\text{-}CH_2]_n-$	chloroprene $CH_2{=}CH\text{-}CCl{=}CH_2$	Synthetic rubber products for wetsuits, insulation

Quick Check

1. Polytetrafluoroethylene, commonly called Teflon, is a non-stick substance used in kitchen products, the aerospace industry, electronics, and communications. It is a polymer that can be represented by the diagram below.

   Is this a homopolymer or a copolymer? Homo

   Circle the repeating unit on the diagram.

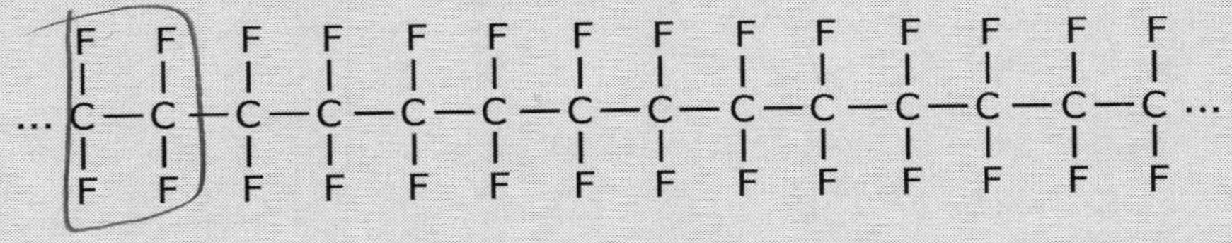

   ```
       F   F   F   F   F   F   F   F   F   F   F   F   F   F
       |   |   |   |   |   |   |   |   |   |   |   |   |   |
   ... C — C — C — C — C — C — C — C — C — C — C — C — C — C ...
       |   |   |   |   |   |   |   |   |   |   |   |   |   |
       F   F   F   F   F   F   F   F   F   F   F   F   F   F
   ```

   segment of Teflon polymer

2. On a molecular level, how does HDPE differ from LDPE?

   HDPE barely has any branches but LDPE has a lot

3. Many plastic pipes, siding, and flooring are made of polyvinyl chloride or PVC. The reaction for its formation is shown below. What type of reaction is this? On the diagram above, circle the repeat unit in this polymer.

   addition

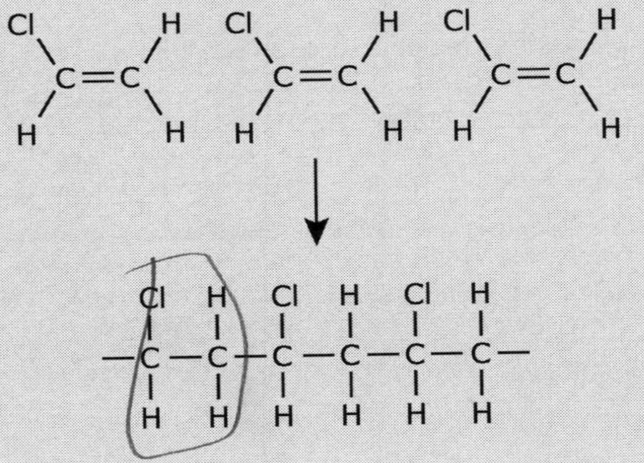

   ```
   Cl       H   Cl       H   Cl       H
     \     /      \     /      \     /
      C=C          C=C          C=C
     /     \      /     \      /     \
   H        H   H        H   H        H

                      ↓

      Cl   H   Cl   H   Cl   H
      |    |   |    |   |    |
    — C —  C — C —  C — C —  C —
      |    |   |    |   |    |
      H    H   H    H   H    H
   ```

4. The symbols shown here are used to distinguish HDPE from LDPE. List two products in your home that are made up of HDPE and two products made of LDPE.

milk jug
shampoo

garbage bag
plastic wrap

Condensation Reactions

Another way to make polymers is through a **condensation reaction**. One such polymer is nylon. It is produced when hexamethylenediamine reacts with adipic acid. For each amine that reacts with a carboxylic acid, a water molecule is eliminated. The monomer in nylon-66 has been circled in Figure 9.3.18.

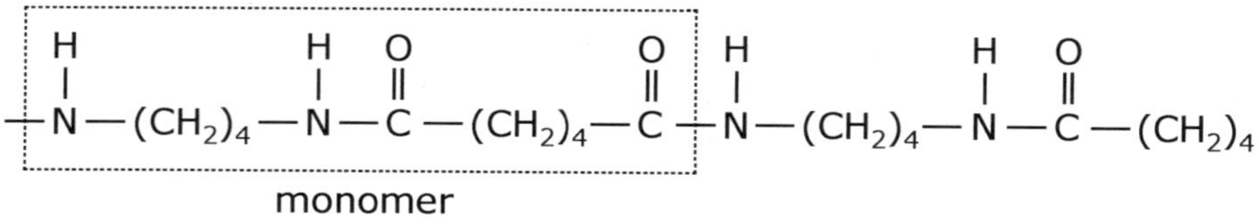

$$\left[-\overset{\overset{\displaystyle H}{|}}{N}-(CH_2)_4-\overset{\overset{\displaystyle H}{|}}{N}-\overset{\overset{\displaystyle O}{\|}}{C}-(CH_2)_4-\overset{\overset{\displaystyle O}{\|}}{C}- \right]_{\text{monomer}} \overset{\overset{\displaystyle H}{|}}{N}-(CH_2)_4-\overset{\overset{\displaystyle H}{|}}{N}-\overset{\overset{\displaystyle O}{\|}}{C}-(CH_2)_4$$

Figure 9.3.18 *Nylon*

Another example of a condensation reaction is found in your body in the process of protein production. The building blocks of proteins are amino acids. An amino acid is an organic molecule containing at least one amino group (–NH_2) and one carboxyl group (–COOH). There are 20 different amino acids in your body used to produce various proteins. The amino group on one amino acid reacts with the carboxyl group on another amino acid. When two amino acids combine, they form a dipeptide and water as shown in the reaction below and in Figure 9.3.19.

amino acid + amino acid → dipeptide + water

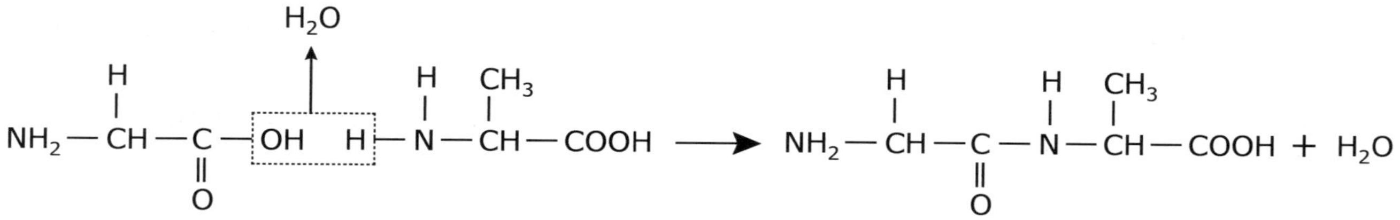

$$NH_2-\overset{\overset{\displaystyle H}{|}}{C}H-\underset{\underset{\displaystyle O}{\|}}{C}-\boxed{OH\quad H}\!\!-\overset{\overset{\displaystyle H}{|}}{N}-\overset{\overset{\displaystyle CH_3}{|}}{C}H-COOH \longrightarrow NH_2-\overset{\overset{\displaystyle H}{|}}{C}H-\underset{\underset{\displaystyle O}{\|}}{C}-\overset{\overset{\displaystyle H}{|}}{N}-\overset{\overset{\displaystyle CH_3}{|}}{C}H-COOH + H_2O$$

(the boxed OH and H are eliminated as H_2O)

Figure 9.3.19 *Formation of a dipeptide*

When many amino acids combine, the structure is called a polypeptide or a protein. One water molecule is eliminated with the formation of each new peptide bond. A protein chain may contain from 50 to thousands of amino acid fragments. A protein is a natural polymer (Figure 9.3.20). Other important polymer molecules in your body include nucleic acids such as DNA and RNA. Deoxyribonucleic acid is one of the largest molecules known, and has a molecular weight of up to several billion amu.

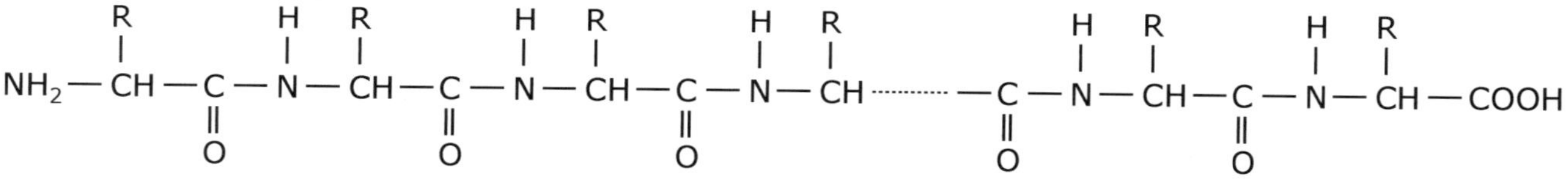

$$NH_2-\overset{\overset{\displaystyle R}{|}}{C}H-\underset{\underset{\displaystyle O}{\|}}{C}-\overset{\overset{\displaystyle H}{|}}{N}-\overset{\overset{\displaystyle R}{|}}{C}H-\underset{\underset{\displaystyle O}{\|}}{C}-\overset{\overset{\displaystyle H}{|}}{N}-\overset{\overset{\displaystyle R}{|}}{C}H-\underset{\underset{\displaystyle O}{\|}}{C}-\overset{\overset{\displaystyle H}{|}}{N}-\overset{\overset{\displaystyle R}{|}}{C}H \cdots\cdots -\underset{\underset{\displaystyle O}{\|}}{C}-\overset{\overset{\displaystyle H}{|}}{N}-\overset{\overset{\displaystyle R}{|}}{C}H-\underset{\underset{\displaystyle O}{\|}}{C}-\overset{\overset{\displaystyle H}{|}}{N}-\overset{\overset{\displaystyle R}{|}}{C}H-COOH$$

Figure 9.3.20 *A protein polymer*

9.3 Activity: Organic Molecules In Every Day Life

Question

What are some common organic compounds you encounter daily?

Background

By now, you should have some appreciation of the wide variety of organic compounds that you encounter daily. The study of organic chemistry is an enormous field responsible for billions of dollars annually in industry. This unit on organic chemistry has been a brief introduction to the world of organic chemistry. In this activity, you will have the opportunity to explore the production and uses of an organic compound based on your area of interest.

Procedure

1. You may work on your own or with a partner. Choose a topic from the list below. Your teacher may suggest additional topics.
   - the accidental discovery of Teflon
   - the production of chlorofluorocarbons and their impact on the upper atmosphere
   - the vulcanization of rubber
   - the production of polyester
   - the uses of inorganic polymers based on silicon instead of carbon
   - the use of petrochemicals as a raw material for the production of many other organic compounds
   - saponification — the production of soaps
   - the presence of methane hydrates off the coast of BC and their potential use as a fuel

2. Research the topic, including information about the uses of this compound currently, how it was discovered, and its chemistry.

Results and Discussion

1. Produce a research paper, poster, computer slide presentation, or other medium to demonstrate your understanding.
2. You may be asked to present your findings to your class.

9.3 Review Questions

1. What is the difference between complete combustion and incomplete combustion? Compare and contrast the reaction conditions and products for each.

2. (a) Which types of reactions do alkanes typically undergo?

   substitution

   (b) Which types of reactions do alkenes and alkynes typically undergo?

   addition

3. In an elimination reaction, state two molecules commonly eliminated.

   water & compounds w/ H^+ ion

4. What happens to the number of atoms bonded to the carbon atom in the skeleton during an addition reaction?

   increased

   A substitution reaction?

   no change

5. What happens during a hydrogenation reaction?

   double bonds become saturated w/ added Hs

   A condensation reaction?

   OH and and H are taken out of an alkane, and a double bond is formed

   A dehydration reaction?

6. Describe the difference between a monomer and a polymer.

   polymer is made of repeating units which are monomers

7. Salicylic acid is both an acid and an alcohol. It can undergo two different esterification reactions.

   (a) When reacted with ethanoic acid (commonly called acetic acid) the common painkiller acetylsalicylic acid (ASA) is formed. This is the active ingredient in Aspirin. In this reaction, the hydroxyl group on salicylic acid reacts with the carboxyl group on the acetic acid. Using the structures shown above and below, draw structural formulas to represent this reaction. Write the name of each molecule underneath each structure.

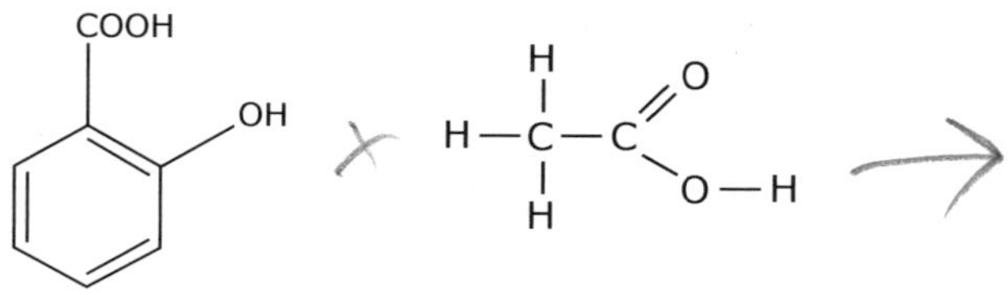

COOH, OH + H—C(H)(H)—C(=O)—O—H →

salycylic acid

ethanoic acid

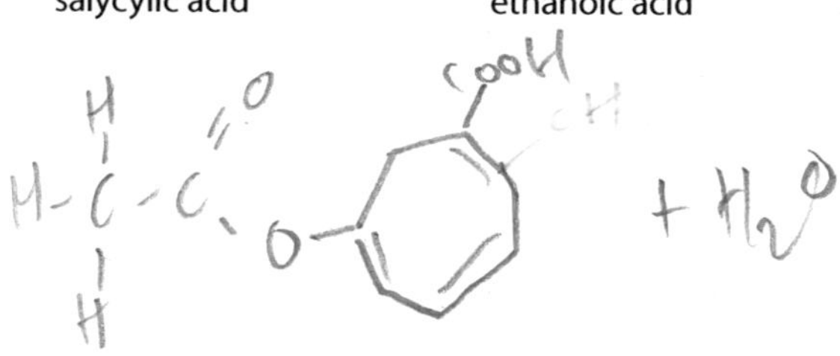

(b) When reacted with methanol, the carboxylic acid part of salicylic acid reacts with the hydroxyl group on the methanol. In this reaction, methyl salicylate is formed, commonly known as oil of wintergreen. Using the structures shown above and below, draw structural formulas to represent this reaction. Write the name of each molecule next to each structure.

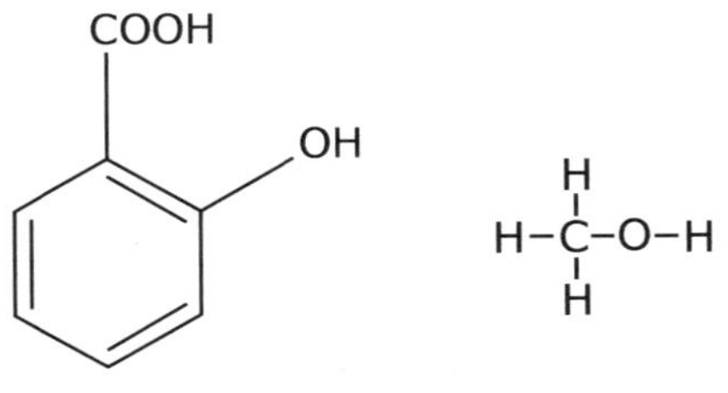

COOH
OH

salicylic acid

H
H–C–O–H
H

methanol

8. Represent the following reactions by drawing skeletal formulas, then state the type of reaction involved.

(a) propene + oxygen

(b) cyclohexane + chlorine

(c) cyclohexene + hydrogen

(d) 1-octanol + ethanoic acid

(e) propyne + hydrogen bromide

9. What is addition polymerization? Give an example of a polymer produced by addition polymerization.

10. What is condensation polymerization. Give an example of a polymer produced by condensation polymerization.

11. Name three naturally occurring polymers.

12. For the following polymers, circle the repeating unit.

(a) polystyrene (Styrofoam)

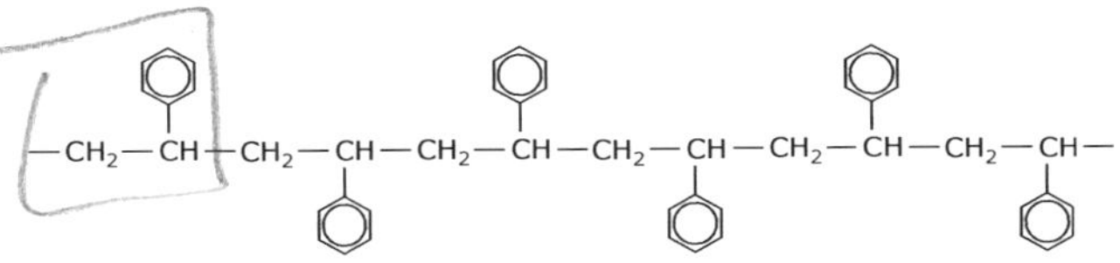

$-CH_2-CH-CH_2-CH-CH_2-CH-CH_2-CH-CH_2-CH-CH_2-CH-$

(b) cellulose (component of cell walls in plant cells)

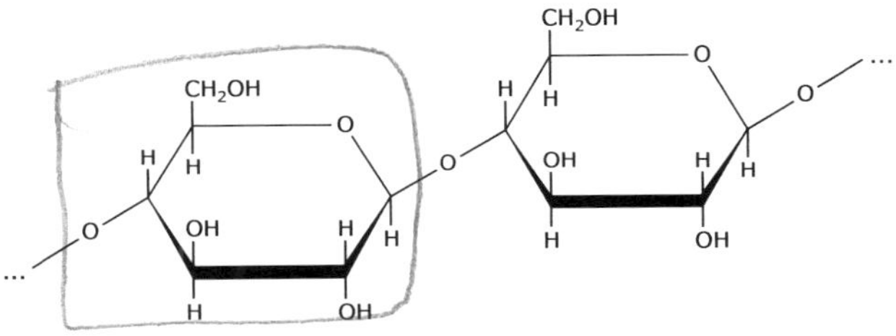

CH_2OH O H H OH H H OH H OH O CH_2OH O H H OH H H OH H OH O ...

(c) natural rubber

CH_2 CH_2-CH_2 CH_2
$C=CH$ $C=CH$
H_3C H_3C

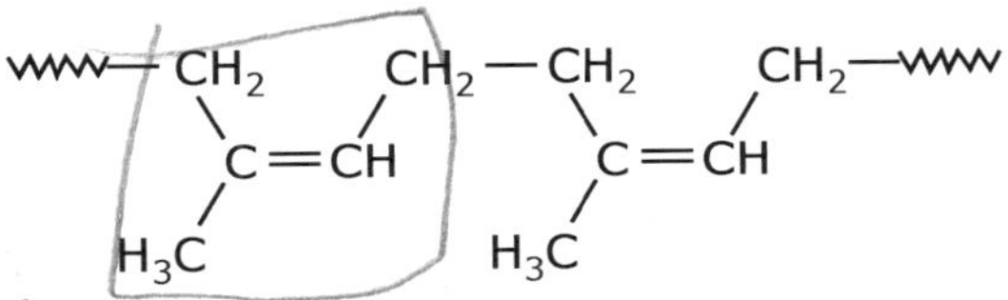

(d) polyvinyl chloride (PVC)

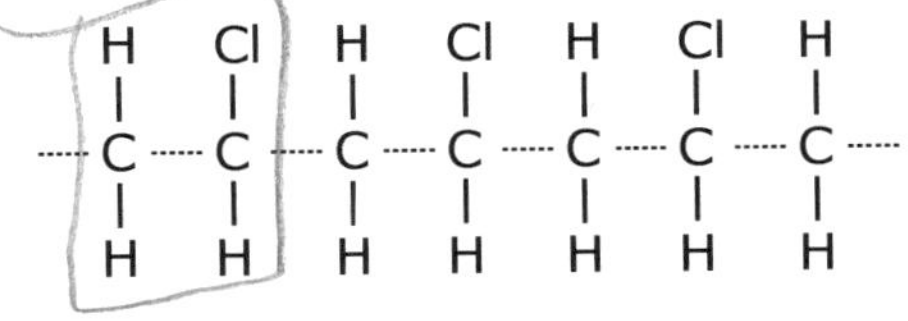

H Cl H Cl H Cl H
C — C — C — C — C — C — C
H H H H H H H

Answer Key

For the most current version of the answer key, scan the appropriate QR code with your mobile device. Or, go to edvantagescience.com, login and select Garfield AP Chemistry 1. The answer keys are posted in each chapter.

Chapter 1

Chapter 2

Chapter 3

Chapter 4

Chapter 5

Chapter 6

Chapter 7

Chapter 8

Chapter 9

Glossary

ΔH notation (4.4) a form of equation-writing that requires that the energy change be written separately following a "$\Delta H =$" expression
***a* and *b* factors** (8.4) factors that account for the attractive forces and the volume that gases demonstrate; the factors vary gas to gas
absolute uncertainty (1.3) refers to how much bigger or smaller a measured value is than an accepted value
accuracy (1.3) the agreement of a particular view with the true value
acid (2.2) one or more hydrogen ions bonded to an anion; special type of molecular compound that can be induced to form ions
actinides (6.1) a series of elements in the inner transition elements that fits between elements 88 and 104 on the periodic table
alcohol (9.2) an organic compound with a hydroxyl group in it
aldehyde (9.2) organic compound containing a carbonyl group at the end of a carbon chain
alkali metal (6.1) atom that has one valence electron in the s sublevel; forms a 1+ ion
alkaline earth metals (6.1) atom that has two valence electrons; forms a 2+ ion
alkane (9.1) hydrocarbon that has only single bonds
alkene (9.1) hydrocarbon containing double bonds
alkyne (9.1) hydrocarbon containing triple bonds
allotropes (2.2) different groupings or arrangements of the same atoms
angular momentum quantum number (5.4) a number that relates to the shape of an atomic orbital
anhydrous (2.4) a form of hydrous salt, but without water
anion (2.4, 4.2, 5.1) negatively charged ion
antibonding orbital (6.7) an orbital with high potential energy, and tend to be unstable
aqueous solution (2.2, 7.1) solution in which water is the solvent
aromatic (9.1) hydrocarbon that contains at least one benzene ring at room temperature (except mercury), is a good conductor of heat and electricity, and is malleable, ductile and flexible
atmospheric pressure (8.1) the force exerted by the atmosphere
atomic mass (5.1) the average mass of an element's atoms
atomic mass unit (amu) (5.1) mass used for determining the weight of atoms, defined as the weight of 1/12 of a carbon-12 atom
atomic number (5.1) a number that represents the total number of protons in the nucleus
atomic orbitals (5.3) the three-dimensional space around the nucleus in which electrons can be found
atomic radius (6.2) distance from the nucleus to the boundary of the surrounding cloud of electrons
Aufbau principle (5.4, 6.7) when orbitals are filling, the lowest energy orbitals available always fill first
Avogadro's hypothesis (3.4, 8.2) equal volumes of different gases measured at the same temperature and pressure have an equal number of particles
Avogadro's number (3.2) number of atoms in a mole; approximately $6.02214179 \cdot 10^{23}$ atoms

B

barometer (8.1) an instrument used to measure atmospheric pressure
base (2.2) any compound containing hydroxide (OH)
benzene ring (9.1) ring-shaped hydrocarbon containing six carbons and six hydrogens, with delocalized electrons
binary compound (2.2, 2.4) compound made of only two elements
Bohr model (6.4) a model that shows the number of electrons in each shell
boiling (2.1) vigorous bubbling that occurs within the body of a liquid as it vaporizes internally
bond energy (4.4) the potential energy of the electrons in an atom
bonding orbital (6.7) an orbital with low potential energy; tends to be stable
Born-Haber cycle (4.5) a hypothetical series of steps that represents the formation of an ionic compound from its constituent elements
Boyle's law (8.2) at constant temperature, the volume occupied by a fixed mass of gas is inversely proportional to its pressure
bright-line spectrum (5.2) a bright, bar code-like pattern that is unique for each element
buoyancy (2.3) upward force exerted on substances immersed in a liquid

C

calorimeter (4.6) An instrument with which to measure calories
calorimeter constant (4.6) the number of joules the entire calorimeter must absorb or release in order to change its temperature by 1(C
capillary action (2.3) tendency for a liquid to rise up in narrow tubes or to be drawn into small openings
carbonyl (9.2) a group with a carbon atom double-bonded to an oxygen atom
cation (2.4, 4.2, 5.1) positively charged ion
Charles's law (8.2) at constant pressure, the volume of a fixed mass of any gas is directly proportional to its Kelvin temperature

chemical properties (2.1) properties that describe interactions between different forms of matter; they include stability, reactivity, toxicity, and flammability

chemical reactivity (4.2) the tendency for a chemical to undergo chemical change

chemical species (2.2) all the particles of matter; atoms, molecules, ions

chemistry (2.1) science concerned with the properties, composition, and behaviour of matter

cis-trans isomers (9.1) [see geometric isomers]

coarse suspension (2.2) a heterogeneous mixture with a dispersed phase and a continuous medium

coefficient (4.1) number that multiplies the entire chemical species that follows

combined gas law (8.2) a relationship that is a combination of Boyle's, Charles's and Gay-Lussac's laws

combustion (4.2) reaction between a hydrocarbon or a carbohydrate with oxygen gas to produce carbon dioxide and water

concentration (3.6) any expression of the proportion of a chemical in a solution

conceptual definition (2.1) explains what operational definitions describe

condensation (2.1) state change from gas to liquid

condensation reaction (9.2) a reaction that creates polymers

conversion factor (1.4) fraction or factor written so that the denominator and

core notation (5.4) a condensed version of electron configuration notation using the previous noble gas to shorten the notation

Coulomb's law (6.3) the relationship between the forces on two charged objects

covalent bond (2.2, 6.4) a shared pair of valence electrons between two atoms

covalent radius (6.2) one-half the distance between the two nuclei in the molecule

crystal field theory (6.7) a theory describing the behaviour of coordination compounds containing partially filled *d*-orbital electrons

crystal lattice (6.4) an ordered, solid, three-dimensional array of anions and cations

cyclic (9.1) ring-shaped

D

Dalton's law of partial pressures (8.3) liquids that have a high vapour pressure will evaporate very readily

data table (1.2) an arrangement of information

decanting (2.3) carefully pouring the liquid off the top and leaving the sediment intact in the original container

decomposition (4.2) reaction involving a complex substance breaking down into simpler substances (not the same as dissociation)

density (3.4) amount of matter in a given volume of an object or material

dependent variable (1.2) the value that responds to the variation

deposition (2.1) state change from gas to solid

derived unit (1.4) a unit composed of two or more units

desiccant (2.4) salts used to keep the air dry in a container

desiccator (2.4) container used to store desiccants

developing a chromatogram (2.3) spraying the chemicals on a chromatogram to form coloured complexes with separated substances so they reveal their location

diamagnetic (6.7) substances that are weakly repelled by a magnetic field

diffusion (8.4) the term used to describe the mixing of one gas through another

dipole-dipole force (4.6, 6.6, 7.2) the attraction between two poles on two polar molecules

dissociate (3.6) when ions in an ionic compound break apart in a solution

dissociation equation (7.3) an equation that represents the separation of the positive and negative ions of a salt by a solvent

distillate (2.3) pure substance created via distillation

distillation (2.3) any process that separates a mixture of substances by using their different vapour pressures or boiling points

domain (6.7) a region of space shared by two orbitals

E

effective nuclear charge (6.3) the reduced charge experienced by the valence electrons

effusion (8.4) the passage of a gas through a tiny orifice into an evacuated chamber

electrolyte (7.3) a solution that conducts electricity well

electron (5.1) negatively charged subatomic particle, found outside the nucleus

electron configuration (5.4) shorthand notation used to describe the locations of electrons in an atom

electronegativity (6.2) the relative ability of a bonded atom to attract shared electrons to itself

empirical formula (3.5) simplest integral ratio of the different types of atoms in the compound

endothermic (4.2) reaction that absorbs heat

endpoint (7.4) the point at which an indicator changes colour during a titration

enthalpy (4.4) potential energy that may be evolved or absorbed as heat

equivalence point (7.4) the point at which the unknown solution is completely reacted during a titration

ether (9.2) organic compound in which two hydrocarbon fragments are attached by an oxygen atom

evaporation (vaporization) (2.1) state change from liquid to gas

excess reactant (4.8) the reactant that remains once the limiting reactant has been completely consumed

excited state (6.3) a higher level of energy for electrons than ground state

exothermic (4.2) reaction that releases energy
expanded notation (1.2) same as standard notation, or writing out the full number
expanded octets (6.5) more than two atoms bonded covalently to satisfy the octet rule
extensive properties (2.1) qualities that are or depend on the amount of the material

F

family/group (6.1) vertical column on the periodic table
filtrate (2.3) the liquid that has passed through the filter after filtration
filtration (2.3) pouring a mixture through a filter to separate different substances
first law of thermodynamics (4.5) energy cannot be created or destroyed, but it can be converted from one form to another
formal charge (6.6) an entirely fictitious charge that is used to defend the most probable Lewis structure of a molecule when several different Lewis structure arrangements are possible
formula mass (3.2) sum of all the masses of the atoms that make up a compound
fractional distillation (2.3) repeated distillation followed by the pure vapour entering a fractionation column; used to separate different substances while in vapour form
freezing (2.1) state change from liquid to solid
froth flotation (2.3) process in which powdered ore is mixed with water; pine oil is added, which adheres to the minerals; air is bubbled though the mixture and the hydrophobic mineral grains are carried to the surface where they are retrieved by skimming them off the top
functional group (9.2) an atom, group of atoms, or organization of bonds in an organic molecule that react in a characteristic manner

G

gas (8.1) a state of matter in which the particles are free to move around, due to weaker intermolecular forces
gas laws (8.1) mathematical relationships between pressure, volume, temperature, and the amount of substance present
Gay-Lussac's law (8.2) at constant volume, the pressure of a fixed mass of any gas is directly proportional to its Kelvin temperature
geometric isomers (9.1) alkenes that have different orientations of groups across a double bond
graph (1.2) representation of data visually
ground state (6.3) the lowest level of energy for an electron

H

halogenation (9.2) an addition reaction where a halogen is added to a compound
halogens (6.1) the elements in group 17
heat (2.1, 4.6) energy transferred from one body to another due to a difference in temperature
heat capacity (4.6) the quantity of energy required to change the temperature of a particular sample of material
heat of combustion (2.1) the energy released when a specified amount of a substance undergoes complete combustion with oxygen; measured in joules per gram
heat of condensation (4.6) the energy required for the phase change from gas to liquid
heat of formation (2.1) the energy released when a substance is formed from its elements; measured in joules per gram
heat of fusion (2.1, 4.6) the energy required to change a particular quantity of a pure solid at its melting point into a liquid
heat of solidification (4.6) the energy required for the phase change from liquid to solid
heat of vaporization (2.1, 4.6) the energy required to evaporate a specific amount of a substance at its boiling point
heterogeneous mixture (2.2) a mixture that does not appear to be uniform throughout
homogeneous mixture (2.2) a mixture that appears to be the same throughout
household products (1.1) products for home use
Hund's rule (5.4, 6.7) when orbitals of equal energy are being filled, the most stable configuration is the one with the maximum number of unpaired electrons with the same spin
hybrid bonding orbital (6.7) the orbital resulting from the valence atomic orbital of one atom merging with that of another
hybrid orbitals (6.6) the product of hybridization
hybridization (6.6) a mathematical process in which standard atomic orbitals combine to form new atomic orbitals
hydrate (2.4) a salt with water molecules in its crystals
hydration (7.3) process of water molecules surrounding solute particles in an aqueous solution
hydration shell (6.6) layer of water molecules surrounding an ion
hydrocarbon (9.1) compound that contains carbon and hydrogen; may also include other elements
hydrogen bond (4.6, 6.6) intense intermolecular force between a tiny electropositive hydrogen atom and a lone pair of electrons; bonds where hydrogen is attached to one of the three smallest diameter, largest electronegativity elements: N, O, or F
hydrophobic (2.3) water-repelling
hydroxyl (9.2) functional group composed of an -OH group

I

ideal gas law (8.2) a law concerning the relationships between temperature, pressure, and volume: $PV = nRT$
immiscible (7.1) not soluble in any proportion

Imperial system of measurements (1.4) a system of units of measurement originally developed in Britain

independent variable (1.2) the value that varies

inertia (2.3) resistance to change in motion

infrared (6.3) a portion of the electromagnetic spectrum with a lower energy and longer wavelength than visible light

inner transition elements (6.1) the two periods that are found below the main section of the periodic table: elements 57 through 71 (lanthanides) and elements 89 through 103 (actinides)

insoluble (7.1) describes substances that do not dissolve in a solvent

intensive properties (2.1) qualities that do not depend on the amount of material

intermolecular forces (4.4, 6.6) attractive forces between molecules and between ions and molecules

internal energy (4.5) the summation of various types of energy within a system

intramolecular bonds (4.4, 6.6) chemical bonds within molecules

ion (2.2, 5.1) charged atom or group of atoms

ion-dipole force (6.6, 7.2) attraction between an ion and a polar molecule

ionic bond (2.2, 6.4) attraction between two oppositely charged ions

ionic compound (2.2) a compound composed of positively and negatively charged atoms held together by their opposite electrical charges

ionic crystal lattice (2.2) long-range, symmetrical packing arrangement for an ionic compound

ionization energy (6.2) the minimum amount of energy required to remove an electron from a gaseous atom or ion

ionization equation (7.3) an equation that represents the solute breaking down into ions

isoelectronic (6.1) able to readily form ions to match the electron configuration of the nearest noble gas

K

kinetic energy (2.1) any form of energy that cannot be stored

kinetic molecular theory (2.1, 8.1) explains what happens to matter when the kinetic energy of particles changes

L

lanthanides (6.1) a series of elements in the inner transition elements that fits between elements 56 and 72 on the periodic table

latent heat (4.6) a heat change that occurs at constant temperature

lattice energy (4.5) the change in enthalpy required for the formation of an ionic compound from the gaseous state

law of conservation of mass (4.1, 4.5) the mass before and after the reaction remains constant

law of constant composition (3.1) all samples of a given compound have the same mass ratios between elements

law of Hess or **Hess's law of heat summation** (4.5) the enthalpy change of a reaction is expressed as the algebraic sum of the enthalpy changes of a series of other reactions that have been manipulated to produce the overall reaction

Lewis structure (6.5) a model that shows the number of valence electrons

limiting reactant (4.8) the reactant that is completely consumed when the reaction is completed

London dispersion forces (4.6, 6.6, 7.2) a weak force that involves instantaneous induced poles of opposite charge on the molecules; intermolecular forces that cause dispersion throughout a sample

lone pairs (6.5) pairs of non-bonding electrons

M

magnetic moment (6.3) created by the combination of spin and charge of the nucleus, causing the nucleus to act like a compass needle, aligning itself north or south when a magnetic field is applied

magnetic quantum number (5.4) a number that gives the orientation in space of a given atomic orbital

main group elements (6.1) the elements in groups 1, 2, 13, 14, 15, 16, 17, and 18 in the periodic table

manometer (8.1) an instrument used to measure the pressure exerted by a gas in a closed container

mantissa (1.2) the decimal portion of a value in scientific notation

mass (2.1, 3.1) amount of matter contained in a thing

mass number (5.1) a number that represents the total number of protons and neutrons in the nucleus

mass spectrometer (3.5) instrument that identifies the mass spectrum of a compound, and in doing so, finds the relative abundance of the particles in the compound

Material Safety Data Sheet (MSDS) (1.1) sheet providing information about hazardous chemicals

matter (2.1) anything that has mass and occupies space

mean free path (8.4) the average distance a particle travels between collisions in a sample of gas

mechanical energy (2.1) any form of energy that enables translational, rotational, and/or vibrational motion

mechanical means of separation (2.3) any form of physical separation that uses gravity, contact forces, or motion to sort out the substances in a mixture

melting (2.1) state change from solid to liquid

melting point (2.1) temperature at which a solid changes to a liquid

metallic radius (6.2) one-half the distance between the two identical nuclei of adjacent atoms in the crystal of a metal

metalloids (6.1) elements with properties intermediate between metals and non-metals; also called semi- metals

metals (6.1) a shiny or lustrous element that is solid

metathesis reaction (4.3) reaction that does not involve electron transfer

mineral (2.3) naturally occurring compound

miscible (7.1) soluble in any proportion
molar mass (3.2) mass of one mole of a given element
molar solubility (7.1) solubility given as a molarity
molar volume (3.4) space occupied by a mole of a given element's or compound's particles
molarity (3.6, 7.3) number of moles of the chemical per litre
mole (3.2) quantity equal to the number of atoms in the atomic mass of any element expressed in grams
mole fraction (8.3) a relationship used to calculate partial pressure
molecular compound (2.2) compound consisting of molecules
molecular dipole (6.6) any molecule that has positive and negative poles
molecular formula (3.5) actual number of each type of atom in each molecule of the compound
molecular mass (3.2) sum of all the masses of the atoms that make up a compound
molecular orbital (MO) model (6.7) a model that enhances our ability to predict molecular structures
molecule (2.2) a neutral group of atoms held together by covalent bonds
monatomic ions (2.4) charged individual atoms
multiple bonds (6.5) when two atoms share more than one pair of electrons covalent bonds
multivalent (2.4) describes an element that has more than one stable ion

N

network covalent solids (6.4) substances held together by covalent bonds that extend throughout the entire sample
neutralization (4.2) reaction between an acid and a base to produce water and a salt
neutron (5.1) subatomic particle with no electric charge, found in the nucleus
neutron number (5.1) a number that represents the total number of neutrons in the nucleus
noble gases (6.1) the elements in group 18
node (6.7) an area of minimal electron density between the nuclei in a σ^* antibonding molecular orbital
non-metals (6.1) elements that are usually gases or brittle solids (bromine excepted), conduct heat and electricity poorly, and range from dull to lustrous and from transparent to opaque
nonelectrolyte (7.3) solution that does not conduct electricity
nuclear magnetic resonance (NMR) (6.3) a method for measuring the change in polarity of many nuclei in a sample
nuclear spin (6.3) the angular momentum of neutrons and protons
nucleus (5.1) dense centre of an atom, made of protons and neutrons

O

operational definition (2.1) definition based on observable characteristics; used to classify things
orbital diagram (5.4) a diagram that depicts electrons and their spin
ordinate (1.2) the exponential portion of a value in scientific notation
ore (2.3) rock containing the desired mineral
organic chemistry (9.1) chemistry involving compounds made of carbon and hydrogen
organic compound (2.2) any compound that has carbon and hydrogen; may also include other elements
oxidation (4.3) an increase in the oxidation state
oxidation number (4.3) the combining capacity of an element, monatomic ion, or a polyatomic ion
oxidation state (4.3) [see oxidation number]
oxidation-reduction reaction (4.3) reaction that involves electron transfer
oxyanion (2.4) an atom and some number of oxygen atoms

P

paramagnetic (6.7) substances that are attracted to a magnetic field
partial pressure (8.3) the pressure contributed by a single gas in a system of many gases
pathway dependent functions (4.5) functions that are dependent on the process used
Pauli exclusion principle (5.4, 6.7) no two electrons in the same atom can be described by the same set of quantum numbers
percentage composition (3.5) percent of an object's mass contributed by each type of atom in the compound
percentage error (1.3) indication of an error of measurement as a percentage of what a value should be
percentage purity (4.8) the purity of a chemical made from a reaction (by mass)
percentage yield (4.8) the amount of product obtained in a reaction, divided by the amount expected, and multiplied by 100
periodic law (6.1) law stating that, if elements are arranged in order of increasing atomic number, a pattern can be seen in which similar properties recur on a regular basis
periodic table (6.1) a table in which the elements are ordered by increasing atomic number and by chemical properties
periodic trends (6.2) consistent and predictable changes in elemental properties
periods (6.1) the horizontal rows on the periodic table
photoelectric effect (6.3) [see photoionization]
photoelectron spectroscopy (PES) (6.3) a process involving the use of a device that focuses a monochromatic beam of X-rays at a solid sample and detects released electrons
photoionization (6.3) ionization caused by a photon

physical properties (2.1) properties that describe the physical characteristics of a material and physical changes (changes in state or form)
physical separation (2.3) separation of chemicals in a mixture that does not involve chemical reaction(s)
polar covalent bond (6.4) a covalent bond in which the electrons are drawn to one side of the molecule, resulting in the molecule having two magnetic poles
polyatomic ion (2.4) a charged group of covalently bonded atoms
polymer (9.2) a very large molecule created by linking smaller ones
potential energy (2.1) stored energy
precipitate (4.1) solid formed from two solutions
precision (1.3) refers to the exactness of a measurement
pressure-volume work (4.5) work done by expanding gases
principal quantum number (5.4) a number that indicates the relative size of an atomic orbital
products (4.1) final substances after a chemical reaction
properties (2.1) qualities common to a thing or group of things
proton (5.1) positively charged subatomic particle, found in the nucleus

Q

quantum numbers (5.4) special numbers that each specify something different about the orbitals and electrons

R

radio waves (6.3) the longest waves in the electromagnetic spectrum
random error (1.3) a group of errors that occurs equally in high and low directions
range uncertainty (1.3) an acceptable range of values within which the true value resides
reactants (4.1) starting substances in a chemical reaction
reactivity (2.1) refers to whether a substance reacts or to its reaction rate
redox reaction (4.3) [see oxidation-reduction reaction]
reduction (4.3) a decrease in the oxidation state
relationship (1.2) in mathematical terms, an equation that shows how the variable quantities depend on each other
relative mass (3.1) comparison between two masses
residue (2.3) the remaining material in the filter (after filtration)
resonance structure (6.5, 9.1, 6.7) type of Lewis structure used to represent delocalized electrons
root mean square velocity (8.4) the average velocity of gas particles in a sample

S

salt (2.2) any ionic compound other than a hydroxide
saturated (7.1, 9.1) a solution in which no more solid can be dissolved
scientific method (1.2) a way of drawing conclusions from experiments
scientific notation (1.2) a way of representing large numbers
sediment (noun) (2.2, 2.3) matter that has fallen or sunk to the bottom of a liquid
sediment (verb) (2.3) to fall or sink to the bottom of a liquid
semi-metals (6.1) elements with properties intermediate between metals and non-metals; also called metalloids
shielding effect (6.3) the reduction in the nuclear charge felt by a valence electron
SI system (1.3) International System of Units; the modern metric system of measurement
significant figures (1.3) a system to decide how many digits to use in a calculation
single replacement (4.2) reaction between a compound and an element so that the element replaces an element of the same type in the compound; the result is a new compound and a different element
slope (1.2) the change in y divided by the change in x in an equation for a straight-line relationship
solubility (7.1) maximum amount of solute that can be dissolved in a given amount of solvent at a particular temperature
soluble (7.1) a solute that can be dissolved in a solvent
solute (2.2, 7.1) the minor component in a mixture; usually what has been dissolved
solution (2.2, 7.1) type of homogeneous mixture in which the mixed chemical species do not form particles greater than 1 nm solution by reacting it with a substance of known concentration
solvation (7.3) process of solvent molecules surrounding solute particles
solvent (2.2, 7.1) the major component in a mixture; usually what dissolves the solute
specific heat capacity (4.6) the quantity of heat required to raise the temperature of a specific quantity of a substance by one degree Celsius
spectroscopy (6.3) a process used to probe matter
spin quantum number (5.4) a number that indicates one of two possible electron spins
standard atmospheric pressure (8.1) the pressure exerted by the atmosphere at sea level
standard solution (3.6, 7.4) solution of known concentration
standard temperature and pressure (STP) (3.4) 0°C and 101.3 Kpa
state function (4.5) functions that are independent from the process used
stoichiometric quantities (4.8) molar ratio that is identical to that predicted in the balanced equation
stoichiometry (3.3) branch of chemistry that deals with quantitative relationships between elements in a compound and between the reactants and products in a chemical reaction
strong acid (7.3) acid that dissociates completely to form an ionic compound
structural formula (3.5) chemical formula showing how the atoms are arranged in a compound

structural isomers (9.1) different structures with the same chemical formula
sublimation (2.1) state change from solid to gas
substituent groups (9.1) chains of carbons that branch off the main chain of carbons
supersaturated (7.1) describes a solution in which there is more dissolved solute than there would normally be
surroundings (4.5) the area around the system
synthesis (4.2) reaction involving two or more simple substances combining into a single complex substance
system (4.5) the studied reaction
systematic error (1.3) a group of measurements that consistently show the same error

T

temperature (1.4, 2.1) a measure of intensity of heat; the average mechanical energy of the particles that compose a material
theoretical yield (4.8) the amount of product predicted to be created from a chemical reaction
thermal energy (2.1) total mechanical energy of an object's or a material's particles
thermochemical equation (4.4) equation that includes the energy change
thermodynamics (4.5) the study of energy changes and the laws governing the conversion of heat into other forms of energy things
titration (7.4) a quantitative analysis method used to determine the concentration of an unknown
torr (8.1) a unit equivalent to mm Hg
transition elements (6.1) the elements in groups 3 through 12 of the periodic table
Tyndall effect (2.2) difference in the dispersion of light when shone through various homogeneous mixtures

U

uncertainty (1.3) a degree of being unsure
unsaturated (7.1, 9.1) when the solute is completely dissolved in the solvent
UV/Vis (6.3) a process involving the absorption of light by valence electrons

V

valence bond theory (6.6) describes the location of bonding and non-bonding, lone electrons in quantum-mechanical orbitals, created by overlap of the standard s, p, d and f orbitals
valence electrons (6.1) the electrons in the outer shell of an atom
valence shell electron pair repulsion theory (VSEPR) (6.6) theory describing the tendency for electrons to reside in a place that minimizes the repulsion between them
vapour (2.1) gas formed by a substance that boils above room temperature
vapour pressure (8.3) the pressure exerted by the vapour of a substance
visible and ultraviolet radiation (6.3) portions of the electromagnetic spectrum with a higher energy and shorter wavelength than infrared (ultraviolet more so than visible light)
volatile (2.1, 8.3) readily evaporates or evaporates at high rates

W

weak acid (7.3) acid that does not dissociate completely, or does not form many ions
weak electrolyte (7.3) solution that does not conduct electricity well
weigh (3.1) to find the weight or to compare the weight of
weighing scale (3.1) measuring instrument for determining the mass or weight of an object
white light (6.3) the sum of all of the wavelengths in the electromagnetic spectrum
Workplace Hazardous Materials Information System (WHMIS) (1.1) a system for communicating information about the safety requirements for working with chemicals

Names, Formulae, and Charges of Some Common Ions

** Aqueous solutions are readily oxidized by air.*
*** Not stable in aqueous solution*

Positive Ions (Cations)			
Al^{3+}	aluminum	Pb^{4+}	lead(IV), plumbic
NH_4^+	ammonium	Li^+	lithium
Ba^{2+}	barium	Mg^{2+}	magnesium
Ca^{2+}	calcium	Mn^{2+}	manganese(II), manganous
Cr^{2+}	chromium(II), chromous	Mn^{4+}	manganese(IV)
Cr^{3+}	chromium(III), chromic	Hg_2^{2+}	mercury(I)*, mercurous
Cu^+	copper(I)*, cuprous	Hg^{2+}	mercury(II), mercuric
Cu^{2+}	copper(II), cupric	K^+	potassium
H^+	hydrogen	Ag^+	silver
H_3O^+	hydronium	Na^+	sodium
Fe^{2+}	iron(II)*, ferrous	Sn^{2+}	tin(II)*, stannous
Fe^{3+}	iron(III), ferric	Sn^{4+}	tin(IV), stannic
Pb^{2+}	lead(II), plumbous	Zn^{2+}	zinc

Negative Ions (Anions)			
Br^-	bromide	OH^-	hydroxide
CO_3^{2-}	carbonate	ClO^-	hypochlorite
ClO_3^-	chlorate	I^-	iodide
Cl^-	chloride	HPO_4^{2-}	monohydrogen phosphate
ClO_2^-	chlorite	NO_3^-	nitrate
CrO_4^{2-}	chromate	NO_2^-	nitrite
CN^-	cyanide	$C_2O_4^{2-}$	oxalate
$Cr_2O_7^{2-}$	dichromate	O^{2-}	oxide**
$H_2PO_4^-$	dihydrogen phosphate	ClO_4^-	perchlorate
CH_3COO^-	ethanoate, acetate	MnO_4^-	permanganate
F^-	fluoride	PO_4^{3-}	phosphate
HCO_3^-	hydrogen carbonate, bicarbonate	SO_4^{2-}	sulphate
$HC_2O_4^-$	hydrogen oxalate, binoxalate	S^{2-}	sulphide
HSO_4^-	hydrogen sulphate, bisulphate	SO_3^{2-}	sulphite
HS^-	hydrogen sulphide, bisulphide	SCN^-	thiocyanate
HSO_3^-	hydrogen sulphite, bisulphite		

Made in the USA
San Bernardino, CA
27 May 2018